Modern
BRAZILIAN PORTUGUESE
Grammar

Modern Brazilian Portuguese Grammar: A Practical Guide is an innovative reference guide to Brazilian Portuguese, combining traditional and function-based grammar in a single volume.

The *Grammar* is divided into two parts. Part A covers traditional grammatical categories such as agreement, nouns, verbs and adjectives. Part B is carefully organized around language functions covering all major communication situations such as establishing identity, making contact and expressing likes, dislikes and preferences.

With a strong emphasis on contemporary usage, all grammar points and functions are richly illustrated with examples. Building on the success of the first edition, this edition also includes:

- An introduction to the history and current status of Brazilian Portuguese
- Notes for Spanish speakers pointing out the main grammatical differences between the two languages
- Additional explanation and exemplification of areas of particular difficulty for learners.

A combination of reference grammar and practical usage manual, *Modern Brazilian Portuguese Grammar* is the ideal source for learners of Brazilian Portuguese at all levels, from beginner to advanced.

John Whitlam is a freelance writer, university lecturer and lexicographer based in Rio de Janeiro. He has authored a number of language teaching books and project-coordinated and co-authored four best-selling bilingual dictionaries of Portuguese and English.

Routledge Modern Grammars

Other books in series:

Modern Brazilian Portuguese Grammar, Second Edition
Modern Brazilian Portuguese Grammar Workbook, Second Edition

Modern French Grammar, Second Edition
Modern French Grammar Workbook, Second Edition

Modern German Grammar, Second Edition
Modern German Grammar Workbook, Second Edition

Modern Italian Grammar, Third Edition
Modern Italian Grammar Workbook, Second Edition

Modern Japanese Grammar
Modern Japanese Grammar Workbook

Modern Korean Grammar
Modern Korean Grammar Workbook

Modern Mandarin Chinese Grammar
Modern Mandarin Chinese Grammar Workbook

Modern Russian Grammar
Modern Russian Grammar Workbook

Modern Spanish Grammar, Second Edition
Modern Spanish Grammar Workbook, Second Edition

Modern BRAZILIAN PORTUGUESE Grammar

A Practical Guide

Second Edition

John Whitlam

Routledge
Taylor & Francis Group
LONDON AND NEW YORK

Second edition published 2017
by Routledge
2 Park Square, Milton Park, Abingdon, Oxon OX14 4RN

and by Routledge
711 Third Avenue, New York, NY 10017

Routledge is an imprint of the Taylor & Francis Group, an informa business

First edition published by Routledge 2011

British Library Cataloguing-in-Publication Data
A catalogue record for this book is available from the British Library

Library of Congress Cataloging-in-Publication Data
Names: Whitlam, John, author.
Title: Modern Brazilian Portuguese grammar : a practical guide / John Whitlam.
Description: 2nd edition. | Milton Park, Abingdon, Oxon ; New York,
NY : Routledge, [2017] |
Includes bibliographical references and index.
Identifiers: LCCN 2016039749| ISBN 9781138646889 (hardback : alk. paper) |
ISBN 9781138646896 (pbk. : alk. paper) | ISBN 9781315627311 (ebook : alk. paper)
Subjects: LCSH: Portuguese language—Grammar. | Portuguese language—Textbooks
for foreign speakers—English. | Portuguese language—Spoken Portuguese.
Classification: LCC PC5444 .W45 2017 | DDC 469.7/981—dc23
LC record available at https://lccn.loc.gov/2016039749

ISBN: 978-1-138-64688-9 (hbk)
ISBN: 978-1-138-64689-6 (pbk)
ISBN: 978-1-315-62731-1 (ebk)

Typeset in Times and Akzidenz Grotesk
by Florence Production Ltd, Stoodleigh, Devon
Printed by CPI Group (UK) Ltd, Croydon CR0 4YY

Contents

Part A Structures

CONTENTS

CONTENTS

Part B   **Functions**

I   *Social contact and communication strategies*   267

CONTENTS

CONTENTS

CONTENTS

Preface to the second edition

My intention when I proposed the first edition of the Routledge *Modern Brazilian Portuguese Grammar* was to write the grammar I wished had existed when I myself first started studying the language more than thirty years ago. At that time, textbooks for English-speaking learners described European Portuguese, with Brazilian variants banished to appendices and footnotes, if mentioned at all. Even there, the information was sketchy and unreliable. Once I came to Brazil, I soon realized I could disregard most of what I had read in the books, especially as far as the spoken language was concerned. I longed for a comprehensive grammar book that dealt exclusively with Brazilian Portuguese and was not afraid to present and discuss the considerable differences between the spoken and written languages without value judgements. It took me thirty years, the last decade of which living in Brazil, to feel qualified enough even to attempt to write one myself.

The reaction to the first edition has been more than gratifying. In the intervening years, Brazil has grown immeasurably in economic importance and global prominence, while the expansion and affordability of mass travel means that more people than ever are able to visit the country for themselves. This has brought something of a boom in the study of specifically Brazilian Portuguese and whereas Portuguese has traditionally been studied as a minor or subsidiary to Spanish in the English-speaking world, it is now available as a major in many universities and colleges.

In this second edition, I have added new information where it may be useful and reformulated some parts of the text in the interests of clarity. One new feature in this second edition is the inclusion of a paragraph at the end of each chapter in the Structures section pointing out major differences between Portuguese and Spanish. These are for the benefit of the many students of Portuguese who already know some Spanish, but they can simply be ignored by those who do not. I have also included a new introduction to Brazilian Portuguese outlining how it has evolved since the discovery of Brazil in 1500 and some of the contemporary issues surrounding the language.

I would like to reiterate my thanks to Dr Beatriz Caldas for her perceptive and thought-provoking comments on the text of the first edition and to Andrea Hartill of Routledge for her continued confidence in me and support throughout. I am also grateful to all the friends, family, students and colleagues in Brazil who have, mostly unwittingly, served as informants for this book. This second edition is dedicated to the memory of Marcelo Affonso.

John Whitlam
Rio de Janeiro
November 2016

Introduction to this book

This book aims to provide a complete and practical guide to the Portuguese language as it is spoken and written in Brazil today. It is divided into two main parts: *Structures* and *Functions*.

Part A – Structures is a concise grammar of Brazilian Portuguese organized in the traditional way, describing the different grammatical features in turn. You can use this section both for systematic study of grammar and for quick reference when you want to know something about a particular form or structure (e.g. the subjunctive forms of a particular verb, how adjectives agree with nouns, when to use **ser** or **estar**, etc.).

Part B – Functions, which is the larger of the two parts, is organized according to the kinds of things you might want to say or write in particular situations in Portuguese, and here you can look up such things as how to apologize, how to say what you like and dislike, how to describe a person, etc. You will find that sometimes the same information is given in both parts of the book, although it is organized in a different way: in Part A by grammatical category and in Part B by linguistic function.

You will often want to refer back and forth between the two parts of the book; indeed, you are encouraged to do so, and to help you find what you are looking for, there are numerous cross-references indicated in the text or by arrows in the margin. There is also an index of words and topics at the back of the book so that you can find information again quickly and easily.

In Brazilian Portuguese there are considerable differences between informal and formal usage and between spoken and written language, and these are pointed out where appropriate. Every attempt has been made to reflect the register of different forms and structures in the content and translation of the numerous example sentences.

Traditional grammatical terms have been used, especially in the *Structures* part, though they are usually explained with reference to English. You can also find an explanation of any grammatical terms you may be unfamiliar with in the *Glossary*.

The following abbreviations have been used:

fem.	feminine
indic.	indicative
imperf.	imperfect
masc.	masculine
pl.	plural

pluperf.	pluperfect
pres.	present
sing.	singular
subj.	subjunctive.

Introduction to Brazilian Portuguese

Brazilian Portuguese vs. European Portuguese

Brazil is a country of a little over 200 million inhabitants, of which 99% have Portuguese as their mother tongue, with most of the remaining 1% proficient in Portuguese as a second language.[1] The process of divergence of Brazilian Portuguese from that spoken in Portugal dates back to the earliest days of the colonization of Brazil, from 1532 onwards. During this period, Portuguese, as spoken at court in Lisbon, was largely exclusive to the ruling elite, the law courts and the Church in Brazil, while the colonization and evangelization of the native population was conducted in the so-called *língua geral* ('general tongue'), a creolized version of the major indigenous language of the coastal region, Tupinambá, with a generous admixture of Portuguese vocabulary. Thus from the earliest times, European Portuguese was seen as the language of authority, used in writing and other formal contexts, while everyday exchanges between settlers and the indigenous population were in the *língua geral* and, increasingly over the course of time, pidgin Portuguese. As the use of Portuguese among the populace increased, it was inevitable that the contact between Portuguese speakers and local populations would lead to a simplification of some aspects of Portuguese grammar in the spoken language, a process that was subsequently compounded by the arrival of large numbers of slaves from Africa and speakers of different regional dialects of Portuguese among the substantial number of new settlers from Portugal attracted by the discovery of gold and diamonds in the interior of Brazil. After the use of Portuguese in the colony became compulsory in 1758 – a measure taken to reassert the authority of the Portuguese crown –, a number of different spoken variants could be identified: those of settlers from different regions of Portugal; those of indigenous tribes living in permanent contact with the Portuguese; that of people of mixed indigenous and Portuguese parentage; that of recently-arrived slaves from Africa; that of people of mixed African and Portuguese parentage; that used for communication between slaves and slave-owners and a hybrid of all these developing in the emerging cities. European Portuguese continued to be the standard used in writing and formal education. Not surprisingly, the spoken language saw the influx of a large number of words of indigenous origin, particularly to name plants, animals and other natural phenomena previously unknown in Europe, as well as the addition of some terms of African origin, and inevitable changes in the pronunciation of the language as a result of its adoption by

---

NOTE   1   The remaining 1% consists of indigenous peoples and a few immigrant communities that use German or Italian dialect as their first language.

3

non-native speakers. Add to this the fact that, between 1538 and 1850, around 70% of the Brazilian population were of indigenous, African or mixed-race origin, the vast majority of them enslaved and illiterate – as against only 30% of Portuguese descent – and it is easy to see why the spoken language of Brazil would develop into a variant distinct not only from the speech of Portugal, but also from the written standard used in the country, which was still largely identical to that of Portugal.

The influence of European Portuguese on the language of Brazil was given new impetus by the transfer of the Portuguese royal court from Lisbon to Rio de Janeiro in 1808 in the wake of Napoleon's invasion of Portugal. This renewed influence was due not so much to the arrival of the court itself, but rather to the influx of some 15,000 Portuguese who followed it to Rio. Its effects were particularly evident in the Portuguese of Rio de Janeiro itself (such as the pronunciation of syllable-final s as [ʃ], still today a distinctive feature of the Rio accent) but Rio's new-found status as royal capital ensured that some of this influence filtered through to other parts of Brazil, too.

Since Brazilian independence in 1822, subsequent waves of non-Portuguese-speaking immigrants (most significantly from Italy, Germany, Syria and Lebanon and Japan) have also had an influence on the syntax, vocabulary and pronunciation of Brazilian Portuguese. In the late 19th century, attempts were made to develop a distinctly Brazilian literary language, culminating in the works of the Brazilian Modernists in the 1920s and 30s, who brought elements of the spoken language into literary usage, giving their writing a distinctly Brazilian flavour. Nevertheless, the syntax of formal written Portuguese as used in official documents, the press and academic circles remained very close to that of Portugal.

There is a school of thought which maintains that, rather than diverging from European Portuguese under the influence of other languages, many so-called Brazilian features have their origins in the 15th century grammar and non-standard dialects of European Portuguese which were preserved in Brazil because of its remoteness from the standardizing dominance of the Lisbon dialect and subsequent linguistic developments there. These kinds of theories are difficult to prove or disprove conclusively, and the truth of the matter is most probably that Brazilian Portuguese has developed its distinctive characteristics through a combination of all these different factors and influences.

Despite the historical links which exist between Brazil and Portugal, the fact is that, for the vast majority of Brazilians today, except those descended from more recent Portuguese immigrants, Portugal is just another distant foreign land with no special significance. The considerable differences in pronunciation, vocabulary and syntax between the two varieties, compounded by the minimal exposure the overwhelming majority of Brazilians have to European Portuguese language and culture, mean that most Brazilians have some difficulty understanding European Portuguese speech. Consequently, on the rare occasions when a European Portuguese speaker appears on Brazilian TV, or when a Portuguese film is shown in Brazil, subtitles are usually provided for the benefit of the Brazilian audience. Interestingly, the reverse is not true: the popularity of Brazilian music and telenovelas in Portugal means that most Portuguese have a good understanding of spoken Brazilian. What is more, it is fair to say that the two varieties are diverging, rather than converging. One reason for this is that as the Brazilian written standard inevitably moves closer to the spoken language, it is becoming ever more distinct syntactically and idiomatically from European. Perhaps even more significant is the fact that the two varieties create neologisms independently, European being heavily influenced by French, Iberian Spanish and to a certain extent British English, while Brazilian is very much influenced by American English. Compare BP *celular* EP *telemóvel* 'cell/mobile phone', BP *tela* EP *ecrã* 'screen',

BP *mouse* EP *rato* '(computer) mouse', BP *AIDS* EP *Sida* 'Aids', BP *terceirizar* EP *externalizar* 'to outsource', BP *homem-bomba* EP *homem kamikaze* 'suicide bomber', BP *time* EP *equipa* '(sports) team', BP *blogueiro* EP *bloguista* 'blogger', etc. Examples of this type run into the hundreds, adding to the already large number of lexical differences between the two variants. Furthermore, there is no single authority similar to the *Académie Française* in French or the *Real Academia* in Spanish that dictates global Portuguese usage.

Brazilian vs. European spelling

The Brazilian Academy of Letters put forward the first proposals for a spelling reform in 1907. The aim was to make spelling more phonetic and less etymological, as at that time Portuguese spelling was still very close to Latin. The proposals were not initially adopted, and even though the Lisbon Academy of Sciences successfully introduced a similar reform in Portugal in 1911, it was another 20 years before Brazil adhered to the changes. The reform did away with all doubled consonants except *rr* and *ss*, many silent consonants and the letters *k* and *y*, replacing them with *qu/c* and *i* respectively. In addition, the combinations *ph*, *rh* and *th* were simplified to *f*, *r/rr* and t respectively, and *ch* to *qu* or *c* in words where it represented that sound (e.g. *chimica* > *química*, *Christo* > *Cristo*). The reform also introduced written accents on proparoxytone words (those with the stress on the third last syllable). The difference in the pronunciation of *e* and *o* before *m* and *n* in such words means that they are spelt with a circumflex accent in Brazilian (e.g. *polêmico*, *crônica*) and an acute accent in European (*polémico*, *crónica*).

In Brazil, a further reform was introduced in 1943 which among other things did away with all silent consonants (except word-initial h). The Portuguese had drawn up new reform proposals of their own in 1940 and this gave rise to a joint Spelling Agreement between the two countries in 1945. However, this agreement was never approved by the Brazilian congress, probably because it would have reintroduced many European features into the spelling which would have been at odds with Brazilian pronunciation, such as the inclusion of silent letters and use of the acute accent instead of the circumflex before *m* and *n* in proparoxytone words. Thus, Brazil continued to abide by its own reform of 1943, introducing further modifications to the rules of accentuation in 1971. Most of these were also adopted in Portugal two years later.

The proponents of a unified spelling continued to pursue their objective through the 1970s and 80s, despite strong resistance or plain indifference to the issue on both sides of the Atlantic, culminating in the Spelling Agreement of 1990 between all the Portuguese-speaking countries under the aegis of the Lisbon Academy of Sciences and the Brazilian Academy of Letters. But after a further five years, only three countries had ratified the agreement, Brazil among them, so it could not be implemented across the Lusophone world. In 2004, the combined heads of state of the recently founded Community of Portuguese-speaking Countries (CPLP) signed a protocol stipulating that the agreement only required ratification by three countries to be imposed on all the others. This condition was met in 2006, but Portugal itself did not ratify the agreement until 2008 against fierce resistance from some academics and writers, who saw the reform as heavily weighted in favour of Brazilian spelling. It is certainly true that the terms of the reform had a much greater impact on European Portuguese than on Brazilian. This may explain why the reform generated far less opposition in Brazil, but it also reveals a lot about Brazilian attitudes to the (written) language. While the issue of spelling reform was hotly debated in the media in Portugal, with hearings and surveys conducted to gauge public opinion and many questioning the legitimacy of the agencies involved to legislate on the language, in Brazil it was presented to the public as a fait accompli and unquestioningly espoused by the mass media. The reform was introduced on 1 January 2009 with a transition period until the end of 2012, later extended to end 2015. It is difficult to see the justification for the expense and confusion caused on both sides of the Atlantic by a reform intended to harmonize spelling when European and Brazilian are so different from one another syntactically, lexically and phonetically. Indeed, the 2009 reform has had to allow some divergent spellings to account for certain divergent pronunciations. Needless to say, the spelling differences that existed pre-reform had never posed any problems for readers of either variant. Meanwhile, the Brazilian Academy of Letters has already announced its intention to introduce further adjustments post-2016.

The Academy publishes the *Vocabulário Ortográfico da Língua Portuguesa*, a list of 381,000 words (5th edition, 2009) which can also be consulted online (http://www.academia. org.br/nossa-lingua/busca-no-vocabulario) to check spellings. However, like any other dictionary, it will never be able to list all the words in the language or stay totally up to date with new vocabulary.

Spoken vs. written Brazilian Portuguese

For the historical reasons outlined above, spoken Brazilian Portuguese has been going its own way since the 16th century, while the written language has remained close to the European standard, particularly in more formal registers. Indeed, it is probably still true to say that the more formal a Brazilian text is, the more it will resemble European Portuguese[2]. In Brazilian, the differences between the spoken and written languages are largely syntactic and have to do in particular with the usage of personal pronouns, prepositions, demonstratives, possessives and, to a lesser extent, the use of certain verb forms and tenses. There are also some issues surrounding the countability of nouns (singular vs. plural).

The approach to teaching Portuguese grammar in Brazilian schools has always been very conservative and there is a strong prescriptive bias in dictionaries and grammars, which has reinforced and perpetuated the gulf between spoken and written language, while also promoting the notion that Portuguese as it is spoken in Brazil is somehow substandard, or plain incorrect. The grammar of the written language is generally regarded with some trepidation by native speakers. If the subject gets onto Portuguese, most Brazilians will describe it as "very difficult" with "a lot of little rules" and many will lament the fact that "Brazilians don't speak Portuguese correctly." This last statement is clearly a misconception engendered by the prescriptivism of school Portuguese classes and the media[3], but the other two reveal how insecure many Brazilians feel about using the written standard, which requires adopting a different syntax and attention to all the "little rules" memorized at school. Needless to say, there is also a great deal of prejudice and elitism surrounding correct use of this standard.

NOTE

2   This is not to say that European Portuguese is a homogeneous entity with no difference between the spoken and written languages. But in European Portuguese – like English – the syntax of spoken and written varieties is essentially the same, a continuum so to speak, with certain constructions perceived as more or less formal.

3   A very lucrative industry has grown up around teaching Portuguese to adults, especially for the purposes of public service selection tests with their promise of a secure job for life. There are countless manuals, websites devoted to grammar queries and a number of famous so-called grammar experts who regularly appear in the media to comment on linguistic issues. In most cases, all of these merely trot out the same old rules; there is little or no acceptance of the fact that grammar may evolve over time.

Any grammar of Brazilian Portuguese written for foreign learners must acknowledge and address the difference between the spoken and written languages because, in order to be able to communicate appropriately in all contexts (spoken and written), the learner must be able to switch between spoken and written syntax in the same way that native speakers do. It is important to note that the distinction spoken vs. written is not synonymous with the distinction informal vs. formal: spoken language is not necessarily informal and written language not necessarily formal. In fact, most spoken or written language – in all languages – is neutral in register, neither markedly informal nor especially formal. Furthermore, there are varying degrees of (in)formality. Of course, the spoken vs. written dichotomy is also flawed because there are many situations where the distinction is difficult to draw, such as delivering a prepared speech or presentation (speaking written language) or writing a text message to a friend (writing spoken language), and contexts where the two modes overlap (advertising copy, dialogue in a novel, film and TV subtitles, popular magazine articles written in conversational style, etc.). But, even with these caveats, spoken vs. written is the most useful distinction to bring to the analysis of Brazilian syntax for foreign learners. Social class and level of education are also irrelevant here: those with access to a good education may become more proficient at using the written standard, but they will still use spoken language syntax in their speech, and this is remarkably uniform across the social spectrum.

The advent of new forms of communication and, in particular, the increased use of writing in informal contexts (messaging, social media, etc.) are leading to a blurring of the once clearly defined boundaries between written and spoken language and consequently to a reduction in the differences between the two modes. While certain elements of spoken language syntax may never be accepted in formal writing and school and public service examinations, informal writing, with a much greater admixture of spoken language features, is gaining ground as a new type of discourse, in popular literature, magazines, advertisements and publicity materials, customer relations, blogs and social media. The democratization of language through these channels will probably end up sweeping away the prejudice and elitism that have beset the language debate in Brazil for so long.

Regional variation vs. national standard

In a vast country like Brazil, it is only natural for there to be a good deal of regional variation, particularly in accent and pronunciation and to a lesser extent in vocabulary, idiom and syntax. Nevertheless, the "educated urban standard" (*norma urbana culta*) spoken in the larger conurbations is remarkably uniform across the country, largely due to the influence of television, a medium very much dominated by the major networks, all of which are based in Rio and São Paulo. Thus, although a great many Brazilian speakers do not palatalize *d* and *t* before an [i] sound, the palatalized pronunciation (as [dʒ] and [tʃ] respectively) has become standard because of its predominance in Rio and São Paulo. Nowadays, the 'standard' is much closer to the São Paulo accent than to that of Rio, which was once considered the model to be emulated when Rio was still the capital of the country. For example, the *paulista* syllable-final s pronounced [s] has long since superseded the *carioca* [ʃ] pronunciation as the standard.

It is this spoken standard that is described in this Grammar, alongside the written language. Too much information can be confusing, so a deliberate decision has been made not to describe non-standard spoken forms and usage, however common they may be in a particular region or among certain groups.

Glossary of grammatical terms

Small capitals indicate that the word is described elsewhere in the Glossary.

Active see **Voice**

Adjectives (see **Chapters 2**, **3** and **5**)
Adjectives are words that describe NOUNS, and they agree in NUMBER (singular or plural) and GENDER (masculine or feminine) with the noun they describe:

> **O apartamento é pequeno.**
> The apartment is small.

> **As casas são espaçosas.**
> The houses are spacious.

Adjectives in Portuguese may also function as NOUNS (see **5.4**) and as ADVERBS (see **5.5**).

Adverbs
Adverbs are words that tell you something about a VERB, an ADJECTIVE or another adverb:

> **Ele sempre atrasa.**
> He's always late.

> **A Júlia é extremamente inteligente.**
> Julia is extremely intelligent.

> **Falam muito rápido.**
> They talk very fast.

Agent
The performer of a verbal action: in an ACTIVE sentence, the agent is typically the SUBJECT of the sentence; in a PASSIVE sentence, the agent (the subject of the corresponding active sentence) is usually introduced by 'by' in English and by **por** in Portuguese.

Antecedent (see **Chapter 10**)
This is the noun to which a RELATIVE CLAUSE pertains, and which usually stands immediately before the relative PRONOUN:

> **O rapaz que está falando com a Cristina é meu primo.**
> The guy who is talking to Cristina is my cousin.

> **O carro que compramos é verde.**
> The car we bought is green.

Articles (see **Chapter 4**)

There are two kinds of article in Portuguese: definite articles: **o**, **a**, **os**, **as** 'the'; indefinite articles: **um**, **uma** 'a(n)':

> **A praia é longe daqui.**
> The beach is a long way from here.

> **Tem uma livraria por aqui?**
> Is there a bookshop around here?

Auxiliary verbs (see **17.3**, **17.4**, **24.1**)

This is the name given to certain very common verbs that regularly combine with other verb forms. For example, in Portuguese **ter** is the perfect auxiliary and combines with the PAST PARTICIPLE to make the compound tenses (see **17.3**).

Clause

A clause is a sentence within a sentence, recognizable because it contains a verb of its own. Clauses that can stand on their own are called main clauses, while those that cannot stand alone and must be combined with a main clause are called subordinate clauses:

> **Se chover, vou ficar em casa**.
> If it rains, I'm going to stay at home.

> **Eu acho que ele tem razão**.
> I think he's right.

In the examples above, **vou ficar em casa** and **eu acho** are the main clauses, while **se chover** and **que ele tem razão** are subordinate clauses.

Conjunctions (see **Chapter 26**)

Conjunctions join words or groups of words. They are words like **e** 'and', **ou** 'or', **mas** 'but', **porque** 'because', etc.:

> **Ele chega amanhã ou depois de amanhã**
> He arrives tomorrow or the day after tomorrow.

> **Ela trabalhou até tarde porque tinha muito o que fazer**.
> She worked late because she had a lot to do.

Demonstratives (see **Chapter 8**)

Demonstratives indicate proximity or remoteness, e.g. **este** 'this', **aquele** 'that'.

Diphthong (see **1.3** and **1.4**)

A diphthong is a sequence of two vowels in the same syllable.

Direct object see **Object**

Gender (see **Chapter 2**)

Portuguese has two genders, masculine and feminine. For example, **a mesa** 'the table' is feminine, while **o carro** 'the car' is masculine. ADJECTIVES, ARTICLES, DEMONSTRATIVES, POSSESSIVES and PRONOUNS must agree in gender with the noun they refer to.

Gerund (see **17.1**)

Gerunds are forms like **estudando** 'studying', **fazendo** 'doing'.

Imperative see **Mood**

Indicative see **Mood**

Indirect object see **Object**

Infinitive (see **Chapter 19**)
This is the base form of the Portuguese verb, as it normally appears in a dictionary, e.g. **cantar** 'to sing', **beber** 'to drink'. In Portuguese, the infinitive can be impersonal or personal: an impersonal infinitive is one that has a general meaning or that has the same SUBJECT as an AUXILIARY or MODAL VERB used with it; a personal infinitive is one that has a SUBJECT of its own:

> **Eles querem voltar.**
> They want to come back.

> **Vamos esperar até eles voltarem.**
> Let's wait until they get back.

In the first example above, **voltar** is an impersonal infinitive with the same subject as **querem**; in the second example, **voltarem** is a personal infinitive with its own subject, **eles**.

Intransitive verb
An intransitive verb is one that cannot take a direct OBJECT, e.g. **ir** 'to go', **dormir** 'to sleep'.

Modal verb (see **24.2**)
A modal verb, or modal AUXILIARY, is one that combines with another verb to express shades of meaning such as desire, possibility, obligation, ability, etc. Examples in Portuguese are: **querer** 'want', **poder** 'can, may, might', **dever** 'should, must', etc.

Mood
In Portuguese it is usual to refer to the indicative (see **Chapter 18**), the subjunctive (see **Chapter 20**) and the imperative (see **Chapter 21**) as different moods of the verb:

> **Ela mora em Sorocaba.**
> She lives in Sorocaba.

> **Tomara que não chova.**
> Let's hope it doesn't rain.

> **Fecha a porta.**
> Close the door.

As a rough guide, the indicative mood is associated with statements and assertions, the imperative with orders and commands, and the subjunctive with a wide range of subordinate CLAUSE usages.

Nouns
Nouns typically denote things, people, animals or abstract concepts, e.g. **mesa**, **João**, **garota**, **camelo**, **beleza**, **razão**.

Number
Portuguese, like English, distinguishes singular and plural number, e.g. **a criança** 'the child' (sing.), **as crianças** 'the children' (pl.).

Object

The object of a verb is a NOUN or PRONOUN that is affected by the action of the verb. It is usual to distinguish between direct objects and indirect objects: a direct object is directly affected by the action of the verb, while an indirect object is indirectly affected:

> **Ela me deu um presente.**
> She gave me a present.

In this sentence, **um presente** is the direct object of the verb **deu** while **me** is the indirect object.

Object pronoun

An object pronoun is a word that substitutes a noun, usually to avoid repetition, and that functions as the OBJECT of a verb. Like objects, object pronouns can be direct or indirect:

> **Ele me ama.**
> He loves me. (*me is the direct object of amar*)

> **Ele me mostrou as fotos.**
> He showed me the photos. (*me is the indirect object of mostrar*)

Passive see **Voice**

Past participle

A past participle is that part of the verb that is used to form the compound perfect and pluperfect tenses (see **17.2**):

> **Ele tinha esquecido.**
> He had forgotten.

> **Não tem sido fácil.**
> It hasn't been easy.

Past participles are also used to form the PASSIVE (see **17.4**) and can function as ADJECTIVES (see **17.5**). In these two cases, they must agree in GENDER and NUMBER with the noun they refer to:

> **alimentos congelados**
> frozen foods

> **A casa foi destruída.**
> The house was destroyed.

Person

A category of personal pronouns (see **Chapter 7**), POSSESSIVES (see **Chapter 9**) and verb forms (see **Chapter 15**) indicating relationship to the speaker. There are three persons: the first person ('I', 'we'), the second person ('you') and the third person ('he', 'she', 'it', 'they').

Possessives (see **Chapter 9**)

Adjectives or pronouns that indicate to whom or to what someone or something belongs:

> **os nossos amigos**
> our friends

> **Esses livros são meus.**
> These books are mine.

Preposition (see **Chapter 25**)

A preposition is a word such as **em** 'in', 'on', 'at', **com** 'with', **entre** 'between' 'among' that gives information about location, time, direction, etc:

> **Ela está em casa.**
> She's at home. (*place*)

> **Eles mudaram para São Paulo.**
> They moved to São Paulo. (*direction*)

> **Trabalhei até meia-noite.**
> I worked until midnight. (*time*)

Pronoun

A pronoun is a word that takes the place of a noun or noun phrase, usually to avoid repetition:

> **Conhece o Felipe? Ele é meu primo.**
> Do you know Felipe? He's my cousin.

> **O seu carro é maior do que o meu.**
> Your car is bigger than mine.

Reflexive (see **Chapter 22**)

A reflexive verb form involves the use of an OBJECT PRONOUN that refers back to the SUBJECT of the verb, e.g. **eu me cortei** 'I cut myself'. However, reflexive verbs in Portuguese have other meanings that do not involve the subject doing something to him-, her- or itself. These are explained in **Chapter 22**.

Relative clause

A relative clause is a group of words within a sentence, containing a verb and introduced by a RELATIVE PRONOUN. The relative pronoun refers back to a preceding noun or pronoun (the ANTECEDENT) and the purpose of the relative clause is to further define that noun or pronoun or to provide additional information about it:

> **Você está vendo aquele homem de terno que está sentado ali?**
> Do you see that man in a suit who's sitting over there?

> **A cidade onde eu moro fica a 100 km daqui.**
> The town where I live is 100 km from here.

Relative pronoun (see **Chapter 10**)

A relative pronoun is a word such as **que**, **quem**, **onde**, etc. that is used to introduce a RELATIVE CLAUSE:

> **Estou gostando muito do livro que estou lendo.**
> I'm really enjoying the book I'm reading.

> **A mulher com quem eu falava é a minha tia.**
> The woman I was talking to is my aunt.

Relative pronouns can often be omitted in English, as the translations above show, but they can never be omitted in Portuguese.

Subject

The subject is the word or group of words in a sentence that designates the person or thing performing the action of the verb:

O português não é difícil.
Portuguese is not difficult.

Susana e Pedro vão casar.
Susana and Pedro are going to get married.

Tense (see **Chapter 18**)

Tenses are different forms of the verb that refer to different times. The present, the future, the imperfect, etc. are traditionally known as the tenses of the verb:

Ele mora em Paris.
He lives in Paris. (*verb in the present tense*)

Ele morou um ano em Londres.
He lived for a year in London. (*verb in the past tense*)

Transitive

A transitive verb is one that has a direct OBJECT, e.g. **tomar (cerveja)** 'to drink (beer)', **conhecer (a Ana)** 'to know (Ana)'.

Triphthong

A sequence of three vowel sounds in the same syllable.

Verb

Verbs usually denote actions or states, but they can also convey other ideas, such as transformations:

Ele trabalha numa fábrica.
He works in a factory.

Eles estão cansados.
They are tired.

Começou a chover.
It started to rain.

Voice

The voice of a verb is either active or passive. When a verb is in the active voice, the SUBJECT is doing the action of the verb; when a verb is in the passive voice, the subject is being affected by the action of the verb:

A cobra mordeu o cachorro.
The snake bit the dog. (*verb in the active voice*)

O cachorro foi mordido por uma cobra.
The dog was bitten by a snake. (*verb in the passive voice*)

Part A

Structures

1

Pronunciation and spelling

The Portuguese alphabet

The Portuguese alphabet comprises the same letters as the English alphabet, but notice how the names of the letters are pronounced:

Letter	Name	Pronunciation	Letter	Name	Pronunciation
A, a	a	[a]	**N, n**	ene	['ɛni]
B, b	bê	[be]	**O, o**	o	[ɔ] or [o]
C, c	cê	[se]	**P, p**	pê	[pe]
D, d	dê	[de]	**Q, q**	quê	[ke]
E, e	e	[ɛ] or [e]	**R, r**	erre	['ɛhi]
F, f	efe	['ɛfi]	**S, s**	esse	['ɛsi]
G, g	gê	[ʒe]	**T, t**	tê	[te]
H, h	agá	[a'ga]	**U, u**	u	[u]
I, i	i	[i]	**V, v**	vê	[ve]
J, j	jota	['ʒɔta]	**W, w**	dábliu	['dablju]
K, k	cá	[ka]	**X, x**	xis	[ʃis]
L, l	ele	['ɛli]	**Y, y**	ípsilon	['ipsilõ]
M, m	eme	['ɛmi]	**Z, z**	zê	[ze]

NOTES

(i) Notice in particular the names of the letters *h*, *j*, *x* and *y*, and take care not to confuse *e* and *i* and *k* and *q*.

(ii) The 'official' pronunciation of the names of the letters *e* and *o* is [ɛ] and [ɔ] respectively, but many Brazilians, notably from São Paulo southwards, pronounce them [e] and [o] respectively (see **1.3.2**).

(iii) The letters *k*, *w* and *y* are normally only used in foreign words and proper names.

(iv) *H* also forms part of the two-letter combinations **ch**, **lh** and **nh** (see **1.2**).

Pronunciation of consonants

The consonants **b**, **f**, **k**, **p** and **v** are pronounced as in English.

Other consonants:

c [k] as in *cap* before *a*, *o* and *u*: **café** [ka'fɛ] 'coffee';
[s] as in *cite* before *e* and *i*: **centro** ['sẽtru] 'centre';
ç [s] as in *cite*: **raça** ['hasa] 'race';
ch [ʃ] as in *shop*: **choque** ['ʃɔki] 'shock';
d [d] as in *day* before *a*, *e*, *o*, *u*: **dado** ['dadu] 'dice';

[dʒ] as in *Jill* before *i* and unstressed final *e*: **dia** ['dʒia] 'day', **sede** ['sedʒi] 'thirst' – see note (i) below;

g [g] as in *game* before *a, o* and *u*: **gás** [gas] 'gas';
[ʒ] as in *measure* before *e* and *i*: **gente** ['ʒẽtʃi] 'people';

gu [gw] as in *Gwyneth* before *a* and *o*: **guarda** ['gwarda] 'guard';
[g] as in *get* before *e* and *i*: **guerra** ['gɛha] 'war' – see note (ii) below;

h silent in word-initial position: **herói** [e'rɔj] 'hero', hora ['ɔra] 'hour', except in some words of foreign origin, where it is pronounced [h] as in English: **hall** [haw] 'hall', **hóquei** ['hɔkej] 'hockey';
see separate alphabetical entries for the two-letter combinations **ch, lh** and **nh**;

j [ʒ] as in *measure*: **já** [ʒa] 'already';

l [l] as in *land* before a vowel: **longe** ['lõʒi] 'far';
[w] as in *how* before a consonant or at the end of a word: **alto** ['awtu] 'high', **mil** [miw] 'thousand';

lh [ʎ] as in *million*: **olho** ['oʎu] 'eye';

m [m] as in *man* before a vowel: **motor** [mo'tor] 'engine';
before a consonant or at the end of a word, it is not pronounced as a separate letter, but merely serves to indicate that the preceding vowel is nasal (see **1.4.1**): **tempo** ['tẽpu] 'time';

n [n] as in *no* before a vowel: **nada** ['nada] 'nothing';
before a consonant or at the end of a word, it is not pronounced as a separate letter, but merely serves to indicate that the preceding vowel is nasal (see **1.4.1**): **pronto** ['prõtu] 'ready';

nh [ỹ] is a nasalized *y* sound, similar to the *ni* in *onion*: **vinho** ['viỹu] 'wine';

qu [kw] as in *quake* before *a* and *o*: **quatro** ['kwatru] 'four';
[k] as in *bouquet* before *e* and *i*: **que** [ke] 'that' – see note (ii) below;

r is pronounced as a single trill, as in Spanish, Italian and Scottish English, between vowels and after most consonants (*b, c, d, f, g, k, p, t, v*): **caro** ['karu] 'expensive', **fraco** ['fraku] 'weak'. The single trill pronunciation may also be considered the standard in syllable-final position, i.e. before another consonant and in word-final position (except in the infinitive form of verbs): **porta** ['pɔrta] 'door', **azar** [a'zar] 'bad luck' – see note (iii) below;
in word-initial position and after the consonants *m* and *n* (indicating a preceding nasal vowel), *l* and *s*, it is pronounced like the English [h] in *hot*: **rio** ['hiu] 'river', **genro** ['ʒẽhu] 'son-in-law', **guelra** ['gɛwha] 'gill', **Israel** [izha'ɛw] 'Israel';
as the final letter of an infinitive verb, it is not usually pronounced at all: **amar** [a'maʳ] 'to love', **fazer** [fa'zeʳ] 'to do, make', **pedir** [pe'dʒiʳ] 'to ask for', though it is usually reinstated as a single trill when the following word starts with a vowel: **fazer isso** [fa'ze 'risu] 'to do this';

rr [h] as in *hot*: **carro** ['kahu] 'car';

s [s] as in *sing* at the beginning of a word, after a consonant or nasal vowel or before a voiceless consonant (*c, f, p, qu, t*): **som** [sõw] 'sound', **urso** ['ursu] 'bear', **tenso** ['tẽsu], **ostra** ['ostra] 'oyster';
[z] as in *zoo* between vowels or before a voiced consonant (*b, d, g, l, m, n, r, v*): **rosa** ['hoza] 'rose', **asma** ['azma] 'asthma';
[s] at the end of a word: **mês** [mes] 'month', **carros** ['kahus] 'cars', except when there is a word following in the same phrase which begins with a vowel or voiced consonant (*b, d, g, l, m, n, r, v*), in which case it is pronounced [z] and the two words are run together: **aquelas árvores** [a'kɛlaz'arvoris] 'those trees', **as mulheres** [azmu'ʎɛris] 'the women', **eles estão** ['elizis'tãw] 'they are' – see note (iv) below;

ss [s] as in *sing*: **isso** ['isu] 'that';

t [t] as in *top* before *a, e, o, u*: **tatu** [ta'tu] 'armadillo';

[tʃ] as in *chip* before *i* and unstressed final *e*: **tia** ['tʃia] 'aunt', **forte** ['fɔrtʃi] 'strong' – see note (i) below;

w pronounced [u], it only occurs in foreign words and proper names: **webcam** [uɛbi'kã] 'webcam', **Woody** ['udʒi] (*American name*). In many Brazilian proper names, it is pronounced [v]: **Wanderlei** [vãder'lei];

x [ʃ] as in *shop* in word-initial position: **xale** ['ʃali] 'shawl'
[s] before a voiceless consonant (*c, f, p, qu, t*): **extra** ['ɛstra] 'extra';
[z] in words beginning *ex-* followed by a vowel and before a voiced consonant (*b, d, g, l, m, n, r, v*): **exame** [e'zami] 'exam', **ex-mulher** [ezmu'ʎɛr] 'ex-wife' – see note (iv) below;
[ʃ] as in *shop* between vowels: **caixa** ['kajʃa] 'box', except in the following cases:
[s] in **auxílio, máximo, próximo, sintaxe, trouxe** and derivatives;
[ks] in **anexo, axila, complexo, fixo, flexão, fluxo, hexa-, léxico, maxilar, nexo, ortodoxo, óxido, oxigênio, paradoxo, reflexo, sexa-, sexo, táxi, tóxico** and derivatives;
[ks] in word-final position: **box** [bɔks] 'booth, stall', **duplex** [du'plɛks] 'duplex apartment', except in the informal use of **ex** as a noun meaning 'ex' (husband, girlfriend, etc.), pronounced [e(j)s];

y pronounced [i], it only occurs in foreign words and proper names: **Nova York** ['nɔva i'ɔrki] 'New York';

z [z] as in *zoo*, though may also be heard as [s] in word-final position: **zebra** ['zebra] 'zebra', **luz** [luz] or [lus] 'light' – see note (iv) below.

NOTES

(i) The pronunciation of *d* and *t* as [dʒ] and [tʃ] respectively before a phonetic [i] sound is a phenomenon called palatalization and is very characteristic of Brazilian Portuguese. While there are many Brazilian speakers who do not palatalize *d* and *t* before [i], the palatalized pronunciation may be regarded as the standard and should be imitated by foreign learners. Palatalization occurs before the letter *i* and before unstressed *e* when it is pronounced as [i], most notably at the end of a word and in the prefix **des-**.

(ii) In some words, the *u* is pronounced as a separate letter before *e* and *i*, e.g. **aguentar** [agwẽ'tar] 'to stand, withstand', **frequente** [fre'kwẽtʃi] 'frequent', **linguiça** [lĩ'gwisa] 'sausage', **quinquagésimo** [kwĩkwa'gɛzimu] 'fiftieth'. Before the 2009 spelling reform, such cases were indicated in writing by placing a diaeresis over the *u* (**ü**), but this convention was abolished in the reform, making it necessary to consult a dictionary when in doubt about the pronunciation.

(iii) There is considerable regional variation in the pronunciation of *r*, especially in syllable-final position, and it is one of the ways of detecting where someone is from. The 'standard' pronunciation of syllable-final *r* is heard in the city of São Paulo and much of the south, while in Rio and Bahia, it is pronounced as a guttural [χ] sound, like the *ch* in the German word *Achtung*: ['pɔʃta, a'zaʒ]. In the interior of São Paulo state, Minas Gerais and much of the midwest, it is realized as a retroflex *r*, similar to the American or British West Country pronunciation of *r* as in *car*: ['pɔɻta, a'zaɻ]. This retroflex pronunciation is considered to be characteristic of people from the countryside. In some regions, word-final *r* is always dropped.

(iv) Syllable-final [s] and [z] are pronounced as [ʃ] and [ʒ] in some parts of Brazil, especially the states of Rio de Janeiro and Pará. This pronunciation once had prestige as being that of the former capital, but is nowadays felt to be a regional phenomenon.

1.3 Oral vowel sounds

1.3.1 *a, i, u*

a [a] as in *father*: **carro** ['kahu] 'car'
i [i] as in *machine*: **fino** ['finu] 'fine'
u [u] as in *rune*: **rua** ['hua] 'street'.

1.3.2   **e and o**

When stressed, the letters *e* and *o* each have two possible pronunciations depending on the particular word[1]:

e   [e] similar to *ay* in *day*: **cedo** ['sedu] 'early', or
    [ɛ] as in *bed*: **cego** ['sɛgu] 'blind';
o   [o] as in *bone*: **cor** [kor] 'colour', or
    [ɔ] as in *top*: **copo** ['kɔpu] 'glass'.

NOTE   1   When stressed *e* or *o* is unaccented, there is no way of knowing which of the two pronunciations is required other than by memorization. A few pairs of words are differentiated only by the pronunciation of the tonic vowel, e.g. **forma** ['fɔrma] 'way, form' vs. **forma** ['forma] 'baking tin, mould', **sede** ['sɛdʒi] 'headquarters, clubhouse' vs. **sede** ['sedʒi] 'thirst'. The pair **o corte** ['kɔrtʃi] 'cut' and **a corte** ['kortʃi] 'court' are also differentiated by gender.

When the rules of accentuation require stressed *e* and *o* to carry a written accent (see **1.7**), the circumflex accent (^) is used to indicate the so-called close pronunciation of each, [e]/[o], and the acute accent (´) to indicate the open pronunciation [ɛ]/[ɔ]:

ê   [e]: **gênero** ['ʒeneru] 'gender, genre', **você** [vo'se] 'you'
é   [ɛ]: **péssimo** ['pɛsimu] 'terrible', **café** [ka'fɛ] 'coffee'
ô   [o]: **eletrônico** [ele'troniku] 'electronic', **robô** [ho'bo] 'robot'
ó   [ɔ]: **hóspede** ['ɔspedʒi] 'guest', **nó** [nɔ] 'knot'.

When unstressed, the pronunciation of *e* and *o* varies according to the position in the word:

e   [e] in most unstressed positions: **exato** [e'zatu] 'exact';
    [i] as in *movie* in word-final position: **mole** ['mɔli] 'soft';
o   [o] in most unstressed positions: **tomate** [to'matʃi] 'tomato';
    [u] as in *into* in word-final position: **sapato** [sa'patu] 'shoe'.[2]

NOTE   2   Many speakers pronounce unstressed *e* and *o* as [i] and [u] respectively in other positions too, and the negative prefix **des-** is always pronounced [dʒis/dʒiz] in normal speech.

The unstressed word-final pronunciation also applies before final **-s**:

cones ['kɔnis] 'cones', **simples** ['sĩplis] 'simple', **patos** ['patus] 'ducks', **falamos** [fa'lamus] 'we speak'.

See also **1.5.10** below on the alternation between [e] and [ɛ] and between [o] and [ɔ] in some words.

1.3.3   **Oral diphthongs**

The following vowel combinations form diphthongs consisting of a vowel + semivowel sound. Notice that the combination of a vowel followed by syllable-final *l* (pronounced [w]) also produces a diphthong:

ai   [aj] as in *Kaiser*: **cais** [kajs] 'quay';
au, al   [aw] like *ow* in *now*: **mau** [maw] 'bad', **mal** [maw] 'badly';

ei	[ej] like *ey* in *hey*: **rei** [hej] 'king';
éi, ei	[ɛj] like *e* in *bed* followed by *y*: **papéis** [pa'pɛjs] 'papers', **ideia** [i'dɛja] 'idea';
eu, el	[ew] like *ay* in *day* followed by *w*: **meu** [mew] 'my', **feltro** ['fewtru] 'felt';
éu, el	[ɛw] like *e* in *bed* followed by *w*: **céu** [sɛw] 'sky', **mel** [mɛw] 'honey';
iu, il	[iw] like *i* in *machine* followed by *w*: **riu** [hiw] '(he) laughed', **vinil** [vi'niw] 'vinyl';
oi	[oj] like *oy* in *boy*: **noite** ['nojtʃi] 'night';
ói, oi	[ɔj] like *o* in *top* followed by *y*: **lençóis** [lẽ'sɔjs] 'sheets', **heroico** [e'rɔjku] 'heroic';
ol	[ɔw] like *o* in *top* followed by *w*: **lençol** [lẽ'sɔw] 'sheet';
ou, ol	[ow] like *ow* in *show*: **sou** [sow] 'I am', **toldo** ['towdu] 'awning';
ui	[uj] like *ewy* in *chewy*: **fui** [fuj] 'I was, I went';
ul	[uw] like *u* in *rune* followed by *w*: **sul** [suw] 'south'.

1.3.4 Oral triphthongs

There are four oral triphthongs that only occur after [g] and [k] (spelt *g* and *q*):

uai	[waj] like *why*: **quais?** [kwajs] 'which ones?';
ual	[waw] like the exclamation *wow*: **qual?** [kwaw] 'which one?';
uei	[wej] like *way*: **averiguei** [averi'gwej] 'I ascertained';
uou	[wow] like the exclamation *whoa*: **averiguou** [averi'gwow] 'he ascertained'.

1.4 Nasal vowel sounds

1.4.1

The nasal vowel sounds are very characteristic of Portuguese and differ from the oral vowel sounds in that, when you pronounce them, you allow air to pass through your nose as well as your mouth. To get the feel of nasal vowels, try saying 'aah!' as you would for the doctor and then, without stopping, push some of the air up through your nose. It should sound something like 'aang', but not quite the same.

There are five nasal vowels in Portuguese, and nasalization is indicated in spelling by placing a tilde (~) above the vowel or by the presence of *m* or *n* following the vowel in the same syllable. The letter *m* is used in word final position[3] and before *b* and *p*, the letter *n* before all other consonants. It is important to note that, in such cases, *m* and *n* are not themselves pronounced as separate sounds, e.g. **campo** 'field' is pronounced ['kãpu], and not *['kãmpu] or *['kampu], **lindo** 'beautiful' is pronounced ['lĩdu], and not *['lĩndu] or *['lindu]:

ã, am, an	[ã]: **ímã** ['imã] 'magnet', **cantar** [kã'tar] 'to sing'; in unstressed word-final position, **am** is pronounced [ãw]: **falam** ['falãw] 'they speak' (see **1.4.2** below);
em, en	[ẽ]: **membro** ['mẽbru] 'member', **venda** ['vẽda] 'sale'; when word-final and stressed, pronounced as a diphthong [ẽj] (see **1.4.2** below);
im, in	[ĩ]: **sim** [sĩ] 'yes', **pintar** [pĩ'tar] 'to paint';
om, on	[õ]: **compra** ['kõpra] 'purchase', **honra** ['õha] 'honour'; when word-final and stressed, pronounced as a diphthong [õw] (see **1.4.2** below);
um, un	[ũ]: **um** [ũ] 'a, one', **uns** [ũs] 'some'.

NOTE   3   There are a few words which end in -*n* such as: **bóton** 'button, badge', **elétron** 'electron', **hífen** 'hyphen', **íon** 'ion', **nêutron** 'neutron', etc.

1.4.2 Nasal diphthongs

The following diphthongs consist of a nasal vowel + semi-vowel sound:

ãe, ãi	[ãj]: **mãe** [mãj] 'mother', **cãibra** ['kãjbra] 'cramp';
ão	[ãw]: **mão** [mãw] 'hand';
	as a verb ending, this diphthong is also spelt **am**: **iam** ['iãw] 'they went';
em	[ẽj]: in stressed word-final position: **trem** [trẽj] 'train', **também** [tã'bẽj] 'also';
õe	[õj]: **põe** [põj] '(he) puts';
om	[õw]: in stressed word-final position: **bom** [bõw] 'good', **marrom** [ma'hõw] 'brown';
ui	[ũj]: this sound only occurs in the word **muito** ['mũjtu] 'much, very'.

1.4.3 Nasal triphthongs

There are two nasal triphthongs that only occur after [g] and [k] (spelt g and q):

uão [wãw]: **saguão** [sa'gwãw] 'lobby';
uõe [wõj]: **saguões** [sa'gwõjs] 'lobbies'.

1.5 Spelling and pronunciation

1.5.1 Unpredictable letter values

Portuguese spelling is largely phonetic in the sense that most letters only have one possible reading in any given position. The exceptions to this are:

(i)   stressed *e* and *o* when they do not carry a written accent: in most cases, you just have to memorize whether the sound is close ([e] or [o]) or open ([ɛ] or [ɔ]) in a particular word (see **1.3.2**);

(ii) **gue/gui** and **que/qui** are usually pronounced [ge/gi] and [ke/ki] respectively, but, in some words, the *u* is pronounced, forming the sounds [gwe/gwi] and [kwe/kwi]. Before the 2009 spelling reform, the *u* was written with a diaeresis (**ü**) in such cases, but this convention was abolished in the reform, making it necessary to check the dictionary when in doubt;

(iii) *x* is usually pronounced [ʃ] between vowels, but there are cases where it is pronounced [z], [s] or [ks] (see **1.2**).

1.5.2 Spelling of verb ending [ãw]

As a matter of convention, the unstressed third person plural verb ending [ãw] is spelt **-am**; when stressed, as in the future tense of all verbs and the present tense of the verbs **ser**, **estar**, **dar** and **ir**, it is spelt **-ão**.

1.5.3 Consonant clusters

The phonology of Brazilian Portuguese is such that two consonant sounds cannot fall together unless the first is [r] or [s/z] (written as *s* or *x*), or the second is [l] or [r]. The combinations [ks] and [kt] are also permissible, in words like **táxi, ficção** and **conectar**, as is the combination [ps] when spelt **pç/pc** in words like **decepção, decepcionar, opção** and **opcional**. Three-consonant combinations of the form [r] or [s/z] + consonant + [l/r] may also occur, as in words like **perplexo, explícito, esdrúxulo**, etc. In words where the spelling presents consonant combinations other than those described above,[4] an extra [i] sound is inserted between the two consonants when the word is pronounced. Examples:

pneu [pi'new] 'tire/tyre'

psicologia [pisicolo'ʒia] 'psychology'

abdicar [abidʒi'kaʳ] 'to abdicate'

abstrato [abis'tratu] 'abstract'

capturar [capitu'raʳ] 'to capture'

ignorar [igino'raʳ] 'to ignore'

significar [siginifi'kaʳ] 'to mean'

objeto [obi'ʒɛtu] 'object'

observar [obiser'vaʳ] 'to observe'

obscuro [obis'kuru] 'obscure'

segmento [segi'mẽtu] 'segment' (pronounced identically to **seguimento**)

submeter [subime'teʳ] 'to submit'

subscrever [subiscre'veʳ] 'to sign, underwrite'.

NOTE | 4 Some speakers also insert the [i] sound between [ks], [kt] and [ps], e.g. **conectar** [koneki'taʳ], **opção** [opi'sãw]

When this extra [i] sound is inserted after *d* or *t*, it causes palatalization:

admirar [adʒimi'raʳ] 'to admire'

advogado [adʒivo'gadu] 'lawyer'

ritmo ['hitʃimu] 'rhythm'

tsunami [tʃisu'nami] 'tsunami'.

1.5.4 Word-final consonants

Native Portuguese words can only end in a vowel or the consonants *l* (pronounced [w]), *m* or *n* (merely indicating the nasality of the preceding vowel), *r*, *s* or *z*. With foreign words and names that end in a consonant other than these, Brazilian speakers automatically add an [i] sound to the end of the word. This is also reflected in the Portuguese spelling of words of foreign origin:

pop ['pɔpi] 'pop'

Ford ['fɔrdʒi] 'Ford' (*with palatalization*)

internet [ĩter'nɛtʃi] 'Internet' (*with palatalization*)

time ['tʃimi] 'team'

clube ['klubi] 'club'.

1.5.5 **Initial *s* + consonant**

The combination *s/x* + consonant is always preceded by a vowel sound in native words, so in non-native words beginning with an *s* + consonant combination, an [i] sound is inserted before the [s]:

> **scanner** [*i*s'kaner] 'scanner' (*also spelt* **escâner**)
>
> **spray** [*i*s'prei] 'spray'
>
> **Sting** [*i*s'tʃĩgi] 'Sting' (*singer*).

1.5.6 **Pronunciation different from spelling**

In everyday Brazilian speech, there are cases where the pronunciation of certain sounds departs from the spelling. Most notable among these are:

(i)   Stressed final vowels followed by *s* or *z* are frequently diphthongized:

> **mas** [majs] 'but' (this is the usual pronunciation of this word)
>
> **gás** [gas] or [gajs] 'gas'
>
> **rapaz** [ha'paz] or [ha'pajz] 'guy, lad'
>
> **vocês** [vo'ses] or [vo'sejs] 'you'
>
> **nós** [nɔs] or [nɔjs] 'we'
>
> **voz** [vɔz] or [vɔjz] 'voice'
>
> **pus** [pus] or [pujs] 'I put'
>
> **produz** [pro'duz] or [pro'dujz] '(it) produces'.

(ii)   The diphthong *ei* is simplified to [e] before [r], [ʃ] and [ʒ]:

> **primeiro** [pri'mero] 'first'
>
> **deixar** [de'ʃaʳ] 'to let, leave'
>
> **beijo** ['beʒu] 'kiss'.

(iii)   The diphthong *ai* is simplified to [a] before [ʃ] (spelt *x*):

> **caixa** ['kaʃa] 'box, cash desk'.

(iv)   The diphthong *ou* is simplified to [o][5]:

> **vou** [vo] 'I go'
>
> **louro** ['loru] 'blond'.

(iv)   The oral vowels, especially *a*, are partially nasalized before *m* or *n* in the following syllable:

> **ano** ['ãnu] 'year'
>
> **sonho** ['sõɲu] 'dream'.

(v)   The infinitive **vir** 'to come' is pronounced with a nasal *i* [vĩ].

NOTE   5   Word-final *ou* is often replaced with *ô* in very informal writing, e.g. **tô fora!** (= **estou fora**) 'count me out!'

1.5.7 | Doubled letters

The only doubled consonants that occur in Portuguese spelling are **rr** and **ss**. These only occur between vowels and contrast in pronunciation with the single letters: **caro** ['karu] 'dear' vs. **carro** ['kahu] 'car', **casar** [ka'zaʳ] 'to marry' vs. **cassar** [ka'saʳ] 'to suspend'.[6]

Doubled vowels are rare in Portuguese. Double *e* occurs in words beginning with *e* to which the prefix **pre** or **re** is added, such as: **preencher** 'to fill out', **reescrever** 'to rewrite' and in a group of verbs ending in -**preender** (corresponding to English -*prehend*) and words derived from them, such as: **apreender** 'to seize', **compreensão** 'understanding', etc. It also occurs in the third person plural verb forms **creem**, **deem**, **leem** and **veem**, from **crer** 'to believe', **dar** 'to give', **ler** 'to read' and **ver** 'to see' respectively. Double *o* occurs in words with the prefix **co-** before an *o*, such as **cooperar** 'to cooperate', **coordenar** 'to coordinate', etc. It also occurs in a few nouns, such as **enjoo** 'nausea' and **voo** 'flight', and in the first person singular present indicative of verbs with an infinitive ending in -**oar**, e.g. **enjoar** > **eu enjoo** 'I get sick/nauseous'. In all these cases, the two vowels are pronounced separately. Doubled vowels also occur in some words of foreign origin, such as: **graal** 'grail', **iídiche** 'Yiddish', **Saara** [sa'ara] 'Sahara', **Teerã** 'Teheran', etc.

NOTE | 6 Note that there are many cognate words in English and Portuguese that originally came from Latin. Whereas English spelling has retained Latin doubled consonants, Portuguese spelling has simplified them, except in the case of **rr** and **ss**. Compare **ilegal** 'illegal', **adição** 'addition', **afetar** 'to affect', **exagerar** 'to exaggerate', etc.

1.5.8 | Word-final vowel elision

Unstressed word-final [a] is elided (i.e. not pronounced) before another word beginning with any unstressed vowel, oral or nasal, and the two words are run together: **rosa amarela** [rɔzama'rɛla] 'yellow rose', **fala errado** [fale'hadu] '(he) speaks incorrectly', **o dia inteiro** [udʒiĩ'teru] 'the whole day', **liga o ar** [ligu'ar] 'turn on the air-conditioning', **raça humana** [hasu'mana] 'human race'. This rule does not apply if the final [a] or the following vowel is stressed: **sofá estofado** [so'fa esto'fadu] 'upholstered couch', **faça isso** ['fasa 'isu] 'do that', **pega uma** ['pɛga 'uma] 'take one'.

Similarly, unstressed word-final [i] and [u] are run together with a following unstressed [i] and [u] respectively, with a slight lengthening of the vowel sound: **me identifiquei** [mi:dẽtʃifi'kej] 'I identified (myself)', **faço um bolo** [fasũ:'bolu] 'I make a cake'.

1.5.9 | Nasal liaison

When stressed word-final [ẽ], [ẽj] or [ĩ] is followed by another word beginning with any vowel sound, stressed or unstressed, the sound [ỹ] (equivalent to **nh**) is inserted to make a liaison between the two vowels: **vem amanhã** [vẽ(j)ỹama'ỹã] 'come tomorrow', **vim hoje** [vĩ'ỹoʒi] 'I came today'.

1.5.10 | Metaphony

Metaphony is a phonological phenomenon whereby there is an alternation between the close [e] and open [ɛ] sounds, both spelt **e**, and between the close [o] and open [ɔ] sounds, both spelt **o**, in different inflected forms of the same word. Metaphony occurs in the following cases:

(i)   In a small group of nouns, where the tonic vowel is pronounced [o] in the singular and [ɔ] in the plural, e.g. **ovo** ['ovu] 'egg' > **ovos** ['ɔvus] 'eggs' – see full list in **3.2.8**;

(ii) In certain adjectives, namely those ending in **-oso**, **posto** 'placed' and derivatives (**disposto**, **oposto**, etc.), **grosso** 'thick, coarse, rude' and **novo** 'new', where the masculine singular form has the close [o] sound while the feminine singular and both masculine and feminine plural have the open [ɔ] sound, e.g. **gostoso** [gos'tozu] > **gostosa** [gos'tɔza], **gostosos** [gos'tɔzus], **gostosas** [gos'tɔzas] 'tasty';

(iii) In nouns and adjectives ending in **-eu(s)** ['ew(s)] in the masculine and **-eia(s)** ['ɛja(s)] in the feminine, e.g.: **ateu** [a'tew] > **ateia** [a'tɛja], **ateus** [a'tews] > **ateias** [a'tɛjas] 'atheist';

(iv) In the third person personal pronouns **ele(s)/ela(s)** and the demonstratives **este(s)/esta(s)**, **esse(s)/essa(s)** and **aquele(s)/aquela(s)**, where the masculine singular and plural forms have the close [e] sound while the feminine singular and plural forms have the open [ɛ] sound, e.g. **ele** ['eli] 'he' > **ela** ['ɛla] 'she', **eles** ['elis] 'they *masc.*' > **elas** ['ɛlas] 'they' *fem.*; **este** ['estʃi] 'this *masc.*' > **esta** ['ɛsta] 'this *fem.*', **estes** ['estʃis] 'these *masc.*' > **estas** ['ɛstas] 'these *fem.*'

(v)   In certain **-ar** verbs with **-e-** or **-o-** in the stem where the vowel is close when unstressed and open when stressed, e.g. **levar** [le'vaʳ] 'to take' > **levo** ['lɛvu] 'I take', **leva** ['lɛva] '(he) takes', **levam** ['lɛvãw] '(they) take'; **tocar** [to'kaʳ] 'to touch' > **toco** ['tɔku] 'I touch', **toca** ['tɔka] '(he) touches', **tocam** ['tɔkãw] '(they) touch' – see note in **16.1**;

(vi) In certain **-er** verbs with **-e-** in the stem where the vowel is close except in the third persons singular and plural of the present indicative: **dever** [de'veʳ] 'to owe', **devo** ['devu] 'I owe' > **deve** ['dɛvi] '(he) owes', **devem** ['dɛvẽ] '(they) owe' – see note in **16.1**.

1.6   Syllabification

1.6.1

Before learning the rules for the use of the written accents, it is important to know how to divide up Portuguese words into their constituent syllables. A syllable may take the following forms: vowel, vowel plus consonant, consonant plus vowel, or consonant vowel consonant:

> **ti-a**
>
> **ap-to**
>
> **sub-mun-do**.

1.6.2

A syllable is only considered to end with a consonant if the next syllable begins with a consonant, i.e. two consonants that fall together, including the doubled consonants **rr** and **ss**, are assigned to separate syllables. The following consonant groups are exceptions to this rule: **ch**, **lh**, **nh**; **bl**, **br**, **cl**, **cr**, **dr**, **fl**, **fr**, **gl**, **gr**, **pl**, **pr**, **tr**; **gu**, **qu** – they are not split and begin a new syllable:

> **ta-char**
>
> **ca-mi-nho**
>
> **ne-gro**
>
> **dis-tin-guir**.

1.6.3

The only two-consonant combination that can appear in syllable-final position is **-ns**. Remember that the *n* is not pronounced as a separate letter, so, phonetically, the syllable ends in a single consonant, e.g. **trans-por-te** [trãs'pɔrtʃi].

1.6.4 Diphthongs and triphthongs are not split:

> **lau-do**
>
> **sa-guão**.

1.7 Stress and written accents

1.7.1 The default position for word stress is the penultimate syllable. Words ending in **-o(s)**, **-a(s)**, **-e(s)**, **-am**, **-em** or **-ens** that are stressed on the penultimate syllable have no written accent. The only exception to this rule is that stressed *i* and *u* may be written with an accent to show that they are to be pronounced separately rather than as part of a diphthong:

> **bracelete** [brase'letʃi] 'bracelet' (*follows rule*)
>
> **desaparecido** [dʒizapare'sidu] 'disappeared' (*follows rule*)
>
> **amam** ['amãw] 'they love' (*follows rule*)
>
> **decidem** [de'sidẽj] 'they decide' (*follows rule*)
>
> **jovens** ['ʒɔvẽs] 'young people' (*follows rule*)
>
> **saída** [sa'ida] 'exit' (*accent used to separate vowel sounds*)
>
> **saúde** [sa'udʒi] 'health' (*accent used to separate vowel sounds*).

1.7.2 Words ending in the following letters are stressed on the last syllable unless another syllable carries a written accent: **i, is, im, ins; u, us, um, uns; l, n, r, x, z; ei, eis; ã, ãs, ão, ãos, ões, ães**:

> **cupins** [ku'pĩs] 'termites'
>
> **urubu** [uru'bu] 'vulture'
>
> **capital** [kapi'taw] 'capital'
>
> **comer** [ko'meʳ] 'to eat'
>
> **cartaz** [kar'taz] 'poster'
>
> **falei** [fa'lej] 'I spoke'
>
> **maçã** [ma'sã] 'apple'
>
> **organizações** [organiza'sõjs] 'organizations'.

The accented forms **éi/éis** are used to differentiate the open diphthongs [ɛj/ɛjs] from the closed **ei/eis** [ej/ejs]:

> **levei** [le'vej] 'I took'
>
> **papéis** [pa'pɛjs] 'papers'.

1.7.3 Words ending in stressed *a*, *e* or *o* (with or without *s*), including monosyllables, are written with an accent on the vowel. The acute accent is used for *a* and for *e* and *o* when they have the open pronunciation [ɛ] and [ɔ]. Close *e* and *o*, [e] and [o], are written with the circumflex accent:

> **pá** [pa] 'shovel'
>
> **café** [ka'fɛ] 'coffee'

vocês [vo'ses] 'you'

cipó [si'pɔ] 'vine'

robô [ho'bo] 'robot'.

Stressed word-final [ẽ(j)] is also marked with an acute accent except in monosyllabic words:

também [tã'bẽ(j)] 'also'

refém [he'fẽ(j)] 'hostage', *pl.* **reféns**, but

trem [trẽj] 'train', *pl.* **trens**.

Some words of this type lose the written accent when a flexional ending is added, as the stressed syllable then becomes the penultimate of the word and, as such, does not require a written accent:

mês [mes] 'month', *pl.* **meses**

francês [frã'ses] 'French', *fem.* **francesa**, *pl.* **franceses**.

1.7.4   Words stressed on the antepenultimate (third from last) syllable are written with an accent on the stressed vowel. The acute is used for *a* (except before *m* and *n*), *i* and *u*, and for *e* and *o* when they represent the open sounds [ɛ] and [ɔ]; the circumflex is used for *a* before *m* or *n*, and for *e* and *o* when they represent the close sounds [e] and [o] (which is always the case before *m* or *n*):

árabe ['arabi] 'Arab, Arabic'

dúvida ['duvida] 'doubt'

lógico ['lɔʒiku] 'logical'

âncora ['ãkora] 'anchor'

polêmico [po'lemiku] 'controversial'.

1.7.5   The same rules apply when a written accent is required on the penultimate syllable of words ending with the letters listed in **1.7.2**:

âmbar ['ãbar] 'amber'

tênis ['tenis] 'tennis, tennis shoes'

órgão ['ɔrgãw] 'organ'.

1.7.6   As stated in **1.7.1**, stressed *i* and *u* may be written with an accent to show that they are to be pronounced separately and not as part of a diphthong (e.g. **saída**, **saúde**). However, the written accent is not used before -*nh* and the letters *l, m, n, r, z, i* and *u* when the latter occur in the same syllable, even though *i* and *u* are pronounced separately in these cases:

rainha [ha'iỹa] 'queen'

cair [ka'iʳ] 'to fall'

caiu [ka'iw] '(he) fell'

ruim [hu'ĩ] 'bad'

Raul [ha'uw] (*proper name*)

juiz [ʒuˈiz] 'judge' cf. the plural **juízes** 'judges' (*which has a written accent because z is no longer in the same syllable as the i*).

The verb **pôr** [poʳ] 'to put' is written with an accent to differentiate it from the preposition **por** [pɔʳ] 'for, by, through', and the verb form **pôde** [ˈpodʒi] '(he) was able to' is written with an accent to differentiate it from the present tense **pode** [ˈpɔdʒi] '(he) can, is able to'. Notice the difference in vowel quality in the pronunciation of these pairs.

The third-person plural forms of the verbs **ter** 'to have' and **vir** 'to come', **têm** 'they have' and **vêm** 'they come', are written with a circumflex accent to differentiate them from the third-person singular forms **tem** '(he) has' and **vem** '(he) comes'. In two-syllable derivatives of these verbs, the third-person singular forms are written with an acute accent and the plurals with a circumflex, e.g. **ele detém** 'he holds' vs. **eles detêm** 'they hold' (from **deter** 'to hold'), **ele convém** 'he concurs' vs. **eles convêm** 'they concur' (from **convir** 'to concur'). But note that, in all these verbs, there is no difference in pronunciation between the third-person singular and plural forms.

1.8 Hyphenation

The hyphen has the following functions in Portuguese:

1.8.1 With unstressed object pronouns

To link a dependent object pronoun to a verb form when the pronoun is placed after the verb (see **7.5**):

> **lavar-se** 'to wash (oneself)'
>
> **agradecendo-lhe** 'thanking him'.

1.8.2 In two-word compounds

To link the elements of two-word compounds consisting of two nouns, two adjectives, a noun and an adjective, an adjective and a noun or a verb stem and a noun:

> **palavra-chave** 'key word'
>
> **azul-claro** 'light blue'
>
> **caixa-forte** 'vault, strongroom'
>
> **baixo-astral** 'gloomy'
>
> **guarda-roupa** 'wardrobe'.

1.8.3 In three-word compounds

To link the elements of three-word compounds (usually with **de** as the second word) used as the names of plants and animals, as well as the following: **água-de-colônia** 'eau de cologne', **do arco-da-velha** (*idiom*) 'far-fetched', **cor-de-rosa** 'pink', **mais-que-perfeito** 'pluperfect' and **pé-de-meia** 'nest egg (*savings*)'. The 2009 spelling reform abolished the hyphens in all other three-word compounds:

> **bico-de-papagaio** 'poinsettia' (*plant*)
>
> cf. **bico de papagaio** 'bone spur' (*medical condition*), 'parrot's beak' (*literal meaning*).

After prefixes

(i)   the prefixes **além-** 'beyond', **aquém-** 'this side of', **bem-** 'well', **ex-** 'ex', **pós-** 'post', **pré-** 'pre', **pró-** 'pro', **recém-** 'newly', **sem-** 'without' and **vice-** 'deputy, vice' are always followed by a hyphen:

> **ex-marido** 'ex-husband'
>
> **pró-China** 'pro-China'.

(ii)   With prefixes ending in a vowel (**aero, agro, alfa, ante, anti, arqui, auto, beta, bio, contra, eletro, entre, extra, foto, geo, giga, hetero, hidro, hipo, homo, infra, intra, iso, lipo, macro, maxi, mega, meso, micro, mini, mono, multi, neo, neuro, paleo, peri, pleuro, poli, proto, pseudo, psico, retro, semi, sobre, supra, tele, tetra, tri, ultra**), a hyphen is inserted if the following element begins with *h* or the same vowel as the last vowel of the prefix:

> **micro-ondas** 'microwave (oven)'
>
> **anti-horário** 'anticlockwise'.

In other cases, the two elements are written together, but note that if the second element begins with *r* or *s*, this is doubled:

> **sobrenatural** 'supernatural'
>
> **contrarrevolução** 'counter-revolution'
>
> **ultrassom** 'ultrasound'.

(iii)   With prefixes ending in *r* (**hiper, inter** and **super**), a hyphen is inserted before *h* or *r*:

> **super-herói** 'superhero'
>
> **inter-racial** 'interracial'
>
> cf. **superfácil** 'really easy'.

(iv)   With prefixes ending in *b* (**ab, ob, sob** and **sub**), a hyphen is inserted before *b*, *h* or *r*:

> **sub-humano** 'subhuman'
>
> **sub-reptício** 'surreptitious'
>
> cf. **submarino** (pronounced [sub*i*ma'rinu] – see **1.5.3**) 'submarine'.

(v)   With the prefix **co**, the hyphen is not used even if the second element begins with *o*. The letter *h* is dropped after **co**:

> **cooperar** 'to cooperate'
>
> **coerdeiro** 'joint heir' (= **co** + **herdeiro**).

(vi)   With the prefixes **pre** and **re**, the hyphen is not used even if the second element begins with *e*:

> **preexistente** 'pre-existing'
>
> **reencontro** 'reunion'.

(vii)   With the prefix **mal**, a hyphen is inserted before a vowel or *h*:

> **mal-assombrado** 'haunted'
>
> **mal-humorado** 'bad-tempered'
>
> cf. **malcriado** 'ill-mannered'.

(viii)   With the prefix **circum**, a hyphen is inserted before a vowel, *h*, *m* or *n*:

circum-navegar 'to circumnavigate'

cf. **circumpolar** 'circumpolar'.

Note that the same prefix is spelt **circun** (with no hyphen) before consonants other than *h*, *m*, *n* and *p*:

circunferência 'circumference'.

1.8.5   Carrying part of a word over to the next line

When breaking a word to carry part of it over to the next line, note that words can only be broken according to the rules of syllable division (see **1.6**) and should not be hyphenated in such a way as to leave a single letter at the end or beginning of a line.

If the word to be broken already contains a hyphen, for one of the reasons described in **1.8.1** to **1.8.4** above, it should be broken immediately after the hyphen and a second hyphen written at the start of the new line.

1.9   Use of capital letters

The following are the chief differences between the uses of initial capitals in Portuguese and English:

1.9.1   No initial capital in Portuguese

Unlike English, Portuguese uses a small initial letter for:

(i)   days of the week and months of the year:

na sexta 'on Friday'

em maio 'in May';

(ii)   nouns and adjectives of nationality, religion and political affiliation:

dois brasileiros 'two Brazilians'

um budista 'a Buddhist'

o islamismo 'Islam'

os republicanos 'the Republicans';

(iii)   the names of languages:

em japonês 'in Japanese';

(iv)   nouns and adjectives derived from proper names:

a teoria marxista 'Marxist theory';

(v)   titles when accompanied by a name, although usage varies:

o presidente *or* **Presidente Lula** 'President Lula'

o rio *or* **Rio Amazonas** 'the Amazon River, the River Amazon'

a rua *or* **Rua Normandia** 'Normandia Street'.

1.9.2 Initial capital in Portuguese

Unlike English, Portuguese uses an initial capital letter for:

(i)   the names of academic disciplines:

um curso de História 'a history course'

um bacharel em Direito 'a law graduate';

(ii)   words like **o Estado** 'the state (national or federal)', **a Igreja** 'the church', **o País** 'the country (i.e. Brazil)', **a Prefeitura** 'the city/local authority', etc. when they refer to a particular institution:

um ofício da Prefeitura 'an official letter from City Hall'.

1.10 Punctuation

The rules for punctuation are largely the same as in English, except for the following:

(i)   Single inverted commas are never used.

(ii)   The dash may be used without inverted commas to indicate a change of speaker in written dialogues:

– Onde você vai?
– Não é da sua conta.

'Where are you going?'
'None of your business.'

The dash is repeated before a verb of saying:

– Onde você vai? – ele perguntou.
– Não é da sua conta – respondi.

'Where are you going?' he asked.
'None of your business,' I replied.

(iii)   Commas are more frequently used in Portuguese than in English as there is a tendency to demarcate every phrase and clause within a sentence.

(iv)   In numerical expressions, a comma is used in place of the decimal point and the thousands are separated by a full stop:

15.742,35   '15,742.35'.

Notes for Spanish speakers

Portuguese has not undergone the loss of Latin initial *f* (cf. **fazer** 'to do', **ferro** 'iron', **folha** 'leaf') nor the diphthongization of *e* and *o* (cf. **tempo** 'time', **porta** 'door'). Vulgar Latin [ʎ] has also been retained between vowels (cf. **agulha** 'needle', **alho** 'garlic', **colher** 'to pick', **filho** 'son', **olho** 'eye') and *b* and *v* have remained separate phonemes, as in English. Portuguese has not palatalized Latin *-ll-* and *-nn-* (cf. **cavalo** 'horse', **ano** 'year'), but it has palatalized single *-n-* in some cases (cf. **sobrinho** 'nephew', **vinho** 'wine'), while in others intervocalic *-l-* and *-n-* have been lost completely (cf. **céu** 'sky, heaven', **dor** 'pain', **pôr** 'to put', **seio** 'breast', **ter** 'to have', **vir** 'to come'). Note that the Spanish endings *-án*, *-ano*, *-ón* and *-ión* are all realized as **-ão** in Portuguese (cf. **alemão** 'German', **são** 'sane, sound', **sabão** 'soap powder', **decisão** 'decision'). Spanish word-initial *ll-* is realized in Portuguese as **ch-** (cf. **chama** 'flame', **chamar** 'to call', **cheio** 'full', **chorar** 'to cry', **chover** 'to rain'), some word-initial *pla-* as **pra-** (cf. **praça** 'square', **praia** 'beach', **prata** 'silver', **prazer** 'pleasure') and some word-initial *y-* as **j/g-** (cf. **já** 'already', **jazer** 'to lie', **gesso** 'plaster', **jugo** 'yoke'). Portuguese retains the contrast between single **s** [z] and double **ss** [s] between vowels (cf. **rosa** ['hɔza] 'rose', **esse** ['esi] 'that') and the sound [kw-] is spelt **qu-** (cf. **qual** 'which', **quanto** 'how much', **frequente** 'frequent'). Brazilian Portuguese has simplified the Latin clusters *-cti-* and *-ct-* to **-ci-/-ç-** and **-t-** respectively (cf. **acionar** 'to activate', **ação** 'action', **ator** 'actor'), and *-pt-* to **-t-** (cf. **aceitar** 'to accept', **adotar** 'to adopt', **ótimo** 'great').

The palatalization of **d** and **t** before an [i] sound can render cognate words unrecognizable for Spanish speakers when pronounced. The nasal vowel sounds are also a distinctive feature of Portuguese and the Portuguese **nh** [ỹ] is not the same sound as the Spanish **ñ** [ɲ].

One important difference in the rules for accentuation is that, in Portuguese, the first vowel of word-final **-ia**, **-io**, **-ua**, **-uo** is not written with an accent when stressed (cf. **dia** 'day', **rio** 'river', **grua** 'crane'), but when the stress falls on the preceding syllable, the latter is accented (cf. **família** 'family', **imaginário** 'imaginary', **promíscuo** 'promiscuous').

2

Gender and gender agreement

2.1 What is grammatical gender?

Every Portuguese noun falls into one of two grammatical categories, called masculine and feminine. The categories are so called because nearly all nouns denoting male beings are masculine, and nearly all nouns denoting female beings are feminine. But all other nouns – those denoting inanimate objects, abstract concepts, etc. – also belong to one of these categories, so, for example, **carro** 'car', **calor** 'heat' and **restante** 'remainder' are all masculine, while **mesa** 'table', **idade** 'age' and **decisão** 'decision' are all feminine.

Except in the case of nouns denoting living beings, there are no semantic clues to the gender of a particular noun. You simply have to memorize the gender of each new noun you learn, but this task is made considerably easier by the fact that certain endings are indicative of a particular gender (see **2.2**).

Grammatical gender is crucial in Portuguese because articles, adjectives, possessives, demonstratives and pronouns have to agree in gender with the noun they are accompanying or replacing, which in most cases means their form or ending changes according to whether the noun is masculine or feminine.

2.2 Rules for determining gender

2.2.1 Nouns that are masculine by form

(i)   Nouns ending in **-o**, including those in **-ão**, are *masculine*, e.g. **livro** 'book', **passeio** 'outing, trip', **cidadão** 'citizen', **cartão** 'card', etc.

Exceptions, all feminine:
- the words **libido** 'libido', **tribo** 'tribe' and **mão** 'hand';
- nouns ending in **-ção/-são** that have English cognates ending in *-tion/-sion*, e.g. **ação** 'action', **nação** 'nation', **decisão** 'decision', **ilusão** 'illusion' etc.;
- nouns ending in **-idão** that have English cognates ending in *-itude*, e.g. **certidão** '(birth) certificate', **multidão** 'crowd', **solidão** 'loneliness';
- words ending in **-o** that are abbreviations of longer feminine nouns, e.g. **foto** 'photo' (from **fotografia**), **moto** 'motorcycle' (from **motocicleta**), etc.;

(ii)   Nouns with the following endings are also *masculine*:
- **-dor/-sor/-tor**, e.g. **cantor** 'singer', **grampeador** 'stapler', **revisor** 'copy editor';
- **-eu/-éu**, e.g. **europeu** 'European', **museu** 'museum', **céu** 'sky, heaven', **réu** 'defendant';

34

- **-ma** when there is an English cognate ending in *-m* or *-ma*, e.g. **cinema** 'cinema', **dilema** 'dilemma', **problema** 'problem', **sistema** 'system'.

2.2.2 Nouns that are feminine by form

(i) The vast majority of nouns ending in **-a** are *feminine*, e.g. **cama** 'bed', **paciência** 'patience', including those ending in -ã which denote a female being, e.g. **alemã** 'German woman', **irmã** 'sister', as well as the words **avelã** 'hazelnut', **lã** 'wool', **maçã** 'apple', **rã** 'frog' and **romã** 'pomegranate'.

> *Exceptions, all masculine*:
> - nouns ending in **-a** that denote human beings and can therefore be masculine or feminine depending on the sex of the person referred to (see **2.2.3**);
> - the words **alerta** 'alert, warning', **cometa** 'comet', **dia** 'day', **mapa** 'map', **planeta** 'planet', **samba** 'samba', **tapa** 'slap', among others;
> - nouns ending in **-ma** when there is an English cognate ending in *-m* or *-ma*, e.g. **drama** 'drama', **pijama** 'pajamas/pyjamas', **poema** 'poem', etc., also **lema** 'motto' and **tema** 'theme, topic';
> - nouns ending in stressed **á**, e.g. **maracujá** 'passion fruit', **sofá** 'sofa', **tamanduá** 'anteater';
> - nouns ending in **-ã** other than those mentioned above, e.g. **balangandã** 'bauble', **divã** 'couch', **o Irã** 'Iran', **o Islã** 'Islam'.

(ii) In addition, nouns with the following endings are *feminine*:
- **-ção** (corresponding to English *-tion*), e.g. **abolição** 'abolition', **fração** 'fraction', **noção** 'notion';
- **-dade**,[1] e.g. **cidade** 'city, town', **idade** 'age', **lealdade** 'loyalty';
- **-gem**,[2] e.g. **bobagem** 'nonsense', **margem** 'bank, shore, margin', **origem** 'origin', **vagem** 'green bean', **viagem** 'journey';
- **-ice**, e.g. **breguice** 'tackiness', **pieguice** 'schmaltz', **tolice** 'foolishness'
- **-idão** (corresponding to English *-itude*), e.g. **imensidão** 'immensity', **lentidão** 'slowness, slow-moving traffic', **vastidão** 'vastness';
- **-ie**, e.g. **barbárie** 'barbarism', **planície** 'plain', **superfície** 'surface, area';
- **-ite**, e.g. **bronquite** 'bronchitis', **celulite** 'cellulite', **elite** 'élite';
- **-são** (corresponding to English *-sion*), e.g. **erosão** 'erosion', **mansão** 'mansion', **previsão** 'forecast', **versão** 'version';
- **-se**, e.g. **análise** 'analysis', **catarse** 'catharsis', **crise** 'crisis', **metamorfose** 'metamorphosis', **tese** 'thesis';
- **-tude**, e.g. **juventude** 'youth', **magnitude** 'magnitude', **virtude** 'virtue'.

NOTES

1 The word **autoridade** is used as a masculine noun when it means 'a (male) official, dignitary'.

2 Except the word **personagem** 'character' (in a book, film, etc.), which can be masculine or feminine.

2.2.3 Nouns that can be both masculine and feminine

In general, words referring to human beings can be either masculine or feminine, depending on the sex of the person referred to. Note that the default gender is masculine when the sex of the person is unknown or irrelevant.

Nouns of this type end in **-ante/-ente/-inte**, e.g. **estudante** 'student', **gerente** 'manager', **ouvinte** 'listener'; **-cida**,[3] e.g. **suicida** 'suicide (victim)'; **-ense**, e.g. **canadense** 'Canadian'; **-ista**, e.g. **dentista** 'dentist'; **-ta**, e.g. **diplomata** 'diplomat', **idiota** 'idiot', **vietnamita** 'Vietnamese' and some other nationalities, such as **belga** 'Belgian', **etíope** 'Ethiopian'.

NOTE | 3   Nouns ending in -**cida** that refer to chemical products are masculine, e.g. **inseticida** 'insecticide'.

Other members of this category are: **caipira** 'hick', **camarada** 'mate, comrade', **chapa** 'buddy', **colega** 'friend, fellow, colleague', **comparsa** 'sidekick, partner in crime', **cúmplice** 'accomplice', **fã** 'fan', **herege** 'heretic', **intérprete** 'interpreter, performer', **mártir** 'martyr', **modelo** '(fashion) model', **personagem** 'character' (*in a story*) and **sósia** 'double, lookalike'.

Note that many originally single-gender nouns become two-gender when used to refer to human beings, e.g. **âncora** 'TV anchor', **bandeirinha** 'linesman', **caixa** 'teller, cashier',[4] **mão de vaca** (*informal*) 'skinflint', **segurança** 'security guard, bodyguard', etc.

NOTE | 4   One of the meanings of **caixa** as a feminine noun is 'cash desk, checkout', but most Brazilians refer to the cash desk or checkout as **o caixa** (masculine).

2.2.4   Single-gender nouns that can refer to both males and females

The following nouns are grammatically masculine only, but can refer to females as well as males: **cônjuge** 'spouse', **indivíduo** 'individual', **ser** 'being'.

The following nouns are grammatically feminine only, but can refer to males as well as females: **criança** 'child', **pessoa** 'person', **testemunha** 'witness', **vítima** 'victim'.

2.2.5   Nouns that are masculine or feminine depending on meaning

Some words can be masculine or feminine depending on the meaning. Here are some common examples:

	As masculine noun	As feminine noun
capital	capital (= *money*)	capital (= *city*)
cara	guy	face
grama	gram (= *measure*)	grass
guia	guide (= *man or book*)	guide (= *woman*); form, slip
moral	morale	morality; moral (*of a story*)
rádio	radio; radium	radio station.

2.2.6   Words that are masculine by implication

The following nouns are masculine by implication, i.e. there is an unexpressed noun (shown below in parentheses) which determines their gender:

(i)   months of the year (**mês**): **abril próximo** 'next April';
(ii)   rivers, seas, mountains (**rio, mar/oceano, monte**): **o Amazonas** 'the Amazon', **o Pacífico** 'the Pacific', **o Matterhorn** 'the Matterhorn';
(iii)   cardinal points (**ponto cardeal**): **ao norte** 'to the north';

(iv)   cars,[5] planes, ships (**carro**, **avião**, **navio**): **um Fiat** 'a Fiat', **um Boeing** 'a Boeing', **o Titanic** 'the Titanic';

(v)   bars, restaurants, hotels (**bar**, **restaurante**, **hotel**): **o Hilton** 'the Hilton', **no McDonald's** 'at McDonald's';

(vi)   TV stations and newspapers (**canal**, **jornal**): **no MTV** 'on MTV', **o New York Times** 'the *New York Times*';

(vii)   sports teams (**time**): **o Corinthians** 'Corinthians', **o Lakers** (*singular*) 'the Lakers';

(viii) letters of the alphabet: **dois fs** 'two fs'.

NOTE   5   Some luxury cars are treated as feminine, e.g. **uma Ferrari**, **uma BMW**, etc.

2.2.7 Words that are feminine by implication

(i)   cities (**cidade**): **toda Paris** 'all of Paris', except when the city name contains the masculine definite article, e.g. **o Cairo**, **o Rio de Janeiro** (*masc.*);

(ii)   streets (**rua**): **na esquina da Visconde** 'on the corner of Visconde';

(iii)   TV networks (**rede**): **na CNN** 'on CNN', **a BBC** 'the BBC';

(iv)   companies, shops, airlines (**empresa**, **loja**, **companhia**): **a Microsoft** 'Microsoft'.

2.2.8 The gender of compound nouns

The gender of a hyphenated compound noun is usually determined by the gender of the first noun in the compound, e.g. **posto-chave** 'key post', which is masculine like **posto**, and **meia-noite**, which is feminine like **noite**. Compounds that begin with a verb stem are masculine, e.g. **guarda-chuva** 'umbrella', **para-brisa** 'windscreen'.

However, compounds referring to people can be masculine or feminine, depending on the sex of the person referred to, regardless of the original gender of the component noun, e.g. **sem-teto** 'homeless person', **cabeça-dura** 'pigheaded person', **porta-voz** 'spokesperson', **relações-públicas** 'PR manager'.

2.2.9 Nouns of either gender

A few nouns can be either masculine or feminine. Relatively common among these are: **diabetes** (also **diabete**) 'diabetes', **suéter** 'sweater' (more often encountered as masculine) and **hélice** 'propeller' (which is more commonly feminine, though can be masculine when referring to the propeller of a ship or boat).

2.3 Feminine forms of nouns and adjectives

Nouns with characteristically masculine endings that denote male human beings usually have corresponding feminine forms that are used to refer to females. And many types of adjective also have distinct feminine forms that must be used when referring to a feminine noun. It makes sense to deal with the feminine forms of nouns and adjectives together because the principles for deriving them are the same and many Portuguese words can function as both nouns and adjectives.

2.3.1 Words ending in *-o*

With nouns and adjectives ending in -o (except those ending in -ão), -o becomes -a, e.g. **médico** > **médica** 'doctor', **filho** > **filha** 'son/daughter', **barato** > **barata** 'cheap', **pequeno** > **pequena** 'small'.

2.3.2 **Words ending in *-ão***

With nouns and adjectives ending in -ão, -ão becomes -ã, e.g. **irmão** > **irmã** 'brother/sister', **alemão** > **alemã** 'German', **são** > **sã** 'sane, healthy'.

Exceptions:

(i)   nouns and adjectives in -ão that describe a person with a particular character trait usually change -ão to -ona, e.g. **brincalhão** > **brincalhona** 'playful (person)', **sabichão** > **sabichona** 'know-all';

(ii)   a few nouns change -ão to -oa: **leão** > **leoa** 'lion/lioness', **leitão** > **leitoa** 'piglet', **patrão** > **patroa** 'boss';

(iii)   **ladrão** 'thief' becomes **ladra** or **ladrona**;

(iv)   the feminine equivalent of the title **São** 'Saint' used before a name is **Santa**. Note that the masculine form is **Santo** before a name beginning with vowel, e.g. **São Francisco**, **Santa Bárbara**, **Santo André**.

2.3.3 **Words ending in *-dor/-sor/-tor***

With nouns ending in -dor/-sor/-tor, -or becomes -ora, e.g. **escritor** > **escritora** 'writer', **professor** > **professora** 'teacher'. This also applies to adjectives: **trabalhador** > **trabalhadora** 'worker, hard-working', **promissor** > **promissora** 'promising', **sedutor** > **sedutora** 'seductive', and the word **senhor** 'Mr., gentleman, sir' > **senhora** 'Mrs., lady, ma'am/madam'.

Exceptions:

(i)   **ator** > **atriz** 'actor/actress', **imperador** > **imperatriz** 'emperor/empress';

(ii)   the noun **embaixador** 'ambassador', which has two feminine forms: **embaixadora** '(female) ambassador' and **embaixatriz** 'ambassador's wife';

(iii)   the adjective **motor** has two feminine forms: **motriz** as in **força motriz** 'driving force', and **motora** as in **coordenação motora** '(physical) coordination';

(iv)   comparatives such as **anterior** 'previous', **inferior** 'lower, inferior', **maior** 'bigger, greater', **melhor** 'better/best', **menor** 'smaller', **pior** 'worse/worst', **posterior** 'subsequent' and **superior** 'upper, superior', do not inflect for gender: **uma ideia melhor** 'a better idea', **a semana anterior** 'the previous week'.

2.3.4 **Words ending in *-eu***

With nouns and adjectives ending in -eu, -eu becomes -eia, e.g. **ateu** > **ateia** 'atheist', **europeu** > **europeia** 'European'. Note that the masculine ending has the close *e* sound [ew] while the feminine has the open *e* sound [ɛja].

Exceptions:

(i)   **judeu** > **judia** 'Jew, Jewish';

(ii)   **ilhéu** 'islander', which ends in accented -éu, becomes **ilhoa**, while **réu** 'defendant' becomes **ré**.

2.3.5 **Words ending in *-ês***

With nouns and adjectives ending in -ês, -ês becomes -esa, losing the written accent, e.g. **chinês** > **chinesa** 'Chinese', **burguês** > **burguesa** 'bourgeois'.

Exceptions: **cortês** 'courteous' and **descortês** 'discourteous', which are invariable.

2.3.6 ## Other feminine forms

(i) -**a**: **deus** > **deusa** 'god/goddess', **espanhol** > **espanhola** 'Spaniard, Spanish', **nu** > **nua** 'naked', **cru** > **crua** 'raw, crude';

(ii) **mau** 'bad' has the feminine form **má**;

(iii) -**essa**: **abade** > **abadessa** 'abbot/abbess', **conde** > **condessa** 'count/countess', **visconde** > **viscondessa** 'viscount/viscountess';

(iv) -**esa**: **barão** > **baronesa** 'baron/baroness', **cônsul** > **consulesa** 'consul', **duque** > **duquesa** 'duke/duchess', **príncipe** > **princesa** 'prince/princess';

(v) -**isa**: **diácono** > **diaconisa** 'deacon/deaconess', **poeta** > **poetisa** 'poet/poetess',[6] **profeta** > **profetisa** 'prophet/prophetess', **sacerdote** > **sacerdotisa** 'priest/priestess';

(vi) -**ina**: **maestro** > **maestrina** 'conductor', **herói** > **heroína** 'hero/heroine';

(vii) the feminine form **presidenta** 'president' exists alongside the more common **presidente**.

NOTE   6   It is now more common to use the form **poeta** (see **2.2.3**) for female poets, just as 'poet' is preferred to 'poetess' in English.

2.3.7 ## Adjectives with no distinct feminine form

Adjectives that end in -**a** (see **2.2.3**), -**e**, -**l**, -**m**, -**r** (except those in -**dor/-sor/-tor**, see **2.3.3**), -**s** (except those in -**ês**, see **2.3.5**) and -**z**, as well as the word **só** 'alone, single', do not have a distinct feminine form. However, two important exceptions are: **bom** > **boa** 'good' and **espanhol** > **espanhola** 'Spanish'.

2.3.8 ## Adjectives with phonetic changes in the feminine

A few types of adjectives, most notably a large group ending in -**oso**, the past participle **posto** 'placed' and its derivatives (**disposto**, **oposto**, etc.) and the words **grosso** 'thick, coarse, rude' and **novo** 'new', have the close [o] sound in the masculine form and the open [ɔ] sound in the feminine, e.g. **gostoso** [gos'tozu] > **gostosa** [gos'tɔza] 'tasty', **grosso** ['grosu] > **grossa** ['grɔsa] 'thick', **oposto** [o'postu] > **oposta** [o'pɔsta] 'opposite'.

2.3.9 ## Agreement of compound adjectives

In compound adjectives consisting of two adjectives linked by a hyphen, only the second takes the feminine form, e.g. **vermelho-escuro** > **vermelho-escura** 'dark red', **luso-brasileiro** > **luso-brasileira** 'Portuguese-Brazilian'. One exception is **surdo-mudo** 'deaf-mute', *fem.* **surda-muda**.

If the second component is a noun, the adjective is uninflected for gender: **uma blusa amarelo-laranja** 'an orange-yellow blouse'.

2.3.10 ## Gender with names of animals

Although there are some commonly used gender-specific words for animals, e.g. **cão** > **cadela** 'dog/bitch', **cavalo** > **égua** 'horse/mare', **boi** > **vaca** 'ox/cow', most animal names have only one gender but can refer to either sex, e.g. **uma cobra** 'a snake', **um rinoceronte** 'a rhinoceros'. The sex can be specified by adding **macho** 'male' or **fêmea** 'female', e.g. **um rinoceronte fêmea** 'a female rhinoceros'.

Notes for Spanish speakers

There are some important differences in gender between the two languages: in Portuguese, all nouns ending in -**agem** are feminine (except **personagem** 'character', which can be masculine when referring to a male), as well as **margem** 'bank, margin' and **origem** 'origin'. Monosyllables ending in -**or** are feminine (e.g. **cor** 'colour', **dor** 'pain', **flor** 'flower'), as are all words ending in -**se** (e.g. **análise** 'analysis', **ênfase** 'emphasis') and the following: **árvore** 'tree', **estante** 'bookcase', **fraude** 'fraud, deception' and **ponte** 'bridge'. The following words are masculine in Portuguese: **costume** 'custom, habit', **legume** 'vegetable', **leite** 'milk', **mel** 'honey', **nariz** 'nose', **sal** 'salt', **sangue** 'blood' and **sinal** 'sign, signal'.

The Spanish endings -*án*, -*ano*, -*ón* and -*ión* are all realized as -**ão** in Portuguese (hence **alemão** 'German', **são** 'sane, sound', **sabão** 'soap powder' are all masculine, while **ação** 'action' and **decisão** 'decision' are both feminine). The feminine ending -*ana* is realized as -**ã** (cf. **alemã** 'German woman', **lã** 'wool', **sã** 'sane, sound (*fem.*)').

3

Number and number agreement

Singular vs. plural

Like their English counterparts, most Portuguese nouns have different forms for singular and plural. Unlike English, most Portuguese adjectives also have plural forms that have to be used when they refer to a plural noun and very many have distinct masculine and feminine plural forms. The rules for forming the plural of nouns and adjectives are the same, so they will be dealt with together.

Forming the plural of nouns and adjectives

The basic rule is that nouns and adjectives ending in a vowel add **-s** to form the plural, e.g. **carro** > **carros** 'car(s)', **casa** > **casas** 'house(s)', **barato/barata** > **baratos/baratas** 'cheap' (*masc./fem.*), **verde** > **verdes** 'green'.

Nouns and adjectives with a distinct feminine form in the singular (see **2.3**) also have a distinct feminine plural, formed by adding **-s** to the feminine singular, e.g. **alemã** > **alemãs** 'German(s)', **brincalhona** > **brincalhonas** 'playful', **professora** > **professoras** 'teachers'. The only exception are feminine nouns ending in **-iz**, which form the plural by adding **-es**: **atriz** > **atrizes** 'actresses'.

Plural of nouns and adjectives ending in -ão

The ending **-ão** becomes **-ões** in most cases, e.g. **decisão** > **decisões** 'decision(s)', **brincalhão** > **brincalhões** 'playful', but there are exceptions:

(i) **-ão** > **-ãos**: **ancião** > **anciãos** 'old, elder(s)', **cidadão** > **cidadãos** 'citizen(s)', **corrimão** > **corrimãos** 'handrail(s), banister(s)', **cristão** > **cristãos** 'Christian(s)', **grão** > **grãos** 'grain(s), bean(s)', **irmão** > **irmãos** 'brother(s)',[1] **mão** > **mãos** 'hand(s)', **pagão** > **pagãos** 'pagan(s)', **são** > **sãos** 'healthy, sane', **vão** > **vãos** 'gap(s); vain' and all nouns in **-ão** that are accented on the last but one syllable, e.g. **bênção** > **bênçãos** 'blessing(s)', **órfão** > **órfãos** 'orphan(s)', **órgão** > **órgãos** 'organ(s)', **sótão** > **sótãos** 'attic(s)';

(ii) **-ão** > **-ães**: **alemão** > **alemães** 'German(s)', **cão** > **cães** 'dog(s)', **capitão** > **capitães** 'captain(s)', **charlatão** > **charlatães** 'charlatan(s)', **escrivão** > **escrivães** 'clerk(s)', **pão** > **pães** 'bread, loaves', **tabelião** > **tabeliães** 'notary(-ies)'.

NOTE   1   See **3.3**.

3.2.2 ## Plural of nouns and adjectives ending in *-l*

The letter -l becomes -is, e.g. **jornal** > **jornais** 'newspaper', **terrível** > **terríveis** 'terrible', but note the following:

(i)   -el and -ol become -éis and -óis respectively when the stress is on the last syllable, i.e. when there is no written accent elsewhere in the word, e.g. **papel** > **papéis** 'paper(s)', **lençol** > **lençóis** 'sheet(s)', **sol** > **sóis** 'sun(s)';

(ii) -il becomes -is if it is the stressed syllable, e.g. **fuzil** > **fuzis** 'rifle(s)', **sutil** > **sutis** 'subtle'; otherwise (i.e. if there is a written accent elsewhere in the word), -il becomes -eis, e.g. **fóssil** > **fósseis** 'fossil(s)', **réptil** > **répteis** 'reptile(s)'.

(iii) Nouns and adjectives ending in -l have no separate feminine form, except for **espanhol/espanhola** 'Spaniard, Spanish', which has the plural forms **espanhóis/espanholas**.

(iv) *Exceptions*: **cônsul** > **cônsules** 'consul(s)', **gol** > **gols** 'goal(s)', **mal** > **males** 'evil(s), harm'.

3.2.3 ## Plural of nouns and adjectives ending in *-m* and *-n*

The letter -m becomes -ns, e.g. **trem** > **trens** 'train(s)', **ruim** > **ruins** 'bad'. The few nouns ending in -n also add -s to form the plural, e.g. **bóton** > **bótons** 'button(s), badge(s)', **hífen** > **hifens** (no accent in the plural, see **1.7.1**) 'hyphen(s)'. Both singular and plural forms are invariable for gender. Remember that *m* and *n* serve merely to indicate that the preceding vowel is nasalized and are not pronounced as separate letters.

3.2.4 ## Plural of nouns and adjectives ending in *-r* and *-z*

Nouns and adjectives ending in -r and -z are made plural by adding -es, e.g. **colher** > **colheres** 'spoon(s)', **voz** > **vozes** 'voices', **melhor** > **melhores** 'better, best', **capaz** > **capazes** 'able'. Nouns and adjectives ending in -dor/-sor/-tor and **senhor** have a separate feminine plural form ending in -as, e.g. **professor/professora** > **professores/professoras** 'teacher(s)'. Note that comparatives such as **anterior** 'previous', **inferior** 'lower, inferior', **maior** 'bigger, greater', **melhor** 'better/best', **menor** 'smaller', **pior** 'worse/worst', **posterior** 'subsequent' and **superior** 'upper, superior' have a plural form ending in -es, but do not inflect for gender.

3.2.5 ## Plural of nouns and adjectives ending in *-s*

Nouns and adjectives ending in -s that consist of a single syllable, and those that are stressed on the last syllable, add the ending -es. Note that many nouns of this type have a written accent in the singular that they lose when the -es ending is added (see **1.7.3**), e.g. **mês** > **meses** 'month(s)', **revés** > **reveses** 'setback(s)', **inglês** > **ingleses** 'English', **país** > **países** (*retains accent separating vowel sounds a-i*) 'country(-ies)'. Adjectives of this type and nouns referring to people have a separate feminine plural form ending in -as, e.g. **português/portuguesa** > **portugueses/portuguesas** 'Portuguese'.[2]

Exceptions: **cais** 'quay(s)' and **xis** '(letter) x(s)', which do not change in the plural.

NOTE   2   The plural form of the adjectives **cortês** 'courteous' and **descortês** 'discourteous', **corteses** and **descorteses**, is invariable for gender.

All other nouns and adjectives ending in **-s** (i.e. those stressed on any syllable but the last) are invariable, the plural being identical to the singular, e.g. **ônibus** > **ônibus** 'bus(es)', **pires** > **pires** 'saucer(s)', **reles** > **reles** 'mere', **simples** > **simples** 'simple'.

3.2.6 Plural of hyphenated compound nouns

With compound nouns consisting of adjective + noun or noun + adjective, both elements are pluralized according to the rules given above, e.g. **longa-metragem** > **longas-metragens** 'feature film(s)', **segunda-feira** > **segundas-feiras** 'Monday(s)', **cachorro-quente** > **cachorros-quentes** 'hotdog(s)'.

With compound nouns consisting of verb stem + noun, invariable word + noun or two repeated elements, the second element only is pluralized, e.g. **guarda-chuva** > **guarda-chuvas** 'umbrella(s)', **abaixo-assinado** > **abaixo-assinados** 'petition(s)', **teco-teco** > **teco-tecos** 'small plane(s)'.

Exception: compounds beginning **sem-** are invariable: **sem-teto** > **sem-teto** 'homeless'.

With compound nouns consisting of noun + noun, usage varies as the second element can be invariable when it limits or defines the first, e.g. **carro-bomba** > **carros-bombas** *or* **carros-bomba** 'car bomb(s)', but the tendency is to make both elements plural. If in doubt, check in a dictionary.

Of course, if neither element can be pluralized, the plural is identical to the singular, e.g. **bota-fora** > **bota-fora** 'send-off(s)' (*verb stem + adverb*), **guarda-costas** > **guarda-costas** 'bodyguard(s)' (*verb stem + already plural noun*).

3.2.7 Plural of hyphenated compound adjectives

With compound adjectives consisting of two adjectives, only the second element is pluralized, e.g. **verde-escuro** > **verde-escuros** 'dark green'.

Exceptions:

(i)   **surdo-mudo/surda-muda** > **surdos-mudos/surdas-mudas** 'deaf-mute' (*masc./fem.*);
(ii)   **azul-marinho** 'navy blue' and **azul-celeste** 'sky blue' are invariable.

Compound adjectives consisting of adjective + noun are invariable, e.g. **verde-garrafa** 'bottle green', **vermelho-cereja** 'cherry red'.

With compound adjectives consisting of adverb or prefix + adjective, only the adjective part is pluralized: **bem-comportado** > **bem-comportados** 'well-behaved'.

3.2.8 Nouns with phonetic changes in the plural

There is a category of masculine nouns that have the close [o] sound in the singular and the open [ɔ] sound in the plural. The most common of these are:

> **caroço** [ka'rosu] > **caroços** [ka'rɔsus] 'pit(s)/stone(s)'; **corvo** ['korvo] > **corvos** ['kɔrvus] 'crows'; **corpo** ['korpu] > **corpos** ['kɔrpus] 'body(-ies)', **esforço** [es'forsu] > **esforços** [es'fɔrsus] 'effort(s)', **fogo** ['fogu] > **fogos** ['fɔgus] 'fire(works)', **imposto** [ĩ'postu] > **impostos** [ĩ'pɔstus] 'tax(es)', **jogo** ['ʒogu] > **jogos** ['ʒɔgus] 'game(s)', **miolo** [mi'olu] 'flesh, crumb, marrow' > **miolos**

[mi'ɔlus] 'brains', **olho** ['oʎu] > **olhos** ['ɔʎus] 'eye(s)', **osso** ['osu] > **ossos** ['ɔsus] 'bone(s)', **ovo** ['ovu] > **ovos** ['ɔvus] 'egg(s), **poço** ['posu] > **poços** ['pɔsus] 'well(s), shaft(s)', **porco** ['porku] > **porcos** ['pɔrkus] 'pig(s)', **porto** ['portu] > **portos** ['pɔrtus] 'port(s)', **posto** ['postu] > **postos** ['pɔstus] 'post(s)', **povo** ['povu] > **povos** ['pɔvus] 'people(s)', **reforço** [he'forsu] > **reforços** [he'fɔrsus] 'reinforcement(s)', **socorro** [so'kohu] > **socorros** [so'kɔhus] 'aid(s)', **tijolo** [tʃi'ʒolu] > **tijolos** [tʃi'ʒɔlus] 'brick(s)'.

3.2.9 Adjectives with phonetic changes in the plural

The same adjectives that have the close [o] sound in the masculine singular and the open [ɔ] sound in the feminine singular (see **2.3.8**), also have the open [ɔ] sound in the masculine and feminine plural, e.g. **gostoso** [gos'tozu] > **gostosa** [gos'tɔza] > **gostosos/gostosas** [gos'tɔzus/gos'tɔzas] 'tasty', **oposto** [o'postu] > **oposta** [o'pɔsta] > **opostos/opostas** [o'pɔstus/o'pɔstas] 'opposite'.

3.3 Plurals referring collectively to males and females

It is an important principle in Portuguese grammar that the masculine plural is used to refer to males and females collectively, as well as to males only. The feminine plural is only used to refer exclusively to females. There is a group of nouns denoting family relationships where the default meaning of the masculine plural includes males and females:

filhos 'children' (= *sons and daughters*) *or* 'sons', **irmãos** 'brother(s) and sister(s)' *or* 'brothers', **netos** 'grandchildren' *or* 'grandsons', **pais** 'parents' *or* 'fathers', **primos** 'cousins' (*of both sexes or just male*), **sobrinhos** 'nephew(s) and niece(s)' *or* 'nephews', **sogros** 'in-laws' *or* 'fathers-in-law', **tios** 'uncle and aunt' *or* 'uncles'.

This should be borne in mind to avoid misunderstandings:

Você tem irmãos?   Do you have any brothers and sisters? (*not just 'brothers'*)

Ela tem dois filhos. She has two children. (*not necessarily both male*)

If it is not clear from the context, the word **homens** 'men' can be added to specify 'males only':

Você tem irmãos homens?   Do you have any brothers?

Ela tem dois filhos homens.   She has two sons.

São cinco irmãos, dois homens e três mulheres.
There are five siblings, two brothers and three sisters.

With **avô/avó** 'grandfather/grandmother', two masculine plural forms are possible: **avôs** meaning 'grandfathers' and **avós** meaning 'grandparents'. As a feminine plural, **avós** means 'grandmothers'.

3.4 Use of singular and plural

There are some differences in the use of singular and plural in Portuguese and English:

3.4.1 Uncountable singular with generic plural meaning

In the spoken language in particular, the singular of otherwise countable nouns is used uncountably with a generic plural meaning:

> **Comprei maçã, laranja e banana.**
> I bought apples, oranges and bananas.

> **O Rafael entende de computador.**
> Rafael knows all about computers.

This uncountable singular form refers to an unspecified number greater than one, as in the first example above, or to a generic category, as in the second. It may be accompanied by a collective quantifier, such as **muito** or **pouco**:

> **Hoje em dia tem muito carro na rua.**
> There are a lot of cars on the roads nowadays.

> **A biblioteca tem pouco livro.**
> The library doesn't have many books.

The formal written language would require the use of the plural in all the above examples: **maçãs**, **laranjas**, **bananas**, **computadores**, **muitos carros**, **poucos livros**.

But note that, in both spoken and written language, the normal singular and plural are used when the number is specified and with quantifiers like **alguns/uns** 'some, a few' and **vários** 'several, a number of':

> **Comi uma maçã.**
> I ate an apple.

> **Temos dois computadores em casa.**
> We have two computers at home.

> **Li vários livros durante as férias.**
> I read a number of books over the vacation.

3.4.2 Uncountable singular in general statements

In the spoken language, the uncountable singular with generic plural meaning often occurs in general statements. Notice that in such cases the noun is used without a definite article even when it is the subject or direct object of the sentence:

> **Criança adora história de fantasma.**
> Children love ghost stories.

> **A Rita odeia barata.**
> Rita hates cockroaches.

NUMBER AND NUMBER AGREEMENT

Written language would require the use of the plural and definite articles in these examples:[3]

As crianças adoram histórias de fantasmas.
A Rita odeia as baratas.

3.4.3 Plural in English, singular in Portuguese

Cutting and holding utensils, items of clothing for the legs and accessories for the eyes and ears (*e.g. scissors, pants, glasses, headphones, etc.*) are plural in English, whereas, in Portuguese, they are singular,[4] e.g. **uma tesoura** 'a pair of scissors, some scissors', **duas calças** 'two pairs of trousers', **esse fone de ouvido** 'these headphones':

Essa bermuda é pequena para mim.
These shorts are too small for me.

3.4.4 Singular to refer to pairs of things

In spoken and informal written language, Brazilian Portuguese uses the singular to refer to body parts and items of clothing that come in pairs, such as eyes, ears, hands, feet, arms, legs, shoes, socks, gloves, contact lenses, etc. Thus, **um sapato** *can* mean 'a shoe',[5] but is much more commonly used to mean 'a pair of shoes':

O Vinícius tem olho azul.
Vinícius has blue eyes.

Quem é aquele rapaz de ombro largo?
Who's that guy with the broad shoulders?

Meu pé está doendo.
My feet are hurting./My foot is hurting.

Você usa lente?
Do you wear contacts?

Ela estava usando uma bota branca.
She was wearing (a pair of) white boots.

Comprei duas sandálias na promoção.
I bought two pairs of sandals on special offer.

NOTES

3 The plural with the definite article would also be used in spoken language if referring to specific children: **As crianças adoram história de fantasma**. 'The children love ghost stories.' In fact, the spoken language can differentiate between general and specific statements (**Criança adora ...** vs. **As crianças adoram ...**) whereas the written language cannot, as the definite article is also required in general statements – see **4.1.4** (i).

4 The word **óculos** 'glasses', though plural in form, is used as a singular noun in the spoken language: **um óculos** 'a pair of glasses', **Gostou do meu óculos novo?** 'Do you like my new glasses?'

5 When referring to one shoe or sock of a pair, **pé** 'foot' is used: **Não acho o outro pé do meu sapato**. 'I can't find my other shoe.' Similarly, **mão** 'hand' is used in the case of gloves: **Perdi uma mão da minha luva**. 'I've lost a glove/one of my gloves.'

3.4.5 **Singular expressing one each**

Portuguese uses the singular rather than the plural when each member of a plural subject has only one of a particular noun:

Os monges raspam a cabeça.
The monks shave their heads.

Todos os homens tiraram o chapéu.
All the men took their hats off.

Você sabe o nome de todos os alunos?
Do you know the names of all the students?

3.4.6 **Singular with family names**

Family names are not pluralized when used to refer to the family members collectively:

os Smith   the Smiths

a mansão dos Marinho   the Marinhos' mansion

3.4.7 **Singular after collective nouns**

Singular collective nouns, such as **grande número de** 'a large number of', **a maioria de** 'the majority of, most', **metade de** 'half of', **uma centena de** 'about a hundred', **um terço de** 'a third of', are usually followed by verbs and adjectives in the singular:[6]

A maioria dos alunos é brasileira.
Most of the students are Brazilian.

Mais da metade dos candidatos é reprovada.
More than half the candidates fail.

Um terço dos operários está disposto a aderir à greve.
A third of the workers are prepared to join the strike.

But the verb **ser** 'to be' is used in the plural when followed by a plural noun:

A maioria dos enfermeiros são mulheres./A maioria dos enfermeiros é mulher.
Most (of the) nurses are women.

NOTE   6   English uses a plural verb in such cases. In British English in particular, singular nouns that denote a collective, such as *family*, *team*, *police*, *company*, etc., are often used with a plural verb (e.g. *How are your family?*). This is never the case in Portuguese.

3.5 # Countability mismatches

3.5.1 **Portuguese plural corresponds to English uncountable singular**

There are a number of nouns where the Portuguese plural corresponds semantically to an uncountable singular in English, e.g. **aplausos** 'applause', **conselhos** 'advice', **dados** 'data', **equipamentos** 'equipment', **evidências** 'evidence', **fofocas** 'gossip', **gírias** 'slang', **imóveis** 'real estate', **informações** 'information', **móveis** 'furniture', **negócios** 'business', **notícias** 'news', **provas** 'proof', **raios/relâmpagos** 'lightning', **softwares** 'software', **talheres** 'cutlery/silverware', **trovões** 'thunder'. The singular of such nouns has to be translated using 'a piece of . . .' or another partitive word, e.g. **um raio** 'a bolt of lightning', **um relâmpago** 'a flash of lightning', **um trovão** 'a clap of thunder':

> **um móvel antigo**
> a piece of antique furniture

> **As informações são armazenadas em CD-ROM.**
> The information is stored on CD-ROM.

> **Ela me deu dois bons conselhos.**
> She gave me two pieces of good advice.

But note that, in the spoken language, nouns such as those listed above are often used in the singular in a generic sense, following the principle explained in **3.4.1**:

> **Brasileiro fala muita gíria**.
> Brazilians use a lot of slang.

> **Sempre peço conselho ao meu pai**.
> I always ask my dad for advice.

> **Não é bom espalhar fofoca**.
> It's not good to spread gossip.

3.5.2 Indefinite article with uncountable nouns

Many nouns that are normally uncountable in English can be used with the indefinite article in Portuguese to mean 'some, an amount of':

> **Ele herdou um dinheiro do avô.**
> He inherited some money from his grandfather.

> **Vai um leitinho no chá?**
> Would you like a little milk in your tea?

3.5.3 Abstract nouns used countably

Similarly, many abstract nouns can be used countably to mean 'an instance of . . .', 'an act of . . .', 'a . . . thing':

> **O assassinato do menino foi uma barbaridade.**
> The murder of the boy was a barbaric act.

> **Ele falou várias idiotices.**
> He said a number of stupid things.

Notes for Spanish speakers

The letter -z is retained before the plural ending (cf. **feliz** > **felizes**, **voz** > **vozes**) while final -l is replaced with -is (cf. **jornal** > **jornais**, **papel** > **papéis**, **fuzil** > **fuzis**). Words ending in -**m** or -**n** in the singular end in -**ns** in the plural (cf. **trem** > **trens**, **hífen** > **hífens**), while the plural endings -*anes*, -*anos* and -*(i)ones* occur in Portuguese as -**ães**, -**ãos** and -**ões** respectively (cf. **alemães** 'Germans', **cidadãos** 'citizens', **melões** 'melons', **decisões** 'decisions'). The use of singular nouns with generic plural meaning is a distinctive feature of spoken Brazilian Portuguese.

4

Articles

4.1 The definite article

In English, the definite article has only one form for all nouns: 'the'. In Portuguese, the form of the definite article depends on the gender and number of the noun it accompanies.

4.1.1 Forms of the definite article

The forms of the definite article are as follows:

	Singular	*Plural*
Masculine	o	os
Feminine	a	as

Examples:

o jornal 'the newspaper'
a casa 'the house'
os homens 'the men'
as mulheres 'the women'.

4.1.2 Pronunciation of the definite articles

The masculine singular and plural forms are usually unstressed and pronounced [u] and [us]. If stress is required for some reason, they are pronounced with the close *o* sound: [o] and [os]. The feminine articles are pronounced [a] and [as], as you would expect.

Note that, when the word following the plural articles begins with a vowel, *h* or a voiced consonant (*b*, *d*, *g*, *l*, *m*, *n*, *r*, *v*), the *s* is pronounced [z] as the article and the word it accompanies are run together, e.g. **os homens** [u'zɔmẽjs], **as mulheres** [azmu'ʎɛris].

4.1.3 Contractions of the definite articles with prepositions

The prepositions **a** 'to', **de** 'of, from', **em** 'at, in, on' and **por** 'by, for, through' combine with the definite articles to form single-word contractions:

Preposition	*Reduced form*	o	os	a	as
a	–	ao	aos	à	às
de	d-	do	dos	da	das
em	n-	no	nos	na	nas
por	pel-	pelo	pelos	pela	pelas

Note also that the preposition **para**, which in the spoken language is usually pronounced [pra], forms the following phonetic contractions with the definite articles: [pru], [prus], [pra], [pras], so **Ele vai para o Rio** 'He's going to Rio' is pronounced ['eli vai pru 'hiu].

4.1.4 Principal differences between the uses of the definite article in Portuguese and English

The use of the definite article in Portuguese largely corresponds to the use of 'the' in English, although there are a number of important differences.

The definite article is used in Portuguese in the following cases where English does not use 'the':

(i)   With nouns used in a general sense:[1]

> **um país caracterizado pela diversidade**
> a country characterized by diversity

> **O leite faz bem à saúde.**
> Milk is good for you.

> **A música brasileira é muito conhecida no exterior.**
> Brazilian music is very well known abroad.

> **Os políticos nem sempre falam a verdade.**
> Politicians don't always tell the truth.

(ii)   With the names of languages, except after verbs closely associated with languages, such as **falar** 'speak', **entender** 'understand', **aprender** 'learn', **estudar** 'study', etc.:

> **O russo é uma língua difícil.**
> Russian is a difficult language.

(iii)   With the names of most countries[2] (e.g. **o Brasil, a China, os Estados Unidos**), some cities (e.g. **o Rio de Janeiro, o Recife, o Cairo, o Porto** 'Oporto'), most Brazilian and American states[3] (e.g. **o Maranhão, a Bahia, o Texas, a Califórnia**) and some neighbourhoods (e.g. **o Leme, a Lapa**).

NOTES

1   But remember that the article is not used with singular nouns used in a generic plural sense in the spoken language – see **3.4.2**.

2   Among the exceptions are: **Portugal, Moçambique** and **Cuba**.

3   Brazilian states not preceded by the article: **Alagoas, Goiás, Mato Grosso, Mato Grosso do Sul, Minas Gerais, Pernambuco, Rondônia, Roraima, Santa Catarina, São Paulo, Sergipe**.

(iv)   With titles when accompanied by a proper name, e.g. **o senhor Ricardo Neves** 'Mr Ricardo Neves', **o presidente Bush**, 'President Bush', **a doutora Sandra** 'Dr Sandra', except when addressing the person in question, e.g. **Bom dia, doutora Sandra** 'Good morning, Dr Sandra'.

(v)   With proper names, e.g. **a Susana, o João, o Pelé, a Gisele Bundchen**. In this case, the article lends a tone of familiarity and is not therefore used with the names of historical figures, nor in more formal written language, such as news reporting. However, it is the norm in the spoken language except when addressing the person directly:

O Bob entende português. Não é mesmo, Bob?
Bob understands Portuguese. Isn't that right, Bob?

(vi) In numerical expressions, such as **na página 22** 'on page 22', **o início do capítulo 6** 'the beginning of Chapter 6', **na Linha 4 do metrô** 'on Line 4 of the metro', etc.

(vii) With the names of meals and seasons,[4] e.g. **depois do café da manhã** 'after breakfast', **na hora do almoço** 'at lunchtime', **na primavera** 'in (the) spring', etc.

O que você comeu no jantar?
What did you have for dinner?

---

4 Note that the days of the week are not normally preceded by the definite article, but its use is obligatory in conjunction with the prepositions **em** and **a** meaning 'on', e.g. **na terça**, **no sábado**, **aos domingos**, etc.

(viii) With the names of companies, shops, bars, restaurants, streets, TV networks and channels, computer programs, sports teams, etc. (see also **2.2.6** and **2.2.7**):

Ela trabalha na Petrobras.
She works for Petrobras.

Comemos no McDonald's.
We ate at McDonald's.

É melhor pegar a Frei Caneca.
It's better to take Frei Caneca (*street*).

O jogo vai passar na Globo.
The game's going to be on Globo TV.

Não consigo abrir o Word.
I can't open Word.

Ele jogou pelo Palmeiras.
He played for Palmeiras.

(ix) Before the possessive adjectives (**meu**, **teu**, **seu**, **nosso**, etc. – see **9.3.6** for full explanation of this usage):

Carimbaram o seu passaporte?
Did they stamp your passport?

(x) The definite article is used in Portuguese where English would use a possessive adjective before a part of the body, item of clothing, accessory or family member belonging to the subject of the sentence:

Ele tirou os óculos.
He took his glasses off.

Coloque a mão na cabeça.
Put your hand on your head.

Perdi o celular.
I've lost my cell phone.

Ela parece com o pai.
She looks like her father.

▶ **9.4** (p. 107); **37.3** (p. 334); **40.3** (p. 351)

4.1.5 | Pronominal use of the definite article

The appropriate form of the definite article may be used pronominally before **de** 'of', **que** 'which, that', an adjective or a possessive referring back to a noun that has been mentioned before, to avoid repetition. This usage is equivalent to the English 'the (. . .) one(s)':

Vi a foto do Davi e a do Pedro.
I saw the photo of Davi and the one of Pedro.

Meu carro é azul. O do meu pai é preto.
My car's blue. My dad's is black.

Tenho que olhar as minhas roupas e separar as que quero levar.
I have to look over my clothes and sort out the ones I want to take.

Os novos modelos são menos volumosos do que os antigos.
The new models are less bulky than the old ones.

Desculpe, confundi a sua mala com a minha.
Sorry, I mistook your suitcase for mine.

4.2 | The indefinite article

The indefinite article (English 'a(n)') also has distinct forms for masculine and feminine in Portuguese. Unlike English, the indefinite article also has plural forms corresponding to English 'some'.

4.2.1 | Forms of the indefinite article

The forms of the indefinite article are as follows:

	Singular	*Plural*
Masculine	**um**	**uns**
Feminine	**uma**	**umas**

Examples:

um livro 'a book'
uma maçã 'an apple'
uns garfos 'some forks'
umas xícaras 'some cups'.

4.2.2 | Contractions of the indefinite article with prepositions

The preposition **em** 'at, in, on' can combine with the indefinite article to form a single-word contraction, but this is not obligatory. The contraction is normally made in speech, but not always in the written language:

	Reduced form	**um**	**uns**	**uma**	**umas**
em	**n-**	**num**	**nuns**	**numa**	**numas**

Similar contractions with **de** 'of, from' (**dum**, **duns**, **duma**, **dumas**) are nowadays rare and should not be imitated. **De** and **um, uns, uma, umas** are usually run together in speech as [dʒũ, dʒũs, 'dʒuma, 'dʒumas], but are written separately.

Principal differences between the uses of the indefinite article in Portuguese and English

The use of the indefinite article in Portuguese largely corresponds to the use of 'a(n)' in English, although there are a number of important differences.

The indefinite article is not normally used in Portuguese in the following cases:

(i)   After the verb **ser** 'to be' when describing a person's nationality, profession or religion:

> **Ela é médica.**
> She's a doctor.

> **Ele é neozelandês.**
> He's a New Zealander.

> **Sou budista.**
> I'm a Buddhist.

▶ **34.6** (p. 317)

(ii)   After the verbs **tornar-se** and **virar** 'to become':

> **um músico que se tornou escritor**
> a musician who became a writer

> **A casa virou museu.**
> The house has become a museum.

(iii)   After the word **como** when it means 'as':

> **Ele trabalha como garçom num restaurante.**
> He works as a waiter in a restaurant.

> **Como advogado, não posso comentar.**
> As a lawyer, I can't comment.

(iv)   Before a noun used as a direct object in a generic sense:

> **Você já comprou passagem?**
> Have you bought a ticket yet?

> **O hotel tem piscina.**
> The hotel has a pool.

> **Não tenho carro.**
> I don't have a car.

(v)   After the prepositions **de** 'with, in' when used to specify someone's characteristics and **sem** 'without':

> **um homem de bengala**
> a man with a walking stick

> **Saí de casa sem guarda-chuva.**
> I came out without an umbrella.

(vi)   When an indefinite noun is used in apposition, usually to a name:

> **Bebeto, antigo jogador da seleção.**
> Bebeto, a former player in the national squad.

Ele nasceu em Porto Feliz, cidade próxima a Sorocaba.
He was born in Porto Feliz, a town near Sorocaba.

4.2.3.2 The indefinite article occurs in Portuguese in the following cases where it is not used in English:

(i)   With abstract and otherwise uncountable nouns when qualified by an adjective:

Ele fala um inglês impecável.
He speaks impeccable English.

Está um tempo horrível lá fora.
It's horrible weather outside.

Ela tem uma paciência incrível.
She has incredible patience.

O filme é de uma beleza arrebatadora.
The film is breathtakingly beautiful.

In informal speech, an adjective may be dispensed with for emphatic effect in expressions like:

Estou com uma fome!
I'm so hungry!

Caiu uma chuva essa noite!
There was one heck of a rainstorm last night!

(ii)   With many abstract nouns to mean one instance:

Acabei dizendo uma besteira.
I ended up saying something stupid.

O que eles fizeram foi uma crueldade.
What they did was cruel/an act of cruelty.

(iii)   Especially in the colloquial spoken language, with normally uncountable nouns to mean 'some', 'a piece of':

Meu pai me deu um dinheiro.
My dad gave me some money.

Comi uma carne e um arroz branco.
I had a piece of meat and some plain rice.

4.2.4   Use of *uns/umas*

The plurals of the indefinite article correspond to the English 'some' in the sense of 'a few', 'a number of':

Passei uns dias em São Paulo.
I spent a few days in São Paulo.

Preciso comprar umas canetas.
I need to buy some pens.

They have a special usage preceding a number in the sense of 'about, around':

Recebi uns dez telefonemas.
I got about ten phone calls.

Deve custar uns cem reais.
It must cost about a hundred reais.

daqui a umas duas semanas
in about two weeks

A festa vai começar a umas oito horas.
The party'll start around eight.

Notes for Spanish speakers

Portuguese has a more complex set of contractions with the definite article, as all four forms of the article form contractions with the prepositions **a**, **de**, **em** and **por**. There is no neuter article in Portuguese: the masculine singular **o** is used before adjectives (e.g. **o bom é que** . . . 'the good thing is . . .', **fazer o possível** 'to do your best', etc.) and the adverb **como** to express 'how . . .' (e.g. **É incrível como ele é ingênuo.** 'It's incredible how naive he is.'). The definite article is used far more extensively in Portuguese in conjunction with proper nouns, most notably with names of people, companies and countries. It can also be used before possessive adjectives.

5

Adjectives and adverbs

Portuguese adjectives agree in gender and number with the nouns they refer to – see **2.3** and **3.2** on the formation of the feminine and plural forms of adjectives.

5.1 Position of adjectives

▶ **36.1.2** (p. 321)

Another important difference between Portuguese and English is that the default position for attributive adjectives is *after* the noun in Portuguese:

> **um livro interessante**
> an interesting book

> **as forças armadas brasileiras**
> the Brazilian armed forces.

This is such an instinctive rule that other types of words, names, etc. are placed after the noun when used adjectivally:

> **tamanho família** 'family size'

> **promoção relâmpago** 'flash sale'

> **uma picape Toyota** 'a Toyota pick-up'.

However, certain types of adjectives can be placed before the noun when their purpose is not to differentiate or specify, but rather to mention an inherent quality of the noun. This kind of stylistic device is mainly confined to the written language, especially journalistic style:

> **na longínqua China**
> in far-away China (*there is no 'nearby China'*)

> **um oásis no meio de um vasto deserto**
> an oasis in the middle of a vast desert (*vastness is an inherent quality of deserts*)

> **uma TV de alta definição**
> a high-definition TV

Adjectives which express a subjective opinion may also be placed before the noun when there is a specifying adjective or other complement following it:

> **Tomamos um excelente vinho francês.**
> We drank an excellent French wine. (*'excellent' is an opinion, 'French' specifies the type of wine*)

É a mais difícil prova de ciclismo do mundo.
It's the world's most difficult cycling event. *('most difficult' is subjective and the noun is further qualified by 'cycling')*

These are questions of style which you can develop a feel for through extensive reading.

5.2 Adjectives that always precede the noun

Certain types of adjectives always precede the noun:

(i)   ordinal numbers and **último** 'last';
(ii) indefinite adjectives and those of quantity, e.g. **cada** 'each every', **qualquer** 'any', **outro** 'other', **muito** 'much, a lot of', etc. (see **Chapter 13**);
(iii) irregular superlatives – see **5.9.3**;
(iv) **chamado** 'so-called', **futuro** 'future',[1] **mero** 'mere'.

NOTE   1   **futuro** is used after the noun in a specialized economic sense, e.g. **o mercado futuro do dólar** 'the dollar futures market'.

5.3 Adjectives with different meanings according to their position

A number of common adjectives have slightly different meanings according to whether they are placed before or after the noun:

	Before noun	*After noun*
antigo	old, former	old-fashioned, antique
	meu antigo professor	**um rádio antigo**
	my former teacher	an old-fashioned radio
bastante	quite a lot	sufficient, enough
	bastante dinheiro	**dinheiro bastante**
	quite a lot of money	sufficient money
belo	fine, good-looking	beautiful
	um belo dia	**uma mulher bela**
	one fine day	a beautiful woman
bom	good (= *general sense*)	good (= *moral sense*)
	um bom livro	**um homem bom**
	a good book	a good man
certo	a certain, one	right (= *correct*)
	a certa altura	**a resposta certa**
	at a certain point	the right answer
determinado	certain, particular	fixed, determined
	um determinado assunto	**um prazo determinado**
	a certain subject	a fixed period of time
diferentes (*pl.*)	different (= *various*)	different (= *not the same*)
	diferentes tipos de vírus	**três tipos diferentes**
	various types of virus	three different types
diversos (*pl.*)	various	diverse, differing
	diversos países	**opiniões diversas**
	various countries	differing opinions

grande	great	big, large
	uma grande atriz	**um carro grande**
	a great actress	a big car
	uma grande decepção	
	a great/big disappointment	
mau	bad (= *general sense*)	bad, evil (= *moral sense*)
	mau tempo	**uma pessoa má**
	bad weather	an evil person
mesmo	same	actual, very
	no mesmo dia	**no dia mesmo do casamento**
	on the same day	on the very day of the wedding
novo	new (= *another*)	new (= *brand new*)
	uma nova folha	**uma bicicleta nova**
	a new sheet of paper	a new bike
pequeno	small, little (*inherently*)	small (= *as opposed to big*)
	see note (i) below	
pobre	poor (= *pitiful*)	poor (= *without money*)
	um pobre órfão	**uma família pobre**
	a poor orphan	a poor family
próprio	own; himself/herself	of one's own
	minha própria casa	**uma casa própria**
	my own house	a house of one's own
	o próprio rei	
	the king himself	
próximo	next, upcoming	nearby
	a próxima edição	**um hospital próximo**
	the next edition	a nearby hospital
puro	pure (= *nothing but*)	pure (= *clean, purified*)
	pura maldade	**água pura**
	pure evil	pure water
semelhante	such	similar
	com semelhante empenho	**uma situação semelhante**
	with such commitment	a similar situation
único	only, single	unique
	uma única chance	**uma chance única**
	a single chance	a unique chance
	a única solução	**ser filho único**
	the only solution	to be an only child
velho	old (= *of long standing*)	old (= *aged*)
	um velho amigo	**um carro velho**
	an old friend	an old car
verdadeiro	real, veritable	true
	o verdadeiro assassino	**uma história verdadeira**
	the real murderer	a true story
	um verdadeiro pesadelo	
	a veritable nightmare	

NOTES

(i) **pequeno** is usually placed before the noun when it is used descriptively or when it refers to inherent smallness:

pequenas empresas
small businesses

Eles moram num pequeno apartamento em Copacabana.
They live in a small apartment in Copacabana.

It is placed after the noun when the smallness is emphasized and there is an idea of contrast with 'big':

Estou procurando um apartamento pequeno.
I'm looking for a small apartment. (*as opposed to a big one*)

(ii) **bom** (= *of good quality*) can be placed after the noun for emphatic contrast:

Faz tempo que não vejo um filme bom.
It's a while since I saw a *good* movie.

(iii) Adjectives are always placed after the noun when they are further qualified:

um carro muito velho
a very old car

uma casa tão pequena
such a small house

um cara bom de garfo
a guy who likes his food (*literally*, 'good with a fork')

(iv) The adjective 'bad' in the sense of 'of low quality, of a low standard' is usually translated with the word **ruim**, which is always placed after the noun. The difference between pre-nominal **mau** and post-nominal **ruim** is that **mau** is a more objective measure of badness, while **ruim** implies a subjective value judgement:

mau tempo
bad weather (*adverse weather conditions*)

tempo ruim
bad weather (*unpleasant weather*).

It follows that only **ruim** can be intensified in this sense:

tempo muito ruim
very bad weather.

After a noun or the verb 'to be', **mau/má** means 'morally bad, evil, mean, nasty'. Other senses of 'bad' are conveyed with **ruim**:

Ele foi tão mau comigo.
He was so mean to me.

Sou ruim em geografia.
I'm bad at geography.

O tempo estava ruim naquele dia.
The weather was bad that day.

▶ **36.1.2** (p. 321)

5.4 Adjectives used as nouns

All adjectives that describe people can be used as nouns in Portuguese, e.g. **um cego** 'a blind man', **uma velha** 'an old woman', **os desempregados** 'the unemployed', **as grávidas** '(the) pregnant women'. In English, you have to add a noun such as 'man, boy; woman, girl; person, people' if there is no distinct word for the noun meaning. However, the masculine plural can have a generic meaning (see **os desempregados** above) corresponding to the English 'the' + adjective:

> **os sem-teto**
> the homeless
>
> **os ricos**
> the rich.

A few adjectives can be used with the masculine singular definite article **o** to mean 'the . . .' as in English:

> **O impensável aconteceu.**
> The unthinkable happened.
>
> **Vou fazer o possível.**
> I'll do what I can. / I'll do my best.

Note also expressions of the type **o bom é . . .** 'the good thing is . . .', **o certo é . . .** 'the right thing (to do) is . . .', **o difícil é . . .** 'the difficult thing/part is . . .', **o importante é . . .** 'the important thing is . . .', etc.:

> **O bom é que, desse jeito, ganhamos tempo.**
> The good thing is that, this way, we gain some time.
>
> **Conhecer pessoas é fácil, o difícil é achar a pessoa certa.**
> Meeting people is easy; the difficult part is finding the right person.

Whereas it is normally necessary in English to add 'one/ones' to an adjective when referring back to a noun mentioned previously, in Portuguese the adjective stands alone, though, of course, it must agree in gender and number with the noun it refers to:

> **Esses pratos são pequenos. Acho que precisamos de maiores.**
> These plates are too small. I think we need bigger ones.
>
> **Gostei da blusa vermelha, mas prefiro a azul.**
> I like the red sweater, but I prefer the blue one.

5.5 Adjectives used as adverbs

A number of adjectives are used in the masculine singular (base) form as adverbs:

	Adverb meaning(s)
adoidado (*colloquial*)	like crazy

> **Dançavam adoidado.**
> They were dancing like crazy.

alto	high; loud(ly)

> **Você consegue alcançar mais alto do que eu.**
> You can reach higher than I can.
>
> **Ele fala muito alto.**
> He talks very loud(ly).

baixo	low; quietly

> **O avião voava baixo demais.**
> The plane was flying too low.

É melhor falar baixo para não acordar as crianças.
You'd best keep your voice down so as not to wake the kids.

barato cheap(ly)

Compramos a casa barato.
We bought the house cheap.

caro a lot (of money); dearly

O anel custou caro.
The ring cost a lot.

Ele vai pagar caro pelo que fez.
He'll pay dearly for what he's done.

direito properly

Você não limpou a pia direito.
You didn't clean the sink properly.

direto direct(ly), straight; all the time (*colloquial*)

Ele foi direto ao assunto.
He went straight to the point.

Ela mata aula direto.
She's always cutting class.

duro hard

Trabalhamos duro para chegar até aqui.
We've worked hard to get this far.

errado[2] wrong

Você escreveu meu nome errado.
You've spelt my name wrong.

NOTE   2   In more formal style: **de forma errada** 'wrongly'

---

firme firmly, steadily

Eles namoram firme há três anos.
They've been going steady (= *dating firmly*) for three years.

forte heavily, hard

Chovia forte na hora do acidente.
It was raining hard at the time of the accident.

Ele bateu forte com a cabeça no chão.
He hit his head hard on the ground.

junto together, along (with)

Meu pai tem que ir a Nova York e minha mãe vai junto.
My dad has to go to New York and my mum's going along.

rápido	fast, quickly
	Não consigo andar tão rápido. I can't walk that fast.
reto	straight (ahead)
	Você segue reto toda a vida. You keep going straight as far as you can go.
só	only, just
	Eu só queria tirar uma dúvida. I'd just like to ask a question.

Other adjectives are used adverbially in the spoken language. Here are some examples:

O nosso time vai ganhar fácil.
Our team's going to win easily.

Pode estacionar aqui tranquilo.
You can park here no problem.

Você está falando sério?
Are you being serious?

Preciso arranjar emprego urgente.
I need to find a job urgently.

5.6 Formation of adverbs of manner

Just as English derives adverbs of manner from adjectives by adding the suffix -*ly*, so Portuguese does the same by adding the ending **-mente** to the feminine form of the adjective, e.g. **lento** 'slow' > **lentamente** 'slowly', **frio** 'cold' > **friamente** 'coldly', **infeliz** 'unfortunate' > **infelizmente** 'unfortunately'.

Note that any written accent the adjective may carry is lost when the **-mente** suffix is added, e.g. **fácil** 'easy' > **facilmente** 'easily', **ingênuo** 'naive' > **ingenuamente** 'naively', and that the adverb derived from **comum** 'common' is spelt **comumente** 'commonly'.

When one adverb of manner follows another, only the second has the **-mente** suffix, e.g. **lenta e cuidadosamente** 'slowly and carefully'.

Another way of expressing an adverb of manner is to use the phrase **de forma** followed by the feminine form of the adjective, e.g. **de forma adequada** 'suitably', **de forma incorreta** 'incorrectly', etc. This type of adverbial sounds more formal than the **-mente** type.

5.7 Position of adverbs and adverbials

Adverbs of time, such as **sempre** 'always', **geralmente** 'usually, generally', **logo** 'soon', and some others, such as **só** 'only', **apenas** 'just', **talvez** 'perhaps', **provavelmente** 'probably', are usually placed between subject and verb, except with the verbs **ser** and **estar** 'to be'. In fact, this is just as in English:

Ela provavelmente volta amanhã.
She's probably coming back tomorrow.

Ele às vezes esquece as coisas.
He sometimes forgets things.

BUT **Ele está sempre bem-vestido.**
He's always well dressed.

Adverbs of manner are usually placed immediately after the verb and before any direct object. This is different from English, which usually places the adverb of manner between subject and verb:

Planejamos cuidadosamente os nossos gastos mensais.
We carefully plan our monthly expenditure.

In both languages, the adverb of manner may be placed after the direct object to give it greater emphasis:

Você tem que planejar os gastos mensais cuidadosamente.
You have to plan your monthly expenditure carefully.

Adverbial phrases normally occur in this position too:

Segui as instruções à risca.
I followed the instructions *to the letter*.

5.8 Comparison of adjectives and adverbs

There is no equivalent to the English *-er/-est* endings in Portuguese; all adjectives and adverbs (except those in listed in **5.9**) are made comparative by preceding them with the word **mais** 'more':

Aquele outro modelo é mais caro.
That other model is more expensive.

Você pode falar um pouco mais devagar?
Can you speak a little more slowly?

Meu irmão é mais novo do que eu.
My brother is younger than me.

A gente se vê mais tarde.
We'll see each other later.

The only difference between the comparative and superlative in Portuguese is that the superlative is normally preceded by the definite article 'the' or a possessive (as in English). In other cases, especially with adverbs, only the context makes it clear whether the sense is comparative or superlative:

Ela é a aluna mais inteligente da sala.
She's the cleverest/smartest student in the class.

meu amigo mais querido
my dearest friend

Aqui o rio é mais largo.
Here, the river is wider. *or* Here, the river is at its widest.

O Renato trabalha mais rápido.
Renato works faster *or* the fastest.

The last two sentences can be phrased differently if it is important to emphasize the superlative meaning:

> **Esse é o ponto mais largo do rio.**
> This is the widest point of the river.

> **Quem trabalha mais rápido é o Renato.**
> The person who works the fastest is Renato.

5.9 Irregular comparative forms

5.9.1 The following adjectives and adverbs have irregular comparative forms:

	Comparative/superlative
bom 'good'; **bem** 'well'	**melhor** 'better/best'
mau, ruim 'bad'; **mal** 'badly'	**pior** 'worse/worst'
grande 'big, great'	**maior** 'bigger/biggest, greater/greatest'
pequeno 'small'	**menor** 'smaller/smallest'
muito 'much, many; a lot'	**mais** 'more/most'
pouco 'little, few'	**menos** 'less/least, fewer/fewest'.

5.9.2 Note that **melhor, pior, maior** and **menor** are the same for masculine and feminine singular, the plural forms being **melhores, piores, maiores** and **menores** for both genders. The words **mais** and **menos** are invariable:

> **Dizem que os vinhos franceses são os melhores do mundo.**
> They say that French wines are the best in the world.

> **Parece que a situação está pior do que imaginávamos.**
> It seems that the situation is worse than we imagined.

> **Vocês precisam de mais toalhas?**
> Do you need more towels?

5.9.3 When used attributively, **melhor, pior, maior** and **menor** are placed *after* the noun with comparative meaning and *before* the noun with superlative meaning:

> **o maior jogador de todos os tempos**
> the greatest player of all time

> **Você tem um número maior?**
> Do you have a bigger size?

5.9.4 When used attributively, **mais** and **menos** are placed before the noun. Only the context makes it clear whether the intended meaning is comparative or superlative, but there is seldom any ambiguity:

> **Você quer mais café?**
> Would you like some more coffee?

> **Ganha quem cometer menos erros.**
> The person who makes the fewest mistakes wins.

5.9.5 To say 'another one/two/three, etc.', **mais** is placed before the number:

> **Essa cerveja desceu muito bem. Acho que vou tomar mais uma.**
> That beer went down very well. I think I'll have another one.

> **O surto de dengue fez mais 15 vítimas.**
> The outbreak of dengue fever has claimed another 15 victims.

5.9.6 To say 'one/two/three, etc. more/less', the phrases **a mais** or **a menos** are placed after the noun:

> **O nosso time tem três pontos a menos que o líder da tabela.**
> Our team is three points behind the league leader.

> **O professor nos deu duas semanas a mais para concluir o trabalho.**
> The teacher gave us two more weeks to complete the assignment.

These phrases can also be used to mean 'one/two/three, etc. too many/few':

> **Tem duas cadeiras a mais na mesa.**
> There are two chairs too many at the table.

> **Aquele cara tem um parafuso a menos.**
> That guy has a screw loose. (*literally*, 'is one screw short')

5.10 The syntax of comparative sentences

▶ **Chapter 37** (p. 329)

5.10.1 'Than' is usually translated **do que**, or less frequently, **que**:

> **Ele já está mais alto do que o pai.**
> He's already taller than his father.

> **Ela ganha menos que eu.**
> She earns less than me.

> **Fui melhor do que esperava na prova.**
> I did better than expected on the test.

5.10.2 Note that, before a numerical expression, 'than' is translated **de** after **mais** 'more' or **menos** 'less':

> **mais de cem mil pessoas**
> more than a hundred thousand people

> **Terminei em menos de uma hora.**
> I finished in less than an hour.

5.10.3 'As . . . as' is translated **tão . . . quanto** (more common) or **tão . . . como**:

> **A irmã é tão talentosa quanto ela.**
> Her sister is as talented as she is.

> **Não estou tão otimista como você.**
> I'm not as optimistic as you are.

5.10.4 'In' after a superlative is translated with the preposition **de**:

> **o prédio mais alto do mundo**
> the tallest building in the world.

5.10.5 Sentences of the type 'the more . . ., the more . . .' are expressed using **quanto mais . . , mais . . .'**:

> **Quanto mais a cachaça envelhece, melhor fica.**
>
> The more cachaça ages, the better it gets.
>
> **Quanto maior a turma, menos tempo o professor pode dedicar a cada aluno.**
> The bigger the class, the less time the teacher can devote to each student.

5.10.6 Note also the expressions **cada vez mais** 'more and more' and **ainda mais** 'even more':

> **cada vez pior/mais tarde/mais difícil**
> worse and worse/later and later/more and more difficult
>
> **ainda maior/mais quente/mais caro**
> even bigger/hotter/more expensive

5.11 The absolute superlative

5.11.1 There is a second type of superlative in Portuguese that is used for emphasis to mean 'really . . .', 'extremely . . .'. It is formed as follows:

(i) Adjectives ending in **-o** or **-e** replace the final vowel with **-íssimo**:

> **belo** > **belíssimo**   **um dia belíssimo**
> a really beautiful day
>
> **interessante** > **interessantíssimo**   **uma palestra interessantíssima**
> an extremely interesting lecture.

(ii) Adjectives ending in **-z** change this to **-c-** before **-íssimo**:

> **feliz** > **felicíssimo**   **Fiquei felicíssimo.**
> I was overjoyed.

(iii) Adjectives ending in **-vel** change this to **-bil-** before **-íssimo**:

> **agradável** > **agradabilíssimo**   **uma tarde agradabilíssima**
> a most pleasant afternoon.

(iv) Irregular forms:

> **bom** 'good' > **ótimo** 'great, really good'
> **mau**, **ruim** 'bad' > **péssimo** 'terrible, really bad'
> **fácil** 'easy' > **facílimo** 'really easy'
> **difícil** 'difficult' > **dificílimo** 'really difficult'
> **pequeno** 'small' > **mínimo** 'tiny, really small'
> **antigo** 'old' > **antiquíssimo** (**quí** pronounced /kwi/) 'ancient, really old'
> **cruel** 'cruel' > **crudelíssimo** 'extremely cruel'
> **pobre** 'poor' > **paupérrimo** 'extremely poor'
> **simpático** 'nice, friendly' > **simpaticíssimo** 'extremely nice/friendly'.

5.11.2 The superlatives **máximo** 'maximum' and **mínimo** 'minimum, least, slightest' are used in a slightly different way:

> **uma velocidade máxima de 200 km/h**
> a maximum speed of 200 km/h

> **O governo aumentou o salário mínimo.**
> The government increased the minimum wage.

> **Não tenho a mínima ideia.**
> I don't have the slightest idea.

5.11.3 The absolute superlative of **amigo** 'friend, friendly' is used as a noun:

> **Ele é amicíssimo do governador.**
> He's really good friends with the governor.

5.11.4 In colloquial speech, 'irregular' absolute superlatives are often created for humorous or emphatic effect. Examples include: **chiquérrimo** 'really fancy/posh' (< **chique** 'fancy/posh'); **magérrimo** 'really thin, incredibly slim' (< **magro** 'thin'); **chatérrimo** 'incredibly boring' (< **chato** 'boring'); **carésimo** 'mega-expensive' (< **caro** 'expensive').[3]

NOTE   3   The form **magérrimo** is also used in the written language even though grammarians list the correct form as **macérrimo**. Non-standard forms, such as **chatérrimo** and **carésimo**, may be used in speech for humorous effect, but the standard forms are the regular **chatíssimo** and **caríssimo**.

5.12 Colloquial intensifiers

In addition to the standard intensifiers, such as **muito** 'very', **tão** 'so', **extremamente** 'extremely', etc., there are a number of ways of intensifying adjectives and adverbs in the colloquial spoken language:

(i)   By adding the prefix **super**, or, less commonly, **hiper** or **ultra**:

> **Aquele hotel é supercaro.**
> That hotel is really expensive.

> **Ele canta superbem.**
> He sings really well.

(ii)   By following the adjective or adverb with one of the many expressions beginning **pra** (< **para**), which range from the mild **pra burro**, **pra caramba** and others, through the stronger **pra cacete**, to the very vulgar **pra caralho**. These expressions can also be used to intensify verbs:

> **Está frio pra cacete.**
> It's damn cold.

> **O José mora longe pra dedéu.**
> José lives miles away.

> **A gente comeu pra caramba no churrasco.**
> We ate a heck of a lot at the barbecue.

(iii)   By using an exclamatory phrase introduced by **que** or **como**:

> **Que desculpa mais esfarrapada!**
> What a lame excuse! / That's such a lame excuse![4]

> **Que bom que você gostou!**
> I'm so glad you liked it!

> **Como você está linda!**
> You look so beautiful!

(iv)   The expression **o/a maior** (*literally*, 'the biggest') is frequently used before a noun in the sense of 'a real . . .', 'a major . . .', 'one hell of a . . .':

> **Tivemos a maior briga.**
> We had a major fight.

> **Levei o maior susto.**
> I got one hell of a fright.

NOTE | 4   This kind of exclamatory sentence is more common, and sounds less affected, in spoken Brazilian Portuguese than English sentences beginning 'What . . .!', 'How . . .!'. For this reason, it is usually more natural to translate them with exclamations containing the words 'such' or 'so'.

5.13 Agreement of adjectives qualifying more than one noun

An adjective that refers to more than one singular noun must be put into the plural when it follows the nouns or a linking verb such as **ser**, **estar** or **ficar**:

> **o mar e céu azuis**
> the blue sea and sky

> **O parque e o lago são lindos.**
> The park and the lake are beautiful.

If the nouns are of different genders, the adjective goes into the masculine plural:

> **o Exército e a Marinha brasileiros**
> the Brazilian army and navy

> **O Sérgio e as irmãs dele estão muito animados com a viagem.**
> Sergio and his sisters are very excited about the trip.

But if the adjective precedes the nouns, it agrees in gender and number with the first noun mentioned:

> **Como é que a religião leva a tanta violência e ódio?**
> How does religion lead to so much violence and hatred?

> **outras festas e feriados**
> other festivals and holidays.

5.14 Singular adjectives qualifying a plural noun

A plural noun may be accompanied by two or more adjectives in the singular when the adjectives refer to different instances of the noun. Look at the following examples:

alunos dos níveis intermediário e avançado
students at intermediate and advanced level(s)

as políticas econômica e orçamentária do governo
the government's economic and budgetary policies.

Notes for Spanish speakers

Portuguese adjectives do not have short forms (cf. **um grande erro** 'a great mistake', **o primeiro dia** 'the first day', **o terceiro mês** 'the third month'). 'Than' is most commonly expressed as **do que** and 'as . . . as' as **tão . . . quanto**. The only possible comparatives of **grande** and **pequeno** are **maior** and **menor** respectively (cf. **o maior quarto** 'the biggest room', **uma casa menor** 'a smaller house') and these words are never used to refer to age. Note that, in Portuguese, when you add **-mente** to the feminine form of an adjective to form an adverb, any written accent the adjective normally carries is dropped (e.g. **econômico** > **economicamente**, **sério** > **seriamente**, etc.).

6

Numbers and numerical expressions

Cardinal numbers

1–100

um, uma	one	**onze**	eleven	**vinte e um**	twenty-one
dois, duas	two	**doze**	twelve	**vinte e dois**	twenty-two
três	three	**treze**	thirteen	**trinta**	thirty
quatro	four	**catorze**	fourteen	**quarenta**	forty
cinco	five	**quinze**	fifteen	**cinquenta**	fifty
seis	six	**dezesseis**	sixteen	**sessenta**	sixty
sete	seven	**dezessete**	seventeen	**setenta**	seventy
oito	eight	**dezoito**	eighteen	**oitenta**	eighty
nove	nine	**dezenove**	nineteen	**noventa**	ninety
dez	ten	**vinte**	twenty	**cem**	a hundred

NOTES

(i) **um** and **dois** are the forms used when counting, in mathematics, phone numbers, etc., or before a masculine noun. Before a feminine noun, the forms are **uma** and **duas**, e.g. **duas casas** 'two houses'. The same applies to compound numbers, e.g. **vinte e uma mulheres** 'twenty-one women'.

(ii) When quoting phone numbers or other series of numbers, the word **meia** (short for **meia-dúzia** 'half a dozen') is normally used instead of **seis** to avoid confusion with **três** 'three':

> **o voo 467** (*read*: **quatro meia sete**)
> flight 467.

(iii) There is a less common variant of **catorze** 'fourteen' spelt **quatorze** and pronounced [kwaˈtorzi].

(iv) The **u** in **cinquenta** 'fifty' is pronounced: [sĩˈkwẽta].

(v) Note that, in compound numbers, twenty-one, twenty-two, etc., the word **e** 'and' is inserted between the ten and the unit.

(vi) **cem** alone translates as 'a hundred' or 'one hundred'. Before a smaller number, **cem** becomes **cento e . . .** , e.g. **cento e trinta e cinco** 'a hundred and thirty-five'.

6.1.2   200–999,999

duzentos -as	two hundred	**setecentos -as**	seven hundred
trezentos -as	three hundred	**oitocentos -as**	eight hundred
quatrocentos -as	four hundred	**novecentos -as**	nine hundred
quinhentos -as	five hundred	**mil**	a/one thousand
seiscentos -as	six hundred	**dois (duas) mil**	two thousand

NOTES

(i) The hundreds from 200 to 900 agree in gender with a following noun, e.g. **duzentas e quarenta páginas** 'two hundred and forty pages'. The masculine form is used in counting and mathematics.

(ii) The word **e** 'and' is inserted between the hundreds and a smaller number, as in English, e.g. **quinhentos e onze** 'five hundred and eleven'.

(iii) **mil** 'thousand' is invariable: **dois mil**, **três mil**, **quatro mil**, etc. Note that 'two thousand' is **duas mil** before a feminine noun, e.g. **duas mil e quinhentas libras** 'two thousand five hundred pounds'.

(iv) **mil** is followed by **e** 'and' before a round multiple of a hundred or a smaller number, e.g. **mil e trezentos** 'one thousand three hundred', **três mil e setenta e cinco** 'three thousand and seventy-five'. In other cases (i.e. when followed by hundreds and smaller units), **e** is not included after **mil**, e.g. **mil oitocentos e cinquenta** 'one thousand eight hundred and fifty', **duzentos e cinquenta mil novecentos e noventa e cinco** '250, 995'.

(v) Note that a full stop (not a comma) is used to separate thousands and hundreds when numbers are written in figures, e.g. **3.460** '3,460', **2.880.000** '2,800,000', etc.

(vi) On cheques and other official documents where a number is written out in words as confirmation of the amount written in figures, the convention is to write 1,000 as **hum mil**.

6.1.3   1,000,000 upwards

um milhão	a/one million	**um bilhão**	a billion
dois milhões	two million	**dois bilhões**	two billion
três milhões	three million	**um trilhão**	a trillion

NOTES

(i) Unlike **cem** and **mil**, **milhão**, **bilhão** and **trilhão** are preceded by **um** and have plural forms ending in -**ões**.

(ii) **milhão**, **milhões**, etc. may be followed by the conjunction **e** before a round number of thousands or a smaller number, but never before thousands and smaller units.

(iii) When used directly before a noun (i.e. when not part of a more complex number), **milhão**, **bilhão** and **trilhão** must be followed by the preposition **de**, e.g. **dois milhões de pessoas** 'two million people', **um bilhão de dólares** 'a billion dollars' (cf. **um milhão e quinhentos mil dólares**).

(iv) Particularly in news reporting, **milhão**, **bilhão** and **trilhão** are frequently abbreviated to **mi**, **bi** and **tri** respectively, e.g. **um déficit de R$ 70 bi** 'a 70 billion real deficit'.

6.2 Ordinal numbers

primeiro	first	**décimo primeiro**	eleventh
segundo	second	**décimo segundo**	twelfth
terceiro	third	**décimo terceiro**	thirteenth
quarto	fourth	**décimo quarto**	fourteenth
quinto	fifth	**décimo quinto**	fifteenth
sexto	sixth	**décimo sexto**	sixteenth
sétimo	seventh	**décimo sétimo**	seventeenth
oitavo	eighth	**décimo oitavo**	eighteenth
nono	ninth	**décimo nono**	nineteenth
décimo	tenth	**vigésimo**	twentieth
vigésimo primeiro	twenty-first	**ducentésimo**	two-hundredth
trigésimo	thirtieth	**trecentésimo**	three-hundredth
quadragésimo	fortieth	**quadringentésimo**	four-hundredth
quinquagésimo [kwĩ-]	fiftieth	**quingentésimo** [kwĩ-]	five-hundredth
sexagésimo [seksa-]	sixtieth	**sexcentésimo**	six-hundredth
septuagésimo	seventieth	**septingentésimo**	seven-hundredth
octogésimo	eightieth	**octingentésimo**	eight-hundredth
nonagésimo	ninetieth	**nongentésimo**	nine-hundredth
centésimo	hundredth	**milésimo**	thousandth
milionésimo	millionth	**bilionésimo**	billionth

NOTES

(i) The ordinal numbers are adjectives that agree with the noun they refer to in gender and number. The feminine and plural are formed according to the usual rules, e.g. **a sétima casa** 'the seventh house'.

(ii) With the two-word ordinals, eleventh to nineteenth, twenty-first, twenty-second, etc., both elements inflect for gender and number, e.g. **a vigésima quinta colocação** 'twenty-fifth place'.

(iii) Ordinal numbers always precede the noun they qualify.

(iv) Ordinal numbers are used as in English, except that they are not used in dates (see **6.4**).

(v) The ordinals 200th–900th are hardly ever used in the spoken language and most native speakers are unfamiliar with them. Their use is avoided by paraphrasing, e.g. **os 500 anos do Brasil** 'Brazil's 500th anniversary'.

(vi) On the rare occasions when larger ordinals are used, note that every element of the number is ordinal in Portuguese whereas, in English, only the last element is ordinal, e.g. **septuagésimo quinto** '75th', **quadringentésimo nonagésimo oitavo** '498th', **terceiro milésimo nongentésimo sétimo** '3,907th', **segundo milionésimo** 'two millionth' etc.

(vi) Ordinals are abbreviated in writing by placing a full stop after the number followed by a superscript *o* or *a* according to gender, e.g. **18.º andar** '18th floor', **a 255.ª colocação** '255th place', **o 5.000.º cliente** 'the 5,000th customer', etc. The full stop is often dropped.

6.3 Collective numbers

6.3.1 Portuguese has some commonly used collective numbers: **dezena** '(group of) ten', **centena** '(group of a) hundred' and **milhar** '(group of a) thousand'. These are nouns and may be used in the singular to express an approximate number, e.g. **uma dezena de pessoas** 'about ten people', but are more commonly found in the plural:

> **centenas de e-mails**
> hundreds of e-mails

> **milhares de quilômetros**
> thousands of kilometers

> **dezenas de visitantes**
> dozens[1] of visitors

> **dezenas de milhares de manifestantes**
> tens of thousands of demonstrators.

NOTE 1 Strictly speaking, the meaning is 'tens' not 'dozens', but 'tens' is not used in this way in English and the number is approximate anyway. The actual word for 'dozen', **dúzia**, refers to a batch of twelve items only and is not used in approximations. Note that it is followed by the preposition **de** before a noun, e.g. **uma dúzia de rosas** 'a dozen roses', **meia dúzia de ovos** 'half a dozen eggs'.

6.3.2 These collective numbers are also used in the expressions **às dezenas** 'in their dozens', **às centenas** 'in their hundreds' and **aos milhares** 'in their thousands':

> **Os refugiados continuam chegando aos milhares.**
> The refugees continue to arrive in their thousands.

6.3.3 Similar to the above are the words **quadra**, **quina** and **sena**, which are used to refer to a series of four, five or six correct lottery numbers respectively:

> **O prêmio da quina foi de 10 milhões.**
> The prize for five correct numbers was 10 million.

6.4 Dates

6.4.1 Unlike English, dates are expressed in Portuguese using cardinal numbers except for the first of the month. The date is usually preceded by the word **dia** 'day' and the preposition **de** is inserted between date and month and between month and year:

> **no dia 5 de maio de 2008**
> on May 5th 2008

> **a partir do dia primeiro de junho**
> from June 1st onwards

> **Hoje é dia 16.**
> Today is the 16th.

6.4.2 In more formal written language, the word **dia** and the definite article are omitted:

> **sua carta de 11 de abril**
> your letter of April 11th.

6.5

Note also that, in letterheads and official documents, the date is always preceded by the name of the place:

Rio de Janeiro, 18 de setembro de 2009

6.4.3 Years are read as if they were numbers, e.g. 1976 = **mil novecentos setenta e seis**, 2016 = **dois mil e dezesseis**.

6.4.4 Centuries are expressed with cardinal numbers in Portuguese:

    o século 21 *or* **XXI** (*read:* **vinte e um**)   'the 21st century'

    no século IV (*read:* **quatro**) **a.C.**   'in the 4th century BC'.

▶ **29.9** (p. 281)

6.5 Clock time

6.5.1 The equivalent of 'o'clock' is **horas**, except in the case of one o'clock, which is **uma hora**:

    Que horas são?
    What time is it?

    São duas horas.
    It's two o'clock. (NB: 'two' meaning 'two o'clock' is always **duas**.)

    É uma hora.
    It's one o'clock. (NB: 'one' meaning 'one o'clock' is always **uma**.)

6.5.2 After prepositions, clock times are preceded by the definite article **as** (or **a** before **uma**). Accordingly, 'at' with clock times is **às** (preposition **a** + **as**) or **à** before **uma**:

    Começo a trabalhar às oito.
    I start work at eight.

    O banco abre das 10h às 16h (= **dez às dezesseis horas**).
    The bank opens from 10 a.m. to 4 p.m.

6.5.3 Minutes past the hour are expressed using the conjunction **e** 'and':

    à uma e vinte
    at 1.20.

6.5.4 'Half past' is expressed . . . **e meia**. Note that there is no equivalent of '(a) quarter' when talking about clock time; use **quinze** 'fifteen':

    às 9h30 (= **nove e meia**)
    at nine thirty / half past nine

    até as 10h15 (= **dez e quinze**)
    until ten fifteen / quarter past ten.

6.5.5 Minutes to the hour are expressed using the preposition **para** 'to':

    às 10h55 (= **cinco para as onze** / **dez e cinquenta e cinco**)
    at five to eleven

das 15h45 (= **quinze para as quatro** / **três e quarenta e cinco**)
from quarter to four.

The verb **faltar** 'to be short/lacking' is often used to say the time when it involves minutes to the hour:

Faltam (or: **São**) **cinco para as quatro.**
It's five to four.

Faltavam dois minutos para a meia-noite.
It was two minutes to midnight.

6.5.6 'Twelve' is translated using **meio-dia** 'midday, noon' or **meia-noite** 'midnight' as appropriate. Note that both words are preceded by the definite article. The word **doze** 'twelve' is only used when expressing time by the 24-hour clock (see **6.5.8**):

ao meio-dia e meia
at 12.30 midday

23h50 (= **dez para a meia-noite** / **onze e cinquenta**)
11.50 at night.

6.5.7 In everyday conversation, the 12-hour clock is used. The part of the day can be specified if necessary, i.e. **da manhã** 'in the morning', **da tarde** 'in the afternoon', **da noite** 'in the evening, at night', **da madrugada** 'in the (early hours of the) morning':

O voo dele chega às sete da noite.
His flight arrives at seven in the evening.

O telefone tocou às três horas da madrugada.
The phone rang at three o'clock in the morning.

6.5.8 The 24-hour clock is used in the spoken language for giving the exact times of flights, appointments, etc. and is frequently used in the written language. Note that 24-hour clock times are still preceded by the article **as**:

o voo das 19h45 (= **dezenove e quarenta e cinco**)
the 19.45 flight

O filme começa às 22h30. (= **vinte e duas e trinta**)
The movie starts at 22.30.

6.6   Fractions

6.6.1 The words for fractions down to a tenth and from a hundredth onwards are the same as the ordinal numbers, except for **um terço** 'a third':

um décimo do PIB
a tenth of GDP

dois terços da população
two thirds of the population.

6.6.2 Fractions between a tenth and a hundredth are expressed using the word **avos** with a cardinal number:

um doze avos do orçamento
a twelfth of the budget

três dezesseis avos
three sixteenths.

6.6.3 'Half a . . .' and '. . . and a half' are translated using the adjective **meio**:

três litros e meio de leite (NB: position of **e meio**)
three and a half litres of milk

Comi meia maçã.
I ate half an apple.

6.6.4 'Half' as a noun and 'half the . . .' are translated using the noun **metade**:

a outra metade do grupo
the other half of the group

Ele comeu metade do bolo sozinho.
He ate half (of) the cake himself.

6.7 Decimal fractions

Decimal fractions are written in Portuguese with a comma in place of the decimal point. This is read **vírgula** 'comma':

0,05   (pronounced: **zero vírgula zero cinco**)

8,75   (pronounced: **oito vírgula sete cinco**).

6.8 Percentages

Percentages are expressed using **por cento** 'per cent':

60% (= sessenta por cento) dos eleitores
60 per cent of voters.

Note that an adjective accompanying a percentage must be masculine plural:

os outros 40% dos alunos
the other 40 per cent of the students

O preço aumentou em espantosos 500%.
The price has gone up by an amazing 500 per cent.

The article **os** is sometimes used before a percentage:

O índice anual de inflação ultrapassou os 10%.
The annual rate of inflation went above 10 per cent.

6.9 Monetary amounts

The currency unit and fractions thereof are separated in speech by **e** 'and', and in writing by a comma:

Custou 8,50 (= oito e cinquenta).
It cost 8.50.

When the unit of currency is specified, the fractions are usually specified too:

Custou R$8,50 (= **oito reais e cinquenta centavos**).
It cost 8 reais 50.

Note that monetary amounts are grammatically plural, the gender depending on that of the currency unit:

Vou te dar outros cem reais.
I'll give you another 100 reais.

Esses cinquenta dólares são suficientes?
Is this 50 dollars enough?

6.10 Monarchs, popes, etc.

With the names of monarchs, popes, etc. ordinal numbers are used up to ten and then cardinals. In both cases, the number is usually written in Roman numerals. Notice that there is no definite article ('the') in these expressions in Portuguese:

Dom Pedro II (Segundo)

Papa Bento XVI (Dezesseis) 'Pope Benedict XVI'

6.11 *N* and *enésimo* as indeterminate numbers

The letter **N**, pronounced ['ɛni], is used as if it were a numeral to refer to an indeterminate number, equivalent to 'umpteen', 'any number of':

Isso pode ocorrer por N motivos. (*also spelt*: **por "n" motivos**)
This can occur for any number of reasons.

The corresponding ordinal is **enésimo** 'umpteenth':

Estou te falando isso pela enésima vez.
I'm telling you this for the umpteenth time.

6.12 Gender and plural of numbers

Numbers are often used as nouns to refer to things that are numbered, such as buses, playing cards, hotel rooms, etc. The gender assigned to the number in such cases depends on what is being referred to:

o três de ouros
the three of diamonds (*playing card*)

É mais rápido pegar a 147.
It's quicker to take the 147. (*bus, feminine because of linha 'bus route'*)

O João mora no 401.
João lives in 401. (*masculine because of apartamento 'apartment'*)

Numbers which end in a vowel or nasal can form a plural by adding -s. Numbers ending in a consonant are invariable:

quatro uns	'four ones'
três noves	'three nines'
dois dez	'two tens'

Notes for Spanish speakers

The number two has distinct masculine and feminine forms in Portuguese (cf. **dois homens** 'two men', **duas mulheres** 'two women'). Compound numbers from 21 to 29 are written as three separate words (cf. **vinte e um**, **vinte e dois**, etc.) being consistent with those beyond 30. Ordinal numbers between 11th and 100th are in relatively common use; those above 100th are rarely encountered, except for **milésimo** 'thousandth'. Dates normally include the word **dia** except in very formal register (cf. **no dia 8 de novembro** 'on November 8th') and the first of the month is always referred to with the ordinal **primeiro** (cf. **no dia primeiro de maio** 'on May 1st').

7

Personal pronouns

Personal pronouns can be further categorized into subject pronouns (e.g. English *I*, *he*, *she*, *we*, *they*) and object pronouns (e.g. English *me*, *him*, *her*, *us*, *them*). An object pronoun can function either as the direct object (like English *me* in 'He hit *me*') or as the indirect object (like English *me* in 'He gave *me* a present'). Personal pronouns also occur after prepositions (e.g. 'behind *me*', 'to *them*' etc.). *I/me* and *we/us* are so-called first person pronouns referring to or including the speaker. *You* is a second person pronoun referring to the person or persons addressed. *He/him*, *she/her*, *it* and *they/them* are all third person pronouns used to refer to people or things other than the speaker and the person addressed.

The usage of personal pronouns in Brazilian Portuguese is quite complex, both in terms of which pronoun should be used and where it should be placed in relation to the verb. Furthermore, personal pronoun usage is one of the areas in which there are considerable differences between the spoken and written languages, making it necessary to learn two sets of rules, especially with regard to third person pronouns.

An overview of all the personal pronouns and their placement is provided in the tables at the end of this chapter – see **7.11**.

7.1 First person pronouns

The forms of the first person pronouns are as follows:

As subject	As object	After preposition	Meaning
eu	**me**	**mim**	I, me
nós	**nos**	**nós**	we, us

NOTES

(i) The object forms **me** and **nos** are unstressed so are pronounced [mi] and [nus] respectively.

(ii) The subject and post-preposition forms of the first person plural pronoun are identical, differing from the object form only in the written stress accent and corresponding stressed pronunciation, [nɔs] or [nɔjs].

(iii) The object forms **me** and **nos** can function as either direct or indirect objects:

A Júlia me beijou.
Julia kissed me.

O professor nos ensinou umas palavras novas.
The teacher taught us some new words.

For the placement of object pronouns, see **7.5**.

7.1.1 *a gente*

In the spoken language, it is extremely common to use the noun phrase **a gente** (*literally* 'the people'[1]) instead of **nós/nos** to mean 'we, us'. Being a singular noun, it is followed by a third person singular verb:

> **A gente mora na próxima rua.**
> We live in the next street.

> **O Paulo vai ajudar a gente.**
> Paulo's going to help us.

> **Quer ir com a gente?**
> Do you want to go with us?

Note that adjectives referring to **a gente** are used in the *masculine singular*, unless the adjective refers to women only, in which case it is feminine singular:

> **A gente está cansado.**
> We're tired.

NOTE   1   The meaning 'we, us' is so established that **a gente** is never used to mean 'the people'. 'The people' is translated **as pessoas** in the sense of 'persons', or **o povo** in the sense of 'populace, nation'.

7.2 'You'

7.2.1 *você/vocês*

The general word for 'you' is **você** when addressing one person and **vocês** when addressing more than one person. The word **você** derives historically from the noun phrase and form of address **vossa mercê** 'your mercy' (and **vocês** from the plural **vossas mercês** 'your mercies'), which has two important implications:

(i)   **você** and **vocês** are followed by verbs in the third person, singular and plural respectively:

> **Você é americano?**
> Are you American?

> **Vocês estão com fome?**
> Are you hungry?

(ii)   As the object of a verb, **você** and **vocês** are placed after it like any other noun object:

> **Considero você meu melhor amigo.**
> I consider you to be my best friend.

> **Pretendo visitar vocês ano que vem.**
> I intend to visit you next year.

7.2.2 *o senhor/a senhora*

However, when talking to an older stranger or a superior, you should use the respectful **o senhor** (*literally*, 'the gentleman') for a man and **a senhora** (*literally*, 'the lady') for a woman. These are also the forms of address used by employees in service positions to address customers. Grammatically, they are obviously nouns so must be followed by a third person verb:

> **A senhora está na fila?**
> Are you in the queue? (*to an older woman you don't know*)

> **Posso falar com o senhor?**
> Can I talk to you? (*to a man to whom you show respect, e.g. a boss or teacher*)

> **Qual o nome do senhor?**
> What's your name, sir? (*to a customer*)

> **A senhora aceita um café?**
> Would you like a coffee, madam? (*to a customer*)

As a rule of thumb, it is appropriate to use **o senhor/a senhora** in cases where in English you might address the person as 'sir' or 'madam, ma'am'.[2] If you are not sure, you can often avoid the problem by not using a subject pronoun at all – as long as you are addressing someone with a question intonation, it is clear that you mean 'you':

> **Quer sentar?**
> Would you like to sit down?

NOTE 2 Although now considered rather old-fashioned, it is not uncommon to hear people address their parents as **o senhor/a senhora**, especially in more conservative areas of Brazil. This usage parallels that of some American English speakers who address their parents as 'sir' and 'ma'am'.

7.2.3 *os senhores/as senhoras*

The titles **o senhor/a senhora** can also occur in the plural: **os senhores** (for males or males and females) and **as senhoras** (for females only), but their use is restricted to only the most formal circumstances. The tendency is to use **vocês** or to omit the subject pronoun altogether:

> **Querem me acompanhar, por favor?**
> Would you follow me, please?

7.2.4 *te* as the object form of *você*

In the spoken language, the second person object pronoun **te** is frequently used as an alternative to **você**. But, as a true unstressed object pronoun, it must be placed immediately before the verb it is associated with, functioning as either a direct or indirect object:

> **Eu te amo.** *or* **Eu amo você.**
> I love you.

> **Te empresto o dinheiro.** *or* **Empresto o dinheiro para você.**
> I'll lend you the money.

See also **7.5** on object pronoun placement.

7.2.5 Third-person object pronouns used to mean 'you'

In the written language, and occasionally in the spoken language, the third person direct object pronouns **o** (for a male), **a** (for a female), **os** (for males or males and females) and

as (for females only) and the indirect object pronouns **lhe** (for one person) and **lhes** (for more than one person) are used to mean 'you' with an equivalent degree of formality to **o senhor/a senhora**, etc.[3] The equivalences are as follows:

Subject	Direct object	Indirect object	Addressee
o senhor	o	lhe	male
a senhora	a	lhe	female
os senhores	os	lhes	males or males and females
as senhoras	as	lhes	females only.

Examples:

Posso ajudá-la?
Can I help you?

Muito prazer em conhecê-lo.
Delighted to meet you.

Em que posso lhe ser útil?
How can I be of service (to you)?

É com enorme prazer que os convidamos ao lançamento do novo livro.
We are delighted to invite you to the launch of the new book.

Vimos apresentar-lhes proposta de reforma do estatuto social.
We hereby submit (to you) a proposal for reform of the company statutes.

See **7.5** on the placement of these object pronouns.

Note that, especially in speech, **o senhor/a senhora** can also be used as the direct or indirect object:

Já vou atender o senhor.
I'll be with you in a moment, sir.

Estaremos enviando à senhora o contrato em duas vias.
We will be sending you two copies of the contract, madam.

NOTE   3   Many grammarians state that **o/a** should be used as the object form of **você** and **os/as** as the object form of **vocês**. However, this does not take account of the fact that Brazilians perceive **o(s)/a(s)** meaning 'you' to be more formal than **você(s)**. The description given here more accurately reflects actual usage.

7.3 Third person pronouns

7.3.1 Forms

Third person pronouns have a stressed form and unstressed direct and indirect object forms:

Stressed form		Unstressed forms		Meaning
		Direct object	Indirect object	
ele	masc. sing.	o	lhe	he, him, it
ela	fem. sing.	a	lhe	she, her, it
eles	masc. pl.	os	lhes	they, them
elas	fem. pl.	as	lhes	they, them

(i) The masculine forms **ele** and **eles** are pronounced with the close *e* sound, ['eli], ['elis], while the feminine forms **ela** and **elas** have the open *e* sound, ['ɛla], ['ɛlas].

(ii) The unstressed object pronouns **o(s)**, **a(s)** and **lhe(s)** are pronounced [u(s)], [a(s)] and [ʎi(s)] respectively.

(iii) The masculine singular pronouns can refer to a male person ('he, him') or any masculine singular noun ('it'), the feminine singular pronouns to a female person ('she, her') or any feminine noun ('it').

(iv) The masculine plural pronouns can refer to two or more males, two or more people of whom at least one is male, any masculine plural noun or a combination of masculine and feminine nouns ('they, them'). The feminine plural pronouns can refer to two or more females, any feminine plural noun or a combination of exclusively feminine nouns ('they, them').

(v) Notice that the indirect object pronouns **lhe/lhes** are not differentiated for gender, so **lhe** can mean '(to) him, her, it' while **lhes** means '(to) them' regardless of gender.

(vi) The third person pronouns contract with the prepositions **de** and **em** as follows: **dele**, **dela**, **deles**, **delas**; **nele**, **nela**, **neles**, **nelas**.

7.3.2 Usage

The stressed forms of the third person pronouns (**ele**, **ela**, **eles**, **elas**) are used as subject pronouns and after prepositions in both the spoken and written languages:

> **Ela gosta de chocolate.**
> She likes chocolate.

> **Vou com eles.**
> I'm going with them.

The unstressed object pronouns are used in the written language and are placed immediately before or after the verb they are associated with (see **7.5**).

Examples with direct object pronoun:

> **A vendedora o acusou de ter roubado uma calça jeans.** (*written*)
> The sales assistant accused him of stealing a pair of jeans.

> **Dei as chaves ao gerente e ele as colocou na gaveta.** (*written*)
> I gave the keys to the manager and he put them in the drawer.

Examples with indirect object pronoun:

> **A mulher alega que a agência lhe ofereceu um trabalho.** (*written*)
> The woman claims that the agency offered her a job.

> **Os pais do menino pediram ao médico que lhes contasse a verdade.** (*written*)
> The boy's parents asked the doctor to tell them the truth.

In the spoken language, the stressed forms of the third person pronouns (**ele**, **ela**, **eles**, **elas**) are also used as object pronouns, being placed after the verb in the noun-object position (like **você(s)** see **7.2.1 (ii)**). This is one of the key differences between spoken and written registers in Brazilian Portuguese:

> **Vejo ela todo dia.** (*spoken*)
> I see her every day.

A gente vai buscar eles no aeroporto. (*spoken*)
We're going to pick them up from the airport.

The indirect object is expressed using the preposition **para**:

Mandei um e-mail para ele. (*spoken*)
I sent him an e-mail.

Falei para as meninas que eu ia escrever para elas. (*spoken*)
I told the girls I'd write to them.

Translation of 'it' and 'they' referring to things

(i)   As the subject of a sentence, 'it/they' referring back to a specific noun is usually untranslated, especially in more formal style. But a pronoun can be used, and often is in informal speech. Even in more formal written style, a subject pronoun may be used to avoid ambiguity:

Que flores são aquelas? – São orquídeas.
'What flowers are those?' – 'They're orchids.'

Você já viu meu celular? (Ele) é novo.
Have you seen my cell phone? It's new.

Conheça o chá verde e entenda como ele ajuda a emagrecer!
Discover green tea and understand how it helps you to lose weight!

(ii) In speech, 'it/them' used as an object pronoun referring back to a specific noun is not usually translated at all, being understood from the context:

Achei o livro interessante e acabei comprando. (*spoken*)
I found the book interesting and ended up buying it.

O que é que você fez com as cartas? – Rasguei e joguei fora. (*spoken*)
'What did you do with the letters?' – 'I tore them up and threw them out.'

Though, again, a pronoun can be used, especially to avoid ambiguity:

Gostou do meu relógio? Ganhei (ele) no meu aniversário.
Do you like my watch? I got it for my birthday.

In writing, the unstressed object pronouns (**o**, **a**, **os**, **as**) would be used in such cases:

O Senado votou a proposta, mas não a aprovou.
The Senate voted on the proposal, but did not approve it.

O Roberto tinha separado uns livros e disse que pretendia vendê-los.
Roberto had set aside some books and said he intended to sell them.

(iii) 'It' is never translated when it stands for an impersonal subject or object, that is, when it has a purely grammatical function and does not refer back to a specific noun:

Está chovendo.
It's raining.

São quatro horas.
It's four o'clock.

É impossível prever o resultado.
It's impossible to predict the result.

Considero errado não ajudá-los.
I feel it's wrong not to help them.

7.3.4 The reflexive pronoun *se*

The reflexive pronoun **se** is an unstressed object pronoun that refers back to a third person subject, including **você(s)** and **a gente**. Among other functions (see **Chapter 22**), it is used when the third person subject and object are the same, i.e. it translates 'himself, herself, itself, themselves', 'yourself, yourselves' when referring to **você(s)** and 'ourselves' when referring to **a gente**. When referring back to a plural subject, it can also have reciprocal meaning, i.e. 'each other':

O menino se enxugou com uma toalha.
The boy dried himself with a towel.

Você se machucou?
Did you hurt yourself?

A gente se conhece há muito tempo.
We've known each other for a long time.

7.4 Use of subject pronouns

7.4.1

Subject pronouns occur in various types of verbless sentences and comparative expressions. This does not always correspond to English usage:

Quem quer sorvete? – Eu!
'Who wants ice cream?' – 'Me!' / 'I do!'

Nós vamos de carro. – Nós também.
'We're going by car.' – 'So are we.' / 'Us too.'

pessoas como eu[4]
people like me

Ele é mais alto do que eu.
He's taller than me.

NOTE   4   The subject pronoun is used after **como** even when, grammatically, it is the object of the sentence, e.g. **Quem diria que escolheriam uma pessoa como eu?** 'Who would have thought they'd choose a person like me?' This also happens in lists, e.g. **Escolheram Paulo, Sérgio e eu.** 'They chose Paulo, Sérgio and me.'

7.4.2

With verbs, subject pronouns are never obligatory in Portuguese and can always be left out if the subject of the verb is clear from the wider context or from the form of the verb itself. For instance, **falo** can only mean '*I* speak' and **falamos** can only mean '*we* speak/spoke' so, in these cases, a subject pronoun is not necessary; however, **falava** can mean 'I spoke', 'he spoke', 'she spoke' or even 'you spoke', so it may well be necessary to specify with a subject pronoun unless the wider context makes it unambiguous who the subject is. In many cases, the inclusion or omission of a subject pronoun is purely a matter of personal preference, but there are a number of factors to take into consideration:

(i)   A subject pronoun is always included when the subject is emphasized for some reason or when there is an idea of contrast:

> **Eu vou decidir quem faz o quê.**
> *I* will decide who does what.

> **Nós falamos português, eles não.**
> *We* speak Portuguese, *they* don't.

(ii) Third person verb forms in particular can be ambiguous, so third person subject pronouns are normally included, at least the first time the subject is mentioned:

> **Ele joga tênis. Você joga também?**
> He plays tennis. Do you play too?

(iii) 'It' as an impersonal subject is never translated into Portuguese (see **7.3.3** (iii)):

> **Está quente hoje.**
> It's hot today.

(iv) Although not actually wrong, it sounds stilted to keep repeating the subject pronoun once the subject has been established. Such repetition would certainly be avoided in writing:

> **Meu nome é Ricardo. Sou brasileiro e moro em São Paulo.**
> My name is Ricardo. I'm Brazilian and I live in São Paulo.

> **Você me liga quando chegar em casa?**
> Will you call me when you get home?

7.5 Placement of unstressed object pronouns

7.5.1 Unstressed object pronouns (**me, te, se, nos, o, a, os, as, lhe, lhes**) have to be placed immediately before or immediately after the verbs they are associated with.[5] When placed after, they are appended to the verb in writing with a hyphen. When there is a straight choice between the two positions, it is generally true that placing the pronoun after the verb sounds more formal than placing it before, although euphony may also be a factor.

NOTE 5 There is another possible position, which is sandwiched between the future stem and the ending in future and conditional verb forms, e.g. **ver-me-iam** 'they would see me', but such forms are perceived as extremely formal/literary and are rarely used nowadays except in the most formal contexts.

7.5.2 The crucial difference between the spoken language and the written language as regards unstressed object pronoun placement is that, in speech, there are no restrictions on placing an object pronoun at the beginning of a sentence or clause, so we can say that **me**, **te** and **nos** are always placed before the verb in the spoken language:

> **Te vejo amanhã.** (*spoken*)
> I'll see you tomorrow.

> **O Pedro vai nos levar até lá.** (*spoken or written*)
> Pedro's going to take us there.

7.5.3 But in written Portuguese, there is a cardinal rule that you must not begin a sentence or clause with an unstressed object pronoun. This means that, if there is no explicit subject, and none of the conditions in **7.5.4** apply, the unstressed object pronoun has to be placed after the verb with a hyphen:

> **Vi-o.** (*written*)   cf. **(Eu) vi ele.** (*spoken*)
> I saw him.

Beijou-a. (*written*)   cf. **Ele/ela beijou ela.** (*spoken*)
He/she kissed her.

7.5.4

However, there are also a number of circumstances in which the unstressed object pronoun has to be placed before the finite verb:

(i)   After a negative (**não** 'not', **nunca** 'never', **nem** 'nor', **ninguém** 'nobody', etc.):

Não o vi. (*written*)   cf. **Não vi ele.** (*spoken*)
I didn't see him.

(ii)   In a relative clause:

a pessoa que o viu (*written*)   cf. **. . . que viu ele** (*spoken*)
the person who saw him

(iii) In any kind of subordinate clause when the subordinating conjunction is immediately followed by the verb and its associated object pronoun:

A vizinha disse que o viu. (*written*)   cf. **. . . que viu ele.** (*spoken*)
The neighbour said she saw him.

Não lembro quando o vi. (*written*)   cf. **. . . quando vi ele.** (*spoken*)
I don't remember when I saw him.

If there is a noun or pronoun subject between the conjunction and the verb, the general rules on pronoun placement apply once more, i.e. the object pronoun may be placed after the verb in more formal written or literary style (see **7.5.5**).

(iv)   After an adverb or adverbial phrase placed before the verb[6] (e.g. **sempre** 'always', **já** 'already', **bem** 'well', **aqui** 'here', **só** 'only', **talvez** 'perhaps', **também** 'also', **provavelmente** 'probably', **geralmente** 'usually', **às vezes** 'sometimes', etc.):

Já o vi. (*written*)   cf. **Já vi ele.** (*spoken*)
I've already seen him.

NOTE   6   The adverb or adverbial must constitute an unbroken sense unit with the object pronoun and verb. If there is a pause after the adverb, represented in writing by a comma, the verb is then considered to be starting a new clause, making it subject to the rule explained in 7.5.3.

(v)   After demonstrative and indefinite pronouns, including quantifiers (e.g. **alguém** 'somebody, someone', **isso** 'that', **muito** 'a lot', **muitos** 'many (people)', **pouco** 'little', **poucos** 'few (people)', **quem** 'who, anyone who, whoever', **todos** 'everyone', **tudo** 'everything', etc.):

Alguém o viu? (*written*)   cf. **Alguém viu ele?** (*spoken*)
Did anyone see him?

(vi)   In sentences starting with an interrogative or exclamatory word:

Quando o viu? (*written*)   cf. **Quando você viu ele?** (*spoken*)
When did you see him?

Como o odeio! (*written*)   cf. **Como odeio ele!** (*spoken*)
How I hate him!

(vii) In exclamations and wishes expressed in the subjunctive (see **20.6**):

Deus te abençoe!
God bless you!

> **Macacos me mordam!**
> Well I'll be damned! (*literally*, may monkeys bite me!)

7.5.5 When the subject of the verb is a noun or personal pronoun and none of the conditions described in **7.5.4** apply, you have the choice of placing the unstressed object pronoun immediately before or immediately after the verb. Broadly speaking, placement before the verb is preferred in less formal written style and especially journalism, whereas in more formal and literary style the pronoun tends to be placed after the verb:

> **A polícia o prendeu.** (*neutral written style*)
>
> **A polícia prendeu-o.** (*formal/literary written style*)
>
> cf. **A polícia prendeu ele.** (*spoken*)
> The police arrested him.

7.5.6 Brazilians will often include a subject pronoun in writing just so that the object pronoun can be placed in the less formal-sounding pre-verbal position without breaking the rule about not starting a sentence with an object pronoun:

> **Eu me vesti e saí. (Vesti-me** *would sound formal/literary*)
> I got dressed (*dressed myself*) and went out.

7.5.7 ## Special forms of the object pronouns *-o, -a, -os, -as*

(i) When appended to an infinitive, the third person object pronouns take the form **-lo**, **-la**, **-los**, **-las**, the final **-r** of the infinitive is dropped and a written accent is added to **-a-** and **-e-** (but not **-i-**):[7]

> **amar** + **o** > **amá-lo** 'to love him/it'
> **escrever** + **a** > **escrevê-la** 'to write it'
> **dividir** + **os** > **dividi-los** (*no written accent on i*[8]) 'to divide them'.

(ii) When appended to a first person plural verb form ending in **-mos**, the third person object pronouns take the form **-lo**, **-la**, **-los**, **-las** and the final **-s** of the verb form is dropped:[9]

> **ajudamos** + **o** > **ajudamo-lo** 'we helped him'
> **vimos** + **as** > **vimo-las** 'we saw them'.

(iii) When appended to a verb form ending in a nasal sound (**-am**, **-em**, **-ão**, **-õe**), the third person object pronouns take the forms **-no**, **-na**, **-nos**, **-nas**:

> **comem** + **o** > **comem-no** 'they eat it'
> **põe** + **as** > **põe-nas** 'he/she puts them'.

NOTES

7 This rule also applies when third person object pronouns are placed between stem and ending in future and conditional verb forms, e.g. **amá-lo-ei** 'I will love him'. See note 6.

8 Except in the case of verbs ending in **-air** or **-uir**, where the i is accented to indicate that it is pronounced separately from the previous vowel, e.g. **para substituí-los** 'to replace them'.

9 This rule also applies when the third person object pronouns are appended to other verb forms ending in **-s** or **-z**, e.g. **fez** + **o** > **fê-lo**, **quis** + **as** > **qui-las**, etc., but such forms sound so antiquated and stilted these days that they are avoided even in very formal/literary writing.

7.5.8   Position of object pronouns with the infinitive

The pronouns **me**, **te**, **se**, **nos** and **lhe(s)** can be placed before an infinitive or appended to it with a hyphen. They are placed before it in speech and neutral written style, and after it in more formal and literary style:

> **Ela pode nos ajudar.** (*speech or neutral written style*)
> She can help us.

> **O filme pode ajudar-nos a entender o que aconteceu.** (*more formal writing*)
> The film may help us to understand what happened.

The pronouns **o**, **a**, **os**, **as** are appended to an infinitive as **-lo**, **-la**, **-los**, **-las** in all styles, in accordance with the rule explained in **7.5.7** (i):

> **Decidi comprá-lo.**
> I decided to buy it.

> **É impossível vê-las a olho nu.**
> It's impossible to see them with the naked eye.

The above construction is often used in the spoken language too, and is obligatory when these pronouns are used to mean 'you' (see **7.2.5**):

> **Temos que ajudá-lo.** (*written or spoken*)
> **Temos que ajudar ele.** (*spoken only*)
> We have to help him.

> **Muito prazer em conhecê-la.**
> Delighted to meet you. (*to a woman in a fairly formal situation*)

In fact, infinitives are subject to the same rules as finite verb forms, i.e. when preceded by a negative, an interrogative word or pronoun subject, the unstressed object pronoun should be placed before the infinitive (see **7.5.4**). As far as the pronouns **o**, **a**, **os** and **as** are concerned, this rule is observed in more formal written language, but not usually in speech and less formal writing, where the appended forms are often used instead:

> **Eu me arrependo de não tê-lo comprado.** (*spoken*)
> **Eu me arrependo de não o ter comprado.** (*written*)
> I regret not buying it.

> **Vitaminas A, C e D: para que servem e onde encontrá-las.** (*spoken and written*)
> **Vitaminas A, C e D: para que servem e onde as encontrar.** (*written*)
> Vitamins A, C and D: what they're for and where to find them.

> **Não tem motivo para eu fazê-lo.** (*spoken*)
> **Não há motivo para eu o fazer.** (*written*)
> There's no reason for me to do it.

Similarly, the unstressed object pronouns **me**, **te**, **se** and **nos** are always placed before the infinitive in speech, even at the start of a clause, whereas in writing the rule given in **7.5.3** applies, requiring the pronoun to be appended:

> **Se adaptar não é impossível, mas é difícil.** (*spoken*)
> **Adaptar-se não é impossível, mas é difícil.** (*written*)
> Adapting is not impossible, but it is difficult.

7.5.9   Position of object pronouns in the perfect tenses

In the spoken language and neutral written language, **me**, **te**, **se**, **lhe(s)** and **nos** are placed between the auxiliary and the past participle:[10]

> **Ele tem se queixado de dores abdominais.**
> He's been complaining of abdominal pains.

The third person pronouns **o**, **a**, **os**, **as** are positioned before or after the auxiliary according to the rules given in **7.5.3–7.5.6**:

> **O presidente o tinha convidado.** (*neutral written style*)
> The president had invited him.

> **Haviam-na ajudado.** (*formal/literary written style*)
> They had helped her.

NOTE | 10 The rules given in **7.5.3–7.5.6** may also be applied to these pronouns in more formal writing, especially **lhe** and **lhes** with third person reference rather than second, which means that they are sometimes placed before the auxiliary. When the rules require the object pronoun to be placed after the auxiliary, it then falls between auxiliary and participle as it does in less formal style, the only difference being that the pronoun is appended to the auxiliary with a hyphen.

7.5.10   Position of object pronouns in the continuous tenses

In the spoken language and neutral written language, **me**, **te**, **se**, **nos** and **lhe(s)**[11] are placed between the auxiliary and the gerund:

> **Estou me preparando para o concurso.**
> I'm preparing myself for the competition.

NOTE | 11 The rules given in **7.5.3–7.5.6** may be applied to these pronouns too in more formal writing, especially **lhe** and **lhes** with third person reference rather than second, which means that they are either placed before the auxiliary or appended to the gerund with a hyphen.

The pronouns **o**, **a**, **os**, **as** are either positioned before the auxiliary or appended to the gerund with a hyphen, according to the rules given in **7.5.3–7.5.6**:

> **O governo o está apoiando.** / **O governo está apoiando-o.**
> The government is supporting him.

> **Estavam esperando-a.**
> They were waiting for her.

Note that object pronouns are always appended to the gerund when it is used adverbially, i.e. not in combination with **estar** or similar auxiliary:

> **Ela apagou o cigarro, esmagando-o com o salto do sapato.**
> She put her cigarette out, crushing it with the heel of her shoe.

7.6   More about indirect pronoun objects

7.6.1

Although the prepositional phrases **a ele(s)** and **a ela(s)** can always be used instead of the indirect object pronouns **lhe(s)** in the written language, there are three cases where a prepositional phrase has to be used:

(i)   When the indirect pronoun is stressed (i.e. when the preposition *to* is used in English):

Dei o dinheiro a ela.
I gave the money to *her*.

cf.   **Eu lhe dei o dinheiro. / Dei a ela o dinheiro.**
I gave her the money.

(ii)   When **lhe** could be ambiguous:

Depois do que o amigo fez, ele prometeu a ela que nunca mais o procuraria.
After what his friend did, he promised her he would never contact him again.

(iii)   When the sentence contains both direct and indirect pronoun objects:

Eu queria que você o encaminhasse a ele.
I'd like you to pass it on to him.

Ele deixou a casa ao irmão, depois de tê-la prometido a nós.
He left the house to his brother after having promised it to us.

7.6.2   As the direct objects 'it, them' are not usually translated in spoken Portuguese (see **7.3.3 (i)**), it is common in the spoken language to form sentences that contain only an indirect object:

Ele trouxe as fotos e mostrou para mim. (*spoken*)
He brought the photos and showed them to me.

Estou com minha bicicleta aqui. Te empresto. (*spoken*)
I have my bike here. I'll lend it to you.

7.6.3   The preposition **em** is used instead of **a/para** when the action of the verb affects the indirect object physically:

Ele deu um beijo nela. (*spoken or written*)
Ele lhe deu um beijo. (*written*)
He gave her a kiss.

7.6.4   The indirect object pronouns can be used to indicate that someone is the beneficiary or victim of an action. In such cases, English uses 'for' with a pronoun or a possessive where Portuguese has the definite article:

Ele me roubou a carteira.
He stole my wallet.

Eles nos consertaram o carro.
They fixed our car (for us).

7.6.5   In a similar usage, indirect **me** can be included in colloquial speech to express the speaker's surprise or annoyance:

Não me quebre esse copo, hein!
Don't go breaking that glass now!

Em vez de quitar as dívidas, ele me compra um carro zero.
Instead of paying off his debts, he only goes and buys a brand-new car.

7.7 Pronouns used with prepositions

7.7.1

As we have seen above, the forms of the personal pronouns used after prepositions are the same as the subject pronouns, except in the case of the first person singular, **mim**:[12]

sem ela
without her

atrás de nós
behind us

contra mim
against me.

NOTE | 12 After **entre** 'between', the rule in writing is that **mim** is to be used immediately after the preposition, e.g. **entre mim e ele** 'between me and him', but the subject form **eu** can be used as the second term, e.g. **entre ele e eu** 'between him and me'. In speech, most people would also use **eu** in the first case: **entre eu e ele**.

7.7.2

Note that the first person singular and plural pronouns combine with the preposition **com** to form the single words **comigo** 'with me' and **conosco** 'with us'. The other pronouns form regular two-word combinations with **com**, e.g. **com você, com eles**.

7.7.3

The third person reflexive pronoun **se** takes the form **si** after prepositions and forms the word **consigo** with the preposition **com**. However, these forms are only used in very formal written language, or when the meaning is impersonal (see **22.6**). In the spoken language and less formal writing, the subject pronoun is used instead, reinforced where appropriate with **mesmo(s)/mesma(s)** '-self, -selves':

Ele prometeu a ele mesmo que não voltaria a fumar.
He promised himself that he would not smoke again.

A Laura se surpreendeu com ela mesma.
Laura was surprised at herself.

Não se deve pensar só em si mesmo. (*impersonal sense*)
One shouldn't think just of oneself.

7.7.4

In colloquial speech, you may hear the familiar forms **ti** (in place of **você**) and **contigo** (in place of **com você**):

Eu vou contigo.
I'll go with you.

7.8 Emphatic uses of object pronouns

7.8.1

In the written language, the preposition **a** + pronoun is also used to emphasize a direct object:

Por que não convidaram a mim?
Why didn't they invite *me*?

Isso não prejudica só a eles, prejudica a nós também.
This doesn't harm just them, it harms us too.

7.8.2   In the spoken language, this is only an issue with the first person object pronouns, as in other cases the pronouns are placed in noun-object position anyway and can simply be pronounced with greater emphasis. In the first person, the subject pronouns **eu** and **nós** are employed in noun-object position:

> **Por que não convidaram eu?**
>
> **Prejudica nós também.**

The same rules apply when a pronoun forms a composite direct object with a noun. Note that, in such cases, the accompanying noun must also be preceded by the preposition **a** in the written language:

> **Convidaram a mim e a três outras pessoas.** (*written*)
> **Convidaram eu e três outras pessoas.** (*spoken*)
> They invited me and three other people.
>
> **Conheci a ele e ao diretor.** (*written*)
> **Conheci ele e o diretor**. (*spoken*)
> I met him and the director.

7.8.3   The above rules also apply when a pronoun is accompanied by **só** 'only, just', **todos/todas** 'all' or **mesmo(s)/mesma(s)** '-self, -selves':

> **Pretendemos ajudar só a ela.** (*written*)
> We intend to help only her.
>
> **Preciso convencer a mim mesmo primeiro.** (*written or spoken*)
> I need to convince myself first.

7.9   Non-standard pronouns

7.9.1   *tu*

The subject pronoun **tu** is often used in place of **você** in very colloquial speech in some regions, but always in combination with third person verb forms. This usage is most widespread in the southernmost part of Brazil, where it may be considered the norm in colloquial spoken language. A small number of speakers in that region also use second person verb forms.

7.9.2   *lhe/lhes* meaning 'you'

In some regions, notably from Rio de Janeiro northwards, **lhe/lhes** are used as both the direct and indirect object form of **você/vocês** and as such are always placed in the less formal position before the verb.

7.9.3   *vós*

The old second person plural pronoun **vós** (unstressed object form: **vos**) is nowadays only encountered in biblical contexts as a form of address used between God and man. It can be likened to the English 'thou' and 'ye'.

See **Appendix V: Second person verb forms** on page 524.

7.10 Other pronominal forms of address

There are some other honorific forms of address which are used in the same way as **você(s)** and **o senhor/a senhora** (see **7.2.1** and **7.2.2**), i.e. as if they were personal pronouns. You may encounter the following:

Vossa Alteza	Your Highness	(to a prince, princess, duke or duchess)
Vossa Eminência	Your Eminence	(to a cardinal)
Vossa Excelência	Your Excellency	(used to address any person of high authority, such as a president, senator, member of congress or parliament, minister, governor, mayor, ambassador or judge)
Vossa Majestade	Your Majesty	(to a king or queen)
Vossa Reverendíssima	Your Grace	(to priests, bishops and other high-ranking clergy)
Vossa Santidade	Your Holiness	(to the Pope)
Vossa Senhoria		used in official communications and business correspondence as a formal term for 'you'. The abbreviation used in writing is **V.Sa.** (plural: **V. Sas.**).

NOTES

(i) These expressions are followed by third person verb forms, e.g. **Vossa Alteza está de acordo?** 'Does Your Highness agree?' or 'Do you agree, Your Highness?'

(ii) They can all occur in the plural, e.g. **como é do conhecimento de Vossas Senhorias ...** 'as you are aware ...'

(iii) Gender agreement depends on the sex of the person addressed, e.g. **Vossa Excelência está enganado, Senador.** 'You are mistaken, Senator.'

(iv) Reflexives and possessives referring to these forms are in the third person (i.e. **se, seu(s)/sua(s)**) and third person object pronouns may also be used to replace them so as to avoid repetition, e.g. **V.Sa. tem direito de reduzir sua jornada diária de trabalho em duas horas, conforme a lei lhe faculta.** 'You may reduce your working day by two hours, as the law entitles you to do.'

7.11 Brazilian personal pronoun usage – quick reference tables

Table 7.11.1 Forms

Subject form	Spoken direct object form	Written direct object form	Spoken indirect object form	Written indirect object form	After preposition
eu 'I'	**me***	**me***	**me*/para mim**	**me***	**mim**
você 'you'	**te*/você**	**você**	**te*/para você**	**a você**	**você**
ele 'he, it'	**ele**	**o***	**para ele**	**lhe*/a ele**	**ele**
ela 'she, it'	**ela**	**a***	**para ela**	**lhe*/a ela**	**ela**
nós 'we'	**nos***	**nos***	**nos*/para nós**	**nos***	**nós**
vocês 'you'	**vocês**	**vocês**	**para vocês**	**a vocês**	**vocês**
eles 'they' *m.*	**eles**	**os***	**para eles**	**lhes*/a eles**	**eles**
elas 'they' *f.*	**elas**	**as***	**para elas**	**lhes*/a elas**	**elas**

* unstressed object pronoun – for guide to placement see Table 7.11.2.

Table 7.11.2 Placement of unstressed object pronouns in spoken, neutral written and formal/literary style

	me, te, se, lhe, nos, lhes	*o, a, os, as*
Finite verb: zero subject	*spoken*: before verb, e.g. **me escutou** *written*: after verb with hyphen, e.g. **escutou-me**	after verb with hyphen, e.g. **escutou-o**
Finite verb: noun or pronoun subject	*spoken/neutral*: before verb, e.g. **ela me escutou** *formal/literary*: after verb with hyphen, e.g. **ela escutou-me**	*neutral*: before verb, e.g. **ela o escutou** *formal/literary*: after verb with hyphen, e.g. **ela escutou-o**
Finite verb: negative, subordinate clause, etc. (see **7.5.4**)	before verb, e.g. **não me escutou**	before verb, e.g. **não o escutou**
Infinitive: after auxiliary, preposition, adjective, etc.	*spoken/neutral*: before infinitive, e.g. **pode me escutar** *formal/literary*: after infinitive with hyphen, e.g. **pode escutar-me**	appended to infinitive as **-lo**, **-la**, **-los**, **-las** (see **7.5.7**), e.g. **pode escutá-lo**
Infinitive: after negative, interrogative, noun or pronoun subject, etc. (see **7.5.4**)	before infinitive, e.g. **pode não me escutar**	*spoken/neutral*: appended to infinitive as **-lo**, **-la**, **-los**, **-las** (see **7.5.7**), e.g. **pode não escutá-lo** *formal/literary*: before infinitive, e.g. **pode não o escutar**
Infinitive: as subject or in isolation	*spoken*: before infinitive, e.g. **se expressar é importante** *written*: after infinitive with hyphen, e.g. **expressar-se é importante**	appended to infinitive as **-lo**, **-la**, **-los**, **-las** (see **7.5.7**), e.g. **expressá-lo é importante**
Perfect auxiliary: zero subject	between auxiliary and participle, no hyphen, e.g. **tinha me escutado**	after auxiliary with hyphen, e.g. **tinha-o escutado**
Perfect tenses: noun or pronoun subject	between auxiliary and participle, no hyphen, e.g. **ela tinha me escutado**	*neutral:* before auxiliary, e.g. **ela o tinha escutado** *formal/literary*: after auxiliary with hyphen, e.g. **ela tinha-o escutado**
Perfect tenses: negative, subordinate clause, etc. (see **7.5.4**)	*spoken/neutral*: between auxiliary and participle, no hyphen, e.g. **não tinha me escutado** *formal/literary*: before auxiliary, e.g. **não me tinha escutado**	before auxiliary, e.g. **não o tinha escutado**
estar + gerund: zero subject	*spoken/neutral*: between auxiliary and gerund, e.g. **está me escutando** *formal/literary*: after gerund with hyphen, e.g. **está escutando-me**	after gerund with hyphen, e.g. **está escutando-o**
estar + gerund: noun or pronoun subject	*spoken/neutral*: between auxiliary and gerund, e.g. **ela está me escutando**	after gerund with hyphen, e.g. **ela está escutando-o**

	formal/literary: after gerund with hyphen, e.g. **ela está escutando-me**	
estar + gerund: negative, subordinate clause, etc. (see **7.5.4**)	*spoken/neutral*: between auxiliary and gerund, e.g. **não está me escutando** *formal/literary*: before auxiliary, e.g. **não me está escutando**	before auxiliary, e.g. **não o está escutando**

Notes for Spanish speakers

There is a strong tendency to use subject pronouns without any particular emphasis or element of contrast, especially in the spoken language. The pronouns **tu** and **vós** and second-person verb forms are not normally used at all, their place taken by **você** and **vocês** followed by third-person verb forms. Polite 'you' is expressed with **o senhor/a senhora**. It is much more common in the spoken language to use **a gente** followed by a third-person singular verb form than the first-person plural **nós**. Unstressed object pronouns may be appended to verbs, including finite verb forms, with a hyphen in formal/literary style, but the normal position in spoken and informal written language is before the main verb, even in the case of infinitives, gerunds and past participles, the object pronoun being inserted between the auxiliary and main verb form in the last two cases. Third-person unstressed object pronouns are only used in the written language; in the spoken language, the subject forms are used disjunctively in noun-object position, and after a preposition to express the indirect object. Object pronouns referring to things are frequently omitted in speech, and combinations of unstressed indirect and direct object pronouns never occur, nor does the pleonastic use of an object pronoun to prefigure or echo a noun object. Third person pronouns form contractions with the prepositions **de** (> **dele, dela, deles, delas**) and **em** (> **nele, nela, neles, nelas**).

8

Demonstratives

8.1 **Introduction**

There are three demonstratives in Brazilian Portuguese, though only two are regularly used in the spoken language. They can be used as adjectives (accompanying a noun) or as pronouns (replacing a noun), but in either case they must agree in gender and number with the noun in question. In addition, there are corresponding neuter forms, which are only used as pronouns and refer to something as yet unidentified or to a fact, an idea, etc.

8.2 **Forms and meaning**

In each case, the masculine singular form ends in -**e**, the feminine singular in -**a**. The plural is formed by adding -**s** to the singular form:

Masc. sing.	Fem. sing.	Masc. pl.	Fem. pl.	Basic meaning
este	**esta**	**estes**	**estas**	this/these
esse	**essa**	**esses**	**essas**	that/those (*near you*)
aquele	**aquela**	**aqueles**	**aquelas**	that/those (*over there*)

NOTES

(i) In all the masculine forms, singular and plural, the stressed first **e** has the close [e] sound, while in the feminine forms it is has the open [ɛ] sound.

(ii) Like the definite article, the demonstratives merge with the prepositions **em** and **de**, e.g. **neste** (= em + este), **nesse** (= em + esse), **naquele** (em + aquele); **deste** (= de + este), **desse** (= de + esse), **daquele** (= de + aquele) etc.

(iii) The preposition **a** merges with **aquele(s)/aquela(s)** to become **àquele(s)/àquela(s)**.

8.3 **Usage**

8.3.1 The fundamental difference between **esse(s)/essa(s)** and **aquele(s)/aquela(s)** is that the former refers to something close to the listener, while the latter refers to something at a distance from both speaker and listener. Compare:

Onde você comprou esse relógio?
Where did you buy that watch (*i.e. the one you are wearing*)?

Você está vendo aquela casa verde?
Can you see that green house (*i.e. over there*)?

8.3.2 The demonstrative **este(s)/esta(s)** is only used in the written language; in the spoken language, **esse(s)/essa(s)** is used instead, with the result that **esse(s)/essa(s)** does duty for both 'this/these' and 'that/those' (*near you*):

> **Caso o pagamento tenha sido efetuado, desconsidere este aviso.**
> If payment has been made, disregard this notice. (*written*)

> **Comprei essa camiseta semana passada.**
> I bought this T-shirt last week. (*spoken*)

To avoid ambiguity, **aqui** or **daqui** may be added to express 'this' and **aí** or **daí** to express 'that' – see **8.5.2**:

> **Esse livro aqui é seu, não é? – Não, esse daí é da Sandra.**
> 'This book's yours, isn't it?' – 'No, that's Sandra's.'

8.3.3 Beyond the spatial realm, **esse(s)/essa(s)** is also used to refer back to something the speaker or listener has mentioned previously:

> **Foi nesse momento que percebi . . .**
> It was at that moment (*i.e. the one I have just mentioned*) that I realized . . .

> **Quando é que você tomou essa decisão?**
> When did you take this decision (*i.e. the one you have just told me about*)?

8.3.4 Similarly, **aquele(s)/aquela(s)** is used to pinpoint something remote in space or time with which both speaker and listener are familiar:

> **Você já esteve naquele shopping novo?**
> Have you been to that new shopping mall yet?

> **Sabe aquelas flores que parecem pompons?**
> You know those flowers that look like pompoms?

Once a noun has been established with **aquele(s)/aquela(s)**, it will then be referred back to with **esse(s)/essa(s)**. Look at the following dialogue:

> – **A nova namorada do Rafa parece aquela atriz que fez "Jogos Vorazes".**
> – **Aquela loura?**
> – **É, essa mesmo. Então, ela parece essa atriz.**
> – **Qual o nome dessa atriz mesmo? Me fugiu agora.**
> 'Rafa's new girlfriend looks like that actress who did *Hunger Games*.'
> 'That blonde one?'
> 'Yes, that's the one. Well, she looks like that actress.'
> 'What's that actress's name again? It's slipped my mind.'

8.3.5 In colloquial speech, **aquele(s)/aquela(s)** can also be used for emphatic effect in the sense of 'you know the kind I mean':

> **Acordei com aquela ressaca hoje.**
> I woke up today with such a hangover.

> **Foi aquele sufoco para achar uma vaga.**
> It was the usual hassle to find a parking space.

8.3.6 The construction **aquele(s)/aquela(s) que . . .** is used to mean 'the one(s) who/that . . .':

> **um programa para aqueles que gostam da natureza**
> an activity for those who enjoy nature

Prefiro essa saia àquela que experimentei antes.
I prefer this skirt to the one I tried on before.

8.3.7 The demonstratives can be used in conjunction with possessives and other indefinite pronouns, as in English:

todos esses problemas
all these problems

aquelas outras meninas
those other girls

O que aconteceu com aquele seu namorado? (*notice placement of possessive*)
What happened to that boyfriend of yours?

8.3.8 Note the expression **um/uma ... desses/dessas** 'one of these ...':

Temos que nos encontrar um dia desses.
We must meet up one of these days.

8.3.9 And also note, in colloquial speech, **um/uma ... daqueles/daquelas** 'a major ...', 'one hell of a ...':

Foi uma correria daquelas para terminar tudo.
It was a major rush to get everything finished.

8.3.10 The feminine singular form **essa** is used pronominally in a number of colloquial expressions, some of which are:

A impressora quebrou? Essa não!
The printer's broken down? Oh no!

Você não pode ficar nessa de sair toda noite.
You can't keep up this business of going out every night.

Essa foi boa!
Good one! (*referring to a joke or witty remark*) or
That's a good one! (*irony indicating disbelief*)

8.3.11 The demonstratives **aquele(s)/aquela(s)** and **este(s)/esta(s)** can be used in combination in formal written language to mean 'the former' and 'the latter' respectively:

A América do Sul foi colonizada por portugueses e espanhóis: aqueles no Brasil e estes nos demais países.
South America was colonized by the Portuguese and the Spanish: the former in Brazil and the latter in the other countries.

8.3.12 In the written language, the convention is that **esse(s)/essa(s)** is used to refer back to things mentioned previously in the text while **este(s)/esta(s)** is used to refer to what follows:

"O Brasil não é para iniciantes." Quem cunhou essa frase foi Tom Jobim.
'Brazil is not for beginners.' It was Tom Jobim who coined that phrase.

Foi Tom Jobim quem cunhou esta famosa frase: "O Brasil não é para iniciantes."
It was Tom Jobim who coined this famous phrase: 'Brazil is not for beginners.'

8.4 Neuter demonstrative pronouns

8.4.1 The corresponding neuter pronouns are: **isto** 'this', **isso** 'this/that' and **aquilo** 'that'. As with **este(s)/esta(s)**, the use of **isto** is confined to the written language (except for occasional emphatic use in speech[1]), so **isso** is used to mean both 'this' and 'that' in the spoken language.

| NOTE | 1 **Isto** is sometimes used in speech as a kind of emphatic form of **isso**, to mean either 'this' or 'that'. Many native speakers are unclear about the semantic distinction between **este(s)/esta(s)/isto** and **esse(s)/essa(s)/isso**, believing the former to be simply a more formal synonym of the latter. |

8.4.2 These pronouns combine with the prepositions **em** and **de** to form **nisto, nisso, naquilo** and **disto, disso, daquilo** respectively. The preposition **a** merges with **aquilo** to become **àquilo**.

8.4.3 These neuter pronouns are used to refer to something concrete that has not yet been identified, or to something abstract, such as a fact, an idea, something a person has just said, etc.:

> **O que é aquilo no céu?**
> What's that in the sky?

> **Por que você disse isso?**
> Why did you say that?

> **É isso que precisamos fazer.**
> That's what we must do.

8.4.4 Notice the difference in meaning between the following pairs of sentences:

> **Aquilo é uma câmera de segurança.**
> That's a security camera. (*that thing is a security camera*)

> **Aquela é uma câmera de segurança.**
> That's a security camera. (*that camera is for security*)

> **Isso é um problema sério.**
> This is a serious problema. (*the fact just mentioned constitutes a serious problem*)

> **Esse é um problema sério.**
> This is a serious problem. (*this problem is a serious one*)

8.4.5 The neuter pronouns can be preceded by **tudo** 'everything' to mean 'all this, all that'. Placing **tudo** after the pronoun gives greater emphasis in colloquial speech:

> **Tudo isso aconteceu muito tempo atrás.**
> This all happened a long time ago.

> **Você vai comer isso tudo?**
> Are you going to eat *all* that?

8.5 Demonstrative adverbs 'here' and 'there'

8.5.1

It is useful at this point to present the words for 'here' and 'there' in Portuguese because they follow the same logic as the demonstratives:

Adverb	Translation	Meaning	Equivalent demonstrative
aqui	here	near me	**este** (written), **esse** (spoken)
aí	there	near you	**esse**
ali	(over) there	within sight	**aquele**
lá	there	remote	**aquele**

NOTES

(i) **aqui**, **aí** and **ali** combine with the preposition **de** to form **daqui** 'from here', **daí** 'from there' and **dali** 'from (over) there'.

(ii) In deictic usage, **ali** refers to a place you can see and thus is often equivalent to 'over there' while **lá** refers to a place that is further away and out of sight. Both may also refer back to a place previously mentioned, but **ali** tends to refer to a more narrowly defined location than **lá**:

Sentei num banco e fiquei ali a tarde inteira, lendo meu livro.
I sat on a bench and stayed there the whole afternoon reading my book.

Ele foi aos EUA e ficou lá três anos.
He went to the US and stayed there for three years.

(iii) As in English, these adverbs can denote location or movement to a location, so may be used in association with both stative verbs and verbs of motion:

O banco é logo ali.
The bank's just over there.

Vou passar aí amanhã.
I'll drop by there tomorrow. (*i.e. where you are*)

(iv) **lá** is often used to mean 'over there' in the sense of 'abroad':

Não temos essa fruta lá.
We don't have this fruit over there. (*i.e. where I'm from*)

8.5.2

In the spoken language, the demonstrative adverbs are often combined with the corresponding adjective or pronoun for precision or emphasis, as is also the case in English:

Você só vai levar essa bolsa aqui?
Are you only taking this bag here?

Não é esse ônibus, é aquele ali.
It's not this bus, it's that one over there.

The adverbs are sometimes preceded by **de** in this usage:

Essa daqui é a minha filha.
This is my daughter.

Bom, isso daí é você que sabe.
Well, that's up to you.

8.5.3

In combination with the preposition **por**, the demonstrative adverbs each have two possible meanings: **por aqui** 'around here' or 'this way', **por aí** 'around there' or 'that way', **por ali** 'around there' or 'that way', **por lá** 'around there' or 'that way':

É por aqui para ir ao museu?
Is it this way to the museum?

A Cristina está por aí?
Is Cristina around? (*said on the phone*)

8.5.4 These adverbs can be combined with other adverbs of place. Notice that the order is the reverse of English: **aqui dentro** 'in here', **aí fora** 'out there', **ali embaixo** 'down there'. The adverb **lá** forms some idiomatic expressions of this type: **lá embaixo** 'downstairs; at the bottom', **lá em cima** 'upstairs; at the top' and **lá fora** 'outside; abroad':

Não estamos escutando nada aqui atrás.
We can't hear anything back here.

Tem outro banheiro lá embaixo.
There's another bathroom downstairs.

8.5.5 There is another demonstrative adverb, **cá** '(to) here', but its use is restricted. It can be used on its own with the verb **vir** 'to come' or in the combination **para cá** with **vir** and other verbs of movement:

Vem cá. / Vem para cá. / Vem aqui. (*spoken*)
Come here.

Acho que ele não volta para cá tão cedo.
I don't think he'll be back here any time soon.

8.5.6 **cá** and **lá** can be considered opposites when expressing proximity:

Chega um pouco mais para cá.
Move up (towards me) a little.

Vai para lá que você está ocupando o sofá todo.
Move over. You're taking up the whole sofa.

Note also the expressions **o lado de cá** 'this side' and **o lado de lá** 'the other side, the far side':

O hotel fica do lado de lá do rio.
The hotel's on the other side of the river.

8.5.7 The demonstrative adverbs also have temporal usages that correspond to their spatial meanings; **aí**, **ali** and **lá** can all mean 'then' while **aqui** is equivalent to 'now' in the expressions **daqui para frente** 'from now on' and **daqui a . . .** 'in . . . time':

Até lá vai estar tudo esquecido.
By then it'll all be forgotten. (*remote time*)

Foi aí que eu descobri a verdade.
It was then that I found out the truth. (*the moment I just mentioned*)

Ela volta daqui a duas semanas.
She'll be back in two weeks' time.

8.5.8 Finally, **aí** or **daí** can have the sense of 'so':

Eles não gostam da gente. E daí?
They don't like us. So what?

Eu não tinha dinheiro, aí eu desisti de ir.
I didn't have any money, so I decided not to go.

Notes for Spanish speakers

The masculine plural forms of the demonstratives are **estes**, **esses** and **aqueles**. When used adjectivally, demonstratives are always placed before the noun they refer to. The forms **este(s)/esta(s)** and **isto** are not used in the spoken language; in speech, **esse(s)/essa(s)** and **isso** are used to translate both 'this/these' and 'that/those (*near you*)'.

9

Possessives

▶ Chapter 40 (p. 347)

9.1 Introduction

Possessives can be used as adjectives (accompanying a noun) or as pronouns (replacing a noun), but in either case they must agree in gender and number with the noun in question. The usage of the possessives differs slightly between the spoken language and the written language, as explained below:

9.2 Forms

Masc. sing.	Fem. sing.	Masc. pl.	Fem. pl.	Basic meaning
meu	**minha**	**meus**	**minhas**	my/mine
seu	**sua**	**seus**	**suas**	your; his, her, its; their; yours, his, hers, its; theirs
nosso	**nossa**	**nossos**	**nossas**	our/ours

9.3 Usage

9.3.1

The possessives shown above can be used adjectivally, i.e. before a noun, or pronominally, i.e. replacing a noun, always agreeing in gender and number with the noun referred to. A peculiarity of Portuguese possessives is that they may be preceded by the definite article when used before a noun (see **9.3.6** below), and must be when used pronominally:

(as) minhas irmãs
my sisters

(os) nossos compromissos
our commitments

O cabelo dela é mais escuro do que o meu.
Her hair is darker than mine.

As casas deles são diferentes das nossas.
Their houses are different from ours.

9.3.2

In the spoken language, **seu(s)/sua(s)** is only used to mean 'your' or 'yours'.[1] 'His' is translated **o(s)/a(s) . . . dele** (*literally*, 'the . . . of him'), 'her' **o(s)/a(s) . . . dela**, 'its' **o(s)/a(s) . . . dele** or **dela** depending on the gender of the noun referred to, and 'their' **o(s)/a(s) . . . deles**, or **o(s)/a(s) . . . delas** referring to females or feminine nouns only:

O Carlos me trouxe no carro dele.
Carlos brought me in his car.

Sua mãe é professora?
Is your mother a teacher?

O tecido parece seda. A cor dele muda dependendo da luz.
The fabric is like silk. Its colour changes depending on the light.

Essas são as minhas meias; as suas estão na outra gaveta.
Those are my socks; yours are in the other drawer.

Os seus filhos são mais novos do que os dela.
Your children are younger than hers.

Aquela não é a bike do Thiago. A dele é vermelha.
That's not Thiago's bike. His is red.

NOTE

1   Because of the bias towards written language grammar in traditional textbooks of Brazilian Portuguese, foreign learners, especially those who have studied Spanish, have a tendency to use **seu(s)/sua(s)** to mean 'his, her, their' when speaking. In conversational situations, Brazilians always take **seu(s)/sua(s)** to mean 'your', which can lead to potentially embarrassing misunderstandings, e.g. **Eu vi a Elaine beijando o seu namorado.** 'I saw Elaine kissing your boyfriend.' (*not* 'her boyfriend'!)

9.3.3

In the written language, **seu(s)/sua(s)** without the definite article is also used to mean 'his', 'her', 'its' or 'their', but **dele/dela/deles/delas** are still preferred if it is not obvious who **seu(s)/sua(s)** refers to. Similarly, **de você** may be used for 'your' to avoid ambiguity:

Eles me convidaram a ficar em sua casa.
They invited me to stay at their house.

A atriz mora num pequeno apartamento com seus dois cachorros.
The actress lives in a small apartment with her two dogs.

o Rio de Janeiro e seus encantos
Rio de Janeiro and its charms

A namorada do Ricardo saiu da casa dele às 7h00.
Ricardo's girlfriend left his house at 7.00. a.m.
(*sua casa could mean 'her house' or even 'their house'*)

Ele quer vender a casa de você.
He wants to sell your house.
(*sua casa could mean 'his (own) house', 'her house' or 'their house'*)

9.3.4

The possessive **seu(s)/sua(s)** is not used for 'your' when addressing more than one person. In that case, it is customary to use **o(s)/a(s) ... de vocês**. Similarly, when talking to someone you address as **o senhor/a senhora**, the appropriate construction is **o(s)/a(s) ... do senhor/da senhora**:

Gente, posso ir no carro de vocês?
Guys, can I go in your car?

A nossa casa é menor do que a de vocês.
Our house is smaller than yours.

Qual o nome da senhora?
What's your name, (madam)?

9.3.5 Note that **nosso(s)/nossa(s)** is often used in combination with **a gente** in the spoken language, though **o(s)/a(s) . . . da gente** is also possible:

> **A gente vai vender o nosso carro.**
> We're going to sell our car.

> **Ele pagou o jantar da gente.**
> He paid for our dinner.

9.3.6 When the possessives are used adjectivally (i.e. before a noun), the inclusion of the definite article is optional. In the spoken language, its inclusion with nouns in subject or object position is a matter of personal preference, whereas after prepositions that contract with the definite article (**a**, **de**, **em**, **por** and **para** – see **4.1.3**), it is always included (e.g. **o nome da minha rua** 'the name of my street', **no nosso caso** 'in our case', **pelo seu próprio bem** 'for your own good', etc.). In more formal written language, it is considered better style to leave the article out before a possessive, even after a preposition, and this is always the case with **seu(s)/sua(s)** when used to mean 'his', 'her', 'its' or 'their':

> **Ela falou de suas viagens à África.** (*neutral writing*)
> She talked about her journeys to Africa.

> **O carro está em meu nome.** (*neutral writing*)
> The car is in my name.

9.3.7 Possessives may also be placed after the noun corresponding to the English 'of mine, of yours, of ours', etc. The forms **dele**, **dela**, **deles** and **delas** are also used in this way:

> **um amigo meu**
> a friend of mine

> **aquela professora sua**
> that teacher of yours

> **alguns pertences dela**
> some belongings of hers

> **vários parentes deles**
> several relatives of theirs.

9.3.8 With a few nouns, such as **foto** 'photo', **lembrança** 'memory, reminder', **notícia** 'news' and **saudade** 'feeling of missing a person or thing', the possessive placed after the noun means 'of me, of you', etc.:

> **Aguardo notícias suas.**
> I look forward to hearing from you. (*literally*, I await news of you)

> **Pode tirar uma foto nossa?**
> Can you take a picture of us?

> **Estou com muitas saudades suas.**
> I really miss you.

9.4 Omission of possessives

▶ **40.3** (p. 351)

9.4.1 When a possessive is used in English to refer back to the subject of the sentence, Portuguese usually uses the definite article instead, especially in the following cases:

(i)   With parts of the body:

> **Coloque as mãos na cabeça.**
> Put your hands on your head.

> **Ela quebrou o braço.**
> She's broken her arm.

(ii)   With items of clothing and personal accessories:

> **Ele tirou o casaco.**
> He took off his jacket.

> **Ela colocou a bolsa na cadeira do lado.**
> She put her bag on the chair next to her.

(iii)   With family members and relatives:

> **Eles puxaram ao pai.**
> They take after their father.

> **Ela vai ficar um tempo com os avós.**
> She's going to stay with her grandparents for a while.

(iv)   With any other noun where it is reasonable to assume that it is the subject's own:

> **Você não pode deixar o carro aqui.**
> You can't leave your car here.

> **Ele rabiscou o telefone num guardanapo.**
> He scribbled his phone number on a napkin.

9.4.2 The definite article may also be used with similar types of noun object, the possessor being expressed as an indirect object pronoun (see **7.6.3**). This construction is primarily used in written language:

> **uma voz que nos dá nos nervos**
> a voice that gets on our nerves

> **O ladrão me roubou algumas joias.**
> The thief stole some jewellery of mine.

9.5 *próprio* 'own'

▶ **40.2** (p. 350)

9.5.1 The possessives may be reinforced with the word **próprio** 'own', which, as a regular adjective, agrees in gender and number with the noun referred to:

> **Apresentei ao chefe as minhas próprias ideias.**
> I submitted my own ideas to the boss.

9.5.2 As expressions with 'own' usually refer back to the subject of the sentence, it is very common to replace the possessive with the definite article, especially when the subject is third person:

> **Ele veio no próprio carro.**
> He came in his own car.

> **Ela nem reconhecia a própria mãe.**
> She didn't even recognize her own mother.

9.5.3 In the sense of '(a) . . . of my/your/his, etc. own', **próprio** is placed after the noun and a possessive is not included in Portuguese:

> **Eles querem uma casa própria.**
> They want a house of their own. / . . . their own house.

> **Ela montou um negócio próprio.**
> She's started up a business of her own. / . . . her own business.

9.6 Possessives after the verb *ser* 'to be'

9.6.1 Possessives may be used after the verb **ser** to mean 'to be mine/yours/his', etc.:

> **Essa caneta é sua? – Não, é dele.**
> 'Is this pen yours?' – 'No, it's his.'

> **Esses papéis são meus.**
> Those papers are mine.

9.6.2 The possessive may be preceded by the definite article when there is an idea of contrast, sometimes expressed in English by saying 'my/your/his, etc. one(s)':

> **Essa caneta é a sua? – Não, é a dele.**
> 'Is this pen yours (your one)?' – 'No, it's his (one).' (i.e. *there are two pens in question*)

9.7 The second person possessive *teu(s)/tua(s)*

The second person possessive **teu(s)/tua(s)** is often heard in colloquial spoken language as an alternative to **seu(s)/sua(s)**:

> **Esse é teu irmão?**
> Is that your brother?

> **Pode deixar tuas coisas aqui.**
> You can leave your stuff here.

9.8 Special use of the possessive *seu(s)/sua(s)*

The possessive **seu(s)/sua(s)** is used before a noun to mean 'you . . .' when addressing a person directly:

> **Seu idiota, olha o que você fez!**
> You idiot, look what you've done!

> **Vocês vão me pagar, seus desgraçados!**
> I'll get you for that, you bastards!

Notes for Spanish speakers

Possessives have only one set of forms in Portuguese, regardless of whether they are used before a noun, after it or referring back to it. When used adjectivally before the noun, they may be preceded by the definite article, and always are after a preposition, except in more formal writing. In speech, **seu(s)/sua(s)** is only used and understood to mean 'your, yours', while 'his', 'hers' and 'their, theirs' are always expressed using **dele**, **dela** and **deles/delas** respectively. Note how the preposition **de** contracts with the third person pronouns. In the written language, **seu(s)/sua(s)** is also used to mean 'his', 'hers', 'its' and 'their, theirs'; the rule generally followed is that the possessive is used without a preceding definite article to refer to the third person and with one to refer to the second person, though the context usually makes the meaning clear.

10

Relative pronouns

Relative pronouns are words like 'who', 'which', 'that' in English which refer back to a preceding noun or pronoun, known as the antecedent, and introduce a so-called relative clause, a group of words within a sentence which further defines the antecedent or provides additional information about it. In English, the relative pronoun can be omitted under certain circumstances (cf. 'the movie we saw' vs. 'the movie that/which we saw'); this can never happen in Portuguese.

The relative pronouns used in Portuguese are:

que	who, which, that
quem	who(m); he/those who, the person/people who
o que	which; what
o/a qual, os/as quais	who, which, that
cujo(s), cuja(s)	whose, of which
quanto(s), quanta(s)	as
onde	where

Their usage and the difference between them is described below.

10.1 *que*

10.1.1 The most versatile relative pronoun is **que**, which can refer to a person or thing, subject or object, translating 'who(m)', 'which' or 'that'. Note that, unlike English, the relative pronoun can never be omitted in Portuguese:

o homem que eu vi
the man (who/that) I saw

Qual é o ônibus que vai ao centro?
Which is the bus that goes to the city centre?

10.1.2 The relative pronoun **que** can be preceded by the simple prepositions **a**, **com**, **de** and **em** (but not when these form part of a compound preposition, see **10.4.2**). The preposition has to be placed before the relative pronoun in Portuguese and the pronoun cannot be omitted:

a moça com que eu falava
the girl (who/that) I was talking to / the girl to whom I was talking

Foi uma decisão de que ele se arrependeria.
It was a decision (which/that) he would regret.

10.2 *quem*

10.2.1 The relative pronoun **quem** can be used instead of **que** after the simple prepositions **a**, **com**, **de**, **em**, **para** and **por** when the relative pronoun refers back to a person. Again, the preposition has to be placed before the relative pronoun in Portuguese and the pronoun cannot be omitted:

> **a moça com quem eu falava**
> the girl (who/that) I was talking to / the girl to whom I was talking

> **a pessoa a quem ela se referia**
> the person (who/that) she was referring to / the person to whom she was referring

10.2.2 In addition, **quem** can combine the function of antecedent and relative with the meaning of 'someone/anyone who . . .', 'he/the one/those who . . .', 'a person/people who . . .':

> **Quem gosta de peixe vai adorar este novo restaurante.**
> Anyone who likes fish will love this new restaurant.

> **Para quem não faz exercício, ela tem bastante fôlego.**
> She has quite a lot of stamina for someone who doesn't exercise.

> **O cachorro me olhou como quem diz: 'Tenha dó.'**
> The dog looked at me as if to say: 'Take pity on me.'

> **Quem roubou o dinheiro foi o mordomo.**
> The one who stole the money was the butler.

10.2.3 It can also be used in this way in emphatic expressions:

> **Quem manda aqui sou eu.**
> I give the orders around here. (= The person who gives the orders here is me.)

> **Quem quebrou o vidro foi o Jorge.**
> It was Jorge who broke the window.

10.3 *o que*

10.3.1 Some grammarians recommend using **o que** as the relative pronoun after **tudo** 'everything' and **nada** 'nothing', but **que** alone is also widely used:

> **O livro contém tudo (o) que se precisa saber sobre Paris.**
> The book contains everything you need to know about Paris.

> **Não entendi nada (o) que ele disse.**
> I didn't understand anything he said.

10.3.2 The pronoun **o que** is also used as a relative referring back to a whole sentence or idea:

> **Ele tirou o primeiro lugar, o que nos surpreendeu.**
> He came first, which surprised us.

> **Ela alega que eu a agredi, o que não é verdade.**
> She claims I attacked her, which is not true.

10.3.3 It can also combine the function of antecedent and relative with the meaning 'what':

> **O que nos falta é dinheiro.**
> What we lack is money.

Você sabe do que estou falando.
You know what I'm talking about.

Ele não entendeu nada do que o professor disse.
He didn't understand any of what the teacher said.

10.4 *o/a qual, os/as quais*

10.4.1 The relatives **o/a qual**, **os/as quais** agree with the noun they refer to in gender and number. They are used instead of **que** to avoid possible confusion, or when the relative pronoun does not immediately follow the antecedent:

Comprei um romance e uma revista, a qual folheei durante o voo.
I bought a novel and a magazine, which I leafed through during the flight.
(*i.e. I only leafed through the magazine*)

Os alunos haviam perdido 60 horas de aula com a greve, as quais eles teriam que repor durante as férias.
The students had missed 60 hours of classes with the strike, which they would have to make up during the vacation.

10.4.2 The relatives **o/a qual**, **os/as quais** are also used after prepositions other than **a**, **com**, **de** and **em**, including compound prepositions:

. . . a data a partir da qual os salários seriam reajustados
. . . the date from which salaries would be increased

O Brasil produziu alguns dos craques mais famosos do mundo, entre os quais Pelé e Ronaldo.
Brazil has produced some of the world's most famous soccer stars, including (*literally*, among which) Pelé and Ronaldo.

10.4.3 The relatives **o/a qual**, **os/as quais** may also be used with the simple prepositions **a**, **com**, **de** and **em**:

a empresa da qual ele é presidente
the company of which he is president

as organizações às quais eles estão ligados
the organizations (which/that) they are linked to.

10.5 *cujo(s), cuja(s)*

10.5.1 The relative pronoun **cujo** behaves like an adjective, agreeing in gender and number with the noun following it. It can refer back to a person or a thing, meaning 'whose', 'of which':

a professora cujo nome me escapa (*written*)
the teacher whose name escapes me

os países cujos cidadãos precisam de visto (*written*)
the countries whose citizens require a visa.

O ônibus bateu num carro, cujos ocupantes escaparam ilesos. (*written*)
The bus hit a car, the occupants of which escaped unhurt.

10.5.2 The relative pronoun **cujo** is not used in the spoken language. Either the construction is avoided, or the relative pronoun **que** is used with the appropriate possessive inserted in the relative clause:

> **a professora que eu esqueci o nome dela** (*spoken*)
> the teacher whose name I forget (*literally*, . . . that I forgot her name)

> **uma casa que o telhado está sendo consertado** (*spoken*)
> a house whose roof is being repaired (*literally*, . . . that the roof is . . .)

10.6 *quanto(s), quanta(s)*

10.6.1 The form **quanto** is used as a relative after **tanto** 'as much'; similarly, **quanto(s)/quanta(s)** are used after **tanto(s)/tanta(s)**:

> **Não recebi tanto quanto pedi.**
> I didn't get as much as I asked for.

> **Faremos tantas tentativas quantas forem necessárias.**
> We will make as many attempts as are necessary.

10.6.2 Note also the expressions **tudo quanto** 'everything which' and **todos quantos** 'all those who':

> **Ela gosta de tudo quanto é esporte.**
> She likes any kind of sport. (*literally*, everything that is sport)

> **A nova terapia traz esperança para todos quantos sofrem de asma.**
> The new therapy brings hope for all those who suffer from asthma.

> **Procurei a minha chave em tudo quanto é lugar.**
> I've looked for my key all over the place. (*idiomatic expression*)

10.7 *onde*

10.7.1 The relative **onde** means 'where':

> **o bairro onde eu moro**
> the neighbourhood where I live

> **Voltamos ao lugar de onde tínhamos saído.**
> We went back to the place (where) we had set out from.

10.7.2 Note that **aonde** (spoken or written) or **para onde** (spoken) should be used when movement to a place is involved. In the spoken language, **aonde** is used interchangeably with **onde**, denoting either location or movement, but this is frowned upon by grammarians and should be avoided in the written language:

> **o restaurante aonde fomos naquela noite**
> the restaurant where we went that night

> **a cidade para onde eles pretendem se mudar**
> the town they're planning to move to

> **o restaurante aonde/onde ele trabalha** (*spoken*)
> the restaurant where he works.

10.8 Note on translating 'when' as a relative

'When' as a relative pronoun should be translated **em que** 'on/in which':

o dia em que ela chegou
the day (when) she arrived

na época em que ainda usávamos a máquina de escrever
in the time when we still used typewriters.

See also **20.3.6** and **20.4.2** on the use of the subjunctive in relative clauses.

11

Interrogatives

Interrogatives are words like 'what', 'who', 'which' that are used to introduce questions. The interrogatives used in Portuguese are the following:

o que	what
que	what
qual, **quais**	which
quem	who
quanto/a	how much
quantos/as	how many
como	how
onde	where
cadê	where is/are
quando	when
por que	why
para que	what for
que tal	how/what about
quão	how

Their usage and the difference between them are described below.

▶ **31.2** (p. 300); **33.4** (p. 309)

11.1   *o que*

11.1.1   The interrogative **o que** means 'what' as a pronoun:

> **O que você disse?**
> What did you say?

> **O que aconteceu?**
> What happened?

> **Do que eles estão falando?**
> What are they talking about?

11.1.2   The **o** is often omitted after a preposition, especially in more formal style:

> **A que se refere essa palavra?**
> What does this word refer to?

> **Quanto ao fax, muitos jovens nem sabem de que se trata.**
> As for the fax, many young people don't even know what it is.

11.1.3 When **o que** falls at the end of a sentence, it is spelt **o quê**. The same applies to **que** after a preposition:

> **Acho que fiz algo errado, mas não sei o quê.**
> I think I did something wrong, but I don't know what.
>
> **Não tem de quê.**
> Don't mention it. (*fixed phrase in response to thanks*)

11.2 *que*

Before a noun **que** translates 'what ...':

> **Que horas são?**
> What time is it?
>
> **Que ônibus temos que pegar?**
> What bus do we have to take?
>
> **Você é de que cidade no Canadá?**
> What town are you from in Canada?

11.3 *qual, quais*

11.3.1 The interrogative **qual** means 'which (one)'. The plural is **quais** 'which (ones)':

> **Qual você prefere?**
> Which (one) do you prefer?
>
> **Quais são as melhores laranjas para fazer suco?**
> Which are the best oranges for making juice?
>
> **Qual dos dois é o seu namorado?**
> Which of the two (of them) is your boyfriend?

11.3.2 They can also be used adjectivally before a noun, but this construction is generally avoided, either by using **qual/quais dos/das ...** or **qual o/a ... que, quais os/as ... que**:

> **Qual livro é o seu? / Qual dos livros é o seu?**
> Which book is yours?
>
> **Quais alunos foram reprovados? / Quais dos alunos foram reprovados? / Quais (são) os alunos que foram reprovados?**
> Which students failed?
>
> **Qual marca você comprou? / Qual a marca que você comprou?**
> Which brand did you buy?

11.3.3 The constructions **qual é ... ?/quais são ... ?** should be used to translate 'what is/are ... ?' when you are asking someone to specify something from among a range of possibilities, as opposed to **o que é/são ... ?**, which is used when asking for a definition. Note that the verb **ser** may be omitted after **qual/quais**:

> **Qual (é) o seu nome?**
> What's your name?
>
> **Quais (são) os motivos do atraso?**
> What are the reasons for the delay?

Compare:

>**O que são células-tronco?**
>What are stem cells?

11.3.4 Notice the use of **qual** in sentences like the following:

>**Qual é a altura do muro?**
>How high is the wall?

>**Qual é o comprimento do rio?**
>How long is the river?

>**Qual é a sua idade?**
>How old are you?

11.4 *quem*

11.4.1 The interrogative **quem** means 'who':

>**Quem pegou a minha caneta?**
>Who's taken my pen?

>**Quem você viu na festa?**
>Who did you see at the party?

>**Com quem ela estava falando?**
>Who was she talking to?

11.4.2 As subject, **quem** is followed by a singular verb, except in the case of the verb **ser** 'to be', which agrees in number with what follows it, as in English:

>**Quem canta essa música?**
>Who sings this song?

>**Quem são aqueles homens ali?**
>Who are those men over there?

>**Quem foram os primeiros habitantes desta região?**
>Who were the first inhabitants of this region?

11.5 *quanto(s)/quanta(s)*

11.5.1 The forms **quanto/quanta** mean 'how much?' and **quantos/quantas** 'how many?'. They can be used adjectivally, before a noun, or pronominally, replacing a noun, but, in either case, they must agree in gender and number with the noun referred to:

>**Quantas horas você levou para vir até aqui?**
>How many hours did you take to get here?

>**Quanto dinheiro você tem na carteira?**
>How much money do you have in your wallet?

>**Vou fritar uns ovos. Quantos você quer?**
>I'm going to fry some eggs. How many do you want?

>**Eu senti tanta dor, você nem imagina quanta.**
>I was in such pain, you can't imagine how much.

11.5.2 Note that **quanto tempo?** translates 'how long':

> **Quanto tempo temos que esperar?**
> How long do we have to wait?

> **Há quanto tempo você estuda português?**
> How long have you been studying Portuguese?

11.5.3 The form **quanto** is used invariably as an adverb meaning 'how much':

> **Quanto você pagou?**
> How much did you pay?

> **Você sabe quanto ele ganha?**
> Do you know how much he earns?

11.5.4 In indirect questions, this adverbial **quanto** is often preceded by the definite article **o**, which adds emphasis:

> **Você sabe o quanto ele ganha?**
> Have you any idea just how much he earns?

> **Fiquei impressionado com o quanto ele envelheceu**.
> I was amazed by how much he had aged.

11.6 *como*

11.6.1 As an interrogative, **como** means 'how?':

> **Como vai?**
> How are you?

> **Como se escreve 'Guaratinguetá'?**
> How do you spell 'Guaratinguetá'?

▶ **42.1.2** (p. 360)

11.6.2 It also translates 'What . . . like?':

> **Como está o tempo aí?**
> What's the weather like there?

> **Como é a sua namorada?**
> What's your girlfriend like? / What does your girlfriend look like?

▶ **36.2** (p. 323)

11.6.3 Used on its own, **como?** can mean 'pardon?' 'sorry?', etc. when you haven't heard or understood what someone has said. The longer form **como é que é?** often expresses impatience or disbelief:

> **Como? Não estou te escutando.**
> Sorry? I can't hear you.

> **Como é que é? Você está me chamando de mentiroso?**
> I beg your pardon? Are you calling me a liar?

11.6.4   Note the use of **como** in sentences like the following:

> **É incrível como esse carro é econômico.**
> It's incredible how economical this car is.

> **Ficamos surpresos como ela falava bem português.**
> We were surprised how well she spoke Portuguese.

11.7   *onde*

11.7.1   The interrogative **onde?** means 'where?', expressing location or direction:

> **Onde você mora?**
> Where do you live?

> **Onde ele vai?**
> Where is he going?

> **De onde ela é?**
> Where is she from?

11.7.2   The form **aonde?** means 'where to?', but in the spoken language it is used interchangeably with **onde** for both location and direction, though this is frowned upon by grammarians:[1]

> **Perguntei-lhe aonde ele ia.**
> I asked him where he was going.

> **Aonde nos encontramos?** (*spoken*)
> Where shall we meet?

NOTE   1   In the spoken language, you will also hear **daonde?** 'where from?': **Você é daonde?** 'Where are you from?'

11.8   *cadê*

11.8.1   The word **cadê** is commonly used in the spoken language to mean 'where is/are ...?'. Note that the word already incorporates the verb 'to be'[2] so is followed immediately by a noun or pronoun. It is normally used to inquire about the temporary location of a person or thing, being synonymous with **onde está/estão ...?**, though it can also be used to ask about the existence of something you expected to find:

> **Cadê a chave do carro?**
> Where is the car key?

> **E o Pedro? Cadê ele?**
> What about Pedro? Where is he?

> **Cadê os serviços públicos correspondentes a todos estes impostos?**
> Where are the public services corresponding to all these taxes?

NOTE   2   The word **cadê** derives from the expression **que é de ...** 'what has become of ...?'.

11.9 *quando*

11.9.1 The interrogative **quando** means 'when?':

> **Quando você chegou?**
> When did you arrive?
>
> **Você sabe quando ela volta?**
> Do you know when she'll be back?
>
> **Desde quando você fuma?**
> Since when have you been smoking?

11.10 *por que*

▶ **42.1.1** (p. 360)

11.10.1 The term **por que** means 'why?'. Note that it is written as two words to differentiate it from **porque** 'because':

> **Por que você não manda um e-mail para ela?**
> Why don't you send her an e-mail?

11.10.2 When it falls at the end of a sentence, **por que** is spelt **por quê**:

> **Ele não para de emagrecer, mas os médicos não sabem por quê.**
> He just keeps losing weight, but the doctors don't know why.

11.11 *para que*

▶ **42.4** (p. 366)

11.11.1 The interrogative **para que** means 'what for?':

> **Para que você precisa de dois carros?**
> What do you need two cars for?

11.11.2 When it falls at the end of sentence, **para que** is spelt **para quê**:

> **Ela me pediu dinheiro emprestado, sem me dizer para quê.**
> She asked me to lend her money without telling me what for.

11.12 *que tal*

11.12.1 The combination **que tal?** means 'how/what about . . .?' and is most frequently used to make a suggestion. It can be followed by a noun or an infinitive, which may have its own subject (see **19.3**):

> **Que tal um cafezinho?**
> How about a coffee?
>
> **Que tal pegar um cachorro?**
> What about getting a dog?
>
> **Que tal vocês alugarem um carro?**
> How about you rent a car?

11.12.2 **Que tal?** can also be used to ask someone's opinion or impression of something:

> **Que tal o bolo? Está gostoso?**
> How's the cake? Is it tasty?

> **Que tal a viagem? Você aproveitou bastante?**
> How was the trip? Did you have a good time?

11.13 *quão*

11.13.1 The word **quão** 'how' is used to quantify adjectives and adverbs, mostly in indirect questions. It is only used in the written language.

> **A enquete revela quão arraigado ainda é o racismo.**
> The survey reveals how deep-rooted racism still is.

> **Quão fiel é a tradução ao original?**
> How faithful is the translation to the original?

11.13.2 In indirect questions, this adverbial **quão** is often preceded by the definite article **o**, which adds emphasis:

> **Resta saber o quão eficaz será esta política.**
> It remains to be seen how effective this policy will be.

11.14 Other points about interrogatives

11.14.1 Note that when an interrogative word is governed by a preposition, this must be placed before the interrogative word, unlike English:

> **De onde você é?**
> Where are you from?

> **Para quem você emprestou o livro?**
> Who did you lend the book to?

> **O restaurante fica aberto até que horas?**
> What time does the restaurant stay open till?

11.14.2 Especially in the spoken language, **... é que ...** is often inserted after an interrogative word, or **... foi que ...** when the main verb is past tense:

> **O que é que aconteceu? / O que foi que aconteceu?**
> What happened?

> **Quem é que você vai convidar?**
> Who are you going to invite?

> **Onde é que eles moram?**
> Where do they live?

> **Quando é que ela ligou? / Quando foi que ela ligou?**
> When did she phone?

> **Por que é que ele vai embora?**
> Why is he leaving?

11.14.3 Unlike English, a pronoun subject precedes the verb even after an interrogative:

> **Onde você está?**
> Where are you?
>
> **O que ele disse?**
> What did he say?

11.14.4 With a noun subject, inversion is optional with intransitive verbs, i.e. when there is no direct object in the sentence:

> **A que horas acaba o filme? / A que horas o filme acaba?**
> What time does the movie end?
>
> **Onde moram os seus pais? / Onde os seus pais moram?**
> Where do your parents live?

Inversion is preferred in the following cases:

(i)   When the verb means 'to be' (**ser, estar, ficar, ir, andar**, etc.):

> **Como vai o seu pai?**
> How is your father?
>
> **Onde fica o banheiro?**
> Where is the bathroom?

(ii)   When the verb is reflexive – see **Chapter 22**:

> **Como se chama essa flor em português?**
> What's this flower called in Portuguese?
>
> **Onde se conheceram os dois?**
> Where did the two of them meet?

(iii)   In indirect questions, especially in careful written style:

> **a cidade onde moram meus pais**
> the town where my parents live
>
> **Eles se perguntam por que não veio ninguém ao enterro.**
> They wonder why no one came to the funeral.
>
> **Precisamos averiguar como se extraviaram os documentos.**
> We must ascertain how the documents went astray.

11.14.5 After **o que** 'what' as the direct object, inversion is optional, provided the meaning is clear:

> **O que disse o médico? / O que (é que) o médico disse?**
> What did the doctor say?

11.14.6 In the spoken language, it is common to place the interrogative expression where the missing information would be in an affirmative sentence:

> **Você vai para casa como?**
> How are you getting home?
>
> **Ele acabou casando com qual das três irmãs?**
> Which of the three sisters did he end up marrying?

> **Ela saiu da empresa por quê?**
> Why did she leave the company?

Interrogatives can be placed before an infinitive to render an impersonal meaning:

> **Por que não proibir o cigarro completamente?**
> Why not ban smoking completely?

> **Como explicar isso a uma criança?**
> How do you explain that to a child?

> **Que computador comprar?**
> Which computer to buy?

They can also be used before an infinitive in the same way as in English, in expressions such as 'how to say', 'what to do', 'which to buy', etc.:

> **Não sei como te agradecer.**
> I don't know how to thank you.

> **Vou perguntar à Julia. Ela vai nos dizer o que fazer.**
> I'll ask Julia. She'll tell us what to do.

> **Estou na maior dúvida qual comprar.**
> I really can't make up my mind which one to buy.

Finally, **o que**, **como** and **por que** can be used after the verbs **ter** 'to have' and **haver** 'there is/are' and before an infinitive to mean 'something to . . .', 'a way of . . .' and 'a reason to . . .' respectively:

> **Não tenho do que me queixar.**
> I don't have anything to complain about.

> **Você tem como entrar em contato com ele?**
> Do you have some way of getting in touch with him?

> **Não há por que desconfiar deles.**
> There's no reason to distrust them.

> **Infelizmente, não tem como.**
> Unfortunately, there's no way / it's impossible.

Notes for Spanish speakers

Interrogative words are not accented in Portuguese and there is no inverted question mark. Note that **qual**, **quando** and **quanto** are spelt with initial **qu**, and 'what?' as a pronoun is usually **o que?**

12

Exclamations

The interrogatives **que**, **quanto(s)/quanta(s)** and **como** are also used in exclamatory sentences. This kind of sentence is used more frequently in spoken Portuguese than the literal English translations might suggest, so alternative translations are also given below.

12.1 *que*

12.1.1 In combination with a noun, **que** means 'what a(n) ... !', 'what ... !':

> **Que ideia!**
> What an idea! / What are you thinking?

> **Que olhos que ele tem!**
> What eyes he has! / He has the most amazing eyes!

> **Que dia bonito!**
> What a nice day! / It's such a nice day today!

12.1.2 When the noun is followed by an adjective, the adjective is often further stressed by preceding it with **mais**:

> **Que tempo mais feio!**
> What horrible weather!

12.2 *quanto(s)/quanta(s)*

12.2.1 Before a noun, **quanto(s)/quanta(s)** basically means 'What a lot of . . . !' though a different translation may be required depending on the noun that follows:

> **Quanta gente!**
> What a lot of people! / Look at all those people!

> **Quantas vezes eu não pensei nisso!**
> The number of times I've thought about that! / I've thought about that so many times!

> **Quanta saudade daquela época!**
> How I miss that time! / I miss that time so much!

12.2.2 The invariable **quanto** can be used as an adverbial in exclamations:

> **Quanto ri!**
> How I laughed! / I laughed so much!

12.3 *como*

The adverbial **como** expresses degree, especially in relation to an adjective, adverb or verb:

Como ele mudou!
How he's changed! / He's changed so much!

Como São Paulo é grande, não é?
São Paulo is so big, isn't it?

Como você fala bem português!
How well you speak Portuguese! / You speak such good Portuguese!

Notes for Spanish speakers

Exclamative words are not accented in Portuguese and there is no inverted exclamation mark. Note that **quanto** is spelt with initial **qu**.

13

Indefinite adjectives and pronouns

The most important indefinite adjectives and pronouns used in Portuguese are the following:

todo(s)/toda(s)	all, every
tudo	everything
ambos/as	both
cada	each
qualquer	any
alguém	somebody/anybody, someone/anyone
algum/alguma	some/any
alguns/algumas	some/any, a few
alguma coisa	something/anything
algo	something/anything
outro(s)/outra(s)	other, others, another
tal	such

Their usage is explained in **13.1** to **13.11** below. Note that this list does not include negative words, which are dealt with separately in **Chapter 14.**

Some indefinite adjectives and pronouns refer specifically to quantity. These are as follows:

muito/a	much, a lot (of)
muitos/as	many, a lot (of)
pouco/a	little
poucos/as	few
tanto/a	so much
tantos/as	so many
mais	more
menos	less, fewer
bastante(s)	plenty (of), quite a lot (of)
vários/várias	several
quanto/a	how much
quantos/as	how many

The usage of these is explained in **13.12** below.

13.1 *todo(s)/toda(s)*

13.1.1 Before a plural noun, **todos/as** means 'all'. Notice that, in Portuguese, the definite article is obligatory in all such cases, whereas, in English, its use depends on whether the expression refers to a specific group or not:

> **todas as crianças**
> all the children *or* all children

> **todos os meus amigos**
> all my friends.

13.1.2 As a pronoun, **todos/as** can combine with other types of pronoun, as well as with verbs:

> **Todos sentimos saudade dele. / Nós todos sentimos … /**
> **Todos nós sentimos … / Sentimos todos …**
> We all miss him.

> **Tem suficiente para todos nós. / … para nós todos.**
> There's enough for all of us. / … for us all.

> **Temos que colocar todas aquelas caixas no carro.**
> We have to put all those boxes into the car.

13.1.3 The form **todos** can also mean 'everyone, everybody' in general. When it is the subject of the verb, only the context makes clear whether the meaning is 'everyone' or 'they all':

> **Todos querem encontrar a felicidade.**
> Everyone wants to find happiness.

> **Ela tem três irmãos. Todos são médicos.**
> She has three siblings. They're all doctors.

13.1.4 In the written language, **todos/as** as an object pronoun is usually preceded by the preposition **a**, even when the verb takes a direct object:

> **Ele cumprimentou a todos.**
> He said hello to everyone.

13.1.5 Before a singular noun, and accompanied by the definite article or equivalent, **todo/a** means 'all', 'the whole':

> **Ele comeu todo o bolo.**
> He ate all the cake. / … the whole cake.

> **Já gastei todo aquele dinheiro.**
> I've already spent all that money.

13.1.6 In the sense described in **13.1.5**, **todo/a** is often placed after the noun:

> **o dia todo**
> all day / the whole day

> **Ele comeu o bolo todo.**
> He ate the whole cake.

13.1.7 Before a singular noun without the article, **todo/a** means 'every':[1]

> **todo dia**
> every day
>
> **Nem toda mulher quer ser mãe.**
> Not every woman wants to be a mother.

NOTE 1 Other translations may be appropriate in particular expressions, e.g. **toda hora** 'all the time', **em todo caso** 'in any case', **todo cuidado é pouco** (*idiom*) 'you can't be too careful'.

13.1.8 The usage described in **13.1.7** has virtually the same meaning as that described in **13.1.1**, and the two possibilities are often used interchangeably:

> **todo dia / todos os dias**
> every day
>
> **toda criança / todas as crianças**
> every child / all children.

3.1.9 Note the idiomatic expression **todo mundo** 'everybody, everyone':

> **Ele se dá bem com todo mundo.**
> He gets along well with everybody.

13.1.10 The form **todo/a** may also be used adverbially before an adjective:

> **Ela ficou toda suja.**
> She got all dirty.

3.2 *tudo*

13.2.1 The pronoun **tudo** means 'everything':

> **Tudo mudou desde então.**
> Everything's changed since then.

13.2.2 It can also translate 'it all / all of it' and 'them all / all of them' referring to things:

> **Ele abriu uma garrafa de vinho e tomou tudo.**
> He opened a bottle of wine and drank it all.

3.2.3 When an adjective is used to qualify **tudo**, it is preceded by the preposition **de**:

> **Ela me culpa por tudo de ruim que aconteceu com ela.**
> She blames me for everything bad that's happened to her.
>
> **Tudo de bom!**
> All the best!

3.2.4 In addition, **tudo** can sometimes be translated 'anything', depending on the context:

> **Tudo é possível.**
> Anything's possible.

13.2.5 In colloquial speech, **tudo** may be used in a dismissive sense to refer collectively to a group of people:

Nenhum dos candidatos presta, é tudo ladrão.
None of the candidates is any good, they're all crooks.

13.3 *ambos/as*

13.3.1 The word **ambos/as** means 'both' and can be used in combination with other pronouns as well as verbs:

Ambos estudam Engenharia.
Both of them study engineering. / They both study engineering.

Eles têm duas filhas, ambas advogadas.
They have two daughters, both (of them) lawyers.

13.3.2 Before a noun, **ambos/as** is always followed by the definite article:

Ambos os países têm armas nucleares.
Both (the) countries have nuclear weapons. / The countries both have nuclear weapons.

13.3.3 When used pronominally as a direct object, **ambos/as** is usually preceded by the preposition **a**:

Conheço a ambos.
I know both of them. / I know them both.

13.3.4 It is rarely used in the spoken language, where it is replaced by **os dois/as duas** 'the two':

Já li as duas revistas.
I've already read both (the) magazines.

Conheço os dois.
I know both of them.

Nós dois falamos português.
We both speak Portuguese. / Both of us speak Portuguese.

13.4 *cada*

13.4.1 The word **cada** means 'each'. It can precede a noun:

Cada funcionário recebe dois uniformes.
Each employee is given two uniforms.

Melhoro um pouco a cada dia.
I get a little better each day.

13.4.2 The pronominal forms are **cada um/cada uma** 'each (one)', or the more formal **cada qual**:

Cada uma delas tem um estilo diferente.
Each one of them has a different style.

Os candidatos aparecem na televisão, cada qual tentando conquistar o eleitor.
The candidates appear on TV, each one trying to win over the voters.

13.4.3 The term **cada um** can also have the general meaning of 'each individual':

Depende do gosto de cada um.
It depends on each individual's taste.

13.4.4 On its own, **cada** can be used adverbially in expressions of quantity, as in English:

Os cartões custam R$4,00 cada.
The cards cost four reais each.

13.4.5 It is also used in expressions of frequency:

Ele faz exame de sangue (a) cada seis meses.
He has a blood test every six months.

13.4.6 And **cada** is used idiomatically to indicate amazement:

Já ouvi cada história.
I've heard the most amazing stories.

Ele vem com cada desculpa!
He comes up with such far-fetched excuses!

13.5 *qualquer*

13.5.1 Before a noun, **qualquer** means 'any' (or 'either' of two) in the sense of 'no matter which'. The plural form **quaisquer** is rarely used in the spoken language:

Você pode pegar qualquer ônibus.
You can take any bus.

Tomaremos quaisquer medidas necessárias para conter a doença.
We will take any measures necessary to contain the disease.

13.5.2 The pronominal form is **qualquer um/qualquer uma** 'any one; either one':

Qual das duas maçãs você quer? – Qualquer uma.
'Which of the two apples do you want?' – 'Either one.'

13.5.3 The term **qualquer um** can also be used with the general meaning of 'anyone':

Qualquer um sabe disso.
Anyone knows that.

13.5.4 On its own, **qualquer** may also be placed after an indefinite noun in the sense of '(just) any old':

Pode usar uma roupa qualquer.
You can wear any old outfit.

Mas este não é um carro qualquer.
But this is no ordinary car.

13.6 | ***alguém***

This is used for 'somebody, someone', or 'anybody, anyone' in questions and conditional sentences:

Preciso de alguém para me ajudar.
I need someone to help me.

Se alguém ligar, anote o telefone.
If anyone calls, note down their phone number.

13.7 | ***algum/alguma, alguns/algumas***

13.7.1 | The forms **algum/alguma**, **alguns/algumas** are used for 'some' before a singular or plural noun, or 'any' in questions and conditional sentences. Note that, before a plural noun, they may also be translated 'a few, a couple of':

Eu vi a Sílvia alguns dias atrás.
I saw Silvia a few days ago.

Você acha que vai ter algum problema?
Do you think there'll be any problem?

A aplicação de gelo no músculo pode trazer algum alívio.
Applying ice to the muscle may bring some relief.

13.7.2 | And they are also used pronominally:

Você tirou fotos na festa? – Tirei algumas.
'Did you take pictures at the party?' – 'I took some/a few.'

Essas camisetas estão em promoção. Gostou de alguma?
Those T-shirts are on special offer. Do you like any of them?

Alguns nascem com talento, outros não.
Some people are born with talent, others are not.

Você leu algum dos livros que te emprestei?
Did you read any of the books I lent you?

13.7.3 | In negative sentences, **algum/alguma**, **alguns/algumas** can follow the noun to express a strongly emphatic negative meaning, 'no . . . whatsoever':

sem dúvida alguma
without any doubt / without a shadow of a doubt

Não há motivo algum para desconfiar dela.
There is no reason whatsoever to suspect her.

13.8 | ***alguma coisa***

13.8.1 | The term **alguma coisa** is used for 'something', or 'anything' in questions and conditional sentences:

Alguma coisa não bate nessa história.
There's something not quite right about this business.

Se quiser que eu explique alguma coisa, é só pedir.
If you want me to explain anything, just ask.

13.8.2 'Something' or 'anything' is often translated as **uma coisa**, especially when followed by an adjective:

> **Eu comi uma coisa na rua.**
> I had something to eat while I was out.

> **Aconteceu uma coisa estranha hoje.**
> Something strange happened today.

13.8.3 When an adjective is used to qualify **alguma coisa**, it may be preceded by the preposition **de**, though this is not obligatory. If the preposition is used, the adjective takes the masculine form:

> **Há alguma coisa de errado aqui. / Há alguma coisa errada aqui.**
> There is something wrong here.

3.9 *algo*

13.9.1 A more formal-sounding word for 'something, anything', **algo** is more often used in the written language, though not exclusively:

> **Os dois escritores têm algo em comum.**
> The two writers have something in common.

13.9.2 As in the case of **alguma coisa** (see **13.8.3**), an adjective qualifying **algo** may be preceded by the preposition **de**, though this is not obligatory:

> **Ela tinha algo (de) muito importante a dizer.**
> She had something very important to say.

13.9.3 The word **algo** is also used adverbially to mean 'somewhat, rather':

> **uma vida algo solitária**
> a somewhat lonely life.

3.10 *outro(s)/outra(s)*

13.10.1 The words **outro(s)/outra(s)** mean 'other'; as pronouns, 'other one(s)', others':

> **As facas não estão nessa gaveta, estão na outra.**
> The knives aren't in that drawer; they're in the other one.

13.10.2 In the sense of 'another (one)', the indefinite article is optional before **outro/outra**, but is usually omitted:

> **Quer outra cerveja?**
> Do you want another beer?

> **Ela viu o namorado beijando outra.**
> She saw her boyfriend kissing another girl.

13.10.3 In the sense of 'another' before a numerical expression, **outros/outras** must be used in the plural in Portuguese, agreeing with the following noun:

> **outras seis semanas**
> another six weeks

> **Onde é que vou arranjar outros cinco mil reais?**
> Where am I going to find another five thousand reais?

13.10.4 Note the expressions **um ao outro/uma à outra** (in the case of two people or things) and **uns aos outros/umas às outras** (in the case of more than two) meaning 'each other, one another'. The preposition **a** may be replaced with other prepositions as appropriate:

> **Os convidados cumprimentaram-se uns aos outros.**
> The guests greeted one another.

> **As meninas não gostam uma da outra.**
> The girls don't like each other.

13.10.5 There is also the expression **um e outro/uma e outra** (used before a singular noun) meaning 'one or two, a couple of':

> **Apenas um ou outro jornal noticiou o fato.**
> Only one or two newspapers reported the incident.

13.11 *tal*[2]

13.11.1 The word **tal** (plural: **tais**) means 'such'.[3] With a singular countable noun, **um(a) tal** means 'such a . . .' in the sense of 'a . . . of this sort', whereas without the indefinite article, **tal** means 'this', i.e. the specific one mentioned earlier:

> **Um tal escândalo é difícil de encobrir.**
> Such a scandal (*or* A scandal such as this) is difficult to cover up.

> **Como é que ele se envolveu em tal escândalo?**
> How did he get involved in this scandal?

> **O clamor foi tal que o presidente foi obrigado a recuar.**
> The outcry was such that the president was forced to back down.

> **frutas tropicais, tais como manga, mamão e abacaxi**
> tropical fruits, such as mango, papaya and pineapple

> **Ele é o chefe e, como tal, tem que assumir a culpa.**
> He is the boss and, as such, has to take the blame.

NOTES

2 In Brazilian grammars, **tal** is classified as a demonstrative, but it is more convenient to deal with it here.

3 Do not confuse this usage of 'such' with 'such' followed by an adjective, where it is the adjective that is being emphasized. In the latter case, the adjective in Portuguese is preceded by **tão** 'so': **Eu não tenho condições de pagar um aluguel tão alto.** 'I can't afford to pay such a high rent.'

13.11.2 The idiomatic expression **um(a) tal de** means 'someone/something called . . .'. A demonstrative or the definite article can be used instead of the indefinite article, with a corresponding change in meaning:

> **Um tal de Rogério ligou querendo falar com você.**
> Someone called Rogério phoned wanting to speak to you.

> **O exame acusou traços de uma tal de efedrina.**
> The test showed up traces of something called ephedrin.

> **Como é que você conheceu essa tal de Cristina?**
> How did you meet this (person called) Cristina?

> **Isso causa o tal de efeito estufa.**
> This causes the so-called greenhouse effect.

13.12 Adjectives and pronouns of quantity

13.12.1 *muito/a, muitos/as*

This is used to mean 'much, many, a lot (of)'. The masculine singular form **muito** is also used invariably as an adverb meaning 'a lot, much', or 'very' before an adjective or adverb:

> **Muitos acreditam que ele é inocente.**
> Many believe he is innocent.

> **Você tem muita paciência.**
> You have a lot of patience.

> **Ela fala muito.**
> She talks a lot.

> **A prova foi muito fácil.**
> The test was very easy.

Depending on the context, the meaning can also be 'too much/many' or 'too' before an adjective or adverb:

> **Não gosto de café assim. Tem muito leite.**
> I don't like coffee like that. There's too much milk in it.

> **O rio é muito largo para atravessar a nado.**
> The river is too wide to swim across.

13.12.2 *pouco/a, poucos/as*

This means 'little, not much, few, not many'. The masculine singular form **pouco** is also used invariably as an adverb meaning 'little, not much', or 'not very' before an adjective or adverb. Note that **pouco(s)/pouca(s)** occur much more frequently in Portuguese than 'little, few' in English because they are often used where in English you would say 'not much, not many'. Also, do not confuse **pouco** 'little, not much' with **um pouco** 'a little, a bit'.

> **Sobrou pouca comida.**
> There wasn't much food left. / There was little food left.

> **Poucos gostaram do filme.**
> Not many people liked the film. / Few (people) liked the film.

> **Ele estuda muito pouco.**
> He studies very little. / He doesn't study very much at all.

> **Achei o argumento dela pouco convincente.**
> I didn't find her argument very convincing.

> **Dormi pouco no avião.**
> I didn't sleep much on the plane.

> **Dormi um pouco no avião.**
> I slept a little on the plane.

13.12.3 *tanto/a, tantos/as*

This means 'so much, so many'. The masculine singular form **tanto** is also used invariably as an adverb:

> **200 CDs? Eu nem imaginava que tinha tantos!**
> 200 CDs? I had no idea I had so many!

> **Choveu tanto ontem que a rua ficou alagada.**
> It rained so much yesterday that the street got flooded.

13.12.4 *mais, menos*

The comparative and superlative forms[4] **mais** 'more, most' and **menos** 'less, least, fewer, fewest' are invariable, even when followed by a noun. Only the context makes it clear whether the meaning is comparative or superlative:

> **Eu tinha muito menos problemas com meu antigo computador.**
> I had a lot less trouble with my old computer.

> **a pessoa que eu mais admiro**
> the person I admire most

> **Quer um pouco mais?**
> Would you like a little more?

NOTE | 4 Both **muito** and **pouco** have absolute superlative forms (**muitíssimo, pouquíssimo**) that are used for additional emphasis (see **5.11**): **Muitíssimo obrigado!** 'Thanks a million!', **São pouquíssimas as chances de uma recuperação**. 'The chances of a recovery are minimal.'

13.12.5 *bastante(s)*

This means 'plenty (of), quite a lot (of), quite a few',[5] though it very rarely occurs in the plural. The singular form **bastante** is also used invariably as an adverb meaning 'plenty, quite a lot', or 'quite' before an adjective or adverb:

> **Você deve tomar bastante água.**
> You should drink plenty of water.

> **Gostamos bastante do hotel.**
> We really liked the hotel.

> **Ela é bastante conhecida como escritora.**
> She's quite well known as a writer.

NOTE | 5 Following a noun, **bastante(s)** can mean 'sufficient'. However, this usage is rare, although the adverbial **o bastante** is more common: **Ela tem conhecimento e experiência bastantes para evitar esse tipo de situação.** 'She has sufficient knowledge and experience to avoid this kind of situation', **O aparelho é compacto o bastante para ser transportado com facilidade.** 'The machine is compact enough to be transported easily.'

13.12.6 *vários/várias*

This is used for 'several':

> **Já estive em Londres várias vezes.**
> I've been to London several times.

Ele não tomou só um uísque, tomou vários.
He didn't have just one whisky, he had several.

13.12.7 *quanto/a, quantos/as*

This is used for 'how much, how many' (see **11.5**).

13.13 Other indefinite adjectives and pronouns

13.13.1 *certo(s)/certa(s)*

This means 'certain'. Note that, in the singular, the indefinite article may be omitted in more formal language and in many fixed expressions:

até certo ponto
to a certain extent

Certo dia, apareceu na porta de casa um policial.
One day, a policeman turned up at my door.

13.13.2 *diversos/diversas*

This is used for 'various, different':

um método usado em diversos países
a method used in various countries.

13.13.3 *tamanho(s)/tamanha(s)*

This means 'such, such great' and is used in the written language:

Sentimo-nos impotentes diante de tamanha injustiça.
We feel impotent in the face of such injustice.

13.13.4 *os/as demais*

This is used for 'the others, the rest', with or without a following noun:

as demais empresas
the other companies

Dois bandidos foram presos, os demais continuam foragidos.
Two bandits were arrested, the others are still on the run.

13.13.5 *demasiado/a, demasiados/as*

This means 'too much, too many'. The masculine singular form **demasiado** is also used invariably as an adverb meaning 'too much, too'. This word is only used in more formal written language:

Deu-se demasiada importância a esse fato.
Too much importance has been attached to this fact.

Um crescimento demasiado rápido poderá gerar inflação.
Too rapid growth may generate inflation.

13.13.6 *outrem*

This means 'another (person)' and is only used in formal writing:

> **Roubo é apropriação ilegal de um bem pertencente a outrem.**
> Theft is illegal appropriation of property belonging to another.

13.14 'Else'

13.14.1 'Else' is translated **mais** when it means 'in addition':

> **tudo (o) mais** 'everything else'
>
> **alguém mais / mais alguém** 'someone else, anyone else'
>
> **mais alguma coisa** 'something else'
>
> **algo mais** 'something else'.

13.14.2 When it means 'different', expressions with **outro** are used:

> **outra pessoa** 'someone else'
>
> **outra coisa** 'something else'
>
> **em outro lugar** 'somewhere else'.

Notes for Spanish speakers

For 'something', **alguma coisa** is much more common than **algo**, especially in the spoken language. Note that Portuguese has the separate pronoun form **tudo** for 'everything'.

14

Negatives

▶ **Chapter 32** (p. 305)

This chapter deals with negative words in Portuguese. These are as follows:

não	not; no
nada	nothing
ninguém	nobody, no one
nunca	never
jamais	never ever
nem	neither, nor; not even
nenhum/nenhuma	no; none, neither
sem	without

There are two basic principles governing the use of negatives in Portuguese:

(i)   unlike English, double (or even triple) negatives are the norm; and

(ii)   when a negative word (**nada**, **ninguém**, **nunca**, **jamais**, **nem**, **nenhum**) occurs after the verb, the verb must be preceded by **não** or another negative word:

> **Não vi nada.**
> I didn't see anything. / I saw nothing.

> **Eu nunca tive nenhum problema.**
> I've never had any problem.

14.1 *não*

14.1.1 In addition to meaning 'no' as a negative response, **não** is used to negate verbs with the meaning of 'not'. Note that it is placed before the verb and that Portuguese does not require the insertion of an auxiliary verb (like 'do' in English) to form the negative:

> **O Jim não fala português.**
> Jim doesn't speak Portuguese.

> **Não a encontrei em casa.**
> I didn't find her at home.

14.1.2 The word **não** is used on its own when the verb is understood. English repeats the auxiliary in such cases:

> **O meu irmão fuma, eu não.**
> My brother smokes, I don't.

14.1.3 The tag question **não é?** is used to render any negative tag question in English:

> **Você sabe chegar lá, não é?**
> You know how to get there, don't you?

> **Nós vamos ter que voltar, não é?**
> We'll have to go back, won't we?

14.1.4 The expression **não ... mais** translates 'not any more'. The synonymous expression **já não** sounds slightly more formal and can be thought of as meaning 'no longer':

> **Ela não mora mais aqui.**
> She doesn't live here any more.

> **Já não se fala em crise.**
> There's no longer any talk of a crisis.

14.2 *nada*

14.2.1 The word **nada** translates 'nothing', or 'anything' after a negative. When it occurs after the verb, the verb must be preceded by **não** or another negative word:

> **Não comi nada hoje.**
> I haven't eaten anything today.

> **Desde então nada mudou.**
> Since then nothing's changed.

> **Ninguém falou nada.**
> No one said anything.

14.2.2 When an adjective is used to qualify **nada**, it may be preceded by the preposition **de**, although this is not obligatory:

> **Não aconteceu nada de novo.**
> Nothing new has happened.

14.2.3 'Nothing else' is translated **mais nada** or **nada mais**:

> **Ele não disse mais nada?**
> Didn't he say anything else?

14.2.4 The word **nada** is also used adverbially to mean '(not) at all':

> **Não dormi nada essa noite.**
> I didn't sleep at all last night.

> **As perspectivas não são nada boas.**
> The prospects are not good at all.

14.2.5 It also occurs in some idiomatic usages:

> **Você estava dormindo? – Dormindo nada, acordei cedo hoje.**
> 'Were you asleep?' – 'No way, I was up early today.'

> **Ir para um hotel? Que nada! Pode ficar aqui em casa.**
> Go to a hotel? Of course not! You can stay here.

14.3 *ninguém*

14.3.1 The word **ninguém** translates 'nobody, no one', or 'anybody, anyone' after a negative:

> **Ninguém acredita em mim.**
> Nobody believes me.

> **Não tem ninguém em casa.**
> There's no one at home.

> **Não contei para ninguém.**
> I didn't tell anyone.

14.3.2 'Nobody else' is translated **mais ninguém** or **ninguém mais**:

> **Você não quer convidar ninguém mais?**
> Don't you want to invite anyone else?

14.4 *nunca*

14.4.1 The word **nunca** is used for 'never':

> **Eu nunca vou esquecer o que aconteceu.**
> I'll never forget what happened.

> **Ele não liga nunca.**
> He never calls.

14.4.2 The expression **nunca mais** means 'never again':

> **Não nos vimos nunca mais.**
> We never saw each other again.

14.4.3 And for 'hardly ever', **quase nunca** is used:

> **Eu quase nunca assisto TV.**
> I hardly ever watch TV.

14.5 *jamais*

This is a more emphatic synonym of **nunca** and might be thought of as meaning 'never ever':

> **Eu jamais faria uma coisa dessas.**
> I would never ever do a thing like that.

> **Você não deve jamais escrever sua senha num e-mail.**
> You should never, ever write your password in an e-mail.

14.6 *nem*

14.6.1 A single **nem** means 'not even'. This idea can be expressed more emphatically with the expression **nem sequer**:

> **Não tive tempo nem de tomar café.**
> I didn't even have time to have breakfast.

> **Nem sei mais onde ela mora.**
> I don't even know where she lives any more.

Ele nem sequer me cumprimentou.
He didn't even say hello to me.

14.6.2 The expression **nem . . . nem . . .** means 'neither . . . nor . . .', or 'either . . . or . . .' after a negative:

Nem o Bruno nem o irmão dele falam inglês.
Neither Bruno nor his brother speak English.

Não tenho aula nem hoje nem amanhã.
I don't have class either today or tomorrow.

14.6.3 On its own, **nem** can also mean 'neither, nor' in expressions of agreement and when giving additional information:

Eu não gosto de filmes de ação. – Nem eu.
'I don't like action movies.' – 'Neither do I.' / 'Nor do I.' / 'Me neither.'

Eu não quero ir, nem você, então não vamos.
I don't want to go, neither do you, so we won't go.

14.6.4 It is also used as a negative before **todo(s)/toda(s)**, **tudo** and **sempre**:

Nem todas as crianças gostam de chocolate.
Not all children like chocolate.

Nem sempre concordo com ele.
I don't always agree with him.

14.6.5 Note the colloquial expression **que nem**, which means 'like':

Ele fala português que nem brasileiro.
He speaks Portuguese like a Brazilian.

14.7 *nenhum/nenhuma*

14.7.1 Before a noun, **nenhum/nenhuma** means 'no', or 'neither' of two. Notice that the negated noun is always singular in Portuguese, whereas it is often plural in English:

O brasileiro não teve nenhuma dificuldade para ganhar a corrida.
The Brazilian had no difficulty winning the race.

Nenhum passageiro ficou ferido no acidente.
No passengers were injured in the accident.

pessoas que não percebem luz em nenhum olho
people who perceive light in neither eye

14.7.2 The word **nenhum/nenhuma** may be placed after the noun for greater emphasis:

Não tivemos problema nenhum.
We had no problem at all.

14.7.3 As a pronoun, **nenhum/nenhuma** means 'none', or 'neither' of two:

Quantas fotos você tirou? – Nenhuma.
'How many photos did you take?' – 'None.'

Nenhum dos gêmeos come carne.
Neither of the twins eats meat.

14.8 *sem*

14.8.1 The word **sem** 'without' is used in combination with the other negative words:

sem nenhum arrependimento
without any regrets / with no regrets

Ela saiu sem dizer nada.
She went out without saying anything.

14.8.2 In phrases without a verb, it often corresponds to the English 'no':

Sem comentários.
No comment.

Aula experimental grátis sem compromisso.
Free trial lesson with no obligation.

14.8.3 Note the common expressions **estar sem** 'to have no' and **ficar sem** 'to go without':

Estou sem dinheiro na carteira.
I have no money in my wallet.

Ficamos um tempão sem nos ver.
We went for ages without seeing each other.

Notes for Spanish speakers

The word for 'nobody, no one' is **ninguém**, which is clearly related to **alguém** 'somebody, someone.'

15

Regular verb conjugations

Introduction to Portuguese verbs: how the system works

Portuguese verb forms consist of a stem and an ending, or inflection. While English verbs have few inflected forms (e.g. speak, speaks, speaking, spoke, spoken), Portuguese verbs have many more, according to the person (I, you, he, we, they, etc.), tense (present, past, future, etc.) and mood (indicative or subjunctive). The pattern of different inflected forms is called conjugation.

While the vast majority of Portuguese verbs inflect according to one of the three regular conjugations, many of the most common verbs of the language have some irregularities that must be memorized.

The job of learning verb forms is made easier by the fact that, in Brazilian Portuguese, it is only necessary to memorize a maximum of four separate forms per tense (the first person singular, for **eu** 'I'; the third person singular, for **você, o senhor/a senhora** 'you', **ele** 'he, it' and **ela** 'she, it'; the first person plural, for **nós** 'we'; and the third person plural for **vocês** 'you', **eles** and **elas** 'they'). In fact, to get by in the spoken language, you only need to remember three forms, as the third person singular is also used with **a gente**, the colloquial alternative for **nós** (see **7.1.1**).

There are only three simple tenses that must be learnt in order to speak Brazilian Portuguese effectively: present, imperfect and preterite[1]. The future tense is hardly ever used in the spoken language and the conditional is usually replaced in speech by the imperfect. The perfect and pluperfect tenses are formed by combining the past participle with the verb **ter** 'to have' (as in English). In addition, there are three subjunctive tenses in frequent use: present, imperfect and future – see **Chapter 20** for an explanation of the nature and use of the subjunctive.

The infinitive and the stem

The verb form shown in dictionaries is the infinitive, e.g. **falar** corresponding to English 'to speak'. The infinitive of virtually all Portuguese verbs[2] ends in either -**ar**, -**er** or -**ir**. This ending immediately shows which conjugation (category of verb) the verb belongs to and which conjugation pattern it follows.

NOTES

1 'Preterite' is the most commonly used name for this tense in English and the one used here, but note that, in Portuguese, the names of all the past tenses – preterite, imperfect, present perfect and pluperfect – include the word 'pretérito'.

2 The only exceptions are the verb **pôr** 'to put' and its derivatives, e.g. **juxtapor, opor, sobrepor**, etc.

5.2.2   A limited number of monosyllabic verbs (e.g. **ir** 'to go', **pôr** 'to put', **ser** 'to be', **ter** 'to have', **ver** 'to see', **vir** 'to come', etc.) cannot be classified according to the above categorization and are irregular in their conjugation.

5.2.3   To isolate the stem of a regular verb – i.e. the element to which the various inflectional endings are added – simply remove the infinitive ending **-ar**, **-er** or **-ir**.

5.2.4   This chapter deals with the conjugation of regular verbs. The uses of the different tenses mentioned here are described in **Chapter 18**.

15.3   Simple tenses: present indicative

5.3.1   The first person singular ending is **-o** for all three conjugations: **falar** 'to speak' > **falo** 'I speak'; **comer** 'to eat' > **como** 'I eat'; **decidir** 'to decide' > **decido** 'I decide'.

5.3.2   The third person singular ending is **-a** for **-ar** verbs, e.g. **falar** > **ele fala** 'he speaks', and **-e** for both **-er** and **-ir** verbs: **comer** > **ele come** 'he eats'; **decidir** > **ele decide** 'he decides'.

5.3.3   The first person plural ending is **-amos** for **-ar** verbs, e.g. **falar** > **falamos** 'we speak'; **-emos** for **-er** verbs, e.g. **comer** > **comemos** 'we eat'; and **-imos** for **-ir** verbs, e.g. **decidir** > **decidimos** 'we decide'.

15.3.4   The third person plural ending is **-am** (pronounced [-ãw]) for **-ar** verbs, e.g. **falar** > **eles falam** 'they speak', and **-em** for both **-er** and **-ir** verbs: **comer** > **eles comem** 'they eat'; **decidir** > **eles decidem** 'they decide'.

▶ **18.1.1** (p. 167)

Table 15.3.1 Summary of present tense endings

	-ar verb: ***falar***	*-er verb:* ***comer***	*-ir verb:* ***decidir***
eu	falo	como	decido
você, ele, ela	fala	come	decide
nós	falamos	comemos	decidimos
vocês, eles, elas	falam	comem	decidem

15.4   Simple tenses: imperfect indicative

5.4.1   In the imperfect tense, there is no distinction between first and third person singular forms, and the endings for **-er** and **-ir** verbs are the same.

5.4.2   The singular ending is **-ava** for **-ar** verbs, e.g. **falar** > **eu/ele falava** 'I/he used to speak', and **-ia** for both **-er** and **-ir** verbs: **comer** > **eu/ele comia** 'I/he used to eat'; **decidir** > **eu/ele decidia** 'I/he used to decide'.

5.4.3   The first person plural ending is **-ávamos** for **-ar** verbs, e.g. **falar** > **falávamos** 'we used to speak', and **-íamos** for both **-er** and **-ir** verbs: **comer** > **comíamos** 'we used to eat'; **decidir** > **decidíamos** 'we used to decide'.

15.4.4 The third person plural ending is **-avam** (pronounced [-'avãw]) for **-ar** verbs, e.g. **falar** > **eles falavam** 'they used to speak', and **-iam** (pronounced [-'iãw]) for both **-er** and **-ir** verbs: **comer** > **eles comiam** 'they used to eat'; **decidir** > **eles decidiam** 'they used to decide'.

▶ **18.1.2** (p. 172)

Table 15.4.1 Summary of imperfect tense endings

	-ar verb: falar	*-er verb: comer*	*-ir verb: decidir*
eu, você, ele, ela	falava	comia	decidia
nós	falávamos	comíamos	decidíamos
vocês, eles, elas	falavam	comiam	decidiam

15.5 Simple tenses: preterite indicative

15.5.1 The first person singular ending is **-ei** for **-ar** verbs, e.g. **falar** > **falei** 'I spoke', and **-i** for both **-er** and **-ir** verbs: **comer** > **comi** 'I ate'; **decidir** > **decidi** 'I decided'. Note that, in all cases, the preterite ending is stressed.

15.5.2 The third person singular ending is **-ou** for **-ar** verbs, e.g. **falar** > **ele falou** 'he spoke'; **-eu** for **-er** verbs, e.g. **comer** > **ele comeu** 'he ate'; and **-iu** for **-ir** verbs, e.g. **decidir** > **ele decidiu** 'he decided'.

15.5.3 The first person plural forms of the preterite are identical to those of the present tense: **falar** > **falamos** 'we spoke'; **comer** > **comemos** 'we ate'; **decidir** > **decidimos** 'we decided'. Only the context makes it clear whether the verb form has present or preterite meaning.

15.5.4 The third person plural ending is **-aram** (pronounced [-'arãw]) for **-ar** verbs, e.g. **falar** > **eles falaram** 'they spoke'; **-eram** (pronounced [-'erãw]) for **-er** verbs, e.g. **comer** > **eles comeram** 'they ate'; and **-iram** (pronounced [-'irãw]) for **-ir** verbs, e.g. **decidir** > **eles decidiram** 'they decided'.

▶ **18.1.3** (p. 169)

Table 15.5.1 Summary of preterite tense endings

	-ar verb: falar	*-er verb: comer*	*-ir verb: decidir*
eu	falei	comi	decidi
você, ele, ela	falou	comeu	decidiu
nós	falamos	comemos	decidimos
vocês, eles, elas	falaram	comeram	decidiram

15.6 Simple tenses: present subjunctive

The present subjunctive is formed by adding the present indicative endings of **-er** verbs to the stem of **-ar** verbs, and the present indicative endings of **-ar** verbs to the stem of **-er** and **-ir** verbs, except in the first person singular, which, in the subjunctive, is always identical in form to the third person singular.

► **Chapter 20** (p. 187)

Table 15.6.1 Summary of present subjunctive endings

	-ar verb: *falar*	*-er* verb: *comer*	*-ir* verb: *decidir*
eu, você, ele, ela	fale	coma	decida
nós	falemos	comamos	decidamos
vocês, eles, elas	falem	comam	decidam

15.7 Simple tenses: imperfect subjunctive

The singular of the imperfect subjunctive, which is the same for first and third persons, is formed by adding the ending **-asse** to the stem of **-ar** verbs, the ending **-esse** to the stem of **-er** verbs and the ending **-isse** to the stem of **-ir** verbs. The first person plural is formed by adding **-mos** to the singular form and a written accent on the first vowel of the combined ending. The third person plural is formed by adding **-m** to the singular form.

► **Chapter 20** (p. 187)

Table 15.7.1 Summary of imperfect subjunctive endings

	-ar verb: *falar*	*-er* verb: *comer*	*-ir* verb: *decidir*
eu, você, ele, ela	falasse	comesse	decidisse
nós	falássemos	comêssemos	decidíssemos
vocês, eles, elas	falassem	comessem	decidissem

15.8 Simple tenses: future subjunctive

In regular verbs, the singular form of the future subjunctive is identical to the infinitive. The first person plural is formed by adding **-mos** to the singular form, the third person plural by adding **-em**.

► **Chapter 20** (p. 187)

Table 15.8.1 Summary of future subjunctive endings

	-ar verb: *falar*	*-er* verb: *comer*	*-ir* verb: *decidir*
eu, você, ele, ela	falar	comer	decidir
nós	falarmos	comermos	decidirmos
vocês, eles, elas	falarem	comerem	decidirem

15.9 Future and conditional tenses

15.9.1

The future and conditional tenses are formed by adding endings to the future stem, which is identical to the infinitive for all verbs except **dizer** 'to say', **fazer** 'to do' and **trazer** 'to bring', which have the future stems **dir-**, **far-** and **trar-** respectively.[3] Note also that the verb **pôr** loses the written accent before the future or conditional endings.

NOTE   3   This also applies to compounds of these verbs, e.g. **contradizer** > **contradir-**, **satisfazer** > **satisfar-**, etc.

15.9.2 The future tense endings for all verbs are: **-ei, -á, -emos, -ão**.

▶ **18.1.4** (p. 170)

Table 15.9.1 Summary of future tense endings

	-ar verb: *falar*	*-er* verb: *comer*	*-ir* verb: *decidir*
eu	falarei	comerei	decidirei
você, ele, ela	falará	comerá	decidirá
nós	falaremos	comeremos	decidiremos
vocês, eles, elas	falarão	comerão	decidirão

15.9.3 The conditional tense endings are the same as those for the imperfect of **-er** and **-ir** verbs but are added to the future stem instead of the present stem. The endings are the same for all verbs: **-ia, -ia, -íamos, -iam**.

▶ **18.1.5** (p. 170)

Table 15.9.2 Summary of conditional tense endings

	-ar verb: *falar*	*-er* verb: *comer*	*-ir* verb: *decidir*
eu, você, ele, ela	falaria	comeria	decidiria
nós	falaríamos	comeríamos	decidiríamos
vocês, eles, elas	falariam	comeriam	decidiriam

15.10 Simple pluperfect tense

There is a simple pluperfect tense that is nowadays only found in very formal written or literary style. The third person plural form of this tense is identical to that of the preterite, and the singular form, which is the same for first and third persons, is derived by removing the final **-m** from the third person plural form. The first person plural is formed by replacing **-m** with **-mos** and adding a written accent to the first vowel of the ending.

Table 15.10.1 Summary of simple pluperfect endings

	-ar verb: *falar*	*-er* verb: *comer*	*-ir* verb: *decidir*
eu, você, ele, ela	falara	comera	decidira
nós	faláramos	comêramos	decidíramos
vocês, eles, elas	falaram	comeram	decidiram

15.11 Stress patterns in regular verbs

In the present indicative and subjunctive of regular verbs, the last vowel of the stem is stressed in the first and third persons singular and the third person plural. In the first person plural the stress shifts to the first vowel of the ending:

> *Pres. indic.* **realizo, realiza, realizamos, realizam**
> *Pres. subj.* **realize, realizemos, realizem.**

In all other tenses, the stress falls on the first syllable of the ending.

15.12 Spelling conventions governing regular verbs

15.12.1 The following spelling rules are applied in the conjugation of regular verbs:

(i)   Verbs ending in **-car**: **-c-** becomes **-qu-** before **-e** (i.e. first person singular preterite and all present subjunctive forms) to preserve the hard *c* sound, e.g. **ficar** > **fiquei**, **fique**.

(ii) Verbs ending in **-çar**: **-ç-** becomes **-c-** before **-e** (i.e. first person singular preterite and all present subjunctive forms) as the cedilla is not required to soften the pronunciation of **c** before **e**, e.g. **abraçar** > **abracei**, **abrace**.

(iii) Verbs ending in **-gar**: **-g-** becomes **-gu-** before **-e** (i.e. first person singular preterite and all present subjunctive forms) to preserve the hard *g* sound, e.g. **pagar** > **paguei**, **pague**.

(iv) Verbs ending in **-cer**: **-c-** becomes **-ç-** before **-o** or **-a** (i.e. first person singular present indicative and all present subjunctive forms) to preserve the soft *c* sound, e.g. **descer** > **desço**, **desça**.

(v)   Verbs ending in **-ger** and **-gir**: **-g-** becomes **-j-** before **-o** or **-a** (i.e. first person singular present indicative and all present subjunctive forms) to preserve the soft *g* sound, e.g. **dirigir** > **dirijo**, **dirija**.

(vi) Verbs ending in **-guer** and **-guir**: **-gu-** becomes **-g-** before **-o** or **-a** (i.e. first person singular present and all present subjunctive forms) as the letter **-u-** is not required before **-o** and **-a** to preserve the hard *g* sound, e.g. **distinguir** > **distingo**, **distinga**.

(vii) Verbs ending in **-ear**: **-e-** becomes **-ei-** when stressed (i.e. the first and third persons singular and third person plural, present indicative and subjunctive), e.g. **passear** > **passeio**, **passeia**, **passeiam**; **passeie**, **passeiem** (cf. **passeamos**, **passeemos**, **passeei**, etc. where the **-e-** of the stem is not stressed).

15.12.2 The following rules apply for the use of the written accent in certain regular verbs:

(i)   In the verbs **saudar** and **reunir**, the letter **u** is accented in those forms that have stem stress (i.e. the first and third persons singular and third person plural, present indicative and subjunctive) to indicate that the two vowels are to be pronounced separately with the stress on **u**, e.g. **saudar** > **saúdo**, **saúda**; **reunir** > **reúno**, **reúne**.

(ii) In the verbs **arruinar**, **proibir** and **coibir**, the letter **i** is accented in those forms that have stem stress (i.e. the first and third persons singular and third person plural, present indicative and subjunctive) to indicate that the two vowels are to be pronounced separately with the stress on **i**, e.g. **arruinar** > **arruíno**, **arruínam**; **proibir** > **proíbo**, **proíbem**.

(iii) In the verbs **aguar**, **desaguar** and **enxaguar**, the letter **a** is accented in those forms that have stem stress (i.e. the first and third persons singular and third person plural, present indicative and subjunctive) to indicate that the stress falls on **a** and not **u**, even though **u** is pronounced in all forms, e.g. **enxaguar** > **enxáguo**, **enxágua**, **enxágue** /ẽ'ʃagwi/.

(iv) The verbs **mobiliar** and **resfolegar** are unusual in that the second from last syllable is stressed in those forms that have stem stress (i.e. the first and third persons singular and third person plural, present indicative and subjunctive) and therefore these forms must be written with an accent: **mobiliar** > **mobílio**, **mobíliam**; **resfolegar** > **resfólego**, **resfólegam**.

15.12.3 Verbs ending in -**air** and -**uir** follow similar rules regarding spelling and accentuation. The forms are as follows (accented forms underlined):

Infinitive	**sair, atribuir**[4]
Pres. indic.	**saio, sai, <u>saímos</u>, saem; atribuo, atribui, <u>atribuímos</u>, atribuem**
Pres. subj.	**saia, saiamos, saiam; atribua, atribuamos, atribuam**
Imperf. indic.	**<u>saía</u>, <u>saíamos</u>, <u>saíam</u>; <u>atribuía</u>, <u>atribuíamos</u>, <u>atribuíam</u>**
Imperf. subj.	**<u>saísse</u>; <u>atribuísse</u>**, etc. (*all forms accented*)
Preterite	**<u>saí</u>, saiu, <u>saímos</u>, <u>saíram</u>; <u>atribuí</u>, atribuiu, <u>atribuímos</u>, <u>atribuíram</u>**
Pluperf.	**<u>saíra</u>; <u>atribuíra</u>**, etc. (*all forms accented*)
Future subj./ Pers. infinitive	**sair, sairmos, <u>saírem</u>; atribuir, atribuirmos, <u>atribuírem</u>**
Past participle	**<u>saído</u>; <u>atribuído</u>**
Gerund	**saindo; atribuindo.**

NOTE 4 An infinitive ending in -**air** or -**uir** is written with an accent when an unstressed third person pronoun is appended to it in the form -**lo**, -**la**, -**los** or -**las** (see **7.5.7**), e.g. **traí-la, substituí-los**, etc.

15.12.4 Verbs ending in -**struir** follow the rules for those ending in -**uir** (see **15.12.3**) but the verbs **construir** and **destruir** have their present indicative third person singular ending in -**ói** and third person plural ending in -**oem**: e.g. **construir** > **constrói** '(he) builds', **constroem** '(they) build'; **destruir** > **destrói** '(he) destroys', **destroem** '(they) destroy'. The same applies to the derivatives **desconstruir** 'to deconstruct' and **reconstruir** 'to rebuild, reconstruct'.

15.12.5 Verbs ending in -**oer** (e.g. **doer, roer**) have a written accent on the third person singular present indicative that ends in -**i** (**dói, rói**), all forms of the imperfect indicative (**roía, roíamos, roíam**), the first person singular of the preterite (**roí**) and the past participle (**doído, roído**).

Notes for Spanish speakers

In the imperfect indicative, the endings of -**ar** verbs are spelt with *v* (cf. **cantava, cantávamos, cantavam**) and there is no written accent on the singular and third person plural endings of -**er** and -**ir** verbs (cf. **comia, comiam**), nor on the same persons of the conditional tense (cf. **cantaria, comeriam**). In the preterite tense, the first and third person singular endings of -**ar** verbs are diphthongs (cf. **cantei, cantou**) and there is a distinction between the third person forms of -**er** verbs (cf. **comeu, comeram**) and those of -**ir** verbs (cf. **decidiu, decidiram**). There is only one set of endings for the imperfect subjunctive, spelt with -**ss**-, but there is also a distinct future subjunctive tense. Portuguese has also preserved an inflected pluperfect indicative tense, used only in formal and literary style, which should not be mistaken for an imperfect subjunctive.

16

Semi-irregular and irregular verbs

16.1 ## Radical-changing verbs

Some groups of verbs of the **-ir** conjugation exhibit a phonetic alternation that is reflected in the spelling of certain forms.[1]

NOTE   1 A similar phonetic alternation is found in **-ar** and **-er** verbs that have **-e-** or **-o-** in the stem, but the spelling is not affected. In all such verbs, **-e-** and **-o-** are pronounced /e/ and /o/ respectively when unstressed. In **-ar** verbs, they become /ɛ/ and /ɔ/ respectively when stressed, e.g. **levar** /le'vaʳ/ > **levo** /'lɛvu/, **leva** /'lɛva/, **levam** /'lɛvãw/; **tocar** /to'kaʳ/ > **toco** /'tɔku/, **toca** /'tɔka/, **tocam** /'tɔkãw/. This alternation does not occur before the nasal letters **m**, **n** and **nh**, nor in the verb **chegar** and those ending in **-ejar**, **-elhar** and **-oar**, where **-e-** and **-o-** are pronounced /e/ and /o/ respectively in all forms. In **-er** verbs, **-e-** and **-o-** are pronounced /e/ and /o/ in the first person singular of the present indicative and all forms of the present subjunctive, changing to /ɛ/ and /ɔ/ respectively in the third persons singular and plural of the present indicative, e.g. **dever** /de've ʳ/ > **devo** /'devu/, **deve** /'dɛvi/, **devem** /'dɛvẽ/; **correr** /ko'heʳ/ > **corro** /'kohu/, **corre** /'kɔhi/, **correm** /'kɔhẽ/. This alternation does not occur before the letter **m**, where **-e-** and **-o-** are pronounced /e/ and /o/ respectively in all forms.

16.1.1 Verbs with **-e-** in the stem: **-e-** changes to **-i-** in the first person singular present indicative and all forms of the present subjunctive (i.e. when stressed before **-o** or **-a** in the next syllable), e.g. **mentir** 'to lie' (irregular forms underlined):

> *Pres. indic.*   <u>**minto**</u>, **mente**, **mentimos**, **mentem**
>
> *Pres. subj.*   <u>**minta**</u>, <u>**mintamos**</u>, <u>**mintam**</u>.
> (*All other forms are regular.*)

Similarly:

> **aderir** 'to adhere', **advertir** 'to warn', **competir** 'to compete', **convergir** 'to converge', **desferir** 'to deal (a blow)', **desmentir** 'to deny', **diferir** 'to differ', **digerir** 'to digest', **divergir** 'to diverge', **divertir** 'to amuse', **ferir** 'to wound, injure', **ingerir** 'to ingest', **preferir** 'to prefer', **proferir** 'to utter', **refletir** 'to reflect', **referir** 'to refer', **repelir** 'to repel', **repetir** 'to repeat', **seguir** 'to follow', **sentir** 'to feel', **servir** 'to serve', **sugerir** 'to suggest', **vestir** 'to dress' and derivatives of these verbs, e.g. **conseguir** 'to get, manage, succeed', **pressentir** 'to sense, anticipate', etc.

16.1.2 Verbs with **-o-** in the stem: **-o-** changes to **-u-** in the first person singular present indicative and all forms of the present subjunctive (i.e. when stressed before **-o** or **-a** in the next syllable), e.g. **dormir** 'to sleep' (irregular forms underlined):

> *Pres. indic.*   **durmo**, **dorme**, dormimos, dormem
>
> *Pres. subj.*   **durma**, **durmamos**, **durmam**.
> (*All other forms are regular.*)

Similarly:

> **cobrir** 'to cover', **descobrir** 'to discover', **encobrir** 'to cover up', **engolir** 'to swallow', **tossir** 'to cough'.

16.1.3 Verbs with -**u**- in the stem: -**u**- changes to -**o**- in the third persons singular and plural of the present indicative (i.e. when stressed before -**e**- in the next syllable), e.g. **subir** 'to go up' (irregular forms underlined):

> *Pres. indic.*   **subo**, **sobe**, subimos, **sobem**.
> (*All other forms are regular.*)

Similarly:

> **consumir** 'to consume', **cuspir** 'to spit', **desentupir** 'to unblock', **entupir** 'to block', **escapulir** 'to slip out', **fugir** 'to escape', **sacudir** 'to shake', **sumir** 'to disappear'.

16.1.4 A group of verbs with -**e**- in the stem change -**e**- to -**i**- in all stressed positions and, by analogy, also in the first person plural of the present subjunctive, e.g. **agredir** 'to attack' (irregular forms underlined):

> *Pres. indic.*   **agrido**, **agride**, agredimos, **agridem**
>
> *Pres. subj.*   **agrida**, **agridamos**, **agridam**.
> (*All other forms are regular.*)

Similarly:

> **cerzir** 'to darn', **denegrir** 'to denegrate', **prevenir** 'to prevent; to warn', **progredir** 'to progress', **regredir** 'to regress', **transgredir** 'to transgress'.

16.1.5 The verb **polir** 'to polish' changes -**o**- to -**u**- in all stressed positions and, by analogy, also in the first person plural of the present subjunctive (irregular forms underlined):

> *Pres. indic.*   **pulo**, **pule**, polimos, **pulem**
>
> *Pres. subj.*   **pula**, **pulamos**, **pulam**.
> (*All other forms are regular.*)

16.2 Semi-irregular verbs

Semi-irregular verbs are those that show irregularities in certain forms but are basically regular.

16.2.1 Verbs ending in -**duzir** and **reluzir** 'to sparkle': these verbs are irregular only in the third person singular of the present indicative, which ends in -**z**, e.g. **produzir** > **produz** '(he) produces', **reluzir** > **reluz** '(it) sparkles'.

16.2.2 Six verbs ending in -**iar** that change -**i**- to -**ei**- in stressed position, e.g. **odiar** 'to hate' (irregular forms underlined):

> *Pres. indic.*   **odeio**, **odeia**, odiamos, **odeiam**
>
> *Pres. subj.*   **odeie**, odiemos, **odeiem**.
> (*All other forms follow regular -ar conjugation.*)

Similarly:

> **ansiar** 'to long for', **incendiar** 'to set alight', **intermediar** 'to intersperse', **mediar** 'to mediate', **remediar** 'to remedy'. All other verbs ending in **-iar** are regular.

16.2.3 The verbs **crer** 'to believe', **ler** 'to read' and their derivatives are irregular only in the present indicative and subjunctive (irregular forms underlined):

> *Pres. indic.* <u>leio</u>, <u>lê</u>, lemos, <u>leem</u>
>
> *Pres. subj.* <u>leia</u>, <u>leiamos</u>, <u>leiam</u>.
> (*All other forms follow regular -er conjugation.*)

16.2.4 The verbs **rir** 'to laugh' and **sorrir** 'to smile' are irregular only in the present indicative and subjunctive (irregular forms underlined):

> *Pres. indic.* <u>rio</u>, <u>ri</u>, rimos, <u>riem</u>
>
> *Pres. subj.* <u>ria</u>, <u>riamos</u>, <u>riam</u>.
> (*All other forms follow regular -ir conjugation.*)

16.2.5 The following verbs are irregular only in the first person singular of the present indicative and all forms of the present subjunctive (irregular forms underlined):

(i) **medir** 'to measure', **pedir** 'to ask' and their derivatives (e.g. **despedir** 'to dismiss', **impedir** 'to stop, prevent'):

> *Pres. indic.* <u>peço</u>, pede, pedimos, pedem
>
> *Pres. subj.* <u>peça</u>, <u>peçamos</u>, <u>peçam</u>;

(ii) **ouvir** 'to hear':

> *Pres. indic.* <u>ouço</u>, ouve, ouvimos, ouvem
>
> *Pres. subj.* <u>ouça</u>, <u>ouçamos</u>, <u>ouçam</u>;

(iii) **perder** 'to lose':

> *Pres. indic.* <u>perco</u>, perde, perdemos, perdem
>
> *Pres. subj.* <u>perca</u>, <u>percamos</u>, <u>percam</u>;

(iv) **valer** 'to be worth':

> *Pres. indic.* <u>valho</u>, vale, valemos, valem
>
> *Pres. subj.* <u>valha</u>, <u>valhamos</u>, <u>valham</u>.

16.3 Irregular verbs

16.3.1 Some tips on memorizing irregular verb forms

(i) The forms of irregular verbs you need to memorize are those of the present indicative, the preterite and, in a few cases, the imperfect.

(ii) The only verbs with an irregular imperfect are: **pôr** 'to put', **ser** 'to be', **ter** 'to have' and **vir** 'to come', and their derivatives (e.g. **compor**, **obter**, **provir**, etc.)

(iii) The present subjunctive forms of irregular verbs can nearly always be derived from the first person singular present indicative by changing the final **-o** to **-a**. For example, **ter** 'to have' > **tenho** 'I have' > *pres. subj.*: **tenha**, **tenhamos**, **tenham**. The only exceptions to this rule are the verbs **dar** 'to give', **estar** 'to be', **haver** 'to have', **ir** 'to go', **saber** 'to know' and **ser** 'to be'.

(iv) The imperfect and future subjunctive forms of all irregular verbs can be derived from the third person plural of the preterite, e.g. **ter** 'to have' > **tiveram** 'they had' > *imperf. subj.*: **tivesse, tivéssemos, tivessem**; *future subj.*: **tiver, tivermos, tiverem**. Note that the first person plural of the imperfect subjunctive of irregular verbs has an acute accent reflecting the open [ɛ] sound (except **ir/ser** – see **16.3.8**).

(v) The simple pluperfect is also derived from the third person plural of the preterite, e.g. **ter** 'to have' > **tiveram** 'they had' > **tivera, tivéramos, tiveram**. Note that the first person plural of the simple pluperfect of irregular verbs has an acute accent reflecting the open [ɛ] sound (except **ir/ser** – see **16.3.8**).

16.3.2 *caber* 'to fit, befit', *saber* 'to know'

Apart from the first person singular of the present indicative, these two verbs follow the same pattern (irregular forms underlined):

Pres. indic.	<u>caibo</u>, **cabe**, **cabemos**, **cabem**
Pres. subj.	<u>caiba</u>, <u>caibamos</u>, <u>caibam</u>
Preterite	<u>coube</u>, <u>coube</u>, <u>coubemos</u>, <u>couberam</u>
Imperf. subj.	<u>coubesse</u>, etc.
Future subj.	<u>couber</u>, etc.
Simple pluperf.	<u>coubera</u>, etc.
Pres. indic.	<u>sei</u>, **sabe**, **sabemos**, **sabem**
Pres. subj.	<u>saiba</u>, <u>saibamos</u>, <u>saibam</u>
Preterite	<u>soube</u>, <u>soube</u>, <u>soubemos</u>, <u>souberam</u>
Imperf. subj.	<u>soubesse</u>, etc.
Future subj.	<u>souber</u>, etc.
Simple pluperf.	<u>soubera</u>, etc.

(*All other tenses follow regular -er conjugation.*)

16.3.3 *dizer* 'to say', *trazer* 'to bring'

These two verbs follow the same pattern in the present tense, diverging in the preterite. Note that both verbs have irregular future stems (irregular forms underlined):

Pres. indic.	<u>digo</u>, <u>diz</u>, **dizemos**, **dizem**
Pres. subj.	<u>diga</u>, <u>digamos</u>, <u>digam</u>
Preterite	<u>disse</u>, <u>disse</u>, <u>dissemos</u>, <u>disseram</u>
Imperf. subj.	<u>dissesse</u>, etc.
Future subj.	<u>disser</u>, etc.
Simple pluperf.	<u>dissera</u>, etc.
Future indic.	<u>direi</u>, etc.
Conditional	<u>diria</u>, etc.
Pres. indic.	<u>trago</u>, <u>traz</u>, **trazemos**, **trazem**
Pres. subj.	<u>traga</u>, <u>tragamos</u>, <u>tragam</u>
Preterite	<u>trouxe</u>, <u>trouxe</u>, <u>trouxemos</u>, <u>trouxeram</u>[2]
Imperf. subj.	<u>trouxesse</u>, etc.
Future subj.	<u>trouxer</u>, etc.
Simple pluperf.	<u>trouxera</u>, etc.
Future indic.	<u>trarei</u>, etc.
Conditional	<u>traria</u>, etc.

(*Remaining forms follow regular -er conjugation.*)

Similarly: **contradizer** 'to contradict', **desdizer** 'to go back on (sth said)'.

NOTE | 2 The letter **x** in these forms is pronounced [s].

16.3.4 *fazer* 'to do, make'

This verb has distinct first and third person singular forms in the preterite. Note that this verb also has an irregular future stem (irregular forms underlined):

Pres. indic.	**faço, faz, fazemos, fazem**
Pres. subj.	**faça, façamos, façam**
Preterite	**fiz, fez, fizemos, fizeram**
Imperf. subj.	**fizesse**, etc.
Future subj.	**fizer**, etc.
Simple pluperf.	**fizera**, etc.
Future indic.	**farei**, etc.
Conditional	**faria**, etc.

(*Remaining forms follow regular -er conjugation.*)

Similarly: **desfazer** 'to undo', **perfazer** 'to make up, complete', **refazer** 'to redo', **satisfazer** 'to satisfy'.

16.3.5 *ter* 'to have', *vir* 'to come'

These two verbs follow the same pattern in the present and imperfect except in the first person plural present indicative. The preterite of both verbs has distinct first and third person singular forms (irregular forms underlined):

Pres. indic.	**tenho, tem, temos, têm**
Pres. subj.	**tenha, tenhamos, tenham**
Imperf.	**tinha, tínhamos, tinham**
Preterite	**tive, teve, tivemos, tiveram**
Imperf. subj.	**tivesse**, etc.
Future subj.	**tiver**, etc.
Simple pluperf.	**tivera**, etc.

Pres. indic.	**venho, vem, vimos, vêm**
Pres. subj.	**venha, venhamos, venham**
Imperf.	**vinha, vínhamos, vinham**
Preterite	**vim, veio, viemos, vieram**
Imperf. subj.	**viesse**, etc.
Future subj.	**vier**, etc.
Simple pluperf.	**viera**, etc.

Similarly: **ater-se a** 'to stick to, abide by'; **conter** 'to contain', **deter** 'to detain', **entreter** 'to entertain', **manter** 'to keep', **obter** 'to obtain', **reter** 'to retain'; **advir** 'to accrue, arise'; **convir** 'to suit, concur', **intervir** 'to intervene', **provir** 'to originate'.

NOTE | The third person singular present indicative of derivatives of **ter** and **vir** is spelt with an acute accent, e.g. **deter** 'to detain' > **ele detém** 'he detains'; **convir** 'to suit' > **convém** 'it suits'.

16.3.6 *ver* 'to see'

The forms of this verb should not be confused with those of **vir** (see **16.3.5**) (irregular forms underlined):

Pres. indic.	**vejo, vê, vemos, veem**
Pres. subj.	**veja, vejamos, vejam**

Imperfect	via, víamos, viam
Preterite	vi, <u>viu</u>, <u>vimos</u>, <u>viram</u>
Imperf. subj.	visse, etc.
Future subj.	vir, etc.
Simple pluperf.	vira, etc.

Similarly: **antever** 'to foresee', **entrever** 'to make out', **prever** 'to predict, anticipate', **rever** 'to see again'.

16.3.7 *pôr* 'to put'

The imperfect stem of this verb is irregular and the preterite has distinct first and third person singular forms (irregular forms underlined):

Pres. indic.	<u>ponho</u>, <u>põe</u>, <u>pomos</u>, <u>põem</u>
Pres. subj.	<u>ponha</u>, <u>ponhamos</u>, <u>ponham</u>
Imperfect	<u>punha</u>, <u>púnhamos</u>, <u>punham</u>
Preterite	<u>pus</u>, <u>pôs</u>, <u>pusemos</u>, <u>puseram</u>
Imperf. subj.	pusesse, etc.
Future subj.	puser, etc.
Simple pluperf.	pusera, etc.

Similarly: **antepor** 'to place before', **compor** 'to compose', **contrapor** 'to counterpose', **depor** 'to give evidence', **descompor** 'to decompose', **dispor** 'to dispose', **expor** 'to expose', **impor** 'to impose', **justapor** 'to juxtapose', **opor** 'to oppose', **pospor** 'to place after', **predispor** 'to predispose', **pressupor** 'to presuppose', **propor** 'to propose', **repor** 'to replace', **sobrepor** 'to overlay', **supor** 'to suppose'.

NOTE | The infinitive of derivatives of **pôr** is spelt without the circumflex accent. However, the accent is used in the third person singular of the preterite, e.g. **compor** 'to compose' > **ele compôs** 'he composed'; **opor-se** 'to oppose' > **ele se opôs** 'he opposed'.

16.3.8 *ir* 'to go', *ser* 'to be'

These two verbs share common forms in the preterite and derived tenses. Both verbs have an irregular present subjunctive and **ser** an irregular imperfect indicative (irregular forms underlined):

Pres. indic.	<u>vou</u>, <u>vai</u>, <u>vamos</u>, <u>vão</u>
Pres. subj.	<u>vá</u>, <u>vamos</u>, <u>vão</u>
Imperfect	ia, íamos, iam
Preterite	<u>fui</u>, <u>foi</u>, <u>fomos</u>, <u>foram</u>
Imperf. subj.	fosse, fôssemos, fossem
Future subj.	for, formos, forem
Simple pluperf.	fora, fôramos, foram

Pres. indic.	<u>sou</u>, <u>é</u>, <u>somos</u>, <u>são</u>
Pres. subj.	<u>seja</u>, <u>sejamos</u>, <u>sejam</u>
Imperfect	<u>era</u>, <u>éramos</u>, <u>eram</u>
Preterite	<u>fui</u>, <u>foi</u>, <u>fomos</u>, <u>foram</u>
Imperf. subj.	fosse, fôssemos, fossem
Future subj.	for, formos, forem
Simple pluperf.	fora, fôramos, foram.

16.3.9 *haver* 'to have'

The imperfect indicative of this verb is regular (irregular forms underlined):

Pres. indic.	<u>hei</u>, <u>há</u>, <u>hemos</u>, <u>hão</u>
Pres. subj.	<u>haja</u>, <u>hajamos</u>, <u>hajam</u>
Preterite	<u>houve</u>, <u>houvemos</u>, <u>houveram</u>
Imperf. subj.	<u>houvesse</u>, etc.
Future subj.	<u>houver</u>, etc.
Simple pluperf.	<u>houvera</u>, etc.

NOTE   The rare verb **reaver** 'to regain, get back' follows the same pattern (initial *h* is dropped after the prefix) but, if encountered at all, it is usually in the infinitive. It cannot form present indicative or subjunctive tenses.

16.3.10 *dar* 'to give'

The imperfect indicative of this verb is regular (irregular forms underlined):

Pres. indic.	<u>dou</u>, <u>dá</u>, damos, <u>dão</u>
Pres. subj.	<u>dê</u>, <u>demos</u>, <u>deem</u>
Imperfect	dava, etc.
Preterite	<u>dei</u>, <u>deu</u>, <u>demos</u>, <u>deram</u>
Imperf. subj.	desse, déssemos, dessem
Future subj.	der, dermos, derem
Simple pluperf.	dera, etc.

16.3.11 *estar* 'to be'

The present indicative and subjunctive of this verb are irregular. The imperfect indicative is regular. The preterite and derived forms are similar to those of the verb **ter** (see **16.3.5**) (irregular forms underlined):

Pres. indic.	<u>estou</u>, <u>está</u>, <u>estamos</u>, <u>estão</u>
Pres. subj.	<u>esteja</u>, <u>estejamos</u>, <u>estejam</u>
Imperfect	estava, etc.
Preterite	<u>estive</u>, <u>esteve</u>, <u>estivemos</u>, <u>estiveram</u>
Imperf. subj.	estivesse, etc.
Future subj.	estiver, etc.
Simple pluperf.	estivera, etc.

NOTE   In the colloquial spoken language, the **es-** part of this verb is hardly ever pronounced (e.g. the present indicative forms are pronounced /tou/, /ta/, /tamos/, /tãw/). This means that the preterite and derived forms sound exactly the same as those of the verb **ter**. The forms without **es-** are never used in writing except to quote speech, although the form **tá** is sometimes seen with its idiomatic meaning of 'OK'.

16.3.12 *poder* 'to be able'

The imperfect indicative of this verb is regular. Note that the third person singular of the preterite is differentiated from that of the present indicative with a cirumflex accent, reflecting the difference in vowel quality: **pode** ['pɔdʒi] vs. **pôde** ['podʒi] (irregular forms underlined):

Pres. indic.	<u>posso</u>, pode, podemos, podem
Pres. subj.	<u>possa</u>, <u>possamos</u>, <u>possam</u>

Preterite	**pude**, **pôde**, **pudemos**, **puderam**
Imperf. subj.	**pudesse**, etc.
Future subj.	**puder**, etc.
Simple pluperf.	**pudera**, etc.

16.3.13 *querer* 'to want

The imperfect indicative of this verb is regular (irregular forms underlined):

Pres. indic.	**quero**, **quer**, **queremos**, **querem**
Pres. subj.	**queira**, **queiramos**, **queiram**
Preterite	**quis**, **quis**, **quisemos**, **quiseram**
Imperf. subj.	**quisesse**, etc.
Future subj.	**quiser**, etc.
Simple pluperf.	**quisera**, etc.

NOTE

The verb **requerer** 'to require; to claim' follows the same pattern in the present indicative and subjunctive, except for the first person singular of the present indicative, which is **requeiro**. But it inflects like a regular -**er** verb in the preterite and derived tenses: **requeri**, **requereu**, **requeresse**, **requerer**, etc.

Notes for Spanish speakers

In verbs with the letters **e** and **o** in the stem, there is phonetic alternation between the open and close pronunciations of these vowels in some -**ar** and -**er** verbs, but no orthographic changes. In -**ir** verbs, there are different patterns of phonetic and orthographic alternation between -**e**- and -**i**- and between -**o**- and -**u**-. The irregular verbs **pôr**, **ter** and **vir** have lost Latin intervocalic -*n*- in the infinitive, but retain vestiges of it in the nasal vowels and **nh** which occur in the conjugation of the present indicative and subjunctive and imperfect indicative tenses.

17

Gerunds, past participles, compound perfect tenses and the passive

17.1 Gerunds

17.1.1 Formation of the gerund

The gerund of all verbs is formed by replacing the final **r** of the infinitive with **-ndo**:

> **falar** 'to speak' > **falando** 'speaking'
>
> **fazer** 'to do' > **fazendo** 'doing'
>
> **ir** 'to go' > **indo** 'going'
>
> **pôr** 'to put' > **pondo** 'putting' (*written accent dropped*).

17.1.2 Use of the gerund

▶ **69.2** (p. 502)

(i) The gerund is used in combination with a number of auxiliary verbs (see **Chapter 24**). Notably, it is used with various tenses of the verb **estar** to form continuous tenses:

> **Estou esperando a resposta dela.**
> I'm waiting for her answer.
>
> **Ele estava vendo televisão quando eu cheguei.**
> He was watching television when I arrived.

(ii) The gerund can also be used adverbially to describe an action that is concurrent with that of the main verb, or with the meaning of 'by . . . ing':

> **Ela passou o fim de semana inteiro pintando a casa.**
> She spent the whole weekend painting the house.
>
> **O ladrão saiu correndo.**
> The thief ran off. (*literally*, 'went off running')[1]

NOTE

1 Note that, whereas English normally uses a verb to express the form of movement and an adverb or preposition to express the direction, Portuguese uses a verb to express the direction and an adverbial expression, often a gerund, to express the form of movement, e.g. **O rio é muito largo para atravessarmos nadando** *or* **a nado**. 'The river is too wide for us to swim across.' **O jogador saiu mancando do campo**. 'The player limped off the field.' **Tivemos que voltar tudo andando** *or* **a pé**. 'We had to walk all the way back.'

Conseguimos voltar para casa pedindo carona com um caminhoneiro.
We managed to get back home by hitching a ride with a truck driver.

Doze presos fugiram da cadeia de Astorga cavando um túnel.
Twelve prisoners escaped from Astorga jail by digging a tunnel.

(iii)   A gerund can also express a causal link, as in English:

O Murilo, precisando de dinheiro, resolveu fazer um empréstimo.
Needing money, Murilo decided to take out a loan.

Conhecendo a Paula, ela não vai desistir tão facilmente.
Knowing Paula, she won't give up that easily.

(iv)   A gerund can have a subject of its own which is different from that of the main verb in the sentence:

As coisas mudam, a gente querendo ou não.
Things change, whether we like it or not.

(v)   A gerund frequently occurs after **mesmo** 'even if/though' and **nem** '(not) even if', with or without its own subject:

Ele ainda tem um forte sotaque francês, mesmo morando no Brasil há 20 anos.
He still has a strong French accent even though he's lived in Brazil for 20 years.

Mesmo você não indo, eu pretendo ir.
Even if you don't go, I plan to go.

Não volto a esse restaurante nem me pagando.
I'm not going back to that restaurant even if they pay me.

(vi)   A gerund may be used after **embora** 'although, though' but only referring to the same subject as the main verb in the sentence:

Embora gostando do curso de Economia, ela quer mudar para Direito.
Although enjoying the economics course, she wants to change to law.

(vii)   The gerund may occur after verbs of perception, such as **ver** 'to see', **ouvir** 'to hear' and **sentir** 'to feel'[2], and similar verbs, such as **flagrar/pegar** 'to catch (sb doing sth)' and **imaginar** 'to imagine'. As in English, the object of the verb of perception is the subject of the gerund:

Ela viu o marido saindo do banco.
She saw her husband coming out of the bank.

Um policial flagrou o adolescente arrombando um carro.
A police officer caught the teenager breaking into a car.

NOTE   2   As in English, verbs of perception may also be followed by an infinitive when a complete action is perceived rather than an ongoing one, cf. **Ela viu o marido sair do banco.** 'She saw her husband come out of the bank.'

17.1.3   **Placement of unstressed object pronouns with the gerund**

(i)   When the gerund is used with an auxiliary verb (see **Chapter 24**), the unstressed pronouns **me**, **te**, **se**, **nos** and **lhe(s)** meaning 'you' are placed between auxiliary and gerund:

Estou te devendo R$50,00.
I owe you 50 reais.

> **A gente vai se falando.**
> We'll be in touch.

(ii) When no auxiliary is present, the same pronouns may be placed before the gerund when it is preceded by a noun or pronoun subject or an adverb, including **não**, **embora**, **mesmo** and **nem**. If none of these elements is present, the pronoun should be appended to the gerund with a hyphen in writing, though in informal speech this rule is usually disregarded:

> **Ela me olhou sem falar nada, aparentemente não me reconhecendo.**
> She looked at me without saying anything, apparently not recognizing me.

> **Mesmo a empresa se dispondo a consertar o produto, o cliente vai pensar duas vezes antes de comprar a mesma marca.**
> Even if the company is willing to repair the product, the customer will think twice before buying the same brand.

> **Meu irmão me apresentou aos outros, empurrando-me delicadamente pelas costas, para que eu desse um passo à frente.** (*written*)
> My brother introduced me to the others, pushing me gently from behind so that I would step forward.

> **O cara veio pra cima de mim, me empurrando e me xingando.** (*spoken*)
> The guy came for me, pushing me and swearing at me.

(iii) The third person pronouns **o**, **a**, **os**, **as**, **lhe** and **lhes**, which are only used in the written language, are always appended to the gerund with a hyphen when it is used adverbially. When used in conjunction with an auxiliary verb, such as **estar**, the rules explained in **7.5.3–7.5.6** apply:

> **Misture as claras à massa despejando-a em pirex untado com manteiga.**
> Blend the egg whites into the batter pouring it into a buttered ovenproof dish.

> **Demonstre ao seu filho que continua amando-o tanto quanto antes.**
> Demonstrate to your child that you still love them as much as before.

> **Ela desconfia que o namorado a está traindo.**
> She suspects her boyfriend is cheating on her.

17.2 Past participles

17.2.1 Regular past participles

With the vast majority of verbs, the past participle is formed regularly, by replacing the final **-ar** of the infinitive with **-ado**, and **-er** and **-ir** with **-ido**:

> **falar** 'to speak' > **falado** 'spoken'

> **comer** 'to eat' > **comido** 'eaten'

> **decidir** 'to decide' > **decidido** 'decided'.

17.2.2 Irregular past participles

The following verbs have irregular past participles:

> **abrir** 'to open' > **aberto** 'opened'

> **cobrir** 'to cover' > **coberto** 'covered'

dizer 'to say' > **dito** 'said'

escrever 'to write' > **escrito** 'written'

fazer 'to do' > **feito** 'done'

pôr 'to put' > **posto** 'put'

ver 'to see' > **visto** 'seen'

vir 'to come' > **vindo**[3] 'come'.

Note that derivatives of these verbs also form irregular participles, e.g. **entreabrir** 'to half-open' > **entreaberto**; **descobrir** 'to discover' > **descoberto**; **contradizer** 'to contradict' > **contradito**; **descrever** 'to describe' > **descrito**; **satisfazer** 'to satisfy' > **satisfeito**; **impor** 'to impose' > **imposto**; **prever** 'to foresee, predict' > **previsto**; **provir** 'to originate' > **provindo**.

NOTE | 3   In the case of the verb **vir** 'to come', the gerund and past participle are identical.

17.2.3   Verbs with both a regular and an irregular past participle

The following verbs have both a regular and an irregular past participle:

aceitar 'to accept' > **aceitado, aceito**

acender 'to light, turn on' > **acendido, aceso**

benzer 'to bless' > **benzido, bento**

concluir 'to complete' > **concluído, concluso**

dispersar 'to disperse' > **dispersado, disperso**

eleger 'to elect' > **elegido, eleito** (similarly: **reeleger** 'to re-elect')

entregar 'to hand over, deliver' > **entregado, entregue**

envolver 'to involve, wrap' > **envolvido, envolto**

enxugar 'to dry, trim down' > **enxugado, enxuto**

excluir 'to exclude' > **excluído, excluso**

expressar 'to express' > **expressado, expresso**

exprimir 'to express' > **exprimido, expresso**

expulsar 'to throw out, expel' > **expulsado, expulso**

extinguir 'to extinguish' > **extinguido, extinto**

fritar 'to fry' > **fritado, frito**

ganhar 'to win, earn' > **ganhado, ganho**

gastar 'to spend, wear out' > **gastado, gasto**

imergir 'to immerse' > **imergido, imerso**

imprimir 'to print' > **imprimido, impresso** (similarly: **reimprimir** 'to reprint')

incluir 'to include' > **incluído, incluso**

inserir 'to insert' > **inserido, inserto**

isentar 'to clear, exempt' > **isentado, isento**

libertar 'to free' > **libertado, liberto**

limpar 'to clean' > **limpado, limpo**

matar 'to kill' > **matado, morto**

morrer 'to die' > **morrido, morto**

pagar 'to pay' > **pagado, pago**

pegar 'to get' > **pegado, pego**

prender 'to fix', 'to arrest' > **prendido, preso**

restringir 'to restrict' > **restringido, restrito**

romper 'to break' > **rompido, roto**

salvar 'to save' > **salvado, salvo**

soltar 'to release' > **soltado, solto**

submergir 'to submerge' > **submergido, submerso**

suprimir 'to do away with' > **suprimido, supresso**

surpreender 'to surprise' > **surpreendido, surpreso**

suspender 'to suspend' > **suspendido, suspenso**.

The basic rule is that the longer, regular form is used with the auxiliaries **ter** and **haver** 'to have' to form the perfect tenses (see **17.3**), while the shorter, irregular form is used as an adjective and with the auxiliaries **ser**, **estar** and **ficar** 'to be' to form passive expressions (see **17.4**):

> **Ela tinha acendido as luzes. / As luzes estavam acesas.**
> She had turned the lights on. / The lights were on.
>
> **Diziam que ele havia matado um homem. / O homem foi morto por uma bala perdida.**
> People said he had killed a man. / The man was killed by a stray bullet.

However, actual usage is not so clear-cut, as explained below:

(i) The following irregular participles are very frequently used instead of the regular forms after **ter** and **haver** in the perfect tenses, especially by more educated speakers and in writing. Such usage sounds rather learned, and the tendency in informal and less educated speech is to use the regular participle, which is perfectly correct according to the basic rule given above:

> **aceito, eleito, entregue, expulso, extinto, ganho, gasto, impresso, pago, pego, salvo, suspenso**

(ii) The following regular participles are much more common than their irregular counterparts even after **ser**, **estar** and **ficar** and as adjectives:

> **concluído[4], envolvido[5], excluído, incluído, inserido, libertado[6], rompido, suprimido**

NOTES

4 The irregular participle **concluso** is only used to refer to legal cases, meaning 'submitted to the judge'.

5 The irregular participle **envolto** is normally only used in the sense of 'wrapped, shrouded'.

6 The irregular participle **liberto** is more commonly used when the sense is figurative: 'freed (from drugs, sin, slavery, etc.)'.

(iii) In the following cases, the regular participles are more common after **ser,** but the irregular ones more common after **estar** and **ficar** and as adjectives:

benzido/bento, enxugado/enxuto, surpreendido/surpreso

(iv) The following regular and irregular participles are roughly equally common after **ser**, while the irregular ones are more common after **estar** and **ficar** and as adjectives:

dispersado/disperso, isentado/isento, restringido/restrito

(v) The remaining verbs in the list above largely follow the basic rule:

acender, expressar, exprimir, fritar, imergir, limpar, matar, morrer, prender, soltar, submergir

17.3 Compound perfect tenses

The compound perfect tenses are formed with the auxiliary verbs **ter** and **haver** 'to have' and the past participle. Note that, in the active compound tenses described in Sections **17.3.1–3**, the past participle is always invariable, ending in **-o**.

17.3.1 The present perfect tense

The present perfect tense is formed by combining the present tense of the verb **ter** 'to have' with the past participle. Note that the meaning of this tense is equivalent to the English present perfect continuous 'have been doing' and not to the present perfect simple 'have done' (see **Chapter 18**):

Tenho lido muito ultimamente.
I've been reading a lot lately.

Tem sido difícil dormir com esse calor.
It's been difficult sleeping with this heat.

17.3.2 The pluperfect tense

The pluperfect tense is formed by combining the imperfect tense of the verbs **ter** or **haver** 'to have' with the past participle. The auxiliary **ter** is much more commonly used and is the only auxiliary used in the spoken language. The auxiliary **haver** is found in more formal or literary written language:[7]

Eu tinha esquecido que hoje era o seu aniversário.
I'd forgotten that today was your birthday.

Até ontem, só 4% dos contribuintes haviam entregue a declaração.
By yesterday, only 4 per cent of taxpayers had submitted their returns.

NOTE   7   Even more formal/literary, and rarely used, is the simple pluperfect – see **15.10**.

17.3.3 Other perfect tenses

The auxiliary **ter** can also be used in other tenses and moods to form compound tenses (see **Chapters 18** and **20**). The more formal/literary auxiliary **haver** also occurs in the cases shown:

ele terá terminado
he will have finished (*future perfect*)

ela teria vindo
she would have come (*conditional perfect*)

Espero que tenham gostado.
I hope they liked it (*perfect subjunctive*)

se isso não tivesse/houvesse acontecido
if this had not happened (*pluperfect subjunctive*)

se tivermos/houvermos terminado até lá
if we've finished by then (*future perfect subjunctive*)

Você poderia ter ligado.
You could have called. (*perfect infinitive*)

17.3.4 Placement of unstressed object pronouns in the compound perfect tenses

(i) The unstressed object pronouns **me**, **te**, **se**, **nos** and **lhe(s)** are normally placed between the auxiliary and the past participle:

Eles tinham nos convidado.
They had invited us.

Tenho me policiado para não comer besteira.
I've been keeping a check on myself so I don't eat junk.

(ii) The unstressed third person pronouns **o**, **a**, **os**, **as**, when used in writing, are placed before or after the auxiliary verb in accordance with the general rules for object prounoun placement given in **7.5.3–7.5.6**:

Haviam-na tratado bem.
They had treated her well.

O Jefferson é muito meu amigo, mas não o tenho visto ultimamente.
Jefferson is a good friend of mine, but I haven't seen him lately.

(iii) The pronouns **me**, **te**, **se**, **nos** and **lhe(s)** are placed according to the same rules as **o**, **a**, **os**, **as** in more formal/literary style. In this more formal style, they may be appended to the auxiliary with a hyphen when placed after it,[8] in the same way as **o**, **a**, **os**, **as**:

Muito tem-se falado a respeito da segurança das informações pessoais.
There has been much talk lately about the security of personal information.

Ele não havia mentido ao delegado. Havia-lhe contado a verdade.
He had not lied to the police inspector. He had told him the truth.

NOTE | 8 Placing these pronouns after the auxiliary effectively puts them in the same position as they normally occupy in neutral and informal style (cf. **17.3.4** (i)) where the hyphen is not used because the object pronoun is felt to be more closely associated with the participle than with the auxiliary. The hyphen is very often omitted in more formal/literary style too, though traditional grammarians would insist it should be used.

17.4 The passive

17.4.1

The passive is formed in exactly the same way as in English, i.e. by combining the relevant person and tense of the verb **ser** 'to be' with the past participle. Note that, in all passive constructions, the past participle must agree in gender and number with the subject of the verb:

Amostras de sangue são colhidas do cordão umbilical.
Blood samples are collected from the umbilical cord.

As garrafas serão recicladas.
The bottles will be recycled.

Ela era admirada pelas outras alunas.
She was admired by the other students.

O dicionário está sendo atualizado.
The dictionary is being updated.

Os mortos já haviam sido enterrados.
The dead had already been buried.

Ser valorizado é importante.
It's important to be appreciated.

17.4.2 The verb **ficar** 'to be, become' may also be used as a passive auxiliary with verbs denoting an involuntary result:

Cinco pessoas ficaram feridas.
Five people were injured.

Tenho medo de ficar preso no elevador.
I'm scared of getting stuck in the lift/elevator.

17.4.3 The past participle can also be combined with the verb **estar** 'to be' to describe a resultant state:

A lista está ordenada alfabeticamente.
The list is ordered alphabetically.

As roupas estavam expostas na vitrine.
The clothes were displayed in the store window.

17.5 Other uses of the past participle

17.5.1 As in English, a past participle can also function as an adjective accompanying a noun and agreeing with it in gender and number:

um relógio quebrado
a broken watch

casas alugadas
rented houses.

17.5.2 Past participles also occur in absolute constructions such as the following:

Dadas as circunstâncias, o governo foi obrigado a recuar.
Given the circumstances, the government was forced to back down.

Dito isso, vamos considerar alguns exemplos.
Having said that/That being said, let's consider some examples.

Terminada a obra, o proprietário deverá solicitar o "habite-se".
Once building work is finished, the owner must apply for the certificate of occupancy.

Eu sabia que o Pedro ia atrasar. Dito e feito! (*idiom*)
I knew Pedro would be late. Sure enough!

A past participle can be used after the preposition **depois de** or its more formal synonym, **após**, to mean 'after being . . .', 'once . . .ed':

Os suspeitos foram soltos duas semanas depois de presos.
The suspects were released two weeks after being arrested.

Depois de dourado o frango, coloque os outros ingredientes.
Once the chicken is browned, add the other ingredients.

Após aberto, mantenha sob refrigeração.
Once opened, keep refrigerated.

Notes for Spanish speakers

The Portuguese gerund has three distinct endings corresponding to the three different conjugations, namely -**ando**, -**endo** and -**indo**, while, like Spanish, the regular past participle has only two, -**ado** for -**ar** verbs and -**ido** for -**er** and -**ir** verbs. Apart from the familiar list of verbs with irregular past participles (**abrir**, **cobrir**, **dizer**, **escrever**, **fazer**, **pôr**, **ver** and **vir**), there are a number of common verbs which have both a regular and an irregular past participle with differing usage. The most frequently used auxiliary for the perfect tenses is **ter**; the use of the verb **haver** as an auxiliary is restricted to formal written style and certain tenses only. Note that the Portuguese present perfect tense (**tenho feito**, etc.) does not correspond in either meaning or usage to the Spanish perfect tense. Except for the third-person pronouns **o**, **a**, **os** and **as**, which are only used in writing, the normal position for other unstressed object pronouns is between the auxiliary and past participle or gerund in the compound tenses. The present and past continuous tenses (**estou/estava fazendo**, etc.) are far more commonly used in Portuguese than in Spanish, especially in the spoken language, broadly corresponding to their use in English.

18

Use of the tenses

This chapter presents the various tenses of the indicative, examining their usage and equivalences in English. The various tenses of the subjunctive are dealt with in **Chapter 20**.

18.1 Simple tenses

Simple tenses are those which consist of a single inflected verb form.

18.1.1 Present indicative

For the forms of the present indicative, see **15.3**.

▶ **69.1** (p. 501); **69.4** (p. 503); **70.1.2** (p. 506); **70.2** (p. 507); **70.3.2** (p. 508); **71.1.2** (p. 512); **71.5** (p. 514)

(i)   The present simple largely corresponds to the present simple in English:

> **Onde você mora?**
> Where do you live?

> **Ela trabalha como professora.**
> She works as a teacher.

(ii) The present simple is also used to describe an action that began in the past and continues in the present. English uses the present perfect tense in such cases:

> **Moramos aqui há três anos.**
> We've lived here for three years.

> **Faz quanto tempo que você estuda português?**
> How long have you been studying Portuguese?

(iii) The present simple may also be used with future reference, either referring to a scheduled event as in English, or in spontaneous statements about the future where English uses 'will':

> **O filme começa às 21h.**
> The movie starts at 9 p.m.

> **De repente a gente se vê mais tarde. Te ligo.**
> Maybe we'll see each other later. I'll call you.

18.1.2 Imperfect indicative

For the forms of the imperfect indicative, see **15.4**.

(i) The imperfect tense is used to describe habitual or repeated action in the past – actions that took place an indefinite number of times. In this usage, it corresponds to the English simple past or expressions with 'used to':

> **Ele falava japonês com os avós.**
> He used to speak Japanese to his grandparents.

> **Naquela época, comíamos pouca carne.**
> At that time, we didn't eat much meat.

► **71.9.1** (p. 516)

(ii) The imperfect tense is also used to 'set the scene' by describing the background to events in the past:

> **Era pleno verão e fazia um calor insuportável.**
> It was the middle of summer and it was unbearably hot.

> **Ela era uma menina alta e magra.**
> She was a tall, thin girl.

► **71.8** (p. 516)

(iii) The imperfect tense can also correspond to the English past continuous 'was/were doing', especially in the written language, where it is preferred stylistically to the imperfect continuous tense – see **18.3.2**:

> **Eles jantavam quando a polícia chegou.**
> They were having dinner when the police arrived.

► **71.10.2** (p. 517)

(iv) The imperfect is also used to describe an action that started at an earlier time in the past and is continuing at the point in the past being discussed; in English, the past perfect or past perfect continuous is used in such cases:

> **A criança não falava desde a morte da mãe.**
> The child had not spoken since the death of its mother.

> **A Sandra me falou que trabalhava como professora havia dez anos.**
> Sandra told me she had been working as a teacher for ten years.

► **71.12** (p. 518)

(v) The imperfect is very frequently used, especially in the spoken language, to replace the conditional tense – see **18.1.5**:

> **Ele disse que vinha à uma.**
> He said he would come at one.

> **Se eu fosse você, deixava assim.**
> If I were you, I'd leave it like that.

► **70.4.3** (p. 510)

18.1.3 Preterite[1]

For the forms of the preterite, see **15.5**.

NOTE 1 'Preterite' is the most commonly used name for this tense in English and the one used here, but note that, in Portuguese, the names of all the past tenses – preterite, imperfect, present perfect and pluperfect – include the word **pretérito**.

(i) The preterite is used to describe one-off actions in the past, and actions that were repeated a finite number of times or which lasted a certain period of time but came to an end. In this usage, it corresponds to the English simple past:[2]

O Paulo caiu da escada e quebrou a perna.
Paulo fell down the stairs and broke his leg.

Fui ao supermercado três vezes num dia.
I went to the supermarket three times in one day.

Eles moraram vinte anos nos Estados Unidos.
They lived for twenty years in the US.

▶ **71.1.1** (p. 512); **71.2** (p. 512); **71.3** (p. 513); **71.11.2** (p. 518)

NOTE 2 The English simple past ('was', 'had', 'went', 'made', 'lived', etc.) can correspond to either the imperfect or the preterite in Portuguese, which makes it difficult for English speakers to grasp the difference between these two tenses. The imperfect sets the scene, giving background information and describing ongoing states and actions that form the backdrop to the main events, which are reported in the preterite. The imperfect is also used to refer to habitual action or action repeated an indeterminate number of times, whereas the preterite describes single acts or those repeated a finite (stated) number of times. The duration of an action is irrelevant; what matters is whether it is viewed as ongoing (imperfect) or finished and complete (preterite).

(ii) The preterite also corresponds to the English present perfect tense. The present perfect meaning is often indicated by the use of the adverb **já** 'already, yet':

Você já almoçou?
Have you had lunch (yet)?

Fui ao supermercado três vezes hoje.
I've been to the supermarket three times today.

Eu nunca provei comida tailandesa.
I've never tried Thai food.

Ele sempre quis ser ator.
He's always wanted to be an actor.

▶ **71.4** (p. 513)

(iii) The preterite is used in Portuguese to describe your first impression of something, where in English the present tense would be used:

O que é que você achou desse sorvete? Gostou?
What do you think of this ice cream? Do you like it?

Você ficou linda nesse vestido!
You look lovely in that dress!

(iv)   The preterite is often used in place of the pluperfect, especially in speech:

Foi aí que percebi que esqueci o passaporte.
It was then I realized I had forgotten my passport.

A companhia aérea informou que o voo foi cancelado.
The airline announced that the flight had been cancelled.

▶ **71.11.2** (p. 518)

(v)   The third person singular of the preterite occurs in some idiomatic uses. It is used in colloquial speech as a kind of imperative:

O exercício é assim: deitou de lado, levantou a perna.
The exercise is like this: you lie on your side and raise your leg.

It can also have the sense of 'once you've . . .':

Comeu, lava o prato.
Once you've eaten, wash your plate.

Procure a tampa premiada: achou, ganhou!
Look for the prize-winning cap: find it and you've won!

▶ **50.4.4** (p. 409)

18.1.4   Future indicative

For the forms of the future indicative, see **15.9**.

The inflected future tense is hardly ever used in the spoken language and is felt to be quite formal, even in writing, although it is much used in news reporting:

Os relógios serão atrasados à meia-noite de sábado para domingo.
The clocks will be put back at midnight on Saturday.

Amanhã, ele prestará depoimento ao procurador da República.
Tomorrow, he will make a statement to the federal prosecutor.

▶ **70.1.3** (p. 507)

In speech and informal writing, the future is expressed by using either the verb **ir** with the infinitive (see **18.4.1**) or the simple present (see **18.1.1. (iii)**).

18.1.5   Conditional

For the forms of the conditional, see **15.9**.

(i)   The conditional corresponds to the English 'would do/be/go etc.':

Se todos colaborassem, o problema seria resolvido.
If everyone did their bit, the problem would be solved.

Mesmo que me pagassem, eu não iria.
Even if they paid me, I wouldn't go.

▶ **70.4.2** (p. 509)

Conditional verb forms have a ponderous and formal ring to them, which means that they are rarely used in the spoken language[3] and are usually avoided by using the imperfect tense instead (see **18.1.2 (v)**) or the imperfect of the verb **ir** plus the infinitive (see **18.4.2**).

3 The conditional tense is used in speech when the conditional meaning might not otherwise be clear from the grammatical or broader context. In addition, the conditional forms of the verbs **ser** 'to be' and **ter** 'to have' are reasonably frequent in the spoken language.

(ii)   There is a special use of the conditional, much used in news reporting, which implies that the action is alleged to be the case, but is uncorroborated:

A casa abrigaria um bingo ilegal.
The house is allegedly home to an illegal bingo parlour.

O senador teria várias contas no exterior.
The senator is alleged to have several accounts abroad.

18.1.6 Pluperfect indicative

For the forms of the simple pluperfect tense, see **15.10**.

The simple pluperfect tense is only encountered in formal/literary writing. In speech and less formal writing, the compound pluperfect tense is used instead – see **18.2.2**.

18.2 Compound tenses

Compound tenses are those which make use of the auxiliary verb **ter** 'to have' in their formation, combining it with the past participle of the main verb. The auxiliary **haver** may be used in place of **ter** to form the pluperfect and future perfect tenses in more formal register. See also **17.2** on the formation of past participles and **17.3** on the formation of compound tenses.

18.2.1 Present perfect indicative

The present perfect tense corresponds in meaning to the English present perfect continuous tense ('have been doing/seeing/reading etc.') denoting an action repeated several times up to and including the present:

Ele tem malhado muito nos últimos meses.
He's been working out a lot in recent months.

Em média, 150 ocorrências por mês têm sido registradas este ano.
On average, 150 incidents a month have been recorded this year. (= 'have been being')

Os dois trabalham muito e quase não têm se visto ultimamente.
They both work a lot and have hardly seen each other lately.

▶ **71.7.1** (p. 515)

Note that, if the sentence gives an indication of how long or since when something has been going on, Portuguese uses the present tense rather than the perfect – see **18.1.1** (ii):

Ele malha muito desde que foi escalado para o papel de Tarzan.
He's been working out a lot since being selected for the role of Tarzan.

18.2.2 **Pluperfect indicative**

(i)   The pluperfect corresponds to the English past perfect 'had done/been/gone etc.':

> **Ele tinha avisado que ia chegar tarde.**
> He had warned that he would arrive late.

> **O ministro rebateu as acusações de que havia mentido.**
> The minister hit back at accusations he had lied.

▶ **71.11.1** (p. 518)

Note that, if the sentence gives an indication of how long or since when something had been going on, Portuguese uses the imperfect tense rather than the pluperfect – see **18.1.2** (iv):

> **O Sérgio trabalhava na empresa desde 1989.**
> Sergio had been working for the company since 1989.

(ii)   The pluperfect is used in less formal register instead of the perfect conditional:

> **Se o Paulo viesse, ele tinha me falado.**
> If Paulo was coming he would have told me.

18.2.3 **Future perfect**

This tense, formed with the inflected future tense of **ter** plus the past participle ('will have done etc.' in English), is normally only encountered in formal writing:

> **Se o governo ceder, os terroristas terão alcançado seu objetivo.**
> If the government gives in, the terrorists will have achieved their objective.

18.2.4 **Perfect conditional**

(i)   The perfect conditional, formed with the conditional of **ter** plus the past participle ('would have done etc.' in English), is mostly used in the written language:

> **Se não fosse a presença de espírito da babá, o bebê teria morrido.**
> If it hadn't been for the nanny's quick thinking, the baby would have died.

In speech and less formal writing, the perfect conditional is usually replaced by the pluperfect – see **18.2.2** (ii).

(ii)   The perfect conditional is very commonly used in news reporting to imply that something is alleged to have happened but is uncorroborated:

> **Segundo o delegado, Silva teria confessado o crime.**
> According to the police chief, Silva supposedly confessed to the crime.

18.3 # Continuous tenses[4]

The continuous tenses are those formed using the auxiliary verb **estar** 'to be' followed by a gerund in the same way as the continuous tenses in English ('to be' plus verb ending in -*ing*).

NOTE   4   Portuguese grammar does not consider these to be separate tenses at all, but rather so-called **locuções verbais** 'verbal phrases'. Clearly, it is only the auxiliary **estar** that actually inflects for tense.

18.3.1 Present continuous

▶ **69.2** (p. 502); **69.4** (p. 503); **71.5** (p. 514)

(i) The use of the present continuous broadly corresponds to that in English:[5]

> **Estou procurando emprego no momento.**
> I'm looking for a job at the moment.

> **Eles estão morando num flat até achar uma casa.**
> They're living in a serviced apartment until they find a house.

But note that the present continuous is not used to talk about future plans and arrangements as it often is in English.

(ii) The present continuous may also describe an action that started in the past and continues in the present, in which case it corresponds to the English present perfect continuous:

> **Estou te esperando há meia hora já.**
> I've been waiting for you for half an hour already.

NOTE 5 There are a few verbs which are commonly used in the present continuous in Portuguese although their equivalents in English are not, such as **achar** 'to think', **acreditar** 'to believe', **gostar** 'to like', **precisar** 'to need' and **querer** 'to want'.

18.3.2 Imperfect continuous

▶ **71.10** (p. 517)

The imperfect continuous broadly corresponds to the past continuous in English, referring to an ongoing action in the past with no clearly defined beginning or end which forms the backdrop to another action or actions:

> **O que é que você estava fazendo no meu quarto?**
> What were you doing in my room?

> **Já estávamos dormindo quando a campainha tocou.**
> We were already sleeping when the doorbell rang.

18.3.3 Preterite continuous

(i) The preterite continuous describes an action that continued for a finite period of time in the past. The completed period in the past is either mentioned or implied in the context, so that the meaning is something like 'spent time doing sth':

> **Ele esteve trabalhando no novo álbum durante um ano.**
> He was working on the new album for a year.

(ii) The preterite continuous does not occur very frequently, especially in speech, because the preterite simple is usually used when talking about an action which continued for a finite period in the past, but the meaning of the particular verb may make it necessary to differentiate continuing from completed action:

> **Ontem estive lendo aquele livro que você me deu. Estou gostando.**
> Yesterday I spent some time reading that book you gave me. I'm enjoying it.
> (in this example, the preterite simple **li** would suggest you read the whole book)

(iii) When talking about the present time, referring to an action which has led up to the present situation, the appropriate translation is 'have been doing/working/studying etc.'. The difference between this tense and the present perfect (see **18.2.1**) is that the preterite continuous denotes a single burst of continuous action whereas the present perfect denotes repeated instances of the same action. Compare:

> **Estive pensando e decidi que não quero mais fazer faculdade**.
> I've been thinking and have decided I don't want to go to college anymore.
> (**Tenho pensado** would mean 'I've been thinking about it over and over')

18.3.4 Future continuous

(i) The future continuous formed with the inflected future tense of **estar** only occurs in more formal writing. In less formal registers, the verb **ir** 'to go' followed by the infinitive **estar** is used to form a future continuous tense. The "correct" usage of the future continuous is to refer to an action which will be going on at the time in the future referred to:

> **Não ligue para ele ao meio-dia, porque ele vai estar almoçando.**
> Don't call him at midday because he'll be having lunch.

(ii) A recent phenomenon, extremely common in telemarketing and customer relations, is the use of the future continuous to refer to a non-continuous future action.[6] This usage is frowned upon by many as being "incorrect" but has become so firmly established in the world of commerce as to be considered the norm:

> **Estaremos lhe enviando um e-mail com os dados para pagamento.** (*written*)
> We will be sending you an e-mail with the details for payment.

> **Vou estar transferindo a sua ligação, senhor.** (*spoken*)
> I'm going to transfer your call, sir.

NOTE | 6 This phenomenon, referred to as **gerundismo**, is a subject of linguistic debate in Brazil. It seems most likely that it has its origin in the over-literal translation into Portuguese of English telemarketing scripts. In English, the future continuous is regularly employed as a more polite-sounding alternative to the rather abrupt future or present simple tenses and is therefore frequently used when addressing customers (cf. 'Will you be requiring anything else, sir?'). It should be said that, although now very firmly established in Portuguese, this usage is restricted to the language of customer relations and not normally encountered in other contexts.

18.4 Periphrastic tenses[7]

Periphrastic tenses are those formed using an auxiliary verb, in this case the verb **ir** 'to go' followed by the infinitive of the main verb.

NOTE | 7 Again, Portuguese grammar does not consider these to be tenses in their own right, but they are included here to complete the picture of verb tense usage.

18.4.1 | ## Periphrastic future

The future tense is expressed in speech and informal writing using the present tense of the verb **ir** 'to go' followed by the infinitive of the main verb.[8] This corresponds not only to 'going to do' in English, but also to 'will do' and 'am/are/is doing' when referring to the future:

> **Vou precisar da sua ajuda.**
> I'll need your help. / I'm going to need your help.

> **Ela vai viajar na segunda.**
> She's going away on Monday.

▶ **70.1.1** (p. 506); **70.3.1** (p. 508)

NOTE | 8 In the written language, it is not uncommon to see the future tense of **ir** used with the infinitive to render the future, e.g. **O governo irá rever a decisão**. 'The government will review the decision.'

18.4.2 | ## Periphrastic conditional

Another way to avoid using the ponderous-sounding conditional tense (see **18.1.5**), also in writing, is to use the imperfect of the verb **ir** followed by the infinitive:[9]

> **Ela disse que ia me ajudar com os preparativos.**
> She said she'd help me with the preparations.

> **Se eu ganhasse na loteria, ia comprar um jatinho.**
> If I won the lottery, I'd buy a private jet.

▶ **70.4.1** (p. 509)

NOTE | 9 In the written language it is not uncommon to find the conditional of the verb **ir** followed by the infinitive, e.g. **Disseram que, se nós não pagássemos, a luz e a água iriam ser cortadas**. 'They said that, if we didn't pay, the power and water would be cut off.'

Notes for Spanish speakers

The simple present, imperfect and preterite tenses are used very much as in Spanish, but note that, as in Latin American varieties of Spanish, the preterite is used where Peninsular Spanish would use the compound perfect tense. The simple future tense is never used in everyday speech in Brazil, and the conditional is largely avoided. In the compound tenses, the default auxiliary is the verb **ter**, which is the only option in the formation of the present perfect, perfect conditional and perfect infinitive. The Portuguese present perfect differs in meaning from the parallel tense in Spanish and there is no compound past anterior tense in Portuguese. With the exception of the preterite continuous, which is equally rare in the two languages, the continuous tenses are more frequently used in Portuguese than Spanish, especially in the spoken language. Periphrastic tense constructions are used in place of the simple future and conditional tenses, especially in informal style.

19

The infinitive

Introduction

19.1.1 In some of its uses, the Portuguese infinitive is equivalent to the English infinitive with or without 'to', as in 'I want *to go*' or 'I must *go*'. However, in many other uses, it translates the English *-ing* form as in 'I prefer *going* by train' or 'before *going* to bed', etc.

19.1.2 Unlike many other languages, where the infinitive cannot by definition have a subject of its own that is different from that of the main verb, Portuguese has a so-called 'personal infinitive', which makes the infinitive an extremely versatile and much-used feature of the language.

19.2 Uses of the infinitive

The infinitive is used in the following ways:

19.2.1 As if it were a masculine noun, as the subject or object of a sentence and after prepositions (see **19.4**), usually corresponding to the English *-ing* form:

> **Viajar é cansativo.**
> Travelling is tiring.

> **Caminhar faz bem à saúde.**
> Walking is good for you.

> **Prefiro ir de ônibus.**
> I prefer going (*or* to go) by bus.

> **Acenda o fósforo antes de abrir o gás.**
> Light the match before turning on the gas.

19.2.2 After the auxiliary verb **ir** to form the periphrastic future tense (see **18.4.1**):

> **Vou falar com ele amanhã.**
> I'll talk to him tomorrow.

19.2.3 After modal verbs, such as **poder** 'to be able to', **dever** 'should', **ter que** 'to have to', **precisar** 'to need to, must' (see **19.5.1**):

> **O presidente deve anunciar sua decisão essa semana.**
> The president is expected to announce his decision this week.

19.2.4 After other verbs, with or without an intervening preposition (see **19.5**):

> **Decidimos voltar ao hotel.**
> We decided to go back to the hotel.

19.2.5   After adjectives and impersonal expressions:

É importante lembrar que isso foi na época da hiperinflação.
It's important to remember that this was in the time of hyperinflation.

Acho arriscado guardar dinheiro em casa.
I think it's risky to keep money at home.

Não adianta fugir.
There's no point (*or* It's no use) running away.

▶ **65.1.9** (p. 483); **65.1.10** (p. 484); **65.2.9** (p. 486)

19.2.6   After interrogatives (see **11.14.7**, **11.14.8**):

Não sei o que fazer.
I don't know what to do.

Como explicar isso a uma criança?
How does one explain that to a child?

19.2.7   In written instructions that are not directed at anyone in particular:

Refogar a cebola e adicionar o molho.
Brown the onions and add the sauce.

19.3   Impersonal vs. personal infinitive

19.3.1   The infinitive can be considered to be 'personal' when it has a subject of its own that is different from that of the main verb. Normally, this subject will be a noun or pronoun placed immediately before the infinitive:

É raro o Pedro atrasar.
It's rare for Pedro to be late.

Ela saiu sem eu saber.
She went out without me knowing.

Eu lembro de você ter me falado.
I remember you telling me. (*literally*, you having told me)

19.3.2   When the subject of the personal infinitive is first or third person plural, the infinitive itself inflects, adding the ending **-mos** for the first person plural and **-em** for the third person plural.[1] As these endings indicate the subject of the infinitive, an explicit pronoun subject is never obligatory, although it is usually included, especially in the spoken language:

É perigoso as crianças brincarem nos trilhos.
It's dangerous for the children to play on the tracks.

NOTE   1   The personal infinitive forms of regular verbs are identical to those of the future subjunctive (see **15.8**), but in the case of irregular verbs the endings are the same but the stems are different, e.g. **fazermos** (infinitive) vs. **fizermos** (future subjunctive). In fact, it is not uncommon to hear native speakers incorrectly use the infinitive of irregular verbs in place of the future subjunctive.

Certas mudanças são necessárias para (nós) podermos assinar o contrato.
Certain changes are necessary for us to be able to sign the contract.

Vocês estão correndo perigo. É melhor ficarem aqui por enquanto.
You are in danger. You'd best stay here for the time being.

19.3.3 The infinitive may have a subject of its own which is not expressed. This occurs with impersonal verbs which never have an explicit subject:

Acho difícil chover amanhã.
I think it's unlikely to rain tomorrow.

É uma pena não haver mais opções de hospedagem na cidade.
It's a pity there aren't more accommodation options in the town.

19.3.4 In most cases, the personal infinitive can be thought of as meaning 'me going', 'you doing', etc. or the more formal equivalent, 'my going', your doing', etc.:

Ele ser budista não atrapalha a nossa relação.
Him being a Buddhist doesn't get in the way of our relationship.

A sociedade os discrimina apesar de (eles) gozarem de igualdade perante a lei.
Society discriminates against them despite them (*or* their) enjoying equality before the law.

19.4 Use of the infinitive after prepositions

19.4.1 Since the personal infinitive can be used to signal a change of subject, prepositional constructions are often used where English requires a conjunction and a subordinate clause:

Ele telefonou antes de nós sairmos.
He phoned before we left.

Você faz o favor de esperar até eu terminar de falar?
Would you be so kind as to wait until I finish speaking?

Não tenho pena deles apesar de serem menores.
I don't feel sorry for them despite the fact that they are under age.

19.4.2 Note that the prepositions **de, em** and **por** should not be contracted with a following article or pronoun when the latter is the subject of an infinitive. Nevertheless, native speakers frequently disregard this rule, especially in speech:

o fato de eles não entenderem a língua (*not* **deles**)
the fact that they don't understand the language

antes de o avião decolar (*not* **do avião**)
before the plane takes off

Não vejo problema em ele visitar a página do filho em redes sociais. (*not* **nele**)
I don't see a problem in him looking at his son's page on social media.

A homofobia não é abordada nas escolas por os professores não saberem lidar com o tema. (not **pelos professores**)
Homophobia is not addressed in schools because teachers do not know how to deal with the topic.

However, the preposition **a** is always contracted with a following article:

O vice-presidente recebeu a delegação chinesa devido ao presidente estar em viagem.
The vice-president welcomed the Chinese delegation due to the president being away.

19.4.3 Purpose is expressed with the preposition **para** '(in order) to' before the infinitive. Again, it can also be used before a personal infinitive signalling a change of subject, equivalent to the English 'for someone/something to do something' or 'so (that) someone/something can/will do something':

Ela me ligou para contar a notícia.
She called me to tell me the news.

Abaixamos a música para não incomodar os vizinhos.
We turned the music down so as not to (or so we wouldn't) bother the neighbours.

Parei o carro para ele descer.
I stopped the car for him to get out (or so he could get out).

Desci a escada de mansinho para ninguém me ouvir.
I crept down the stairs so that no one would hear me.

▶ **42.5.1** (p. 366)

19.4.4 The preposition **por** followed by the infinitive often requires the translation 'because' plus clause in English:

Ele não consegue emagrecer por não fazer exercício.
He doesn't manage to lose weight because he doesn't do any exercise.

Ela nos tratou assim por sermos estrangeiros.
She treated us like that because we're foreigners.

▶ **42.2.2** (p. 362)

19.5 Verbs followed by the infinitive

▶ Chapter 24 (p. 216); 33.6 (p. 310)

19.5.1 The following verbs are followed by the infinitive without an intervening preposition:

(i) The modal verbs **conseguir** 'to manage to, succeed in', **dever** 'should, to be due to', **poder** 'to be able to', **precisar** 'to need to', **querer** 'to want to', **saber** 'to know how to', **ter que** 'to have to':

Quero ficar em casa.
I want to stay at home.

(ii) Impersonal verbs and expressions, such as **convém** 'it is appropriate to', **vale a pena** 'it is worth', **não adianta** 'it's no use, there's no point', etc.:

Cabe a você tomar uma decisão.
It's up to you to take a decision.

(iii) The verbs **adorar** 'to love (to)', **ameaçar** 'to threaten to', **aparentar** 'to appear to', **buscar** 'to seek to', **cogitar** 'to contemplate'[2], **costumar** 'to be in the habit of',

decidir 'to decide to', **desejar** 'to wish to', **detestar** 'to hate (to)', **escolher** 'to choose to', **esperar** 'to hope to', **evitar** 'to avoid', **fingir** 'to pretend to', **lamentar** 'to regret', **merecer** 'to deserve to', **odiar** 'to hate (to)', **ousar** 'to dare to', **parecer** 'to seem to', **preferir** 'to prefer to', **pretender** 'to intend to, plan to', **procurar** 'to try to, seek to', **prometer** 'to promise to', **resolver** 'to decide to', **sentir** 'to be sorry to', **tentar** 'to try to', among others:

> **Com quem deseja falar?**
> Who do you wish to speak to?

2   Also used with the preposition **em: cogitar em fazer** 'to contemplate doing'.

(iv)   In more formal style, verbs of saying and believing, such as: **acreditar** 'to believe, think', **afirmar** 'to affirm, state', **alegar** 'to claim', **desmentir/negar** 'to deny', **dizer** 'to say', **pensar** 'to think', etc. Some of these can also be followed by an infinitive in English while others cannot:

> **Ele diz estar arrependido.**
> He says he's sorry.

> **Eu acreditava ter boas chances de ser contratado.**
> I thought I had a good chance of being hired.

(v)   The verbs **ir** 'to go' and **vir** 'to come'. Note that a destination can be inserted between these verbs and the infinitive. The verb **ir** is also used as the auxiliary for the periphrastic future tense (see **19.2.2**):

> **Vieram nos visitar.**
> They came to visit us.

> **Ela foi à padaria comprar pão.**
> She's gone to the bakery to buy bread.

(vi)   The verbs **ouvir** 'to hear', **sentir** 'to feel', **ver** 'to see' and **deixar** 'to let', **fazer** 'to make', **mandar** 'to tell, order', which take a direct object before the infinitive (see **19.6**).

(vii)   With an indirect object: **impossibilitar a alguém fazer** 'to make it impossible for someone to do', **permitir a alguém fazer** 'to allow/enable someone to do', **possibilitar a alguém fazer** 'to enable someone to do', **recomendar a alguém fazer** 'to recommend someone do':

> **Isso lhe permitiu expandir seus negócios.**
> This enabled him to expand his business.

19.5.2   The following verbs are followed by the preposition **a** and the infinitive:

(i)   **aprender a** 'to learn to', **atrever-se a** 'to dare to', **chegar a** 'to get/go as far as', **começar a** 'to start/begin to', **comprometer-se a** 'to commit yourself to, undertake to', **continuar a**[3] 'to continue to, go on', **custar a** 'to take a while to', **decidir-se a** 'to make up your mind to', **demorar a** 'to take a long time to', **limitar-se a** 'to limit yourself to', **passar a** 'to switch to, come/get to', **resolver-se a** 'to resolve to', **voltar a** 'to (do) again, go back to (doing)', among others:

3   The verb **continuar** is more often followed by the gerund, especially in the spoken language: **Ele continuou falando.** 'He went on talking.'

Ele chegou a desconfiar da própria mãe.
He got as far as distrusting his own mother.

Passamos a usar margarina em vez de manteiga.
We've gone over to using margarine instead of butter.

(ii) With a direct object: **aconselhar alguém a** 'to advise someone to', **ajudar alguém a** 'to help someone to', **convencer alguém a** 'to persuade/convince someone to', **convidar alguém a** 'to invite someone to', **ensinar alguém a** 'to teach someone to', **forçar alguém a** 'to force someone to', **incentivar alguém a** 'to encourage someone to' **levar alguém a** 'to cause/lead/bring someone to', **obrigar alguém a** 'to force/oblige someone to', among others:

Não sei o que a levou a fazer isso.
I don't know what caused her to do this.

► **65.1.11** (p. 484)

19.5.3 The following verbs are followed by the preposition **de** and the infinitive:

(i) **acabar de** 'to have just, to finish',[4] **combinar de** 'to arrange to', **deixar de** 'to stop, to fail to', **encarregar-se de** 'to undertake to', **esquecer de** 'to forget to', **ficar de** 'to say you will (do)', **lembrar de** 'to remember to',[5] **parar de** 'to stop', **terminar de** 'to finish', **tratar de** 'to see to (it that)', among others:

Ficamos de sair no domingo.
We said we'd go out on Sunday.

(ii) With a direct object: **demover alguém de** 'to dissuade someone from', **impedir alguém de** 'to stop/prevent someone (from)', **proibir alguém de** 'to forbid someone to':

Ninguém vai me impedir de ver meus filhos.
No one is going to stop me seeing my children.

(iii) With an indirect object: **lembrar a alguém de** 'to remind someone to':

Preciso lembrar ao Bruno de pagar a conta de luz.
I must remind Bruno to pay the electricity bill.

NOTES

4 Although **acabar de** can be used to mean 'to finish (doing something)', it is more commonly used in the preterite to mean 'have/has just': **Eles acabaram de chegar.** 'They've just arrived.'

5 Note the difference between **lembrar de fazer** 'to remember to do' and **lembrar de ter feito** 'to remember doing': **Você lembrou de comprar leite?** 'Did you remember to buy milk?' **Não lembro de ter visto esse filme.** 'I don't remember seeing this movie.'

19.5.4 The following verbs are followed by the preposition **em** and the infinitive:

(i) **contentar-se em** 'to be content to', **empenhar-se em** 'to put your mind to, strive to', **pensar em** 'to think of':

Estou pensando em comprar um carro.
I'm thinking of buying a car.

(ii)   The preposition **em** is also used after nouns and adjectives expressing emotion, e.g. **feliz em** 'happy to', **prazer em** 'pleasure to', **triste em** 'sad to', etc.:

> **Fiquei contente em saber que você está bem.**
> I was glad to hear that you are well.

> **Prazer em conhecê-lo.**
> Pleased to meet you.

19.5.5   The following verbs are followed by the preposition **para** and the infinitive:

(i)   **pedir para** 'to ask to':

> **Ela pediu para sair da mesa.**
> She asked to leave the table.

(ii)   With indirect object: **dizer/falar a alguém para** 'to tell someone to', **pedir a alguém para** 'to ask someone to'[6]. In the spoken language, these constructions are simplified to **dizer/falar para alguém fazer**, **pedir para alguém fazer** using the personal infinitive:

> **O médico falou para eu não tomar sol.**
> The doctor told me not to go out in the sun.

> **Pedi às crianças para me ajudarem.**
> I asked the children to help me.

NOTE   6   The personal infinitive may be used after **para** in this construction, especially with the verb **pedir**. In formal written language, the verb **pedir** is also used with a subjunctive clause **pedir que alguém faça** 'to ask that someone do sth': **Pedimos que V. Sa. reembolse essa quantia.** 'We would ask that you reimburse this amount.'

19.6   Cases where either the impersonal or personal infinitive may be used

19.6.1   After the verbs of perception **ver** 'to see', **ouvir** (colloquially also **escutar**) 'to hear' and **sentir** 'to feel', as well as some other verbs, such as **deixar** 'to let', **fazer** 'to make' and **mandar** 'to tell, to order', a noun object can be construed either as the object of these verbs or as the subject of a following infinitive, which means that the infinitive can be either impersonal or personal. In fact, this is only an issue when the noun object is third person plural or combined with a pronoun to make first person plural:

> **Ele viu os ladrões pularem (*or* pular) o muro.**
> He saw the thieves jump over the wall.

> **Não deixaram a mim e aos meus amigos entrarmos (*or* entrar).**
> They didn't let me and my friends go in.

▶ 53.1.5 (p. 422)

19.6.2   When the object of the first verb is an unstressed pronoun, the following infinitive can only be impersonal:

> **Ela nos mandou fechar a porta.**
> She told us to shut the door.

19.6.3 But when the pronouns **eles** or **elas** are used in noun-object position in the spoken language (see **7.3.3**), they are followed by the personal infinitive:

> **Manda elas entrarem.** (*spoken*)
> Tell them to come in.

19.6.4 Note that 'let me ...' is translated **deixa eu** with the personal infinitive in the spoken language, and **deixe-me** with the impersonal infinitive in the written language:

> **Deixa eu ver.** (*spoken*)
> Let me see.
>
> **Deixe-me explicar de outra forma.** (*written*)
> Let me explain in another way.

19.7 Personal infinitive with the same subject as the main verb

19.7.1 There are a number of cases where the personal infinitive may optionally be used even though it has the same subject as the main verb:

(i) When the infinitive expression precedes the main verb, usually introduced by a preposition:

> **Sem fazermos barulho, abrimos a porta e entramos na casa.**
> Without making a noise, we opened the door and went into the house.

(ii) When the infinitive expression is some distance away from the verb it depends on:

> **Começaram, depois de muita discussão, a derrubarem a parede.**
> They started, after much discussion, to knock the wall down.

19.7.2 Otherwise, if the infinitive is closely preceded by the verb it depends on, even with an intervening preposition, it remains impersonal, though an exception to this is that the inflected personal infinitive[7] is obligatory when the infinitive verb is reflexive or passive, although this rule is not always applied in the spoken language. Compare:

> **Os dois passaram seis meses sem falar com ninguém.**
> The two of them went for six months without speaking to anyone.
>
> **Os dois passaram seis meses sem se falarem.** (*reflexive*)
> The two of them went for six months without speaking to each other.
>
> **Nós nos disfarçamos para não sermos reconhecidos.** (*passive*)
> We disguised ourselves so as not to be recognized.

NOTE 7 Of course, inflection of the infinitive can only occur in the first and third persons plural.

19.8 Position of object pronouns with the infinitive

For the position of object pronouns with auxiliaries and the infinitive, see **7.5.8**.

19.8.1 When an infinitive occurs at the beginning of a clause, any unstressed object pronoun associated with it, including the reflexive **se**, has to be appended to it with a hyphen in the written language. This is in fact the same rule that applies to the placement of unstressed object pronouns with finite verb forms[8] – see **7.5.3**:

> **Proteger-se do sol é fundamental.**
> Protecting yourself from the sun is essential.

19.8.2

In accordance with the rules given in **7.5.4**, if the infinitive is preceded by a noun or pronoun subject, a negative or interrogative word or an adverb, any unstressed object pronoun associated with it, including the third-person pronouns **o**, **a**, **os** and **as**, should be placed before it:[9]

> **Acho difícil a polícia nos ajudar.**
> I think it unlikely the police will help us.

> **Aprendi a não me preocupar com o que os outros pensam.**
> I've learned not to worry about what other people think.

> **Quero converter o arquivo para o Word, mas ainda preciso descobrir como o fazer.**
> I want to convert the file to Word, but I still need to figure out how to do it.

NOTES

8   And as with finite verb forms, the rule is disregarded in the spoken language, where unstressed object pronouns are always placed before the infinitive, even at the beginning of a clause.

9   In fact, with the third-person pronouns, this rule is frequently broken and the pronouns are appended to the infinitive as **-lo**, **-la**, **-los** and **-las** even after the elements mentioned, which sounds less formal than placing them before the infinitive.

9.8.3

After a preposition and in expressions involving an adjective or similar, the unstressed pronouns **me**, **te**, **se**, **nos** and **lhe(s)** are placed before the infinitive in speech and non-formal writing, and are appended to it with a hyphen in more formal style. The third-person unstressed object pronouns are always appended:

> **Foi um grande erro nos comprometer a isso.** (*non-formal*)
> **Foi um grande erro comprometer-nos a isso.** (*formal*)
> It was a big mistake committing ourselves to this.

> **Depois de se casar, ela foi morar no interior.** (*non-formal*)
> **Depois de casar-se, ela foi morar no interior.** (*formal*)
> After marrying, she went to live in the country.

> **Ao verem-na sair, os fotógrafos se amontoaram em volta dela.**
> On seeing her come out, the photographers crowded around her.

19.9   # Other uses of the infinitive

9.9.1

Some adjectives, most notably **fácil** 'easy', **difícil** 'difficult', **duro** 'hard', **bom** 'good', **ruim** 'no good, hard', **agradável** 'nice' and **desagradável** 'unpleasant', may be followed by the preposition **de** and the infinitive:

> **Esta porta é difícil de abrir.**
> This door is difficult to open.

cf.   **É difícil abrir esta porta.**
> It's difficult to open this door.

> **O carro é ruim de dirigir.**
> The car's no good to drive.

19.9.2 Nouns followed by an infinitive in English, in expressions such as 'time to go', 'a chance to win', 'the way to succeed', etc., are followed by the preposition **de** before the infinitive in Portuguese:

> **É hora de irmos para casa.**
> It's time for us to go home.

> **Preciso achar uma maneira de recuperar os dados.**
> I need to find a way to recover the data.

19.9.3 The preposition **por** preceding an infinitive can also mean 'yet to be done, yet to happen':

> **Ainda tem quatro páginas por traduzir.**
> There are still four pages to be translated.

> **O melhor está por vir.**
> The best is yet to come.

19.9.4 An infinitive may be introduced by **ao** (preposition **a** + article **o**), which is equivalent to the English 'on doing, when doing'. This construction is only used in the written language, and may also sometimes be translated 'in/by doing':

> **Ao entrarem na igreja, tiraram o chapéu.**
> On entering the church, they took off their hats.

> **O árbitro errou ao não expulsar o jogador.**
> The referee made a mistake in not sending the player off.

19.9.5 The preposition **a** alone can introduce an infinitive with a passive meaning. The passive infinitive may also be used:

> **as regras a respeitar** *or* **as regras a serem respeitadas**
> the rules to be respected.

It is also found in some idiomatic phrases:

> **a julgar pela reação da população**
> to judge from public reaction

> **três países, a saber, Inglaterra, França e Itália**
> three countries, namely, England, France and Italy

> **a seguir**
> as follows

> **Não tem nada a ver comigo.**
> It has nothing to do with me.

> **A persistirem os sintomas, o médico deverá ser consultado.**[10]
> If symptoms persist, consult your doctor. (*health warning printed on over-the-counter medicines*)

NOTE   10 You also see **Ao persistirem os sintomas** . . . which could be construed as meaning 'Upon symptoms persisting . . .', but most grammarians argue that this is simply an incorrect use of **ao** for **a**.

19.9.6 Very occasionally, the infinitive may be accompanied by an article:

> **o cantar dos pássaros**
> the singing of the birds

> **num piscar de olhos**
> in the blink of an eye.

19.10 Perfect infinitive

19.10.1 The perfect infinitive consists of the infinitive of the auxiliary **ter** followed by the past participle of the verb in question. In some of its uses, it is equivalent to the English perfect infinitive 'to have done/gone/eaten etc.', in others it translates the English perfect gerund 'having done/gone/eaten etc.':

> **É uma honra ter trabalhado com vocês nesse projeto.**
> It's an honour to have worked with you on this project.

> **Apesar de ter estudado muito, o Sérgio foi reprovado na prova.**
> Despite having studied hard, Sergio failed the test.

19.10.2 The perfect infinitive is more frequent in Portuguese than its English equivalent because it has to be used in cases where the action of the infinitive precedes that of the main verb of the sentence. In English, the perfect infinitive or gerund is usually replaced by the present infinitive or gerund in such cases:

> **Ele foi preso por ter roubado um carro.**
> He was arrested for stealing a car. (*literally*, for having stolen)

> **Apesar de ter nascido em Portugal, ela se considera brasileira.**
> Despite being born in Portugal, she considers herself Brazilian. (*literally*, having been born)

> **Eu não lembro de você ter me falado isso.**
> I don't remember you telling me that. (*literally*, you having told)

19.10.3 The perfect infinitive follows the same rules as the present infinitive with regard to the use of the inflected personal form. The rules on unstressed object pronoun placement are the same as for the finite compound perfect tenses – see **17.3.4**:

> **Em muitos países, as pessoas se casam sem terem se conhecido pessoalmente.**
> In many countries, people get married without having met each other in person.

> **O livro é excelente; só me arrependo de não o ter lido antes.**
> The book is excellent; I just regret not reading it before.

Notes for Spanish speakers

The use of the Portuguese impersonal infinitive is very similar to that of its equivalent in Spanish, though note that unstressed object pronouns normally precede the infinitive except in formal written style. When the infinitive is introduced by an auxiliary verb, any object pronoun precedes the infinitive, not the auxiliary (cf. **não posso me queixar**, **essa notícia deve te surpreender**, **vamos nos encontrar**, etc.). The personal infinitive is unique to Portuguese and does away with the need to use a conjunction and subordinate clause when there is a change of subject. Personal infinitive constructions occur very frequently in everyday speech and writing and are much preferred to the type of subjunctive clauses that Spanish has to employ.

20

The subjunctive

20.1 Introduction

20.1.1 The subjunctive forms of verbs could be described as expressing hypothetical actions and situations, as opposed to the real ones expressed by the indicative. In English, the subjunctive is little used, only occurring in isolated cases like 'long *live* the king', 'the judge recommended he *do* community service' and 'if I *were* you'. But the Portuguese subjunctive is in frequent and systematic use as certain syntactic and semantic contexts require it. These contexts will be examined below.

20.1.2 There are three simple subjunctive tenses in Portuguese: present (see **15.6**), imperfect (see **15.7**) and future (see **15.8**). Using these tenses of the auxiliary **ter** (see **16.3.5**) and a past participle, it is also possible to form a perfect, pluperfect and future perfect subjunctive:[1]

Pres. subj.	**eu fale, eu coma, eu decida**, etc.
Imperf. subj.	**eu falasse, eu comesse, eu decidisse**, etc.
Future subj.	**eu falar, eu comer, eu decidir**, etc.
Perfect subj.	**eu tenha falado/comido/decidido**, etc.
Pluperf. subj.	**eu tivesse falado/comido/decidido**, etc.
Future perfect subj.	**eu tiver falado/comido/decidido**, etc.

NOTE   1   In the case of the pluperfect and future perfect subjunctive, the auxiliary **haver** may also be used in more formal writing.

20.1.3 The subjunctive mainly occurs in subordinate clauses, i.e. after the conjunction **que** 'that'[2] and some others. These are clauses that cannot stand on their own, but depend on a main clause, which is usually in the indicative. There are a few special uses of the subjunctive in main clauses, and these will be dealt with at the end of this chapter.

NOTE   2   The conjunction 'that' is often omitted in English, but **que** can never be left out in Portuguese, except in a few very formal turns of phrase.

20.2 Sequence of tenses

20.2.1 When the subjunctive occurs in a subordinate clause, its tense is usually determined by the tense of the main verb (i.e. the verb in the main clause). If the main verb is present, future or present perfect, the subordinate verb is usually in the present or future subjunctive; if the main verb is imperfect, preterite, conditional or pluperfect, the subordinate verb goes into the imperfect subjunctive. This relationship is called the sequence of tenses. Compare the following examples:

Ela quer que eu a ajude.
She wants me to help her.

Ela queria que eu a ajudasse.
She wanted me to help her.

Se eu tiver dinheiro suficiente, vou comprar um computador novo.
If I have enough money, I'll buy a new computer.

Se eu tivesse dinheiro suficiente, compraria um computador novo.
If I had enough money, I'd buy a new computer.

20.2.2 This rule of 'sequence of tenses' applies equally to the auxiliary **ter**, the compound tenses being used if the action of the subjunctive verb occurred before that of the main verb:

Espero que você tenha aproveitado a sua estadia.
I hope you('ve) enjoyed your stay.

Era surpreendente que ninguém tivesse pensado nisso antes.
It was surprising that no one had thought of that before.

20.2.3 In fact, the 'sequence of tense' rules are sometimes broken. This occurs when the main verb is present tense but the subjunctive verb refers to an imperfect (ongoing) or conditional action in the past, in which case the imperfect subjunctive is used. It also occurs when a preterite tense is used with reference to the present and is then followed by a present subjunctive. Study the examples:

É provável que ele conhecesse o agressor.
It's probable he knew his attacker.

Duvido que eles tivessem ganho sem a ajuda do juiz.
I doubt they would have won without the referee's help.

Fiquei contente que os alunos estejam gostando das aulas.
I'm glad the students are enjoying the classes.

20.2.4 The future subjunctive is used to refer to potential future action or events that have not yet taken place at the time of speaking and may not necessarily happen at all, most notably after certain temporal conjunctions and in relative and conditional clauses which refer to the future. See sections **20.4** and **20.5.1** below.

20.3 The present or imperfect subjunctive in subordinate clauses

The present or imperfect subjunctive (according to the sequence of tenses) is used in the following types of subordinate clauses:

20.3.1 After impersonal phrases that express doubt, an opinion or value judgement[3], such as **é possível/impossível que** 'it's possible/impossible that', **é provável que** 'it's likely that', **é importante que** 'it's important that', **é bom que** 'it's good that', **é uma pena que** 'it's a pity that', **convém que** 'it is appropriate that', etc.:

É duvidoso que a nova política resolva o problema.
It is doubtful that the new policy will solve the problem.

NOTE 3 Such expressions may also occur after the verb **achar** 'to think': **Acho possível que ele seja o assassino.** 'I think it's possible he's the murderer.'

Não me importa que as pessoas não gostem de mim.
It doesn't matter to me that people don't like me.

▶ **47.1.5** (p. 394); **61.1.2** (p. 465)

20.3.2 After certain verbs, when the subject of the subordinate clause is different from that of the main clause, e.g. **aconselhar que** 'to advise that', **adorar que** 'to love that', **conseguir que** 'to get (sb to do sth)', **deixar que** 'to allow that', **desejar que** 'to wish that', **detestar que** 'to hate that', **esperar que** 'to hope/expect that', **exigir que** 'to demand that', **gostar que** 'to like (sb to do)', **impedir que** 'to prevent, stop', **insistir que** 'to insist that', **mandar que** 'to order that', **obrigar que** 'to make it compulsory that', **odiar que** 'to hate that', **pedir que** (see **19.5.5**) 'to ask that', **permitir que** 'to allow that', **precisar que** 'to need (sb to do sth)', **proibir que** 'to forbid that', **querer que** 'to want (sb to do sth)', **sugerir que** 'to suggest that', etc.:

Eu queria que ele me acompanhasse.
I wanted him to go with me.

A oposição tentou impedir que o projeto de lei fosse votado.
The opposition tried to stop the bill being put to the vote.

Espero que você tenha se divertido.
I hope you had a good time.

▶ **33.6** (p. 310); **46.1.4** (p. 388); **56.4.1** (p. 445); **56.4.2** (p. 446); **57.3.3** (p. 450); **60.2.1** (p. 461); **65.1.10** (p. 484); **68.1.10**, **68.1.12** (p. 496)

20.3.3 After phrases expressing an emotional reaction to the content of the subordinate clause, including **lamentar que** 'to regret that', **temer que** 'to fear that', **ter medo de que** 'to be afraid that', **surpreender-se que** 'to be surprised that', etc.:

Surpreendeu-a que ele pensasse assim.
It surprised her that he should think that.

Estamos contentes que o caso tenha sido resolvido.
We are glad that the case has been resolved.

Ela tinha medo de que ele contasse a verdade.
She was afraid he might tell the truth.

▶ **58.2.1** (p. 454); **61.1.4**, **61.1.5** (p. 466); **63.1.3** (p. 472)

20.3.4 After the verbs **duvidar** 'to doubt' and **negar** 'to deny', **imaginar** 'to imagine' and **supor** 'to suppose' when they posit an unreal situation, verbs of thinking and believing in the negative[4] and expressions that negate such as **não (é) que** '(it's) not that', **não (é) porque** '(it's) not because', **é falso que** 'it is false that' and **é mentira que** 'it's a lie that', as well as to express things that turned out to be untrue:

Duvido que ele volte tão cedo.
I doubt he'll be back in a hurry.

Imagine que você pudesse viajar de graça para qualquer lugar do mundo. Aonde iria?
Imagine you could travel for free to anywhere in the world. Where would you go?

NOTE   4   It is not uncommon to hear the subjunctive used after the affirmative of **acreditar** though the indicative is more frequent.

Não acredito que ela seja capaz de fazer uma besteira dessas.
I don't believe she's capable of doing something so stupid.

Não é que eu não goste dele, é que não temos afinidade.
It's not that I don't like him, it's just that we have nothing in common.

Pensei que ela fosse bater em mim.
I thought she was going to hit me.

▶ **48.1.2**, **48.1.3** (p. 398); **54.2.1** (p. 428); **54.2.3** (p. 430)

20.3.5 Note that the subjunctive is also used in clauses introduced by nouns derived from the adjectives and verbs mentioned above:

a possibilidade de que o governo aumente as taxas de juros
the possibility that the government may raise interest rates

Ele gritava na esperança de que alguém o ouvisse.
He was shouting in the hope that someone would hear him.

Há receio de que as negociações acabem fracassando.
There is concern that talks may end up breaking down.

20.3.6 After a relative pronoun when the relative clause describes a type of person or thing that may or may not exist rather than someone or something specific. The antecedent of the relative clause is usually an indefinite noun or pronoun or a negative word:

Precisamos de um recepcionista que fale inglês.
We need a receptionist who speaks English.

Ele procurava alguém que o ajudasse a montar um negócio.
He was looking for someone who would help him set up a business.

Não há ninguém que me compreenda.
There's no one who understands me.

Ele recebeu várias ofertas de emprego, mas nada que o empolgasse.
He got several job offers, but nothing that excited him.

20.3.7 After the following conjunctions: **a fim de que** 'in order that', **a menos que** 'unless', **a não ser que** 'unless', **ainda que** 'even though', **antes que** 'before', **caso** 'if', **contanto que** 'provided (that)', **desde que** 'as long as, provided (that)'[5], **embora** 'although', **mesmo que** 'even if/though', **nem que** 'even if', **para que** 'in order that', **sem que** 'without':

Ele prometeu ajudar os pobres caso ganhasse a eleição.
He promised to help the poor if he won the election.

Qualquer dia serve, desde que seja à tarde.
Any day is fine as long as it's in the afternoon.

Embora o anel fosse caríssimo, ele insistiu em comprá-lo.
Although the ring was extremely expensive, he insisted on buying it.

Não vamos conseguir fugir sem que nos vejam.
We won't manage to escape without them seeing us.

NOTE | 5   **desde que** is also used with the indicative meaning 'since' in the temporal sense: **Não vejo o Paulo desde que voltou do Canadá**. 'I haven't seen Paulo since he got back from Canada.'

▶ **42.5.2** (p. 367); **42.5.4**, **42.5.5** (p. 368)

20.3.8 The conjunctions **até que** 'until' and **de maneira que/de modo que** 'so that' are followed by the subjunctive when the subordinate clause refers to an unfulfilled action:[6]

> **Ela se posicionou de maneira que todos a vissem.**
> She positioned herself so that everyone would see her.

> **O aeroporto permanecerá fechado até que o tempo melhore.**
> The airport will remain closed until the weather improves.

NOTE | 6 The same conjunctions are followed by an indicative when the subordinate verb refers to something that is actually happening or happened, e.g. **A janela bateu com força de modo que o vidro quebrou.** 'The window slammed so hard that the glass broke.'

20.3.9 After adjectives and adverbs preceded by **por** or **por mais** in the sense of 'however ... it may be':

> **Por incrível que pareça, eles sobreviveram.**
> Incredible as it may seem, they survived.

> **Por mais que tentasse, ele não conseguiu.**
> As hard as he tried/Try as he might, he did not succeed.

20.3.10 After interrogatives followed by **quer que** with the meaning '. . . ever', e.g. **o que quer que** 'whatever', **quem quer que** 'whoever', **onde quer que** 'wherever', etc.:

> **Ele aceita ajuda de quem quer que seja para atingir seus objetivos.**
> He accepts help from whoever it may be to achieve his objectives.

> **Ela era assediada pelos fãs aonde quer que fosse.**
> She was besieged by fans wherever she went.

20.4 The future or imperfect subjunctive in subordinate clauses

The future subjunctive is used to refer to potential future action or events that have not yet taken place at the time of speaking and may not necessarily happen at all. The grammatical contexts in which it occurs are described below. The sequence of tenses (see **20.2** above) requires that the imperfect subjunctive be used instead when a potential future event is referred to from a past perspective, i.e. in relation to the action of a main verb in a past tense – see **20.4.5**.

20.4.1 The future subjunctive is used after the following conjunctions of time when the main verb of the sentence refers to the future and the action of the subordinate verb has not happened yet[7]: **assim que** 'as soon as', **como** 'as', **depois que** 'after', **enquanto** 'while, as long as', **logo que** 'as soon as', **quando** 'when', **sempre que** 'whenever':

> **Vamos sair assim que a novela terminar.**
> Let's go out as soon as the soap ends.

NOTE | 7 The same conjunctions are followed by the indicative when the subordinate verb refers to present or past action that actually happens or happened, e.g. **Ela me ligou assim que chegou em casa**. 'She called me as soon as she got home.' **Visito minha avó sempre que posso**. 'I visit my grandma whenever I can.'

Fique à vontade para personalizar o seu quarto como quiser.
Feel free to personalize your room as you like.

Não vou dormir enquanto ela não chegar em casa.
I'm not going to bed until she gets home.

Mande notícias quando você tiver tempo.
Send news when you have time.

20.4.2 The future subjunctive is also used in relative clauses (i.e. after the relative pronouns described in **Chapter 10**) to refer to a potential action that may occur at some undefined time in the future:

Qualquer coisa que você precisar, é só pedir.
(If there's) anything you need, you only have to ask.

Vocês podem comer quanto vocês quiserem.
You can eat as much as you want.

É melhor a gente pegar o primeiro ônibus que aparecer.
We'd best take the first bus that comes along.

O curso universitário que você escolher vai definir a sua carreira.
The university course you choose will define your career.

20.4.3 After the headless relatives **quem** 'who', **o que** 'what' and **onde** 'when', the future subjunctive gives the idea of 'ever':

Quem ganhar esse jogo vai para a final.
Whoever wins this game goes through to the final.

Pode sentar onde quiser.
You can sit wherever you like.

20.4.4 The future subjunctive is also used after **quanto mais** 'the more' when it refers to the future:

Quanto mais você treinar, mais rápido pega o jeito.
The more you practise, the quicker you'll get the hang of it.

20.4.5 In the cases described in **20.4.1** to **20.4.4** above, the subordinate verb goes into the imperfect subjunctive if the main verb is in the past (see **20.2**). In this case, the subordinate verb describes an action which has not yet taken place in relation to the action of the main verb:

Ele disse que ia ligar assim que chegasse.
He said he would call as soon as he arrived.

Resolvemos pegar o primeiro ônibus que aparecesse.[8]
We decided to take the first bus that came along.

NOTE | 8   At the time described in this sentence, a bus has not yet come along and it is still uncertain how things will develop. Using the preterite indicative in the relative clause (. . . **o primeiro ônibus que apareceu**) would mean that a bus actually came and the speaker took it.

20.5 The subjunctive in conditional clauses

▶ **49.1.1** (p. 401); **Chapter 50** (p. 405); **65.1.1** (p. 481); **65.1.3** (p. 482); **65.2.7** (p. 486)

20.5.1 The future subjunctive is used after the conjunction **se** 'if' when the main clause refers to future time:

Se quiser mais informações, clique aqui.
If you want more information, click here.

Se ganharmos o próximo jogo, avançamos para a fase eliminatória.
If we win the next game, we go forward to the knockout stage.

20.5.2 The imperfect subjunctive is used after the conjunction **se** to express an unreal condition. The main verb is either imperfect or conditional (in more formal writing) in such cases:

Se tivéssemos o dinheiro, comprávamos um carro novo.
If we had the money, we'd buy a new car.

Se não fosse o empréstimo, a empresa teria que fechar as portas.
If it weren't for the loan, the company would have to close down.

20.5.3 Both conditional and main clause can contain a compound tense to express an impossible condition:

Se o Palmeiras tivesse vencido, teria garantido o campeonato.
If Palmeiras had won, it would have had the championship sewn up.

Se eu soubesse, não tinha vindo.
If I'd have known, I wouldn't have come.

20.5.4 The imperfect subjunctive is also used after **como se** 'as if', regardless of the tense of the main verb:

Ele fala com os funcionários como se fossem crianças.
He talks to the employees as if they were children.

20.5.5 The conditional **se** 'if' can be used with indicative tenses if the sense requires it:

Se você está sem dinheiro, posso te dar emprestado.
If you don't have any money, I can lend you some.

Se te magoei, peço desculpas.
If I hurt you, I apologize.

20.5.6 Do not confuse the above conditional usages with **se** meaning 'if, whether', which introduces an indirect question and is followed by the indicative:

Não sei se ele vai poder nos ajudar.
I don't know if he'll be able to help us.

20.6 The subjunctive in main clauses

20.6.1 The present subjunctive is used for the formal imperative (see **Chapter 21**):

Assine aqui.
Sign here.

20.6.2 The present subjunctive is also used in third person wishes, sometimes introduced by **que**:

> **Deus te abençoe!**
> (May) God bless you!
>
> **Que os seus desejos se realizem!**
> May your wishes come true!

20.6.3 The first person plural of the present subjunctive expresses an exhortation 'Let us . . .'. This is replaced in the spoken language and informal writing by the auxiliary **vamos** followed by the infinitive:

> **Vejamos alguns exemplos.** (*written*)
> Let us look at some examples.
>
> **Vamos pedir uma pizza.** (*spoken*)
> Let's order a pizza.

▶ **65.2.1** (p. 484); **68.1.5** (p. 495)

20.6.4 The subjunctive must be used after the adverb **talvez** 'perhaps'. The tense used depends on the sense, with the imperfect subjunctive functioning as if it were an imperfect indicative or conditional:

> **A outra opção talvez seja melhor.**
> The other option is perhaps better.
>
> **Talvez fosse assim naquela época.**
> Perhaps that's how things were at that time.
>
> **Se você tivesse explicado melhor, talvez eu tivesse entendido.**
> If you had explained it better, perhaps I would have understood.

▶ **47.1.2** (p. 393)

20.6.5 The present subjunctive is also used after the expression **tomara que** 'let's hope (that)' and its literary synonym **oxalá que**:

> **Tomara que não chova!**
> Let's hope it doesn't rain!

▶ **60.2.2** (p. 462); **60.3** (p. 462)

20.7 Idiomatic uses of the subjunctive

20.7.1 The present and future subjunctives of the same verb are combined in expressions of the following type:

> **seja como for**
> be that as it may
>
> **venha o que vier**
> come what may
>
> **Haveremos de conseguir, custe o que custar.**
> We shall succeed, whatever the cost.

Note also the expression **quer queira ou não** 'like it or not':

> **Quer queira ou não, a realidade é essa.**
> Like it or not, that is the reality of the situation.

20.8 Subjunctive vs. infinitive

In some of the usages described above (**20.3.1–3**, **20.3.5** and after **antes**, **até**, **para** and **sem**), a personal infinitive construction could be used instead of a subjunctive clause. Generally speaking, where a choice exists, the subjunctive construction sounds more formal and, consequently, a personal infinitive construction is more likely to be favoured in speech.

20.9 Avoidance of the subjunctive in colloquial speech

There is a definite tendency to avoid the subjunctive in colloquial speech and the indicative is often used where formal grammar calls for a subjunctive. This is particularly true when the subordinate verb refers to past or present facts and events that are beyond doubt:

> **Que pena que ela não veio!** (*for* . . . **que ela não tenha vindo**)
> What a pity she didn't come!

> **Fiquei surpreso que ele não ganhou o jogo.** (*for* . . . **que ele não tenha ganho . . .**)
> I'm surprised he didn't win the game.

> **Que bom que você está aqui!** (*for* . . . **que você esteja . . .**)
> It's great that you're here!

Notes for Spanish speakers

Although the rules for the use of the subjunctive are basically very similar in the two languages, Portuguese has a future subjunctive tense in addition to present and imperfect subjunctives. The future subjunctive is used to refer to as yet unfulfilled future action after certain temporal conjunctions, in conditional clauses and in relative clauses where Spanish uses the present subjunctive or present indicative (in conditional clauses). In cases where a personal infinitive construction is possible instead of a subjunctive clause, Portuguese prefers this, especially in the spoken language and non-formal style.

21

The imperative

For addressing one person, Brazilian Portuguese has a familiar imperative, which is used in the spoken language and in informal writing, and a formal imperative, which is used in formal speech and writing. There is also a plural imperative form used for addressing more than one person in all situations.

21.1 Familiar imperative

21.1.1 The familiar imperative form is identical to the third person singular of the present indicative.[1] It is used in most spoken language situations except when particular formality is called for (see **21.2.1**) and in informal writing:

> **Fala a verdade!**
> Tell the truth!
>
> **Vem aqui!**
> Come here!

NOTE   1   The only exceptions are the verbs **ser** and **estar**, which only have the formal imperative forms **seja** and **esteja**. The familiar imperative is the original second person imperative (**tu** form), which has survived even though other second person verb forms are no longer used.

21.1.2 Unstressed object pronouns are positioned immediately before the verb form:

> **Me dá o seu e-mail.**
> Give me your e-mail address.
>
> **Te cuida.**
> Take care of yourself.

21.1.3 The familiar imperative can also occur in the negative in very colloquial speech, although the present subjunctive is more usual in prohibitions (see **21.2.3**):

> **Não fica pegando no meu pé.**
> Don't keep going on at me.
>
> **Não esquece de comprar leite.**
> Don't forget to buy milk.

21.2 Formal imperative

21.2.1
The third person singular of the present subjunctive is used as a formal imperative. This form is used in speech with people you would address as **o senhor/a senhora** and in written orders and instructions:

Abra aqui.
Open here.

Entre.
Come in.

21.2.2
Unstressed object pronouns are appended to polite imperative forms with a hyphen[2]:

Certifique-se de que o aparelho está desligado na tomada.
Make sure the appliance is unplugged.

Deixe-me citar alguns exemplos.
Allow me to quote some examples.

NOTE   2   In fact, it is not uncommon to hear and read hybrid forms in which an unstressed object pronoun is placed before a formal imperative, e.g. **me desculpe!** 'sorry!'. This occurs most frequently in speech where the formal imperative may be used to address, e.g. a customer, but placing an object pronoun after it would sound overly formal and pedantic.

21.2.3
In prohibitions (negative imperative sentences) the present subjunctive is used even in informal speech:

Não esqueça de ligar para o Eduardo.
Don't forget to call Eduardo.

Não pise na grama.
Do not step on the grass.

21.2.4
In prohibitions, unstressed object pronouns are placed between the adverb of negation and the verb form:

Não se preocupe.
Don't worry.

Nunca se esqueça disso.
Never forget that.

21.3 Plural imperative

When addressing more than one person, the third person plural of the present subjunctive is used as an imperative in both informal and formal registers. Unstressed object pronouns are appended to the imperative form with a hyphen or placed between the adverb of negation and the imperative in prohibitions:

Passem por aqui, por favor.
Come this way, please.

Fiquem à vontade.
Make yourselves at home.

Sentem-se.
Sit down.

Não se encabulem.
Don't be shy.

For third and first person imperatives, see **20.6.2** and **20.6.3**.

Notes for Spanish speakers

The formation of the familiar and formal imperatives is the same as in Latin American Spanish, but note that unstressed object pronouns are placed before the familiar imperative, not after it.

22

Reflexive verbs

Introduction

The English term 'reflexive verb' denotes a verb that is accompanied by a pronoun object referring back to the subject, i.e. the subject and the object of the verb are the same. In English, this type of verb is only used when the subject does something to himself/herself (e.g. *I cut myself*, *they blamed themselves*, etc.), whereas, in Portuguese, verbs that are reflexive in form have a number of different meaning patterns, of which the truly reflexive usage is just one.

22.2 | Reflexive object pronouns

The reflexive object pronouns are as follows:

Subject pronoun	Corresponding reflexive pronoun
eu	**me**
você **ele** **ela**	**se**
nós	**nos**
vocês **eles** **elas**	**se**

The reflexive pronouns are subject to the same rules of placement as other unstressed object pronouns[1] (see **7.5**).

NOTE   1   When the first person plural reflexive pronoun **nos** is appended to a first person plural verb form in more formal written style, the final **-s** of the verb form is dropped, e.g. **sentamo-nos** 'we sat down', **pusemo-nos a trabalhar** 'we set to work'.

Note that the third person reflexive pronoun **se** as also used to refer back to **a gente** meaning 'we':

A gente se comprometeu a ajudar.
We've committed ourselves to helping.

22.3 Meaning patterns of reflexive verbs

22.3.1 Reflexive use

This usage corresponds to the use of reflexive verbs in English, e.g. **lavar-se** 'to wash one-self', **cortar-se** 'to cut oneself'. There are also many Portuguese reflexive verbs that involve doing something to oneself and that do not have 'myself, yourself', etc. in the translation:

> **Ele se escondeu atrás de uma árvore.**
> He hid behind a tree. (*literally*, He hid himself . . .)

> **Eles se vestem muito bem.**
> They dress very well. (*literally*, They dress themselves . . .)

> **Nós nos identificamos com os personagens.**
> We identify with the characters. (*literally*, We identify ourselves . . .)

Note that the reflexive pronoun can also be the indirect object:

> **Ela tem que se aplicar duas injeções por dia.**
> She has to give herself two injections a day.

22.3.2 Reciprocal use

When the subject is plural, the reflexive pronoun can have a reciprocal meaning:

> **Vi os dois se beijando.**
> I saw the two of them kissing (each other).

> **Não entendo por que vocês dois se gostam tanto.**[2]
> I don't understand why you two like each other so much.

> **A gente mal se conhece.**
> We hardly know each other.

This reciprocal meaning can be made more explicit with the addition of **um ao outro** (when two people are involved) or **uns aos outros** (when more than two are involved – see **13.10.4**):

> **Foi uma oportunidade para nós nos conhecermos uns aos outros.**
> It was a chance for us to get to know one another.

The reflexive pronoun can also be the indirect object:

> **Nós nos compramos o mesmo presente de Natal.**
> We bought each other the same Christmas present.

NOTE   2 The verb **gostar** 'to like' is peculiar in that the reflexive pronouns can be used with reciprocal meaning even though the object is usually introduced with the preposition **de**.

22.3.3 Intransitive meaning

Many reflexive verbs correspond to intransitive verbs in English, especially those that indicate a change of some kind:

> **a relação que se desenvolveu entre eles**
> the relationship that has developed between them

A doença se espalha rapidamente pelo corpo.
The disease quickly spreads through the body.

O sol se põe por volta das seis horas.
The sun sets around six o'clock.

22.3.4 Change of emotional state

There are many reflexive verbs that denote a change of emotional state, usually translated into English with a passive:

Eu me surpreendi com a reação dele.
I was surprised at his reaction.

Não se estresse.
Don't get stressed out.

In informal speech, such reflexive verbs tend to be replaced by the verb **ficar** 'to be, to get' with the corresponding past participle:

Eu fiquei surpreso com a reação dele.
Não fique estressado.

22.3.5 Change of physical position

There is also a class of reflexive verbs that denote a change of bodily position, e.g. **sentar-se** 'to sit down', **ajoelhar-se** 'to kneel down', **deitar-se** 'to lie down', **levantar-se** 'to get up, stand up':

O padre se ajoelhou diante do altar.
The priest knelt before the altar.

In informal speech, these verbs are usually used intransitively, without the reflexive pronoun:

Levantei da mesa e fui embora.
I got up from the table and left.

22.3.6 Conventionally reflexive verbs

There are a number of verbs that are simply reflexive by convention and do not fall into any particular meaning pattern, e.g. **arrepender-se** 'to be sorry', **recusar-se** 'to refuse', **gabar-se** 'to boast', etc.

22.4 Impersonal *se*-construction

22.4.1 Most normally non-reflexive verbs can be used in the third person in combination with the reflexive pronoun **se** to form a general statement. With verbs that are otherwise intransitive, this **se** may be thought of as meaning 'one, they, people', etc., although, in strictly syntactic terms, it is still an unstressed object pronoun and must be positioned according to the rules given in **7.5**. The verb is always singular:

Come-se bem nos restaurantes do bairro.
One eats well in the local restaurants.

Naquela época, não se saía na rua à noite.
At that time, people didn't go out at night.

É importante que se responda a qualquer comunicação recebida.
It is important that one should reply to any communication received.

22.4.2 With verbs that are transitive, the **se**-construction is best translated by making the verb passive in English:

um tipo de peixe que se chama surubim
a type of fish that is called surubim

Aqui se fala inglês. (*on a sign*)
English spoken here.

22.4.3 More formal grammar requires a third person plural verb if the grammatical subject is plural:[3]

a necessidade de se criarem novas regras
the need for new rules to be devised

Vendem-se apartamentos. (*on a sign or advertisement*)
Apartments for sale.

NOTE 3 A singular verb is widely used in such cases in both speech and writing. This is quite justifiable linguistically, as the use of the **se**-construction with intransitive verbs demonstrates that native speakers perceive it to be an impersonal construction in which **se** acts as a kind of surrogate subject. What traditional grammarians identify as the subject of a reflexive verb, native speakers perceive as the object of a transitive verb with the impersonal singular subject **se**.

22.4.4 When the **se**-construction is used with a modal auxiliary verb, **se** precedes or follows the modal (according to the rules on object pronoun placement). The modal verb itself is singular, though it can be plural if the grammatical subject is plural and there is no preposition between the modal and the following infinitive:

Não se deve/devem destruir as florestas. (*plural subject, no preposition*)
The forests should not be destroyed.

Tende-se a subestimar as dificuldades. (*preposition before main verb*)
People tend to/There is a tendency to underestimate the difficulties.

Não se pode fumar aqui. (*intransitive main verb*)
You cannot smoke here.

22.4.5 The impersonal **se**-construction has a slightly formal ring to it and its use in informal speech is therefore limited, other than in certain set phrases, such as: **Nunca se sabe.** 'You never know.' It is especially common in scientific and academic writing where an objective tone is called for. In such contexts, it is often preferred to the more cumbersome passive.

22.5 Reflexive verbs in the spoken language

There is a definite tendency away from reflexive verbs in the spoken language. Apart from the cases noted above (**22.3.4**, **22.3.5**), there are verbs that are used reflexively in more formal language and non-reflexively in everyday speech, such as **casar(-se)** 'to get married', **divorciar(-se)** 'to get divorced', **esquecer(-se)** 'to forget', **lembrar(-se)** 'to remember', among others.

22.6 Other reflexive pronouns

22.6.1 The unstressed reflexive pronoun **se** has a corresponding stressed form **si**, which is used after prepositions. Note that the preposition **com** 'with' combines with **si** to form the single word **consigo**:

> **Deve-se sempre questionar a si mesmo.**
> One should always question oneself.

> **Cada passageiro pode levar consigo uma peça de bagagem.**
> Each passenger may take one piece of luggage with them.

22.6.2 In formal grammar, **si** and **consigo** should be used to refer back to any third person subject, including **você(s)**, but in practice they are only used in impersonal sentences or general statements with an indefinite subject (such as the two examples given in **22.6.1**). When the subject is a specific person or persons, the stressed reflexive pronoun is replaced by the appropriate non-reflexive pronoun, sometimes followed by **mesmo(s)/mesma(s)** '-self, -selves':

> **Você vai ter que cuidar de você mesmo.**
> You will have to take care of yourself.

> **O presidente leva a primeira dama junto com ele quando viaja.**
> The president takes the first lady along with him when he travels.

22.6.3 In the first person, the stressed pronouns **mim** and **nós** (in combination with **com**, **comigo** and **conosco**) may also be used reflexively:

> **Fiquei decepcionado comigo mesmo.**
> I was disappointed with myself.

> **Temos que conservar este patrimônio para nós e os nossos filhos.**
> We must preserve this heritage for ourselves and our children.

Notes for Spanish speakers

Reflexive verbs are much less common in Portuguese than in Spanish, especially in the spoken language, where verbs that are reflexive in more formal register are frequently used non-reflexively, i.e. as simple intransitive verbs. The impersonal **se**-construction is also largely confined to formal writing. Constructions such as *se me cae/ocurre/olvida/pierde algo*, etc. are unknown in Portuguese, not least because strings of consecutive unstressed object pronouns are only encountered in extremely formal writing and older literature.

23

Ser, estar and *ficar*

23.1 ## Introduction

As explained in detail below, the verbs **ser** and **estar** both mean 'to be' but have different uses. The verb **ficar** also translates 'to be' in certain circumstances, so it will also be dealt with in this chapter.

23.2 ## *ser*

▶ **16.3.8** (p. 155)

23.2.1
The verb **ser** is used to define the subject, so it is the verb to use when the verb 'to be' is followed by a noun that identifies the subject:

Esse é o meu marido.
This is my husband.

Sou jornalista.[1]
I'm a journalist.

A baleia é um mamífero.
The whale is a mammal.

Era um dia como qualquer outro.
It was a day like any other.

▶ **Chapter 34** (p. 312); **Chapter 35** (p. 319); **38.1.4** (p. 338); **41.2.3** (p. 358)

NOTE   1   When the verb **ser** is followed by a noun that describes the subject's profession, nationality or religion, the indefinite article is not used in Portuguese (see **4.2.3.1 (i)**).

23.2.2
The verb **ser** can also be followed by a pronoun in this identifying function, but note that **ser** always agrees with what follows it, not what precedes:

Quem é? – Sou eu.
'Who is it?' – 'It's me.'

Quem fala? – É Bob.
'Who's speaking?' – 'It's Bob.'

O maior problema são os mosquitos.
The biggest problem is/are the mosquitoes.

23.2.3 It follows that **ser** is used with adjectives that describe an inherent and/or permanent characteristic of the subject:

> **Os dois irmãos são altos.**
> Both brothers are tall.
>
> **O verão é quente no Brasil.**
> The summer is hot in Brazil.

▶ **36.1.2** (p. 321); **36.7** (p. 326)

23.2.4 In addition, **ser** is used with adjectives that denote human qualities when the meaning is 'behave in a . . . way':

> **Ela foi muito simpática comigo.**
> She was very nice to me.
>
> **Ele pode ser teimoso às vezes.**
> He can be stubborn at times.

▶ **36.8** (p. 326)

23.2.5 And it is also used to describe permanent location in the case of things that do not normally move, such as buildings, geographical features, etc.; **ficar** may also be used in this sense:

> **Por favor, onde é a Biblioteca Nacional?**
> Excuse me, where is the National Library?
>
> **A minha rua é logo aqui, à direita.**
> My street is just here, on the right.

▶ **39.1.3** (p. 341)

23.2.6 The verb **ser** is also used to identify the time when something occurs:

> **O meu aniversário é na semana que vem.**
> My birthday is next week.
>
> **Isso foi logo depois da morte do pai dela.**
> That was just after the death of her father.

▶ **39.2** (p. 342)

23.2.7 It is also used in expressions of time by the clock, dates and distance:

> **Eram dez para a meia-noite.**
> It was ten to midnight.
>
> **Hoje é dia oito.**
> Today is the eighth.
>
> **São cinco quilômetros daqui até a praia.**
> It's five kilometres from here to the beach.

23.2.8 And it is also used with a past participle to form the passive (see **17.4.1**):

> **O serviço será incluído na conta.**
> The service charge will be included in the bill.

23.3 *estar*

23.3.1 The verb **estar** describes a temporary state and is therefore used with adjectives that denote such states:

> **Estávamos muito cansados.**
> We were very tired.
>
> **Estou pronto para sair.**
> I'm ready to go out.

▶ **36.3** (p. 324)

23.3.2 It is also used with adjectives that describe the speaker's perception of someone or something, such as the appearance, feel, taste, etc. In fact, **estar** can also translate 'to look', 'to feel', 'to taste' in certain circumstances:

> **Você está linda hoje!**
> You look lovely today!
>
> **Essa sopa está muito salgada.**
> This soup is/tastes very salty.
>
> **Está quente aqui dentro.**
> It's/It feels hot in here.

▶ **36.4** (p. 325)

23.3.3 It follows that **estar** can only be followed by a noun when the noun is being used metaphorically to describe a temporary state or sensation:

> **Eu estava um caco depois da aula de aeróbica.**
> I was a wreck after the aerobics class.
>
> **A cozinha está um brinco.**
> The kitchen is spotless.

23.3.4 The verb **estar** is also used with adjectives and nouns to describe temporary weather conditions:

> **Estava uma tarde linda.**
> It was a lovely afternoon.
>
> **Está muito frio hoje.**
> It's very cold today.

▶ **36.9** (p. 327)

23.3.5 It is also used to express the temporary location of living beings and things that are easily moved around:

> **Você sabe onde está a chave do carro?**
> Do you know where the car key is?
>
> **Ele estava na minha frente na fila do supermercado.**
> He was in front of me in the supermarket queue/line.

▶ **39.1.1** (p. 340)

23.3.6 In addition, it is used when referring to a level:

> **Hoje o dolar está a R$3,50.**
> Today the dollar is at R$3.50.

23.3.7 And **estar** is used with a past participle to describe a resultant state (see **17.4.3**):

> **O serviço está incluído.**
> Service is included.

23.4 *ficar*

23.4.1 The verb **ficar** can be used as an alternative to **ser** when expressing permanent location; **ser** could also be used in the following examples:

> **Porto Alegre fica no sul do Brasil.**
> Porto Alegre is in the south of Brazil.

> **Onde fica o banheiro?**
> Where is the bathroom?

▶ **39.1.3** (p. 341)

23.4.2 Before an adjective, **ficar** marks a transition to a new state, usually as a reaction to something else. It often translates 'to get, become', but should be used to translate 'to be' when a change of emotional state is implied – see also **23.6.6** below:

> **O chefe vai ficar furioso quando souber disso.**
> The boss is going to be furious when he hears about this. (*i.e. get furious*)

> **Não fique triste.**
> Don't be sad. (*i.e. Don't get sad*)

▶ **41.1.1** (p. 354); **41.1.2** (p. 355)

23.4.3 Like **estar**, **ficar** can only be followed by a noun used metaphorically to describe a new state:

> **Meu cabelo vai ficar um lixo com essa chuva.**
> My hair's going to be a proper mess with this rain.

23.4.4 Like **estar**, **ficar** can be used to talk about the appearance, sound, taste or feel of something, but while **estar** refers to a state (see **23.3.2**), **ficar** refers to the resultant effect:

> **Ele fica muito charmoso de terno.**
> He looks very fetching in a suit.

> **Essa sopa fica ainda mais gostosa de um dia para o outro.**
> This soup tastes even better the next day.

23.4.5 Also, **ficar** can be followed by a past participle to express an involuntary passive result (see **17.4.2**):

> **Ficamos presos no elevador.**
> We got stuck in the lift/elevator.

23.5 **Adjectives used with either *ser* or *estar***

23.5.1 Some adjectives can be used with either **ser** or **estar**, depending on whether an inherent/ permanent or temporary feature is being described:

Ele sempre foi magro.	vs.	**Ele estava magro quando o vi.**
He's always been thin.		He was thin when I saw him.

23.5.2 Often, the criterion is inherent quality (**ser**) vs. speaker's perception (**estar**):

Meu pai é velho.	vs.	**Meu pai está velho.**
My father is old.		My father is looking old.
Você é louco.	vs.	**Você está louco.**
You're crazy. (*in general*)		You're being/acting crazy.

23.5.3 The words **rico** 'rich' and **pobre** 'poor' are usually used with **ser**, although **estar** can be used to describe a temporary situation:

> **O avô dela era rico.**
> Her grandfather was rich.

> **Estou pobre no momento.**
> I'm poor (= *broke*) at the moment.

23.5.4 The words **vivo** 'alive' and **morto** 'dead' are used with **ser** when describing a person's historical status ('living vs. no longer living')[2] and with **estar** when describing their current state ('alive vs. dead'). There is some variation in usage, and **estar** is generally more common, especially with **morto**:

> **Se o cantor ainda fosse vivo, teria hoje 90 anos.**
> If the singer were still living, he'd be 90 now.

> **Há quem acredita que Michael Jackson esteja vivo.**
> There are people who believe Michael Jackson is alive.

23.5.5 The words **casado** 'married', **divorciado** 'divorced', **separado** 'separated' and **solteiro** 'single' are used with **ser** when citing a person's formal marital status and with **estar** when describing current relationship status:[3]

> **Eles são casados há muitos anos.**
> They've been married for many years.

> **Atualmente ela está solteira.**
> She's currently single.

NOTES

2 The word **falecido** 'deceased', the standard euphemism for **morto**, is always used with **ser**: **Meus pais já são falecidos.** 'My parents are already deceased.'

3 **estar casado** tends to mean 'to be in a committed relationship' though not officially married.

23.6 **Translating 'was/were' and 'has/have been'**

When it comes to translating 'was/were' and 'has/have been' into Portuguese, the choice of the correct verb (**ser**, **estar** or **ficar**) in the correct tense (imperfect, preterite or present perfect) can be difficult for English speakers. Here are some tips.

23.6.1 Imperfect of *estar* (*estava, estávamos, estavam*)

Used to 'set the scene' in the past by describing the temporary state or location of people and things at the time of the events being reported. It is also used to convey the speaker's own sensory perceptions, i.e. 'was/were' in the sense of 'looked, seemed, sounded, tasted, felt, smelt':

Eu tinha trabalhado o dia inteiro e estava muito cansado.
I had been working the whole day and was very tired.

Estava muito quente no dia do casamento.
It was very hot on the day of the wedding.

A chave estava na fechadura da porta.
The key was in the lock of the door.

Pedi uma sopa mas estava horrível.
I ordered some soup but it was/tasted horrible.

A Sandra estava linda na festa.
Sandra looked lovely at the party.

23.6.2 Imperfect of *ser* (*era, éramos, eram*)

Used to 'set the scene' in the past by describing the permanent characteristics of people and things that feature in the events being reported. Also used to report time by the clock, dates, the permanent position of things that cannot be moved around and the identity of the people and things mentioned:

Ele era um homem alto e magro.
He was a tall, thin man.

Era quase meia-noite quando chegamos em casa.
It was almost midnight when we got home.

Era inverno e estava frio naquela noite.
It was winter and it was cold that night.

O banheiro era do outro lado do corredor.
The bathroom was on the other side of the hallway.

Era o Cláudio no telefone, perguntando se a gente quer sair hoje à noite.
It was Claudio on the phone, asking if we want to go out tonight.

Note that the imperfect of **ser** also translates 'used to be':

Aquele prédio era um teatro antigamente.
That building used to be a theatre.

O Pedro era meu melhor amigo, mas acabamos nos afastando.
Pedro used to be my best friend, but we ended up drifting apart.

23.6.3 Imperfect of *ficar* (*ficava, ficávamos, ficavam*)

Can be used in the sense of 'was/were' to describe the permanent location of something that cannot normally be moved around, as an alternative to the imperfect of **ser**:

O hotel ficava muito longe da praia.
The hotel was a very long way from the beach.

23.6.4 **Preterite of *estar* (*estive, esteve, estivemos, estiveram*)**

Used to report a person or movable thing being in a particular location or state for a finite period of time in the past. Whereas the imperfect of **estar** sets the scene of where and how people and things were when the main events happened, the preterite is used when 'being' itself is the main event reported:

> **Estive em São Paulo semana passada.**
> I was in São Paulo last week (= I went to SP and back in the course of last week).

> **Estivemos com o Paulo ontem à noite.**
> We saw Paulo last night. (*literally*, We were with Paulo last night)

> **A Ângela esteve doente durante uma semana.**
> Angela was sick for a week.

Note that the preterite of **estar** can also translate 'has/have been' when talking about where someone has been. In this sense, it is usually accompanied by the adverb **já**, literally 'already':

> **Já estivemos em Paris duas vezes.**
> We've been to Paris twice.

23.6.5 **Preterite of *ser* (*fui, foi, fomos, foram*)**

Used to describe a one-off event in the past and also a person's behaviour on a particular occasion. It is also used to define what a person or thing was for a finite period; in this usage, it differs from the imperfect in that the imperfect either sets the scene or emphasizes that someone or something 'used to be' but is no longer, whereas the preterite simply reports that a period of 'being' happened:

> **Como foi a prova? – Foi bem difícil.**
> 'How was the test?' – 'It was really difficult.'

> **O atendente foi grosso comigo.**
> The attendant was rude to me.

> **Santos Dumont foi um aeronauta, esportista e inventor brasileiro.**
> Santos Dumont was a Brazilian aviator, sportsman and inventor.

> **Meu pai foi jogador durante dez anos.**
> My dad was a soccer player for ten years.

The preterite can also translate 'has/have been', particularly in conjunction with the adverbs **já** 'already, yet, ever', **sempre** 'always' and **nunca** 'never':

> **Esse prédio já foi muitas coisas, inclusive uma igreja.**
> This building has been a lot of things, including a church.

> **Ela sempre foi muito simpática comigo.**
> She's always been very friendly towards me.

23.6.6 **Preterite of *ficar* (*fiquei, ficou, ficamos, ficaram*)**

Used to translate 'was/were' when reporting an emotional reaction to events:

> **Quando subimos ao Cristo Redentor, ficamos maravilhados com a vista.**
> When we went up to the statue of Christ, we were blown away by the view.

> **Fiquei contente em saber que você está bem.**
> I was glad to hear you're well.

23.6.7 Present perfect of *estar* (*tenho/tem/temos/têm estado*)

Translates 'has/have been' when describing being in a temporary location or state on repeated occasions up to and including the present:

> **Tem estado muito quente ultimamente.**
> It's been very hot lately.

> **Tenho estado quinzenalmente em São Paulo.**
> I've been going to São Paulo every two weeks.

23.6.8 Present perfect of *ser* (*tenho/tem/temos/têm sido*)

Translates 'has/have been' when describing the nature of a person or thing since an undefined point in the past up to and including the present:

> **Não tem sido fácil me adaptar à vida aqui.**
> It hasn't been easy for me to adapt to life here.

> **O gerente do hotel tem sido muito solícito em tentar resolver o problema, mas até agora sem sucesso.**
> The hotel manager has been very obliging in trying to solve the problem, but so far without success.

23.7 Idiomatic expressions with *ser*

23.7.1 *ser com alguém*

This is used for 'to be meant for someone; to be someone's department':

> **É comigo?**
> Do you mean me? / Do they mean me? / Are you talking to me?

> **É com você, Renata.**
> Over to you, Renata. (*on TV show*)

> **Os aplausos eram com o diretor.**
> The applause was for the director.

> **Futebol não é comigo.**
> Soccer's not my strong point. / It's no use asking me about soccer.

> **Abrir conta é com o gerente.**
> Opening an account is a matter for the manager.

23.7.2 *ser de*

This is used for 'to be from (a place)', 'to be made of (a material)' and 'to be one to (do something)'. **Ser de alguém** means 'to be somebody's, belong to somebody':

> **Você é de onde?**
> Where are you from?

> **As casas eram de madeira.**
> The houses were built of wood.

O Zé não é de beber.
Zé is not one to drink.

De quem é essa bolsa? – É da Rita.
'Whose bag is this?' – 'It's Rita's.'

▶ **36.5** (p. 325)

23.7.3 *é para (alguém) fazer*

This is used informally for 'someone is supposed to do':

É para pagar primeiro?
Are you/we supposed to pay first?

Era para todos estarem aqui às nove.
Everyone was supposed to be here at nine.

23.7.4 *é*

This can follow another verb as a form of emphasis:

Quero é voltar para casa.
To go home is what I want.

Estamos é cansados.
Tired is what we are.

23.7.5 *é que*

This can be inserted between subject and verb as a form of emphasis:

Eu é que tenho que bancar tudo.
It's me who has to pay for everything.

Oportunidades é que não faltam.
There's no shortage of opportunities. / It's not opportunities that are lacking.

23.8 Idiomatic expressions with *estar*

23.8.1

On its own, **estar** can also mean 'to be in (at home or work), to be there, to be present':

A Lúcia está por favor? (*on the phone*)
Is Lucia there please?

O meu chefe não estava ontem.
My boss wasn't in yesterday.

23.8.2 *estar com*

The expression **estar com** is used as follows:

(i)   To mean 'to have' when talking about things you have on you and illnesses:

Você está com a chave de casa?
Have you got the house key?

> **Ele estava com dengue.**
> He had dengue fever.

► **40.5.2** (p. 352)

(ii) To mean 'to be' with ages:

> **Ela está com quantos anos?**
> How old is she?

(iii) To mean 'to have on' with clothing, etc.:

> **Ela estava com uma saia vermelha.**
> She had a red skirt on.

(iv) To mean 'to be' in the following expressions: **estar com fome** 'to be hungry', **estar com sede** 'to be thirsty', **estar com sono** 'to be sleepy', **estar com frio** 'to be cold', **estar com calor** 'to be hot', **estar com medo** 'to be frightened', **estar com ciúme(s)** 'to be jealous', **estar com vergonha** 'to be embarrassed'. Note also the expression **estar com vontade de fazer** 'to feel like doing':

> **Estou com fome. Vamos comer alguma coisa?**
> I'm hungry. Shall we have something to eat?

23.8.3 *estar sem*

The expression **estar sem** is used as the negative of **estar com** in usages (i), (iii) and some of the expressions in (iv) above:

> **Estou sem dinheiro.**
> I have no money (on me).

> **Ela estava sem sutiã.**
> She had no bra on.

> **Tentei comer, mas estava sem fome.**
> I tried to eat, but I didn't feel hungry.

23.8.4 *estar para fazer*

This is used for 'to be due to do, to be meaning to, to be soon to do':

> **O bebê está para nascer.**
> The baby is due (to be born).

> **Estou para te ligar há semanas.**
> I've been meaning to call you for weeks.

23.8.5 *estar por fazer*

This means 'to be yet to do':

> **O pior ainda estava por vir.**
> The worst was yet to come.

> **Muitas dúvidas ainda estão por ser esclarecidas.**
> Many doubts are yet to be clarified.

23.8.6   *estar fazendo*

This is used for 'to be doing' (see **17.1.2**).

23.9   Other meanings and idiomatic uses of *ficar*

23.9.1   The verb **ficar** can be used with an adjective following to mean 'to get, to become, to go':

> **O nosso planeta está ficando cada vez mais quente.**
> Our planet is getting hotter and hotter.

> **Ele está ficando careca.**
> He's going bald.

23.9.2   It can also mean 'to stay' in a location or at someone's house, a hotel, etc.:

> **Fica aqui enquanto eu vou buscar o seu irmão.**
> Stay here while I go and pick up your brother.

> **Você pode ficar lá em casa.**
> You can stay at our place.

23.9.3   It can be used to mean 'to come out, turn out':

> **As fotos ficaram ótimas.**
> The photos came out out really well.

23.9.4   *ficar com*

The expression **ficar com** can be used in the following ways:

(i)   To mean 'to keep (for oneself)':

> **Vou ficar com uma cópia para mim.**
> I'm going to keep a copy for myself.

(ii)   To mean 'to get' with reference to something you are given or an illness:

> **Cada um fica com uma porcentagem do lucro.**
> Each one gets a percentage of the profit.

> **Fiquei com dor de barriga de tanto comer.**
> I got stomach ache from eating so much.

(iii) In the expressions in **23.8.2 (iv)** to mean 'get': **ficar com fome** 'to get hungry', **ficar com sede** 'to get thirsty', **ficar com sono** 'to get sleepy', **ficar com frio** 'to get cold', **ficar com calor** 'to get hot', **ficar com medo** 'to get frightened', **ficar com ciúme(s)** 'to get jealous', **ficar com vergonha** 'to get embarrassed':

> **Estou ficando com sono.**
> I'm getting sleepy.

23.9.5   *ficar fazendo*

The expression **ficar fazendo** can be used in the following ways:

(i)   To mean 'to keep doing':

> **Ele fica me ligando sem parar.**
> He keeps calling me non-stop.

(ii)   To mean 'to go on doing':

> **Ficamos conversando até altas horas da madrugada.**
> We went on talking into the small hours.

(iii)   To mean 'to be/sit/stand there doing':

> **Quando saí, as crianças ficaram acenando na porta.**
> When I left, the children stood there waving at the door.

> **Ele fica assistindo TV o dia inteiro.**
> He sits there watching TV all day long.

23.9.6 *ficar de fazer*

This can be used for 'to arrange to do, say you will do':

> **Ficamos de sair na sexta à noite.**
> We arranged to go out on Friday night.

> **Eles ficaram de me ligar assim que chegassem.**
> They said they'd call me as soon as they arrived.

Notes for Spanish speakers

Although the usage of **ser** and **estar** is very similar in the two languages, one important difference is that Portuguese employs **ser** or **ficar** to indicate permanent location, while **estar** is only used for temporary location. The verb **ficar** corresponds in meaning to the Spanish *quedar* but has a wider range of uses. Phrases expressing physical sensations ('hungry', 'cold', 'sleepy', 'frightened', 'embarrassed', etc.) and illnesses are constructed with **estar com** in Portuguese when referring to a temporary state; the verb **ter** is only used in such expressions to refer to permanent feelings and afflictions (e.g. **Ele tem medo de aranha**. 'He's afraid of spiders.'). **Estar com** is also frequently used as an alternative to **ter** to express age. Note that, in normal everyday speech, the initial **es-** in forms of the verb **estar** is not pronounced and frequently omitted in very informal writing (text messages, etc.).

24

Verbs used in auxiliary, modal and impersonal constructions

24.1 ## Auxiliary constructions

An auxiliary construction is one in which a 'helper' verb is used to give a particular nuance of meaning to a following main verb. In the auxiliary constructions described below, the main verb appears in the infinitive or gerund form.

For the use of the verbs **ser**, **estar** and **ficar** as auxiliaries, see **Chapter 23**. For the use of **ter** and **haver** as perfect tense auxiliaries, see **17.3**.

24.1.1 ### *acabar*

The verb **acabar** + gerund or (more formal) **acabar por** + infinitive 'end up doing, eventually do':

Acabamos dormindo no chão.
We ended up sleeping on the floor.

A polícia acabou prendendo o ladrão.
The police eventually caught the thief.

O réu acabou por confessar o crime.
The defendant eventually confessed to the crime.

24.1.2 ### *acabar de* + infinitive

Although this can mean 'to finish doing', the sense is more often 'to have just done'. In the spoken and less formal written language, the preterite of **acabar** is used to mean 'has/have just' and the pluperfect to mean 'had just'; in more formal registers, the present and imperfect tenses respectively are used:

Eu acabei de chegar.
I've just arrived.

Ele tinha acabado de jantar.
He had just had dinner.

A editora Sol acaba de publicar uma coletânea de suas poesias.
The publisher Sol has just published a collection of his poems.

Brasília acabava de ser construída.
Brasilia had just been built.

Você já acabou de comer?
Have you finished eating?

▶ **71.6.1** (p. 514)

24.1.3   *andar* + gerund

The present and imperfect tenses translate as 'have been (doing)' and 'had been (doing)' respectively:

O que é que você anda fazendo?
What have you been doing (lately)?

O político foi assassinado porque andava ameaçando contar tudo o que sabia.
The politician was murdered because he had been threatening to tell everything he knew.

The preterite of **andar** can also occur with the gerund, meaning 'have been doing' or 'had been doing' depending on whether the context is present or past:

Andei pensando no que você falou e eu concordo.
I've been thinking about what you said and I agree.

▶ **71.7.2** (p. 515)

24.1.4   *haver de* + infinitive

This is used for 'shall/will surely' (emphatic future). It is a very formal/literary usage which expresses a kind of wish. The verb **haver** is often in the future tense:

Dias melhores hão de vir!
Better days will surely come!

Se Deus quiser, haveremos de conseguir.
God willing, we shall succeed.

24.1.5   *ir* + infinitive

This is used for 'be going to do, will do' and other expressions of future intent, as well as 'go to do, go and do' where 'go' expresses actual movement:

Vou me encontrar com ela amanhã.
I'm meeting her tomorrow.

Ele foi ao supermercado comprar café.
He's gone to the supermarket to buy coffee.

24.1.6   *ir* + gerund

This is used for 'keep doing, get on with doing, go along doing':

Pode ir fazendo as malas que nós vamos viajar.
You can get on with packing because we're going on a trip.

Ela foi fazendo papéis pequenos durante cinco anos.
She went along playing small roles for five years.

Como vai a vida? – Ah, vou levando.
'How's life?' – 'Oh, I keep jogging along.'

24.1.7 *vir* + infinitive

This is used for 'come to do, come and do':

Ele vem nos visitar de vez em quando.
He comes to visit us from time to time.

24.1.8 *vir a* + infinitive

This is used for 'come to do, end up doing, turn out to do':

um político que, um dia, viria a ser presidente
a politician who, one day, would end up being president

Isso pode vir a comprometer a imagem da empresa.
This may turn out to damage the company's image.

24.1.9 *vir* + gerund

This is used for 'have been doing':

Os alunos vêm reclamando já há algum tempo.
The students have been complaining for some time now.

O setor vinha crescendo 2% ou mais a cada mês.
The sector had been growing 2% or more every month.

O Marco vem vindo. (*idiomatic use*)
Marco is just coming. / Marco is on his way.

▶ **71.7.2** (p. 515)

24.1.10 *viver* + gerund

This is used for 'to be always doing something':

Ela vive perdendo as chaves.
She's always losing her keys.

Os dois viviam brigando.
The two of them were always fighting.

The verb **viver** can also be used in this sense before an adjective or prepositional phrase:

O Zeca vive duro.
Zeca's always broke.

Minha irmã vive de mau humor.
My sister's always in a bad mood.

24.2 Modal constructions

24.2.1 *poder*

▶ **45.5.3** (p. 386); **47.1.7 (iv)** (p. 395); **52.1.1** (p. 416); **53.1.1**, **53.1.2** (p. 420); **65.1.5** (p. 482); **65.2.4** (p. 485); **66.1.5** (p. 489); **66.1.6** (p. 490); **68.1.11** (p. 496)

The verb **poder** + infinitive is used for 'can, be able to', referring to possibility, availability and permissibility:

> **O tempo pode mudar de uma hora para outra.**
> The weather can change from one moment to the next.

> **Acho que não vou poder ir.**
> I don't think I'll be able to go.

> **Você não pode levar isso na bagagem de mão.**
> You can't take this in your hand luggage.

Note that, in the spoken language, the third person singular **pode** can be used impersonally:

> **Pode estacionar aqui?**
> Is it OK to park here?

The verb **poder** can also translate 'may, might', referring to both possibility and permissibility:

> **Não coloque essas taças na máquina de lavar louça que podem quebrar.**
> Don't put those wine glasses in the dishwasher as they may break.

> **Posso sentar aqui?**
> May I sit here?

In more formal written language, the future tense of **poder** is used with the meaning of 'may, might':

> **As Bolsas poderão voltar a registrar altas a partir do mês que vem.**
> Stock markets may start to pick up again from next month.

Take care with the translation of 'could':

> **Você poderia/podia solicitar uma bolsa de estudos.** (*conditional or imperfect for conditional*, see **18.1.5**)
> You could apply for a scholarship.

> **O tenista estava lesionado e não podia jogar.** (*imperfect*)
> The tennis player was injured and could not play.

> **O tenista se machucou e não pôde terminar o jogo.** (*preterite*)
> The tennis player injured himself and could not finish the match.

Here are some examples of **poder** followed by the perfect infinitive:

> **Ele pode ter ligado enquanto eu não estava.**
> He may have called while I was out.

> **Poderíamos/Podíamos ter sido arrastados pela correnteza.**
> We could have been swept away by the current.

There is also an idiomatic usage of **poder** + perfect infinitive meaning 'should have':

> **Você não poderia/podia ter feito isso.**
> You shouldn't have done that.

24.2.2 *conseguir*

▶ **52.1.2** (p. 417)

The verb **conseguir** + infinitive is used for 'can, be able to' (physical ability), 'manage to, succeed in':

> **Não consigo abrir a porta.**
> I can't get the door open.

> **O Jorge queria ser ator e conseguiu.**
> Jorge wanted to be an actor and succeeded.

> **Finalmente conseguimos convencê-la.**
> We finally managed to persuade her.

24.2.3 *saber*

▶ **43.6** (p. 373); **52.2.1** (p. 419)

The verb **saber** + infinitive is used for 'can, be able to' (learned skills), 'know how to':

> **Ele não sabe nadar.**
> He can't swim.

> **Eu sei contar até dez em alemão.**
> I can/I know how to count to ten in German.

> **Ela não soube me dizer o nome da empresa.**
> She was unable to tell me the name of the company.

24.2.4 *querer*

▶ **56.1.1** (p. 439); **68.1.7** (p. 495); **68.1.13** (p. 497)

The verb **querer** + infinitive is used for 'want to':

> **Você quer jantar com a gente?**
> Do you want to have dinner with us?

> **Eu sempre quis conhecer Salvador.**
> I've always wanted to visit Salvador.

> **Coma quanto quiser.**
> Eat as much as you want.

The imperfect also does duty for the conditional and can mean 'would like to':

> **Eu queria te pedir um favor.**
> I'd like to ask you a favour.

> **Eu queria muito ter conhecido a sua mãe.**
> I would very much like to have/I really wish I'd met your mother.

24.2.5 *desejar*

▶ **56.1.5** (p. 442); **68.1.9** (p. 496)

The verb **desejar** + infinitive means 'wish to, would like to', a more formal and polite synonym of **querer**:

> **Com quem deseja falar?**
> Who do you wish to speak to?

> **Novas oportunidades estão se abrindo a todos os que desejarem participar.**
> New opportunities are opening up for all those who wish to participate.

24.2.6 *ter que*

▶ **45.1.1** (p. 382); **45.5.2** (p. 386); **46.1.2** (p. 387); **46.3.2** (p. 390); **65.1.7** (p. 483); **65.2.4** (p. 485); **67.1.3** (p. 492)

The expression **ter que** + infinitive is used for 'have to':[1]

> **Temos que estar lá às 9h00.**
> We have to be there at 9.00 a.m.

> **Tiveram que arrombar a porta.**
> They had to break the door down.

> **Você teria que fazer tudo de novo.**
> You would have to do it all again.

NOTE | 1 There is an alternative form **ter de** + infinitive that is only used in more formal written style, e.g. **Uma mulher teve de ser carregada pelas escadas até uma ambulância.** 'A woman had to be carried down the stairs to an ambulance.'

The third person singular is often used with an impersonal meaning in the spoken language:

> **Tem que pagar adiantado?**
> Do you/we have to pay in advance? (= *Does one . . . ?*)

The imperfect can be used idiomatically to mean 'should have':

> **Você tinha que ver a cara dele!**
> You should have seen his face!

24.2.7 *dever*

▶ **45.1.3** (p. 383); **45.5.1** (p. 385); **49.1.7** (p. 403); **65.1.6** (p. 483); **65.2.5** (p. 485)

The verb **dever** + infinitive is used for 'should, must', expressing obligation or supposition:

> **Você deve ir ao médico.**
> You should see a doctor.

> **Devemos chegar por volta do meio-dia.**
> We should arrive around midday.

> **Você não deve mexer no computador.**
> You must not touch the computer.

Eles não devem terminar hoje.
They're not likely to finish today.

It can also translate as 'be expected to, be due to, be to, be supposed to':

O preço do petróleo não deve cair tão cedo.
The price of oil is not expected to fall any time soon.

O presidente deve fazer uma declaração amanhã.
The president is (due) to make a statement tomorrow.

As câmeras de segurança devem inibir os assaltantes.
Security cameras are supposed to deter robbers.

In more formal writing, the future tense of **dever** is commonly used with the above meanings:

A Polícia Federal deverá abrir um inquérito.
The Federal Police is to open an inquiry.

The conditional, or its less formal substitute, the imperfect, can mean 'ought to, should' when talking about a moral obligation, or something that ought to happen but does not:

A escola deveria/devia avisar os pais quando isso acontece.
The school ought to notify parents when this happens. (*but they don't*).

cf. **A escola deve avisar os pais quando isso acontece.**
The school should/must notify parents when this happens.

Notice the meanings of **dever** followed by the perfect infinitive:

Ela deve ter esquecido.
She must have forgotten. (*supposition*)

Ele não deve ter recebido a mensagem.
He can't/must not have got the message. (*supposition*)

Eu deveria/devia ter telefonado.
I ought to/should have phoned. (*unfulfilled obligation*)

24.2.8 *precisar*

▶ **45.1.2** (p. 383); **45.5.2** (p. 386); **46.1.1** (p. 387); **46.3.1** (p. 389)

The verb **precisar** + infinitive is used for 'need to, must, have to':

Preciso ir, senão vou atrasar.
I must go, otherwise I'll be late.

Vocês não precisam me esperar.
You don't need to wait for me. / You needn't wait for me.

The imperfect can sometimes be translated 'should have':

Você precisava ver a bagunça naquela cozinha!
You should have seen the mess in that kitchen!

The third person singular is often used in an impersonal way:

> **Precisa marcar hora?**
> Is it necessary to make an appointment?
>
> **Um presente para mim? Não precisava!**
> A present for me? You shouldn't have! (= *it wasn't necessary*)

24.3 Impersonal uses of certain verbs

Impersonal verb constructions are those without a specific subject. In English, the grammatical subject of such constructions is usually 'it' as in 'it's raining', 'it takes four hours to get there', etc. In Portuguese, such verbs do not have an explicit subject and only occur in the third person singular or infinitive form. The following four verbs have important impersonal uses:

24.3.1 *haver*

When used impersonally, the verb **haver** can have the following meanings:

(i) 'There is/are'. In the spoken language, **haver** is usually replaced by **ter** in this meaning (see **24.3.2**):

> **Há várias formas de alcançar o mesmo objetivo.**
> There are several ways of achieving the same objective.
>
> **Se houver algum problema, ligue para este número.**
> If there is any problem, call this number.
>
> **É melhor haver um garçom para cada mesa.**
> It's better for there to be one waiter for each table.

▶ **38.1.2** (p. 337)

(ii) The present tense form **há** can also mean 'for', denoting a period of time that started in the past and continues in the present. This is combined with a present tense in Portuguese, although English requires the perfect (see **18.1.1**(ii)). The verb **fazer** can also be used with this meaning – see below:

> **Moramos no Rio há cinco anos. / Há cinco anos que moramos no Rio.**
> We've been living in Rio for five years.

▶ **69.4.1** (p. 503); **69.4.3** (p. 504)

(iii) The imperfect form **havia** combines with an imperfect tense[2] to render the English pluperfect (see **18.1.2**):

> **Naquela altura, morávamos no Rio havia cinco anos.**
> At that point, we had been living in Rio for five years.

▶ **71.12** (p. 518)

NOTE   2   However, this rule is only observed in formal writing. In speech, **há** is used instead, e.g. **morávamos no Rio há cinco anos**.

(iv)   With a past tense verb, the meaning of **há** is 'ago'[3]:

> **Eles mudaram para os EUA há seis meses.**
> They moved to the USA six months ago.

> **A empresa foi fundada há meio século.**
> The company was founded half a century ago.

> **Você lembra o que estava fazendo há exatos cinco anos?**
> Do you remember what you were doing exactly five years ago?

▶ **71.2** (p. 512)

NOTE   3   Another way of expressing 'ago' is with the word **atrás** 'back': **seis meses atrás** 'six months ago/back'. Very often in speech and occasionally in writing, both **há** and **atrás** are used: **há seis meses atrás**. Though extremely common, this construction is frowned upon as pleonastic by grammarians.

(v)   In the written language, **havia** is used when the point of reference is already in the past[4]:

> **A casa tinha sido destruída por um incêndio havia três meses.**
> The house had been destroyed by a fire three months earlier.

NOTE   4   In the spoken language, the present tense **há** is often used, or **antes** 'before' placed after the time expression, e.g. **três meses antes**.

24.3.2   *ter*

In the spoken language, **ter** is used instead of **haver** to mean 'there is/are':

> **Vai ter churrasco no domingo.**
> There's going to be a barbecue on Sunday.

> **Tem leite na geladeira.**
> There's milk in the fridge.

> **Tinha uma viatura da polícia parada na frente da casa deles.**
> There was a police car stopped outside their house.

▶ **38.1.1** (p. 336)

24.3.3   *fazer*

The verb **fazer** is used impersonally as follows:

(i)   To mean 'for' as a less formal alternative to **haver** (see **24.3.1 (ii)** and **(iii)**):

> **Faz anos que eu não vejo a Patrícia.**
> I haven't seen Patricia for years. / It's been years since I saw Patricia.

> **Ele não dorme faz uma semana.**
> He hasn't slept for a week.

> **Fazia seis meses que eles não se falavam.**
> They hadn't spoken to each other for six months.

▶ **69.4.2** (p. 502); **71.12** (p. 518)

(ii)   In expressions to do with the weather and temperature:

> **Fez sol ontem.**
> It was sunny yesterday.

> **Não costuma fazer frio aqui.**
> It doesn't usually get cold here.

> **Amanhã vai fazer quarenta graus.**
> It's going to be forty degrees tomorrow.

24.3.4   *dar*

The verb **dar** is used impersonally with a number of different meanings, especially in the spoken language:

(i)   'to be possible', often followed by **para** + infinitive '(for sb) to do':

> **Amanhã não vai dar. Tenho compromisso.**
> Tomorrow's impossible. I've got an appointment.

> **Dá para você falar um pouco mais alto?**
> Could you speak up a bit?

> **Não deu para ver tudo em dois dias.**
> It wasn't possible to see everything in two days.

▶ **52.1.3** (p. 417); **53.1.3** (p. 421)

(ii)   'there is/are' in the sense of 'there occur(s)':

> **Se der algum problema, te aviso.**
> If there's any problem, I'll let you know.

> **Eu sabia que ela ia desistir, e não deu outra.**
> I knew she'd back out, and that's exactly what happened.

> **Deu zebra no jogo de ontem.**
> There was an upset in yesterday's game.

(iii)   'to be enough':

> **Coloquei duas xícaras de arroz. Você acha que dá para quatro pessoas?**
> I've put in two cupfuls or rice. Do you think that's enough for four people?

> **Com R$50,00 dá? – Dá sim.**[5]
> 'Is 50 reais enough?' – 'Yes, it is.'

(iv)   **dar tempo** 'to be time':

> **Você acha que vai dar tempo de fazer tudo?**
> Do you think there'll be time to do everything?

NOTE   5   The preposition **com** is frequently omitted in colloquial speech: **R$50,00 dá?**

Notes for Spanish speakers

Note that, after the verb **ir**, there is no intervening preposition before an infinitive, and there is a difference of meaning between **vir fazer** 'to come to/and do' and **vir a fazer** 'to end up doing, turn out to do'. To express physical ability to do something, Portuguese uses the modal **conseguir** rather than **poder**. The modal verb **dever** never takes a preposition before a following infinitive. The impersonal forms **há** and **havia**, from the verb **haver**, are used in expressions of time in preference to the more informal-sounding **faz** and **fazia**, from the verb **fazer**, while the equivalent of *hay* 'there is/are' is **há** in the written language and **tem** in speech. Note also the extremely common impersonal use of the verb **dar** to mean 'to be possible'.

25

Prepositions

25.1 Basic prepositions: *a, com, de, em, para, por*

▶ **39.3** (p. 343)

25.1.1 *a* 'to, at'

Remember that the preposition **a** combines with the definite article and the demonstratives **aquele(s)/aquela(s)** and **aquilo** to form the following contractions: **ao(s)**, **à(s)**, **àquele(s)/àquela(s)** and **àquilo** (see **4.1.3**, **8.2 (iii)** and **8.4.2**).

The main uses of the preposition **a** are as follows:

(i)   To introduce an indirect object:

> **Uma moradora mostrou aos repórteres os estragos causados pela chuva.**
> A local resident showed reporters the damage caused by the rain.

> **Se tiver alguma dúvida, pergunte a um funcionário.**
> If you have any queries, ask a member of staff.

NOTE | In informal spoken language, the preposition **para** is preferred in this usage.

(ii)   To indicate movement 'to':

> **Foram ao banco tirar dinheiro.**
> They went to the bank to get some money out.

> **O ministro será enviado a Washington.**
> The minister will be sent to Washington.

NOTE | In informal spoken language, the prepositions **para** and **em** are preferred in this usage.

(iii)   To indicate position 'at':

> **Estavam sentados à mesa.**
> They were sitting at the table.

> **O ônibus parou ao sinal fechado.**
> The bus stopped at the red light.

NOTE | In informal spoken language, the preposition **em** is preferred in this usage.

(iv)   To indicate 'at' with clock time and age – note the use of the definite article:

O show começa às 20h.
The concert starts at 8.00 p.m.

Ela ganhou sua primeira medalha aos 17 anos.
She won her first medal at 17.

(v)   To indicate 'in' with parts of the day – note the use of the definite article:

Você estuda à tarde?
Do you go to school in the afternoon?

(vi)   To indicate 'at' with prices, rates, speeds, etc.

postais a R$2,00 cada
postcards at R$2 each

O dólar está a R$3,50 hoje.
The dollar is at 3.50 reais today.

O caminhoneiro andava a 130 km/h.
The truck driver was going at 130 km/h.

(vii)   In expressions of distance, untranslated in English:

A cidade fica a 200 km da capital.
The town is 200 km from the capital.

Você está a que distância da praça?
How far are you from the square?

(viii)   In scores, 'to' or untranslated in British English:

O nosso time ganhou 3 a 0.
Our team won 3 (to) 0.

(ix)   Before an infinitive, it can have the sense of 'if':

A persistirem os sintomas, procure orientação médica.
If symptoms persist, seek medical advice.

A julgar pela cor avermelhada do céu, beirava umas seis horas.
Judging by the reddish colour of the sky, it was getting on for about six o' clock.

(x)   Note that the the contraction **ao** is used before an infinitive to mean '(up)on/when doing':

Ao entrarem na casa do suspeito, os policiais encontraram armas e drogas.
On entering the suspect's house, the police found guns and drugs.

os erros mais comuns que os brasileiros cometem ao falar inglês
the most common mistakes Brazilians make when speaking English.

(xi)   In a number of idiomatic expressions:

a lápis/tinta 'in pencil/ink'; **a pé/cavalo** 'on foot/horseback'; **à mão** 'by *or* to hand'; **dia a dia** 'day by day'; **pouco a pouco** 'little by little'; **frente a frente** 'face to face'; **daqui a uma semana/dois dias**, etc. 'in a week's/two days', etc. time'; **falar aos berros** 'to shout'; **aos prantos** 'in tears'; **à brasileira/francesa** 'Brazilian-/French-style', etc.

25.1.2 *com* 'with'

The main uses of the preposition **com** are as follows:

(i)   To indicate 'with', denoting accompaniment or instrument:

> **Quer ir com a gente?**
> Do you want to come with us?

> **Arrombaram a caixa com um pé de cabra.**
> They broke open the box with a crowbar.

(ii)   To denote accompanying circumstances, sometimes translated 'with':

> **Acordei com dor de cabeça.**
> I woke up with a headache.

> **Ela gosta de dormir com a luz acesa.**
> She likes to sleep with the light on.

> **Reduza a velocidade com chuva.**
> Reduce your speed in wet weather.

(iii)   To indicate 'to, towards, at' when referring to a person's attitude to someone or something:

> **Ela sempre foi muito simpática comigo.**
> She's always been very nice to me.

> **O que ele fez comigo não tem desculpa.**
> There's no excuse for what he did to me.

> **Ficamos chocados com a notícia.**
> We were shocked at the news.

25.1.3 *de* 'of, from'

Remember that the preposition **de** combines with the definite article and the demonstratives **este(s)/esta(s), esse(s)/essa(s), aquele(s)/aquela(s), isto, isso, aquilo** and the adverbs **aqui, aí** and **ali** to form the following contractions: **do(s), da(s), deste(s)/desta(s), desse(s)/ dessa(s), daquele(s)/daquela(s), disto, disso, daquilo, daqui, daí, dali** (see **4.1.3**, **8.2 (ii)**, **8.4.2** and **8.5.1 (i)**).

The main uses of the preposition **de** are as follows:

(i)   It is used for 'of' in all senses:

> **a costa do Brasil**
> the coast of Brazil

> **um dos melhores romances dos últimos anos**
> one of the best novels of recent years

> **um pedaço de bolo e um copo de leite**
> a piece of cake and a glass of milk.

(ii)   The English genitive ('s) must be rendered using **de** in Portuguese:

> **o livro do Ricardo**
> Ricardo's book

duas semanas de férias
two weeks' holiday/vacation

o jornal de ontem
yesterday's newspaper

Essas roupas são das crianças.
Those clothes are the children's. / Those clothes belong to the children.

(iii) The preposition **de** is also used to indicate other attributes, such as nature, purpose, material, age, size, price, etc.:

um filme de ação
an action movie

uma máquina de lavar roupa
a washing machine

uma blusa de algodão
a cotton blouse

uma menina de 15 anos
a 15-year-old girl

um homem de mais de dois metros de altura
a man more than two metres tall

um apartamento de três quartos
a three-bedroom apartment.

(iv) It is also used for 'from' in all senses:

Ele é da Bahia.
He's from Bahia.

O banco abre das 10h às 16h.
The bank opens from 10 a.m. to 4 p.m.

(v) It is used for 'out of' and 'off':

Ela tirou uma caneta da bolsa.
She took a pen out of her bag.

Ele caiu da moto e quebrou a perna.
He fell off his motorbike and broke his leg.

(vi) It also means 'by' with means of transport:

Fica a dez minutos de táxi.
It's ten minutes away by taxi.

Vamos de ônibus ou de avião?
Shall we go by bus or by air?

(vii) It is also used for 'by' when referring to authorship:

uma peça de Shakespeare
a play by Shakespeare / a Shakespeare play

Essa música não é do Caetano?
Isn't this song by Caetano Veloso?

(viii) It is used for 'with' or 'in' when describing a person's appearance or dress:

um homem de bigode
a man with a moustache

a mulher de chapéu
the woman in the hat

a moça de preto
the girl in black

Você fica mais jovem de cabelo curto.
You look younger with short hair.

Tem que ir de terno e gravata?
Do we have to go in a suit and tie?

(ix)   It is used for 'in', 'on', etc. after a superlative:

a maior fábrica da América Latina
the biggest factory in Latin America

a melhor faixa do álbum
the best track on the album.

(x)   It is used for 'in' with parts of the day, as a less common alternative to **a**:[1]

de manhã 'in the morning'; **de tarde** 'in the afternoon'; **de noite** 'at night'

(xi)   It is used for 'with, for', referring to the cause:

Eles pulavam de alegria.
They were jumping for joy.

Ele está tremendo de frio.
He's shivering with cold.

(xii)   Before an infinitive it can mean 'from doing' indicating a cause:

Fiquei com dor de barriga de tanto rir.
I got stomach ache from laughing so much.

(xiii)   It can have a partitive meaning with no direct equivalent in English:

Os medicos fizeram de tudo para salvar o paciente.
The doctors did all they could to save the patient.

Chega de lamúrias! Temos que reagir!
Enough whining! We have to fight back!

(xiv)   It is also used in certain idiomatic expressions:

de dia 'in/during the day(time)'; **de frente/costas para** 'facing/with your back to'; **de propósito** 'on purpose'; **de cabeça para baixo** 'upside down', etc.

NOTE   1   'in the morning' is always with **de**: **de manhã**, but with **tarde** and **noite** either preposition can be used.

25.1.4   *em* 'in, at, on'

Remember that the preposition **em** combines with the definite and indefinite articles and the demonstratives **este(s)/esta(s)**, **esse(s)/essa(s)**, **aquele(s)/aquela(s)**, **isto**, **isso**, **aquilo** to form the following contractions: **no(s)**, **na(s)**, **num**, **nuns**, **numa(s)**, **neste(s)/nesta(s)**, nesse(s)/nessa(s), naquele(s)/naquela(s), nisto, nisso, naquilo (see **4.1.3**, **4.2.2**, **8.2 (ii)** and **8.4.2**).

The main uses of the preposition **em** are as follows:

(i) As an all-purpose preposition of location when the exact position is not further specified, **em** can translate as 'in', 'at' or 'on':

Na Itália comem muita massa.
In Italy they eat a lot of pasta.

Ela leciona na Universidade Federal.
She teaches at the Federal University.

O jantar está na mesa.
Dinner is on the table.

(ii) As a preposition of movement, **em** translates 'into, onto' in all registers, but in the spoken language only it is also used to mean 'to':

Ela subiu na bicicleta e saiu pedalando.
She got onto her bike and rode off.

Quantas vezes por semana você vai na academia? (*spoken*)
How many times a week do you go to the gym?

(iii) In colloquial speech, **no/na** can be used with personal names or the names of professions to mean 'at/to . . .'s (house)', 'at/to the . . .':

Vou dormir na Júlia hoje à noite.
I'm going to sleep at Julia's tonight.

Ele vai no dentista amanhã.
He's going to the dentist('s) tomorrow.

(iv) The preposition **em** is also used for 'in' with years, months and seasons:

em 2010
in 2010

O ano letivo começa em março.
The school year starts in March.

Faz muito calor no verão.
It's very hot in (the) summer.

(v) It is used for 'on' with days of the week[2] and dates:

Ela volta na sexta.
She'll be back on Friday.

nos sábados
on Saturdays

Ele nasceu no dia 12 de fevereiro.
He was born on February 12th.

NOTE   2   In more formal speech and writing, the preposition **a** may be used with days of the week when the plural is used to denote a regular occurrence, e.g. **Ele trabalha aos sábados.** 'He works on Saturdays.' In the everyday speech of some regions of Brazil, the preposition **de** is used with the name of the day in the singular to convey this meaning, e.g. **Ele trabalha de sábado.** As in English, days of the week in the singular are often used adverbially without a preposition in the spoken language, e.g. **Ela volta sexta.** 'She'll be back Friday.'

(vi) It is also used for 'by' when referring to the margin of increase or decrease:

> **O preço do petróleo aumentou em 50% nos últimos seis meses.**
> The price of oil has increased by 50 per cent in the last six months.

(vii) It introduces an indirect object which is affected physically or metaphorically by the action of the verb:

> **Ela deu um beijo no filho.**
> She gave her son a kiss.

> **Os brasileiros deram uma surra no time adversário.**
> The Brazilians thrashed the opposing team.

(viii) It is used before an infinitive after expressions of emotion:

> **Muito prazer em conhecê-la!**
> Delighted to meet you!

> **Fiquei triste em saber que você está passando por tantas dificuldades**.
> I was sad to hear that you're going through such a hard time.

25.1.5 *para* 'for, to'

Remember that, in colloquial speech, the preposition **para** is pronounced /pra/[3] and is run together with the definite articles **o(s)** and **a(s)** as /pru(s)/ and /pra(s)/ (see **4.1.3**).

The main uses of the preposition **para** are as follows:

(i) It means 'for' when referring to beneficiary, purpose, time limit and frame of reference:

> **Preciso comprar um presente para minha mãe.**
> I need to buy a present for my mother.

> **A maior parte da safra é para exportação.**
> Most of the crop is for export.

> **Esse trabalho é para amanhã.**
> This assignment is for tomorrow.

> **Ele é muito alto para a idade dele.**
> He's very tall for his age.

(ii) It also means 'to' when referring to permanent destination:

> **Mudaram para São Paulo.**
> They moved to São Paulo.

> **Ela vai embora para Londres.**
> She's leaving for London.

(iii) In informal spoken language, **para** is used for 'to' when referring to a temporary destination[4] or introducing an indirect object (in place of the more formal **a**):

NOTES

3 Although considered non-standard, the spelling **pra** is often seen in advertisements, informal writing and increasingly in literature.

4 In the spoken language, **para** and **em** are used more or less interchangeably to mean 'to'. Before a place name, **para** is more usual, e.g. **Vamos para Brasília amanhã.** 'We're going to Brasilia tomorrow.', though **em** is also heard.

Eles foram para o shopping. (*spoken*, **para** + **o** *pronounced* /pru/)
They went to the mall.

Pergunta para a sua irmã se ela quer ir junto. (*spoken*, **para** + **a** = /pra/)
Ask your sister if she wants to come along.

Ela contou tudo para a polícia. (*spoken*, **para** + **a** = /pra/)
She told the police everything.

(iii)   Before an infinitive, **para** is used to mean '(in order) to'. Before a personal infinitive, it can also translate 'so (that)':

O Jorge ligou para a Sandra para dar uma satisfação.
Jorge called Sandra to explain himself.

O motorista parou o ônibus para a gente descer.
The driver stopped the bus for us to get off/so we could get off.

Desci a escada de mansinho para ninguém me ouvir.
I crept down the stairs so no one would hear me.

(iv)   It is also used in some idiomatic expressions:

para mim 'in my opinion, for me'; **não é para menos** 'it's not surprising'; **para tanto** 'for that purpose', 'to that end'; **não é para tanto** 'there's no need (for that)', 'it's not such a big deal'; **para quê?** what for?, etc.

25.1.6   *por* 'by, for, around'

Remember that the preposition **por** combines with the definite article to form the following contractions: **pelo(s)**, **pela(s)** (see **4.1.3**).

The main uses of the preposition **por** are as follows:

(i)   It is used for 'by' when introducing the agent of a passive verb, and for the means or criterion by which something is done, dimensions and the factor in multiplication and division:

O quadro foi pintado por um menino de oito anos.
The picture was painted by an eight-year-old boy.

Vou te mandar as fotos por e-mail.
I'll send you the photos by e-mail.

O material de reciclagem é separado por tamanho.
The recycling material is sorted by size.

A mesa tem três metros de comprimento por dois de largura.
The table is three metres long by two metres wide.

Temos que dividir o total por quatro.
We have to divide the total by four.

(ii)   It is also used for 'by' when indicating the part held on to:

Ele me puxou pelo braço.
He pulled me by the arm.

Segure a corda pelas pontas.
Hold the rope by the ends.

(iii)   It means 'for' when indicating an exchange or substitution, price, reason, cause and past or future periods of time:

> **Quero trocar essa camiseta por uma branca.**
> I want to exchange this T-shirt for a white one.

> **O meu irmão pode assinar por mim?**
> Can my brother sign for me? (*i.e. on my behalf*)

> **Pagaram cinco milhões pela casa.**
> They paid five million for the house.

> **Ele foi preso por excesso de velocidade.**
> He was arrested for speeding.

> **Temos que lutar pelos nossos direitos.**
> We must fight for our rights.

> **Ele joga pelo Lakers.**
> He plays for the Lakers.

> **Ela vai estudar na França por seis meses.**
> She's going to study in France for six months.

(iv)   It is used for 'because of', 'over' or 'out of' when indicating a cause:

> **Eles brigaram por dinheiro.**
> They argued over money.

> **Ela matou o marido por ciúmes.**
> She killed her husband out of jealousy.

(v)   It also means 'per', 'a(n)' when indicating a rate:

> **cem reais por pessoa**
> one hundred reais per person

> **duas vezes por semana**
> twice a week.

(vi)   It means 'around' when indicating location or movement around a place:

> **Tem uma agência do correio por aqui?**
> Is there a post office around here?

> **Ele andava pelo escritório, cumprimentando a todos.**
> He would go around the office saying hello to everyone.

(vii)   Before an infinitive, **por** can mean 'because'. English requires a clause in such cases:

> **Ela enfrenta mais resistência por ser mulher.**
> She faces more resistance because she's a woman.

> **Ela cansou do marido por ele não ajudar em casa.**
> She got fed up with her husband because he didn't help out around the house.

(viii)   It is also used in some idiomatic expressions:

> **por mim** 'as far as I'm concerned'; **por mim, tudo bem** 'it's fine by me'; **vai por mim** 'take it from me', 'mark my words'; **por aqui/ali** 'this/that way'; **por onde?** 'which way?'; **por isso** 'so', 'that's why'; **por isso mesmo** 'for that very reason'; **por completo** 'completely'; **por extenso** 'in full'; **por ordem alfabética** 'in alphabetical order'; **por sorte** 'luckily'; **pelo menos** 'at least', etc.

25.2 Other simple (one-word) prepositions

ante (*formal*) 'faced with', 'as against':

> **ante a ameaça de perderem clientes**
> faced with the threat of losing clients

> **Foram registradas 15 ocorrências em julho, ante 25 registradas no mesmo mês do ano passado.**
> Fifteen incidents were recorded in July, as against 25 in the same month last year.

após (*written*) 'after':

> **após a morte do presidente**
> after the president's death

> **dia após dia**
> day after day.

até 'until, by, as far as, up to, to':

> **Eles vão ficar até amanhã.**
> They're staying until tomorrow.

> **Temos que terminar até sábado.**
> We've got to finish by Saturday.

> **Pego um ônibus até Sorocaba e depois um táxi.**
> I take a bus as far as Sorocaba and then a taxi.

> **Podem custar até mil reais.**
> They can cost up to a thousand reais.

> **Não tivemos nenhum problema até agora.**
> We haven't had any problems up to now/so far.

conforme 'according to':

> **conforme o prometido**
> as promised. (= *according to what was promised*)

contra 'against' (*all senses*):

> **Votaram contra a proposta.**
> They voted against the proposal.

> **o jogo contra a Itália**
> the game against Italy

> **Coloquei a escada contra a parede.**
> I put the ladder up against the wall.

desde 'since', '(starting/ranging) from':

> **Ele trabalha aqui desde 1975.** (*NB: present tense*)
> He's been working here since 1975.

> **A loja vende de tudo, desde clipes até pianos de cauda.**
> The shop sells everything, from paperclips to grand pianos.

durante 'during', 'for':

> **durante a semana**
> during the week

> **Tivemos que ficar em pé durante quatro horas.**
> We had to stand for four hours.

entre 'between, among':

> **entre os melhores restaurantes de São Paulo**
> among the best restaurants in São Paulo

> **entre 7h e meia-noite**
> between 7.00 a.m. and midnight

> **Qual a relação entre eles?**
> What's the relationship between them?

exceto 'except':

> **a Grã-Bretanha, exceto a Irlanda do Norte**
> Great Britain, except Northern Ireland.

fora 'apart from':

> **Todo mundo concordou, fora o Sérgio.**
> Everyone agreed, apart from Sergio.

mediante (*formal*) 'through, by means of':

> **O candidato pode se inscrever mediante pagamento de uma taxa de R$50,00.**
> Candidates can register by paying a R$50 fee.

perante (*formal*) 'before, in the eyes of';

> **igualdade perante a lei**
> equality before the law

> **o desgaste do governo perante a opinião pública**
> the damage to the government in the eyes of public opinion.

salvo (*formal*) 'save, barring':

> **Salvo mudança de última hora, o show será aberto por Madonna.**
> Barring a last-minute change, the show will be opened by Madonna.

segundo 'according to':

> **segundo as últimas previsões**
> according to the latest predictions.

sem 'without, with no':

> **Saí de casa sem dinheiro.**
> I left home with no money/without any money.

sob 'under, beneath' (*mainly figurative uses*), 'amid':

> **O bar está sob nova direção.**
> The bar is under new management.

> **Sob aplausos, o diretor entrou no palco.**
> Amid applause, the director came out on stage.

sobre 'on, over' (*physical location*), 'about, on':

> **Havia uma colcha vermelha sobre a cama.**
> There was a red bedspread on the bed.

> **um documentário sobre tartarugas**
> a documentary about/on turtles

> **Eles ganham comissão sobre as vendas.**
> They earn commission on sales.

visto (*formal*) 'in view of, considering':

> **visto a representatividade do Brasil no Mercosur**
> in view of Brazil's weight within Mercosur.

25.3 Compound prepositions of place

▶ **39.3** (p. 343)

abaixo de 'below' (*location or degree*):

> **abaixo da superfície do mar**
> below the surface of the sea

> **bem abaixo da média**
> well below average.

acima de 'above' (*location or degree*):

> **uma pessoa acima de qualquer suspeita**
> a person above all suspicion

> **Ele tinha um corte acima do olho esquerdo.**
> He had a cut above his left eye.

além de 'beyond', 'apart from, in addition to':

> **além do horizonte**
> beyond the horizon

> **Além de tocar piano, ela fala vários idiomas.**
> In addition to playing the piano, she speaks several languages.

atrás de 'behind', 'after':

> **O menino se escondeu atrás da porta.**
> The little boy hid behind the door.

> **A polícia está atrás dela.**
> The police are after her.

através de 'across, through', 'through (*a person*)':

> **a transmissão de sinais através do espaço**
> the transmission of signals through space

> **Ele conseguiu o emprego através de um amigo.**
> He got the job through a friend.

debaixo de (*written*) 'under, beneath':

> **debaixo da cama**
> under the bed.

defronte a (*formal/literary*) 'before, in front of':

> **As pessoas passavam defronte ao caixão.**
> The people filed past before the coffin.

dentro de 'inside, within' (*space or time*):

> **O caixa eletrônico fica dentro do banco.**
> The ATM machine is inside the bank.

> **O vale-desconto tem que ser usado dentro de seis meses.**
> The discount voucher has to be used within six months.

embaixo de 'under, underneath':

> **embaixo da mesa**
> under the table.

em cima de 'on, on top of':

> **em cima da geladeira**
> on top of the fridge.

em frente de/a (also **na frente de/a**) 'in front of':

> **Conseguimos uma vaga em frente ao restaurante.**
> We found a parking place in front of the restaurant.

NOTE | 'in front of me/you/us' is translated **na minha/sua/nossa frente**.

---

em meio a 'amid, in the midst of' (*literal and figurative*):

> **O helicóptero pousou em meio a uma nuvem de poeira.**
> The helicopter landed amid a cloud of dust.

> **O ministro renunciou em meio a boatos de que teria aceito propinas.**
> The minister resigned amid rumours that he had taken bribes.

fora de 'outside':

> **Ele mora fora da cidade.**
> He lives outside the city.

longe de 'a long way from, far from' (*literal and figurative*):

> **longe de mim criticar os outros, mas ...**
> far be it from me to criticize other people, but ...

> **A sua casa fica longe da estação de metrô?**
> Is your house far from the subway station?

perto de 'near, close to' (*literal and figurative*):

> **O banco é perto da igreja.**
> The bank is near the church.

> **A empresa tem perto de 20 mil funcionários.**
> The company has close to 20,000 employees.

por baixo de 'under' (*suggesting movement or a wide expanse*):

> **Os canos passam por baixo do piso.**
> The pipes run under the floor.

por cima de 'over' (*suggesting movement or a wide expanse*):

> **O atacante chutou por cima da trave.**
> The striker's shot went over the crossbar.

por trás de 'behind' (*suggesting movement, also figurative*):

> **A ferrovia passa por trás das casas.**
> The railway runs along behind the houses.

> **Ninguém sabe quem está por trás dos atentados.**
> No one knows who is behind the attacks.

25.4 Compound prepositions of time

antes de 'before':

> **antes do meio-dia**
> before midday.

depois de 'after':

> **depois do almoço**
> after lunch.

quando de (*written*) 'at the time of':

> **Ela tinha dez anos quando da queda do Muro de Berlim.**
> She was ten years old at the time of the fall of the Berlin Wall.

25.5 Other compound prepositions

acerca de (*formal*) 'about, concerning':

> **informações acerca do andamento do plano**
> information about the progress of the plan.

a favor de 'in favour of':

> **Alguns brasileiros são a favor da pena de morte.**
> Some Brazilians are in favour of the death penalty.

ao invés de 'instead of':

> **Ao invés de melhorar, o tempo só piorava.**
> Instead of improving, the weather just kept getting worse.

a par de 'up to date with, aware of', 'in addition to, alongside' (*formal*):

> **O ministro mantinha o presidente a par dos acontecimentos.**
> The minister kept the president up to date with developments.

> **A par de intercâmbios culturais, discutiram assuntos comerciais.**
> In addition to cultural exchanges, they discussed trade matters.

apesar de 'despite, in spite of':

> **Ele conseguiu, apesar das dificuldades.**
> He succeeded, despite the difficulties.

▶ **51.1.6** (p. 413)

a respeito de 'about, concerning':

> **Qual a sua opinião a respeito dessa questão?**
> What is your opinion concerning this issue?

de acordo com 'according to':

> **de acordo com as últimas informações**
> according to the latest information.

devido a 'due to, owing to':

> **A conta chegou atrasada devido à greve dos correios.**
> The bill arrived late due to the postal strike.

diante de 'in the face of, faced with':

> **O governo precisa tomar uma atitude diante dessa situação.**
> The government must take action in the face of this situation.

em direção a 'towards':

> **Ela começou a andar em direção à porta.**
> She started to walk towards the door.

em nome de 'on behalf of':

> **Em nome de todos, quero agradecer ao nosso anfitrião.**
> On behalf of everyone, I would like to thank our host.

em prol de 'in aid of, in the interests of':

> **O cantor lançou uma campanha em prol de crianças carentes.**
> The singer launched a campaign in aid of children in need.

em relação a 'in relation to, regarding':

> **Qual é a sua opinião em relação a esses acontecimentos?**
> What is your opinion regarding these events?

em vez de 'instead of':

> **Podemos nos encontrar na quinta em vez de quarta?**
> Can we meet on Thursday instead of Wednesday?

em virtude de (*formal*) 'by virtue of, in view of':

> **Em virtude do grande sucesso da peça, a atriz alcançou a fama nacional.**
> By virtue of the great success of the play, the actress achieved nationwide fame.

graças a 'thanks to':

> **A empresa detém 60% do mercado, graças ao sucesso desta marca.**
> The company has a 60 per cent market share thanks to the success of this brand.

junto a (*formal*) 'with, from':

> **É preciso solicitar um alvará junto à Prefeitura.**
> It is necessary to apply for a permit from City Hall.

para com (*written*) 'towards':

> **a intolerância para com os outros**
> intolerance towards others.

por causa de 'because of':

> **O aeroporto foi fechado por causa do mau tempo.**
> The airport was closed because of the bad weather.

NOTE | 'because of me/you/us' translates as **por minha/sua/nossa causa**.

---

por conta de 'on account of':

> **por conta da greve**
> on account of the strike

por meio de 'through, by means of':

> **por meio desta** (*in formal letter*)
> herewith

> **Por meio desse processo, é possível conservar os alimentos por mais tempo.**
> By means of this process, it is possible to keep foods for longer.

Notes for Spanish speakers

Though the preposition **a** is preferred in written style, **para** is used in the spoken language to mean 'to' before an indirect object or destination. Similarly, the spoken language replaces locative uses of **a** with **em** (cf. **sentado à mesa** *written* vs. **sentado na mesa** *spoken*), and the latter is also used as a preposition of destination in speech (cf. **fomos ao cinema** *written* vs. **fomos no cinema** *spoken*). The preposition **em** is also used to introduce the indirect object when the action of the verb affects the indirect object physically or metaphorically (e.g. **ele deu um soco no policial** 'he punched the police officer', **o pai passou um sermão no meu irmão** 'Dad gave my brother a lecture', etc.).

26

Conjunctions

26.1 Coordinating conjunctions

26.1.1 Additive conjunctions

e 'and':

> **mãe e filha**
> mother and daughter

> **Ele tentou e conseguiu.**
> He tried and succeeded.

não só . . . mas também *or* **ainda, não só . . . senão também, não só . . . como também** 'not only . . . (but) also':

> **Ela não só chegou atrasada, mas ainda me pediu para pagar o táxi.**
> She not only arrived late, she also asked me to pay her taxi fare.

nem 'nor, or' (*after a negative*):

> **Ele não é inteligente, nem bonito.**
> He's not clever, or good-looking.

nem . . . nem 'neither . . . nor', 'not . . . either . . . or':

> **Não vou ter tempo, nem nesse fim de semana nem no outro.**
> I won't have time, either this weekend or next.

tanto . . . como 'both . . . and':

> **tanto em português como em espanhol**
> in both Portuguese and Spanish.

26.1.2 Alternative conjunctions

ou 'or':

> **Você prefere chá ou café?**
> Would you rather have tea or coffee?

ou . . . ou 'either . . . or':

> **Podemos nos encontrar ou na sexta ou no sábado.**
> We can meet either on Friday or on Saturday.

26.1.3 | Adversative conjunctions

mas 'but':

> **Acho que não vou ganhar, mas vou tentar.**
> I don't think I'll win, but I'll try.

▶ **51.1.1** (p. 411)

mas sim 'but' (*signalling a complete contrast after a negative*):

> **Isso não é um luxo, mas sim uma necessidade.**
> This is not a luxury, but a necessity.

mesmo assim 'even so':

> **A temperatura deve cair. Mesmo assim, não há previsão de chuva.**
> The temperature is expected to drop. Even so, no rain is forecast.

porém (*written*) 'but, yet, however':

> **Porém, a realidade é outra.**
> Yet the reality is different.

▶ **51.1.2** (p. 411)

Other adversative conjunctions used in more formal written language are: **contudo**, **entretanto**, **no entanto** and **todavia**, all meaning 'however', and **não obstante** 'nevertheless, notwithstanding'.

▶ **51.1.3** (p. 412)

26.1.4 | Conclusive conjunctions

aí (*spoken*) 'so, so then':

> **Ela não estava, aí eu deixei um recado.**
> She wasn't in, so I left a message.

daí 'so, so then'; 'hence' (*in more formal writing*):

> **E daí?**
> So what?

> **A dengue pode matar. Daí a importância das medidas de prevenção.**
> Dengue fever can kill. Hence the importance of preventive measures.

então 'so, then':

> **Temos muito que fazer, então é melhor a gente começar logo.**
> We've got a lot to do, so we'd best get started right away.

por isso (que) 'so, for this reason, that is why':

> **Eu quase nunca uso meu carro. Por isso decidi vendê-lo.**
> I hardly ever use my car. That's why I've decided to sell it.

portanto (*mostly written*) 'so, therefore':

> **Existem cobras venenosas nesta região, portanto é preciso tomar cuidado.**
> There are poisonous snakes in this region, so care should be taken.

Other conclusive conjunctions are: **consequentemente**, **por conseguinte** (*formal*) 'consequently'.

26.2 Subordinating conjunctions

26.2.1 Complementizers

26.2.1.1 *que* 'that'

The word **que** 'that' introduces an indirect statement, in some cases followed by a subjunctive verb (see **Chapter 20**). Note that the conjunction 'that' is frequently omitted in English, whereas **que** is obligatory in Portuguese:[1]

> **Eu acho que vai chover.**
> I think it's going to rain.

> **É importante que ela saiba a verdade.**
> It is important she (should) know the truth.

The **que** clause is often linked to the main clause with a preposition when the introductory element requires one and the appropriate translation in English is often 'the fact that':

> **Tenho certeza de que ele disse segunda-feira.**
> I'm sure he said Monday.

> **O médico insistiu em que a culpa não era do hospital.**
> The doctor insisted (on the fact) that it was not the hospital's fault.

> **Estou acostumado a que as pessoas olhem para mim na rua.**
> I'm used to the fact that people look at me in the street.

The conjunction **que** can also be followed by **sim** and **não** to mean 'so' or 'not', or to abbreviate a positive or negative indirect statement:

> **Espero que sim.**
> I hope so.

> **Acho que não.**
> I don't think so. / I think not.

> **Eu perguntei se era para levar roupa de cama, e ela falou que sim.**
> I asked if we should take bedding, and she said yes. / . . . she said we should.

> **Você acha que ele vai ligar? Eu aposto que não.**
> Do you think he'll call? I bet he won't.

NOTE 1   In fact, there are cases where omitting **que** is permissible to avoid repetition of the conjunction and in certain fixed turns of phrase, but such cases are extremely rare and limited to the most formal registers.

26.2.1.2 *se* **'if, whether'**

The word **se** 'if, whether' introduces an indirect question:

> **Não sabemos se ele vai ou não voltar.** (*notice placement of* **ou não**)
> We don't know whether he's coming back or not.

> **Vou perguntar ao Eduardo se ele quer ir.**
> I'll ask Eduardo if he wants to go.

26.2.2 ## Causal conjunctions

▶ **42.2** (p. 361)

como 'as, since':

> **Como eles não têm carro, fiquei de levá-los no meu.**
> As they don't have a car, I said I'd take them in mine.

já que 'since':

> **Já que você não tem nada que fazer, vem me ajudar aqui.**
> Since you don't have anything to do, come over here and help me.

na medida em que 'inasmuch as':

> **A política fracassou na medida em que não resolveu os problemas.**
> The policy failed inasmuch as it did not solve the problems.

pois 'as, for, because':

> **Os médicos não querem trabalhar em hospitais públicos, pois os salários são muito baixos.**
> Doctors do not want to work in public hospitals as salaries are very low.

porque 'because':

> **Desistimos de ir porque ia ficar muito caro.**
> We decided not to go because it was going to be too expensive.

que 'as'. This is a distinct usage from that of the subordinating **que** described above and is only really used in the spoken language to signal a vague causal connection. It can sometimes mean 'as' or 'while', but often it has no equivalent in English:

> **Leva um guarda-chuva que é capaz de chover.**
> Take an umbrella as it might rain.

> **Você fica aqui que eu vou ali no caixa eletrônico.**
> You stay here while I go over there to the ATM.

> **Não vai ter aula amanhã que o professor falou.**
> There's no class tomorrow, the teacher said so.

uma vez que (*written*) 'since, given that':[2]

> **A situação se agrava uma vez que nenhuma das partes está disposta a recuar.**
> The situation is getting worse given that neither side is prepared to back down.

NOTE 2 When followed by the subjunctive, **uma vez que** means 'provided that'.

Other causal conjunctions used in writing are: **dado que** 'given that', **visto que** 'seeing that, in view of the fact that', **posto que** 'given the fact that, considering that'.

Temporal conjunctions

The following temporal conjunctions require the future or imperfect subjunctive when the action of the temporal clause has not yet happened at the time of the main action, and the indicative when it has:

assim que, **logo que** 'as soon as':

> **Pode pedir para ele me ligar assim que chegar?**
> Can you ask him to call me as soon as he gets in?

> **Ele me ligou assim que chegou.**
> He called me as soon as he got in.

depois que 'after':

> **O comitê se reunirá depois que o presidente voltar de viagem.**
> The committee will meet after the chairman gets back from his trip.

> **Depois que construíram o prédio em frente, não tínhamos mais vista.**
> After they built the building opposite, we no longer had a view.

enquanto 'while', 'as long as':

> **O piloto diz que, enquanto estiver motivado, continuará na Fórmula 1.**
> The driver says that, as long as he's motivated, he'll stay in Formula 1.

> **As mulheres ficaram vendo TV enquanto os homens preparavam o jantar.**
> The women sat watching TV while the men fixed dinner.

quando 'when':

> **Ela disse que ia me avisar quando chegasse.**
> She said she would let me know when she arrived.

> **Quando alguém entra, toca um sino.**
> When someone comes in, a bell rings.

sempre que 'whenever':

> **Eu vou estar do seu lado sempre que você precisar de mim.**
> I will stand by you whenever you need me.

> **Ele me ajuda sempre que eu preciso.**
> He helps me whenever I need it.

The same applies to expressions such as **toda vez que** 'every time (that)', **cada vez que** 'each/every time (that)', **a primeira/segunda**, etc.[3] / **próxima/última vez que** 'the first/second, etc./next/last time (that)':

> **Toda vez que arranco, o carro morre.**
> Every time I move off, the car stalls.

NOTE   3   In expressions such as 'It's the second time I've seen this film', 'This is the first time I've been to Brazil', Portuguese uses the present tense in place of the English perfect: **É a segunda vez que vejo esse filme. É a primeira vez que venho ao Brasil.**

A próxima vez que ele fizer isso, vou chamar a polícia.
Next time he does that, I'm going to call the police.

antes que 'before' is always followed by the present or imperfect subjunctive:

Tivemos que fazer várias concessões antes que o acordo fosse firmado.
We had to make various concessions before the agreement was signed.

até que 'until' is followed by the present or imperfect subjunctive when the action of the 'until' clause is not yet actual fact, and by the indicative when it is:

Ela tinha que cuidar do irmão até que a mãe voltasse do trabalho.
She had to look after her brother until her mother got back from work.
(*i.e. she had been instructed to, or she used to have to, as long as her mother was not back*)

Ela teve que cuidar do irmão até que a mãe voltou do trabalho.
She had to look after her brother until her mother got back from work.
(*i.e. on that occasion she looked after him until her mother actually got home*)

desde que 'since'[4] is followed by the preterite referring to an action that occurred at a single point in the past, and by the present or imperfect indicative referring to an action that started in the past and continues at the time of speaking:

Ela mora sozinha, desde que ficou viúva em 2002.
She has been living alone since she was widowed in 2002.

Desde que estuda na faculdade, o inglês dele vem melhorando.
Since he's been studying at university, his English has been improving.

agora que 'now (that)':

Agora que ele aprendeu a nadar, vai à piscina todos os dias.
Now he's learnt to swim, he goes to the pool every day.

mal 'no sooner . . . than', 'hardly . . . when':

Mal sentamos para jantar, o telefone tocou.
No sooner had we sat down to dinner than the phone rang.

ora . . . ora (*literary*) 'now . . . now', 'one moment . . . , the next . . .', 'sometimes . . . sometimes':

A peça ora faz rir, ora comove.
The play makes you laugh one moment and moves you the next.

NOTE   4   **desde que** meaning 'as long as, provided that' is followed by the subjunctive.

Concessive conjunctions

ainda que 'even if, even though', followed by the present/imperfect subjunctive:

Ainda que a história não seja muito original, o filme é divertido.
Even though the story is not very original, the film is entertaining.

apesar de que 'despite the fact that', followed by the indicative:

> **Os negócios vão bem, apesar de que o país está em plena recessão.**
> Business is going well, despite the fact that the country is in the middle of a recession.

▶ **51.1.6** (p. 413)

embora 'although', followed by the present/imperfect subjunctive:

> **Estamos otimistas, embora ainda haja vários obstáculos a superar.**
> We are optimistic, although there are still a number of obstacles to overcome.

▶ **51.1.4** (p. 412)

por mais que 'as much as', **por ... que** '. . . as it may', followed by the present/imperfect subjunctive:

> **Por mais que eu goste dele, não quero começar um namoro.**
> As much as I like him, I don't want to start a relationship.

> **Por incrível que pareça, ela sobreviveu.**
> Incredible as it may seem, she survived.

quer ... quer, **quer ... ou** 'whether ... or ...', followed by the present/imperfect subjunctive:

> **Quer queira ou não, ela vai ter que arrumar emprego.**
> Whether she likes it or not, she'll have to find a job.

se bem que 'even though, though', followed by the indicative:

> **O aluguel é caro, se bem que é razoável para aquele bairro.**
> The rent is expensive, though it's reasonable for that neighbourhood.

In formal written language, **se bem que** may also be followed by the subjunctive.

▶ **51.1.7** (p. 413)

seja ... seja ... 'be it ... or', 'whether (it be) ... or':

> **O pagamento tem que ser à vista, seja em reais, seja em dólares.**
> Payment must be in full, whether in reais or dollars.

sem que 'without', followed by the present/imperfect subjunctive:

> **Seria impossível eles saírem sem que ninguém os visse.**
> It would be impossible for them to get out without anyone seeing them.

só que 'only, except (that)', followed by the indicative:

> **Eu sei que ela mora nessa rua, só que não lembro que número.**
> I know she lives in this street, only I can't remember which number.

▶ **51.1.8** (p. 414)

26.2.5 Contrastive conjunctions

enquanto 'while, whereas':

> **Ela optou por Exatas, enquanto a irmã estuda Letras.**
> She went for sciences, while her sister is studying literature.

ao passo que (*written*) 'whereas':

> **O desempenho escolar das meninas está melhorando, ao passo que o dos meninos piora a cada ano.**
> Girls' academic performance is improving, whereas that of boys gets worse every year.

26.2.6 Conditional conjunctions

a não ser que, a menos que 'unless', followed by the present/imperfect subjunctive:

> **Um estrangeiro residente no Brasil não pode votar, a não ser que se naturalize.**
> A foreigner resident in Brazil cannot vote unless he/she becomes naturalized.

▶ **50.4.8** (p. 410)

caso 'if', followed by the present/imperfect subjunctive:

> **O candidato promete, caso ele ganhe a eleição, acabar com a corrupção.**
> The candidate promises to put an end to corruption if he wins the election.

▶ **50.4.1** (p. 408)

contanto que (*formal*) 'provided (that)', followed by the present/imperfect subjunctive:

> **Ele concordou em ser entrevistado, contanto que não filmassem o rosto dele.**
> He agreed to be interviewed, provided they did not film his face.

▶ **50.4.5** (p. 409)

desde que 'as long as, providing (that)', **uma vez que** 'once, provided that', followed by the present/imperfect subjunctive:

> **Vocês podem continuar assistindo TV, desde que abaixem o volume.**
> You can carry on watching TV as long as you turn the volume down.

▶ **50.4.5**, **50.4.6** (p. 409)

mesmo que 'even if, even though', followed by the present/imperfect subjunctive:

> **Mesmo que me oferecessem mais dinheiro, não aceitaria as condições.**
> Even if they offered me more money, I would not accept the conditions.

▶ **50.4.9** (p. 410); **51.1.5** (p. 412)

nem que 'even if', followed by the present/imperfect subjunctive:

> **Quando eu quero algo eu consigo, nem que seja a última coisa que eu faça.**
> When I want something I get it, even if it's the last thing I do.

se 'if', usually followed by the future/imperfect subjunctive (see **20.5**):

> **Se eu precisar, ele vai me ajudar.**
> If I need it, he will help me.

> **Se eu precisasse, ele me ajudaria.**
> If I needed it, he would help me.

▶ **Chapter 50** (p. 405)

26.2.7 Comparative conjunctions

assim como 'just like/as', 'as well as':

> **Ele passava as próprias camisas, assim como sua mãe tinha ensinado.**
> He would iron his own shirts, just as his mother had taught him.

> **O espaço abriga exposições e palestras, assim como outros eventos.**
> The venue is home to exhibitions and lectures, as well as other events.

como 'as, like':

> **uma pessoa como eu**
> a person like me

> **Tudo aconteceu exatamente como ele descreveu.**
> Everything happened exactly as he described.

como se 'as if', followed by the imperfect subjunctive:

> **Ela gritou comigo, como se a culpa fosse minha.**
> She shouted at me, as if it were my fault.

do jeito que (*spoken*) 'the way (that)':

> **Ele não vai durar muito, do jeito que ele bebe.**
> He won't last long the way he drinks.

do que 'than':

> **Foi mais difícil do que imaginávamos.**
> It was more difficult than we imagined.

feito 'like' (*colloquial*):

> **Ela estava correndo para todos os lados feito uma barata tonta.**
> She was running around in all directions like a headless chicken. (*literally*, a dizzy cockroach)

que nem 'like' (*informal*):

> **Ele fala português que nem brasileiro.**
> He speaks Portuguese like a Brazilian.

> **Que nem minha mãe dizia, tudo se ajeita com o tempo.**
> Like my mum used to say, time heals all wounds.

tanto quanto/como 'as much as', **tão . . . quanto/como** 'as . . . as':

> **Eu não malho tanto quanto meu irmão.**
> I don't work out as much as my brother.

> **Ela canta tão bem como toca violão.**
> She sings as well as she plays the guitar.

26.2.8 Proportional conjunctions

à medida que 'as', 'inasmuch as':

> **À medida que envelhecemos, ficamos mais sábios.**
> As we get older, we get wiser.

> **As taxas de juros irão baixar à medida que os preços também caírem.**[5]
> Interest rates will go down inasmuch as prices also fall.

conforme 'as':

> **Conforme você vai jogando, o jogo fica cada vez mais difícil.**
> As you go on playing, the game gets more and more difficult.

quanto mais . . . mais 'the more . . . the more':

> **Quanto mais ele se dedica à carreira, menos tempo sobra para a família.**
> The more he devotes himself to his career, the less time is left over for his family.

NOTE 5 Note the use of the future subjunctive (or imperfect after a past tense main verb) when, in addition the idea of proportionality, there is also conditionality.

26.2.9 Conformative conjunctions

conforme 'in accordance with what, as'.

> **Fizemos a experiência conforme o professor explicou.**
> We did the experiment as the teacher had explained.

segundo 'according to what':

> **Segundo dizem, ela é milionária.**
> According to what people say, she's a millionaire. / She's said to be a millionaire.

26.2.10 Final conjunctions

These conjunctions are all followed by present/imperfect subjunctive when they have final meaning:

a fim de que (*written*) 'so that, in order that':

> **Temos que redobrar os cuidados, a fim de que isso não volte a acontecer.**
> We must take greater care in order that this does not happen again.

para que 'in order that':

> **É preciso tomar uma atitude para que essas espécies não desapareçam.**
> Action is needed in order that these species do not disappear.

de forma que, de maneira que, de modo que 'so that, such that':

É importante aumentar o consumo de forma que a economia cresça.
It is important to increase consumer spending so that the economy grows.

26.2.11 Consecutive conjunctions

de forma que, de maneira que, de modo que 'so that, with the result that', followed by the indicative:

O consumo aumentou, de maneira que a economia cresceu.
Consumer spending increased with the result that the economy grew.

tão ... que 'so ... that', tanto que 'so much that':

Eu me sentia tão fraco que nem conseguia sair da cama.
I was feeling so weak I couldn't even get out of bed.

Ele insistiu tanto que eu acabei cedendo.
He insisted so much I ended up giving in.

26.2.12 Explanatory conjunction

sendo que '(with) ... ing', followed by the indicative:

Dez pessoas foram levadas ao hospital, sendo que duas em estado grave.
Ten people were taken to hospital, two being in serious condition.

As propostas são votadas pelos membros do comitê, sendo que o presidente só vota em caso de empate.
Proposals are voted on by the members of the committee, (with) the chairman only voting in the event of a tie.

26.3 Preposition vs. conjunction

The temporal conjunctions **antes que** 'before', **depois que** 'after' and **até que** 'until', the concessive **apesar de que** 'despite the fact that' and **sem que** 'without', and the final conjunction **para que** 'in order that' are replaced by the corresponding preposition (**antes de, depois de, até, apesar de, sem** and **para** respectively) when the subjects of the main and subordinate clauses are one and the same:

Comemos um lanche antes de voltar para casa.
We had a snack before we went home.

By employing the personal infinitive, the prepositions can be used instead of the corresponding conjunctions even when the subjects of the two clauses are different, and there is a marked preference for using this prepositional construction, especially in the spoken language:

Vamos arrumar aqui antes de os convidados chegarem.
Let's clear up here before the guests arrive.

Seria impossível eles saírem sem ninguém os ver.
It would be impossible for them to get out without anyone seeing them.

26.4 Gerund vs. conjunction

The idea of 'although, even though, even if' is frequently rendered using **mesmo** followed by a gerund, especially in the spoken language:

Mesmo indo de táxi, chegamos atrasados.
Even though we went by taxi, we got there late.

Mesmo ele me implorando, eu não vou.
Even if he begs me, I'm not going.

Notes for Spanish speakers

When the subjects of the main and subordinate verbs are different, Portuguese has the option of using the prepositions **antes de**, **apesar de**, **até**, **depois de**, **para, por** and **sem** followed by a personal infinitive construction instead of using the corresponding conjunction with a subordinate clause, and this is the option generally preferred in less formal style, especially in speech. Note that subordinate clauses referring to as yet unfulfilled future actions usually require a verb in the future subjunctive tense.

27

Word order

Word order in statements

The order of words in statements is largely the same as in English,[1] apart from the following cases:

NOTE   1   Obvious exceptions are the position of attributive adjectives with respect to the nouns they qualify (see **5.1**) and the position of unstressed object pronouns (see **7.5**).

(i)   Adverbs of manner cannot be placed between subject and verb as they often are in English. In Portuguese, the neutral position for an adverb of manner (i.e. when it is has no special emphasis on it) is immediately after the verb and preceding any direct object:

> **Ela abriu cuidadosamente a caixa.**
> She carefully opened the box.

This rule on adverb placement applies equally to short prepositional phrases that function as adverbials, notably indirect objects introduced by **a** or **para**:

> **O professor deu aos alunos os resultados da prova.**
> The teacher gave the students the results of the test.

The adverb or adverbial phrase can be placed after the direct object when it is to be given special emphasis. Compare the following:

> **Ele fala muito bem inglês.** (*no special emphasis, or emphasis on **inglês***)
> He speaks English very well.

> **Ele fala inglês muito bem.** (*emphasis on **muito bem***)
> He speaks English *really well*.

> **O João escreveu à namorada uma carta.**
> João wrote his girlfriend a letter.

> **O João escreveu uma carta à namorada.**
> João wrote a letter to his girlfriend.

(ii)   When the subject of an intransitive verb is a new piece of information, it is usually placed after the verb. This has the effect of placing greater emphasis on the subject, and is often equivalent to starting a sentence with 'There' in English:

> **Ligou um tal de Ricardo.**
> Someone called Ricardo called. / There was a call from a Ricardo.

> **Vai cair um toró a qualquer momento.**
> There's going to be a downpour any minute now.

> **Apareceu um homem que se dizia o pai dela.**
> A man turned up claiming to be her father.

> **Acabou a luz.**
> The power's gone out.

(iii) In journalistic style, it is not uncommon to use this device to create greater impact:

> **Morre em São Paulo, aos 56 anos, ex-ator global Flávio Guarnieri.**
> Former Globo TV actor, Flávio Guarnieri, dies in São Paulo, aged 56.

> **Foi lançado ontem às 19h05, horário de Brasília, da base aérea de Kourou, que pertence à Agência Espacial Europeia, na Guiana Francesa, o novo satélite Amazonas.**
> The new Amazonas satellite was launched yesterday at 7.05 p.m. Brasilia time from the Kourou airbase in French Guyana, which belongs to the European Space Agency.

27.2 Word order in questions

Unlike English, subject and verb are not normally inverted in questions in Portuguese. The only difference between a yes–no question and a statement is the question intonation in speech and the question mark in writing:

> **Ele fala português.**
> He speaks Portuguese.

> **Ele fala português?**
> Does he speak Portuguese?

However, inversion does occur in the following cases:

(i) When the question is introduced by an interrogative word and the verb is **ser**, **estar**, **ficar** or a verb with equivalent meaning. If the subject is a pronoun, inversion is optional:

> **Como andam os negócios?**
> How's business?

> **Onde ele está?** *or* **Onde está ele?**
> Where is he?

(ii) In very formal writing:

> **Tinha Marx uma teoria sistemática e completa das crises do capital?**
> Did Marx have a systematic and complete theory of the crises of capital?

27.3 Word order in indirect questions

In indirect questions introduced by an interrogative word, the subject and verb are usually inverted when the subject is a noun and the verb is intransitive or means 'to be':

> **Você sabe a que horas sai o voo?**
> Do you know what time the flight leaves?

> **Ele me perguntou onde estava a escritura da casa.**
> He asked me where the deeds of the house were.

28

Word formation

Diminutives

Formation of the diminutive

The diminutive form of nouns and adjectives is formed as follows:

(i) With nouns and adjectives that end in unstressed **-o**, **-a** or **-e**, this final vowel is replaced with the ending **-inho** or **-inha** according to the gender of the word:

> **dedo** 'finger' > **dedinho** 'little finger'
>
> **casa** 'house' > **casinha** 'little house'
>
> **dente** 'tooth' (*masc.*) > **dentinho** 'little tooth'
>
> **fome** 'hunger' (*fem.*) > **fominha** 'slight hunger'
>
> **saco** 'bag' > **saquinho** 'little bag, sachet'
>
> (*NB: change of -c- to -qu- to preserve hard c sound*)
>
> **bonito** 'handsome, good-looking' > **bonitinho** 'cute'
>
> **bonita** 'pretty' > **bonitinha** 'cute'
>
> **quente** 'warm' > **quentinho/quentinha** 'nice and warm'
>
> **brega** 'tacky, naff' > **breguinha** 'slightly tacky, naff'
>
> (*NB: change of -g- to -gu- to preserve hard g sound*).

(ii) The ending **-inho/-inha** is also added to nouns and adjectives ending in **-s** or **-z**:

> **japonês** 'Japanese man' > **japonesinho** 'little Japanese guy'
>
> **voz** 'voice' (*fem.*) > **vozinha** 'little voice'.

(iii) With all other nouns, i.e. those ending in a stressed vowel, a nasal vowel, **-l**, **-m**, or **-r**, the ending **-zinho/-zinha** is added to the word. This also applies to nouns ending in **-io** or **-ia**:

> **papel** 'paper' (*masc.*) > **papelzinho** 'scrap of paper'
>
> **mão** 'hand' (*fem.*) > **mãozinha** 'little hand'
>
> **trem** 'train' (*masc.*) > **trenzinho** 'little/toy train'
>
> (*NB: change of -m to -n before the diminutive ending*)
>
> **flor** 'flower' (*fem.*) > **florzinha** 'little flower'
>
> **tia** 'aunt' > **tiazinha** 'auntie'
>
> **melhor** 'better' > **melhorzinho/melhorzinha** 'a little better'.

(iv)   As the spoken stress is always on the **i** of the diminutive ending, any other written accents are dropped:

> **café** 'coffee' > **cafezinho** 'small black coffee'
>
> **só** 'alone' > **sozinho** 'all alone'
>
> **pássaro** 'bird' > **passarinho** 'little bird, birdie'.

(v)   With nouns ending in **-l** and those ending in **-ão**, the plural stem (plural form minus **-s**) is used before the diminutive ending when the diminutive itself is pluralized:

> **animal** 'animal' > **animalzinho** 'little animal', *but*
>
> **animais** 'animals' > **animaizinhos** 'little animals'
>
> **pão** 'bread' > **pãozinho** 'bread roll', *but*
>
> **pães** 'loaves' > **pãezinhos** 'bread rolls'
>
> **botão** 'button, bud' > **botãozinho** 'little button, little bud', *but*
>
> **botões** 'buttons, buds' > **botõezinhos** 'little buttons, little buds'.

28.1.2   Meaning of the diminutive

The diminutive of a noun is often used simply to denote smallness:

> **Tem uma manchinha nessa camisa.**
> There's a little stain on this shirt.
>
> **Ele anota tudo num livrinho.**
> He notes everything down in a little book.

However, it very often connotes cuteness, affection or pleasantness, as does 'little' in English:

> **Adoro pezinho de bebê.**
> I love babies' little feet.
>
> **Estou com saudades da minha mãezinha.**
> I miss my little old mum.
>
> **Que tal uma cervejinha gelada?**
> What about a nice cold beer?

Some diminutive nouns have become lexicalized with a specific meaning (although this does not exclude their use as true diminutives):

> **carrinho** 'toy car', 'cart/trolley' (but can also mean 'little car')
>
> **cafezinho** 'small black coffee'
>
> **bondinho** 'cable car'.

Diminutive adjectives have the connotation of 'nice and . . .', 'nicely . . .' or having a quality to exactly the desirable degree:

> **A roupa já está sequinha.**
> The laundry is already good and dry.

Está quentinho ao pé da lareira.
It's nice and warm by the fire.

Aquela mesa que compramos cabe direitinho ao lado do sofá.
That table we bought fits in exactly next to the sofa.

A roupa estava dobradinha em cima da cama.
The clothes were nicely folded on the bed.

Prontinho!
All done!

The diminutive can also be used to temper the degree of an unpleasant quality:

Está friozinho lá fora.
It's chilly outside.

A filha deles é feinha.
Their daughter's rather plain.

A festa foi chatinha.
The party was a bit dull.

28.2 Augmentatives

28.2.1 Formation of the augmentative

The augmentative of nouns and adjectives is formed as follows:

(i) With nouns and adjectives that end in unstressed **-o**, **-a** or **-e**, this final vowel is replaced with the ending **-ão** or **-ona** according to the gender of the word:

dedo 'finger' > **dedão** 'thumb, big toe'

mesa 'table' > **mesona** 'big table'

peixe 'fish' (*masc.*) > **peixão** 'big fish'

bonito 'handsome, good-looking' > **bonitão** 'very good-looking'

bonita 'pretty' > **bonitona** 'gorgeous'

grande 'big' > **grandão/grandona** 'really big'.

(ii) With other nouns, the ending **-zão/-zona** is added to the word. This also applies to nouns ending in **-io** or **-ia**:

pai 'father' (*masc.*) > **paizão** 'dedicated father'

mãe 'mother' (*fem.*) > **mãezona** 'dedicated mother'

tio 'uncle' > **tiozão** 'middle-aged man trying to be cool'

sol 'sun' > **solzão** 'hot sun, bright sunshine'.

(iii) Some nouns ending in **-l** and **-r** add **-ão/-ona**:

papel 'paper' (*masc.*) > **papelão** 'cardboard'

colher 'spoon' (*fem.*) > **colherona** 'large spoon(ful)'.

(iv)   As the spoken stress is always on the augmentative ending, any other written accents are dropped:

> **pé** 'foot' > **pezão** 'big foot'.

(v)   In some cases, feminine nouns become masculine in the augmentative form:

> **cabeça** 'head' > **cabeção** 'big head'
>
> **mão** 'hand' (*fem.*) > **mãozão** 'big hand'
>
> **mulher** 'woman' > **mulherão** 'striking woman'.

(vi)   In general, the augmentative form is less predictable than the diminutive and there are some irregular augmentatives in frequent use:

> **casa** 'house' > **casarão** 'mansion, big house'
>
> **voz** 'voice' > **vozeirão** 'powerful voice'
>
> **homem** 'man' > **homenzarrão** *or, colloquially,* **homão** 'imposing man'.

28.2.2   Meaning of the augmentative

The augmentative is mainly used for emphasis, when stressing the large size of something or the powerful impression it makes:

> **Que narigão!**
> What a huge nose!
>
> **Aquela estante é pesadona.**
> That bookcase is really heavy.
>
> **Ele bate um bolão.**
> He plays a mean game of football.

Some augmentatives have become lexicalized with a distinct meaning:

> **caixa** 'box' > **caixão** 'coffin, casket'
>
> **papel** 'paper' > **papelão** 'cardboard'
>
> **sacola** 'carrier bag' > **sacolão** 'fruit and vegetable market'
>
> **mochila** 'backpack, rucksack' > **mochilão** 'backpacking tour'.

28.3   The appreciative suffix *-aço*

The suffix **-aço** is added to nouns to express appreciation:

> **Que golaço!**
> What a great goal!
>
> **Foi um jogaço.**
> It was a fantastic game.

28.4   The depreciative suffix *-eco*

The suffix **-eco** is added to a few nouns to express contempt:

> **um filmeco** 'a really bad movie, a turkey'
>
> **um jornaleco** 'a low-quality newspaper, a rag'.

28.5 Verbal nouns ending in *-ada/-ida*

28.5.1 Formation

The feminine form of the past participle (see **17.2**) can be used as a noun:

> **olhar** 'to look' > **uma olhada** 'a look'
>
> **ler** 'to read' > **uma lida** 'a read'.

28.5.2 Usage

Such nouns are normally combined with the verb **dar** to mean 'to have/take a . . .':

> **dar uma olhada** 'to have/take a look'
>
> **dar uma deitada** 'to have a lie-down'
>
> **dar uma dormidinha** 'to have/take a little snooze'.

If the verbal noun has an object, it is introduced with the preposition **em**:

> **Dei uma lida no jornal.**
> I had a read of the newspaper.
>
> **Vou dar uma limpadinha nesses vidros.**
> I'm going to give these windows a bit of a clean.

28.6 Instrumental nouns ending in *-ada*

28.6.1 Formation

The ending **-ada** can be added to nouns denoting objects, to mean 'a blow with a . . .':

> **martelo** 'hammer' > **uma martelada** 'a blow with a hammer'
>
> **pedra** 'stone' > **uma pedrada** 'a blow with a stone'
>
> **faca** 'knife' > **uma facada** 'a wound with a knife'
>
> **pau** 'stick, club' > **uma paulada** 'a blow with a stick'.

28.6.2 Usage

Such nouns are mainly used in the following constructions:

(i)   **dar uma . . . em alguém/algo** 'to hit someone/something with a . . .':

> **O assaltante deu uma coronhada no gerente do banco.**
> The robber pistol-whipped the bank manager.

(ii) **levar uma . . .** 'to be/get hit with a . . .':

> **O jogador levou uma bolada na cara.**
> The player got hit in the face with the ball.

(iii) **a . . . s, com uma . . .** 'with . . .':

> **Os aldeões mataram a cobra a pauladas.**
> The villagers killed the snake by hitting it with sticks.
>
> **O ator agrediu um fotógrafo com uma cabeçada.**
> The actor head-butted a photographer.

28.7 ## Collective nouns ending in *-ada*

28.7.1 ### Formation

The ending **-ada** can be added to nouns denoting living beings to form collective nouns:

criança 'child' > **criançada** 'kids'

mulher 'woman' > **mulherada** 'women'

rapaz 'lad, guy' > **rapaziada** 'lads, guys' (*notice extra* **i** *here*)

cachorro 'dog' > **cachorrada** 'dogs'.

28.7.2 ### Usage

Such nouns are mainly used with the definite article or as forms of address. They are informal and can sometimes have an overtone of contempt, but not necessarily:

Levamos a criançada para tomar sorvete.
We took the kids to get ice cream.

A mulherada adora filme romântico.
The ladies love romantic movies.

Vamos embora, rapaziada.
Let's get going, lads.

Part B

Functions

I

Social contact and communication strategies

29

Making social contacts

This chapter contains the most useful expressions used by Brazilians to establish social contacts, such as when greeting or introducing people, taking leave, using the phone or writing letters. Many of these are set phrases; others are constructions that vary according to context. Reference is made to register where appropriate, so you will know whether a certain expression is formal or informal, or whether it tends to be used more in the spoken or written language.

29.1 Greeting someone

The most common greetings are:

Bom dia.
Good morning.

Boa tarde.
Good afternoon.

Boa noite.
Good evening.

Oi!
Hi!/Hey!

Olá!
Hello!

Tudo bem?
Hi! How are you?

The first three greetings are neutral, and can be used in both formal and familiar address. **Oi!** is informal, whereas **Olá!** is neutral. **Tudo bem?** is fairly informal. Some greetings can be combined, such as **Olá, bom dia**. 'Hello, good morning.'

Bom dia, **Boa tarde** and **Boa noite** may also be said when taking leave, especially in more formal situations, in which case they are equivalent to 'Have a nice day', 'Have a nice afternoon', 'Have a nice evening / Good night' respectively.

You will also hear an array of other informal greetings, mainly used by younger people, such as:

E aí?
What's up?

Beleza?
All right?

Tudo joia? / Tudo certo?
Everything OK?

Fala . . . ! (*followed by the person's name or a form of address such as **meu** or **cara**, equivalent to 'man', 'mate' 'buddy'*)
Hey . . . , what's happening?

In both formal and informal situations, it is customary to shake hands, not only when you are first introduced, but also on subsequent meetings. Between friends and in informal social situations, opposite sexes kiss each other on the cheek (on both cheeks in Rio and further north, on one cheek in São Paulo and the south). On first meeting, opposite sexes may shake hands, particularly when one or both are older. Female friends kiss each other on the cheek, while male friends shake hands while patting each other on the back, or place one arm around the other's shoulder while patting his chest affectionately. Good friends of both sexes may also embrace, and male relatives (and sometimes good friends) kiss each other, regardless of age.

29.2 Conveying greetings

29.2.1

Brazilians are quite assiduous about conveying greetings. To pass on greetings to a third person, use:

Informal:

> **Manda um abraço para o Ricardo.** (*from a man to a man, or to someone you know less well*)
> Say hi to Ricardo from me.

> **Manda um beijo para a Sueli.** (*to someone you know very well, not usually used from a man to a man*)
> Give my love to Sueli.

More formal:

> **Dê lembranças aos seus pais.**
> Give my regards to your parents.

> **Dê lembranças minhas à sua família.**
> Give my regards to your family.

Formal:

> **Estenda meus cumprimentos a todos.**
> Extend my compliments to all.

▶ **Chapter 21** (p. 196)

29.2.2

To pass on someone else's greetings, use the following:

Informal:

> **O Paulo mandou um abraço.** (*from a man to a man, or when the relationship is less close*)
> Paulo says hi.

A Cristina mandou um beijo. (*between close friends or relatives, not usually between male friends*)
Cristina sends her love.

More formal:

O meu pai mandou lembranças.
My father sends regards.

When conveying a greeting from someone who is with you (e.g. when talking to a third party on the phone), the present continuous is used in the above expressions:

O Vinícius está mandando um abraço. Ele está aqui do meu lado.
Vinicius is saying hi. He's here next to me.

29.2.3 To respond to a greeting from a third party, you should always say thank you (**obrigado** if said by a male, **obrigada** if said by a female) and you may return an informal greeting as follows:

Manda outro para ele/ela.
Send him/her mine, too.

29.3 Asking people how they are

29.3.1 To ask someone how he or she is, use the following expressions:

Informal:

Tudo bem? / Tudo bom?
How's things?

Tudo bem com você?
You doing OK?

Você está bem?[1]
Are you well?

Está bom/boa?
Are you OK?

Como é que (você) está?
How are you?

E aí?
What's up?

More formal:

Como vai?
How are you?

NOTE 1 Remember that, in informal spoken language, the verb **estar** and all its conjugated forms are pronounced without the initial **es**-, so **está** and **estou** are pronounced /ta/ and /to/ respectively.

29.3.2 To reply to the above expressions, use the following:

Informal:

> **Tudo bem.**
> Fine.
>
> **Estou bem.**
> I'm OK.
>
> **Tudo ótimo.**
> Really well.
>
> **Tudo joia. / Tudo certo. / (Tudo) beleza.**
> Great.

Formal:

> **Vou bem, obrigado** (*male speaker*) / **obrigada** (*female speaker*).
> I'm fine, thanks.

Any of these expressions can be followed by **E você?** 'And you?' 'How about you?'. If things are not so good, you can use one of the following expressions:

> **Mais ou menos.**
> So so.
>
> **Vou levando.**
> I'm getting by.
>
> **Não posso me queixar.**
> Can't complain.
>
> **Está indo.**
> OK, I suppose.

29.3.3 To ask how someone else is, use:

> **Como vai a sua mãe?**
> How's your mother?
>
> **Como vão os seus filhos?**
> How are your children?
>
> **E o seu irmão?**
> How about your brother?
>
> **E as gêmeas?**
> What about the twins?

29.4 Introducing yourself and others

29.4.1 Introducing yourself

Standard expressions are:

> **Sou . . .**
> I'm . . .

> **Meu nome é . . .**
> My name is . . .

Or formally:

> **Apresento-me. Meu nome é . . .**
> I'll introduce myself. My name is . . .
>
> **Deixe eu me apresentar.**
> Allow me to introduce myself.

29.4.2 | Introducing others

Using the neutral register you can say:

> **Essa é a minha esposa.**
> This is my wife.
>
> **Esse é o Tiago.**
> This is Tiago.
>
> **Você já conhece a Ana?**
> Have you met Ana? / Do you know Ana?
>
> **Deixe eu apresentar meu pai.**
> Let me introduce my dad.
>
> **Quero te apresentar o meu primo, Bruno.**
> I'd like to introduce you to my cousin, Bruno.

If you have already met the person you are being introduced to, you can say:

Informal:

> **A gente já se conheceu.**
> We've already met.
>
> **A gente já se conhece.**
> We already know each other.
>
> **A gente já foi apresentado.**
> We've already been introduced.

Formal:

> **Já nos conhecemos.**
> We've already met. / We already know each other.
>
> **Já fomos apresentados.**
> We've already been introduced.

The standard greetings in an introduction are:

Informal:

> **Oi, tudo bem?**
> Hi, how are you?

Neutral register:

> **Prazer.**
> Nice to meet you.

Formal:

> **Como vai?**
> How do you do?

> **Muito prazer.**
> Very nice to meet you.

> **Prazer em conhecê-lo** (*to a male*) / **conhecê-la** (*to a female*).
> It's a pleasure to meet you.

When taking leave of someone you have just met for the first time, you can say:

> **Foi um prazer.**
> It was nice meeting you.

To which the standard response is:

> **O prazer foi meu.**
> The pleasure was mine.

29.5 Taking leave

Common leave-taking expressions are:

> **Tchau.**
> Bye.

> **Até logo.** (*slightly formal*)
> Goodbye.

> **Boa noite.** (*when leaving for the night or going to bed*)
> Goodnight.

> **A gente se vê.** (*informal*)
> Be seeing you.

> **A gente se vê amanhã.** (*informal*)
> See you tomorrow.

> **A gente se vê por aí.** (*informal*)
> See you around.

The preposition **até** can be combined with an expression of time corresponding to 'see you . . .':

> **Até amanhã.**
> See you tomorrow.

> **Até a semana que vem.**
> See you next week.

> **Até sábado.**
> See you Saturday.

Até já.
See you shortly.

Até daqui a pouco.
See you in a bit.

Até a próxima.
See you next time.

Até mais.
See you.

29.6 Expressing wishes

29.6.1 Wishing someone a good trip

Boa viagem!
Have a good trip!

Aproveite!
Have a good time!

Divirta-se! / Divirtam-se!
Enjoy yourself! / Enjoy yourselves!

29.6.2 Wishing someone well

Boa sorte!
Good luck!

Tudo de bom!
All the best!

Te cuida (aí)!
Take care (of yourself)!

Felicidades! / Muita felicidade!
Be happy!

Muita saúde!
Be healthy!

29.6.3 Wishing someone a good sleep or rest

Bom descanso!
Have a good rest!

Durma bem!
Sleep well!

Durma com os anjos!
Sweet dreams!

29.6.4 Wishing someone better

Melhoras!
Get well! / Get better!

29.6.5 Drinking a toast and telling someone to enjoy their meal

Saúde!
Cheers!

À nossa!
Here's to us!

Aos noivos!
To the bride and groom!

Bom apetite! (*said when encountering someone who is eating or by waiting staff when serving food*)
Enjoy your meal!

29.6.6 More examples of wishes with *bom/boa*

Bom fim de semana!
Have a nice weekend!

Bom trabalho!
Hope work goes OK!

Boa aula!
Have a good class!

Bom passeio!
Have a nice day out!

29.6.7 To return the good wishes, say:

Informal:

(Para) você também.
You too.

More formal:

Igualmente.
Likewise. / The same to you.

29.7 Congratulating somebody

The general word for congratulating is:

Parabéns!
Congratulations!

More formally, you can say:

Meus parabéns!
My congratulations!

Other informal expressions that can be used when congratulating someone are:

Você merece!
You deserve it!

Que máximo!
Fantastic!

Toca aqui!
High five!

Você arrasou! / Você arrebentou!
You were awesome! / You rocked!

Mandou bem!
Good one!

Muito bem!
Well done! / Good job!

Specific expressions used on special occasions are:

Feliz Natal!
Merry Christmas!

Feliz Ano Novo!
Happy New Year!

Feliz Páscoa!
Happy Easter!

Parabéns! / Feliz aniversário!
Happy Birthday!

Note that **Parabéns!** is much more common than **Feliz Aniversário!** as a formula for wishing someone a happy birthday. This is borne out in the expressions **dar os parabéns a alguém** 'to wish someone a happy birthday' and **cantar parabéns** 'to sing happy birthday'.

29.8 Using the phone

29.8.1 Answering the phone

The word for 'hello?' on the phone is **alô?**:

Alô? Quem fala?
Hello? Who's speaking?

29.8.2 Asking to speak to someone

Informal:

A Karina está, por favor?
Is Karina there, please?

O Fábio está por aí?
Is Fabio around?

Me passa a sua irmã.
Put your sister on, would you?

Formal:

> **Queria falar com o gerente, por favor.**
> I'd like to speak to the manager, please.

> **Poderia falar com o Dr. Sérgio, por favor?**
> Could I speak to Dr Sérgio, please?

29.8.3 Asking who is calling

To ask callers to identify themselves, use:

> **Quem fala?**
> Who's speaking?

> **Com quem eu falo?**
> Who am I speaking to?

> **De onde fala?**
> Who's speaking? (*when it is a business call*)

> **Quem quer falar?**
> Who shall I say is calling?

> **Quem gostaria? / Quem deseja?** (*more formal*)
> Who shall I say is calling?

29.8.4 Identifying yourself

To identify who is calling say:

> **É o Pedro.**
> It's Pedro.

> **Quem fala é a Sandra.**
> This is Sandra speaking.

> **Sou eu.**
> That's me.

> **É ele/ela.**
> Speaking. (*when an unknown caller has asked for you by name*)

29.8.5 Asking callers if they wish to leave a message

> **Quer deixar recado?**
> Would you like to leave a message?

> **Posso dar um recado para ele/ela?**
> Can I give him/her a message?

> **Algum recado?**
> Any message?

29.8.6 Leaving a message

> **Posso deixar um recado para ele/ela?** (*polite*)
> Can I leave him/her a message?

Poderia dar um recado para ele/ela? (*more formal*)
Could you give him/her a message?

Faça o favor de dizer a ele/ela que . . . (*more formal*)
Please would you tell him/her that . . .

Você pode falar para ele/ela que . . . (*neutral*)
Can you tell him/her that . . .

Fala para ele/ela que . . . (*informal*)
Tell him/her that . . .

O senhor / Você pede para ele/ela me ligar? (*polite*)
Would you ask him/her to call me?

Fala para ele/ela me ligar. (*informal*)
Tell him/her to call me.

29.8.7 ## Asking for an extension number or department

Ramal 596 (cinco nove meia), por favor.
Extension 596, please.

Poderia me passar o departamento de vendas, por favor?
Could you put me through to the sales department, please?

29.8.8 ## Asking the caller to hold on

Informal:

Só um minutinho. / Momentinho.
Just a minute.

Formal:

Momento, por favor.
Just a moment, please.

Aguarde na linha.
Hold the line.

Vou passar a ligação (para . . .).
I'll put you through (to . . .).

Vou passar a Dra. Maira.
I'm putting you through to Dr Maira.

29.8.9 ## Talking to an operator

Quero fazer uma ligação interurbana/internacional.
I want to make a long-distance/international call.

Como é que eu faço para fazer uma ligação para fora?
How do I go about making an external call?

O número é o 2577 8901.
The number is 2577 8901.

Qual é o DDD/DDI de . . . ? (*pronounced* **dê-dê-dê** *and* **dê-dê-i**)
What's the area code/country code for . . . ?

Qual o número da operadora?
What's the number of the long-distance carrier?

Quero fazer uma ligação a cobrar.
I want to make a collect call/a reverse-charge call.

29.8.10 Problems

Não consigo completar a ligação.
I can't get through.

Toca, toca, mas ninguém atende.
There's no answer.

Está dando ocupado.
I get the busy signal/engaged tone.

Está ocupado.
It's busy/engaged.

É uma gravação.
It's a recorded message.

Para falar com um dos nossos atendentes, digite 9.
To speak to one of our operators, press 9.

Estava falando com . . . , e a ligação caiu.
I was speaking to . . . , and I/we got cut off.

Não estou te ouvindo.
I can't hear you.

A ligação está ruim/péssima.
It's a bad/terrible line.

Se cair, é porque minha bateria está fraca.
If we get cut off, it's because my battery's dying.

NOTE | In Brazil, phone numbers are read in single figures, pairs, or a combination of both, so a number like 2539 2680 could be read **dois-cinco-três-nove – dois-meia-oito-zero**, or **vinte e cinco – trinta e nove – vinte seis – oitenta**, or **dois-cinco-três-nove – vinte e seis – oitenta**, or **vinte e cinco – trinta e nove – dois-meia-oito-zero**. Note that, when read as a single digit, 6 is always **meia** and 0 **zero**. Three-digit numbers may be read as a single number, e.g. **ramal 479 (quatrocentos e setenta e nove** *or* **quatro-sete-nove**) 'extension 479'. Area codes are read as single numbers preceded by 0, e.g. **011** (**zero onze**), and you will often hear, for example, **zero operadora onze**, **zero operadora vinte e um**, etc., which means that you should insert the two-digit code of the long-distance carrier of your choice between the zero and the area code.

29.8.11 Arranging to meet someone

Common expressions are:

Vamos nos encontrar hoje à noite/na quinta?
Shall we meet tonight/on Thursday?

Que tal nos encontrarmos mais tarde?
How about meeting up later?

A gente podia se encontrar no shopping. (*informal*)
We could meet at the mall.

Oito horas/segunda-feira está bom para você?
Is eight o'clock / Monday okay with you?

De manhã não dá, tem que ser à tarde.
The morning's no good, it'll have to be in the afternoon.

Qualquer coisa, te ligo/me liga.
If there's any problem, I'll call you/call me.

29.8.12 Saying goodbye on the phone

The same expressions shown in **29.5** can be used to say goodbye on the phone, **tchau** being the most common.

At the end of a social phone call, it is customary to say **um abraço** (between male friends and to people you don't have a very close friendship with) or **um beijo** (between close friends and family members, except between male friends). The standard response to both expressions is:

Outro.
Same to you.

At the end of business calls, it is customary to say **bom dia/boa tarde/boa noite** 'have a nice day/afternoon/evening' according to the time of day, and you may also hear:

Disponha!
Any time! / At your service! / It's a pleasure to help you.

Obrigado/a pela preferência.
Thank you for choosing us. / Thank you for your custom.

29.9 Writing letters and e-mails

As in English, there are special turns of phrase associated with formal correspondence whatever the medium, but even business e-mails to strangers tend to be less formal in style than letters.

29.9.1 Date

It is usual practice in a letter is to put the name of the place where the writer is before the date, although this may be dispensed with when writing on headed notepaper:

Rio de Janeiro, 5 de fevereiro de 2009

Notice the format of the date and the lower-case initial letter in the names of the months.

29.9.2 Salutation

The most common forms of salutation in formal and business correspondence are:

Very formal:

> **Senhores** (*to a company or collective recipient*)
> Dear Sirs
>
> **Prezados senhores** (*to a company or collective recipient*)
> Dear Sirs
>
> **Senhor**
> Dear Sir
>
> **Prezado Senhor**
> Dear Sir
>
> **Senhora**
> Dear Madam
>
> **Prezada Senhora**
> Dear Madam
>
> **Senhor(a)**
> Dear Sir/Madam

Formal:

> **Prezado Sr. Ricardo Teixeira**
> Dear Mr Teixeira[2]
>
> **Prezada Sra. Raquel Maia**
> Dear Ms Maia
>
> **Prezado cliente**
> Dear Customer

Less formal:

> **Prezado Sr. Ricardo**
>
> **Prezada Sra. Raquel**

---

2   See **34.1.1** on the use of names in Brazil.

In formal business correspondence, the salutation is usually followed by a colon (:) or no punctuation. In less formal correspondence (see below), the salutation is followed by a comma. Notice the abbreviations **Sr.** (= **senhor**) 'Mr' and **Sra.** (= **senhora**) 'Ms'. These may be substituted by other titles as appropriate, e.g. **Dr.** (= **Doutor**), **Dra.** (= **Doutora**) and **Professor(a)** for a teacher.

Neutral level (*to someone you do not know well in a business letter or e-mail*):

> **Prezado Ricardo**
> Dear Ricardo
>
> **Prezada Raquel**
> Dear Raquel
>
> **Prezada Professora Lúcia**
> Dear Lúcia (*to a teacher*)

Once you have established a personal relationship with the addressee, use **caro/a** 'dear':

Caro Ricardo
Dear Ricardo

Cara Raquel
Dear Raquel.

In informal communications to family or friends, use **querido/a** 'dear':

Querido tio
Dear Uncle

Querida Ângela
Dear Angela

Queridos amigos
Dear friends.

In e-mails, even business e-mails, less formal greetings may be used, such as:

Bom dia, Ricardo
Hi Ricardo

Olá, Raquel
Hi Raquel

Oi, Carlos
Hi Carlos.

29.9.3 Common phrases used in formal and business correspondence

29.9.3.1 Acknowledging receipt of a letter or e-mail

Acuso/Acusamos recebimento de sua carta de 9 de março.
I/We acknowledge receipt of your letter of March 9th.

Agradecemos sua carta de 24 de novembro último.
Thank you for your letter dated 24 November.

Em resposta/Em atenção à sua carta de 19 de julho último, . . .
In response to/Further to your letter of July 19th, . . .

Agradeço/Agradecemos o seu e-mail/o seu contato.
Thank you for your e-mail/for contacting me/us.

29.9.3.2 Stating the purpose of a letter or e-mail

Venho pela presente pedir a V.Sa. que . . .
I am writing to ask you to . . . (*letter only*)

Dirigimo-nos a V.Sas. para perguntar-lhes se . . .
We are writing to inquire whether . . .

Tomo a liberdade de escrever a V.Sa. para . . .
I am taking the liberty of writing to you to . . .

Temos a satisfação de informar-lhes que . . .
We are pleased to inform you that . . .

NOTE │ In formal communications, 'you' is translated as **V.Sa.** (= **Vossa Senhoria**) when addressing an individual, and as **V.Sas.** (= **Vossas Senhorias**, plural) when addressing a collective recipient, such as a company. These forms of address require a third person verb and are considered to be masculine for purposes of agreement unless the recipient is known to be female. **V.Sa.** may be replaced in direct object function by the unstressed pronouns **o** (for a male), **a** (for a female) and in indirect object function by **lhe**; **V.Sas.** may be replaced by **os** (direct object) or **lhes** (indirect object). The corresponding possessive is **seu(s)/sua(s)**.

29.9.3.3 Expressing regret for something

Lamentamos informar que ...
We are sorry to inform you that ...

Infelizmente, não poderemos ...
Unfortunately, we are unable to ...

29.9.3.4 Expressing pleasure at something

Tenho/Temos a satisfação de informar-lhes que ...
I/We are pleased to inform you that ...

É com muito prazer que anunciamos ...
We are very pleased to announce ...

29.9.3.5 Requesting something

Peço a gentileza de me enviar ...
Please send me ...

Solicitamos o obséquio de nos enviarem ...
Please send us ...

Agradeceria/Agradeceríamos se me/nos fornecessem ...
I/We would be grateful if you could supply me/us with ...

29.9.3.6 Enclosures and attachments

Anexo/Anexamos ...
I/We enclose ... (*in letter*) *or* I/We attach ... (*in e-mail*)

Segue anexa uma cópia do contrato.
Please find enclosed/attached a copy of the contract.

Note that **anexo** must agree in gender and number with the noun denoting the enclosure, and the verb **seguir** must agree in number, e.g. **Seguem anexas as informações solicitadas.** 'Please find enclosed the information requested.' Alternatively, you can use **em anexo**, which is invariable:

Uma cópia do contrato segue em anexo.
A copy of the contract is enclosed/attached.

29.9.4 Closing a letter or e-mail

To wind up a formal or business communication, the following phrases may be used:

Aguardo/Aguardamos seu contato.
I/We look forward to hearing from you.

Aguardamos uma breve resposta.
We look forward to hearing from you soon.

Agradeço/Agradecemos a atenção.
Thanking you for your attention

Agradeço/Agradecemos antecipadamente *or* **desde já.**
Thanking you in advance.

Coloco-me/Colocamo-nos à disposição para qualquer esclarecimento.
I/We would be happy to provide you with any further information.

For formal closures, use the following:

Atenciosamente,
(Yours) sincerely, / Yours faithfully,

Cordialmente,
(Yours) sincerely, (*slightly less formal than the above*).

NOTE | **Atenciosamente** is often abbreviated to **Att** in short e-mails.

To wind up a personal communication, use the following:

É isso aí por enquanto.
All for now.

To close a personal communication, use the following:

Um abraço, (*between male friends, or to a personal or business acquaintance*)
Regards, / All the best,

Um beijo, (*to close friends and family members*)
Love,

Both the above closures may be pluralized. **Abraços / Beijos**. In e-mails and text messages, the following abbreviations are used:

Abç / Abs

Bjo / Bjs

30

Basic strategies for communication

In any language, there are a number of words and phrases that serve simply to initiate conversation, to keep it going and to structure it. The sections below list and give information about the most common such words and phrases used by Brazilians in everyday communication.

30.1 Attracting someone's attention and responding to a call for attention

30.1.1 The words most commonly used to attract someone's attention are:

Por favor. 'Excuse me.'

Alô! 'Hey!'

Moço! 'Excuse me!' (*to a young man or male in a service role, e.g. a waiter*)

Moça! 'Excuse me!' (*to a young woman or female in a service role*)

Senhor! 'Excuse me, sir!' (*to an older man or male customer*)

Senhora! 'Excuse me, madam!' (*to an older woman or female customer*)

Senhorita! 'Excuse me, miss!' (*respectful address to teenage girl*)

The most versatile of these is **por favor** (*literally*, 'please') which can be used to address a stranger in the street, attract the attention of a waiter or sales assistant, begin an inquiry at an information desk, etc. **Alô**, like its English equivalent 'hey!', should be used with care as it can sound rude.

Por favor, a senhora sabe onde fica a rua Samambaia?
Excuse me, do you know where Samambaia Street is, please?

Por favor, traz o cardápio para a gente.
Excuse me, could you bring us the menu?

Por favor, esse livro está a quanto?
Excuse me, how much is this book?

Moça, vê dois chopes, por favor.
Waitress, two draft beers, please.

Senhor! Esqueceu o guarda-chuva!
Excuse me, sir! You forgot your umbrella!

30.1.2

The most common ways of responding to a call for attention are:

More formal:

> **Pois não?** 'Yes, sir/madam?' / 'Can I help you?'
>
> **Diga.** 'Yes?'
>
> **O que é que você manda?** 'What can I do for you?'
>
> **Pode falar.** 'Go ahead.'

Informal:

> **Fala.** 'Yes?'
>
> **Oi.** 'Yes?'

30.2 Starting up a conversation

When starting up a conversation, it is customary to begin with the person's name, usually preceded by the interjection ô:

> **Ô Geraldo, tenho um assunto para falar com você.**
> Geraldo, there's something I want to talk to you about.
>
> **Ô Laura, deixa eu te perguntar uma coisa.**
> Laura, let me ask you something.

Alternatively, you can open the sentence with **escuta** 'listen' or **vem cá** (*literally*, 'come here') 'listen':

> **Escuta, eu queria te perguntar uma coisa.**
> Listen, I wanted to ask you something.
>
> **Vem cá, deixa eu te falar uma coisa.**
> Listen, let me tell you something.

30.3 Requesting repetition and responding

30.3.1

To ask someone to repeat something you haven't heard properly, use one of the following expressions:

> **Como?** 'Pardon?' / 'Sorry?'
>
> **Oi?** 'Sorry?'
>
> **O que é que foi?** 'What was that?'
>
> **O que foi que você disse?** 'What did you say?' (*more polite*)
>
> **O que é que falou?** 'What did you say?' (*informal*)
>
> **Como é que é?** 'I beg your pardon?' (*expresses shock or impatience*)

In informal conversation, you may also hear **o quê?** 'what?' but, like its English equivalent, this can sound rude so should be used with care. Of the expressions listed above, **como?** is the most versatile.

30.3.2 To answer a request for repetition, speakers will either repeat the exact words said previously or use a paraphrase, but this may be introduced by:

> **Eu disse que . . .** 'I said (that) . . .'
>
> **Falei que . . .** 'I said (that) . . .'
>
> **Eu estava dizendo/falando que . . .** 'I was saying (that) . . .'.

A yes–no question may be repeated by introducing it with **se** 'if, whether' or with **Perguntei se . . .** 'I asked whether . . .':

> **– Quer mais suco?**
> 'Would you like some more juice?'
>
> **– O que é que foi?**
> 'What was that?'
>
> **– Se você quer mais suco.** *or* **Perguntei se você quer mais suco.**
> 'I asked if you wanted some more juice.'

An imperative may be repeated by using **para você** followed by the infinitive. This can be preceded by **Eu disse/falei . . .** 'I told you . . .':

> **– Apaga a luz.**
> 'Turn the light off.'
>
> **– Como?**
> 'Pardon?'
>
> **– Para você apagar a luz.** *or* **Falei para você apagar a luz.**
> 'I told you to turn the light off.'

30.4 Making sure you understand and are understood

30.4.1 The following phrases may be used when you do not understand:

> **Desculpe, não entendi.**
> Sorry, I don't understand.
>
> **Desculpe, mas não falo muito bem português.**
> Sorry, but I don't speak Portuguese very well.
>
> **Dá para repetir, por favor?**
> Could you repeat that, please?
>
> **Pode falar mais devagar, por favor?**
> Can you speak more slowly, please?
>
> **Não peguei a primeira parte.**
> I didn't get the first part.

30.4.2 To ask the meaning of a word or phrase say:

> **O que quer dizer . . . ?**
> What does . . . mean?
>
> **O que significa a palavra . . . ?**
> What does the word . . . mean?

O que significa essa palavra?
What does this word mean?

O que é que você quer dizer com . . . ?
What do you mean by . . . ?

Como é 'paquerar' em inglês?
What's 'paquerar' in English?

30.4.3 If you are lost for a word, you can use the impersonal phrase **Como se diz . . . ?** 'How do you say . . . ?':

Como se diz 'webcam' em português?
How do you say 'webcam' in Portuguese?

30.4.4 To check whether people have understood what you have said, you can use the following phrases, which people will also ask you:

Entendeu?
Do you understand?

Deu para entender?
Were you able to understand?

30.5 Signalling that you understand the speaker and are following what is being said

You can signal that you are following what someone is saying to you by using the following expressions:

É. 'Yes.'

Pois é. 'Yes, that's right.' / 'Yes, I know.'

É isso. 'That's it.'

(Mas) é isso aí. '(But) that's just the thing.'

Aí é que está. 'That's the point.'

Com certeza. 'Quite right.' / 'Sure.' / 'Definitely.'

Sem dúvida. 'Definitely.'

De fato. 'Indeed.' / 'Certainly.'

Certo. 'Right.'

Exato. 'Exactly.'

Perfeito. 'Understood.'

Lógico. 'Of course.'

Entendi. 'I understand.' / 'I see.'

Sei. 'I know.'

É mesmo? 'Really?'

Que bom. 'That's good.'

Legal. 'That's nice (of/for you).'

Ótimo! 'Great!'

You can also use more emotive expressions, such as:

Mentira! 'You're kidding!'

Jura? 'Really?'

Não! 'No!'

Ai, que horror! 'Oh, how awful!'

Não acredito! 'I don't believe it!'

Não me diga! 'You don't say!'

Nossa! 'Gosh!'

Vix!, Vixe! 'Oh dear!'

Gente! 'Gee!', 'Blimey!'

Caramba! 'Damn!'

Que coisa! 'What a thing to happen!'

Meu Deus! 'My goodness!'

Ai meu Deus! 'Oh my God!'

30.6 Asking how to pronounce or spell a word

30.6.1 To ask how to pronounce a word, use the phrase **Como se pronuncia . . . ?** 'How do you pronounce . . . ?':

Como se pronuncia o seu sobrenome?
How do you pronounce your surname?

30.6.2 To ask someone to spell a word, you can use the phrase **Como se escreve?** 'How do you spell it?' or a sentence containing the verb **soletrar** 'to spell (out)':

Como se escreve o seu nome?
How do you spell your name?

Pode soletrar, por favor?
Can you spell that, please?

▶ **22.4** (p. 201)

30.7 Interrupting a speaker

To interrupt someone during the course of a conversation, use one of the following expressions with **desculpar** 'to excuse':

Desculpe (*formal*)/**Desculpa** (*informal*)**, mas . . .**
Excuse me, but . . .

Desculpe/Desculpa interromper, mas . . .
Sorry to interrupt, but . . .

Desculpa eu te cortar, mas . . .
Sorry to cut in on you, but . . .

Desculpe/Desculpa, cortei você.
Sorry, I interrupted you.

▶ **Chapter 21** (p. 196)

30.8 **Fillers**

Fillers are short words or phrases that are used to fill gaps in the conversation, when you are hesitating, pausing for thought, trying to remember something, deciding what to say next, etc. In English, we use words like 'well', 'well then', 'you know', 'right', etc. Brazilians use the following words and expressions:

> **bom** 'well', 'right'/'ok', 'now then'
>
> **então** 'so', 'yes, well . . .', 'now'
>
> **é que** 'it's just that'
>
> **é o seguinte** 'the thing is'
>
> **o negócio é o seguinte** 'the thing is' (*informal*)
>
> **olha** 'look'
>
> **sabe** 'you know'
>
> **veja bem** 'well, you see' (*more formal*)
>
> **ou seja** 'in other words'
>
> **quer dizer** 'I mean'
>
> **aliás** 'in fact', 'actually'
>
> **na verdade** 'actually'
>
> **para falar a verdade** 'to tell the truth', 'to be honest'
>
> **tipo** 'like', 'sort of' (*very informal*)
>
> **tipo assim** 'so like' (*very informal*).

The word **bom** can be used as an opening or to express hesitation:

> **Bom, deixe eu esclarecer a situação.**
> Well, let me clarify the situation.
>
> **Bom, vamos começar?**
> OK, shall we start?
>
> **O que é que você acha? – Bom, não sei.**
> 'What do you think?' – 'Well, I don't know.'

The word **então** can mean 'so' but may also be used as an opening, 'well so . . .':

> **Então, meu nome é Valdir, sou o gerente de vendas.**
> Well, so my name is Valdir and I'm the sales manager.

The expression **é que** is used to introduce a reason or explanation:

> **É que eu estava pensando no que você falou.**
> The thing is, I was thinking about what you said.
>
> **É que temos que tomar uma atitude.**
> The thing is, we have to do something.

The phrases **é o seguinte** and, more informally, **o negócio é o seguinte** can also be used in this way, or as general openers:

> **É o seguinte: você vai querer viajar com a gente esse fim de semana?**
> The thing is this: do you want to go away with us this weekend?

> **O negócio é o seguinte: onde é que nós vamos?**
> The thing is, right, where are we going to go?

The terms **olha** 'look', **sabe** 'you know', **entende?/entendeu?** 'you see?' 'know what I mean?' are used as follows:

> **Olha, não posso prometer nada.**
> Look, I can't promise anything.

> **Olha, eu não achei tão ruim assim.**
> I didn't find it that bad, if you really want to know.

> **Eu gosto dela, sabe, mas às vezes me irrita.**
> I like her, right, but sometimes she gets on my nerves.

The expression **veja bem** 'well, you see' introduces an explanation and sounds slightly more formal:

> **Veja bem, o Brasil é um país imenso, muito maior do que a Inglaterra.**
> Well, you see, Brazil is a huge country, much bigger than Britain.

The phrase **ou seja** 'in other words', 'which means' is used as follows:

> **A empresa quebrou, ou seja, estamos todos na rua.**
> The company's gone bust, which means we're all out of a job.

The expression **quer dizer** 'I mean' introduces a correction, qualification or further explanation:

> **Ele chega no sábado, quer dizer, domingo.**
> He gets here on Saturday, I mean, Sunday.

> **Vou terminar o trabalho essa semana, quer dizer, vou tentar.**
> I'm going to finish the job this week, well, at least, I'm going to try.

> **O dono vai vender a casa, quer dizer, temos que arranjar outro lugar para morar.**
> The owner is going to sell the house, which means we have to find somewhere else to live.

The word **aliás** has four uses: (1) to introduce an incidental comment 'by the way, actually'; (2) to qualify what you have just said 'in fact, actually'; (3) to expand on what you have just said 'what's more'; and (4) to correct a mistake 'or rather, I mean':

> **Quero aprender francês. Aliás, você não conhece algum professor?**
> I want to learn French. By the way, you don't know any teachers, do you?

> **Não comprei a passagem ainda. Aliás, nem sei se vou mais.**
> I haven't bought the ticket yet. In fact, I don't know if I'm going to go any more.

> **Ela é simpática. Aliás, ela é muito inteligente também.**
> She's nice. What's more, she's really clever, too.

Ele faz aniversário em março, aliás, em abril.
His birthday's in March, or rather, April.

The expressions **na verdade** 'actually' and **para falar a verdade** 'to be honest' are used as follows:

Na verdade, não sou daqui. Nasci em Curitiba.
Actually, I'm not from here. I was born in Curitiba.

Nós preferimos sentar lá dentro, na verdade.
We'd prefer to sit inside, actually.

Para falar a verdade, não gosto muito de futebol.
To be honest, I don't like soccer very much.

The expressions **tipo** 'like, sort of' and **tipo assim** 'I mean like' are frequently heard, especially in the speech of young people, but would sound strange coming from a foreign learner:

Ele falou para a gente estar lá tipo nove horas.
He said for us to be there, like, at nine.

Ela me olhou, tipo, quem é você?
She looked at me, like, who are you?

Vamos comprar umas coisinhas, tipo salgadinhos, queijo, frios . . .
Let's buy some little things, like snacks, cheese, cold meats . . .

Eu acho, tipo assim, se ele fez isso, é porque ainda gosta de você.
I think, like, if he did that, it's because he still likes you.

Mas, tipo assim, fiquei chateado, sabe?
But I mean, like, it pissed me off, you know?

30.9 Changing the subject

Common expressions are:

Por falar nisso . . .
By the way . . .

Por falar em . . .
Talking about . . . / On the subject of . . .

Isso me lembra . . .
That reminds me . . .

Mudando de assunto, . . .
Changing the subject, . . .

Voltando ao que eu/a gente/você falava antes, . . .
Going back to what I was/we were/you were saying before, . . .

Mudando da água para o vinho, . . .
Changing the subject completely, . . .

Voltando à vaca fria, . . . (*informal*)
Going back to the previous subject, . . .

30.10 Formal development of a topic

30.10.1 Opening remarks

To present a new topic formally, in the course of a lecture, talk or a very formal discussion, there are a number of expressions that can be used as opening remarks. Among these are:

> **Em primeiro lugar . . .** 'First of all . . .'
>
> **Primeiramente . . .** 'Firstly . . .'
>
> **Para começar . . .** 'To start with . . .'
>
> **Antes de mais nada . . .** 'First of all . . .'
>
> **Quero/Queria mencionar . . .** 'I want to/I'd like to mention . . .'
>
> **Quero falar sobre . . .** 'I want to talk about . . .'
>
> **Quero examinar . . .** 'I want to look at/consider . . .'.

30.10.2 Introducing further points

> **Além disso** 'In addition', 'Besides . . .'
>
> **Também . . .** 'Also . . .'
>
> **Pois bem . . . / Ora bem . . .** 'Well now . . .'
>
> **Vejamos agora . . .** 'Now let's look at . . .'
>
> **Vamos tratar agora de . . .** 'Let us now deal with . . .'.

30.10.3 Establishing a sequence

The following words are used to establish a sequence between various points:

> **Em primeiro lugar . . .** 'First of all . . .'
>
> **Primeiro/Segundo/Terceiro, . . .** 'Firstly/Secondly/Thirdly, . . .'
>
> **Por último, . . .** 'Lastly, . . .'
>
> **Aí . . .** 'Then . . .'
>
> **Depois . . .** 'Then . . .'
>
> **A seguir . . .** 'Next . . .'
>
> **Prosseguindo . . .** 'Moving on . . .'
>
> **Mais adiante vamos ver . . .** 'Further on we shall see . . .'.

30.10.4 Establishing references

To establish references between part of an argument or between information shared between the speaker and listener with a related point, the following phrases are used:

> **No que se refere a . . .** 'With reference/regard to . . .'
>
> **No que diz respeito a . . .** 'As far as . . . is/are concerned'
>
> **Com referência a . . .** 'With reference to . . .'

Em relação a . . . 'With respect to . . .'

Quanto a . . . 'As for . . . , as regards . . .'.

The expressions listed above are also encountered in formal letters:

Com referência a sua carta de 20 de novembro, . . .
With reference to your letter of 20 November, . . .

Em relação à sua proposta . . .
With regard to your proposal . . .

No que se refere à forma de pagamento . . .
With regard to the form of payment . . .

30.10.5 Giving examples

To give examples and illustrate a point, use the following:

Por exemplo . . . 'For example . . .'

Para dar/citar um exemplo . . . 'To give/quote an example . . .'

Vejamos o exemplo de . . . 'Let us take the example of . . .'

Para exemplificar, . . . / Para ilustrar, . . . 'To illustrate (what I mean), . . .'

A título de ilustração, . . . 'By way of an illustration, . . .'

Para você ter uma ideia, . . . 'To give you an idea, . . .'

Assim . . . 'Thus . . .'

Assim, por exemplo . . . 'Thus, for example . . .'

Como . . . 'Like . . .'

Tais como . . . 'Such as . . .'.

30.10.6 How to explain yourself

To indicate you are about to explain something again, in new terms, use the following:

Isto é . . . 'That is to say . . .'

Ou seja . . . 'Or, in other words . . .'

Isso quer dizer que . . . 'That means that . . .'

Isso significa que . . . 'That means that . . .'

Em outras palavras . . . 'In other words . . .'

Vou explicar. 'I'll explain.' / 'Let me explain.'

Vou esclarecer. 'I'll clarify that.' / 'Allow me to clarify.'

O que quero dizer é que . . . 'What I mean is that . . .'.

30.10.7 How to ask for and give the floor

To ask to speak in the course of a formal meeting, you can use the following expressions:

Com licença. 'Excuse me.'

Se vocês permitirem . . . 'If you'll allow me . . .'

Peço a palavra. 'May I say something?'

A palavra está com . . . '(*Name*) has the floor.'

Dou/Cedo a palavra a . . . 'I give the floor to (*name*).'

Pediu a palavra . . . '(*Name*) has asked to speak.'

30.10.8 Summarizing and concluding

To summarize and abbreviate different points in an argument and to conclude a presentation, use the following expressions:

Resumindo . . . 'Summing up . . .'

Em resumo . . . 'In short . . .' / 'To sum up . . .'

Em poucas palavras . . . 'To sum up in a few words . . .'

Concluindo . . . / Para concluir . . . 'To conclude . . .'

Em conclusão . . . 'In conclusion . . .'

Finalmente . . . 'Finally . . .'

Por último . . . 'Lastly . . .'

Como último ponto . . . 'As a final point . . .'

Só quero acrescentar que . . . 'I'd just like to add that . . .'

Não posso deixar de dizer que . . . 'I should just say that . . .'.

II

Giving and seeking factual information

31

Asking questions and responding

31.1   Yes–no questions

31.1.1   Yes–no questions are formulated in the same way as statements, the only difference being the question intonation in speech and the question mark in writing. There is no subject-verb inversion as happens in English and some other languages:

> **Ele é italiano.**
> He's Italian. (*statement*)
>
> **Ele é italiano?**
> Is he Italian? (*question*)

31.1.2   When replying to yes–no questions, the main verb of the question is repeated in the appropriate person and negated with **não** if necessary:

> **Você fala português? – Falo.**
> 'Do you speak Portuguese?' – 'Yes.'
>
> **Você fala chinês? – Não falo.**
> 'Do you speak Chinese?' – 'No.'

31.1.3   Although **não** 'no' can be used on its own to answer a question, **sim** 'yes' is not normally used in this way. But both **não** and **sim** can be added to the repeated verb to add emphasis or to make the answer sound less abrupt:

> **Você é americano? – Não, não sou. / Não sou, não.[1] / Não.**
> 'Are you American?' – 'No, I'm not.' / 'I'm not, no.' / 'No.'
>
> **Vocês foram para a festa? – Fomos sim. / Fomos.**
> 'Did you go to the party?' – 'Yes, we did.' / 'Yes.'

NOTE   1   It is quite common in informal speech to repeat the **não** after the verb, e.g. **não sei não** 'I don't know', **não quero não** 'I don't want it/to', etc. Some speakers omit the first **não**, e.g. **sei não, quero não**, etc.

31.1.4   When an auxiliary verb occurs in the question, it is the auxiliary that is repeated in the answer:

> **Posso usar seu telefone? – Pode.**
> 'Can I use your phone?' – 'Yes.'
>
> **Você vai contar para ele? – Vou.**
> 'Are you going to tell him?' – 'Yes.'

31.1.5 If the question contains the word **já** 'already, yet, ever', **já** is used to give an affirmative answer:

> **Você já provou comida tailandesa? - Já.**
> 'Have you ever tried Thai food?' – 'Yes, I have.'

> **Quem já esteve no Brasil? – Eu já.**
> 'Who's been to Brazil?' – 'I have.'

31.1.6 When you simply want to endorse something that has been said or move the conversation along, the equivalent to 'yes' is **é** (*literally*, 'it is'):

> **Os brasileiros comem muita carne. – É, com certeza.**
> 'Brazilians eat a lot of meat.' – 'Yes, they certainly do.'

> **É, então, vamos começar a aula.**
> Yes, so, let's start the lesson.

31.2 Content questions

▶ Chapter 11 (p. 115)

31.2.1 Content questions are those that contain a question word, such as 'what', 'where', 'who', etc. These can be formed in Portuguese in the same way as in English, with the question word in initial position, but there is no inversion of subject and verb when the subject is a pronoun:

> **Onde você foi ontem à noite?**
> Where did you go last night?

> **Quantas vezes por semana ele vai para São Paulo?**
> How many times a week does he go to São Paulo?

> **Por que não jantamos fora?**
> Why don't we go out for dinner?

31.2.2 When the subject is a noun, inversion can take place and usually does when the verb means 'to be' (**ser**, **estar**, **ficar**, etc.) or with the verb **ter** 'to have':

> **Como vai o seu irmão?**
> How is your brother?

> **Quantos anos tem a sua irmã?**
> How old is your sister?

31.2.3 When a question word is accompanied by a preposition, the preposition is placed at the beginning of the sentence, not the end:

> **De que vocês estão falando?**
> What are you talking about?

> **Com quem ela vai casar?**
> Who's she going to marry?

> **Para quem você deu a chave?**
> Who did you give the key to?

31.2.4 In the spoken language, it is common to insert **... é que ...** (*literally*, 'is it that') after the question word, especially in the case of **o que** 'what' and **quando** 'when':

O que é que você falou?
What did you say?

Quando é que ela volta?
When is she coming back? / When is it she's coming back?

NOTE | In colloquial speech, **o que é que** . . . is pronounced /kiki/, so, for example, **o que é que foi?** 'what's the matter?' is pronounced /kiki foi/.

31.2.5 When the main verb is in the preterite tense, . . . **é que** . . . is often replaced by . . . **foi que** . . . (*literally*, 'was it that'):

O que foi que você falou?
What did you say? / What was it you said?

31.2.6 In colloquial speech, the question word can be inserted in the position where the missing information would be in a statement, and this is the norm when you are asking for repetition or confirmation of something you have already been told. In the latter case, the question word would be more heavily stressed, as in English:

Ela volta quando?
When is she coming back?

Você é de que cidade nos Estados Unidos?
What town are you from in the USA?

Você combinou com eles a que horas mesmo?
What time did you arrange to meet them again?

31.3 Follow-up questions

31.3.1 Follow-up questions can be introduced with **e** (*literally*, 'and'), which, in this case, means 'and/but what about . . . ?':

Como vai? – Eu estou bem. E você?
'How are you?' – 'I'm fine. And you?'

E seu pai? Ele já melhorou?
And how about your dad? Is he better now?

E o Pedro? Ele vai dormir onde?
But what about Pedro? Where's he going to sleep?

31.4 Rhetorical questions

31.4.1 Rhetorical questions are introduced with **Será que** . . . , which can be thought of as meaning 'I wonder if . . .':

Será que ela esqueceu?
I wonder if she's forgotten?

Será que você pode me ajudar um pouco?
I wonder if you can help me a minute?

31.4.2 The expression **será que** can also be used in combination with question words:

Aonde será que ele foi?
I wonder where he's gone? / Where do you suppose he's gone?

Quanto tempo será que vamos ter que esperar?
How long will we have to wait, I wonder? / How long do you suppose we'll have to wait?

31.5 Tag questions

31.5.1 The most versatile tag question is **não é?**,[1] which can be appended to any statement when you expect an affirmative answer:

Você é americano, não é?
You're American, aren't you?

Ele chegou ontem, não é?
He arrived yesterday, didn't he?

Você deve ir no médico, não é?
You should go to the doctor, shouldn't you?

NOTE   1   Often shortened to **né?** in colloquial speech.

31.5.2 It can also be appended to negative statements:

Você não falou nada para ninguém, não é?
You didn't tell anyone anything, did you?

Ela não é brasileira, não é?
She's not Brazilian, is she?

31.5.3 The positive tag **é?** has the sense of 'so . . . , is it?/are you?/did they?', etc.:

Você é americano, é?
So you're American, are you?

Ele chegou ontem, é?
So he arrived yesterday, did he?

Ela sabe ler chinês, é?
So she can read Chinese, can she?

31.5.4 In colloquial speech, tag questions are formed in a similar way to English, i.e. the finite verb of the sentence is repeated and changed from positive to negative or negative to positive:

Você tem carro, não tem?
You have a car, don't you?

Ele não vai voltar, vai?
He's not coming back, is he?

Você pode pegar o trem, não pode?
You can take the train, can't you?

31.6 Negative questions

As in English, a negative question usually expects a negative answer, but can sometimes be used to convey surprise or annoyance or to make a tentative inquiry:

Você não entende português?
Don't you understand Portuguese?

Você não terminou ainda?
Haven't you finished yet? (= *you should have*)

Você não trancou o carro?
Didn't you lock the car? (= *how careless of you*)

Você não acha melhor ligar para os seus pais?
Don't you think you'd better call your parents?

31.7 Polite questions

A question to a stranger can always be introduced with **por favor** 'excuse me' (see **30.1.1**) and then **o senhor/a senhora pode me dizer . . . ?** 'Can you tell me . . . ?' when addressing an older person, or **você pode me dizer . . . ?** 'Can you tell me . . . ?' when addressing someone of the same age or younger:

Por favor, você pode me dizer onde fica o Teatro Municipal?
Excuse me, can you tell me where the Municipal Theatre is, please?

Por favor, a senhora sabe que ônibus vai até a Praça da República?
Excuse me, do you know which bus goes to the Praça da República?

31.8 Other ways of answering questions

31.8.1 Affirmative responses

As pointed out in **31.1.3**, **sim** is not usually used on its own as an affirmative response. The following are other ways of answering in the affirmative:

Claro. 'Of course.'

Claro que (+ *repeated verb*), e.g.:

Você gosta dela? – Claro que gosto. 'Do you like her? – Of course I do.'

Claro que sim. 'Yes, of course.'

Lógico. 'Of course.'

Com certeza. 'Definitely.' / 'Certainly.'

Sem dúvida. 'Definitely.'

Pode crer. (*informal*) 'Sure is/are/do/does etc.'

Boto fé. (*informal*) 'I can well believe it.', 'I bet.'

31.8.2 Negative responses

The most common negative responses are:

Claro que não. 'Of course not.'

Lógico que não. 'Of course not.'

De jeito nenhum. 'Not at all.' / 'No way.' / 'Certainly not.'

Imagina! 'You must be kidding!'

Que nada! 'Not at all!' / 'You're kidding, right?'

Nada disso! 'Nothing of the kind!', 'Not at all!'

Não mesmo! 'Definitely not!'

Fala sério! 'Be serious!', 'Come off it!'

Não vem com essa! / Sem essa! 'Don't give me that!', 'Come off it!'

Deus (que) me livre! 'Heaven forbid!'

Examples:

Você se importa se eu sentar aqui? – Claro que não.
'Do you mind if I sit here?' – 'Of course not.'

Você ficou chateado comigo? – De jeito nenhum.
'Did I upset you?' – 'Not at all.'

Você vai convidar o Cláudio? – De jeito nenhum!
'Are you going to invite Claudio?' – 'No way!' / 'Certainly not!'

Devolveram o seu dinheiro? – Imagina!
'Did they give you your money back?' – 'You must be kidding!'

A obra já terminou? – Que nada! Falta muito ainda.
'Is the building work finished?' – 'Not at all! There's still a long way to go.'

Você está a fim da Tatiana? – Deus me livre!
'Do you have a thing for Tatiana?' – 'God, no!'

32

Negating

See **Chapter 14** for negative words and how to use them.

See **Chapter 31** on how to give negative answers.

32.1 Negating adjectives

32.1.1 Negative prefixes

The two most frequent negative prefixes for adjectives are **in**- (which becomes **im**- before **b** and **p**, **i**- before **l** and **ir**- before **r**, as in English) and **des**-. Of these, **des**- is still productive in that it is occasionally used to create new adjectives:

in-:

incapaz	incapable
impossível	impossible
ilógico	illogical
irrelevante	irrelevant

des-:

desconhecido	unknown
desconfortável	uncomfortable
desocupado	unoccupied
despreocupado	unworried, unconcerned.

32.1.2 Other negativizers

When there is no negative adjective beginning with **in**- or **des**-, the usual device is to use **pouco** as a negativizer:

pouco convincente	unconvincing
pouco original	unoriginal
pouco interessante	uninteresting
pouco atraente	unattractive.

In a few cases, **não** is used,[1] usually corresponding to the English 'non':

objeto voador não identificado	unidentified flying object
quarto não fumante	non-smoking room
países não alinhados	non-aligned countries.

NOTE   1   Since the 2009 spelling reform, such adjectives are no longer spelt with a hyphen.

32.2 Negating nouns

não is also used to negate certain nouns,[2] corresponding to 'non' in English:

não fumante	non-smoker
não proliferação	non-proliferation
não violência	non-violence.

NOTE   2   Since the 2009 spelling reform, such nouns are no longer spelt with a hyphen.

32.3 Negating verbs

The prefix **des-** negates the meaning of a verb, and is often used productively, corresponding to the English 'un-':

desfazer	to undo
desamarrar	to untie
deszipar	to unzip (*a file*)
desconvidar	to 'uninvite' (*someone you have already invited*).

33

Reporting

33.1 Direct vs. indirect speech

An important function in language is to report what other people have said. This may be done by reproducing the exact words expressed by the speaker (direct speech) or, more often, by reporting his or her words in an indirect way (indirect speech). Direct speech, introduced by a verb such as **dizer** 'to say', is commonly found in fiction writing in the form of dialogue:[1]

> – **Vamos para casa** – **disse Antônia.**
> 'Let's go home,' said Antonia.

But particularly in the spoken language, it is much more common to use indirect speech.

NOTE   1   For the punctuation of dialogue in Portuguese, see **1.10.**

33.2 Indirect speech

There are basically three types of indirect speech: indirect statements, indirect questions and indirect commands/requests. An indirect statement reports a statement made by another person, usually introduced with a reporting phrase such as **ele disse que** 'he said that'; an indirect question reports a question asked by another person, usually introduced by a reporting phrase such as **ela perguntou se** 'she asked if/whether'; and an indirect command/request reports an instruction or request made by another person, usually introduced with a reporting phrase such as **ele nos mandou** 'he told us to' or **ela me pediu para** 'she asked me to'.

In Portuguese, as in English, the tense of the verb used in indirect speech may differ from that used in direct speech, depending on the time relations and continued validity of the indirect speech. Consider the following examples:

> *Her actual words*: **Eu gosto de chocolate.** 'I like chocolate.'
> **Ela disse que gosta de chocolate.**
> She said she likes chocolate.
> **Ela disse que gostava de chocolate.**
> She said she liked chocolate.
>
> *His actual words*: **Eu vou ligar para você.** 'I'll call you.'
> **Ele falou que vai ligar para mim.**
> He said he'll call me.
> **Ele falou que ia ligar para mim.**
> He said he'd call me.

In the first example of each pair, the present tense **gosta** 'likes' and the future tense **vai ligar** 'will call' are preserved in indirect speech because the statements 'she likes' and 'he'll call' are still valid in relation to the time when they are reported. The change of tense to **gostava** 'she liked' and **ia ligar** 'would call' in the second example of each pair indicates the reported statements are no longer relevant to the present time, or that the person reporting is skeptical about their validity. Portuguese and English work in the same way in this respect.

Furthermore, as the conversion of **eu** 'I' to **ele** 'he' and **você** 'you' to **mim** 'me' in the above example shows, other elements of the sentence may also change when reporting in indirect speech, but the same changes, including the choice of verb tense, are made in both Portuguese and English.

33.3 Reporting statements

33.3.1 Verbs used to introduce reported statements

The verb **dizer** 'to say' is probably the verb most commonly used to introduce a reported statement, although, in the spoken language, the verb **falar** (*literally,* 'to speak') is also used in the sense of 'to say' and is more frequent than **dizer**. Among other verbs used to introduce reported statements are **acrescentar** 'to add', **afirmar** 'to state', **alegar** 'to claim, allege', **comentar** 'to comment', **explicar** 'to explain', **mencionar** 'to mention', as well as others that reveal the intention of the statement, such as **esperar** 'to hope', **garantir** 'to assure', **negar** 'to deny', **prometer** 'to promise', etc.

33.3.2 Conjunction used to introduce reported statements

The conjunction used to introduce reported statements is **que** 'that' and, unlike in English, it can never be omitted in Portuguese:

> **A Patrícia falou que vinha.**
> Patricia said she was coming.

> **Ele me garantiu que ia devolver a bicicleta antes do meio-dia.**
> He assured me he'd return the bike before midday.

33.3.3 Use of tenses in reported statements

As pointed out in **33.2**, Portuguese and English follow the same rules regarding the use of tenses in indirect speech. But note the following:

(i)   The English 'would' is expressed in Portuguese using the conditional, the imperfect or the imperfect of the auxiliary verb **ir** plus the infinitive.[2] The conditional itself (other than that of the verb **ser**) sounds ponderous and formal and is usually avoided in speech and informal writing. In these registers, the imperfect is used instead (see **18.1.2** (v)) or the imperfect of **ir** followed by an infinitive:

NOTE   2   A fourth possibility may be encountered in the written language: the conditional of the verb **ir** followed by an infinitive, e.g. **Ele disse que iria voltar**. 'He said he would be back.'

> **Ele disse que voltaria.** (*more formal*)

> **Ele disse que voltava.** (*informal and speech*)

> **Ele disse que ia voltar.** (*neutral*)
> He said he'd be back.

(ii)   When the reporting verb is past tense, and the action of the indirect speech happened at an earlier time still, English requires the pluperfect where Portuguese often uses the simple preterite, especially in speech, even though the pluperfect may also be used:

> **Alegaram que o computador foi roubado.**
> They claimed that the computer had been stolen.

Mood in reported statements

▶ **20.3** (p. 188)

Some reporting verbs require the use of the subjunctive in the reported statement, e.g. **duvidar** 'to doubt', **esperar** 'to hope', **negar** 'to deny', etc. (see **20.3.2**, **20.3.4**):

> **O governo negou que tivesse chegado a um acordo com os terroristas.**
> The government denied that it had reached an agreement with the terrorists.

> **O técnico espera que o time se classifique para a final.**
> The coach hopes that the team gets through to the final.

Notice that the sequence of tenses rule (**20.2**) can be broken after **negar** when the reported statement is still valid:

> **O ministro negou que o governo vá revogar a lei.** (*not* **fosse revogar**)
> The minister denied that the government is going to repeal the law.

Reporting questions

▶ **Chapter 11** (p. 115)

In the case of indirect questions, the reporting verb is usually **perguntar** 'to ask', or a synonymous word or expression, such as **querer saber** 'want to know', and the conjunction **se** 'if, whether' or another interrogative word (see **Chapter 11**). The same rules on verb tenses apply as in indirect statements:

> **Ele perguntou se queríamos sair com ele.**
> He asked if we wanted to go out with him.

> **Ela queria saber a que horas a festa vai começar.**
> She wanted to know what time the party's going to start.

Note that, in reported questions, a noun subject is normally placed after the finite verb if the latter would otherwise fall at the end of the sentence. This rule does not apply if the subject is a personal pronoun:

> **Ela perguntou onde era o banheiro.**
> She asked where the bathroom was.

> **Ele queria saber quantos anos tinha a minha mãe.**
> He wanted to know how old my mother was.

> **Ela perguntou onde você estava.**
> She asked where you were.

33.5 ## Reporting yes and no answers

The conjunction **que** is used before **sim** and **não** to report a yes or no answer. Notice that, in English, this often corresponds to the repetition of an affirmative or negative auxiliary:

> **Ele disse que não.**
> He said no.

> **Ela respondeu que sim.**
> She answered yes.

> **Ele quer ir? – Ele diz que não.**
> 'Does he want to go?' – 'He says he doesn't.'

> **Quando perguntei a ela se ia voltar logo, ela respondeu que sim.**
> When I asked her if she would be back soon, she replied that she would.

33.6 ## Reporting commands and requests

The most common verbs used for reporting commands are **mandar** 'to order, instruct, tell' and **dizer/falar** 'to tell'. The constructions used with these verbs are **mandar alguém fazer** and **dizer/falar para alguém fazer**:

> **Ele falou para a gente esperar aqui.** (*spoken*)
> He told us to wait here.

> **Ela disse para você ligar mais tarde.**
> She said for you to call her later.

> **Eles me mandaram sair da sala.**
> They instructed me to leave the room.

▶ **19.5** (p. 179)

Other reporting verbs require a subjunctive construction, e.g. **exigir que alguém faça** 'to demand that someone do', **insistir que alguém faça** 'to insist that someone do', **ordenar a alguém que faça** 'to order someone to do', **querer que alguém faça** 'to want/expect someone to do':

> **Ele exigiu que eu pedisse desculpas.**
> He demanded that I apologize.

> **Ordenaram à polícia que reviste todos os torcedores que entrarem no estádio.**
> They have ordered the police to search all fans entering the stadium.

> **Ela quer que você ligue para ela.**
> She wants you to call her.

▶ **20.3.2** (p. 189)

Indirect requests are usually introduced by the reporting verb **pedir** 'to ask'. **pedir** forms a number of different constructions depending on the meaning and degree of formality:

(i)   **pedir para fazer** 'to ask to do':

> **Ele pediu para usar o telefone.**
> He asked to use the phone.

(ii)   **pedir a alguém para fazer** (*neutral level*), **pedir para alguém fazer** (*informal speech*) and **pedir a alguém que faça** (*formal*) 'to ask someone to do':

> **Ela me pediu para comprar leite.** (*neutral*)

> **Ela pediu para eu comprar leite.** (*informal spoken*)[3]
> She asked me to buy milk.

> **Ela pediu ao assistente que entregasse a carta em mãos.** (*formal*)
> She asked her assistant to deliver the letter by hand.

▶ **19.5** (p. 179)

Other verbs that introduce a reported command/request are: **aconselhar que alguém faça** 'to advise that someone should do', **solicitar que alguém faça** 'to request that someone does', **sugerir que alguém faça** 'to suggest that someone should do':

> **Ele aconselhou que eu não pedalasse sem capacete.**
> He advised that I shouldn't cycle without a helmet.

> **Ela sugeriu que voltemos amanhã.**
> She suggested that we come back tomorrow.

Observe, as in the second example above, that, after reporting verbs such as **exigir**, **ordenar** and **sugerir**, the sequence of tense rules (see **20.2**) are broken if the indirect command/request is still valid.

NOTE   3   You will also hear native speakers say **Ela pediu para mim comprar leite**, which is considered non-standard and incorrect.

34

Asking and giving personal information

In this chapter you will learn different ways of asking and giving personal information, such as name, nationality, place of origin, occupation, marital and professional status, religious, political and other types of affiliation. You will also learn how to say your age and when and where you were born, and to ask for similar information from others.

34.1 Name

34.1.1 Use of names in Brazil

The traditional Portuguese practice of including the mother's maiden name before the father's family name, and the subsequent addition of the husband's family name, means that, over the course of several generations, a Brazilian's family name can become quite long and complex, with two, three, four or even more separate elements. On the other hand, some people opt for a single family name, and waves of immigrants of various nationalities have brought with them their own naming traditions. Thus, to simplify matters, given names are used far more widely than in the English-speaking world. For example, in Brazil, you would refer to and address a doctor with the title **Doutor(a)** followed by the doctor's given name rather than the family name, e.g. **Dr. Ricardo**, **Dra. Márcia**. Note also that you do not address a married woman using her husband's surname. Similarly, when asked your name, you are usually expected to give only your first name unless otherwise specified. If your family name is required, you will be asked **de quê?** after you give your first name or, for example, **John de quê?** 'John what?'. You may also be asked **nome completo?** 'full name?'.

A single family name may be the preferred form of address in the work environment, especially when a person has a very common given name. In such cases, the person is addressed and referred to only by the family name, but this is for convenience rather than formality, and is not perceived to be any more formal than addressing someone by their given name.

When respect is to be shown, e.g. to an older person and/or someone you would address as **o senhor/a senhora** (see **7.2**), it is customary to precede the person's given name with **senhor** (usually abbreviated in speech to **seu**) for males and **dona** for females:

> **Pode entrar, senhor/seu Pedro.**
> You may go in, Mr . . . (*family name would be used here in English*)

> **Bom dia, dona Sandra.**
> Good morning, Mrs/Ms . . . (*family name would be used here in English*).

312

These titles may be replaced by others, such as **doutor(a)** for medical doctors and other liberal professionals, e.g. lawyers, or **professor(a)** for teachers. In direct address, the title alone can be used:

>**Professor, vai ter prova hoje?**
>Sir, will we be having a test today?

Young children address their teachers as **tio/tia** (*literally*, 'uncle/aunt') and also use this form of address for all unrelated adults:

>**Tia, você viu a minha mãe?**
>Miss, have you seen my mum?

34.1.2 Giving and asking names

To say your name, use the expression **(o) meu nome é . . .** 'my name is . . .'. By changing the possessive pronoun (see **Chapter 9**) you can ask and give other people's names:

>**Meu nome é Carla.**
>My name is Carla.

>**Qual (é) o seu nome?**
>What's your name? (*neutral*)

>**Qual (é) o nome do senhor?**
>Can I have your name please, sir? (*formal*)

>**O nome dela é Bianca.**
>Her name's Bianca.

Notice that the verb **é** can be omitted after **qual**.

▶ **Chapter 9** (p. 105)

There is also the reflexive verb **chamar-se** 'to be called', which may be used in giving and asking people's names:

>**Eu me chamo Antônio.**
>I'm called Antonio.

>**O pai dela se chama Eduardo.**
>Her father's called Eduardo.

▶ **Chapter 22** (p. 199)

34.1.3 Other expressions to do with names

>**O nome da senhora?**
>Your name please, madam? (*formal*)

>**Qual o seu sobrenome?**
>What's your surname/family name?

>**O sobrenome dele é Ferreira.**
>His surname is Ferreira.

>**O nome completo, por favor.**
>Your full name, please.

Como se escreve?
How do you spell that?

Pode soletrar, por favor?
Could you spell that, please?

34.2 Nationality and place of origin

▶ **16.3.8** (p. 155); **23.2** (p. 204)

34.2.1 To state your own or someone else's nationality, use the verb **ser** with the appropriate adjective of nationality. Note that adjectives of nationality are written with a lower-case initial letter in Portuguese:

Sou americano.
I'm American.

O Luís é argentino.
Luís is Argentinian.

Note also:

Você é de que nacionalidade?
What nationality are you?

Sou de nacionalidade brasileira.
I am Brazilian by nationality. / My nationality is Brazilian.

34.2.2 To say where you or others come from, use the verb **ser** followed by the preposition **de** 'from':

Sou do Texas.
I'm from Texas.

A Sara é de Londres.
Sara is from London.

To ask where someone comes from, use **de onde . . . ?** with the verb **ser**:

De onde você é? (*neutral*)
Você é de onde? (*informal*)
Where are you from?

De onde eles são? (*neutral*)
Eles são de onde? (*informal*)
Where are they from?

34.3 Marital status

▶ **16.3.8** (p. 155); **23.2** (p. 204)

When stating or inquiring about legal marital status, use the verb **ser**:

Sou solteiro.
I'm single.

Ela é casada?
Is she married?

The verb **estar** can also be used with adjectives denoting marital status, but refers to a person's current, unofficial status and/or a subjective assessment of it:

> **Estou solteiro no momento.**
> I'm single at the moment.

> **Eles estão casados.**
> They're in a committed relationship.

In official situations, you may be asked:

> **Estado civil?**
> Marital status?

To which you may reply with a single word, for example:

> **solteiro/a** 'single', **casado/a** 'married', **divorciado/a** 'divorced', **separado/a** 'separated', **desquitado/a** 'legally separated', **viúvo/a** 'widowed'.

34.4 Age

▶ **16.3.5** (p. 154); **16.3.11** (p. 156)

To refer to someone's age, Portuguese uses the verb **ter** 'to have' or, more colloquially, **estar com** (*literally*, 'to be with'):

> **Quantos anos você tem?** (*neutral*)
> **Você tem quantos anos?** (*informal*)
> **Você está com quantos anos?** (*informal*)
> How old are you?

> **Tenho trinta anos.**
> **Estou com trinta anos.**
> I'm thirty years old.

> **Quantos anos tem sua irmã?**
> **Sua irmã tem quantos anos?**
> **Sua irmã está com quantos anos?**
> How old is your sister?

> **Minha mãe tem cinquenta e cinco.**
> **Minha mãe está com cinquenta e cinco.**
> My mum's fifty-five.

Alternative ways of asking someone's age are:

> **Que idade você tem?**
> **Você tem que idade?**
> **Você está com que idade?**
> What age are you?

When talking about turning a particular age or having a birthday, the verb to use is **fazer**:

> **Vou fazer trinta e cinco esse ano.**
> I'm going to be thirty-five this year.

> **Ela fez oitenta em janeiro.**
> She turned eighty in January.

O Vitor faz aniversário em junho.
Vitor's birthday is in June.

Other age expressions:

Ele deve ter uns quarenta anos.
He must be about forty.

Ela está na casa dos cinquenta.
She's in her fifties.

A filha deles está com vinte e poucos anos.
Their daughter is in her early twenties.

Ele está beirando os setenta.
He's pushing seventy.

34.5 Date and place of birth

Reference to date and place of birth is made with the verb **nascer**, normally in the preterite tense.

34.5.1 Date of birth

Em que data você nasceu?
Você nasceu em que data?
What date where you born?

Nasci no dia 8 de novembro de 1975.
I was born on November 8th, 1975.

In official situations, you are more likely to be asked:

Qual a sua data de nascimento?
What's your date of birth?

Or just:

Data de nascimento?
Date of birth?

34.5.2 Place of birth

Onde você nasceu?
Você nasceu onde?
Where were you born?

Nasci na Inglaterra.
I was born in England.

In official situations, you are more likely to be asked:

Lugar de nascimento?
Place of birth?

34.6 Occupation, status or rank, religious, political and other affiliations

▶ **16.3.8** (p. 155); **23.2** (p. 204)

34.6.1   To say what your or someone else's occupation is, use the verb **ser**:

> **Sou engenheiro.**
> I'm an engineer.

> **A Sandra é médica.**
> Sandra is a doctor.

Note that the indefinite article is not used in Portuguese when stating a person's occupation.

To ask what someone's occupation is, say:

> **Qual (é) a sua profissão?**
> What job do you do?

> **Em que você trabalha? / Você trabalha em quê?**
> What work do you do?

> **Que trabalho você faz?**
> What job do you do?

> **O que você faz como trabalho?**
> **Você faz o que como trabalho?**
> What do you do as a job?

> **O seu pai trabalha em quê?**
> What does your father do?

You can also ask: **O que você faz na vida?** 'What do you do for a living?'

To say that someone works as something, use **trabalhar de** or **como**:

> **Ele está trabalhando de garçom numa pizzaria.**
> He's working as a waiter in a pizza restaurant.

> **Trabalho como assessora de um político.**
> I work as an aide to a politician.

Notice that no indefinite article is used in Portuguese after **de** or **como** in this sense.

34.6.2   To ask and give information about status and rank, religion and political and other affiliations, use **ser**:

> **Ela é chefe da Contabilidade.**
> She's the head of the Accounts department.

> **Ele é oficial da Marinha.**
> He's an officer in the Navy.

> **O João é budista.**
> João is a Buddhist.

> **A Sônia é petista.**
> Sonia is a supporter of the Workers' Party (PT).

Notice that the articles are not used in Portuguese in all such cases.

34.6.3 In Brazil, it seems that everyone, regardless of age or gender, has a favourite soccer team. Brazilian teams have an associated noun/adjective which is used to describe a fan of that team and may be used after the verb **ser**:

> **Eles são flamenguistas.**
> They are Flamengo fans.

> **Você é corintiano?**
> Are you a Corinthians fan?

Alternatively, you can just use the name of the team after the verb **ser** and this is what you do with non-Brazilian team names:

> **Meu irmão é Bayern de Munique.**
> My brother's a Bayern Munich fan.

> **No basquete, sou Lakers.**
> In basketball, I'm a Lakers fan.

To ask someone what team they follow, you can use the verb **ser** or the expression **torcer por** 'to support, root for':

> **Qual é o seu time? / Você torce por que time?**
> Which team do you support/root for?[1]

NOTE | 1 You may well be asked this question in Brazil. Unless otherwise specified, the reference is to soccer. Saying you don't have a team or don't like soccer is often met with bemusement.

35

Identifying people and things

▶ **16.3.8** (p. 155); **23.2** (p. 204)

35.1 Identifying yourself and others

To say who you are or who someone is, use the verb **ser** 'to be':

Sou Leandro Ferreira.
I'm Leandro Ferreira.

Ela é Marta Penteado.
She is Marta Penteado.

Eles são os meus pais.
They are my parents.

If the purpose of the identification is to introduce somebody, then **ser** is usually preceded by a demonstrative pronoun:

Essa é a minha esposa.
This is my wife.

Esse é o meu irmão.
This is my brother.

Esses são os meus filhos.
These are my children.

To ask who someone is, use **quem** followed by **ser**:

Quem é ele?
Who's he?

Quem são aquelas pessoas?
Who are those people?

Note that the verb **ser** agrees in person and number with what follows it.

If you think you know who someone is and you simply want to make sure, you can say:

Você é a Susana?
Are you Susana?

O senhor é o seu Rafael?
Are you Mr . . . ? (*formal: surname would be used here in English*)

319

> **Esse é o seu professor?**
> Is that your teacher?

Identifying things

To identify something, use the verb **ser** and the interrogative pronoun **qual?** 'which (one)' or **quais?** 'which (ones)':

> **Qual é a sua bolsa?**
> Which is your bag?

> **(É) a preta.**
> (It's) the black one.

> **Quais são as xícaras de café?**
> Which are the coffee cups?

> **(São) aquelas ali.**
> (They're) the ones over there.

> **O que é isso?**
> What's this/that?

> **É um saca-rolhas.**
> It's a corkscrew.

> **Essa é a sua chave?**
> Is this/that your key?

Remember that, in spoken Portuguese, the demonstratives **esse(s)/essa(s)/isso** are used to mean both 'this/these' and 'that/those (near you)' (see **8.3**). Notice that **isso** is used when you are not yet sure what something is, and **esse(s)/essa(s)**, with gender and number agreement, when the nature of the thing is already clear. Compare:

> **Isso é uma bicicleta dobrável.**
> This is a folding bicycle. (= *This object is a bicycle that folds up.*)

> **Essa é uma bicicleta dobrável.**
> This is a folding bicycle. (= *This bicycle is one that folds up.*)

36

Describing

36.1 ## Referring to a subject's nature or identity

36.1.1 ### *ser* + adjective

▶ **16.3.8** (p. 155); **23.2** (p. 204)

When referring to a subject's inherent nature or identity, as in 'The Earth is round', 'Paula is intelligent', 'This is a portable cooking stove', we use the verb **ser** 'to be', with an adjective (words like **redondo** 'round', **inteligente** 'intelligent', **portátil** 'portable', which tell us what a noun is like). Remember that adjectives must agree in gender (masculine or feminine) and number (singular or plural) with the noun they refer to:

A Terra é redonda.
The Earth is round.

A Paula é inteligente.
Paula is intelligent.

Isso é um fogão portátil.
This is a portable cooking stove.

São Paulo é muito grande.
São Paulo is very big.

Esse livro é interessante.
This book is interesting.

Esse é o Vinícius. Ele é o meu irmão.
This is Vinicius. He's my brother.

É um filme de terror.
It's a horror movie.

36.1.2 ### Position of the adjective

▶ **5.1** (p. 57); **5.2** (p. 58); **5.3** (p. 58)

When an adjective is used in combination with a noun, it is usually placed after the noun in Portuguese. However, some short descriptive adjectives regularly precede the noun and, with some adjectives, there is a difference of meaning depending on whether the adjective is placed before or after the noun (see **5.1**):

um homem grande 'a big man'

um grande homem 'a great man'

uma oportunidade única 'a unique opportunity'

uma única oportunidade 'a single opportunity'.

With most other adjectives, placement after the noun is the norm, especially when the adjective serves to differentiate the noun. It follows that certain types of adjective, which differentiate by virtue of their meaning, will always be placed after the noun, e.g. those of nationality, colour, shape, nature, purpose, etc.:

um navio francês 'a French ship'

uma enfermeira australiana 'an Australian nurse'

roupa branca 'white clothes, whites'

um rosto oval 'an oval face'

políticas sociais 'social policies'

um brinquedo educativo 'an educational toy'.

Some kinds of descriptive adjectives may be placed before the noun for stylistic reasons. In general, an adjective placed before the noun refers to an inherent, rather than distinctive, characteristic of the noun, or to a subjectively perceived quality. Often, the same noun is further qualified by a defining adjective or expression:

as famosas praias do Rio de Janeiro
Rio de Janeiro's famous beaches (*i.e. all Rio's beaches are famous*)

cf. **As praias famosas do Rio são Copacabana e Ipanema.**
Rio's famous beaches are Copacabana and Ipanema. (*as opposed to the less famous ones*)

Tomamos um excelente vinho francês.
We drank an excellent French wine. (***excelente** is not used to differentiate here, but rather as a subjective comment on the wine*)

um vasto deserto de areia branca
a vast desert of white sand (*'vastness' is an inherent quality of deserts*)

uma divertida comédia de Woody Allen
an amusing comedy by Woody Allen (***divertida** is a subjective comment by the writer as well as being inherent to comedies*).

Except in the case of adjectives that are always placed before the noun (see **5.2**) or that change meaning according to their position (see **5.3**), it is advisable always to place the adjective after the noun until you have acquired a good feel for the language.

36.1.3 ### Other verbs used in descriptions

Of course, as in English, there are a large number of other verbs that may be used to describe people, places and things. The verb **ter** 'to have' is perhaps one of the most common:

Ele tem olhos azuis.
He has blue eyes.

A cidade tem um clima ameno.
The town has a mild climate.

A pousada tem muito charme.
The guest house has a lot of charm.

36.2 | Enquiring about a subject's nature or appearance

▶ **11.6** (p. 118); **16.3.8** (p. 155); **23.2** (p. 204)

To ask what someone or something is like, use the construction **como** + **ser** + noun:

Como é a sua namorada?
What's your girlfriend like?

Como eram os seus pais?
What were your parents like?

Como era o hotel?
What was the hotel like?

Como é o vestido que você comprou?
What's the dress like that you bought?

Note that, **como é/são . . .** can refer to a subject's appearance, nature or both. If you want to specify, you can say:

Como é o seu irmão fisicamente?
What does your brother look like?

Como era sua avó como pessoa?
What was your grandmother like as a person?

Como se parece um tamanduá?
What does an anteater look like?

Que aspecto tem um abacate maduro?
What does a ripe avocado look like?

Another useful expression is **Que tipo de . . .** 'what kind/sort/type of . . .':

Que tipo de pessoa é o seu chefe?
What's your boss like?

Que tipo de filme é?
What kind of movie is it?

Questions about the size, colour or shape of things must include the preposition **de** in Portuguese:

De que cor é o seu carro?
What colour is your car?

De que tamanho era o apartamento?
What size/How big was the apartment?

A mesa é de que formato?
What shape is the table?

36.3 Describing a state or condition

▶ **16.3.11** (p. 156); **23.3** (p. 203)

36.3.1 To refer to a subject's temporary state or condition, rather than its inherent properties, use the verb **estar** 'to be':

A Ana está feliz.
Ana is happy.

O ônibus estava lotado.
The bus was packed.

Esse sapato está novo ainda.[1]
These shoes are still as good as new.

O Celso está doente.
Celso is ill.

Meus pais estão bem.
My parents are well.

NOTE 1 They look new, or are as new. Cf. **Esse sapato é novo**. 'These shoes are (brand) new.'

Sometimes **estar** is used to emphasize a state or condition of the subject that may also be considered to be an inherent property:

Ela está bonita.
She looks pretty.

Ela é bonita.
She is pretty.

O pai deles está jovem ainda.
Their father is still youthful.

O pai deles é jovem ainda.
Their father is still young.

You sometimes hear sentences such as:

A novela não está chata, é chata.
The telenovela is not just going through a boring phase, it's boring period.

36.3.2 To ask about someone's general well-being, use **como** + **ir**:

Como vai a sua mãe?
How's your mother?

Como vão as crianças?
How are the kids?

If there is some question about the person's state of health, use **como** + **estar**:

Como está a sua mãe?
How's your mother? (*i.e. is she better?*)

Como estava o Zé?
How was Zé? (*i.e. when you saw him or spoke to him*)

Compare these three sentences:

> **Como é o seu irmão?**
> What's your brother like?

> **Como vai o seu irmão?**
> How's your brother? (*i.e. what's he doing these days?*)

> **Como está o seu irmão?**
> How's your brother? (*since his accident, illness, divorce, etc.*)

36.4 Descriptions involving an unspoken comparison

▶ **16.3.11** (p. 156); **23.3** (p. 206)

estar is also used when the sentence implies a comparison with other moments in time:

> **O filho dela está grande.**
> Her son's big. (*bigger than when I last saw him*)

> **A cidade estava muito suja.**
> The city was very dirty. (*it used to be clean or cleaner*)

> **Estou gordo, preciso emagrecer.**
> I'm fat, I need to lose weight. (*I've gained weight recently*)

36.5 Asking and saying what something is made of

▶ **16.3.8** (p. 155); **23.2** (p. 204)

36.5.1 To ask someone what material something is made of, use sentences such as:

> **O anel é de quê?**
> What's the ring made of?

> **De que são feitas essas esculturas?**
> What are those sculptures made (out) of?

> **São de ouro?**
> Are they (made of) gold?

36.5.2 To describe what something is made of, use **ser** followed by the preposition **de**:

> **O bracelete é de prata.**
> The bracelet is (made of) silver.

> **São de plástico.**
> They're (made of) plastic.

> **É feito de couro.**
> It's made out of leather.

36.6 Describing events

To say what an event was like, either **ser** or **estar** can be used. **Ser** gives the description a more objective tone, while **estar** refers much more to the speaker's subjective impression. It follows that **estar** can only be used if the speaker has had first-hand experience of the event. In addition, when a one-off past event is being described, **ser** is used in the preterite, while **estar** is normally used in the imperfect because it is conveying the background 'feel' of the event:

> **A aula foi interessante.**
> The class was interesting. (*Anybody would have found it interesting*)

> **A aula estava interessante.**
> The class was interesting. (*I found it interesting*)

> **A noite foi divertida.**
> The evening was fun. (*Everybody enjoyed themselves*)

> **A noite estava divertida.**
> The evening was fun. (*I enjoyed myself*)

When asking someone about a past event, it is more common to use **ser**:

> **Como foi a festa?**
> How was the party?

When the event described is less clear-cut, the preposition **de** is inserted before the noun:

> **Como foi de viagem?**
> How was your trip?

> **Como foi de Natal?**
> How was your Christmas?

An alternative way of asking about an event is to use **que tal . . . ?** without a verb:

> **Que tal o casamento?**
> How was the wedding?

> **Que tal a viagem?**
> What was your trip like?

36.7 Describing facts or information

▶ **16.3.8** (p. 155); **23.2** (p. 204)

Facts and information are described using **ser**, even when it is the speaker's own subjective opinion:

> **Isso é muito interessante.**
> That's very interesting. (*e.g. what you just told me*)

> **O que aconteceu com eles foi horrível.**
> What happened to them was awful.

36.8 Describing a person's character and attitude

▶ **16.3.8** (p. 155); **23.2** (p. 204)

A person's character is inherent and therefore described using **ser**:

> **Ela é muito delicada.**
> She's very thoughtful.

> Ele é um cavalheiro.
> He's a gentleman.

The verb **ser** is also used to describe a person's attitude at a particular point in time:

> Ele foi muito gentil conosco.
> He was very kind to us.

> Não precisa ser grosso comigo.
> There's no need to be rude to me.

36.9 Describing the weather

▶ **16.3.4** (p. 154); **16.3.11** (p. 156); **23.3** (p. 206)

To describe the weather, Portuguese uses either **estar** 'to be' or **fazer** (*literally*, 'to do'), followed by a noun (e.g. **frio**, **calor**, **sol**, **bom tempo**) when talking about a particular point in time:

> Amanhã vai fazer/estar sol.
> It's going to be sunny tomorrow.

> Está (fazendo) um dia lindo.
> It's a lovely day.

When talking in general terms about the climate, only **fazer** can be used with nouns:

> Faz muito calor aqui no verão.
> It's very hot here in the summer.

To describe the weather at a particular point in time, **estar** + adjective can also be used:

> Está abafado hoje.
> It's humid today.

> Ontem estava mais quente.
> It was hotter yesterday.

> Está nublado.
> It's cloudy.

To make more general statements about the climate, use **ser** + adjective:

> É quente na Amazônia.
> It's hot in the Amazon.

> As noites são frias na serra.
> The nights are cold in the mountains.

To ask what the weather or climate is like, use phrases such as the following:

> Como está o tempo hoje?
> What's the weather like today?

> Que tempo está fazendo lá fora?
> What's the weather like outside?

> Como é o tempo/clima no Japão?
> What's the weather/climate like in Japan?

Que tempo faz na Escócia?
What's the weather like in Scotland?

Está (fazendo) muito frio?
Is it very cold? (*at the moment*)

Faz muito calor?
Is it very hot? (*in general*)

37

Making comparisons

▶ **5.8** (p. 64); **5.9** (p. 65); **5.10** (p. 66)

This chapter presents the most common constructions used by Brazilians to compare things. For ease of reference, these have been grouped into three main categories: comparisons of inequality, those of equality and comparisons involving more than two objects.

37.1 Comparisons of inequality

37.1.1 *mais* + adjective + *do que*; *menos* + adjective + *do que*

Comparisons of inequality, as in 'taller than', 'more expensive than', 'less interesting than', are expressed in Portuguese with the word **mais** 'more', for superiority, or **menos** 'less' for inferiority. 'Than' is translated **do que** or, less commonly, just **que**:

> **O Leo é mais alto do que o irmão.**
> Leo is taller than his brother.

> **O meu computador foi mais caro do que o seu.**
> My computer was more expensive than yours.

> **O terceiro livro da série é muito menos interessante do que os outros dois.**
> The third book in the series is much less interesting than the other two.

As in English, if the context makes it clear, there is often no need to express the whole comparison:

> **O Leo é mais alto.**
> Leo is taller.

> **O terceiro livro da série é menos interessante.**
> The third book in the series is less interesting.

37.1.2 *mais* + adverb + *do que*; *menos* + adverb + *do que*

The same constructions are used to compare adverbs:

> **Meu pai anda mais devagar do que eu.**
> My dad walks more slowly than I do.

> **Ela fala português menos fluentemente do que o irmão.**
> She speaks Portuguese less fluently than her brother.

37.1.3 **Irregular comparisons**

Remember that some adjectives and adverbs have irregular comparative forms. The most common are:

bem 'well', **bom** 'good'	**melhor** 'better'
mal 'badly', **mau/ruim** 'bad'	**pior** 'worse'
grande 'big, large, great'	**maior** 'bigger, larger, greater'
pequeno 'small'	**menor** 'smaller'

Ela canta melhor do que eu.
She sings better than me.

O tempo estava pior do que no dia anterior.
The weather was worse than on the previous day.

O Brasil é muito maior do que a Argentina.
Brazil is much larger than Argentina.

Meu novo carro é menor.
My new car is smaller.

37.1.4 *mais* + noun + *do que*; *menos* + noun + *do que*

Both **mais** and **menos** can be used as invariable adjectives preceding nouns:

Ela tem mais dinheiro do que a irmã.
She has more money than her sister.

Ele sabe mais português do que eu.
He knows more Portuguese than I do.

Este ano houve menos assaltos do que no ano passado.
This year there were fewer muggings than last year.

37.1.5 Verb + *mais do que*; verb + *menos do que*

Both **mais** and **menos** can also be used to qualify verbs:

Meu irmão come mais do que eu.
My brother eats more than me.

Gastamos menos com roupa do que com comida.
We spend less on clothes than on food.

37.1.6 *mais/menos* + adjective/adverb/noun + *do que* + clause

The second element of the comparison may be a clause:

Foi mais barato do que eu achava.
It was cheaper than I thought.

Vieram menos pessoas do que esperávamos.
Fewer people came than we expected.

Ela está falando inglês melhor do que falava antes.
She's speaking English better than she did before.

Ele é mais velho do que aparenta.
He's older than he looks.

mais/menos de + numerals

In comparisons involving numerals, use **mais/menos de**:

Ela tem menos de trinta anos.
She's less than thirty years old.

Faz mais de um ano que não vejo os meus pais.
It's more than a year since I saw my parents.

37.2 Comparisons of equality

tão + adjective/adverb + *quanto/como*

Comparisons of equality involving adjectives and adverbs are expressed with the construction **tão ... quanto/como** 'as ... as':

O irmão do Bruno é tão bonito quanto ele.
Bruno's brother is as good-looking as he is.

Esse apartamento é tão grande como o outro.
This apartment is as big as the other one.

Ela dança tão graciosamente quanto a irmã.
She dances as gracefully as her sister.

Você fala espanhol tão bem como você fala português?
Do you speak Spanish as well as you do Portuguese?

The construction **tão ... quanto** may also be used colloquially without a second element, meaning 'just as ...':

Já provei xampus caros, mas esse barato é tão bom quanto.
I've tried expensive shampoos, but this cheap one is just as good.

tanto + noun + *quanto/como*

Comparisons of equality involving a noun require this construction with **tanto ... quanto/como**, in which **tanto** agrees in gender (masculine or feminine) and number (singular or plural) with the noun it refers to. In this construction, **quanto** is invariable and more frequent than **como**:

Como ator, ele fez tanto sucesso quanto o irmão.
As an actor, he has had as much success as his brother.

Hoje tinha tantos clientes como ontem.
Today there were as many customers as yesterday.

Verb + *tanto quanto/como*

When comparing two subjects in terms of an action (i.e. a verb), use **tanto quanto/como** 'as much as'. In this construction, **quanto** is more frequent than **como**:

Ela bebe tanto quanto o marido.
She drinks as much as her husband does.

Nunca ri tanto como hoje à noite.
I've never laughed as much as I have tonight.

37.2.4 *tão* and *tanto* in non-comparative expressions

Without the second element of the comparison, **tão** means 'so' and **tanto** 'so much':

Eu não sabia que ela falava inglês tão bem.
I didn't know she spoke English so well.

O filhinho deles é tão bonitinho!
Their little boy is so cute!

Eu já liguei para ele tantas vezes!
I've already called him so many times!

Rimos tanto!
We laughed so much!

Note that **tão** also translates 'such (a)' before an attributive adjective:

Nunca vi um filme tão engraçado.
I've never seen such a funny movie.

O programa traz matérias tão interessantes.
The show presents such interesting stories.

Both **tão** and **tanto** can be followed by a **que** clause expressing a consequence:

Ele fala tão rápido que não entendo nada.
He talks so fast (that) I can't understand a word.

O voo atrasou tanto que perdemos a conexão.
The flight was delayed so much we missed our connection.

Eu estava com tanta sede que tomei um litro de água de uma vez só.
I was so thirsty (that) I drank a litre of water in one go.

Note also another type of construction with a similar meaning using the preposition **de**:

Ele não conseguia falar de tão bêbado.
He was so drunk he couldn't speak.

Fiquei sem ar de tanto rir.
I was laughing so much I couldn't catch my breath.

37.2.5 Other ways of expressing equality

Comparisons of equality may also be expressed with:

(i)   **igual (a)**[1] 'the same (as), identical (to), just like':

Elas se vestem igual.
They dress the same.

NOTE   1   The preposition **a** is very often omitted in informal speech: e.g. **Ele é igual papagaio: repete tudo**. 'He's just like a parrot: repeats everything.'

Os homens não pensam igual às mulheres.
Men don't think the same way as women.

Ele é igual ao pai.
He's just like his father.

Meu tênis é igual ao seu.
My trainers are the same as yours.

As duas casas são iguais.
The two houses are the same.

The similarity can be further emphasized by using the diminutive **igualzinho (a)** 'exactly the same (as)':

Ela fez uma tatuagem igualzinha à do namorado.
She got a tattoo exactly the same as her boyfriend's.

(ii) **o mesmo (que)** / **a mesma coisa (que)** 'the same (as), the same thing (as)':

Perguntei a várias pessoas, mas todas falaram o mesmo.
I asked several people, but they all said the same.

Pedir ajuda não é a mesma coisa que desistir.
Asking for help is not the same as giving up.

(iii) **igualmente** 'just as, equally':

As duas coisas são igualmente importantes.
The two things are equally important.

O segundo romance dela é igualmente envolvente.
Her second novel is just as gripping.

(iv) **do mesmo jeito** 'the same way':

Se jogarmos do mesmo jeito na final, vamos ganhar com certeza.
If we play the same way in the final, we'll definitely win.

Você pode comprar o livro online, mas, com o frete, vai ficar caro do mesmo jeito.
You can buy the book online, but with the shipping it'll be just as expensive.

(v) **parecer-se** 'to be/look alike', **parecer-se com** (*written*) / **parecer** (*spoken*) 'to be/look like':

Os gêmeos se parecem muito, mas não são idênticos.
The twins look very much alike, but they are not identical.

O novo modelo não se parece em nada com o antigo.
The new model is nothing like the old one.

Ele parece o Brad Pitt.
He looks like Brad Pitt.

These verbs are most commonly used to refer to appearance, but they can also be used to refer to the sound, taste, smell or feel of something:

Quando ela canta, parece a Whitney Houston.
When she sings she sounds like Whitney Houston.

O tecido parecia seda de tão suave.
The fabric was so soft it felt like silk.

(vi) **lembrar** 'to look/sound/taste/smell/feel like', **assemelhar-se a** (*formal*) 'to resemble':

> **A banda lembra um pouco os Beatles.**
> The band sound a little like the Beatles.

> **O projeto do restaurante foi pensado para se assemelhar a um bistrô parisiense.**
> The design of the restaurant was intended to resemble a Parisian bistro.

(vii) **parecido (com)** 'similar (to)', **semelhante (a)** (*more formal*) 'similar to':

> **Os dois idiomas são muito parecidos.**
> The two languages are very similar.

> **É um problema semelhante ao que enfrentamos no ano passado.**
> It's a problem similar to the one we faced last year.

(viii) **como/que nem/feito** (*informal*) 'as, like' used in similes:

> **Dormi como uma pedra.**
> I slept like a log.

> **Ele é burro que nem uma porta.**
> He's as thick as two short planks/dumb as a post.

> **Que nem aquela viagem que fizemos, lembra?**
> Like that trip we went on, do you remember?

> **Com a onda de assaltos, a polícia anda feito barata tonta.**
> With the wave of robberies, the police are running around like headless chickens.
> (*literally,* 'like a dizzy cockroach')

37.3 Comparing more than two objects

▶ **4.1** (p. 50)

37.3.1 Definite article + *mais/menos* + adjective

To express superlatives such as 'the highest', 'the most expensive', 'the least interesting', when comparing more than two objects, Portuguese uses the definite article followed by the comparative form of the adjective:

> **O Monte Everest é a montanha mais alta do mundo.**
> Mount Everest is the highest mountain in the world.

> **Esse relógio é o mais caro da loja.**
> This watch is the most expensive one in the shop.

> **É um dos melhores restaurantes de São Paulo.**
> It's one of São Paulo's best restaurants.

> **Os dois últimos livros da série são os menos interessantes.**
> The last two books in the series are the least interesting.

Notice that the frame of reference is introduced with the preposition **de** in Portuguese, whereas English normally uses 'in' or another preposition:

> **a cidade mais populosa do país**
> the most populous city in the country

a melhor faixa do álbum
the best track on the album.

The definite article may be replaced by a possessive in superlative expressions:

Ele é meu melhor amigo.
He's my best friend.

Esse é nosso modelo mais vendido.
This is our best-selling model.

37.3.2 Omission of the definite article

The definite article is omitted in some sentences of this type, particularly:

(i)   With adverbs:

Quem cantou melhor foi a primeira.
It was the first girl who sang best.

Dos três irmãos, o Carlos se parece mais com o pai.
Of the three brothers, Carlos looks most like his father.

(ii) Following **estar** or **ficar**:

Em casa quem está mais interessado em esportes é a minha mãe.
In our house the person most interested in sports is my mum.

Eu é que fiquei mais decepcionado.
I was the most disappointed.

38

Expressing existence and availability

This chapter deals with the ways of saying 'there is/are . . .', 'there was/were . . .', 'do you have . . . ?', etc. in Portuguese.

38.1 Asking and answering questions regarding existence

38.1.1 *tem, tinha, vai ter . . .*

▶ **16.3.5** (p. 154); **24.3.2** (p. 224)

In everyday speech and some informal writing, the word for 'there is/are . . .' is **tem**. This is the third person singular of the verb **ter**, which in this meaning is used impersonally and always in the singular.

> **Tem uma farmácia por aqui?**
> Is there a pharmacy around here?

> **Tem duas na outra rua.**
> There are two in the next street.

> **Não tem.**
> No, there isn't.

Notice that, in negative sentences such as 'there aren't any, there isn't one', 'any' and 'one' are not translated in Portuguese unless there is particular emphasis:

> **Eu ia comer pão, mas não tem.**
> I was going to eat bread, but there isn't any.

> **Eu procurava uma livraria, mas não tem nenhuma por aqui.**
> I was looking for a bookshop, but there's not (a single) one around here.

Examples using other tenses of **tem**:

> **Tinha muita fila no banco?**
> Was there much of a queue/line at the bank?

> **Teve uma briga feia na boate.**
> There was a nasty fight at the club.

> **Vai ter churrasco no domingo.**
> There's going to be a barbecue on Sunday.

> **Compra salame italiano, se tiver.**
> Buy Italian salami if there is any.

38.1.2 *há, havia, haverá . . .*

▶ **16.3.9** (p. 156); **24.3.1** (p. 223)

In more formal speech and writing, 'there is/are . . .' is translated **há**. This is the third person singular of the verb **haver**, which, like **tem**, is used impersonally and always in the singular in this meaning:

> **Há vários problemas a serem resolvidos.**
> There are several problems to be resolved.

> **Há quantos candidatos por vaga?**
> How many applicants are there for each place?

> **Não há nenhuma possibilidade de ganhar.**
> There is no possibility of winning.

Examples in other tenses and forms:

> **É possível que haja uma reunião no mês que vem.**
> It is possible that there will be a meeting next month.

> **Se houver algum problema, ligue para este número.**
> If there is any problem, call this number.

> **Houve um debate acalorado no Senado.**
> There was a heated debate in the Senate.

> **Havia mais de 30.000 pessoas no jogo de ontem.**
> There were more than 30,000 people at yesterday's game.

> **Deve haver uma solução.**
> There must be a solution.

38.1.3 *existe/existem*

The verb **existir** can also be used in pre-subject position to mean 'there is/are'. Unlike **tem** and **há**, **existir** has to agree in number (singular or plural) with what follows. **Existir** refers to the existence of something in general and is not used to refer to a specific location or event:

> **Existe um departamento específico que trata desses assuntos.**
> There is a specific department that deals with these matters.

> **Existem pessoas que acreditam em reencarnação.**
> There are people who believe in reincarnation.

> **Existe a possibilidade de ter sido um engano?**
> Is there the possibility that it was a mistake?

> **Não existe carro voador.**
> There's no such thing as a flying car.

Given the semantic restrictions mentioned above, **existir** is only really used in the present and imperfect in this meaning, although the subjunctive tenses may also be encountered:

> **Existiam poucos lugares onde se sentia seguro.**
> There were few places where it felt safe.

Não existia polícia na época.
There was no police force at the time.

Duvido que exista outra cidade igual.
I doubt there's any other city like it.

ser

▶ **16.3.8** (p. 155); **23.2** (p. 204)

When talking about how many people there are in a group, the verb used is **ser**:

Quantos somos?
How many of us are there?

Somos seis.
There are six of us.

The preposition **em** is sometimes inserted before the number in this usage:

Lá em casa éramos em seis irmãos.
There were six of us brothers and sisters in my family.

The verb **ser** can be used in other numerical expressions to mean 'there are . . .':

Eram 200 candidatos para uma vaga.
There were 200 applicants for one vacancy.

São 500 ligações por hora.
There are 500 phone calls an hour.

Describing facilities

To ask and say what facilities there are in a place, use either impersonal **tem** or **há**, meaning 'there is/are . . .', or the verb **ter** 'to have':

O hotel tem piscina?
Does the hotel have a pool?

Tem dois bares no hotel. (*spoken*)
Há dois bares no hotel. (*written*)
There are two bars in the hotel.

Todos os apartamentos têm ar-condicionado.
All the rooms have air conditioning.

Tem cofre no quarto?
Is there a safe in the room?

Expressing availability

tem

To ask or say whether something is available or not, use **tem** (see **38.1.1**):

Tem quarto com vista para o mar?
Are there any rooms with a sea view?

Sinto muito, mas não tem.
I'm very sorry, but there aren't any.

Não tinha nada.
There was nothing.

Notice that, when asking how much of something is available, the preposition **de** is used:

Quanto tem de leite?
How much milk is there?

38.3.2 *ter*

The personal verb **ter** 'to have' may also be used to talk about availability, but, in the singular, it only differs from the impersonal **tem** if you include the subject pronoun **você**:

Tem café descafeinado?
Do you have/Is there decaffeinated coffee?

Você tem trocado?
Do you have any small change?

When talking about availability in a shop, hotel, etc. the plural of **ter** may also be used:

Vocês têm protetor solar?
Do you have sunblock?

38.3.3 *dispor de, contar com, possuir*

In more formal contexts, **dispor de**, **contar com** and **possuir** are often used with the meaning of 'to have':

O Brasil dispõe de um dos mais modernos sistemas bancários do mundo.
Brazil has one of the world's most modern banking systems.

O hotel conta com quatro quadras de tênis.
The hotel has four tennis courts.

O carro possui câmbio manual de cinco marchas.
The car has a five-gear manual transmission.

39

Expressing location and distance

This chapter examines all the various expressions used in Portuguese to refer to location and distance, including verbs such as **estar**, **ser** and **ficar**, all meaning 'to be', prepositions and other less common forms.

39.1 Expressing location

39.1.1 *estar*

▶ **16.3.11** (p. 156); **23.3** (p. 206)

To ask or talk about the location of a living being or an object that can be moved around, the verb **estar** is used. Questions are usually introduced by the interrogative **onde?** 'where?':[1]

Onde está a Júlia?
Where is Julia?

Ela está em casa.
She's at home.

Onde vocês estavam?
Where were you?

Estávamos no jardim.
We were in the garden.

Onde está o seu cachorro?
Where's your dog?

Ele está lá fora, no quintal.
He's out in the yard.

Onde estão as chaves do carro?
Where are the car keys?

Estão em cima da mesa.
They're on the table.

NOTE   1   In colloquial speech, you will often hear **aonde** in this usage, but formal grammar only allows **aonde** when motion is involved, i.e. it is supposed to mean 'where . . . to?' and not 'where . . . at?'.

340

39.1.2 *cadê . . . ?*

In colloquial speech, 'where is/are . . . ?' is often expressed using **cadê . . . ?** Note that **cadê** already incorporates the verb[2], so is followed immediately by the subject:

> **Cadê o controle remoto?**
> Where's the remote control?

> **Cadê os outros?**
> Where are the others?

> **Cadê ele?**
> Where is he?

> **E a chave? Cadê?**
> What about the key? Where is it?

---

2   It is derived from **que é de . . .?** 'what has become of . . .?'

The word **cadê?** is normally used with reference to living beings and objects that can be moved around, i.e. as an alternative to **onde está/estão . . .?**, though it can also be used with permanent fixtures that you are having difficulty locating:

> **Cadê o banheiro?**
> Where's the bathroom? (*there must be one in here somewhere*)

39.1.3 *ser, ficar*

▶ **16.3.8** (p. 155); **23.2** (p. 204); **23.4** (p. 207)

To ask or talk about the location of an object that does not normally move around, use the verbs **ser** or **ficar**. Of the two, **ficar** tends to be used more with buildings and geographical features, but **ser** can always be substituted in such cases:

> **Onde é/fica o banco mais próximo?**
> Where is the nearest bank?

> **É/Fica na praça principal.**
> It's on the main square.

> **Onde são/ficam as cataratas de Iguaçu?**
> Where are the Iguaçu Falls?

> **São/Ficam no sul, na fronteira com a Argentina.**
> They're in the south, on the border with Argentina.

> **O banheiro é/fica lá em cima.**
> The bathroom is upstairs.

39.1.4 *encontrar-se*

This verb is often used to mean 'to be' in more formal contexts, usually in writing. It more often refers to temporary location, though it may also refer to permanent location in the sense of 'be found, can be found':

> **Atualmente, o presidente se encontra em Nova York.**
> The president is currently in New York.

A bola já se encontrava fora da linha.
The ball was already over the line.

No centro da cidade encontram-se os melhores restaurantes.
The best restaurants are found in the centre of the city.

39.1.5   *estar situado/localizado*

The expressions **estar situado/localizado** 'to be situated/located' and their more formal alternatives, **situar-se** and **localizar-se**, are also used to describe location. Note that **situado** and **localizado** have to agree in gender (masculine or feminine) and number (singular or plural) with the subject:

A cidade está situada num vale.
A cidade se situa num vale. (*more formal*)
The town is situated in a valley.

O hotel está localizado a cinco minutos do aeroporto.
O hotel se localiza a cinco minutos do aeroporto. (*more formal*)
The hotel is located five minutes from the airport.

39.1.6   *em que lugar (de) . . . ?*

To ask whereabouts in a country or city, use **em que lugar de. . . ?**:

Você nasceu em que lugar da Inglaterra?
Whereabouts in England were you born?

Você mora em que lugar do Rio?
Whereabouts in Rio do you live?

39.1.7   *em que altura (de) . . . ? / na altura de*

To specify the exact location in a street or along a road, use the noun **altura**:

A livraria fica em que altura da Paulista?
Whereabouts along the Avenida Paulista is the bookshop?

Eu estava na altura da igreja quando dei por falta da carteira.
I'd got as far as the church when I noticed I was missing my wallet.

Houve um acidente na Via Dutra, na altura de Lorena.
There has been an accident on the Dutra Highway outside Lorena.

39.2   Asking and saying where an event will take or took place

▶ **16.3.8** (p. 155); **23.2** (p. 204)

To ask or say where an event, such as a meeting or party, will take or took place, use the verb **ser**:

Onde vai ser a reunião?
Where is the meeting going to be?

Vai ser na diretoria.
It'll be in the boardroom.

A festa foi na minha casa.
The party was at my house.

Indicating precise location

▶ **Chapter 25** (p. 227), especially **25.3** (p. 238)

To indicate precise location, we need the Portuguese equivalent of words like 'in', 'on'.'at', 'under', 'behind', etc. These words are called prepositions, and they sometimes combine with other words to form phrases that express location or some other notion, for example distance (see **39.4**). Following are some of the most important.

a

The preposition **a** is used in a number of set phrases and complex prepositions:

a quinze quilômetros daqui 'fifteen kilometres from here' (see **39.4**)

à esquerda/direita 'on/to the left/right'

ao lado 'next door; nearby'

ao lado de 'next to'.

Note that 'at', as in 'at the library', 'at the bank', is usually translated with the preposition **em** in Portuguese: **na biblioteca**, **no banco**. When expressing close proximity, the preposition **a** is used in more formal style, while **em** is used in colloquial speech: **Eles estavam sentados à** (*colloquially*, **na**) **mesa.** 'They were sitting at the table.'

abaixo de

The preposition **abaixo de** 'below' is normally found in more formal registers and figurative senses:

a legenda abaixo da foto
the caption below the photo.

acima de

The preposition **acima de** 'above', is normally found in more formal registers and figurative senses:

Ele sofreu um corte acima do olho esquerdo.
He suffered a cut above his left eye.

atrás de

This means 'behind':

A casa deles fica atrás da igreja.
Their house is behind the church.

de

The preposition **de** occurs as the last element in a number of compound prepositions of location:

ao lado de 'next to'

atrás de 'behind'

embaixo de 'under'

em cima de 'on top of, on'

em frente de 'in front of'

longe de 'a long way from'

na frente de 'in front of'

no final de 'at the end of'

no fundo de 'at the back/bottom of'

nos fundos de 'at the back/rear of'

perto de 'near to'.

39.3.6 *em*

The word **em** serves as a kind of default preposition of location in Portuguese and may translate 'at', 'in' or 'on':

Comprei isso na farmácia.
I bought this at the pharmacy.

O jantar está na mesa.
The dinner is on the table.

A chave estava no meu bolso.
The key was in my pocket.

The prepositions **no/na** are also used in colloquial speech before the name of a person or profession to mean 'at . . .'s (house)', 'at the . . .'s':

Eu estive na Sônia ontem.
I was at Sonia's yesterday.

O Paulo está no dentista.
Paulo's at the dentist('s).

The preposition **em** is also used in the following compound prepositions:

em cima de	on top of, on, above
em frente de/a	in front of, opposite
na frente de[3]	in front of.

NOTE | 3   Note that 'in front of me/you/us' is translated **na minha/sua/nossa frente**.

39.3.7 *embaixo de*

This means 'under, underneath':

O cachorro estava dormindo embaixo da mesa.
The dog was asleep under the table.

39.3.8 *entre*

When expressing location, **entre** translates into English as 'between' or 'among', depending on the context:

> **Arujá fica entre São Paulo e São José dos Campos.**
> Arujá is between São Paulo and São José dos Campos.

> **Pequenas flores brotavam entre as árvores.**
> Small flowers were sprouting among the trees.

39.3.9 *sobre*

The basic meaning of **sobre** is 'over', but it can also translate 'on', 'on top of' in the sense of 'covering':

> **A casa estava abandonada, com lençóis sobre os móveis.**
> The house was deserted, with sheets over the furniture.

> **Coloque um papel-toalha sobre a mancha.**
> Place a paper towel over the stain.

39.3.10 Location may also be expressed with the adverbs **aqui** 'here', **aí** 'there (*where you are*)', **ali** 'over there' and **lá** 'there (*at a place that is out of sight*)' (see **8.5**):

> **Aqui está o dinheiro.**
> Here is the money.

> **A Lúcia está aí com você?**
> Is Lucia there with you?

> **A estação é logo ali.**
> The station is just over there.

> **O meu pai está lá em Búzios.**
> My dad's away in Buzios.

39.4 **Indicating distance**

To indicate distance from something, use **estar**, **ser**, **ficar** or another verb as appropriate (see **39.1**), followed by the preposition **a** and a phrase signalling distance:

> **Feira de Santana fica a 116 km de Salvador.**
> Feira de Santana is 116 km from Salvador.

> **O hotel é a cinco minutos da praia.**
> The hotel is five minutes from the beach.

> **Estamos a mais ou menos uma hora do Rio.**
> We're about an hour away from Rio.

Note also the question **a que distância ... ?** 'how far?':

> **A que distância fica o aeroporto?**
> How far away is the airport?

> **A que distância estamos da sua casa?**
> How far are we from your house?

The preposition **a** is not required with **perto** 'near, close by' and **longe** 'far away':

O supermercado é perto/pertinho.
The supermarket is close by/really close.

Estamos perto da praia?
Are we near the beach?

Não, a praia é longe daqui.
No, the beach is a long way from here.

To ask how far a place is, you can also ask questions such as these:

São quantos quilômetros daqui a Parati?
How many kilometres is it from here to Parati?

São quantos minutos de carro de Copacabana até o centro?
How many minutes' drive is it from Copacabana to the centre?

Dá quanto daqui até Porto Alegre?
How far is it from here to Porto Alegre?

É longe?
Is it far?

É perto?
Is it nearby?

Dá para ir a pé?
Is it within walking distance?

40

Expressing possessive relations

This chapter examines the forms used by Brazilians to express possession and to enquire about possession. The notes below explain the uses of possessive adjectives and pronouns and a range of other constructions associated with this function.

▶ **Chapter 9** (p. 105)

40.1 Expressing ownership and possession

40.1.1 Using possessives

40.1.1.1 *meu(s)/minha(s), seu(s)/sua(s), nosso(s)/nossa(s)*

The words **meu(s)/minha(s)** 'my', **seu(s)/sua(s)** 'your' and **nosso(s)/nossa(s)** 'our' are followed by a noun or noun phrase and must agree in gender (masculine or feminine) and number (singular or plural) with the thing possessed:

Minha chave, por favor.
My key, please.

Os seus óculos estão na mesa.
Your glasses are on the table.

Nosso carro enguiçou.
Our car has broken down.

These three possessive adjectives may be preceded by the definite article with no change of meaning. The definite article is optional except after the prepositions **a**, **de**, **em**, **para** and **por**, when it is always included in informal registers:[1]

a chave do meu quarto
the key to my room

as fotos da nossa viagem
the photos of our trip

Coloca isso na sua bolsa.
Put this in your bag.

NOTE 1 These are the prepositions that form phonetic contractions with the definite article (see **4.1.3**). Note that, in more formal writing, it is considered good style to omit the definite article, even after these prepositions.

40.1.1.2 *dele, dela, deles, delas, de vocês*

In the spoken language and often in writing too (see **40.1.6**), 'his', 'her', 'their' and 'your' (referring to more than one person), are expressed by placing the definite article before the noun and **dele**, **dela**, **deles/delas** or **de vocês** respectively after it:

> **Conheci a esposa dele.**
> I met his wife.

> **Gostei da roupa dela.**
> I like her outfit.

> **É o carro deles?**
> Is it their car?

> **as minhas irmãs e os filhos delas**
> my sisters and their children

> **Vamos para a casa de vocês?**
> Shall we go to your house?

40.1.1.3 *um ... meu/umas ... dele, etc.*

When the noun is preceded by an indefinite article, as in 'a friend of mine', 'some letters of his', etc., the possessives are placed after the noun. The words **meu**, **seu** and **nosso** must agree in gender (masculine or feminine) and number (singular or plural) with the noun:

> **Encontrei um amigo meu na rua.**
> I met a friend of mine in the street.

> **Uma prima deles morreu no acidente.**
> A cousin of theirs was killed in the accident.

> **Achei umas cartas dele numa gaveta.**
> I found some letters of his in a drawer.

40.1.1.4 *o meu, o seu, o dele ...*

The possessives may be used without a noun referring back to something that has already been mentioned. In this case, the possessives must be preceded by the definite article, which has to agree in gender and number with the noun being referred back to. The possessives **meu**, **seu** and **nosso** must also agree in gender and number with this noun:

> **Gosto da minha bicicleta, mas prefiro a sua.**
> I like my bike, but I prefer yours.

> **O nosso quarto é maior do que o de vocês.**
> Our room is bigger than yours.

> **Sua redação está ótima. A minha está horrível.**
> Your composition is really good. Mine is awful.

> **Coloquei a minha bolsa, a sua e a dela no meu carro.**
> I've put mine, yours and her bags in my car.

> **As passagens não estão na minha bolsa, estão na sua.**
> The tickets aren't in my bag, they're in yours.

40.1.1.5 *ser meu, ser dele, etc.*

The possessives can be used after the verb **ser** (without the definite article) to mean 'to be mine, to be his', etc. The words **meu**, **seu** and **nosso** have to agree in gender and number with the noun they refer back to:

> **Essa caneta é dele.**
> This pen is his.

> **O apartamento é alugado, mas os móveis são nossos.**
> The apartment is rented, but the furniture is ours.

> **Essas coisas são suas?**
> Are these things yours?

When you want to describe ownership of different items of the same type, the definite article is included before the possessive to emphasize the contrast:

> **Essa é a sua caneta e essa é a minha.**
> This is your pen and this is mine/my one.

> **Essas são as nossas toalhas e aquelas são as de vocês.**
> These are our towels and those are yours/your ones.

40.1.2 *ser de* + noun

The phrase **ser de** can also be used before a noun to express possession. In this case, the English noun usually has an 'apostrophe *s*':

> **Aquele carro é do Júlio.**
> That car is Julio's.

> **O gato preto é da vizinha.**
> The black cat is the neighbour's.

> **Esse quarto é das crianças.**
> This room is the children's.

40.1.3 *de* + noun

When the possessor is a noun or noun phrase, it is introduced with the preposition **de** in Portuguese. Although this **de** is equivalent to 'of' in English, the possessive phrase often corresponds to an 'apostrophe *s*' genitive or a noun placed before another in English:

> **Conheci a mãe do meu namorado ontem.**
> I met my boyfriend's mother yesterday.

> **A economia do Brasil não para de crescer.**
> Brazil's economy / The economy of Brazil just keeps growing.

> **Abri a janela do quarto.**
> I opened the bedroom window.

40.1.4 *pertencer a*

Ownership may also be expressed with the verb **pertencer a** 'to belong to', which is used in more formal language[2]:

> **O terreno pertence à Prefeitura.**
> The land belongs to the City.

NOTE   2   **Pertencer a** is more formal than 'belong to' in English. In less formal contexts, 'belong to' can be translated using **ser de** (see **40.1.2**), e.g. **Aquele carro é do vizinho**. 'That car belongs to the neighbour.'

Ninguém sabe a quem pertence o carro abandonado.
Nobody knows who the abandoned car belongs to.

40.1.5 *ser propriedade de*

In formal written language, ownership is sometimes expressed with the phrase **ser propriedade de** or **ser de propriedade de** 'to be the property of, to be owned by':

A empresa é de propriedade de um inglês.
The company is owned by an Englishman.

Os museus são propriedade do Estado.
The museums are owned by the State.

40.1.6 *seu(s)/sua(s)* meaning 'his', 'her', 'its' or 'their' in written language

In the written language, **seu(s)/sua(s)** is used without the definite article before it to mean 'his', 'her', 'its' or 'their'. It is only used in this meaning when there is no possible ambiguity about who it refers to; otherwise it is replaced by **dele**, **dela** or **deles/delas** as appropriate (see **40.1.1.2**):

O ministro e sua esposa jantaram com o presidente.
The minister and his wife had dinner with the president.

Os donos da empresa fizeram tudo em seu poder para evitar a falência.
The owners of the company did everything in their power to avoid bankruptcy.

É importante controlar a inflação em sua origem.
It is important to control inflation at its origin.

In normal speech, **seu(s)/sua(s)** is always used and understood to mean 'your' and so using it to refer to a third person can lead to potentially awkward misunderstandings.

40.2 Emphasizing possessive relations

▶ **9.5** (p. 108)

Possessive relations can be emphasized with the adjective **próprio** 'own'. This can be placed between a possessive and the noun:

Vou bancar o projeto com meu próprio dinheiro.
I'm going to fund the project with my own money.

Você não prefere dormir na sua própria cama?
Wouldn't you rather sleep in your own bed?

A própria mãe dele o entregou à polícia.
His own mother turned him over to the police.

The adjective **próprio** can also be placed after an indefinite noun with the meaning of '. . . of one's own'. In this case, no possessive is used:

o sonho da casa própria
the dream of owning your own home

Nenhum dos amigos tem carro próprio.
None of the friends has a car of their own.

40.3 Expressing possessive relations involving parts of the body, personal effects and close family members

▶ **9.4** (p. 107)

In sentences such as 'I washed my face', 'he stood there with his hands in his pockets', 'she took her lipstick out of her bag', 'they adore their father', etc., where the possessive refers back to the subject of the sentence and occurs before a noun denoting a part of the body or clothing, a personal effect or a close family member, Portuguese normally uses the definite article (**o**, **a**, **os** or **as** 'the') instead of a possessive:

> **Lavei o rosto.**
> I washed my face.

> **Ele ficou parado com as mãos nos bolsos.**
> He stood there with his hands in his pockets.

> **Ela tirou o batom da bolsa e retocou os lábios.**
> She took her lipstick out of her bag and redid her lips.

> **Eles adoram o pai.**
> They adore their father.

40.4 Asking whose something is

To ask whose property something is, as in 'whose is this?', use the construction **de quem** + **ser** + noun/noun phrase/pronoun:

> **De quem é isso?**
> Whose is this?

> **De quem é esse celular?**
> Whose mobile phone is this? / Whose is this mobile phone?

> **De quem são aqueles livros?**
> Whose books are those? / Whose are those books?

> **De quem será essa caneta?**
> I wonder whose pen this is?

> **Você sabe de quem são essas chaves?**
> Do you know whose keys these are?

Questions about ownership can also be asked using a possessive:

> **Essa bolsa é sua?**
> Is this bag yours? (*when there is one bag*)

> **Essa bolsa é a sua?**
> Is this bag yours? (*when there are several bags*; see **40.1.1.5**)

> **A mala vermelha é sua, não é?**
> The red suitcase is yours, isn't it?

351

40.5   Other ways of expressing possession

40.5.1 *ter*

▶ **16.3.5** (p. 154)

To ask and answer questions regarding possessions as in 'Have you got a . . . ?', 'I have one/two . . .', etc., Portuguese normally uses the verb **ter** 'to have':

> **Você tem cinco reais?**
> Do you have five reais?

> **Não tenho nada de dinheiro.**
> I haven't got any money.

> **Quantos filhos vocês têm?**
> How many children do you have?

> **Temos três.**
> We have three.

40.5.2 *estar com, estar sem*

▶ **16.3.11** (p. 156); **23.3** (p. 206)

Temporary possession, as in having something on you, may also be expressed with **estar com** 'to have':

> **Você está com as chaves de casa?**
> Do you have the house keys (on you)?

> **Estou com vinte reais no bolso.**
> I've got twenty reais in my pocket.

> **Não estou com meu passaporte.**
> I don't have my passport on me.

The opposite meaning can be expressed with **estar sem** 'to have no . . .':

> **Estou sem relógio.**
> I don't have a watch on.

> **Você está sem documento?**
> Don't you have any ID on you?

> **Ele estava sem um tostão.**
> He didn't have a penny on him.

40.5.3 *ser dono/a de, possuir*

Another way to denote possession is to use **ser dono/a de** 'to own' and, in more formal contexts, **possuir** 'to have, possess, own'[3]:

Ela é dona de quatro apartamentos em Santos.
She owns four apartments in Santos.

A empresa possui laboratório próprio na Alemanha.
The company has its own laboratory in Germany.

NOTE

3 The verb **possuir** can translate 'to possess, to own', but it is most commonly used simply as a more formal synonym of **ter**, e.g. **A aeronave possui seis saídas de emergência**. 'The aircraft has six emergency exits.'

41

Expressing changes

In English, transformations are expressed in a number of ways, which are not always interchangeable. Consider, for example, the following sentences:

> He *got* furious with me.
>
> Our movements *become* slower with age.
>
> We *were* devastated by the news.
>
> The prince *turned into* a frog.
>
> What he said *made* me sad.
>
> The film *turned* him into a star.

Portuguese also uses different verbs to express ideas such as these. As in English, these verbs are not always interchangeable, as you will see from the examples below.

41.1 Talking about changes of state and appearance

41.1.1 *ficar* + adjective

▶ **23.4** (p. 207)

Changes of state and appearance are normally expressed using the verb **ficar** 'to get, to become, to go, to turn', followed by an adjective. These changes may be sudden, as in:

> **Ele ficou furioso comigo.**
> He got furious with me.

Or they may be gradual, as in:

> **Meu irmão já está ficando careca.**
> My brother's already going bald.

Or habitual, as in:

> **Sempre que falamos nisso, eu fico deprimido.**
> Whenever we talk about this, I get depressed.

Note that **ficar** is used with the same kinds of adjectives as **estar**, the former expressing changing into a state and the latter expressing being in a state:

> **Ele ficou animado com a ideia.**
> He got enthusiastic about the idea.

Ele está animado com a ideia.
He is enthusiastic about the idea.

The verb **ficar** + adjective often expresses a change in the subject's state or condition in response to events. When talking about the past or future, English usually uses the verb 'to be' in such circumstances even though a change of state or condition took or will take place. However, in Portuguese, the verb **ficar** must be used in such cases. This is particularly true when expressing changes in a person's emotional state as a result of an event:

Quando ela souber disso, vai ficar muito feliz.
When she hears about this, she'll be really happy.

Ficamos arrasados com a notícia.
We were devastated by the news.

O novo estádio vai ficar pronto ano que vem.
The new stadium will be ready next year.

As Portuguese focuses on the transformation and English on the result, the preterite of **ficar** will often be translated with the present tense of 'to be' in English:

Fiquei contente que você tenha vindo.
I'm glad you came.

Essa foto ficou ótima.
This photo is really good.

When describing the appearance of something, the verb 'to look' will often be more appropriate in English than 'to be':

Essa saia ficou ótima em você.
That skirt looks great on you.

Ele ficou horrível com a cabeça raspada.
He looks horrible with his head shaved.

A sala ficou muito melhor depois de pintada.
The living room looks much better now it's been decorated.

41.1.2 *ficar com*

The verb **ficar** is used idiomatically with the preposition **com** and a series of nouns, such as **fome**, **sede**, **sono**, **medo**, **raiva**, etc., to express a change of state:

Estou ficando com sono.
I'm getting sleepy.

Se você ficar com sede, pega água na geladeira.
If you get thirsty, get some water from the fridge.

Eles ficaram com medo e saíram correndo.
They got scared and ran off.

41.1.3 *tornar-se* **+ adjective**

The verb **tornar-se** 'to become' is a more formal synonym of **ficar** in this sense:

Com a idade, os movimentos se tornam mais lentos.
Our movements become slower with age.

Este tipo de crime tem se tornado frequente ultimamente.
This type of crime has become frequent lately.

Com a abertura do mercado, o consumidor se tornou mais exigente.
As the market has opened up, consumers have become more demanding.

O acordo não se tornou público.
The deal was not made public.

41.1.4 *tornar* + noun/pronoun + adjective

When talking about changing the state or appearance of something else, use the verb
tornar 'to make' with a noun or pronoun object and an adjective:

A correnteza forte torna a travessia ainda mais perigosa.
The strong current makes the crossing all the more dangerous.

O jornal contém muitas fotos, tornando-o mais atraente.
The newspaper contains a lot of pictures, making it more attractive.

The adjective is usually placed before the noun object when the latter is complex or
emphasized:

O piloto soma 95 pontos, tornando remota a chance de ser alcançado.
The driver has a total of 95 points, making the chances of being caught remote.

A vitória esmagadora tornou desnecessário um segundo turno.
The landslide victory has made a second round of voting unnecessary.

Notice that, in sentences such as the following, 'it' is not translated in Portuguese:

A tecnologia tornou possível piratear longas-metragens em DVD.
Technology has made it possible to pirate feature films on DVD.

41.1.5 *deixar* + noun/pronoun + adjective

Literally meaning 'to leave', **deixar** focuses on the effect that something has on someone
or something. In this sense **deixar** is less formal-sounding than **tornar**, and can also be
used with reference to the effect on someone's emotional state:

O que ele falou me deixou triste.
What he said made me sad.

Esse novo sabão deixa as toalhas muito macias.
This new soap powder makes the towels really soft.

O novo projeto promete deixar o metrô mais rápido e confortável.
The new project promises to make the subway faster and more comfortable.

41.1.6 **Other verbs denoting a change of state**

There are many verbs derived from adjectives that denote a change of state, e.g. **melhorar** 'to get better', **piorar** 'to get worse', **engordar** 'to get fat, put on weight', **emagrecer** 'to get thin/slim, lose weight', **envelhecer** 'to get old(er)', **esquentar** 'to get warm(er)/hot(ter)', **esfriar** 'to get cold', **resfriar** 'to get colder', etc.:

Toma o seu café que vai esfriar.
Drink your coffee or it'll get cold.

A situação está piorando cada vez mais.
The situation is getting worse and worse.

Conforme vou envelhecendo, vou engordando.
As I get older, I'm getting fatter.

There are also many reflexive verbs that denote a change of emotional state, e.g. **surpreender-se** 'to be surprised', **animar-se** 'to get enthusiastic', **decepcionar-se** 'to be disappointed', **espantar-se** 'to be amazed', etc:

Nós nos surpreendemos com o que ela disse.
We were surprised at what she said.

Não adianta você se exaltar.
It's no use you getting worked up.

This type of reflexive verb is often substituted in the spoken language by **ficar** followed by the relevant past participle, e.g. **ficar surpreso**, **ficar animado**, **ficar decepcionado**, **ficar espantado**, etc.

Similarly, there are many verbs used with a noun or pronoun object that denote a change made to someone or something else, e.g. **melhorar** 'to improve', **aperfeiçoar** 'to perfect', **decepcionar** 'to disappoint', **animar** 'to encourage', etc.

41.2 # Talking about changes of status, nature and identity

41.2.1 *tornar-se* **+ noun**

The verb **tornar-se** 'to become' can also be followed by a noun indicating a change of status. Like 'to become' in English, **tornar-se** has a slightly formal tone:

Ela se tornou a primeira tenista a ganhar uma medalha de ouro olímpica.
She became the first tennis player to win an Olympic gold medal.

O livro vendeu bem, tornando-se um best seller nos Estados Unidos.
The book has sold well, becoming a bestseller in the USA.

When the noun following is indefinite, the word for 'a' or 'an' is omitted in Portuguese:

Ele se tornou padre.
He became a priest.

However, **um/uma** is included if the noun is further qualified by an adjective or other phrase:

Ela se tornou uma cirurgiã famosa.
She's become a famous surgeon.

O filme se tornou um clássico do cinema italiano.
The film has become a classic of Italian cinema.

41.2.2 *virar* + noun

Although sometimes interchangeable with **tornar-se**, **virar** 'to become, turn into' is used in all registers and focuses on the outcome of the change as perceived by the speaker, rather than the process of change as undergone by the subject. Note that, as with **tornar-se**, the noun following **virar** is not preceded by the indefinite article (**um/uma**) in Portuguese unless it is further qualified:

Ela virou budista.
She's become a Buddhist. (*i.e. so I've heard*)

cf. **Ela se tornou budista.**
She's become a Buddhist. (*i.e. she went through the process*)

The verb **virar** can also indicate a total change of nature or identity, which **tornar-se** cannot:

A antiga estação ferroviária virou museu.
The former railway station has become a museum.

O príncipe virou sapo.
The prince turned into a frog. (*literally*, a toad)

Se você tocar no carro dele, ele vira bicho.
If you touch his car, he goes wild. (*literally*, becomes an animal)

41.2.3 *ser* + noun

In sentences referring to career aspirations, such as 'He wants to become a professional footballer', 'She's studying to become a lawyer', 'I'm thinking of becoming a doctor', etc., where 'become' can be replaced by 'be' in English, Portuguese uses **ser** 'to be':

Ele quer ser jogador profissional.
He wants to become/be a professional footballer.

Ela está estudando para ser advogada.
She's studying to become/be a lawyer.

Estou pensando em ser médico quando crescer.
I'm thinking of becoming/being a doctor when I grow up.

41.2.4 *transformar-se em*; *transformar* + noun/pronoun + *em*

To express a change of nature or identity from one thing to another, you can also use **transformar-se em** 'to turn into, be turned into'. It is sometimes interchangeable with **virar**, but focuses more on the process rather than the result. Note that, as with **virar** and **tornar-se**, the noun following the preposition **em** is not preceded by the indefinite article (**um/uma**) unless it is further qualified:

Depois das 11 horas, o restaurante se transforma em boate.
After 11 o'clock, the restaurant turns into a nightclub.

O jogo se transformou numa acirrada batalha.
The game turned into a hard-fought battle.

> **O vilão do filme se transformava em lobisomem.**
> The villain of the movie would turn into a werewolf.

Similarly, the construction **transformar** + noun/pronoun + **em** 'to turn someone/something into' expresses a change made to someone or something else:

> **Eles transformaram o quarto de hóspedes em estúdio de gravação.**
> They turned the guest room into a recording studio.

> **O novo filme do ator deve transformá-lo em astro de Hollywood.**
> The actor's new movie should turn him into a Hollywood star.

41.2.5 *fazer de* + noun/pronoun + noun

Instead of 'to make A into B', Portuguese says **fazer de A B**. The meaning is similar to **transformar** above:

> **Fizeram da caixa uma cama para o cachorrinho.**
> They made the box into a bed for the puppy.

> **Essa proeza fez dele um mito.**
> This feat made him a legend.

41.3 Other verbs that express change

In more formal and literary contexts, you may also come across the verbs **transfigurar-se em** 'to be transformed into', **transfigurar** + noun/pronoun + **em** 'to transform something into', **converter-se em** 'to become, turn into, convert into' and **converter-se a** 'to convert to':

> **No filme, a cidade se transfigura num mundo onírico.**
> In the movie, the city is transformed into a dreamlike world.

> **O escritor transfigura realidade em poesia.**
> The writer transforms reality into poetry.

> **A obra de J.K. Rowling se converteu em mina de ouro.**
> J.K. Rowling's work has turned into a goldmine.

> **Ele resolveu se converter ao islamismo.**
> He decided to convert to Islam.

42

Expressing cause, effect and purpose

As in English, there are many different ways of expressing cause, effect and purpose in Portuguese. Some of the constructions are simple and not unlike those in English. Others are more complex and may require more detailed study.

42.1 Enquiring about cause

To enquire about the cause or reason for something, Portuguese uses a number of expressions, the most common of which are:

> **por que . . . ?** 'why . . . ?'
>
> **como . . . ?** 'how . . . ?', 'how come . . . ?'
>
> **como é que . . . ?** 'how . . . ?', 'how come . . . ?'
>
> **por que motivo/razão?** 'for what reason?'
>
> **qual (é) o motivo/a razão?** 'what's the reason?'

42.1.1 Of these, **por que . . . ?** is the most common and neutral:

> **Por que você falou isso?**
> Why did you say that?
>
> **Por que ele chegou tão cedo?**
> Why did he get here so early?
>
> **Você não foi por quê?**
> Why didn't you go?

Note that **quê** is spelt with a circumflex accent when it falls at the end of the sentence and that **por que . . . ?** 'why . . . ?' is spelt as two words to differentiate it from **porque** 'because'.

42.1.2 The expressions **como . . . ?** and **como é que . . . ?** usually convey surprise and disapproval, the longer form being more emphatic:

> **Como você faz uma coisa dessas?**
> How could you do something like that?
>
> **Como é que você sabe?**
> How do you know?
>
> **Como é que não convidaram a gente?**
> How come they didn't invite us?

42.1.3 The expression **por que motivo/razão?** is more formal and less commonly used. Notice that, in speech, **motivo** is more common as a translation of 'reason' than **razão**:

> **Por que motivo ela saiu da empresa?**
> For what reason did she leave the company?

> **O governo introduziu essas medidas por que razão?**
> For what reason did the government introduce these measures?

42.1.4 In the expression **qual (é) o motivo/a razão?** the verb **é** is optional after **qual**. The word **motivo** can be followed by the preposition **de**, **razão** by **de** or **para**:

> **Qual o motivo de ele ter perdido o jogo?**
> What is the reason he lost the game?

> **Qual a razão para tanto auê?**
> What is the reason for so much fuss?

42.2 Giving reasons and expressing relationships of cause and effect

► **26.2.2** (p. 247)

To give reasons and explain relationships of cause and effect, Portuguese uses expressions such as the following:

> **porque** 'because'
>
> **até porque / mesmo porque** 'because anyway'
>
> **por . . .** 'because of . . .', 'for . . .'
>
> **por causa de . . .** 'because of . . .'
>
> **por conta de** 'on account of . . .', 'because of . . .'
>
> **pelo fato de que** 'because of the fact that . . .'
>
> **devido a . . .** 'due to, owing to . . .'
>
> **dever-se a** 'to be due to'
>
> **como . . .** 'as, since . . .'
>
> **já que . . .** 'as, since . . .'
>
> **visto que . . .** 'seeing that . . .'
>
> **dado que . . . / posto que . . .** 'given that . . .'
>
> **na medida em que . . .** 'inasmuch as . . .'
>
> **pois** 'as, because'
>
> **é que . . .** 'the thing is . . .'
>
> **o negócio é que . . .** 'the thing is . . .'
>
> **o negócio é o seguinte** 'the thing is this'.

42.2.1 Of these, **porque** is the word most commonly used for giving reasons and establishing links between cause and effect:

Porque eu não quero.
Because I don't want to.

Porque sim.
Because I say so.

Ele não foi porque não tinha dinheiro.
He didn't go because he didn't have any money.

The expressions **até porque** and **mesmo porque** 'because anyway' are used to give an overriding reason:

Não posso comparar o livro e o filme, até porque não vi o filme ainda.
I can't compare the book and the movie, because anyway I haven't seen the movie yet.

42.2.2 The expression **por . . .** can be used with a noun to signal a causal relationship in some contexts, but it is also frequently used with an infinitive, which may be a personal infinitive when the subject of the infinitive is different from that of the main verb. This construction is more common in writing than speech and usually requires the translation 'because' with a clause in English:

Todos acabam se dando mal por alguns baderneiros.
Everyone ends up suffering because of a few troublemakers.

Ele não quis gravar entrevista por medo de represálias.
He did not want to be interviewed for fear of reprisals.

Este projeto foi escolhido por ser o mais barato.
This project was chosen because it is the cheapest.

O país está em melhor situação hoje por o governo ter quitado a dívida externa.[1]
The country is better off today because the government paid off the foreign debt.

42.2.3 The expressions **por causa de . . .** 'because of . . .', **por conta de . . .** 'on account of . . .' and **devido a . . .** 'due to, owing to' are used in similar contexts, the first being the most common in the spoken language:[2]

Não pudemos ir por causa da chuva.
We couldn't go because of the rain.

A economia estava paralisada por conta da crise política.
The economy was at a standstill on account of the political crisis.

O aeroporto foi fechado devido ao mau tempo.
The airport was closed due to the bad weather.

NOTES

1   Notice that the preposition **por** is not contracted with the following definite article in this sentence because it governs the whole infinitive phrase **o governo ter quitado** and not just the noun **o governo**. See **19.4.2**.

2   In very colloquial speech, you may hear the conjunctions **por causa que** 'because', **por conta que** 'on account of the fact that' and **devido que** 'due to the fact that', but these are non-standard usages and should not be imitated.

Note that 'because of me/you/us' translates as **por minha/sua/nossa causa**, and 'on my/your/our account' as **por minha/sua/nossa conta**:

Vim até aqui por sua causa.
I came all the way here because of you.

Se há erros de digitação no documento, não são por minha conta.
If there are typing mistakes in the document, they're not down to me.

42.2.4

The expression **dever-se a** is used in more formal contexts, predominantly in writing:

O sucesso das medidas se deve ao apoio da população.
The success of the measures is due to public support.

Isso se deve ao fato de que as empresas não têm acesso à informação.
This is due to the fact that companies do not have access to information.

42.2.5

The expression **como . . .** introduces a reason that is then followed by a clause explaining the consequence, and is placed at the beginning of the sentence:

Como quinta é feriado, as pessoas vão viajar na quarta à noite.
As Thursday is a holiday, people will travel on Wednesday evening.

Como ele não falava português, tivemos que arranjar um intérprete.
Since he didn't speak Portuguese, we had to get hold of an interpreter.

42.2.6

The expression **já que . . .** 'as, since . . .' is similar in meaning to **como . . .** , but the **já que** clause can also be placed after the main clause:

Já que você vai ao supermercado, compra papel higiênico.
Since you're going to the supermarket, buy toilet paper.

Vou aproveitar para perguntar, já que vou estar com eles.
I'll take the opportunity to ask as I'm going to be seeing them.

The expressions **visto que . . .** 'in view of the fact that, seeing that . . .', **dado que . . .** and **posto que . . .** , both meaning 'given that . . .', are used in a similar way, but are restricted to more formal registers, predominantly in writing:

Uma solução pacífica é difícil de alcançar, dado que/posto que nenhuma das partes está disposta a fazer concessões.
A peaceful solution is difficult to achieve given that neither side is prepared to make concessions.

A construção de casas populares está paralisada, visto que os recursos não têm sido repassados pela Prefeitura.
The building of social housing is at a standstill in view of the fact that funds have not been put in place by the city council.

The expression **na medida em que . . .** 'inasmuch as' is similarly formal:

Concretizar uma separação não é nada fácil, na medida em que a vida a dois induz a uma relação de dependência emocional.
Going as far as an actual separation is not at all easy inasmuch as living as a couple leads to a relationship of emotional dependence.

42.2.7

The word **pois** 'as, because, for' is mainly used in the written language. The **pois** clause always comes after the main clause:

É difícil se manter a par dos avanços da tecnologia, pois as coisas mudam muito rápido.
It is difficult to keep up to date with advances in technology as things change very quickly.

Ele não joga amanhã, pois está fora de forma.
He's not playing tomorrow as he is unfit.

42.2.8 The expression **é que . . .** is used in the spoken language to mean 'the thing is that . . .', 'you see . . .' when introducing an explanation:

É que não dormi muito bem essa noite.
The thing is, I didn't sleep very well last night.

É que temos que tomar cuidado.
You see, we have to be careful.

The expressions **o negócio é que . . .** 'the thing is that . . .' and **o negócio é o seguinte** 'the thing is this' are very common ways of introducing an explanation in colloquial speech:

O negócio é que tem que estar lá às sete.
The things is, we have to be there at seven.

O negócio é o seguinte: eu não tive tempo para ler tudo.
The thing is this: I didn't have time to read it all.

42.3 Other ways of expressing relationships of cause and effect

Relationships of cause and effect can be expressed in several other ways, such as the following:

42.3.1 By using particular verbs such as **causar**, **provocar**, **ocasionar** 'to cause', **dar origem a**, **originar** 'to give rise to', **acarretar** 'to bring (with it)', **desencadear** 'to spark, trigger':

O cigarro pode causar câncer.
Smoking can cause cancer.

As chuvas provocaram 14 mortes.
The rains have caused 14 deaths.

O incêndio foi ocasionado por um curto-circuito.
The fire was caused by a short circuit.

Essas observações deram origem às primeiras inquietações sobre o efeito estufa.
These observations gave rise to the first concerns about the greenhouse effect.

o livro que originou a polêmica
the book that gave rise to the controversy

A saída do ministro desencadeou uma crise política.
The minister's exit from office sparked a political crisis.

O preço deve aumentar em 10%, o que acarretará uma queda nas vendas.
The price is set to rise by 10 per cent, which will bring a drop in sales.

42.3.2   By using noun phrases such as **a razão pela qual/o motivo pelo qual . . .** 'the reason (that) . . .', **a razão/o motivo por que . . .** 'the reason why . . .', **por razões/motivos** + adjective, **por razões/motivos de** + noun 'for reasons (of)', **em razão de** 'because of', 'on the grounds of', **graças a** 'thanks to':

> **O motivo pelo qual ela renunciou continua desconhecido.**
> The reason why she resigned is still unknown.

> **Ele não pôde comparecer por motivos de saúde.**
> He was unable to attend for health reasons.

> **O aeroporto foi fechado por razões de segurança.**
> The airport was closed for security reasons.

> **O Brasil atrai investidores em razão do tamanho de seu mercado.**
> Brazil attracts investors because of the size of its market.

> **Conseguimos graças à sua ajuda.**
> We succeeded thanks to your help.

42.3.3   By using linking words and phrases such as:

> **por isso (que)** 'so', 'that is why'
>
> **assim** 'so', 'thus'
>
> **sendo assim / assim sendo** 'so', 'therefore'
>
> **aí** 'so' (*informal*)
>
> **daí** 'so then', 'hence'
>
> **portanto** 'therefore'
>
> **pois** 'therefore'
>
> **consequentemente**, **por conseguinte** 'consequently'
>
> **de modo/maneira/forma que** 'so', 'with the result that'
>
> **de tal modo/maneira/forma que** 'to such an extent that', 'in such a way that'.

These expressions can be used in the following ways:

> **Eu estava sem celular, por isso que não te liguei.**
> I didn't have my mobile phone on me, that's why I didn't call you.

> **Não tínhamos dinheiro para sair, e assim ficamos em casa.**
> We couldn't afford to go out, and so we stayed at home.

> **O jogador foi suspenso por 180 dias. Sendo assim, ele não pode ser convocado para a seleção.**
> The player was suspended for 180 days. Therefore, he cannot be selected for the national squad.

> **Eu não sabia o que fazer, aí eu liguei para você.**
> I didn't know what to do, so I called you.

> **Eu passei dois anos no Canadá, daí eu decidi dar aula de inglês.**
> I spent two years in Canada, so then I decided to give English lessons.

> **A situação se agrava a cada dia. Daí a urgência de tomar uma atitude.**
> The situation is getting worse by the day. Hence the urgent need to take action.

Faz frio no inverno, portanto as casas têm calefação.
It is cold in winter, therefore houses are heated.

São muitos os perigos. É preciso, pois, precaver-se.
There are many hazards. It is necessary, therefore, to take precautions.

Os ingressos já se esgotaram. Consequentemente, a bilheteria está fechada.
Tickets have already sold out. Consequently, the ticket office is closed.

O carro quebrou, de forma que tiveram que voltar de ônibus.
The car broke down, so they had to come back by bus.

A moda pegou de tal maneira que as fabricantes não conseguem suprir a demanda.
The fashion has caught on to such an extent that manufacturers are unable to meet demand.

42.4 Enquiring about purpose

Purpose is often associated in Portuguese with the preposition **para**, just as cause is sometimes associated with **por**. To enquire about purpose, the most common phrase is **para que ...?** 'what ... for?':

Para que você precisa de tanto dinheiro?
What do you need so much money for?

Para que ele fez isso?
What did he do that for?

Você quer que eu te empreste o carro para quê?
What do you want to borrow the car for?

Note that **quê** is spelt with a circumflex accent when it falls at the end of the sentence.

42.5 Expressing purpose

To express purpose, Portuguese uses a number of constructions, the most common of which involve the preposition **para**.

42.5.1 *para* + infinitive

The preposition **para** is followed by the ordinary impersonal infinitive when the subjects of the infinitive and main verb are the same:

A Ana ligou para me contar a novidade.
Ana called to tell me the news.

Tivemos uma reunião para acertar os detalhes.
We had a meeting to agree on the details.

When the subject of the infinitive is different from that of the main verb, a personal infinitive is used. An infinitive is made personal simply by placing a noun or pronoun subject before it, but in the first and third persons plural, the flectional endings -**mos** and -**em** respectively must also be appended to it, either in addition to, or instead of, a pronoun subject:

Vou trazer as fotos aqui para você ver.
I'll bring the photos here for you to see.

Fecha a porta para o cachorro não entrar.
Close the door so the dog doesn't come in.

Fomos a São Paulo para eu conhecer os pais dela.
We went to São Paulo for me to meet her parents.

Ele trouxe o tabuleiro para (nós) jogarmos xadrez.
He brought the board for us to play chess.

Saí de casa na ponta dos pés para meus pais não perceberem.
I tiptoed out of the house so my parents wouldn't notice.

42.5.2 *para que* + subjunctive

In more formal written language, **para** + personal infinitive is often replaced by **para que** + subjunctive:

Desligue o freezer para que descongele.
Turn off the freezer so that it defrosts.

Para que isso aconteça, é preciso arrecadar fundos.
In order that this should happen, funds must be raised.

Remember that the rules on sequence of tenses (see **20.2**) require that the imperfect subjunctive is used after **para que** if the main verb is preterite, imperfect or conditional:

O técnico desligou o freezer para que descongelasse.
The technician turned off the freezer so that it would defrost.

Para que isso acontecesse, era preciso arrecadar fundos.
In order that this should happen, funds had to be raised.

42.5.3 *para* + noun

When followed by a noun or pronoun, **para** indicates the beneficiary of the action or its purpose:

Preciso comprar um presente para a minha mãe.
I need to buy a present for my mother.

Preparamos uma surpresa para você.
We've got a surprise for you.

O melhor café é cultivado para exportação.
The best coffee is grown for export.

42.5.4 *de modo/maneira/forma que* + subjunctive

These expressions are synonymous with **para que** and are predominantly used in the written language to mean 'so that':

O governo comprou dólares de modo que a cotação da moeda subisse.
The government bought dollars so that the price of the currency would go up.

Compare the use of these conjunctions with the subjunctive, as here, and with the indicative as shown in **42.3.3**. With the subjunctive they express the purpose; with the indicative they express the actual result. Compare:

O governo comprou dólares de modo que a cotação da moeda subiu.
The government bought dollars with the result that the price of the currency went up.

42.5.5 *a fim de* + infinitive/*a fim de que* + subjunctive

These are more formal synonyms of **para** + infinitive/**para que** + subjunctive. They are used almost exclusively in formal writing to mean 'in order to'/'in order that':

Vacinaram as crianças a fim de protegê-las da doença.
They vaccinated the children in order to protect them from the illness.

Ele escondeu a arma do crime a fim de que a polícia não a descobrisse.
He hid the murder weapon in order that the police would not find it.

42.5.6 *com o objetivo de* + infinitive; *com o propósito de* + infinitive; *com o intuito de* + infinitive; *com a intençao de* + infinitive

The expressions **com o objetivo de** 'with the aim of' and **com o propósito de** 'with the purpose of' are used with an infinitive to express the objective of an action. Intent is expressed by **com o intuito de** 'with intent to' and **com a intenção de** 'with the intention of'. These two are more or less synonymous, but the first is more formal:

Vieram ao Brasil com o objetivo de comprar um terreno na Bahia.
They came to Brazil with the aim of buying a plot of land in Bahia.

Ela saiu da empresa com a intenção de montar um negócio próprio.
She left the company with the intention of setting up a business of her own.

III

Putting events into a wider context

43

Expressing knowledge

To express knowledge, Portuguese uses two different verbs, **saber** and **conhecer**, 'to know'. Their uses are clearly differentiated by native speakers, as you will see from the examples below.

▶ **16.3.2** (p. 153)

43.1 Expressing knowledge of a fact

To express knowledge or ignorance of a fact and, generally, to say that one has or does not have information about something, the verb to use in Portuguese is **saber**. Remember that **saber** is irregular in the first person singular of the present: **eu sei** 'I know':

Você sabe onde está o Bernardo?
Do you know where Bernardo is?

Não sei.
I don't know.

Eu sei disso.
I know that.

Você sabia que a Cristina casou?
Did you know that Cristina got married?

Sabia, sim.
Yes, I did (know).

Não sei o nome dele.
I don't know his name.

In more formal written language, 'not to know, be unaware of' can be expressed using the verbs **desconhecer** or **ignorar**:[1]

A polícia desconhece a identidade do assassino.
The police do not know the identity of the murderer.

Muitos ignoram que é proibido vender bebida alcoólica a menores.
Many are unaware that selling alcohol to minors is forbidden.

NOTE | 1 The verb **ignorar** is only used with the meaning of 'not to know' in formal writing. It is more commonly used in all registers to mean 'to ignore'.

Note also the following more colloquial expressions:

Sei lá.
I don't know (*emphatic*). / No idea. / Don't ask me.

Sei lá onde ele foi.
I don't know where he went.

Sei lá, acho que estou ficando velho.
I don't know, I must be getting old.

Não tenho a mínima ideia.
I haven't the slightest idea.

Vou saber?
How should I know? (*expressing annoyance*)

Nunca se sabe.
You never know.

Quem sabe?
Who knows?

Quem sabe ele não te liga mais tarde?
You never know, he might call you later.

43.2 Saying that one knows a person, a place or an object

To say that you know or do not know a person, place or an object, the verb to use in Portuguese is **conhecer**. This verb is a regular **-er** verb, but remember that the second **c** must take a cedilla before **o** or **a** to preserve the soft *c* sound, e.g. **eu conheço**.

Você conhece a Marta?
Do you know Marta?

Conheço ela muito bem. (*spoken*)
I know her very well.

A gente se conhece há anos.
We've known each other for years.

Você conhece Paris?
Do you know Paris? *or* Have you ever been to Paris?[2]

Não conheço essa fruta.
I don't know that fruit. (= *I'm not familiar with it*)

NOTE   2   The verb **conhecer** is frequently used in this sense of 'go to, visit'. Other examples: **Você precisa conhecer a minha casa**. 'You must visit my house.' **Não conheço Londres**. 'I've never been to London.'

43.3 Cases in which both *saber* or *conhecer* can be used with a difference of meaning

The verb **saber** can be used with a person, place or thing when the meaning is 'do you know the one I'm talking about?':

Sabe a Cristina? Então, ela casou.
You know Cristina? Well, she got married.

Compare the meanings of **saber** or **conhecer** in the following examples:

> **Você sabe a capital do Tocantins?** (*a Brazilian state*)
> Do you know the capital of Tocantins? (*i.e. the name of it*)

> **Você conhece a capital do Tocantins?**
> Do you know the capital of Tocantins? (*i.e. do you know your way around it?*) or
> Have you ever been to the capital of Tocantins?

43.4 Expressing knowledge of a subject

To say that you know or do not know about a subject, for example computers, physics, etc., use the verb **entender** (*literally*, 'to understand') followed by the preposition **de**:

> **Você entende de computadores?**
> Do you know about computers?

> **O Pedro entende de física.**
> Pedro knows all about physics.

43.5 Expressing knowledge of a language

To say that you know or don't know a language, use **saber**:

> **Você sabe francês?**
> Do you know French?

> **Ele não sabe nada de português.**
> He doesn't know any Portuguese.

43.6 Expressing knowledge of a skill

To say that you know or don't know how to do something, use **saber** followed by an infinitive:

> **Ela não sabe costurar.**
> She doesn't know how to sew.

> **Você sabe nadar?**
> Do you know how to swim? / Can you swim?

> **Ele nem sabe ligar o computador.**
> He doesn't even know how to turn the computer on.

43.7 Getting to know, becoming acquainted with or meeting someone

These ideas are expressed in Portuguese using **conhecer**:

> **Eu a conheci em 2003.**
> I met/got to know her in 2003.

> **Foi uma oportunidade de conhecê-los melhor.**
> It was an opportunity to get to know them better.

When talking about two or more people getting to know each other, use the reflexive form **conhecer-se**:

> **Como é que vocês dois se conheceram?**
> How did you two meet?

> **Nós nos conhecemos na faculdade.**
> We met at university.

43.8 Hearing or finding out about something

To say that you heard or found out about something, use **saber**:

> **Você soube o que aconteceu comigo ontem?**
> Did you hear what happened to me yesterday?

> **Eu soube do Marcelo.**
> I heard it from Marcelo. *or* I heard about Marcelo.

> **Procura saber onde ela mora.**
> Try and find out where she lives.

In colloquial speech, the expression **ficar sabendo** is often used in this sense:

> **Fiquei sabendo que você está namorando.**
> I heard you're seeing someone.

> **Se meu pai ficar sabendo, estou frito.**
> If my dad finds out, I've had it.

The imperative **fique/fica sabendo** is used in the sense of 'I'll have you know', 'for your information':

> **Fique sabendo que a culpa não foi minha.**
> I'll have you know it wasn't my fault.

44

Remembering and forgetting

This chapter examines the use of verbs of remembering and forgetting in Portuguese and the constructions associated with them.

44.1 Remembering

The usual verb for remembering in Portuguese is **lembrar**. In the sense of 'to remember', there are two possible constructions with **lembrar**: either it is used as a straightforward verb, with or without a direct object, or it is used as a reflexive verb, **lembrar-se**, in which case the object has to be introduced with the preposition **de** (see examples below). In some cases, the two constructions are interchangeable, in others they are not.

44.1.1 *lembrar/lembrar-se* with no direct object

When there is no direct object mentioned, the simple and reflexive verbs can be used interchangeably:

> **Não lembro. / Não me lembro.**
> I don't remember.

> **Estou tentando lembrar. / Estou tentando me lembrar.**
> I'm trying to remember.

> **Não sei se você lembra. / Não sei se você se lembra.**
> I don't know if you remember.

Note that, in English, we often say 'I can't remember' instead of 'I don't remember'. In Portuguese, the verb meaning 'can' is not translated unless it carries particular emphasis, as in:

> **Não consigo me lembrar.**
> I just can't remember.

44.1.2 *lembrar* + noun; *lembrar-se de* + noun

When the direct object is a noun or noun phrase, both constructions are possible. The simple **lembrar** + noun tends to be used when talking about remembering a piece of information or fact and when talking about the act of retrieving something from your memory or memorizing something, while the reflexive **lembrar-se de** tends to be used when the focus is on the content of the memory. For this reason, **lembrar-se de** is preferred when remembering a person, place or past experience:

> **Você lembra o nome dele?**
> Can/Do you remember his name?

287345 – lembre esse número!
287345 – remember that number!

Eu me lembro daquele dia.
I remember that day.

Você lembra o que ele disse?
Do you remember what he said? (= *Can you remember it?*)

Você se lembra do que ele disse?
Do you remember what he said? (= *Do you keep it in mind?*)

Você se lembra do Paulo?
Do you remember Paulo?

The distinction between these two constructions is further blurred by the fact that there is a tendency in the spoken language to drop reflexive pronouns (see **22.5**), so the non-reflexive **lembrar** is often heard with a prepositional object:

Você lembra do Paulo?

44.1.3 *lembrar-se de* + pronoun

When the direct object is a personal pronoun, **lembrar-se de** is the only possible construction:

Você se lembra de mim?
Do you remember me?

Não me lembro dela.
I don't remember her.

But, once again, the reflexive pronoun is often dropped in the spoken language:

Você lembra de mim?

44.1.4 *lembrar que* + clause; *lembrar-se que* + clause

The construction **lembrar que** + clause tends to refer to a simple fact that you retrieve from your memory:

Eu lembro que a porta estava trancada quando cheguei.
I remember that the door was locked when I got here.

Você lembrou que temos um aniversário para ir hoje?
Have you remembered that we've got a birthday party to go to today?

The reflexive **lembrar-se que** + clause tends either to mean 'keep in mind that' or to give the idea of reminiscing:

Eles devem se lembrar que é preciso manter silêncio durante a prova.
They should remember that silence must be observed during the exam.

Eu me lembro que passamos o dia na praia com uns amigos.
I remember that we spent the day on the beach with some friends.

Once again, the reflexive pronoun is often dropped in colloquial speech, especially when the verb is imperative:

> **Lembra que você não pode usar o dicionário.**
> Remember that you're not allowed to use the dictionary.

Sometimes the subjunctive is required in the **que** clause when **lembrar** is negative and the content of the **que** clause is therefore in doubt:

> **Eu não me lembro que ele estivesse aqui naquela noite.**
> I don't remember that he was here that night.

> **Eu não me lembro que ela tenha dito isso.**
> I don't remember she said that.

44.1.5 *lembrar de* + infinitive

The verb **lembrar** can be followed by the preposition **de** and an infinitive to mean 'to remember to do':

> **Você lembrou de comprar leite?**
> Did you remember to buy milk?

> **Ele nunca lembra de apagar a luz.**
> He never remembers to turn the light off.

Note that 'remember to . . .' as a reminder is usually translated **não esqueça de** . . . 'don't forget to . . .':

> **Não esqueça de comprar pão!**
> Remember to buy bread!

44.1.6 *lembrar(-se) de ter* + past participle

Both **lembrar** and **lembrar-se** can be followed by the preposition **de**, the infinitive of the perfect auxiliary **ter** and a past participle to mean 'to remember doing':

> **Eu lembro de ter visto esse filme.**
> I remember seeing this movie.

> **Você se lembra de ter andado de bicicleta na sua infância?**
> Do you remember riding a bike in your childhood?

The infinitive **ter** can have a different subject to that of **lembrar**:

> **Eu não lembro de você ter falado isso.**
> I don't remember you saying that.

> **Ele se lembrava de os policiais terem entrado na casa.**
> He remembered the police coming into the house.

44.1.7 Other verbs of remembering

44.1.7.1 *recordar(-se) de*

The verb **recordar** 'to recall' works in the same way grammatically as **lembrar**, but, as its translations suggest, it is a more formal/literary word:

> **Recordo que acordei cedo naquele dia.**
> I recall that I woke up early that day.

> **Ele ainda se recordava daqueles momentos de felicidade.**
> He still recalled those happy moments.

44.1.7.2 *decorar, memorizar*

The verb **decorar** means 'to memorize', 'to learn by heart', while **memorizar** means 'to memorize' in the sense of 'retain in one's memory':

> **Decore a senha do seu cartão.**
> Memorize the PIN number for your card.

> **Os comandos do programa são fáceis de memorizar.**
> The program's commands are easy to memorize.

44.1.7.3 *reter, gravar*

The verbs **reter** 'to retain, remember, memorize' and **gravar** 'to remember, memorize' are synonymous, but **gravar** is more colloquial:

> **Tenho dificuldade para reter números de telefone.**
> I find it difficult to remember phone numbers.

> **Não consigo gravar o nome das pessoas.**
> I can't memorize people's names.

44.1.7.4 *relembrar*

The verb **relembrar** means 'to remember' in the sense of 'to reminisce about, to relive':

> **Os veteranos se reuniram para relembrar os velhos tempos.**
> The veterans met up to remember old times.

44.2 Reminding

The verb **lembrar** is also used in a number of constructions with the sense of reminding someone else of something.

44.2.1 *lembrar a* + noun/pronoun + *que* + clause

In the sense of 'remind', **lembrar** is followed by the preposition **a**:

> **Você lembra ao Cadu que ele tem que ligar para o banco?**
> Will you remind Cadu that he has to call the bank?

> **Ela me lembrou que o encanador vinha às três.**
> She reminded me that the plumber was coming at three.

Sentences without a **que** clause are also possible:

> **Isso me lembra: precisamos comprar café.**
> That reminds me: we need to buy coffee.

Você me lembra?
Will you remind me?

In more formal language, **lembrar** is sometimes used without a noun or pronoun object to introduce a **que** clause:

O presidente lembrou que a constituição não permitia tal atitude.
The president recalled that the constitution did not allow such a move.

44.2.2 *lembrar a* + noun/pronoun + *de* + noun

This construction means 'to remind a person about something':

Por que você não me lembrou da festa hoje à noite?
Why didn't you remind me about the party tonight?

44.2.3 *lembrar a* + noun/pronoun + *de* + infinitive

This construction means 'to remind a person to do':

Você me lembra de pagar a conta de luz?
Will you remind me to pay the electricity bill?

Tive que lembrar à faxineira de colocar o lixo para fora.
I had to remind the cleaner to put the rubbish out.

44.2.4 *lembrar* + noun/pronoun + *a* + noun/pronoun

With this construction, it is the appearance or sound of something or someone that is reminiscent of a person or thing, 'to remind someone of something/someone':

Ela me lembra a minha tia.
She reminds me of my aunt.

O namorado dela não te lembra aquele ator?
Doesn't her boyfriend remind you of that actor?

In this sense, **lembrar** can also occur without an indirect object:

Petrópolis lembra uma cidade europeia.
Petropolis is reminiscent of a European town.

A banda lembra os Beatles.
The band sounds like the Beatles.

44.2.5 *fazer* + noun/pronoun + *lembrar* + noun/pronoun

This construction has a similar meaning to the previous one, i.e. 'to remind someone of something/someone', except that, in this case, it is not a direct resemblance that is referred to, but the memory that something evokes:

Essa música me faz lembrar aquele verão que passamos na Itália.
This song reminds me of that summer we spent in Italy.

Isso fez o Marco lembrar um filme que tinha visto.
This reminded Marco of a film he had seen.

44.3 Forgetting

The verb used to express forgetting, **esquecer**, has the same two constructions as **lembrar**, i.e. **esquecer** and **esquecer-se de**. In this case, the difference is more one of register: **esquecer-se de** sounds slightly more formal than **esquecer**, but, just as with **lembrar**, the tendency to drop the reflexive pronoun in informal speech means that a hybrid construction – **esquecer de** – is often heard.

44.3.1 *esquecer* with no direct object

> **Não esqueça!**
> Don't forget!

> **Não vou esquecer.**
> I won't forget.

> **Ele deve ter esquecido.**
> He must have forgotten.

> **Eu tinha que pagar aquela conta hoje e esqueci.**
> I was supposed to pay that bill today and I forgot.

44.3.2 *esquecer* + direct object

> **Ele esqueceu meu aniversário.**
> He forgot my birthday.

With a pronoun object, there is a preference for using the **de** construction in less formal language, often without the reflexive pronoun:

> **Ela já (se) esqueceu dele.**
> She's already forgotten him.

The direct object may be a clause:

> **Não devemos esquecer que os jovens são o futuro deste país.**
> We should not forget that young people are the future of this country.

> **Esqueci onde coloquei os óculos.**
> I've forgotten where I put my glasses.

44.3.3 *esquecer de* + infinitive

This construction means 'to forget to do something':

> **Esqueci de te dizer que encontrei o seu irmão no fim de semana.**
> I forgot to tell you that I met your brother at the weekend.

> **Não esqueça de trancar a porta.**
> Don't forget to lock the door.

44.3.4 Forgetting to bring something

The verb **esquecer** can also be used in the sense of 'leave behind':

> **Você esqueceu o guarda-chuva?**
> Did you forget your umbrella?

In Portuguese, the sentence with **esquecer** can also contain an indication of where the object was left:

> **Esqueci minha carteira em casa.**
> I've left my wallet at home.

> **Não esqueça a roupa no varal.**
> Don't (forget and) leave the clothes out on the line.

In English, we usually use 'to leave' when the place is mentioned and this is also possible in Portuguese, using **deixar** 'to leave':

> **Deixei a mochila no ônibus.**
> I left my backpack on the bus.

45

Expressing obligation and duty

This chapter deals with the ideas of obligation and duty and the verbs and expressions associated with them.

45.1   Expressing obligation and duty with regard to oneself and others

To express obligation and duty with regard to oneself and others, Portuguese uses the following verbs, all followed by the infinitive:

45.1.1   *ter que* + infinitive

The verb **ter que** 'to have to' is one of the most frequent verbs used in the expression of obligation and duty and is used with present, past or future reference. Its use usually implies that the obligation involved stems from outside the speaker, that is, from external circumstances:

> **Tenho que sair.**
> I have to go out.

> **Você não tem que ir.**
> You don't have to go.

> **Vamos ter que fazer tudo de novo.**
> We'll have to do it all again.

> **Ela teve que voltar para casa a pé.**
> She had to walk back home.

> **Eu tinha que acordar cedo no dia seguinte.**
> I had to get up early the next day.

The difference between the preterite and the imperfect, which can both mean 'had to' in English, is that the preterite implies that the action was actually done while the imperfect suggests it had not yet been done at the time referred to:

> **Eu tive que ir ao banco.**
> I had to go the bank. (*and I did*)

> **Eu tinha que ir ao banco.**
> I had to go to the bank. (*but, at that point, I hadn't been yet*)

There is a more formal variant of **ter que**, **ter de**, which is mostly restricted to the written language:

> **O governo teve de recuar nesse ponto.**
> The government had to back down on this point.

45.1.2 *precisar* + infinitive

The verb **precisar** 'to need to' is used when the obligation is seen as stemming from the speaker, as a physical, mental or moral need. In the first persons singular and plural of the present tense, it is often equivalent to the English 'must'. In other persons and tenses, the translation is usually 'have/had to':

> **Preciso tomar banho.**
> I need to/must take a shower.

> **Precisamos tomar cuidado.**
> We need to/must be careful.

> **Eu precisei parar para descansar.**
> I had/needed to stop for a rest.

In negative sentences meaning 'don't have to', **precisar** refers to the absence of need rather than absence of obligation:

> **Você não precisa me esperar.**
> You don't have/need to wait for me.

> **Você não precisava comprar um presente.**
> You didn't have/need to buy a present.

> **Não preciso trabalhar hoje.**
> I don't have/need to work today.

45.1.3 *dever* + infinitive

The modal verb **dever** 'must, should' expresses a strong obligation, often moral or legal. With this meaning, it is mainly used in the present tense:

> **Você deve entregar essa carteira à polícia.**
> You should/must hand that wallet in to the police.

> **Eles não devem tocar no computador.**
> They must/should not touch the computer.

> **Vocês não devem entrar na sala de aula.**
> You must not go into the classroom.

It is also used in the conditional, or the imperfect in place of the conditional. In this case, **dever** expresses a moral obligation with the implication that what should happen does not, or vice versa:

> **Vocês não deveriam/deviam estar aqui dentro.**
> You shouldn't be in here. (*but you are*)

> **O governo deveria tomar uma atitude.**
> The government should take action. (*but it probably won't*)

> **Eu devia pedir desculpas.**
> I ought to apologize. (*but I'm not sure I will*)

45.1.4 *é para* + personal infinitive

This expression is commonly used in the spoken language to mean 'be supposed to' and is usually found in the present or imperfect tense:

> **É para a gente esperar aqui.**
> We're supposed to wait here.

> **Era para eles estarem aqui às oito.**
> They were supposed to be here at eight.

> **É para levarmos alguma coisa?**
> Are we supposed to take anything?

45.2 Enquiring whether one is obliged to do something

When enquiring whether you are obliged to do something, the normal verb to use is **ter que** + infinitive (see **45.1.1**):

> **Tenho que informar a idade?**
> Do I have to give my age?

> **Temos que subir a pé?**
> Do we have to walk up?

> **Você vai ter que fazer tudo de novo?**
> Will you have to do it all again?

45.3 Expressing obligation in an impersonal way

Obligation is sometimes expressed in an impersonal way, without reference to a specific person. In spoken Portuguese, the third person singular form of **ter que** (see **45.1.1**) and **precisar** (see **45.1.2**) are frequently used with no subject to refer to a general obligation that applies to everyone, usually in the present tense:

> **Tem que deixar a chave na recepção.**
> You have to leave the key at reception.

> **Tem que marcar hora?**
> Do you have to make an appointment?

> **Precisa pagar primeiro?**
> Do you have to pay first?

> **Precisa pagar no caixa.**
> You have to pay at the cash desk.

Similarly, the expression **é para** can be followed by an impersonal infinitive with general reference:

> **É para deixar a porta aberta?**
> Is the door supposed to be left open?

In more formal language, impersonal obligations may be expressed using the verb **dever** (see **45.1.3**) in the impersonal **se** construction or the expression **é preciso** + infinitive:

> **Deve-se proteger a floresta.**
> The forest must be protected.

> **Não se deve mexer em direitos adquiridos.**
> One should not meddle with established rights.

> **É preciso lembrar que o povo indígena falava tupi naquela época.**
> It should be remembered that the indigenous people spoke Tupi at that time.

45.4 Other ways of expressing obligation and duty

Obligation and duty are also expressed through the following constructions:

> **estar** *or* **ser/ver-se**[1] **obrigado a** 'to be forced to', 'to be obliged to'

> **ter (a) obrigação de** 'to have an obligation to', 'to be under an obligation to'

> **estar** *or* **ver-se na obrigação de** 'to be obliged to'

> **sentir-se na obrigação de** 'to feel obliged to'.

Examples:

> **Ele se viu obrigado a sair da empresa.**
> He was forced to leave the company.

> **O Estado tem obrigação de proteger os cidadãos.**
> The state has an obligation to protect citizens.

> **Ele se sentia na obrigação de dar satisfações ao pai.**
> He felt obliged to explain himself to his father.

NOTE | 1 **Estar** refers to an ongoing obligation established in law whereas **ser/ver-se** refers to a momentary obligation in a particular set of circumstances.

45.5 Expressing unfulfilled obligation

The verbs presented in this chapter can also be used to express unfulfilled obligation, as in sentences such as 'You should have helped your brother', 'You weren't supposed to say anything to him'.

45.5.1 *deveria/devia* + *ter* + past participle

The conditional or, less formally, the imperfect tense of **dever** is followed by the perfect infinitive to refer to something that ought to have been done but was not, or vice versa:

> **Você devia ter ajudado o seu irmão.**
> You should have helped your brother.

> **Deveriam ter sondado a opinião pública.**
> They should have sounded out public opinion.

> **Você não devia ter contado para ninguém.**
> You shouldn't have told anyone.

45.5.2 | *tinha que/precisava/era para* **+ infinitive**

In colloquial speech, the imperfect tense of the verb phrases **ter que**, **precisar** and **ser para** are used with an infinitive to express what should or should not have happened, or what was or was not supposed to happen:

> **Você não tinha que falar nada para ele.**
> You weren't supposed to say anything to him.
>
> **Você precisava ver a cara dele!**
> You should have seen his face!
>
> **Era para você entregar isso ontem.**
> You were supposed to hand this in yesterday.
>
> **Não era para eles saberem.**
> They weren't supposed to know.

45.5.3 | *podia ter* **+ past participle**

The imperfect of the verb **poder** can also be used with a perfect infinitive to express unfulfilled obligation with a tone of indignation. Notice that the positive form means 'could have' while the negative can mean 'should not have':

> **Você podia pelo menos ter ligado!**
> You could at least have called!
>
> **Você não podia ter feito isso!**
> You shouldn't have done that! / I can't believe you did that!
>
> **Eles não podiam ter dado para trás!**
> They can't possibly have pulled out!

46

Expressing needs

This chapter deals with different ways of expressing needs. In the sections below you will learn to express needs in a personal way, through the Portuguese equivalent of phrases such as 'I have to . . .', 'I need to . . .', 'we need you to . . .', 'they need it', and also in an impersonal way through expressions such as 'one has to . . .', 'one needs to . . .', 'it is necessary'.

46.1 Expressing needs with regard to oneself and others

To express needs or lack of need with regard to oneself or others, Portuguese normally uses the verb **precisar** 'to need' as follows.

46.1.1 *precisar* + infinitive

The verb **precisar** + infinitive means 'to need to':

> **Preciso falar com você.**
> I need to talk to you.

> **Precisamos achar um lugar para morar.**
> We need to find a place to live.

> **Eles precisavam ganhar dinheiro.**
> They needed to earn money.

> **Você não precisa se preocupar comigo.**
> You don't need to worry about me.

Note that, unlike the English 'need', the verb **precisar** also occurs in the continuous tenses with the sense of 'to be in need of':

> **Estou precisando desabafar.**
> I need to get things off my chest.

46.1.2 *ter que* + infinitive

The verb phrase **ter que** 'to have to' expresses a strong need where there is little alternative:

> **A impressora quebrou. Vou ter que comprar outra.**
> The printer's broken down. I'll have to buy another one.

> **Temos que correr, senão vamos perder o avião.**
> We have to hurry, otherwise we'll miss the plane.

> **Você teria/tinha que comer mais, está muito magro.**
> You should eat more, you are too thin.

46.1.3 *precisar que* + subjunctive

This construction is used when the subject of the main verb is different from that of the complement verb, i.e. when someone needs someone else to do something:

> **Preciso que você me ajude.**
> I need you to help me.

> **Precisamos que vocês estejam aqui às sete.**
> We need you to be here at seven.

> **Eu precisava que você me falasse isso.**
> I needed you to tell me that.

> **Não preciso que você me lembre disso.**
> I don't need you to remind me of that.

46.1.4 *precisar de* + noun/noun phrase/pronoun

> **Preciso de sossego para estudar.**
> I need peace and quiet to study.

> **Ela disse que não precisava de nada.**
> She said she didn't need anything.

> **Não precisei do guarda-chuva afinal.**
> I didn't need the umbrella after all.

> **Preciso de você.**
> I need you.

Note that the verb **precisar** also occurs in the continuous tenses in the sense of 'be in need of':

> **Estou precisando de férias.**
> I'm in need of a holiday/vacation.

46.1.5 *ter necessidade de* + noun/pronoun/infinitive

The expression **ter necessidade de** means 'to have a need for/to, need' and may be followed by a noun, pronoun or verb in the infinitive. Note that the subject may be a person or a thing:

> **Casos mais graves têm necessidade de cirurgia corretiva.**
> More serious cases require corrective surgery.

> **As pessoas têm necessidade de interagir com as outras.**
> People have a need to interact with others.

46.1.6 *necessitar* + infinitive; *necessitar que* + subjunctive; *necessitar de* + noun/pronoun

The verb **necessitar** 'to require' forms the same grammatical constructions as **precisar**, being a more formal synonym of the latter:

> **A empresa necessita crescer para sobreviver.**
> The company needs to grow in order to survive.

O tiro livre indireto necessita que outro jogador toque na bola.
The indirect free kick requires another player to touch the ball.

Necessitamos de uma nova estratégia de marketing.
We require a new marketing strategy.

46.2 Asking people about their needs

The verb **precisar** (see **46.1**) is also used to ask people about their needs:

Você precisa trocar dinheiro?
Do you need to change money?

Você precisa que eu te acompanhe?
Do you need me to go with you?

Vocês vão precisar de mim?
Are you going to need me?

Você precisou do dicionário afinal?
Did you need the dictionary in the end?

Você está precisando de alguma coisa do supermercado?
Do you need anything from the supermarket?

Note also the use of **precisar de** with certain question words, as in:

Do que você precisa?
What do you need?

De qual você precisa?
Which one do you need?

Você precisa de quanto tempo?
How much time do you need?

Para que você precisa disso?
What do you need it for?

46.3 Expressing needs in an impersonal way

To ask and answer questions about needs in an impersonal way, that is, without reference to a specific person, we use the following expressions:

46.3.1 *precisar* + infinitive

In colloquial speech, the third person singular of the verb **precisar** is used without an explicit subject to refer to a general requirement:

Precisa reservar mesa?
Is it necessary to book a table?

Precisava enfrentar fila.
You had to queue up/stand in line.

46.3.2 *ter que* + infinitive

In colloquial speech, the third person singular of **ter que** is used without a subject to express a strong need:

> **Não tem ônibus que vá para lá, tem que ir de táxi.**
> There aren't any buses that go there, you have to go by taxi.

46.3.3 *precisar de* + noun/noun phrase

In colloquial speech, the third person singular of **precisar de** is used without a subject to express a general requirement, equivalent to the English impersonal 'you need':

> **Precisa de documento para entrar?**
> Do you need ID to get in?

> **Precisa de muita paciência.**
> It takes a lot of patience.

46.3.4 *ser preciso* + infinitive

This is a more formal way of expressing a need when no specific person is involved:

> **É preciso tomar cuidado.**
> Care must be taken.

> **Foi preciso chamar os bombeiros.**
> The fire brigade had to be called.

> **Seria preciso emendar a Constituição.**
> The Constitution would need to be amended.

46.3.5 *ser preciso* + noun

The expression **ser preciso** 'to be necessary' can also be followed by a noun, but note that the word **preciso** remains unchanged, even if the following noun is feminine:

> **É preciso disposição para enfrentar o shopping na véspera de Natal.**
> You need enthusiasm to face the shopping mall on Christmas Eve.

> **Foi preciso muita coragem para combater o preconceito que existia.**
> A good deal of courage was needed to fight the prejudice that existed.

46.3.6 *ser preciso que* + subjunctive

> **É preciso que o governo intervenha.**
> The government must intervene.

> **Para isso, será preciso que a economia volte a crescer.**
> For this, the economy will need to start growing again.

46.3.7 *ser necessário* + infinitive / *ser necessário* + noun / *ser necessário que* + subjunctive

The word **necessário** is synonymous with **preciso** in impersonal expressions of need and enters into the same constructions, the only difference being that, when followed by a noun, **necessário** usually agrees in gender and number with this noun:

É necessária uma nova política ambiental.
A new environmental policy is needed.

São necessárias medidas drásticas.
Drastic measures are called for.

Talvez seja necessário adiar a reunião.
It may be necessary to postpone the meeting.

Não seria necessário que o presidente se pronunciasse.
It would not be necessary for the president to make a statement.

46.3.8 *há/tem necessidade de* + noun/pronoun/infinitive

This expression means 'there is a need to/for' and may be followed by a noun, pronoun or infinitive. **Há** is used in more formal register while **tem** is more prevalent in everyday speech:

Há necessidade de médicos no interior.
There is a need for doctors in the countryside.

Tem gente que posta fotos de animais maltratados. Tem necessidade disso?
There are people who post pictures of mistreated animals. Is that really necessary?

This expression frequently occurs in the negative:

Para o ministro da Justiça, não há necessidade de mudar a legislação atual.
In the view of the Justice minister, there is no need to change current legislation.

46.3.9 *ser o caso de* + infinitive

The sense of this expression is 'the situation calls for doing . . .', 'it is appropriate to . . .':

Não seria o caso de chamar um médico?
Shouldn't we/they call a doctor?

Acho que é o caso de as duas partes buscarem o meio-termo.
I think the two sides need to seek a compromise.

46.4 Expressing strong need

There are stronger synonyms of **preciso** and **necessário** that can be used in similar constructions to express even stronger need. Among these are **essencial** 'essential', **imprescindível** 'crucial, vital', **indispensável** 'indispensable, vital', **fundamental** 'imperative, essential':

É essencial ter carro.
It's essential to have a car.

É imprescindível que o debate seja o mais extenso possível.
It is crucial that the debate should be as wide-ranging as possible.

Pontualidade é fundamental.
Punctuality is imperative.

47

Expressing possibility and probability

Saying whether something is considered possible, probable or impossible

There are many ways of expressing degrees of possibility and probability in Portuguese. Here are some of the most commonly used expressions in the spoken language:

> **pode ser** 'maybe, it could be'
>
> **talvez** 'perhaps, maybe'
>
> **de repente** 'maybe'
>
> **provavelmente** 'probably'
>
> **é possível/impossível** 'it's possible/impossible'
>
> **não é possível** 'it's not possible'
>
> **é difícil** 'it's unlikely', **acho difícil** 'I think it's unlikely'.

pode ser

The expression **pode ser** is used as a reponse to a question or statement, meaning 'maybe', 'could be':

> **Acho que vai chover. – Pode ser.**
> 'I think it's going to rain.' – 'Could be.'
>
> **Você vai ver a Ana amanhã? – Pode ser.**
> 'Are you going to see Ana tomorrow?' – 'Maybe.'

It can also be followed by **que** + subjunctive to express a possibility:

> **Pode ser que ele chegue amanhã.**
> He might arrive tomorrow.
>
> **Pode ser que ela tenha esquecido.**[1]
> She might have forgotten.

NOTE   1   In colloquial speech, the indicative is often used when referring to the past: **pode ser que ela esqueceu.**

The expression **não pode ser** can be used to mean 'that's impossible' or to express exasperation:

> **Cem reais por um computador novo? Não pode ser!**
> A hundred reais for a brand new computer? That's impossible!

> **Não pode ser que você ainda goste dele!**
> You can't possibly still like him!

> **Você esqueceu a chave? Não pode ser!**
> You've forgotten the key? I don't believe it!

47.1.2

talvez

The word **talvez** 'perhaps' may also be used in a verbless sentence as a reponse or comment:

> **Quando é que ele volta? – Talvez na semana que vem.**
> 'When is he back?' – 'Maybe next week.'

> **Devíamos ter ligado antes. – É, talvez.**
> 'We should have called beforehand.' – 'Yes, maybe.'

When it precedes a verb, **talvez** requires the subjunctive. In this case, the tense of the subjunctive depends on the time referred to:

> **Talvez seja melhor esperar.**
> Perhaps it's better to wait.

> **Talvez ele estivesse com vergonha.**
> Perhaps he was embarrassed.

> **Talvez fosse prudente contratar um advogado.**
> Perhaps it would be wise to hire a lawyer.

> **Talvez eles tenham tentado e não conseguido.**
> Perhaps they tried and didn't succeed.

47.1.3

de repente

In colloquial speech, **de repente** is frequently used with the meaning of 'maybe'. Unlike **talvez**, it can be followed by a verb in the indicative:

> **Qual seria um bom dia para você? – Quarta, de repente.**
> 'What would be a good day for you?' – 'Wednesday, maybe.'

> **De repente ela ligou enquanto a gente estava na rua.**
> Maybe she called while we were out.

> **Você tem uma chave de fenda de repente?**
> Do you have a screwdriver maybe?

47.1.4

provavelmente

The word **provavelmente** 'probably' can be used as a response or as a sentence adverb, as in English:

> **Você vai estar aqui no fim de semana? – Provavelmente.**
> 'Are you going to be here at the weekend?' – 'Probably.'

> **Provavelmente eles vão passar o Natal na Europa.**
> They're probably going to spend Christmas in Europe.

47.1.5   é possível/impossível and não é possível

These expressions can all be used as responses:

> **Você acha que ele vai atrasar? – É possível.**
> 'Do you think he'll be late?' – 'It's possible.'

> **Será que ele nos paga o jantar? – Impossível!**
> 'I wonder if he'll buy us dinner?' – 'Impossible!'

They can also be followed by **que** and a clause containing a subjunctive verb:

> **Não é possível que todas as lojas estejam fechadas.**
> It's not possible that all the shops are closed.

> **É impossível que ela seja eleita.**
> It's impossible that she'll be elected.

> **Era possível que o tempo só fosse piorar.**
> It was possible that the weather would just get worse.

The term **não é possível** can also express exasperation:

> **O ar-condicionado pifou de novo? Não é possível!**
> The air conditioning's broken down again? I don't believe it!

47.1.6   é difícil / acho difícil

The word **difícil** is often used with the sense of 'unlikely'. It is used most commonly in the constructions **é difícil** 'it's unlikely' and **acho difícil** 'I think it's unlikely', both of which can be followed by a personal infinitive construction or **que** + subjunctive:

> **Você acha que o Flamengo vai ganhar o campeonato? – Acho difícil.**
> 'Do you think Flamengo will win the championship?' – 'I think it's unlikely.'

> **É difícil ele vir aqui hoje. / É difícil que ele venha aqui hoje.**
> He's unlikely to come here today.

> **Acho difícil meu pai emprestar o carro para a gente.**
> I think it's unlikely my dad will lend us the car.

> **Acho difícil que ele continue no time.**
> I think he's unlikely to stay on the team.

47.1.7   Other expressions of possibility and probability

(i)   **provável/pouco provável que** + subjunctive 'likely/unlikely that':

> **É provável que o presidente seja reeleito.**
> It's likely that the president will be reelected.

> **Acho pouco provável que eles se classifiquem para a final.**
> I think it's unlikely that they'll get through to the final.

(ii)   **possivelmente** 'possibly', mostly used in writing:

> **É uma descoberta que possivelmente mudará o mundo.**
> It is a discovery that may possibly change the world.

(iii) **dificilmente**, usually used with the future or conditional to express improbability:

> **Dificilmente ela vai ganhar da campeã mundial.**
> She's unlikely to beat the world champion.
>
> **Tal solução dificilmente seria aceita pelo queixoso.**
> Such a solution would be unlikely to be accepted by the plaintiff.

(iv) **poder** + infinitive can be used in the sense of 'may, might':

> **Pode chover mais tarde.**
> It may rain later.
>
> **Ele pode ter esquecido.**
> He may have forgotten.

In the written language, the future tense of **poder** is often used with the meaning of 'may':

> **A greve poderá causar transtornos.**
> The strike may cause disruption.

(v)   **ser capaz de** + infinitive is also used to mean 'may, might', particularly in speech:

> **Ela é capaz de atrasar.**
> She may be late.
>
> **Leva um guarda-chuva que é capaz de chover mais tarde.**
> Take an umbrella as it might rain later.

In colloquial speech, **é capaz** can also be followed by **que** + subjunctive:

> **É capaz que ela atrase.**
> She may be late.

(vi) expressions containing the word **chance** 'chance'. Notice the use of the plural in Portuguese:

> **Temos boas chances de ganhar o campeonato.**
> We have a good chance of winning the championship.
>
> **A proposta tem poucas chances de ser aprovada.**
> The proposal has little chance of being approved.
>
> **Resta saber se o plano tem alguma chance de êxito.**
> It remains to be seen whether the plan has any chance of success.

(vii) **a tendência é** + personal infinitive/**que** + present subjunctive 'the likelihood is that . . .':

> **A tendência é o tempo piorar.**
> The likelihood is that the weather will get worse.
>
> **A tendência é que as montadoras reduzam a produção ainda mais.**
> The likelihood is that car manufacturers will cut back production still further.

(vii) **existe a possibilidade de** + personal infinitive/**de que** + present subjunctive 'there is the possibility of/that':

> **Existe a possibilidade de o Brasil ser atingido por um tsunami?**
> Is there the possibility of Brazil being hit by a tsunami?

> **Existe a possibilidade de que a queda do dólar seja apenas temporária**.
> There is the possibility that the fall in the dollar rate is only temporary.

(ix) **não tem/há como** + personal infinitive 'there's no way . . .'. The verb **há** is used in more formal written style. The expression can also be used on its own to mean 'there's no way (that will happen)':

> **Não tem como o plano dar errado.**
> There's no way the plan can go wrong.

47.2 Enquiring whether something is considered possible or impossible

In addition to using the expressions introduced above in questions, you can also ask about the possibility or likelihood of something using the expressions **será que . . . ?** 'I wonder if . . .', 'do you suppose . . .?' or **você acha que . . . ?** 'do you think (that) . . . ?':

> **Será que eles esqueceram?**
> I wonder if they've forgotten?

> **Será que vamos conseguir?**
> I wonder if we'll manage it?

> **Você acha que ele ganha?**
> Do you think he'll win?

> **Você acha que ela não quis vir?**
> Do you think she didn't want to come?

These expressions can also be combined with question words, as in:

> **Quanto será que custa?**
> I wonder how much it costs?

> **Aonde você acha que ele foi?**
> Where do you think he's gone?

48

Expressing certainty and uncertainty

48.1 Saying how certain one is of something

48.1.1 Strong certainty

To express strong certainty, Portuguese uses expressions such as the following:

não tem/há a menor dúvida (que/de que) 'there is absolutely no doubt (that)'

não tenho a menor dúvida (de/(de) que) 'I have absolutely no doubt (about/that)'

sem dúvida 'without a doubt'

sem dúvida alguma 'with no doubt whatsoever'

sem sombra de dúvida 'without a shadow of a doubt'

com certeza 'definitely', 'certainly'

certamente 'certainly', 'surely'

certo 'certain', 'guaranteed'

é certo que . . . 'it's certain that . . .', 'certainly'

claro 'of course'

é claro que . . . 'of course . . .'

lógico 'of course'

é lógico que . . . 'of course . . .'

tenho certeza (que/de que . . .) 'I'm sure (that . . .)'

tenho certeza absoluta (que/de que . . .) 'I'm positive (that . . .)'

estou convencido (que/de que . . .) 'I'm convinced (that . . .)'.

Examples:

Você tem certeza? – Absoluta!
'Are you sure?' – 'Positive!'

É claro que não vão aparecer.
Of course they're not going to show up.

Foi incêndio criminoso mesmo? – Não tem a menor dúvida disso.
'Was it really arson?' – 'There's absolutely no doubt about it.'

Ela é a melhor jogadora, sem dúvida alguma.
She's the best player, no doubt whatsoever.

A vitória da oposição é quase certa.
An opposition victory is almost certain.

É certo que o prédio vai ser derrubado.
It's certain that the building will be pulled down.

Estou convencido de que foi apenas um erro.
I'm convinced it was just a mistake.

48.1.2 Weak certainty

acho que . . . 'I think . . .'

acho que sim/não 'I think so.' / 'I don't think so.'

Examples:

O Paulo está em casa, não é? – Acho que sim.
'Paulo's at home, isn't he?' – 'I think so.'

Acho que o nosso time vai ganhar.
I think our team is going to win.

Seu pai vai te dar o dinheiro? – Acho que não.
'Is your dad going to give you the money?' – 'I don't think so.'

Notice that, in Portuguese, 'I don't think . . .' is usually translated **acho que . . . não . . .**
when referring to something you think is not the case:

Acho que ele não é burro.
I don't think he's stupid. (= *I'm pretty sure he is not stupid*)

The construction **não acho que** means 'it is not the case that I think . . .' and is followed
by the subjunctive:

Não acho que ele seja burro, nunca falei isso.
I don't think he's stupid, I never said that.

48.1.3 Uncertainty

não sei se . . . 'I don't know whether . . .'

não sei bem . . . 'I'm not sure . . .'

não tenho certeza 'I'm not sure'

não tenho certeza de + pronoun 'I'm not sure of + pronoun'

não tenho certeza (de) que . . . 'I'm not sure that . . .'

não é certo que + subjunctive 'it's not certain that'

duvido 'I doubt it'

duvido que + subjunctive 'I doubt that . . .'

estou na dúvida (se) 'I'm not sure' / 'I'm in two minds' (whether)

estou numa dúvida cruel 'I can't make up my mind'

estou dividido (entre) 'I'm torn (between)'

pode ser (**que** + subjunctive) 'maybe (. . .)' (see **47.1.1**)

talvez (+ subjunctive) 'perhaps (. . .)' (see **47.1.2**)

de repente 'maybe' (see **47.1.3**).

Examples:

Não sei se eu vou.
I don't know if I'm going.

Não sei bem o que fazer.
I'm not sure what to do.

Você acha que ele vai nos ligar? – Duvido.
'Do you think he'll call us?' – 'I doubt it.'

Não tenho certeza disso.
I'm not sure of that.

Estou na dúvida se vou ou não na festa.
I'm not sure whether to go to the party or not.

Pretendo fazer uma faculdade, mas estou dividido entre Direito e Administração.
I plan to get a degree, but I'm torn between law and business.

Você acha que ela gostou de mim? – De repente.
'Do you think she liked me?' – 'Maybe.'

The expressions **não é certo que** . . . 'it's not certain that . . .' and **duvido que** . . . 'I doubt that . . .' are followed by a subjunctive:

Duvido que ele apareça.
I doubt he'll show up.

Não é certo que eles terminem a tempo.
It's not certain that they'll finish in time.

The expression **não tenho certeza de que** . . . may be followed by the subjunctive, but is more often followed by an indicative verb, especially in the spoken language:

Não tenho certeza de que ela vai me ouvir.
I'm not sure she'll listen to what I have to say.

48.1.4 Negative certainty

não 'no'

claro que não 'of course not'

lógico que não 'of course not'

eu não acho 'that's not what I think'.

Examples:

> **Devolveram o dinheiro? – Lógico que não.**
> 'Did they return the money?' – 'Of course not.'

> **Claro que não vão aceitar isso.**
> Of course they won't accept that.

> **Eles são apenas amigos. – Eu não acho.**
> 'They're just friends.' – 'That's not what I think.'

48.2 Enquiring about certainty or uncertainty

The following expressions are commonly used to enquire about certainty or uncertainty:

> **Você tem certeza?** 'Are you sure?'

> **Você tem certeza absoluta?** 'Are you absolutely sure?'

> **Você tem certeza (de) que . . .?** 'Are you sure that . . .?'

> **Você acha?** 'Do you think so?'

> **Você acha que . . .?** 'Do you think . . .?'

Examples:

> **Você tem certeza que trancou a porta?**
> Are you sure you locked the door?

> **Vai chover. – Você acha?**
> 'It's going to rain.' – 'Do you think so?'

49

Expressing supposition

49.1 Common expressions of supposition

To express supposition, as in 'If they come . . .', 'Suppose he asks you for the money', 'Imagine you won the lottery', 'They must be there by now', there are a range of words and expressions in Portuguese, of which the most common are the following:

49.1.1 *se* + future subjunctive / *se* + imperfect subjunctive

▶ 20.5 (p. 193)

The first of these two expressions with **se** implies that the supposition is more plausible than the second and, in this case, **se** + future subjunctive is followed by a clause in the present simple tense[1]:

> **Se ele te pedir em casamento, você aceita?**
> If he proposes, do you say yes?

NOTE   1   The periphrastic future **vai aceitar** could also occur in the main clause, but it would make the sentence less of a supposition and more of a straightforward conditional: 'if he proposes, will you say yes?'.

The construction **se** + imperfect subjunctive is followed by a clause in the conditional, imperfect, or the imperfect of the verb **ir** followed by an infinitive and expresses a more hypothetical situation:

> **Se ele te pedisse em casamento, você aceitaria/aceitava/ia aceitar?**
> If he proposed, would you say yes?

In this example, the conditional **aceitaria** sounds quite formal, while the imperfect **aceitava** and **ia aceitar** are neutral in register.

49.1.2 *vamos supor que* + subjunctive / *supondo que* + subjunctive

The expression **vamos supor que** 'let's suppose that, suppose' is the most common way of positing a hypothetical situation. It can be followed by the present subjunctive referring to a likely supposition or by the imperfect subjunctive referring to an unlikely supposition.

> **Vamos supor que ele peça dinheiro para você. Você empresta?**[2]
> Suppose he asks you for money. Do you lend him any?

NOTE   2   Again, **você vai emprestar?** could also be used. See previous note.

**Vamos supor que ele pedisse dinheiro para você. Você emprestaria/
emprestava/ia emprestar?**
Suppose he asked you for money. Would you lend him any?

Notice that the tenses used to ask what would happen in such a case are the same as those used after the 'if' clauses in **49.1.1**.

In colloquial spoken language, hypothetical scenarios are often drawn using the present tense to make them more vivid. In such cases, **vamos supor** is often used without a conjunction connecting it to the rest of the sentence:

Vamos supor: você depara com um ladrão na sua casa. O que você faz?
Supposing: you come across a thief in your house, what do you do?

An alternative way of introducing a supposition, more used in the written language, is with **supondo que** + subjunctive, which is followed by the same tenses as **vamos supor que**:

Supondo que isso fosse tecnicamente possível, será que compensaria?
Supposing this was technically possible, would it be worth the expense?

In more formal written language, the form **suponhamos que . . .** 'let us suppose that . . .' is used in place of **vamos supor que . . .**:

Suponhamos que os republicanos ganhem a eleição.
Let us suppose the Republicans win the election.

49.1.3 *imagine/imagina que* + subjunctive

The formal or familiar imperative of the verb **imaginar** 'to imagine' can also be followed by a **que** + subjunctive clause to posit a hypothetical situation. Again, the present subjunctive indicates a plausible supposition, the imperfect subjunctive a less plausible one:

Imagine que você queira comprar uma casa, por exemplo.
Imagine you want to buy a house, for example.

Imagina que você tivesse ganho na megasena. O que você faria com o dinheiro?
Imagine you had won the lottery. What would you do with the money?

49.1.4 *digamos que* + subjunctive

This expression means 'let's say (that)' and can be used to introduce a supposition[3]. Again, the present subjunctive is used if the supposition is quite plausible and the imperfect subjunctive if it is more far-fetched:

Digamos que você esteja acampando e precisa recarregar seu celular.
Let's say you're camping and need to recharge your cell phone.

Digamos que fosse possível viver para sempre. Você queria?
Let's say it were possible to live forever. Would you want to?

NOTE   3   Note that **digamos que** is also used to mean 'let's just say . . .', in which case it is followed by a verb in the indicative, e.g. **Não estou desempregado. Digamos que estou entre empregos**. 'I'm not unemployed. Let's just say I'm between jobs.'

49.1.5 *faz de conta que* + indicative

In colloquial speech, you can also use the familiar imperative expression **faz de conta** 'pretend, make believe' followed by **que** and an indicative verb to express a supposition:

> **Faz de conta que você está me conhecendo pela primeira vez.**
> Pretend you're meeting me for the first time.

49.1.6 *vai que* + indicative

The colloquial expression **vai que** ... 'supposing ...' is followed by the indicative:

> **Vai que ele se recusa, e aí?**
> Supposing he refuses, then what?

> **É melhor levar guarda-chuva. Vai que chove.**
> You'd best take an umbrella. Suppose it rains.

49.1.7 *dever* + infinitive

The modal verb **dever** 'must, should'[4] followed by an infinitive expresses supposition:

> **Ela deve estar doente.**
> She must be ill.

> **Devemos chegar por volta do meio-dia.**
> We should arrive around noon.

It can also be used in the negative:

> **A casa está toda fechada. Não deve ter ninguém morando lá.**
> The house is all closed up. There can't/must not be anyone living there.[5]

> **A meta não deve ser difícil de alcançar se todo mundo colaborar.**
> The target should not be difficult to achieve if everyone pitches in.

NOTES

4   'must' is used for suppositions about the present, 'should' for suppositions about the future and 'must have' for suppositions about the past.

5   English usually switches to 'can't' to express a negative supposition, though some speakers use 'must not'.

It can be followed by a perfect infinitive to express a supposition about an event in the past:

> **Eles devem ter esquecido.**
> They must have forgotten.

> **Ele já deve ter chegado.**
> He must have got there by now.

> **O Pedro não deve ter recebido a nossa mensagem.**
> Pedro can't/must not have got our message.

But note that the imperfect tense of **dever** is used for a supposition about an ongoing state of affairs in the past:

> **O assaltante era muito novo; devia ter uns 12 anos.**
> The mugger was very young; he must have been about 12.

The verb **dever** can also be followed by the verb **estar** and a gerund to express a supposition about an action in progress:

Eles devem estar dormindo.
They must be asleep.

Ela deve estar achando que a gente não vai.
She must be thinking we're not coming.

49.1.8 Future formed with *ir* + infinitive used to express a supposition

As in English, the future formed with **ir** + infinitive can be used to express a confident supposition about the present:

Ela vai estar em casa agora.
She'll be at home now.

Eles não vão estar trabalhando hoje.
They won't be working today.

50

Expressing conditions

This chapter deals with conditions and conditional sentences, normally expressed in Portuguese with the word **se** 'if'. In the following sections, you will learn to express basic conditions such as 'If I have the money, I'll go with you', 'If I had the money, I'd go with you', 'If I had had the money, I would have gone with you'. You will also learn the Portuguese equivalent of other conditional forms, such as 'provided (that)', 'as long as', 'on condition (that)'.

▶ **20.5** (p. 193)

50.1 Open conditions

Open conditions are those that may or may not be fulfilled, e.g. 'If it rains . . .', or that may or may not be true, e.g. 'If it is as you say. . .'. In English, the word 'if' is followed by the present tense in open conditions.

50.1.1 *se* + future subjunctive + future/present indicative: 'if A happens, B will happen'

Here, the verb in the **se**-clause refers to a future event that may not happen, so the tense used in Portuguese is the future subjunctive. The main clause will normally contain a future tense formed with **ir** + infinitive or the simple future tense in more formal written contexts. The **se**-clause normally precedes the main clause, but may also follow it:

Se chover, vou ficar em casa.
If it rains I'll stay at home.

Se eu tiver tempo, vou ligar para ele amanhã.
If I have time I'll call him tomorrow.

Se perder esse jogo, o time não escapará do rebaixamento.
If it loses this game the team will not escape relegation.

In informal speech, the present tense is often used in the main clause even though future action is referred to:

Se eu tiver o dinheiro, vou com você.
If I have the money I'll go with you.

Se chover muito, o rio transborda.
If it rains a lot the river will overflow.[1]

NOTE   1   This sentence could also mean 'if it rains a lot, the river overflows' – see **50.1.2**.

> **Se não chegarem às nove, começamos sem vocês.**
> If you don't arrive at nine, we'll start without you.

The main clause may also be an imperative or a question:

> **Se você encontrar o Sérgio, fala para ele me ligar.**
> If you meet Sergio tell him to call me.
>
> **O que você vai fazer se ganhar o prêmio?**
> What will you do if you win the prize?

The future subjunctive of **ter** may be combined with a past participle in the **se**-clause to refer to a completed action:

> **Se tiver terminado esse trabalho até amanhã, eu vou com você.**
> If I've finished this job by tomorrow, I'll go with you.

50.1.2 *se* + future subjunctive + present indicative: 'if A happens, B happens'

The main clause may express a general statement rather than a single event. In this case, the main clause is in the present indicative and the **se**-clause has the sense of 'whenever':

> **Se deixar a janela aberta, entra morcego.**
> If you leave the window open, bats come in.
>
> **Se o projeto for aprovado, é encaminhado ao Presidente para sanção ou veto.**
> If the bill is passed, it is sent to the president for approval or veto.

50.1.3 *se* + present indicative + present indicative

The word **se** can be followed by the present indicative when the situation expressed in the **se**-clause is already the case at the time of speaking. In such cases, the main clause is normally in the present tense too:

> **Se é assim, não tem muito o que fazer.**
> If that's the way it is, there's not a lot we can do.
>
> **Se está doendo tanto assim, é melhor chamar a ambulância.**
> If it's hurting that much, we'd better call an ambulance.
>
> **Se ele não quer ir, é porque ele é preguiçoso.**
> If he doesn't want to go it's because he's lazy.

50.1.4 *se* + verb in the past

A past tense may be used in the **se**-clause when the reference is to something that has already happened. The verb in the main clause can be in any appropriate tense:

> **Se ela chegou de viagem ontem à noite, ela deve estar cansada.**
> If she got back from her trip last night, she must be tired.
>
> **Se ele já estava de mau humor, é melhor não incomodá-lo de novo.**
> If he was already in a bad mood, you'd better not bother him again.

50.2 Remote and unreal conditions

Remote and unreal conditions present a scenario that is either unlikely or impossible, as in 'If you explained it to him, he would probably understand', 'If she were just a bit taller she could be a model'.

Remote and unreal conditions are expressed in Portuguese by using the imperfect subjunctive in the **se**-clause. The choice of tense used in the main clause depends on the degree of formality, the conditional sounding formal, the imperfect indicative or the imperfect indicative of **ir** + infinitive less so:

(i)   Less formal examples using the imperfect or **ir** + infinitive in the main clause:

Se você explicasse para ele, ele provavelmente entendia/ia entender.
If you explained (it) to him, he'd probably understand.

Se ela fosse um pouquinho mais alta, podia/ia poder ser modelo.
If she was just a bit taller she could be a model.

(ii) A more formal example showing the conditional or **ir** + infinitive[2]:

Se o governo melhorasse a qualidade de ensino, supriria/ia suprir a falta de mão de obra qualificada.
If the government improved the quality of education it would alleviate the shortage of skilled labour.

NOTE | 2   In formal written style, the conditional of **ir** + infinitive is often encountered, i.e. in the example: **iria suprir**.

50.3 Unfulfilled conditions

An unfulfilled condition is one that cannot possibly be fulfilled because the opportunity has already past, as in 'If I'd have known I would have come yesterday', 'If you hadn't spent all that money we wouldn't be in debt now'.

50.3.1 se + pluperfect subjunctive + perfect conditional/pluperfect

Unfulfilled conditions are expressed in Portuguese by using the pluperfect subjunctive in the **se**-clause. If the main clause also refers to the past, the tense used is the perfect conditional or, in less formal registers, the pluperfect:

Se você tivesse me pedido, eu teria/tinha te emprestado o dinheiro.
If you had asked me I would have lent you the money.

Se ele não tivesse bebido naquela noite, nada disso teria/tinha acontecido.
If he hadn't had a drink that night, none of this would have happened.

When the verb in the **se**-clause refers to an ongoing state of affairs rather than a single action, the imperfect subjunctive is used instead of the pluperfect:

Se não fosse o Zeca, minha irmã teria/tinha morrido afogada.
If it hadn't been for Zeca, my sister would have drowned.

> Se eu soubesse na época o que sei agora, nunca teria/tinha entrado nessa.
> If I'd known then what I know now, I'd never have got into this.

50.3.2 *se* + pluperfect subjunctive + conditional/imperfect/ imperfect of *ir* + infinitive

The verb of the main clause can be conditional (formal), imperfect or infinitive after the imperfect of **ir** when it refers to the present time:

> Se você não tivesse gasto todo aquele dinheiro, não estaríamos/ estávamos/íamos estar endividados agora.
> If you hadn't spent all that money, we wouldn't be in debt now.

> Se nós não tivéssemos ajudado, eles teriam/tinham/iam ter muito o que fazer ainda.
> If we hadn't helped out, they'd still have a lot to do.

50.4 Other conditional expressions

50.4.1 *caso* + present/imperfect subjunctive

The word **caso** + present/imperfect subjunctive is a slightly more formal synonym of **se** meaning 'if, in the event that, should . . .'. The present subjunctive is used when the main verb is present or future, the imperfect when the main verb is past or conditional:

> A greve será inevitável caso o sindicato não ceda.
> The strike will be inevitable if the union does not back down.

> A empresa a ameaçou de demissão caso ela se recusasse a trabalhar aos domingos.
> The company threatened her with dismissal should she refuse to work on Sundays.

50.4.2 Gerund instead of a *se*-clause

In colloquial language, the gerund (words such as **virando** 'turning', **sabendo** 'knowing') can be used to express open conditions:

> Virando aqui à esquerda, você já vai ver a igreja na sua frente.
> Turning left here, you'll see the church ahead of you.

> Sabendo inglês, você vai conseguir um emprego melhor.
> Knowing English, you'll be able to get a better job.

50.4.3 Imperative instead of a *se*-clause

The imperative can be used to express a condition in informal speech, especially in warnings or threats:

> Faz isso e você vai se arrepender.
> Do that and you'll be sorry.

> Atrase mais uma vez e você vai para o olho da rua.
> Be late one more time and you'll be out on your ear.

▶ **21.1** (p. 196)

50.4.4 Preterite + preterite

A verb in the preterite tense can be followed by a second preterite in informal language to express a condition and a consequence. The verbs in this construction are always in the third person singular without an explicit subject, but the implied subject is the general 'you' and the meaning is 'If you do X, then Y happens':

Quebrou, pagou.
If you break it, you pay for it.

Bobeou, dançou.
If you drop your guard, you've had it. / If you snooze, you lose.

This often corresponds to the English use of imperatives in the language of advertising:

Raspou, ganhou!
Scratch and win! (*advertisement for scratch card lottery*)

50.4.5 *desde que/contanto que* + present/imperfect subjunctive

These expressions correspond to the English 'as long as', 'provided (that)', 'providing (that)'. Of the two, **contanto que** is more formal. In both cases, the present subjunctive is used when the main verb is present or future and the imperfect subjunctive when the main verb is past:

Você pode vir qualquer dia, desde que seja à tarde.
You can come any day as long as it's in the afternoon.

Ele aceitou a proposta, contanto que pagassem as despesas dele.
He accepted the proposal provided they paid his expenses.

50.4.6 *uma vez que* + present/imperfect subjunctive

The expression **uma vez que** 'once' also has a conditional meaning:

O governo declarou que negociaria com os guerrilheiros, uma vez que depusessem as armas.
The government declared it would negotiate with the guerrillas once they laid down their arms.

In addition, **uma vez** can precede a past participle in this sense:

Uma vez cadastrado, você pode acessar todo o conteúdo do site.
Once registered, you can access all the content on the site.

50.4.7 *com a condição de* + infinitive; *sob a condição de* + infinitive; *com a condição (de) que* + present/imperfect subjunctive; *sob a condição de que* + present/imperfect subjunctive

These expressions mean 'on condition of doing' when followed by the infinitive and 'on condition that' when followed by the subjunctive. The forms with **com** are slightly more frequent:

Ele foi posto em liberdade com a condição de não se envolver com política.
He was set free on condition that he did not get involved in politics.

> **Eles só concederam entrevista sob a condição de que o local não fosse revelado.**
> They only agreed to an interview on condition that the location would not be revealed.

50.4.8 *a não ser que/a menos que* + present/imperfect subjunctive

These expressions correspond to the English 'unless'. The phrase **a menos que** is more formal and less common than **a não ser que**. Both are normally followed by the present subjunctive, but may be followed by the imperfect subjunctive in a past context (e.g. indirect speech) or when the main verb is conditional:

> **Vou ficar aqui, a não ser que você prefira que eu vá embora.**
> I'll stay here, unless you prefer me to leave.

> **Ele não faria isso, a menos que fosse idiota.**
> He wouldn't do that unless he were an idiot.

50.4.9 *mesmo que* + present/imperfect subjunctive; *mesmo* + gerund

The expression **mesmo que** translates 'even if, even though':

> **Ela não poderia participar, mesmo que quisesse.**
> She could not take part even if she wanted to.

> **Eles vão levar o campeonato, mesmo que percam esse jogo.**
> They will take the championship even if they lose this game.

In the spoken language, this same idea is more often expressed by placing **mesmo** before a gerund:

> **Eles vão levar o campeonato, mesmo perdendo esse jogo.**
> They'll take the championship even if they lose this game.

> **Mesmo estudando muito, ele não vai passar na prova.**
> Even if he studies really hard, he won't pass the exam.

The gerund can have a different subject from the main verb:

> **Vou casar com ele, mesmo meus pais não gostando.**
> I'm going to marry him even if my parents don't like it.

> **Mesmo nós dois empurrando, o carro não quis sair do lugar.**
> Even with the two of us pushing, the car wouldn't budge.

51

Expressing contrast or opposition

This chapter deals with the concept of contrast and the words and expressions associated with this. Contrast between different ideas is expressed in English through the use of words such as 'but', 'though', 'although', as in 'I don't speak Spanish, but I can get by', 'Although the sun's hot today, there's a nice breeze'.

51.1   Common expressions of contrast or opposition

51.1.1   *mas*

The word **mas** 'but' is the one most commonly used to express contrast. Note that many Brazilians pronounce it /majs/:

> **Não falo espanhol, mas consigo me virar.**
> I don't speak Spanish, but I can get by.

> **Ele pode ser chato às vezes, mas, no fundo, ele é boa pessoa.**
> He can be annoying at times, but basically he's a good person.

When a negative clause is followed by a positive one that expresses a complete contrast, the form **mas sim** 'but rather' is used, especially in the written language:

> **A intenção deles não é instruir, mas sim divertir o público.**
> Their intention is not to educate, but rather to entertain the audience.

> **Não se trata de uma biografia, mas sim de um romance biográfico.**
> It's not a biography, but rather a biographical novel.

51.1.2   *porém*

The word **porém** 'yet, though, however' marks a stronger contrast than **mas** and is mainly used in the written language. It can be placed at the start of its clause or sentence or in second place separated by commas for greater emphasis:

> **O documentário é chocante, porém instigante.**
> The documentary is shocking, yet thought-provoking.

> **Ele adora o Brasil. Porém, não deixa de sentir saudades de sua terra natal.**
> He loves Brazil. Though he still misses his homeland.

> **Essa prática é proibida por lei. A realidade, porém, é outra.**
> This practice is banned by law. However, the reality of the situation is different.

51.1.3   *contudo, entretanto, no entanto, todavia*

These words all signal a strong contrast and are formal in register, being used mainly in the written language. Like **porém**, they may be placed at the start of the sentence, but most often occur in second position separated by commas:

> **Há vários problemas. O mais grave, no entanto, é a violência.**
> There are a number of problems. The most serious, however, is violent crime.

> **O português e o espanhol são muito parecidos. Contudo, existem diferenças fundamentais entre os dois idiomas.**
> Portuguese and Spanish are very similar. However, there are fundamental differences between the two languages.

51.1.4   *embora* + subjunctive

The word **embora** 'although' is followed by the present subjunctive when the main verb is present or future and by the imperfect subjunctive when the main verb is past tense. Although this construction is used in the spoken language, it is not frequently used in colloquial speech.

> **Embora o sol esteja forte hoje, tem uma brisa agradável.**
> Although the sun is hot today, there is a nice breeze.

> **Embora fosse doloroso, tiveram que voltar ao local do crime.**
> Although it was painful, they had to return to the scene of the crime.

It can also occur without a following verb:

> **Embora cansados, conseguiram chegar ao cume da montanha.**
> Though tired, they managed to reach the summit of the mountain.

51.1.5   *mesmo que* + subjunctive, *mesmo* + gerund

The expression **mesmo que** 'even if, even though' is followed by the present or imperfect subjunctive according to the usual sequence of tenses:

> **Mesmo que seja difícil, vou tentar.**
> Even though it's difficult, I'm going to try.

> **Eu não iria, mesmo que me implorassem.**
> I wouldn't go even if they begged me.

In the spoken language, **mesmo** is used with a gerund to convey this meaning:

> **Mesmo chovendo, vou sair.**
> Even if it's raining, I'm going to go out.

> **O jantar foi ótimo, mesmo tendo sido improvisado.**
> The dinner was excellent even though it had been thrown together.

Also, **mesmo** can be used without a following verb in this contrastive sense:

> **Mesmo exausto, ele conseguiu terminar a corrida.**
> Even though he was exhausted, he managed to finish the race.

> **Mesmo com dinamite não conseguiram arrombar o cofre.**
> Even with dynamite they were unable to break open the safe.

51.1.6   *apesar de* + noun/pronoun/infinitive; *apesar de que* + indicative/subjunctive

The expression **apesar de** 'despite, in spite of' can be followed by a noun, a pronoun or an infinitive when the subject of the infinitive is the same as that of the main verb:

> **Gostamos da viagem apesar do mau tempo.**
> We enjoyed the trip despite the bad weather.

> **Apesar disso, o time ganhou o campeonato.**
> Despite that, the team won the championship.

> **Achei o filme interessante, apesar de não entender tudo.**
> I found the movie interesting despite not understanding everything.

It can also be followed directly by an adjective:

> **Apesar de doente, ele continua animado.**
> Despite being ill, he remains cheerful.

Also, **apesar de** can be followed by a personal infinitive when the subject of the infinitive is different from that of the main clause or when the infinitive construction precedes the main clause:

> **Apesar de a proposta ter o apoio do governo, dificilmente será aprovada.**
> Despite the proposal having the support of the government, it's unlikely to be approved.

The expression **apesar de que** 'despite the fact that' is usually followed by a verb in the indicative, unless the following clause refers to a potential, rather than actual, state of affairs, in which case the subjunctive is used:

> **Ele foi eleito prefeito, apesar de que muitos não gostam dele.**
> He was elected mayor even though many people don't like him.

> **Ninguém consegue bater o recorde, apesar de que alguns tenham tentado.**
> No one can break the record, despite the fact that some may have tried.

51.1.7   *se bem que* + indicative/subjunctive

The phrase **se bem que** 'though, although' is usually followed by the indicative expressing an actual fact:

> **Gosto de jogar tênis, se bem que não jogo muito bem.**
> I like playing tennis, although I don't play very well.

> **O tempo estava ótimo, se bem que esfriava à noite.**
> The weather was great, although it got cold at night.

The expression **se bem que** is very common in the spoken language and usually adds an afterthought, a reservation, regarding what has just been said. This can also be a response to what someone else has just said:

> **O Grajaú é um bairro legal, não é? – É, se bem que é meio fora de mão.**
> 'Grajaú is a nice neighbourhood, isn't it?' – 'Yes, it's a bit out of the way, though.'

> **Duvido que ele apareça. Se bem que nunca se sabe, não é?**
> I doubt he'll show up. Mind you, you never know, do you?

In formal writing, **se bem que** is often used at the start of a sentence to mean 'although' and, in this case, is followed by the subjunctive:

Se bem que não se soubesse na época, a doença era transmitida por ratos.
Although it was not known at the time, the disease was spread by rats.

51.1.8 *só que*

The expression **só que** 'only, except (that)' is commonly used in the spoken language to voice a reservation[1]. When followed by a verb, the verb is indicative:

Ela vem essa semana sim, só que na sexta em vez de hoje.
She *is* coming this week, only on Friday instead of today.

Eu gosto dele, só que ele me cansa um pouco.
I like him, except that I find him a bit wearing.

No domingo tem churrasco no clube. – É, só que eu tenho que trabalhar.
'On Sunday there's a barbecue at the club.' – 'Yeah, only I have to work.'

NOTE   1 The expression **só que não**, often abbreviated to **sqn** in text messages and social media posts, is equivalent to the humorous use of 'not!' in English to signal irony, e.g. **Estou adorando, só que não**. 'I'm loving it, not!'

51.1.9 *já*

The adverb **já** placed at the beginning of a sentence marks a strong contrast with the previous statement. This usage is mainly found in writing:

Os brasileiros adoram futebol. Já os americanos, nem tanto.
Brazilians love soccer. Americans, on the other hand, are not so keen.

Ela é a favor da ideia. Já o pai dela pensa diferente.
She is in favour of the idea. Her father, on the other hand, thinks differently.

51.1.10 Other ways of expressing contrast or opposition

Here are some other expressions that are commonly used to express contrast or opposition:

por um lado 'on the one hand'

por outro lado 'on the other hand'

pelo contrário 'on the contrary'

muito pelo contrário 'quite the reverse'

ao contrário do que ... 'contrary to what ...'

em compensação 'on the other hand, though'

em contrapartida 'meanwhile' (*formal*)

mesmo assim 'even so'

enquanto 'while'

ao passo que 'whereas' (*formal*)

senão 'otherwise'

caso contrário 'otherwise'.

Examples:

Por um lado, entendo a posição dele.
On the one hand, I understand his position.

Por outro lado, acho que ele extrapolou.
On the other hand, I think he went too far.

Eu não achei o filme chato. Pelo contrário, achei bem interessante.
I didn't find the movie boring. On the contrary, I thought it was really interesting.

Ele gostou? – Muito pelo contrário, odiou.
'Did he like it?' – 'Quite the reverse, he hated it.'

Ao contrário do que se pode pensar, muitos brasileiros nunca viram uma praia.
Contrary to what you might think, many Brazilians have never seen a beach.

O nosso bairro é meio fora de mão. Em compensação, é tranquilo.
Our neighbourhood is rather out of the way. It's quiet, though.

Em contrapartida, a economia argentina não anda tão bem.
Meanwhile, the Argentinian economy is not faring so well.

As obras estão bem avançadas. Mesmo assim, ainda há muito o que fazer.
Construction work is well under way. Even so, there is still a lot to do.

Os brasileiros gostam de futebol, enquanto os americanos preferem beisebol.
Brazilians like soccer, while Americans prefer baseball.

Mais de 45% da energia consumida no Brasil provêm de fontes renováveis, ao passo que a média nos países desenvolvidos é de cerca de 10%.
More than 45 per cent of the energy consumed in Brazil comes from renewable sources, whereas the average in the developed countries is around 10 per cent.

Anda logo, senão perdemos o ônibus.
Get a move on, otherwise we'll miss the bus.

O governo deve tomar uma atitude. Caso contrário, a situação só vai piorar.
The government should take action. Otherwise the situation will just get worse.

52

Expressing capability and incapability

52.1 Enquiring and making statements about capability or incapability

52.1.1 *poder* + infinitive

The verb **poder** 'to be able to' is the most general word for expressing capability. It can express mental or technical capability and capability as determined by circumstances. The modal verb **poder** + infinitive is also used to express permission, possibility and requests, which are dealt with elsewhere in this book.

> **Você vai poder me buscar no aeroporto?**
> Will you be able to pick me up from the airport?

> **Você pode me ajudar? – Posso, sim.**
> 'Can you help me?' – 'Yes, I can.'

> **Não posso imaginar nada pior.**
> I can't imagine anything worse.

> **Eu não poderia/podia morar longe da minha família.**
> I couldn't live a long way away from my family.

> **Você não vai poder dormir depois desse café.**
> You won't be able to sleep after that coffee.

> **A aeronave pode chegar até duas vezes a velocidade do som.**
> The aircraft can reach up to twice the speed of sound.

The preterite of **poder** means that the subject actually succeeded or failed in carrying out the action of the verb:

> **Não puderam salvar o menino.**
> They were unable to save the boy. (*i.e. they tried but failed*)

> **Eu pude convencê-lo.**
> I was able to convince him. (*and he changed his mind*)

The imperfect of **poder** indicates a lack of capability in the past:

> **Não podiam salvar o menino.**
> They couldn't save the boy. (*i.e. because they did not have the capability*)

> **Eu achava que podia convencê-lo.**
> I thought I could convince him. (*but might not actually have done so*)

52.1.2 *conseguir* + infinitive

Although **conseguir** + infinitive often translates as 'to manage to do, to succeed in doing', it also corresponds to 'can, be able to' especially when talking about physical ability. In other cases, **conseguir** is more emphatic than **poder**, suggesting that a certain amount of effort has gone into trying to carry out a specific action, whereas **poder** refers more to a natural capability:

> **Você consegue alcançar aquela prateleira?**
> Can you reach that shelf?

> **Não consigo encontrar a rua nesse mapa.**
> I can't manage to find the street on this map.

> **Você conseguiu terminar tudo?**
> Did you manage to get everything finished?

> **Eles não conseguiam abrir a porta.**
> They were not managing to get the door open. (*but they may have subsequently*)

> **Eles não conseguiram abrir a porta.**
> They didn't manage to get the door open. (*so they gave up*)

52.1.3 *dar para* + infinitive

The verb **dar** can be used impersonally to mean 'to be possible'. As an impersonal verb, it only occurs in the third person singular form or the infinitive, but it may be used in all tenses. Generally, when used in a statement, **dar para** refers to a first person subject 'I, we' or a general 'you' subject. In a question, it will usually refer to a general subject or specifically to the person asked. This is a colloquial expression and extremely common:

> **Dá para entender? – Dá, sim.**
> 'Can you understand?' – 'Yes, I can.'

> **Deu para sentir a diferença?**
> Could you tell the difference?

> **Não dá para dormir com esse barulho.**
> It's impossible to sleep with this noise.

> **Se desse, eu comprava um carro novo.**
> If I could, I'd buy a new car.

The subject may be specified by using a personal infinitive after **dar para**:

> **Não dá para eu atender agora.**
> I can't come to the phone/door now.

> **Deu para vocês se entenderem?**
> Were you able to understand each other?

Note that **dar** can also be used without a following infinitive to mean 'to be possible/OK':

> **Dá para você na terça? – Na terça não dá para mim, mas na quarta dá.**
> 'Is Tuesday OK for you?' – 'Tuesday doesn't work for me, but Wednesday's OK.'

52.1.4   *ter como* + infinitive

The verb **ter** can be used personally or impersonally in this expression. With a personal subject, the literal sense is 'to have a way to . . .' but the expression is largely interchangeable with **poder**:

> **Você tem como me emprestar um dinheiro?**
> Could you lend me some money? / Is there any way you could lend me some money?

> **Não tenho como voltar para casa.**
> I have no way of getting home. / I can't get home.

The same idea can be expressed by using the impersonal third person singular of **ter** followed by a personal infinitive, or an impersonal infinitive if the statement is general. In this impersonal usage, the verb **há** is preferred in more formal written style:

> **Tem como você me emprestar um dinheiro?**
> Could you lend me some money?

> **Não tem como dormir com esse barulho.**
> It's impossible to sleep with this noise.

> **Não há como negar a influência da língua inglesa no cotidiano do brasileiro.**
> There's no denying the influence of the English language on the daily life of Brazilians.

The infinitive can be omitted if clear from the context:

> **Quero baixar o documento no meu celular. Tem como?**
> I want to download the document onto my cell phone. Is there a way to do that?

> **Você me empresta um dinheiro? - Desculpa, não tem como.**
> 'Will you lend me some money?' – 'Sorry, I can't.'

52.1.5   **Using a single verb to express capability or incapability**

With some verbs, especially those to do with the senses, such as 'see', 'hear', 'feel', and some others, such as 'remember', 'find', the verb 'can' may be used in English but not usually in Portuguese. Instead, Portuguese uses the present or past continous of these verbs to convey this sense (except in the case of **lembrar** 'remember' – see example below):

> **Não estou enxergando nada.**
> I can't see anything.

> **Você está me ouvindo?**
> Can you hear me?

> **Ele estava sentindo a vibração do motor.**
> He could feel the vibration of the engine.

> **Não estou achando os óculos.**
> I can't find my glasses.

> **Não lembro o nome dele.**
> I can't remember his name.

52.1.6 *ser capaz de* **+ infinitive**

The expression **ser capaz de** 'to be capable of, able to' can refer either to the skill or ability required to do something or the moral capacity to do something:

> **Ele é capaz de ficar dias sem comer.**
> He's capable of going for days without eating.

> **Ela disse que seria capaz de reconhecer o homem que a agrediu.**
> She said she'd be able to recognize the man who attacked her.

> **Você seria capaz de matar alguém para se defender?**
> Would you be capable of killing someone to defend yourself?

52.2 Enquiring and making statements about learned abilities

52.2.1 *saber* **+ infinitive**

To enquire and make statements about learned abilities, as in 'Can you play the piano?', 'She can't swim', Portuguese uses the verb **saber**, literally 'to know (how to)', not **poder**:

> **Você sabe tocar piano?**
> Can you play the piano?

> **Sei tocar um pouco, sim.**
> Yes, I can play a bit.

> **Ela não sabe nadar?**
> Can't she swim?

> **Sabe sim.**
> Yes, she can.

52.2.2 **Present**

Learned abilities are often expressed by simply using the present tense:

> **Ele cozinha muito bem.**
> He cooks very well. / He's a good cook.

> **Ela fala chinês fluentemente.**
> She speaks Chinese fluently.

53

Seeking and giving permission

53.1 Seeking permission

To seek permission, as in 'May/Can I come in?', 'Let me come in', 'Do you mind if I come in?', Portuguese uses a number of verbs and expressions, of which the most common are the following:

53.1.1 *poder* + infinitive

Using **poder** 'can, may' is the most straightforward way of asking permission:

> **Posso entrar?**
> May/Can I come in?

> **Posso deixar a minha bolsa aqui?**
> Can I leave my bag here?

> **Podemos estacionar aqui?**
> Can we park here?

> **Podemos ver o cardápio, por favor?**
> Can we see the menu, please?

To make a more formal and polite request, the conditional tense of **poder** may be used:

> **Poderia falar com o Sr. Ricardo Tavares, por favor?**
> Could I speak to Mr Ricardo Tavares, please?

> **Nós poderíamos nos encontrar para falar do assunto?**
> Could we meet to discuss the matter?

53.1.2 *pode* + infinitive

In the spoken language, the third person singular of **poder** is used without an explicit subject to convey the general meaning of 'Is it OK to . . . ?':

> **Pode deixar a bicicleta aqui? – Pode.**
> 'Is it OK to leave my bike here?' – 'Yes.'

> **Pode fumar aqui? – Não pode.**
> 'Is it OK to smoke here?' – 'No, it's not allowed.'

> **Pode pegar um folheto desses?**
> Is it OK to take one of these leaflets?

53.1.3 *dá* + infinitive

In colloquial speech, the third person singular of the verb **dar** 'to give' is used impersonally to mean 'is it OK?'. It is followed by an infinitive, which may be a personal infinitive with the subject **eu** 'I' or **a gente** 'we':

> **Dá para estacionar aqui? – Dá, sim.**
> 'Is it OK to park here?' – 'Yes, it is.'

> **Dá para eu usar o banheiro?**
> Is it all right if I use the bathroom?

> **Dá para a gente deixar as coisas aqui?**
> Can we leave our stuff here?

> **Dá para repetir, por favor?**
> Could you repeat that, please?

53.1.4 *dá licença, com licença*

The expression **dá licença** means 'excuse me' and is said when you are about to do something that may be considered rude. It can be pronounced with question intonation if you really want the other person's permission, but usually it is pronounced with statement intonation as you go ahead with what you intend to do.

> **Dá licença, vou descer aqui.**
> Excuse me, I'm getting off here. (*could you let me through?*)

> **Dá licença um minutinho, eu preciso atender o telefone.**
> Excuse me a moment, I have to answer the phone.

Brazilians also say **dá licença** when taking up an offer or invitation that might cause inconvenience or be considered intrusive. For example, when you invite a Brazilian into your home, he or she will normally say **dá licença** while walking through the door. Similarly, if you invite a Brazilian guest to sit down, he or she will say **dá licença** while doing so. It is also said in situations such as helping yourself to food offered by your host, joining or leaving others at a shared table, asking to get by when someone is in your way, etc. The expression can also be used with a subject pronoun:

> **Vocês me dão licença que vou pegar a sobremesa.**
> Excuse me while I go and get the dessert.

> **O senhor me dá licença um pouquinho?**
> Would you excuse me a moment, sir?

The expression **com licença** is more or less synonymous with **dá licença**, except that it sounds more perfunctory and 'entitled', i.e. rather than theoretically asking for permission, you are assuming it is given:

> **Com licença, senhoras e senhores.**
> Excuse me, ladies and gentlemen.

> **Com licença, por aqui, senhor.**
> This way please, sir, if you don't mind.

deixar + infinitive

The verb **deixar** 'to let' can be used in two ways to ask permission:

(i) With the imperative of **deixar** followed by **eu** 'I' + infinitive. Either the formal or the familiar imperative may be used, as in speech both **deixe** and **deixa** are run together with **eu** and pronounced /dejʃew/ with equal stress on the two syllables:

> **Deixa eu dar uma pensada.**
> Let me think about it.

> **Deixe eu explicar para o senhor.**
> Let me explain, sir.

In this construction, **eu** is the subject of a personal infinitive. In formal grammar, the formal imperative should be followed by the object pronoun **me**, but this construction (e.g. **deixe-me explicar**) is only found in formal writing.

(ii) By using **você me deixa/vocês me deixam** + infinitive? 'will you let me . . . ?' with question intonation, as in:

> **Você me deixa segurar o bebê um pouco?**
> Will you let me hold the baby for a minute?

> **Vocês deixam a gente ficar aqui?**
> Will you let us stay here?

importar-se/incomodar-se se + future subjunctive; *importar-se/incomodar-se que* + present subjunctive

The verbs **importar-se** and **incomodar-se** both mean 'to mind' and are practically interchangeable. If there is any difference, it is that **importar-se** implies having an intellectual or moral objection, while **incomodar-se** refers to physical inconvenience. Both verbs can be used in two possible constructions: with **se** followed by a future subjunctive 'do you mind if I . . .' or with **que** followed by a present subjunctive, 'do you mind me . . . ing':

> **Você se importa se eu me sentar aqui?**
> Do you mind if I sit here?

> **Você se incomoda que eu fume?**
> Do you mind me smoking?

> **Vocês se importam se eu for embora mais cedo?**
> Do you mind if I leave early?

> **Você se incomoda se ele deixar a bicicleta aqui?**
> Do you mind if he leaves his bike here?

Giving permission

When giving permission in reponse to a request made with **poder** (**53.1.1**, **53.1.2**) or **dar** (**53.1.3**), the simplest response is to repeat the verb in the third person singular:

> **Posso entrar? – Pode.**
> 'Can I come in?' – 'Yes.'

> **Pode estacionar aqui? – Pode.**
> 'Is it OK to park here?' – 'Yes.'

Dá para pagar com cartão? – Dá.
'Is it OK to pay with a card?' – 'Yes.'

Other responses you may use to give permission are:

claro 'yes, of course'

fique/fica à vontade 'feel free'

não faça cerimônia 'don't stand on ceremony'

por favor 'please do', 'go ahead'

está bom 'OK', 'all right' (*pronounced* [ta bõw])

tudo bem 'all right', 'it's fine'

tá 'OK' (*the spoken form of* **está**)

toda 'of course' (*response to* **dá licença**)

com toda 'of course' (*response to* **com licença**).

Examples:

Posso usar o banheiro? – Claro, fique à vontade.
'May I use the bathroom?' – 'Of course, feel free.'

Sentem, amigos, não façam cerimônia.
Sit down, everybody, don't stand on cerimony.

Você se importa se eu ligar o ventilador? – Não, por favor.
'Do you mind if I turn on the fan?' – 'No, go ahead.'

Deixa eu dar uma olhada no seu dicionário. – Está bom.
'Let me have a look in your dictionary.' – 'All right.'

Você se incomoda que eu fume? – Não, tudo bem.
'Do you mind me smoking?' – 'No, it's fine.'

Só um minutinho. – Tá.
'Just a moment.' – 'OK.'

Com licença. – Com toda.
'Excuse me.' – 'Of course.'

53.3 Stating that permission is withheld

When denying permission in response to a request made with **poder** (**53.1.1**, **53.1.2**) or **dar** (**53.1.3**), the simplest response is to repeat the verb in the third person singular with the negative **não**, which may be repeated:

Posso deixar a bolsa aqui? – Não pode, não.
'Can I leave my bag here?' – 'No, you can't.'

Pode estacionar aqui? – Não, não pode.
'Is it OK to park here?' – 'No, it isn't.'

Dá para usar o telefone? – Não, não dá não.
'Is it OK to use the phone?' – 'No, it's not.'

Other expressions are:

>**sinto muito, mas . . .** 'I'm sorry, but . . .'
>
>**desculpe/desculpa, mas . . .** 'sorry, but . . .'
>
>**eu prefiro que não** 'I'd rather you didn't'
>
>**é proibido** 'it's not allowed'
>
>**infelizmente** 'unfortunately', 'I'm afraid . . .'
>
>**de jeito nenhum** 'certainly not'.

Examples:

>**Posso estacionar aqui? – Sinto muito, mas aqui é proibido.**
>'Can I park here?' – 'I'm sorry, but it's not allowed here.'
>
>**Pode me ajudar? – Desculpe, mas não dá.**
>'Can you help me?' – 'I'm sorry, but I can't.'
>
>**Você se incomoda se eu fumar? – Eu prefiro que não.**
>'Do you mind if I smoke?' – 'I'd rather you didn't.'
>
>**Posso deixar a mala aqui? – Infelizmente não dá.**
>'Can I leave my suitcase here?' – 'I'm afraid that's not possible.'
>
>**Você me deixa dirigir o seu carro? – De jeito nenhum!**
>'Will you let me drive your car?' – 'Certainly not!'

Signs normally use the word **proibido**, followed by an infinitive, to signal that something is not allowed:

>**É proibido fumar.**
>No smoking.
>
>**Proibido estacionar.**
>No parking.

54

Asking and giving opinions

54.1 ## Asking someone's opinion

The following are the verbs and constructions most commonly used to ask people their opinion:

54.1.1 ### achar

The most frequent verb in this context is **achar** 'to think'. The constructions used to ask someone's opinion are:

> **O que (é que) você acha?** 'What do you think?'
>
> **O que (é que) vocês acham?** 'What do you think?' (*to more than one person*)
>
> **O que você acha de . . . ?** 'What do you think of . . . ?'
>
> **O que vocês acham de . . . ?** 'What do you think of . . . ?' (*to more than one person*)
>
> **Você acha que . . . ?** 'Do you think (that) . . . ?'

Examples:

> **Vamos sair? O que é que você acha?**
> Shall we go out? What do you think?
>
> **O que você achou do filme?**
> What did you think of the movie?
>
> **O que vocês acharam da minha sugestão?**
> What did you think of my suggestion?
>
> **Você acha que vai chover?**
> Do you think it's going to rain?

The expression **o que você(s) acha(m) de . . .** can be followed by a personal infinitive to put forward a suggestion:

> **O que você acha de a gente jantar fora?**
> What do you think about us eating out? / How about us eating out?
>
> **O que vocês acham de eu convidar o Tom?**
> What do you think about me inviting Tom? / How about me inviting Tom?

When asking for someone's first impression of something, e.g. something they are eating or something they are seeing or have just seen for the first time, the preterite of **achar** is normally used in Portuguese:

> **O que é que vocês acharam do bolo?**
> What do you think of the cake? (*i.e. that you are eating*)

> **Olha meu vestido novo. O que é que você achou?**
> Look at my new dress. What do you think?

The subjunctive is occasionally used after **você acha que ... ?** 'do you think that ... ?'. The use of the subjunctive implies that the person asking the question does not think so:

> **Você acha que ele seja o melhor candidato?**
> Do you think he's the best candidate? (*because I don't think so*)

> **Você acha que ele é o melhor candidato?**
> Do you think he's the best candidate? (*impartial question*)

54.1.2 *pensar*

The verb **pensar** 'to think' refers more to the process of thinking and is therefore not used to ask for someone's impression of something, as is the case with **achar**, but rather to ask for their considered opinion on a subject. The construction commonly used is:

> **O que (é que) você pensa de/sobre/a respeito de ... ?**
> 'What do you think about ... ?'

Examples:

> **O que você pensa dos últimos avanços da tecnologia?**
> What do you think about the latest advances in technology?

> **O que vocês pensam a respeito do aborto?**
> What do you think about abortion?

The question **você pensa que ... ?** 'do you think (that) ... ?' differs from **você acha que ... ?** in that, instead of asking for a person's own individual feeling about something, you are asking for a considered view based on objective data:

> **Você pensa que o presidente vai ser reeleito?**
> Do you think the president will be re-elected? (*based on the data available*)

> **Você acha que o presidente vai ser reeleito?**
> Do you think the president will be re-elected? (*in your personal opinion*)

54.1.3 *acreditar, crer*

The verbs **acreditar** and **crer** both mean 'to believe' and can be used to ask a person's opinion. Of the two, **acreditar** is much more frequent:

> **Você acredita que as novas medidas vão surtir efeito?**
> Do you believe the new measures will be effective?

> **Você crê que houve motivação política no crime?**
> Do you believe that the crime was politically motivated?

As with **achar** (see **54.1.1**), the subjunctive may be used in the **que** clause to imply scepticism on the part of the speaker. When used after **acreditar** and **crer**, the subjunctive changes the intention of the question from asking for an opinion to asking whether the person actually believes that the statement is true:

> **Você acredita que ele é inocente?**
> Do you think he's innocent? (*i.e. what's your view?*)

> **Você acredita que ele seja inocente?**
> Do you believe he's innocent? (*i.e. do you believe claims that he is innocent?*)

54.1.4 *opinar*

The verb **opinar** 'to give an opinion' is more formal and is often used in interviews and similar situations. The following are typical examples of its use:

> **O senhor quer opinar sobre os últimos acontecimentos?**
> Would you like to give us your view on the latest developments?

> **Você pode opinar sobre essa questão?**
> Could you give us your opinion on this issue?

54.1.5 *qual (é) a sua opinião?*

This phrase, meaning 'what is your opinion?', sounds rather formal and is more likely to be used in an interview or survey than in everyday conversation. Note that the verb **é** is optional after **qual**. The phrase is normally followed by the prepositions **sobre** 'on, about' or **a respeito de** 'concerning':

> **Qual a sua opinião a respeito?**
> What's your opinion on that?

> **Qual é a sua opinião sobre esse projeto?**
> What is your opinion about this project?

54.1.6 Other ways of asking for someone's opinion

The following expressions may also be used to ask someone's opinion:

> **Na sua opinião, o que/como/qual ... ?** 'In your opinion, what/how/which ... ?'

> **Como você vê isso?** 'How do you see this?'

> **Você concorda comigo (que ...)?** 'Do you agree with me (that ...)?'

> **Você não acha (que ...)?** 'Don't you think (that ...)?'

> **Queria ouvir a sua opinião sobre ...** 'I'd like to hear your opinion on ....'.

54.2 Expressing opinions

Personal opinions can be conveyed simply by asserting an idea directly, using an indicative verb:

> **O Rio é uma cidade linda**.
> Rio is a beautiful city.

> **Os brasileiros são muito bem-humorados.**
> Brazilians are very good-humoured.

In addition, there are certain verbs and expressions that are associated more specifically with opinions, the most common of which are:

54.2.1 *achar*

The verb **achar** 'to think' is found in set phrases, such as:

>**acho que ...** / **eu acho que ...** 'I think (that) ...'
>
>**achamos que ...** / **nós achamos que ...** 'we think (that) ...'
>
>**acho que sim** 'I think so'
>
>**acho que não** 'I don't think so'
>
>**eu não acho** 'that's not what I think'.

Examples:

>**Acho que deveríamos tentar.**
>I think we ought to try.
>
>**O Rafael chega hoje? – Acho que sim.**
>'Is Rafael arriving today?' – 'I think so.'
>
>**Você acha que vai chover? – Acho que não.**
>'Do you think it's going to rain?' – 'I don't think so.'
>
>**Acho que vai chover. – Eu não acho.**
>'I think it's going to rain.' – 'I don't.'

Note that the English 'I don't think ...' has two possible interpretations, which call for different translations in Portuguese. Compare the following sentences:

>**Eu acho que não vai chover.**
>I don't think it's going to rain. (*i.e. in my opinion, it will not rain*)
>
>**Eu não acho que vai chover.**
>I don't think it's going to rain. (*i.e. I don't agree that it will rain*)

After **não acho que ...** the subjunctive may be used when you want to disagree with a statement previously made by someone else:

>**O Brasil vai ganhar a Copa. – Eu não acho que o Brasil ganhe.**
>'Brazil will win the World Cup.' – 'I don't think Brazil will win.'
>
>**Acho que ela gostou do presente. – Eu não acho que ela tenha gostado.**
>'I think she liked the present.' – 'I don't think she liked it.'
>
>**Acho que ele estava com vergonha. – Eu não acho que ele estivesse com vergonha.**
>'I think he was embarrassed.' – 'I don't think he was embarrassed.'

When saying what you think of a person or thing, **achar** can be used with a noun or pronoun object followed by an adjective. This is equivalent to the use of 'to find' as in 'I found the movie boring', 'I find him unbearable', but also translates 'I think something/someone is ...':

>**Achei o filme chato. / Achei chato o filme.**
>I found the movie boring *or* I thought the movie was boring.

Acho ele insuportável. (*spoken*)
I find him unbearable *or* I think he's unbearable.

Achamos o restaurante muito caro. / Achamos muito caro o restaurante.
We found the restaurant very expensive *or* We thought the restaurant was very expensive.

An infinitive can be used in this construction in place of a noun/pronoun:

Acho melhor trancar a porta.
I think it's better to lock the door.

Achei fácil chegar na casa dele.
I found it easy to get to his house.

Notice that the word 'it' is not translated in the above example. The infinitive may also be a personal one with its own subject:

Acho estranho ele ter falado isso.
I find it strange that he said that *or* I think it's strange he said that.

Achamos um absurdo eles serem tratados desse jeito.
We found it outrageous them being treated like that.

Finally, note that it is more common to use the preterite tense of **achar** when giving your first impression of something (see **54.1.1**):

Achei lindo o seu cabelo assim.
I think your hair looks lovely like that.

<h3>54.2.2   pensar</h3>

The verb **pensar** 'to think' is used when giving a reasoned opinion based on objective facts:

Penso que a educação é essencial para o crescimento econômico do país.
I think education is essential for the country's economic growth.

Pensamos que ele é a pessoa certa para este cargo.
We think that he is the right person for this post.

Note the difference between **eu pensava que . . .** 'I used to think, I was thinking, I had been thinking, I thought (until I discovered otherwise) that' and **eu pensei que . . .** '(in response to something that happened) I thought that . . .': **eu pensava que** is followed by the imperfect or conditional indicative; **eu pensei que** can be followed by these indicative tenses when there is a degree of certainty in what you are thinking, but is followed by the imperfect subjunctive when what you are thinking turns out to be mistaken:

Eu pensava que ele era um cara sério.
I used to think that he was a reliable guy.

Quando ele disse isso, pensei que ele era um cara sério.
When he said that, I thought he was a reliable guy.

Pensei que ele fosse um cara sério, mas acabei me decepcionando.
I thought he was a reliable guy, but I ended up being disappointed.

Quando vi as nuvens, pensei que ia chover.
When I saw the clouds, I thought it was going to rain. (*and it did*)

Pensei que fosse chover hoje, mas não caiu uma gota.
I thought it was going to rain today, but there wasn't a drop.

54.2.3 *acreditar, crer*

These verbs, which both mean 'to believe', can be used to give an opinion. Of the two, **acreditar** is much more common, while **crer** sounds quite formal:

Eu acredito que o chefe tinha razão.
I believe/think that the boss was right.

Acredito que sim.
I believe so.

Creio que não.
I don't believe so.

A subjunctive may be used in the **que** clause after these verbs, and always is when they are in the negative:

Acredito que essa seja a melhor solução.
I believe this is the best solution.

Não creio que isso seja um problema.
I don't believe this is a problem.

54.2.4 *considerar*

The verb **considerar** 'to consider, regard, feel' is used in the same way as **achar**. Here are some examples:

Considero o João meu melhor amigo.
I consider João (to be) my best friend.

Consideramos prudente diversificar as aplicações.
We consider it wise to diversify your investments.

Considero um absurdo ele ter sido absolvido.
I consider it an outrage that he has been acquitted.

Eu me considero uma pessoa compreensiva.
I regard myself as being an understanding person.

Considero que o governo precisa fazer mais na área da saúde.
I feel that the government needs to do more in the area of healthcare.

The expression **não considero/consideramos que** is followed by the subjunctive:

Não consideramos que isso constitua crime.
We do not feel that this constitutes a crime.

54.2.5 Other ways of expressing an opinion

Here are some other phrases commonly used to express opinions:

na minha opinião 'in my opinion'

para mim, ... 'for me, ...', 'as far as I'm concerned'

a meu ver 'in my view'

por mim 'if it was me', 'if it was down to me'

se dependesse de mim 'if it was up to me'.

Examples:

Na minha opinião, ele não passa de um vigarista.
In my opinion, he's nothing more than a conman.

Para mim, ele é um dos melhores jogadores de todos os tempos.
As far as I'm concerned, he's one of the best players of all time.

O presidente agiu corretamente, a meu ver.
The president acted correctly, in my view.

Por mim, essa lei teria sido abolida há muito tempo.
If it was down to me, this law would have been abolished a long time ago.

Se dependesse de mim, o cara estava na cadeia.
If it was up to me, the guy would be in jail.

54.3 Reporting on other people's opinions

54.3.1

To report on other people's opinions, the verbs **achar**, **pensar**, **acreditar**, **crer** and **considerar** can all be used with a third person subject. The verb **dizer** 'to say' or, more colloquially, **falar**, can also be used to report other people's opinions:

Ele disse que gostou do filme.
He said he liked the movie.

Ela achou o livro interessante.
She found the book interesting.

54.3.2 Other expressions used for reporting on the opinions of others

para ele/ela/eles, . . . 'as far as he is/she is/ they are concerned'

segundo . . . 'according to . . .'

na opinião de . . . 'in . . .'s opinion'

se dependesse de . . . 'if it were up to . . .'.

Examples:

Para ele, o resultado foi marmelada.
As far as he is concerned, the result was a fix.

Segundo moradores do bairro, é perigoso sair à noite.
According to residents of the neighbourhood, it is dangerous to go out at night.

Na opinião do técnico, o jogador não mereceu ser expulso.
In the coach's opinion, the player did not deserve to be sent off.

Se dependesse dela, a boate seria interditada.
If it were up to her, the nightclub would be closed down.

55

Expressing agreement, disagreement and indifference

55.1   Expressing agreement

55.1.1   Set phrases

There are a number of set phrases used to express agreement. Below is a list of the most common:

tá 'OK, all right, right'

está bem 'all right', 'very well'

está certo 'OK, all right, right'

tudo bem 'fine'

por mim, tudo bem 'it's fine by me'

está bom 'OK', 'fine'

ótimo 'great'

beleza 'great', 'cool' (*informal*)

é 'yes'

pois é 'that's right'

certo 'right'

exato 'exactly'

é isso 'that's it'

é isso aí 'that's right'

aí é que está 'that's (just) the point'

claro/lógico 'of course'

com certeza 'definitely', 'for sure'

sem dúvida 'without a doubt'.

In all those expressions that contain the verb form **está**, this is normally pronounced /ta/ in everyday conversation. The extremely common expression **tá** 'OK', which is originally derived from **está**, is never pronounced **está** and is therefore written as **tá**. The expression **está bem** is only used in more formal contexts and the **es-** part is usually pronounced. It can be thought of as the more formal equivalent of **tá**. The word **é** is used for 'yes' when simply endorsing what someone has said.

Examples:

> **Que tal pegar um cineminha? – Tá/está bom/tudo bem.**
> 'What about catching a movie?' – 'OK/all right/fine.'

> **Eu te encontro às sete. – Tá/está bom/está certo.**
> 'I'll meet you at seven.' – 'OK/all right/right.'

> **Precisamos pintar a casa. – É, eu sei.**
> 'We must paint the house.' – 'Yes, I know.'

> **O governo não faz nada. – Pois é/é isso/é isso aí.**
> 'The government doesn't do anything.' – 'That's right.'

> **Deveriam melhorar o transporte coletivo. – Exato.**
> 'They should improve public transport.' – 'Exactly.'

> **Se ele não perguntar, nunca vai saber. – Claro/lógico.**
> 'If he doesn't ask, he'll never know.' – 'Of course.'

> **Isso vai dar a maior confusão. – Com certeza/sem dúvida.**
> 'This is going to cause real trouble.' – 'Definitely/without a doubt.'

55.1.2 *concordar*

The verb **concordar** 'to agree' is also used to express agreement:

> **(Eu) concordo.** 'I agree.'

> **Concordo com você.** 'I agree with you.'

> **Concordo plenamente.** 'I totally agree.'

> **Concordo em gênero, número e grau.** 'I couldn't agree more.'

55.1.3 *ter razão*

The expression **ter razão** means 'to be right' and is used in a number of phrases to express agreement:

> **(Você) tem razão.** 'You're right.'

> **(Você) tem toda a razão.** 'You're quite right.'

> **(Você) está coberto/a de razão.** 'You're absolutely right.'

55.2 Expressing disagreement

The words and phrases most commonly used in the expression of disagreement are the following:

> **não** 'no'

> **não sei** 'I don't know'

> **não sei bem** 'I'm not sure'

> **de jeito nenhum** 'certainly not', 'no way'

> **você acha?** 'do you think so?'

> **eu não acho** 'I don't think so', 'that's not what I think'

> **não é verdade** 'that's not true'

não é isso 'it's not that'

(você) está errado/a 'you're wrong'

(você) está enganado/a 'you're mistaken'

não concordo (com você/isso) 'I don't agree (with you/that)'

discordo totalmente (disso) 'I disagree completely (with that)'

como assim? 'what do you mean?'

imagina! 'come off it!'

que nada! 'come off it!', 'no way!'

(que) bobagem! '(what) nonsense!'

isso é balela! 'that's bull!', 'that's rubbish!' (the word **balela** is not offensive)

Examples:

> **Então você vai comigo? – Não sei. / Não sei bem.**
> 'So you're coming with me?' – 'I don't know.' / 'I'm not sure.'

> **Vou levar o seu carro. – De jeito nenhum!**
> 'I'm going to take your car.' – 'Certainly not!'

> **Ela é um pouco estranha. – Você acha? / Eu não acho.**
> 'She's a bit strange.' – 'Do you think so?' / 'I don't think so.'

> **Você está com ciúmes. – Não é isso. / Não é verdade.**
> 'You're jealous.' – 'It's not that.' / 'That's not true.'

> **É culpa sua. – Como assim?**
> 'It's your fault.' – 'What do you mean?'

> **Ela está a fim de você. – Imagina!**
> 'She has a thing for you.' – 'Come off it!'

> **Ele falou que é ator. – Que nada! Ele trabalha no supermercado.**
> 'He said he's an actor.' – 'No way! He works at the supermarket.'

> **Dizem que o mundo vai acabar ano que vem. – Bobagem!**
> 'They say the world's going to end next year.' – 'Nonsense!'

55.3 Asking about agreement and disagreement

To ask people whether they agree or disagree with something, we use expressions such as the following:

(você) concorda? 'do you agree?'

(você) não concorda? 'don't you agree?'

(você) concorda comigo? 'do you agree with me?'

você acha? 'do you think so?'

você não acha? 'don't you think?'

está bom? 'is that OK?'

tá? 'OK?'

beleza? 'OK?', 'cool?' (*informal*)

certo? 'right?'

tudo bem? 'is that OK?'

se você está de acordo 'if you're in agreement', 'if it's OK with you'.

Examples:

Deviam reembolsar o dinheiro, não concorda comigo?
They should refund the money, don't you agree with me?

Você não acha melhor voltar amanhã?
Don't you think it would be better to come back tomorrow?

Te ligo mais tarde, está bom?/tá?/certo?/tudo bem?
I'll call you later, all right?/OK?/right?/is that OK?

Se você está de acordo, podemos começar amanhã.
If it's OK with you we can start tomorrow.

55.4 | Expressing indifference

To express indifference, use expressions such as the following:

(para mim,) tanto faz 'I don't mind', 'it makes no difference (to me)'

por mim . . . 'I don't mind', 'it's fine by me'

não importa 'it doesn't matter'

não me importa/não importa para mim 'it doesn't matter to me'

dá no mesmo 'it comes to the same thing'

não interessa 'it makes no difference'

não me interessa 'I don't care'

e daí? 'so what?'

(não) estou nem aí (para . . .) 'I couldn't care less (about . . .)'

estou me lixando (para . . .) 'I couldn't care less (about . . .)'.

Examples:

Você quer água ou suco? – Tanto faz.
'Do you want water or juice?' – 'I don't mind.'

Que tal jantarmos fora? – Por mim . . .
'How about we go out for dinner?' – 'Fine by me.'

Tem que escrever em letra de forma? – Não importa.
'Do you have to write it in block capitals?' – 'It doesn't matter.'

Não sei se pago com cheque ou com cartão. – Dá no mesmo.
'I don't know whether to pay by cheque or by card.' – 'It comes to the same thing.'

Mas eu não fiz por mal. – Não interessa.
'But I didn't mean any harm.' – 'It makes no difference.'

Ele está puto com você. – E daí?
'He's furious with you.' – 'So what?'

Não estou nem aí para o que eles acham.
I couldn't care less what they think.

IV

Expressing emotional attitudes

56

Expressing desires and preferences

56.1 ## Expressing desires

To express desire, Portuguese normally uses the following verbs and expressions:

> **querer** 'to want'
>
> **gostaria de** 'would like'
>
> **estar com/ter vontade de** 'to feel like'
>
> **estar a fim de** 'to feel like', 'to be in the mood for'
>
> **desejar** 'to wish'
>
> **tomara (que . . .)** 'let's hope so/(that . . .)'
>
> **quem (me) dera** 'if only', 'I wish'.

56.1.1 ### *querer*

▶ **16.3.13** (p. 157)

The verb **querer** 'to want' is probably the most frequently used to express desires, either present or past. To say what you want now, you can use:

(i) The present tense, for example:

> **Quero um suco de laranja, por favor.**
> I want an orange juice, please.
>
> **Queremos conhecer Paris.**
> We want to visit Paris.

(ii) The future tense formed with **ir**, as an alternative to the present tense when the actual thing you want will be brought or will occur at some point in the future. This construction is often used when ordering in restaurants:

> **Vou querer um misto quente.**
> I'll have a toasted ham and cheese sandwich.
>
> **Vou querer assistir aquele documentário hoje à noite.**
> I want to watch that documentary tonight.

(iii) **queria/queríamos**: this is equivalent to 'would like' or 'wanted' in that it is less direct and abrupt than **quero/queremos** and therefore used when you want to sound more polite[1]:

> **Eu queria uma água sem gás, por favor.**
> I'd like a still mineral water, please.

> **Eu queria te perguntar uma coisa.**
> I wanted to ask you something.

> **Nós queríamos alugar um barco.**
> We'd like to rent a boat.

> **Queria falar com o Cláudio, por favor.**
> I'd like to speak to Claudio, please.

NOTE | 1 However, when asking for things, **quero** is not considered as blunt or rude as 'I want' in English.

When talking about the past, the imperfect of **querer** is used to talk about recurring desires or those that were unfulfilled, at least at the time referred to:

> **Ele sempre queria sair com a gente.**
> He was always wanting to go out with us.

> **Nós queríamos conhecer Paris.**
> We wanted to visit Paris. (*i.e. that was our as yet unfulfilled intention at the time*)

The preterite of **querer** refers to something that you have wanted to do or that you wanted to do and actually did:

> **Ele sempre quis ser médico.**
> He's always wanted to be a doctor.

> **Quisemos conhecer Paris.**
> We wanted to visit Paris. (*and that's why we went there*)

The imperfect **queria** is also used in place of the conditional[2] to express an unfulfilled desire or wish relating to the present:

> **Ai, eu queria ser rico!**
> Oh, I wish I was rich!

The construction **queria ter** + past participle expresses an unfulfilled desire or wish relating to the past:

> **Eu queria ter visto a cara dele.**
> I would like to have seen his face. / I wish I'd seen his face.

> **Queríamos ter ficado mais tempo.**
> We would like to have stayed longer. / We wish we'd stayed longer.

NOTE | 2 The actual conditional form **quereria** is extremely rare in the modern language.

56.1.2 *gostaria de*

The conditional of **gostar** is used with the preposition **de** and an infinitive to express a wish or a polite request[3]:

> **Eu gostaria de ter uma casa na praia.**
> I'd like to have a house at the beach.

> **Gostaríamos de agradecer a sua hospitalidade.**
> We'd like to thank you for your hospitality.

> **Eu gostaria de ouvir sua opinião sobre os últimos acontecimentos.**
> I'd like to hear your opinion on the latest developments.

> **Gostaria de ter conhecido o seu pai.**
> I would like to have met your father.

NOTE | 3   As a formula for expressing a polite request, **gostaria de** is quite formal and is not used in everyday situations, where **quero** or **queria** would be used instead as equivalents of 'I'd like to'.

56.1.3 *estar com/ter vontade de* + infinitive

These expressions mean 'to feel like' and they can only be used before an infinitive. The first, **estar com**, is used to talk about a momentary desire, while **ter** is used to talk about a lasting or recurrent desire.

> **Estou com vontade de tomar sorvete.**
> I feel like (eating) ice cream.

> **Ela estava com vontade de desistir.**
> She felt like giving up.

> **Às vezes tenho vontade de mudar de vida.**
> Sometimes I feel like changing everything about my life.

> **Não tenho vontade de passar por aquilo tudo de novo.**
> I don't feel like going through all that again.

The verb **ficar** can be used instead of **estar com/ter** to signal a change from not wanting to wanting:

> **Quando tomo café, fico com vontade de fumar.**
> When I drink coffee I feel like smoking.

> **Depois da viagem à Argentina, fiquei com vontade de conhecer outros países.**
> After the trip to Argentina, I felt I wanted to visit other countries.

The expression **dar vontade de** is used either with or without an explicit subject with the meaning of 'make (me) want to'. It may be preceded by the unstressed pronouns **me** and **te** in colloquial speech and the third person pronoun **lhe** in more formal contexts, but it is also used without a pronoun object:

> **Quando tomo café, me dá vontade de fumar.**
> When I drink coffee, I feel like smoking.

> **O frio dá vontade de ficar em casa.**
> The cold makes you want to stay at home.

Não te dá vontade de gritar?
Doesn't it make you want to scream?

Ele senta no jardim quando lhe dá vontade.
He sits in garden when he feels like it.

56.1.4 *estar a fim de* + infinitive/noun/pronoun

The expression **estar a fim de** 'to feel like, be in the mood for/to' is more colloquial than **estar com vontade**, and refers to mood rather than desire. It is usually followed by an infinitive:

Não estou a fim de trabalhar hoje.
I don't feel like working today. / I'm not in the mood for work today.

Estou a fim de dançar.
I feel like dancing. / I'm in the mood for dancing.

Unlike **estar com/ter vontade de**, **estar a fim de** can be followed by a noun or pronoun:

Estou a fim de novas experiências.
I'm in the mood for new experiences.

Não estou muito a fim de comida japonesa.
I'm not really feeling like Japanese food.

Note that **estar a fim de** is used in colloquial speech to refer to a person you feel attracted to, 'to have a thing for, fancy':

Ele está a fim da Letícia.
He has a thing for Leticia.

56.1.5 *desejar*

The verb **desejar** 'to wish' is a more formal synonym of **querer**. It can also be used in the sense of 'would like to' but is not normally used to express one's own wishes. It is most commonly used to address customers and strangers:

Podemos entregar em casa se desejar.
We can deliver it to your home if you wish.

Quem deseja falar com ele?
Who shall I tell him is calling? (*on the phone*)

56.1.6 *tomara (que* + present subjunctive)

The expression **tomara que ...** means 'let's hope (that) ...' and is followed by a verb in the present subjunctive:

Tomara que você consiga!
Let's hope you succeed!

Tomara que não chova!
Let's hope it doesn't rain!

The word **tomara** can also be used on its own as a response:

> **Se tudo correr bem, a obra fica pronta essa semana. – Tomara!**
> 'If all goes well, the construction work will be finished this week.' – 'Let's hope so!'

quem (me) dera + imperfect subjunctive

The phrase **quem (me) dera** followed by a verb in the imperfect subjunctive conveys a wish for something unrealistic with the sense of 'if only', 'I wish'. Notice that it is used without a conjunction[4]:

> **Quem dera todas as provas fossem assim tão fáceis!**
> If only/I wish all the tests were that easy!

> **Quem me dera isso tudo nunca tivesse acontecido!**
> If only/I wish all this had never happened!

It can also be used alone as a response:

> **Você não recebe auxílio-alimentação? – Quem dera!**
> 'Don't you get a meal allowance?' – 'I wish!'

NOTE | 4 Though some native speakers say **quem dera que** or **quem dera se**.

Enquiring about desires

The same verbs as above can be used to enquire about desires:

Informal:

> **O que é que você quer fazer?**[5]
> What do you want to do?

> **Você gostaria de morar no interior?**
> Would you like to live in the country?

> **O que é que você está com vontade de comer?**
> What do you feel like eating?

> **Você está a fim de sair?**
> Do you feel like going out?

NOTE | 5 **Você quer . . .?** does not necessarily sound as blunt as 'do you want . . .?' in English and can also be equivalent to 'would you like . . .?' in non-formal contexts.

Formal:

> **O senhor deseja aguardar?**
> Do you wish to hold? (*on the phone*)

> **O que vocês desejam tomar?**
> What would you like to drink?

> **Gostaria de deixar recado?**
> Would you like to leave a message?

56.3 **Expressing preferences and enquiring about preferences**

56.3.1 *preferir*

▶ **16.1.1** (p. 150)

The verb most used for expressing preferences, both in statements and in questions, is **preferir** 'to prefer'. Remember that the second **e** of **preferir** changes to **i** when there is an **o** or an **a** in the next syllable, e.g. **prefiro** 'I prefer'. Like **querer**, it can also be followed by an infinitive:

> **Você prefere chá ou café?**
> Do you prefer tea or coffee?

> **Prefiro café.**
> I prefer coffee.

> **O que é que você prefere fazer?**
> What do you prefer to do?

> **Prefiro sair para tomar um drinque.**
> I prefer to go out for a drink.

> **Qual você prefere?**
> Which one do you prefer?

> **Como prefere a carne?**
> How do you prefer your steak?

> **Prefiro malpassada.**
> I prefer it rare.

Note also the use of **preferir** with the preposition **a**:

> **Prefiro o cinema ao teatro.**
> I prefer the cinema to the theatre.

> **Prefiro cerveja a vinho.**
> I prefer beer to wine.

> **Prefiro o vermelho ao azul.**
> I prefer the red (one) to the blue.

When expressing a preference about the immediate future, English uses 'I would prefer . . .', while Portuguese uses the simple present tense of **preferir**:

> **Eu prefiro ir sozinho.**
> I'd prefer to go on my own.

> **Você quer café? – Prefiro chá, se tiver.**
> 'Would you like coffee?' – 'I'd prefer tea if you have it.'

> **Você prefere sentar lá fora?**
> Would you prefer to sit outside?

The conditional **preferiria**, or the less formal-sounding imperfect **preferia** in place of the conditional, is used when the preference is unfulfilled and in true conditional sentences:

Você preferiria morar em outro país?
Would you prefer to live in another country? (*if you could*)

Se eu fosse pegar um bicho de estimação, preferia gato a cachorro.
If I was going to get a pet, I'd prefer a cat to a dog.

These tenses of **preferir** can also be followed by a perfect infinitive expressing an unfulfilled preference about the past, often equivalent to 'I wish I had . . .':

Eu preferia não ter vindo.
I'd have preferred not to come. / I'd rather not have come. / I wish I hadn't come.

56.3.2 *gostar mais de*

The construction **gostar mais** 'to like more/better', 'to like most/best' is an alternative way to express a preference. The noun, pronoun or infinitive that follows is preceded by the preposition **de**:

De qual você gosta mais?
Which one do you like better/best?

Gosto mais da verde.
I like the green one more/most.

Gosto mais de surfar na Internet do que assistir TV.
I like surfing the Internet more than watching TV.

56.3.3 *ir de*

The colloquial expression **ir de** followed by a noun can also be used to express a preference. The meaning is 'to go for' when different options are on offer:

Vinho tinto ou branco? – Acho que vou de tinto.
'Red or white wine?' – 'I think I'll go for red.'

De sobremesa fui de sorvete.
For dessert I went for ice cream.

56.4 Expressing desires and preferences involving others

56.4.1 *querer/preferir que* + subjunctive

Desires and preferences involving others, as in 'I want you to come with me' and 'I'd rather you didn't tell anyone', are expressed in Portuguese with a construction involving a subjunctive verb in a **que** clause. Look at the following examples:

Quero que você me acompanhe.
I want you to come with me.

Eu queria que você me ajudasse.
I wanted you to help me.

Prefiro que você não conte para ninguém.
I'd rather you didn't tell anyone.

Prefiro que você fale com ele.
I'd prefer you to talk to him.

Eu preferiria/preferia que você não me telefonasse no trabalho.
I'd prefer you didn't call me at work.

56.4.2 *gostaria que* + subjunctive; *desejar que* + subjunctive

The words **gostaria** 'would like' and **desejar** 'to wish, would like' can be followed by the same construction:

Gostaria que você me falasse a verdade.
I would like you to tell me the truth.

O senhor deseja que feche a janela?
Would you like me to close the window, sir?

57

Expressing likes and dislikes

57.1 ## How to say you like or dislike someone or something

The verb **gostar** 'to like' is the one most commonly associated with likes and dislikes. It can occur on its own when it is clear from the context who or what you are talking about; otherwise it is followed by the preposition **de** and then a noun, a pronoun or an infinitive:

> **Você gosta de frutos do mar? – Gosto muito.**
> 'Do you like seafood?' – 'Yes, very much.'

> **Não gosto do irmão dela.**
> I don't like her brother.

One peculiarity of **gostar**, as well as other verbs of liking and disliking, is that it is normally used in the preterite tense when you are giving your first impression of something, for example when trying some food, or commenting on a friend's appearance. The present tense is used more to refer to general likes and dislikes or when you have had some time to form an opinion. Look at these examples:

> **A sopa está boa? – Eu gostei.**
> 'Is the soup good?' – 'I like it.'

> **Que tal essa camiseta azul? – Não gostei.**
> 'What about this blue T-shirt?' – 'I don't like it.'

> **Ele é um banana. – "Banana", gostei!**
> 'He's a wimp.' – '"Wimp", I like it!'

57.1.1 ### *gostar de* + noun/pronoun

The expression **gostar de** can be followed by a noun or pronoun to say what or who you like:

> **Gosto muito da Sílvia.**
> I really like Silvia.

> **Gostamos deles.**
> We like them.

> **Não gosto de repolho.**
> I don't like cabbage.

Remember that the preterite tense is used to express first impressions:

> **Gostei do seu novo visual.**
> I like your new look.

Não gostei desse sorvete.
I don't like this ice cream.

Note that 'it/them' is not usually translated when referring to things:

Você come sushi? – Ai, eu não gosto.
'Do you eat sushi?' – 'Oh no, I don't like it.'

Esses copos são lindos. – É, eu também gostei muito.
'These glasses are beautiful.' – 'Yes, I really like them, too.'

57.1.2   *gostar de* + infinitive

The expression **gostar de** can also be used with an infinitive to say that you like or liked doing something:

Eu gosto de assistir televisão.
I like watching television.

Não gostamos de dormir com a janela fechada.
We don't like sleeping with the window closed.

57.2   Enquiring about likes and dislikes

The verb **gostar** can also be used in questions to ask others about their likes and dislikes:

Você gosta de tomar banho de mar?
Do you like going in the sea?

Vocês gostam de peixe?
Do you like fish?

Você não gosta do irmão dela?
Don't you like her brother?

The preterite tense is used when asking about a person's first impression:

Você gostou do meu relógio?
Do you like my watch?

Que tal o bolo? Gostaram?
How's the cake? Do you like it?

É a sua primeira vez no Brasil. E aí, gostou?
It's your first time in Brazil. So, do you like it?

Often, **gostar** is combined with question words:

De qual você gostou?
Which one do you like? / Which one did you like?

O que é que vocês gostam de fazer nos fins de semana?
What do you like doing at weekends?

Por que você não gostou?
Why didn't you like it? / Why don't you like it?

57.3 ## Other ways of expressing likes and dislikes

57.3.1 ### *adorar, amar*

The verb **adorar** 'to love, like very much' is used to express a strong liking. It is followed directly by a noun, pronoun or infinitive:

> **Eu adoro dançar.**
> I love dancing.

> **Adoro chocolate.**
> I love chocolate.

> **Ela te adora.**
> She adores you.

> **O Jaime adora o mar.**
> Jaime loves the sea.

> **Estou adorando meu novo emprego**.
> I'm loving my new job.

Like **gostar**, **adorar** is usually used in the preterite to convey a first impression:

> **Adorei o seu sapato!**
> I love your shoes!

> **Essa cor ficou ótima na parede. Adorei.**
> That colour looks great on the wall. I love it.

The verb **amar** means 'to love' in the true sense, but is also used in colloquial speech for very emphatic expressions of liking:

> **Eu te amo.**
> I love you.

> **Eu amo aquele filme.**
> I just love that movie.

> **Amei o seu apartamento!**
> I just love your apartment!

57.3.2 ### *não gostar, desgostar, odiar, detestar*

The idea of disliking is usually expressed with the negative of **gostar**:

> **Não gosto de futebol.**
> I dislike soccer.

> **Não gosto de atrasar.**
> I dislike being late.

The verb **desgostar** 'to dislike' is rarely used and, when it is, it is normally combined with **não**, as in the following example:

> **Eu não desgosto dele, mas não temos nenhuma afinidade.**
> I don't dislike him, but we have nothing in common.

Stronger dislike may be expressed with **odiar** and **detestar**, both meaning 'to hate'. Both verbs can be followed by a noun, pronoun or infinitive. Remember that the **i** of **odiar** becomes **ei** in those forms that are stressed on the stem, e.g. **eu odeio** 'I hate', **ele odeia** 'he hates', **eles odeiam** 'they hate', but **nós odiamos** 'we hate':

> **Odeio acordar cedo.**
> I hate getting up early.

> **Detesto vinho doce.**
> I hate sweet wine.

> **Por que é que você me odeia tanto?**
> Why do you hate me so much?

Like **gostar** and the other verbs of liking and disliking, these verbs are used in the preterite tense to convey a first impression:

> **O que é que você achou dessa cor? – Odiei.**
> 'What do you think of this colour?' – 'I hate it.'

▶ **16.2.2** (p. 151)

<h2>57.3.3   Verbs of liking and disliking followed by que</h2>

Verbs such as **gostar**, **adorar**, **odiar** and **detestar** can also be followed by a **que** clause with a verb in the subjunctive to talk about facts that you like or dislike:

> **Eu gosto que ele me traga presentes.**
> I like him bringing me presents. / I like (the fact) that he brings me presents.

> **Ela não gostava que os filhos brincassem na rua.**
> She didn't like her children playing in the street.

> **Adoro que me papariquem.**
> I love people pampering me.

> **Eu ia detestar que meu marido me tratasse assim.**
> I would hate my husband to treat me like that.

<h2>57.3.4   curtir</h2>

The colloquial verb **curtir** is much used to mean 'to enjoy', 'to like'. It can be followed by a noun, pronoun or infinitive expressing what it is you enjoy or like:

> **Não curto baladas.**
> I don't like/enjoy clubbing.

> **Você curte assistir série?**
> Do you like/enjoy watching TV series?

When the object of the verb is a person, the idea is 'enjoy time with':

> **Uma das vantagens de ser solteiro é que você pode curtir seus amigos.**
> One of the advantages of being single is that you can enjoy time with your friends.

The verb **curtir** can also be used on its own in the sense of 'enjoy yourself, have a good time':

> **Ele não quer namorar, só quer curtir.**
> He doesn't want a relationship, he just wants to have fun.

> **Não vou estudar durante as férias. Quero é curtir.**
> I'm not going to study during the vacation. What I want is to enjoy myself.

Note that **curtir** is the verb used for 'to like' in the internet sense[1]:

> **Visite e curta nossa página no Facebook!**
> Visit our Facebook page and like it!

NOTE | 1 Hence the associated noun **curtidas** 'likes', although the English word 'likes' is also used.

57.3.5 *amarrar-se em*

This is a colloquial expression used by younger people with the sense of 'to be/get into'. The object can be a noun, pronoun or infinitive:

> **Me amarro em comida japonesa.**
> I'm into Japanese food.

> **O Douglas se amarra em surfar.**
> Douglas is into surfing.

With a person as object, it can mean 'to fall for':

> **Me amarrei em você da primeira vez que te vi.**
> I fell for you the first time I saw you.

57.3.6 *uma delícia, delicioso, gostoso*

The expression **uma delícia** and the adjective **delicioso** can be used to refer to food, like 'delicious' in English, but also to any pleasant sensation. Note that both are used with **ser** when making a general statement and with **estar** when commenting on a particular situation:

> **As sobremesas daquele restaurante são uma delícia.**
> The desserts in that restaurant are delicious.

> **Esse bolo está uma delícia.**
> This cake is delicious.

> **Acho uma delícia ficar deitado à beira da piscina.**
> I think it's lovely to lie beside the pool.

> **Você precisa dar um mergulho. A água está deliciosa hoje.**
> You should go for a dip. The water's lovely today.

> **É delicioso no inverno sentar ao pé da lareira.**
> It's lovely in winter to sit by the fire.

The word **gostoso** can be used in the same way:

> **Essa sopa está muito gostosa.**
> This soup is very tasty.

É gostoso sentar no jardim à noite.
It's nice to sit in the garden in the evening.

57.3.7 Miscellaneous expressions

A range of other colloquial expressions can be used to express likes and dislikes. The following are among the most common:

É ótimo/maravilhoso! 'It's great/wonderful!'

É legal. 'It's nice.'

É superlegal! 'It's really nice!'

É (muito) bacana. 'It's (really) cool.'

É maneiro. 'It's cool.'

É um luxo! 'It's great!'

Irado! 'Awesome!' (*slang used by young people*)

É (muito) agradável/desagradável. 'It's (very) pleasant/unpleasant.'

É horrível. 'It's horrible.' (*talking about an object or in a general statement*)

Está horrível. 'It's horrible.' (*talking about the food you are eating, the current weather, etc.*)

Não aguento . . . 'I can't bear/stand . . .'

Ele é simpático/legal. 'He's friendly/nice.'

Ela é insuportável. 'She's unbearable.'

58

Expressing surprise

Portuguese uses a range of expressions to indicate surprise. Many of these are set phrases or exclamations, while others are complete sentences.

58.1 Set expressions

Ah, é? 'Oh yes?'

Verdade? 'Really?'

Jura? 'Really?'

Sério? 'Really?'

Fala sério! 'You're kidding, right?'

Mentira! 'No!' 'You're kidding!'

Que bom! 'That's great!'

É estranho isso. 'It's strange, that.'

Não me diga! 'You don't say!'

Gente! 'Heavens!'

Nossa! 'Gosh!'

Não pode ser! 'That's impossible!'

Que coisa! 'What a thing to happen!'

Que horror! 'How awful!'

Não acredito! 'I don't believe it!'

Meu Deus! 'My goodness!' 'My God!'

Meu Deus do céu! 'Oh my God!'

58.2 ## Expressing surprise with regard to someone or something

58.2.1 ### Saying you are surprised

In addition to the word **surpreso** (or, less commonly, **surpreendido**) 'surprised', you can use other adjectives to express different degrees of surprise[1], such as:

abismado	'astounded'
atônito	'astonished'
boquiaberto	'speechless'
chocado	'shocked'
estarrecido	'stunned', 'aghast'
horrorizado	'horrified'
impressionado	'amazed'
pasmo	'staggered'
passado	'taken aback', 'flabbergasted'
perplexo	'dumbfounded'

NOTE 1 The English translations given are not necessarily exact correspondences, but merely intended to give an idea of the meaning and intensity of each word.

All of the above can be used with the verb **estar** to describe a state of surprise, but they often occur with the preterite of **ficar** with present reference when you mean you have been surprised by something you have just heard or witnessed. All of them can be followed by the preposition **com** corresponding to 'at, by':

Nossa, fiquei passado com essa notícia.
Gosh, I'm flabbergasted by that news.

Nem sei o que falar. Fiquei pasmo.
I don't even know what to say. I'm staggered.

These adjectives of surprise can also be followed by a clause introduced by **que** 'that' and containing a verb in the subjunctive in more formal written style, but usually in the indicative in less formal contexts and speech[2]:

Estou surpreso que ele tenha dito isso. / . . . que ele disse isso.
I'm surprised he said that.

NOTE 2 In these kinds of sentences, the subjunctive has a similar more formal ring to it as does the use of 'would' or 'should' in such sentences in English, e.g. 'I'm surprised he would have said that' vs. 'I'm surprised he said that'.

58.2.2 ### *surpreender(-se)*

The reflexive form of the verb **surpreender** can be used as an alternative to **ficar surpreso** to express the idea of being surprised. As with **ficar surpreso**, it can also be followed by the preposition **com** or a **que** clause:

> **Comprei uns livros online e me surpreendi com a rapidez da entrega.**
> I bought some books online and was surprised by the promptness of the delivery.

The verb **surpreender** can also be used in the third person with the object pronoun **me** and a following personal infinitive or **que** clause containing a verb in the subjunctive to mean 'it surprises me that':

> **Me surpreende ele não falar inglês / que ele não fale inglês.**
> It surprises me he doesn't speak English.

Another expression using this verb is **o que me surpreende é** 'what surprises me is', which can also be followed by a personal infinitive or a **que** clause with a verb in the indicative:

> **O que me surpreendeu foi ela ser tão jovem / que ela era tão jovem.**
> What surprised me was her being so young / that she was so young.

58.2.3 *estranhar*

The verb **estranhar** means 'to find (it) strange' and can be used to express surprise, typically in the present continuous or preterite tenses followed by a personal infinitive or a **que** clause with a verb in the subjunctive or often, less formally, the indicative:

> **Estou estranhando o Cláudio não ter aparecido.**
> I find it strange Claudio hasn't shown up.

> **Estranhei ele não aparecer / que ele não aparecesse / que ele não apareceu.**
> I found it strange him not showing up / that he didn't show up.

The verb **estranhar** can also be followed by a noun:

> **Estamos estranhando o comportamento dela.**
> We're finding her behaviour strange.

58.2.4 *ser estranho/incrível* + personal infinitive/subjunctive

These constructions, meaning 'it's strange/incredible that . . .' can be used to express surprise at a fact. In Portuguese there are two possible constructions: the first involves the personal infinitive and is preferred in the spoken language; the second, involving a **que** + subjunctive clause, has a more formal ring to it:

> **É estranho ele não ter chegado ainda.**
> It's strange he hasn't got here yet.

> **É incrível eles pensarem assim.**
> It's incredible that they think like that.

> **Era estranho ela estar lá sem o marido.**
> It was strange her being there without her husband.

> **É estranho que o presidente não tenha sido informado.**
> It is strange that the president was not informed.

> **É incrível que um médico formado não soubesse disso.**
> It's amazing that a trained doctor did not know that.

In the last example, the verb **soubesse** is imperfect subjunctive referring to an ongoing state of affairs in the past even though the main verb is present tense, which would normally be followed by a present subjunctive. Compare this with the previous example, where a perfect subjunctive is used to refer to a single event in the past.

58.3 Saying that something is not surprising

There are a number of expressions which may be used to say that something is not surprising. The following are the most common:

58.3.1 *não surpreende/não admira*

These two expressions both mean '(it) is not surprising', **não admira** being more formal than **não surpreende**. Both can be preceded by an explicit subject:

> **O resultado da votação não surpreendeu.**
> The result of the vote was no surprise.

> **A oposição ganhou a eleição, o que não admira, já que o país estava em recessão.**
> The opposition won the election, which is not surprising, given that the country was in recession.

Both expressions can also be followed by a personal infinitive or a **que** clause containing a verb in the subjunctive:

> **Não surpreende o governo agir dessa forma.**
> It's not surprising the government should act in this way.

> **Não admira que ela tenha preferido renunciar.**
> It's not surprising she preferred to resign.

58.3.2 *não é para menos*

This expression means 'it's not surprising', 'it's no wonder' and can be used alone or followed by a **que** clause with a verb in the indicative:

> **Estou muito cansada. – Não é para menos. Você não parou o dia inteiro**.
> 'I'm very tired.' – 'It's no wonder. You haven't stopped all day.'

> **Não é para menos que o Rio de Janeiro é apelidado de Cidade Maravilhosa**.
> It's no wonder Rio de Janeiro is nicknamed the 'Wonderful City'.

58.3.3 *pudera*

The exclamation **pudera** means 'no wonder':

> **Estou com dor de barriga. – Pudera! Você comeu igual a um porco!**
> 'I have stomach ache.' – 'No wonder! You ate like a pig!'

 também

In informal conversation, **também** is often used in sentence-initial position as a response in the sense of 'yes, well (that's hardly surprising)':

> **Estou meio bêbado. – Também, né? Quem mandou você tomar quatro caipirinhas?**
> 'I'm kind of drunk.' – 'Yes, well, who forced you to have four caipirinhas?'

59

Expressing satisfaction and dissatisfaction

Expressing satisfaction

There are a number of set phrases used to express satisfaction:

Isso! 'That's it!' 'That's right!'

Ótimo! 'Great!'

É ótimo/a. 'It's great.'

Está ótimo. 'That's great.'

Perfeito! 'Perfect!'

Maravilha! 'Fantastic!'

Beleza! 'Great!' 'Brilliant!' 'Cool!'

Excelente! 'Excellent!'

Valeu! 'Good one!' 'Nice one!'

Está bom. 'That's fine.' 'That's enough.'

Está bom assim. 'That's fine like that.' 'That's enough.'

Chega. 'That's enough.'

Gostei. 'I like it/them.'

Acho ótimo. 'I think it's fine.'

Estou (muito) satisfeito/a com . . . 'I'm (very) pleased with . . .'

Estou/fiquei contente. 'I'm happy, pleased.'

Isso! is used, for example, when showing someone how to do something, or when the other person is trying to work out exactly what it is you want:

Agora clica em 'Enviar'. Isso!
Now click on 'Send'. That's it!

– Quero uma passagem para Tera . . . Teras . . .
– Teresópolis?
– Isso!
'I'd like a ticket to Tera . . . Teras . . .'
'Teresópolis?'
'That's it!'

Valeu! is a colloquial expression used when someone does or says something that you appreciate. It is often used as an informal word for 'thank you', like 'cheers!' in English:

> **Eu te deixo na estação. – Valeu, obrigado.**
> 'I'll drop you at the station.' – 'Nice one, thanks.'

Está ótimo and **Acho ótimo** can be used when you really find something excellent, but they are also used to reassure the other person that you are satisfied:

> **Sinto muito, mas só tem água. – Está ótimo.**
> 'I'm really sorry, but there's only water.' – 'That's fine.'

> **Você acha que com doze latas de cerveja dá? – Acho ótimo.**
> 'Do you think twelve cans of beer will be enough?' – 'I think that's fine.'

59.2 Expressing dissatisfaction

Dissatisfaction is commonly expressed with phrases such as:

> **Não gostei.** 'I don't like it/them.', 'I didn't like that.'

> **Não gosto assim.** 'I don't like it like that.'

> **Isso não está certo.** 'That's/This is not right.'

> **(Isso) não dá.** '(That's) It's not on.', '(That's) It's unacceptable.'

> **É pessimo/a.** 'It's terrible.' (*hotel, service, etc.*)

> **Está horrível.** 'It's horrible.' (*food, etc.*)

> **Não é isso que eu quero/queria.** 'That/this is not what I want/wanted.'

> **Não foi isso que eu pedi.** 'This isn't what I ordered/asked for.'

> **Não estou (nada) satisfeito.** 'I'm not (at all) satisfied.'

> **Estou muito decepcionado.** 'I'm very disappointed.'

> **Deixa (muito) a desejar.** 'It leaves a lot to be desired.'

> **Isso não vai ficar assim.** 'You haven't heard the last of this.'

Não gostei can be used for example when you don't like the food you have been served, or when you don't like an item offered to you in a shop. But it can also be used when you didn't like something that was said or done:

> **Esse peixe está com um gosto estranho. Não gostei.**
> This fish tastes funny. I don't like it.

> **Ela me chamou de mentiroso. Não gostei.**
> She called me a liar. I didn't like that.

59.3 Enquiring about satisfaction or dissatisfaction

The following expressions are commonly used to enquire about satisfaction or dissatisfaction:

> **Está tudo bem?** 'Is everything OK?'

> **Está bom assim?** 'Is it all right like that?'

Tudo bem aí? 'Everything OK?'

O que é que você acha? 'What do you think?'

Que tal . . . ? 'How is . . . ?'

Está satisfeito/a (agora)? 'Are you satisfied (now)?'

É isso que você quer? 'Is that what you want?'

Era isso que você queria? 'Was that what you wanted?'

Foi isso que você pediu? 'Was this/that what you ordered/asked for?'

In the question 'What do you think?', the preterite tense is often used when asking for a person's first impression of something:

Comprei esse vestido hoje. O que é que você achou?
I bought this dress today. What do you think of it?

Que tal . . . ? followed by a noun can be used to ask how someone is finding something:

Que tal o seu hotel?
What's your hotel like? / How's your hotel?

Que tal a pizza?
How's the pizza?

60

Expressing hope

60.1 Saying what one hopes or others hope to do

To express this idea, Portuguese uses the verb **esperar** 'to hope' followed by an infinitive:

Espero estudar Direito.
I hope to study law.

O Sérgio espera passar na prova.
Sergio hopes to pass the test.

Esperamos receber o dinheiro amanhã.
We hope to receive the money tomorrow.

60.2 Expressing hope with regard to others

When the expression of hope involves a subject other than that of the main verb, as in 'We hope you enjoy yourselves', the following constructions are used:

60.2.1 *esperar que* + subjunctive

This is by far the most frequent way of expressing hope involving others and is used in all registers. When the hope expressed refers to the present or future, the verb in the **que** clause must be in the present subjunctive:

Espero que não chova.
I hope it doesn't rain.

Esperamos que vocês se divirtam.
We hope you enjoy yourselves.

Meus pais esperam que eu estude Medicina.
My parents hope I will study medicine.

Hope with regard to something in the past is expressed with the present tense of **esperar** and, in formal grammar, with the perfect subjunctive in the **que** clause. In colloquial speech, the preterite indicative is usually used instead:

Espero que você tenha se divertido. (*formal*)
Espero que você se divertiu. (*colloquial*)
I hope you enjoyed yourself.

Espero que eles tenham conseguido achar o lugar. (*formal*)
Espero que eles conseguiram achar o lugar. (*colloquial*)
I hope they managed to find the place.

461

To say what you or others hoped or were hoping would happen, use **esperar** in the imperfect indicative and the verb in the **que** clause in the imperfect subjunctive:

> **Eu esperava que você chegasse mais cedo.**
> I was hoping you'd arrive earlier.

> **Ela esperava que a convidassem também.**
> She hoped they'd invite her too.

> **Esperávamos que eles tivessem esquecido.**
> We were hoping they had forgotten.

Notice the use of the pluperfect subjunctive in the last example to express something you hoped had happened before the time referred to.

60.2.2 *tomara que* + subjunctive

The expression **tomara que** 'let's hope (that)' may be used to express hope about the present, the future or the past.

> **Tomara que não chova.**
> Let's hope it doesn't rain.

> **Tomara que ela goste.**
> Let's hope she likes it.

> **Tomara que eles tenham chegado sãos e salvos.**
> Let's hope they got there safe and sound.

When expressing hope about the past, as in the last example, the preterite indicative is very often used in colloquial speech:

> **Tomara que eles chegaram sãos e salvos.** (*colloquial*)

60.3 Expressing hope in response to a question or statement

To express hope in response to a question or statement from someone else, you can use the following expressions:

> **Espero que sim.** 'I hope so.'

> **Espero que não.** 'I hope not.'

> **Espero.** 'I hope so.'

> **Tomara!** 'Let's hope so!'

> **Tomara que sim.** 'Let's hope so.'

> **Tomara que não.** 'Let's hope not.'

Examples:

> **Será que vamos poder ir também? – Espero que sim.**
> 'I wonder if we'll be able to go too?' – 'I hope so.'

> **Acho que ele esqueceu. – Espero que não.**
> 'I think he's forgotten.' – 'I hope not.'

Será que você tirou a nota que precisava? – Espero.
'Do you think you got the grade you needed?' – 'I hope so.'

Tenho certeza que você vai conseguir. – Tomara (que sim)!
'I'm sure you'll succeed.' – 'Let's hope so!'

Será que tem prova hoje? – Tomara que não.
'I wonder if we're having a test today?' – 'Let's hope not.'

61

Expressing sympathy

This chapter explains how to tell someone that you are sorry or glad about something that has happened to them, e.g. the loss of a job or a promotion.

61.1 Saying one is sorry about something

61.1.1 Set phrases

Que pena! 'What a pity!'

É uma pena. 'It's a pity.'

Sinto muito. 'I'm sorry (to hear that).'

É lamentável. 'It's a terrible shame.'

Lamento muito/profundamente. 'I am deeply saddened.'

Que horror! 'How awful!'

Que tristeza! 'How sad!'

Coitado/a! 'Poor thing!'

Coitado/a de você! 'Poor you!'

Coitada da Júlia! / Coitada da sua mãe! 'Poor Julia!' / 'Your poor mother!'

Coitadinho/a! 'Poor little thing!'

Sinto muito can be used as a response to any kind of sad news, including bereavement. **Lamento muito/profundamente** are more formal expressions of regret.

Coitado/a has to agree in gender (masculine or feminine) and number (singular or plural) with the person or persons referred to. On its own, it can refer to the person you are talking to or the person you are talking about, but you can specify by appending a noun or pronoun with the preposition **de**, as shown above. The diminutive **coitadinho/a** is used in response to less serious situations or when referring to a child or pet, for example. It can also be used sarcastically when you think the person is trying to win sympathy for no good reason.[1] Note that when the diminutive is used in informal speech, it is often abbreviated to **tadinho/a**.

NOTE   1   This usage gives rise to expressions such as **fazer-se de coitadinho** 'to play the victim'.

For condolences, use the set phrases:

> **Meus pêsames.** 'My condolences.'
>
> **Meus sentimentos (a você e à sua família).** 'My sympathies (to you and your family).'

61.1.2 *que pena/é uma pena* + infinitive; *que pena/é uma pena* + *que* + subjunctive/indicative

The expressions **que pena** 'what a pity' and **é uma pena** 'it's a pity' can be followed by an infinitive:

> **Que pena derrubar aquele prédio lindo!**
> What a pity to pull down that lovely building!
>
> **É uma pena jogar fora toda essa comida.**
> It's a pity to throw all this food away.

The infinitive may also be personal, i.e. have its own subject:

> **Que pena a Regina não ter vindo!**
> What a pity Regina didn't come!
>
> **É uma pena ele ser tão teimoso.**
> It's pity he's so stubborn.

Alternatively, both expressions can be followed by a **que** clause. In formal grammar, particularly in the written language, the **que** clause must contain a verb in the subjunctive, but in colloquial speech the indicative is normally used instead:

> **Que pena que a Regina não tenha vindo/não veio!**
> What a pity Regina didn't come!
>
> **É uma pena que ele seja/é tão teimoso.**
> It's a pity he's so stubborn.

When followed by a **que** clause, **é uma pena** is often shortened to just **pena que**:

> **Pena que eles não tenham conseguido/não conseguiram.**
> Pity they didn't succeed.

61.1.3 *sinto/sentimos muito por* + noun phrase

The verb **sentir** 'to be sorry' can be followed by the preposition **por** and a noun phrase:

> **Sinto muito pela morte do seu pai.**
> I'm so sorry about the death of your father.
>
> **Sentimos muito pelo acidente que você sofreu.**
> We're very sorry about your accident.
>
> **Sinto muito pelo que aconteceu com o seu filho.**
> I'm so sorry about what happened to your son.

Note that, when talking about someone's death, the preterite of **sentir** can be used without **por** to mean 'was/were sorry to hear about':

Senti muito a morte da sua tia.
I was sorry to hear about the death of your aunt.

▶ **16.1.1** (p. 150)

61.1.4   *sinto/sentimos muito* + personal infinitive; *sinto/sentimos muito* + *que* + subjunctive

The verb **sentir** can also be followed by a personal infinitive or a **que** clause with a subjunctive verb to express sympathy about a fact. The subjunctive construction sounds more formal, with the present subjunctive used to refer to the present or future and the perfect subjunctive to refer to a past event:

Sinto muito você estar doente.
Sinto muito que você esteja doente.
I'm very sorry (to hear) that you are ill.

Sentimos muito você ter perdido o emprego.
Sentimos muito que você tenha perdido o emprego.
We're very sorry (to hear) that you've lost your job.

61.1.5   *lamentar* + noun phrase/infinitive/personal infinitive; *lamentar* + *que* + subjunctive

The verb **lamentar** 'to regret' is used in the same grammatical constructions as **sentir** as an expression of concern, but it is more formal and perfunctory than **sentir** and tends to be used to express consternation rather than direct sympathy. Consider these examples:

Lamentamos muito seu descontentamento.
We are very sorry to hear that you are not satisfied.

Lamento saber sobre o ocorrido.
I am sorry to hear about what happened.

Lamentamos a chuva ter estragado a festa.
Lamentamos que a chuva tenha estragado a festa.
We regret that the rain spoilt the celebrations.

61.2   Saying one is glad about something

61.2.1   Set phrases

Que bom! 'I'm so glad!', 'That's good!'

Que ótimo! 'That's great!'

Que maravilha! 'That's fantastic!'

Ainda bem! 'Just as well!'

Menos mal! 'That's something at least!'

Fico contente que ... 'I'm glad ...', 'I'm pleased ...'

Que alívio! 'What a relief!'

É um alívio (que ...) 'It's a relief (that ...)'

Graças a Deus! 'Thank goodness!' 'Thank God (for that)!'

Ainda bem is used as a response to news that things turned out well in the end, while **menos mal** is the response to a positive development in an otherwise negative situation:

> **Bati com o carro, mas não me machuquei. – Ainda bem!**
> 'I crashed my car, but I wasn't hurt.' – 'Just as well!'

> **Ontem eu estava péssimo, mas hoje melhorei um pouco. – Menos mal!**
> 'Yesterday I was feeling awful, but today I'm a little better.' – 'That's something!'

All these expressions can be followed by a **que** clause. **Que bom!**, **Que ótimo!** and **Que maravilha!** may be followed by a subjunctive in the **que** clause, but the indicative is much more common in everyday speech. **Fico contente que ...** and **É um alívio que ...** are usually followed by the subjunctive, although the indicative is also heard in colloquial speech. The other expressions are followed by the indicative:

> **Que bom que você veio!/que você tenha vindo!**
> I'm so glad you came.

> **Que ótimo que você foi promovido!/que você tenha sido promovido!**
> It's great that you've been promoted!

> **Que maravilha que vocês vão casar!/que vocês casem!**
> It's fantastic that you're getting married!

> **Ainda bem que está tudo bem.**
> Just as well that everything is OK.

> **Umas cem pessoas ficaram desabrigadas por conta das enchentes. Menos mal que finalmente parou de chover.**
> Around a hundred people have been made homeless by the floods. It's something at least that it's finally stopped raining.

> **Fico contente que você tenha gostado/que você gostou.**
> I'm glad you liked/enjoyed it.

> **Que alívio que eles estão bem!**
> What a relief that they're OK!

> **É um alívio que ninguém tenha ficado ferido/que ninguém ficou ferido.**
> It's a relief that no one was injured.

> **Graças a Deus que ninguém ficou ferido.**
> Thank Goodness nobody was injured.

Que bom/ótimo/maravilha/alívio! and **É um alívio** can also be followed by an infinitive:

> **Que bom você estar aqui!**
> I'm so glad you're here!

> **Que maravilha ganhar um prêmio desses!**
> How fantastic to win a prize like that!

> **É um alívio ele ter voltado para casa.**
> It's a relief that he's come home.

62

Apologizing and expressing forgiveness

62.1 Apologizing

62.1.1 Set phrases

Desculpa. 'Sorry.'

Desculpe. 'Sorry.' (*formal*)

Desculpem. 'Sorry.' (*to more than one person*)

Desculpa/desculpe o atraso. 'Sorry I'm late.'

Desculpe a demora. 'Sorry to keep you waiting.' 'Sorry for the delay.'

Desculpa qualquer coisa. 'Sorry if I/we put you to any trouble.'

Perdão. 'Sorry.'

(Me) perdoa. 'Forgive me.'

Sinto muito. 'I'm very sorry.'

Foi mal. 'Sorry.' 'My bad.' (*colloquial*)

Foi sem querer. 'I didn't mean to.' 'It was an accident.'

Não fiz/foi por mal. 'I didn't mean any harm.'

Não (me) leve a mal. 'Don't take it the wrong way.' 'Don't take it to heart.'

Desculpa/e/em and **Perdão** can be used as polite ways of apologizing to strangers, e.g. for bumping into someone. They can also be used for more serious apologies to people you know. **Sinto muito** is used for less spontaneous apologies, usually for something quite serious. **Foi mal** is a more colloquial expression of apology.

Desculpa qualquer coisa is a polite formula, usually said when leaving someone's house after a visit, or on parting when you think that the other person may have been inconvenienced or embarrassed in some way.

▶ **Chapter 21** (p. 196)

62.1.2 | Excuse/reason for the apology

The expressions above are often followed, or sometimes preceded, by a sentence giving an excuse or reason for the apology:

> **Desculpa, sentei no seu lugar.**
> Sorry, I sat in your place.

> **Não aceitamos cartão, senhor. Desculpe.**
> We don't take credit cards, sir. Sorry.

> **Ih, pisei no seu pé. Foi mal, cara.**
> Oops, I stepped on your toe. Sorry about that, mate/buddy.

> **Sinto muito, mas não vou poder ir com você.**
> I'm really sorry, but I won't be able to go with you.

62.1.3 | *Desculpa / Desculpe / Desculpem* + infinitive

▶ **Chapter 21** (p. 196)

The various set forms of **desculpar** can be followed by an infinitive in sentences such as 'Sorry to bother you', 'Sorry I woke you up'. This infinitive can have its own subject when it is necessary to specify:

> **Desculpe incomodar, mas posso pedir uma informação?**
> Sorry to bother you, but can I ask you something?

> **Desculpa eu ter te acordado.**
> Sorry I woke you up.

> **Desculpem nós termos atrasado tanto.**
> Sorry we are so late.

62.1.4 | *Sinto muito* + infinitive

▶ **16.1.1** (p. 150)

Sinto muito is also followed by an infinitive:

> **Sinto muito não poder te emprestar o dinheiro.**
> I'm really sorry I can't lend you the money.

> **Sentimos muito não estar aí com você.**
> We're sorry for not being there with you.

It can be a perfect infinitive when referring to something in the past:

> **Sinto muito não ter te falado antes.**
> I'm really sorry I didn't tell you before.

62.1.5 | Formal apologies

A more formal way of apologizing is to use the expression **pedir desculpas por . . .** 'to apologize for . . .':

> **Peço desculpas pelo meu comportamento.**
> I apologize for my behaviour.

Pedimos desculpas pelo transtorno.
We apologize for the inconvenience.

Pedimos-lhes as mais sinceras desculpas.
Please accept our sincerest apologies.

In formal writing, such as business correspondence, the verb **lamentar** may be used instead of **sentir**:

Lamentamos informar que, por motivos que fogem ao nosso controle, . . .
We regret to inform you that, for reasons beyond our control, . . .

62.2 Expressing forgiveness

To grant forgiveness, the following set expressions may be used:

Tudo bem. 'It's fine.' 'It's all right.'

Não foi nada. 'It was nothing.'

Nada. 'It's OK.'

Está bom. 'It's OK.'

Não importa. 'It doesn't matter.'

Não tem importância. 'It doesn't matter.'

Não tem problema. / Sem problema. 'No problem.'

Não faz mal. 'Never mind.' 'No harm done.'

Imagina. 'Don't be silly.'

Tranquilo. 'It's cool.'

Relaxa. 'Relax.' 'Don't worry about it.'

Deixa pra lá. 'Never mind.' 'Forget about it.'

Esqueça. 'Forget it.'

63

Expressing fear or worry

Common expressions of fear

The idea of being or getting frightened or worried is normally expressed in Portuguese using the following words and phrases:

>   **estar com medo/ter medo** 'to be scared/afraid/frightened'
>
>   **ficar com medo** 'to get scared/afraid/frightened'
>
>   **dar medo** 'to be scary/frightening'
>
>   **estar assustado** 'to be frightened'
>
>   **ficar assustado/assustar-se** 'to get frightened'
>
>   **estar preocupado** 'to be worried'
>
>   **ficar preocupado** 'to get worried'
>
>   **preocupar-se (com . . .)** 'to worry (about . . .)'.

estar com/ter medo (*de* + noun/pronoun/infinitive)

The difference between **estar com medo** and **ter medo** is that the first expresses a momentary fear while the second expresses a general fear. Both may be followed by the preposition **de** and a noun, pronoun or infinitive referring to the thing feared:

>   **Estou com medo de pular na água.**
>   I'm scared to jump into the water.
>
>   **Tenho medo de cachorro.**
>   I'm afraid of dogs.
>
>   **Você tem medo de avião?**
>   Are you afraid of flying?
>
>   **Você não está com medo?**
>   Aren't you frightened?
>
>   **Não tenho medo de morrer.**
>   I'm not afraid of dying.

These expressions can also be followed by a personal infinitive:

>   **Estou com muito medo de ele descobrir a verdade.**
>   I'm very afraid of him finding out the truth.

> **Você não tem medo de os seus filhos se envolverem com drogas?**
> Aren't you afraid of your children getting into drugs?

> **Estou com medo de eles terem se perdido.**
> I'm afraid that they may have got lost.

63.1.2 *ficar com medo* (*de* + noun/pronoun/infinitive)

The phrase **ficar com medo** highlights the transition from not being scared to being scared, e.g. in response to something that happens. When talking about the present, it is equivalent to 'to get scared/afraid/frightened' in English, but when talking about the past or the future, it is often equivalent to 'to be scared/afraid/frightened':

> **Quando escurece, fico com medo.**
> When it gets dark I get scared.

> **Depois de ser assaltado, ele ficou com medo de sair de casa.**
> After being mugged, he was afraid to go out of the house.

> **Você acha que vai ficar com medo?**
> Do you think you'll be frightened?

63.1.3 *estar com/ficar com/ter medo* (*de*) *que* + subjunctive

These constructions can be followed by a **que** clause meaning 'to be scared/afraid/frightened that . . .'. The verb in the **que** clause has to be in the subjunctive: the present subjunctive referring to present or future time and the imperfect subjunctive when the whole sentence is set in the past:

> **Eles estavam com medo de que os ladrões voltassem.**
> They were afraid the thieves would come back.

> **Temos medo que os nossos filhos sofram preconceito.**
> We are afraid that our children may suffer prejudice.

This is a slightly more formal alternative to the personal infinitive construction explained in **63.1.1**.

63.1.4 *dar medo* (*de* + noun/pronoun/infinitive)

The expression **dar medo** 'to be scary/frightening' can have a specific or non-specific subject:

> **Aquele cachorro dá medo.**
> That dog is frightening.

> **Dá medo olhar para baixo.**
> It's scary to look down.

> **O avião balançou muito? – É, deu medo.**
> 'Was the flight very bumpy?' – 'Yes, it was scary.'

The pronouns **me** and **te** may be used to specify who is frightened:

> **Não te deu medo?**
> Weren't you scared? / Didn't it scare you?

> **Só de pensar nisso me dá medo.**
> It frightens me just to think about it.

The expression **dar medo de** + noun/pronoun/infinitive means 'to make one scared of/ to do', 'to put one off (doing)':

> **Esse tipo de notícia dá medo de viajar.**
> That type of news story puts you off travelling.

> **Aquela experiência me deu medo de cachorro.**
> That experience made me frightened of dogs.

63.1.5 *estar assustado; ficar assustado/assustar-se*

The word **assustado** means 'frightened' in the sense of 'startled', 'shaken' 'alarmed', a more physical feeling of fear:

> **Os moradores do bairro estão assustados com o aumento da criminalidade.**
> Residents of the neighbourhood are alarmed at the increase in crime.

> **Fiquei assustado quando ouvi o grito.**
> I got a fright when I heard the scream.

> **Eu me assustei quando eu vi o quanto ele envelheceu.**
> I got a fright when I saw how much he had aged.

The expression **ficar assustado** is slightly more informal than **assustar-se**, but the meaning is the same.

63.1.6 *estar/ficar preocupado*

The phrases **estar/ficar preocupado** 'to be/get worried' can be followed by the preposition **com**:

> **Estou preocupado com o Marcelo.**
> I'm worried about Marcelo.

> **Minha mãe fica preocupada se eu não ligar.**
> My mum gets worried if I don't call.

> **Ele estava muito preocupado.**
> He was very worried.

63.1.7 *preocupar-se*

The expression **preocupar-se** 'to be worried, to worry' can also be followed by the preposition **com**:

> **Não se/te preocupe.**
> Don't worry.

> **Você não precisava se preocupar.**
> You needn't have worried.

> **Não se preocupem comigo.**
> Don't worry about me.

63.2 Other ways of expressing fear

The following sentences illustrate other common expressions used to convey the idea of fear:

> **O meu medo é que eles se percam.**
> What I'm afraid of is that they'll get lost. / My fear is that . . .

> **A nossa preocupação é que ele dê para trás.**
> What we're worried about is that he'll back out. / Our worry is that . . .

> **Dizem que a sucuri consegue engolir uma pessoa. – Que medo!**
> 'They say that anacondas can swallow people.' – 'Scary!'

> **Eu estava morrendo de medo.**
> I was really scared.

> **Morro de medo de aranha.**
> I'm petrified of spiders.

> **Levei/tomei um susto!**
> I got such a fright!

> **Que susto!**
> That/You made me jump! / That/You gave me such a fright!

> **Você me deu um susto!**
> You frightened the life out of me!

> **Tenho pavor de altura.**
> I'm terrified of heights.

> **Eles ficaram apavorados.**
> They were terrified.

63.3 More formal expressions of fear

63.3.1 *receio, receoso*

The more formal word **receio** refers to fear, concern or misgivings about what may happen in the future. It commonly occurs in the expressions **estar com receio de** and **ter receio de**, both of which may be followed by a noun, pronoun, infinitive or **que** clause containing a verb in the subjunctive. Use **estar com** to refer to a momentary concern and **ter com** to refer to an ongoing one:

> **Temos receio do que os outros pensam de nós.**
> We are concerned about what others think of us.

> **Estamos com receio de montar um negócio e não dar certo.**
> We're afraid of starting a business and it not working out.

> **Estou com receio de que o financiamento seja negado.**
> I'm afraid the mortgage will be declined.

The related adjective **receoso** 'concerned, fearful' may also be used after the verbs **estar** and **ficar** and followed by the same constructions as above:

> **Depois da notícia do acidente, fiquei receoso de pegar avião.**
> After the news about the crash, I was apprehensive about flying.

Estamos receosos de que não concluam a obra a tempo.
We're concerned they won't complete the construction work in time.

temer

The verb **temer** 'to fear' can be followed by a noun, pronoun, infinitive or **que** clause with a verb in the subjunctive:

Os ilhéus temem o mar.
The islanders fear the sea.

Ele não teme ser preso.
He doesn't fear being arrested.

Temo que a crise econômica mal tenha começado.
I fear the economic crisis may hardly have started.

Note also the expression **temer por** 'to fear for':

Os refugiados temiam por suas vidas.
The refugees feared for their lives.

64

Expressing gratitude

Expressing gratitude

Set phrases

The following are the words and phrases most commonly used to express gratitude in Portuguese:

Obrigado/a. 'Thank you.' 'Thanks.'

Muito obrigado/a. 'Thank you very much.'

Muitíssimo obrigado/a. 'Thank you very much indeed.'

Obrigadão. 'Thanks a lot.'

Valeu. 'Cheers.' 'Thanks.'

Agradeço/Agradecemos. 'I/We thank you.'

Agradecido/a. 'Much obliged.'

É muita gentileza sua. 'It's very kind of you.'

É muito gentil da sua parte. 'It's very kind of you.'

Te agradeço muito. 'I'm very grateful to you.'

Agradeço muito a você/vocês todos. 'I'm very grateful to you/you all.'

Agradeço do fundo do meu coração. 'I thank you from the bottom of my heart.'

Não sei como agradecer. 'I don't know how to thank you.'

Só tenho que agradecer. 'All I can do is to say thank you.'

Meus/Nossos agradecimentos (a . . .) 'My/Our thanks (to . . .)'

Grato. (*in correspondence*) 'Many thanks.'

Obrigadão and **valeu** are colloquial expressions, mainly used by younger people.

Obrigado/a por **+ noun/infinitive**

Obrigado/a is by far the most common word for 'Thank you' or 'Thanks', used in both formal and informal contexts. The masculine form **obrigado** is used by males and the feminine form **obrigada** by women. It can be followed by the preposition **por**:

Obrigado pelo seu e-mail.
Thank you for your e-mail.

> **Obrigado pela presença.**
> Thank you for coming. (*said to guests attending an event*)

The preposition **por** can also introduce an infinitive. Very often this is a perfect infinitive referring to a past action:

> **Obrigado por ter ligado.**
> Thanks for calling.

> **Muito obrigado por me apoiar sempre.**
> Thank you very much for always supporting me.

The infinitive may also be personalized with **você** or **vocês**:

> **Obrigado por você ter me ajudado tanto.**
> Thank you for helping me so much.

> **Obrigado por vocês terem montado essa surpresa para mim.**
> Thank you for arranging this surprise for me.

64.1.3 *agradecer*

The verb **agradecer** 'to thank, be grateful, appreciate' sounds more formal as an expression of thanks. It is also much used in the written language. More often than not, the person to whom the thanks are addressed is not explicitly mentioned, since it is implicit that the thanks are addressed to the listener or reader. The thing you are expressing gratitude for either follows the verb immediately or is introduced by the preposition **por**. The construction with **por** is less formal than that without:

> **Agradecemos a/pela ajuda.**
> We are grateful for your help.

> **Agradeço o/pelo carinho.**
> I appreciate your warmth and affection.

> **Quero agradecer o excelente artigo sobre a saúde pública.**
> I would like to thank you for the excellent article on public healthcare.

> **Agradecemos sua carta de 9 de novembro último.**
> Thank you for your letter dated November 9th.

The person to whom thanks is being given is introduced with the preposition **a**:

> **Agradeço aos meus pais o/pelo apoio que me deram.**
> I am grateful to my parents for the support they have given me.

> **Agradeço a todos (por) esse lindo presente.**
> I am grateful to you all for this lovely present.

To say 'I thank you for doing . . .' with a following infinitive, three constructions are possible: **agradecer** + **a** + noun/pronoun + infinitive, **agradecer** + **a** + noun/pronoun + **por** + infinitive, **agradecer** + **por** + noun/pronoun + infinitive. The infinitive will very often be a perfect infinitive referring to a past action:

> **Agradeço a você ter me convidado.**
> **Agradeço a você por ter me convidado.**

Agradeço por você ter me convidado.
I thank you for inviting me. / I appreciate you inviting me.

Of these three sentences, the first is the most formal and the third the least formal.

Note that **agradecer** can also translate 'to say thank you' in sentences such as:

Mandei umas flores para agradecer.
I sent some flowers to say thank you.

Agradeça aos seus pais por mim/da minha parte.
Say thank you to your parents for/from me.

Ele nem agradeceu.
He didn't even say thank you.

64.1.4 Expressions of gratitude in formal correspondence

There are a number of set phrases used to express gratitude in formal correspondence:

Agradeço/agradecemos a sua carta de 17 de maio último.
Thank you for your letter of May 17th.

Grato por sua carta solicitando informações sobre nossos produtos.
Thank you for your letter requesting information about our products.

Agradeceria/agradeceríamos se me/nos enviasse(m) a atual lista de preços.
I/we would be grateful if you would send me/us the current price list.

Agradeço/agradecemos desde já.
Thanking you in advance.

Agradeço/agradecemos a atençao.
Thanking you for your attention.

64.2 Responding to an expression of gratitude

In English, it is not considered necessary to respond to thanks, although, depending on the individual speaker and the circumstances, people say things such as 'You're welcome', 'That's OK', 'Don't mention it'. Brazilians usually say something in response to thanks, however brief. The following is a list of the most commonly used expressions:

Nada. 'OK.' 'That's OK.'

De nada. / Por nada. 'You're welcome.'

Não tem de quê. 'Don't mention it.' (*formal, rather old-fashioned*)

Imagina! 'Don't be silly!' 'No need to thank me!'

Obrigado/a eu. 'Thank *you*.' (*returning thanks*)

Eu que agradeço. 'It's me who should be thanking you.'

Você não precisa me agradecer. 'There's no need to thank me.'

V

The language
of persuasion

65

Giving advice and making suggestions

Giving advice and making suggestions that do not involve the speaker

65.1.1 *se eu fosse você* + conditional/imperfect/imperfect of *ir* + infinitive

The phrase **se eu fosse você, . . . / se fosse você, eu . . . / eu, se fosse você, . . .** 'if I were you' is one of the most common expressions for giving advice and making suggestions that do not involve the speaker. The advice itself is expressed using the conditional (rather formal), the imperfect (informal) or the imperfect of the verb **ir** 'to go' followed by an infinitive (neutral register):

> **Se fosse você, eu tentaria/tentava/ia tentar falar com ele.**
> If I were you, I'd try talking to him.

> **Se eu fosse você, não iria/ia.**[1]
> If I were you, I wouldn't go.

> **Eu, se fosse você, arranjaria/arranjava/ia arranjar outro emprego.**
> If I were you, I'd find another job.

Alternative expressions with a similar meaning and construction are:

> **No seu lugar, eu . . .** *or*
> **Se eu estivesse no seu lugar, . . . / Se estivesse no seu lugar, eu. . . / Eu, se estivesse no seu lugar, . . .**
> If I were in your situation . . . / If it was me, . . .

Examples:

> **No seu lugar, eu não o perdoaria/o perdoava/ia perdoá-lo.**
> If it was me, I wouldn't forgive him.

> **Eu, se estivesse no seu lugar, tomaria/tomava/ia tomar um empréstimo.**
> If it was me, I'd take out a loan.

NOTE | 1   When the main verb is **ir** 'to go', the **ir** + infinitive construction is obviously impossible.

481

65.1.2 *Por que você(s) não . . . ?* + present

Por que você(s) não . . . ? 'Why don't you . . . ?' is another common expression used for giving advice and making suggestions:

> **Por que você não compra um computador novo?**
> Why don't you buy a new computer?

> **Por que vocês não assistem um filme?**
> Why don't you watch a movie?

> **Por que você não volta na terça?**
> Why don't you go/come back on Tuesday?

65.1.3 *E se você(s) . . . ?* + future/imperfect subjunctive

E se você(s) . . . ? 'What if you . . . ?' can be followed by a future subjunctive to make a straightforward suggestion or by an imperfect subjunctive to make a more tentative one:

> **E se você me mandar o arquivo por e-mail?**
> What if you e-mail me the file?

> **E se vocês mudassem para mais perto da sua filha?**
> What if you moved/were to move closer to where your daughter lives?

65.1.4 Imperative

▶ **Chapter 21** (p. 196)

The imperative can be used to give advice and suggestions. In speech you will nearly always use the familiar imperative to give advice, but the formal imperative may be encountered in written advice and suggestions:

> **Compra! Está muito barato.**
> Buy it! It's really cheap.

> **Meu primo é advogado. Liga para ele!**
> My cousin is a lawyer. Give him a call!

> **Faça o check-in online e economize tempo.** (*written*)
> Check in online and save time.

65.1.5 *Você(s) podia(m) . . .* + infinitive

Você(s) podia(m) . . . 'You could . . .'. This is the imperfect of **poder** used in place of the conditional. The conditional **poderia(m)** could also be used, but it would sound rather formal.

> **Você podia usar o terceiro quarto como escritório.**
> You could use the third bedroom as an office.

> **Vocês podiam alugar um carro e fazer uns passeios.**
> You could rent a car and go on some trips.

65.1.6 *Você(s) deve(m)/devia(m) . . . + infinitive*

Você(s) deve(m) . . . 'You must/should . . .' expresses a forceful recommendation:

Você deve procurar um médico.
You must/should see a doctor.

Você(s) devia(m) . . . 'You ought to . . .' (imperfect for conditional) expresses a less forceful suggestion. Note that the conditional **deveria(m)** could also be used here, but would sound rather formal.

Vocês deviam conhecer o Nordeste.
You ought to/should visit the northeast of Brazil.

Você não devia deixar sua carteira jogada na mesa.
You shouldn't leave your wallet lying around on the table.

65.1.7 *Você tem/vocês têm que . . . + infinitive; você(s) tinha(m) que . . . + infinitive*

Você tem/vocês têm que . . . 'You must/have to . . .' is used in colloquial speech to make a strong recommendation:

Se vocês forem a Salvador, têm que comer acarajé.
If you go to Salvador, you must have *acarajé* (bean fritters).

Você tem que conhecer a minha prima, ela é uma figura.
You must meet my cousin, she's a real character.

The recommendation can be made less emphatic by using the imperfect **tinha(m) que**:

Você tinha que perguntar para o meu pai. Ele deve saber.
You ought to ask my dad. He should know.

65.1.8 *Você precisa/vocês precisam . . . + infinitive; você(s) precisava(m) . . . + infinitive*

The verb **precisar** 'must, need to' can also be used to make a strong recommendation:

Você precisa conhecer minha amiga, Júlia.
You must meet my friend, Júlia.

Again, the imperfect can be used to make a less emphatic recommendation:

Vocês precisavam transformar esse quarto em escritório.
You ought to turn this bedroom into an office.

65.1.9 *É melhor (você/vocês) . . . + infinitive*

É melhor . . . 'It's better/best to . . .' can be followed by a simple infinitive when giving general advice that also applies to the person addressed:

É melhor ir de táxi.
It's better to go by taxi.

É melhor não deixar objetos de valor no quarto.
It's best not to leave valuables in the room.

But a personal infinitive can also be used after **É melhor** when giving specific rather than general advice:

> **É melhor você pedir desculpas.**
> It's best if you apologize. / You'd best apologize.

> **É melhor vocês deixarem as coisas aqui.**
> You'd best leave your stuff here.

65.1.10 *É bom (você/vocês) . . . + infinitive*

É bom . . . 'It's a good idea to . . .' can be followed by a simple infinitive when giving a general recommendation that also applies to the person addressed:

> **É bom fechar as janelas antes de sair.**
> It's a good idea to close the windows before going out.

> **É bom você salvar tudo na nuvem.**
> It's a good idea to save everything to the cloud.

65.1.11 *Aconselho você(s) a + infinitive*

Aconselho você(s) a . . . 'I (would) advise you to . . .' is a slightly more formal way of giving advice:

> **Aconselho você a não andar de bicicleta sem capacete.**
> I advise you not to ride a bike without a helmet.

> **Aconselho vocês a lerem as instruções com muita atenção.**
> I advise you to read the instructions very carefully.

65.1.12 *Sugiro que você(s) . . . + subjunctive*

Sugiro que você(s) . . . 'I (would) suggest you . . .', from the verb **sugerir**, is followed by the present subjunctive:

> **Sugiro que você volte amanhã.**
> I suggest you come back tomorrow.

> **Sugiro que vocês não deixem as janelas abertas.**
> I would suggest you don't leave the windows open.

Sugiro can be followed by an infinitive when making a general suggestion:

> **Sugiro fazer uma lista das pendências.**
> I suggest making a list of the outstanding items.

65.2 Suggesting a course of action involving the speaker

65.2.1 *Vamos + infinitive*

Vamos . . . followed by the infinitive means 'Let's . . .' when pronounced with statement intonation:

> **Vamos pedir uma pizza.**
> Let's order a pizza.

Vamos descansar um pouco.
Let's take a little rest.

When pronounced with question intonation, **Vamos . . .** is equivalent to 'Shall we . . . ?':

Vamos pedir uma pizza?
Shall we order a pizza?

Vamos descansar um pouco?
Shall we take a little rest?

65.2.2 First person plural of the present subjunctive

In more formal style, especially in writing, the first person plural of the present subjunctive is used to make a suggestion, equivalent in meaning and formality to the English 'Let us . . .':

Vejamos alguns exemplos.
Let us look at some examples.

Oremos.
Let us pray.

65.2.3 *Por que não . . . ?* + present

Por que não . . . ? may used with a first person plural verb or, more colloquially, with **a gente** and a third person singular verb to make a suggestion involving the speaker:

Por que não dividimos um prato?
Why don't we share a main course?

Por que é que a gente não chama o Fábio?
Why don't we invite Fábio?

65.2.4 *Podíamos/A gente podia . . .* + infinitive

Podíamos . . . or, more colloquially, **A gente podia . . .** 'We could . . .' is also used to make a suggestion:

A gente podia jantar fora.
We could go out for dinner.

Podíamos ir de táxi.
We could go by taxi.

65.2.5 *Devíamos/Tínhamos que . . . ; A gente devia/tinha que . . .* + infinitive

Devíamos/Tínhamos que . . . or, more colloquially, **A gente devia/tinha que . . .** is used for 'We should . . .':

A gente tinha que ir ao supermercado.
We ought to go to the supermarket.

Devíamos contratar um recepcionista.
We should hire a receptionist.

In more formal register, the conditional **deveríamos** or **teríamos que** may be used in place of the imperfect.

65.2.6 *Que tal nós . . . / Que tal a gente . . . + infinitive*

Que tal nós . . . ? or, more colloquially, **Que tal a gente . . . ?** 'What about if we . . . ?', 'How about we . . . ?' is followed by an infinitive. Remember that the infinitive takes the ending **-mos** after **nós**:

> **Que tal nós contratarmos um serviço de bufê?**
> What about if we hire a caterer?

> **Que tal a gente ir ao shopping?**
> How about we go to the mall?

65.2.7 *O que é que você acha de nós/da gente + infinitive; O que é que você acha se nós/a gente + subjunctive*

O que é que você acha de nós/da gente . . . ? 'What about us . . . ?' is followed by an infinitive. Remember that, after **nós**, the infinitive takes the ending **-mos**:

> **O que é que você acha da gente comer peixe hoje?**
> What about us having fish today?

> **O que é que você acha de nós convidarmos a Rita?**
> What about us inviting Rita?

O que é que você acha se nós/a gente . . . ? 'What do you think if . . . ?' is followed by a future subjunctive to express a straightforward suggestion and by an imperfect subjunctive to express a more tentative one:

> **O que é que você acha se nós pedirmos uma garrafa de vinho?**
> What do you think about ordering a bottle of wine?

> **O que é que você acha se a gente pintasse o quarto de verde?**
> What do you think about painting the bedroom green?

65.2.8 *E se . . . ? + subjunctive*

E se . . . ? 'What if . . . ?' is followed by a future subjunctive to express a straightforward suggestion and by an imperfect subjunctive to express a more tentative one:

> **E se mudarmos a mesa de lugar?**
> What if we move the table somewhere else?

> **E se a gente pegasse um táxi?**
> What if we took a cab?

65.2.9 *É melhor nós/a gente . . . + infinitive*

É melhor nós/a gente . . . 'It's better/best if we . . .' is followed by an infinitive. Remember that, after **nós**, the infinitive takes the ending **-mos**:

> **É melhor a gente ir à pé.**
> It's best if we walk.

> **É melhor nós procurarmos um advogado.**
> We'd better get a lawyer.

65.3   Asking for advice and suggestions

65.3.1   Question word + present tense

This is the simplest way of asking for advice or suggestions, equivalent to the English 'question word + shall/should I . . . ?':

> **O que é que eu faço?**
> What shall I do?

> **Onde eu coloco os copos?**
> Where should I put the glasses?

> **Quem é que a gente convida?**
> Who shall we invite?

65.3.2   Question word + *poder* + infinitive

> **O que é que eu posso fazer?**
> What can I do?

> **Como é que eu posso negar sem ofendê-los?**
> How can I say no without offending them?

65.3.3   Question word + conditional/imperfect/imperfect of *ir* + infinitive

> **O que você faria/fazia/ia fazer?**
> What would you do?

> **Qual você compraria/comprava/ia comprar?**
> Which one would you buy?

Such questions can be expanded with the phrases **se fosse você** 'if it was you' or **no meu lugar** 'in my place':

> **Como você responderia/respondia/ia responder a isso se fosse você?**
> How would you answer that if it was you?

> **Qual você escolheria/escolhia/ia escolher no meu lugar?**
> Which one would you choose in my place?

65.3.4   *aconselhar, recomendar, sugerir*

The verbs **aconselhar** 'to advise', **recomendar** 'to recommend' and **sugerir** 'to suggest' may be used to ask for advice or suggestions:

> **O que você me aconselha?**
> What do you advise me to do?

> **O que você me recomenda?**
> What you recommend I do?

> **O que você sugere (que eu faça)?**
> What do you suggest (I do)?

66

Making requests

Common expressions of request

por favor; por gentileza; favor

The expression **por favor** means 'please' when making a request. In making requests to strangers it is used as in English, but in making informal requests to family and friends, it is not normally used, and using it in such situations can sound overbearing and insistent. Instead, the softening effect of 'please' in English is rendered by means of a questioning intonation (see **66.1.2**):

> **Aguarde na linha, por favor.** (*to a stranger*)
> Hold the line, please.

> **Me passa o sal?** (*to friend or family*)
> Will you pass me the salt, please?

A more formal and polite variant of **por favor** is **por gentileza**:

> **Só um momento, por gentileza.**
> Just a moment, please.

> **Qual o nome da senhora, por gentileza?**
> What's your name please, madam?

Favor + infinitive is equivalent to the English 'Kindly . . .', 'Please . . .' and is usually seen on signs:

> **Favor não fumar.**
> Please do not smoke.

> **Favor fechar a porta.**
> Kindly close the door.

Present tense used to express a request

A request can be expressed using a question in the present tense. This is equivalent to the English 'Will/Would you . . . ?' and can be used in most situations. When addressing strangers it is normally accompanied by **por favor** 'please' (see **66.1.1**):

> **Você leva essa sacola?**
> Will you carry this bag?

> **Você me ajuda um pouco?**
> Would you help me a minute?

O senhor assina aqui, por favor?
Would you sign here, please, sir?

66.1.3 Imperative

▶ **Chapter 21** (p. 196)

As in English, using the imperative is a fairly abrupt way of making a request, even if it is accompanied by **por favor** 'please'. Generally speaking, the familiar imperative is used in speech with people you would address as **você**, while the formal imperative is used with people you would address as **o senhor/a senhora**, e.g. a customer, and always in writing, e.g. on notices:

Para com isso!
Stop that!

Me dá esse copo!
Give me that glass!

Certifique-se de que a sua poltrona está na posição vertical.
Make sure your seat is in the upright position. (*announcement or notice*)

Since the familiar imperative is identical to the third person singular of the present tense, there is no difference in form between requests expressed in the familiar imperative and those expressed in the present tense, as shown in **66.1.2**, except that the latter may include the subject pronoun **você**. The difference is in the intonation, which can range from a brusque imperative tone to a polite question intonation depending on the circumstances:

Para aqui!
Stop here!

(Você) para aqui?
Will you stop here?

66.1.4 *faça/faz o favor de* + infinitive

The expression **faça/faz o favor de** + infinitive 'kindly . . .' is used to make polite requests, usually to strangers. It can have a connotation of impatience when used in speech:

Faça o favor de usar o e-mail informado no anúncio.
Kindly use the e-mail address given in the advertisement.

Garçom, faça/faz o favor de passar um pano nessa mesa.
Waiter, do you think you could give this table a wipe?

66.1.5 *(Você) pode . . . ?* + infinitive

(Você) pode . . . ? is used to mean 'Can/Could you . . . ?':

Pode vir aqui um pouco?
Can you come here a minute?

Pode dar um recado para ela?
Could you give her a message?

Você pode me deixar na rodoviária?
Can you drop me at the bus station?

66.1.6 *(Você) poderia ... ?* + infinitive

The conditional **(Você) poderia ... ?** 'Could you ... ?' is used in more formal situations where a greater degree of politeness is called for. As this expression is normally used to address strangers, the pronoun **você** is usually left out:

> **Poderia me passar a Contabilidade?**
> Could you put me through to the Accounts department?

> **Poderia me dizer de onde sai o ônibus para Parati?**
> Could you tell me where the bus to Parati goes from?

66.1.7 *Você se importa/incomoda de ... ?* + infinitive

Você se importa/incomoda de ... ? 'Would you mind ... ?' is followed by the infinitive:

> **Você se importa de me mandar as fotos por e-mail?**
> Would you mind sending me the pictures by e-mail?

> **Você se incomoda de me explicar como funciona?**
> Would you mind explaining to me how it works?

Note that **importar** seems to be more common than **incomodar** in this usage.

66.1.8 Formal written requests

There are a number of formulae used for making requests in formal contexts, especially in business correspondence. These usually involve the verbs **pedir** 'to ask', **solicitar** 'to request' or **agradecer** 'to be grateful, to appreciate'. The examples below are typical of such requests:

> **Pedimos a gentileza de nos enviarem seu catálogo mais recente.**
> Please send us your latest catalogue.

> **Solicitamos o obséquio de nos informarem os termos e condições de frete.**
> Please advise us of your shipping terms.

> **Agradeceria se me enviasse seu material de vendas.**
> I would be grateful if you would send me your sales literature.

67

Giving directions, instructions and orders

67.1 ## Giving directions and instructions

67.1.1 ### The present tense

▶ **15.3** (p. 144)

In the spoken language, directions and instructions are often given using the present tense, with or without the subject pronoun **você**:

> **Você continua reto até o segundo sinal e aí vira à esquerda.**
> You keep going straight as far as the second set of traffic lights and then turn left.

> **Você desce na próxima estação.**
> You get off at the next station.

> **Você paga no caixa e depois entrega a ficha no balcão.**
> You pay at the cash desk and then hand over the ticket at the counter.

07.1.2 ### The imperative

▶ **Chapter 21** (p. 196)

The familiar imperative has the same form as the third person singular of the present tense, so directions given in the imperative are the same as those given in the present except for the inclusion of the pronoun **você**:

> **Entra aqui à direita.**
> Turn right here.

> **Desce em frente à Prefeitura.**
> Get off outside the Town Hall.

> **Vai na padaria e compra oito pães.**
> Go to the bakery and buy eight bread rolls.

The formal imperative may occasionally be used when giving directions to customers and strangers verbally, but it is always used in written instructions:

> **Siga em frente até o segundo semáforo e depois vire à esquerda.**
> Continue straight ahead until the second set of traffic lights and then turn left.

> **Desembarque na Estação Sé e faça transferência para Linha 3.**
> Get off at Sé station and change onto Line 3.

Não perca o seu bilhete.
Do not lose your ticket.

Feche todos os aplicativos e reinicie o computador.
Close all applications and restart the computer.

67.1.3 *ter que* + infinitive

Spoken directions and instructions sometimes contain the expression **ter que** 'to have to'. Remember that, in colloquial speech, the third person singular can be used without an explicit subject to give a general instruction:

Você tem que pagar no caixa e depois pedir no balcão.
You have to pay at the cash desk and then order at the counter.

Tem que pegar senha e esperar o número.
You have to take a ticket and wait for your number.

67.1.4 The infinitive

The infinitive is often used as an alternative to the formal imperative in written instructions such as operating manuals, recipes, etc.:

Abrir o registro de gás e regular o botão de controle de chama de acordo com a necessidade.
Turn on the gas supply and adjust the flame control knob as required.

Colocar o feijão numa bacia grande e deixar de molho por 3 horas.
Place the beans in a large basin and leave to soak for 3 hours.

67.2 Giving orders

67.2.1 The imperative or the present tense

▶ **15.3** (p. 144); **Chapter 21** (p. 196)

As with directions and instructions, orders may be given in the imperative or using the present tense.

Sai daqui!
Get out!

Cala a boca!
Shut up!

Me larga!
Let go of me!

Você vai embora daqui agora!
You get out of here now!

Spoken orders are normally given using the familiar imperative, as in the examples above. The formal imperative is encountered in written orders, such as:

Pare
Stop (*on a road sign*)

Retire seu cartão.
Remove your card.

67.2.2   The future tense with *ir* + infinitive

The future tense formed with the verb **ir** 'to go' + infinitive can also be used to give an order:

> **Você não vai mais sair com esse rapaz, ouviu?**
> You will not go out with that boy again, do you hear?

> **Você vai me obedecer!**
> You will do as you're told!

67.2.3   *Vê se você* + present tense; *Trata/Trate de* + infinitive

Vê se você . . . 'Make sure you . . .' is a colloquial expression used to give orders:

> **Vê se você não volta tarde.**
> Make sure you don't get home late.

> **Vê se você arruma esse quarto já!**
> Get this room tidied up now!

Trata/Trate de + infinitive is a slightly more formal expression with a similar meaning 'See to it that . . .':

> **Trata de cortar esse cabelo!**
> See to it that you get that hair of yours cut!

> **Trate de resolver isso o mais rápido possível.**
> See to it that you get this sorted out as soon as possible.

68

Making an offer or invitation and accepting or declining

68.1 ## Making an offer or invitation

68.1.1 ### *convidar, pagar*

Invitations can be made with the verb **convidar** 'to invite':

> **Quero convidar você para jantar lá em casa.**
> I'd like to invite you to dinner at our house.

> **Não precisa pagar nada. Convido você. / Você está convidado.**
> You don't need to pay anything. It's my treat.

An offer to treat someone can also be expressed with the verb **pagar**:

> **Vamos nesse bar. Eu te pago um chope.**
> Let's go into this bar. I'll buy you a beer.

> **Quero pagar o seu almoço.**
> I want to treat you to lunch.

68.1.2 ### Imperative

▶ **Chapter 21** (p. 196)

The imperative can be used to make an invitation. An oral invitation to one person will usually be expressed with the familiar imperative:

> **Senta aqui e toma um drinque com a gente.**
> Sit down here and have a drink with us.

The formal imperative may be encountered in written invitations:

> **Venha conhecer o nosso showroom.**
> Come and visit our showroom.

68.1.3 ### Present simple

The present simple can be used to make a spontaneous offer, usually in response to the situation. It is equivalent to the use of 'will' or ''ll' in English, or 'shall/should' in a question:

> **Você está precisando de dinheiro? Eu te empresto.**
> Do you need money? I'll lend you some.

Não te preocupe. A gente ajuda.
Don't worry. We'll help.

A Sandra deixa você na estação, não é, Sandra?
Sandra will drop you at the station, won't you, Sandra?

Coloco a sua mala no carro?
Shall I put your suitcase in the car?

68.1.4 *Deixa que eu* + present

In colloquial speech, **Deixa que eu . . .** 'Leave it, I'll . . .' can be used to offer to do something that the other person is intending to do:

Deixa que eu pago.
No, that's OK. I'll get this.

Deixa que eu levo a sua mala.
Here, let me carry your suitcase.

68.1.5 *Vamos* + infinitive

An invitation that includes the speaker can be expressed with **Vamos . . .** 'Let's . . .' followed by an infinitive. With a question intonation, the meaning is 'Shall we . . . ?':

Vamos sair amanhã à noite.
Let's go out tomorrow night.

Vamos comer pizza?
Shall we have pizza?

68.1.6 *Por que não . . . ?* + present

Por que não . . . ? is used to mean 'Why don't . . . ?':

Por que você não dorme lá em casa?
Why don't you stay over at our place?

Por que você não janta com a gente?
Why don't you have dinner with us?

68.1.7 Present of *querer* + infinitive/noun

The verb **querer** 'to want' is used in informal invitations and offers. In more formal situations, it would sound rather abrupt.

Tem churrasco aqui hoje. Quer vir?
We're having a barbecue here today. Do you want to come?

Você quer uma água?
Do you want a glass of water?

The question is often phrased in the negative to make it sound more persuasive:

Você não quer deixar a bolsa aqui?
Don't you want to leave your bag here?

68.1.8 Present of *aceitar* + noun

The verb **aceitar** 'to accept' is used when offering something in a formal or polite way. Depending on the person addressed, it can be preceded by **você(s)**, **o senhor/a senhora** or no explicit subject:

> **Aceita um cafezinho? – Aceito.**
> 'Would you like a coffee?' – 'Yes, thank you'.

> **Vocês aceitam uma bebida?**
> Would you like something to drink?

68.1.9 Present of *desejar* + infinitive/noun

The verb **desejar** 'to wish to/for' is used for formal and polite invitations and offers. It can be regarded as a more formal synonym of **querer** (see **68.1.5**) and is often equivalent to 'would like' in English:

> **Deseja deixar um telefone de contato?**
> Do you wish to leave a contact number?

> **O senhor deseja uma sobremesa?**
> Would you like a dessert, sir?

68.1.10 *querer que* + subjunctive

This construction can be used for both informal and more formal invitations and offers:

> **Você quer que a gente leve alguma coisa?**
> Do you want us to bring anything?

> **O senhor quer que chame um táxi?**
> Would you like me to call a taxi, sir?

68.1.11 *poder* + infinitive

The modal verb **poder** 'can' followed by an infinitive may also be used to make formal or informal offers and invitations:

> **Pode ficar aqui se quiser.**
> You can stay here if you like.

> **Posso deixar vocês no shopping se quiserem.**
> I can drop you at the mall if you want.

68.1.12 *queria/gostaria que* + imperfect subjunctive

The words **queria** and **gostaria** both mean 'I would like'. Of the two, **gostaria** sounds more heartfelt or more formal. Both are followed by **que** + imperfect subjunctive to express a polite invitation:

> **Eu queria que você viesse conhecer a minha casa.**
> I'd like you to come and visit my home.

> **Gostaríamos que vocês estivessem presentes no nosso casamento.**
> We'd like you to be present at our wedding.

68.1.13 *queria/gostaria de* + infinitive

Both **queria** and **gostaria de** can be followed by an infinitive as another way of phrasing an invitation or offer:

> **Queríamos convidar vocês para um jantar aqui em casa.**
> We'd like to invite you to dinner here at our house.

> **Gostaria de oferecer meus serviços como guia.**
> I'd like to offer my services as a guide.

68.1.14 *Tenho/Temos o prazer de* + infinitive

Tenho/Temos o prazer de . . . 'I/We are pleased to . . .' is an expression commonly used in formal invitations and offers, especially in writing:

> **Tenho o prazer de convidar você para o lançamento do meu livro.**
> I am pleased to invite you to the launch of my book.

> **Temos o prazer de oferecer a você um produto de altíssima qualidade.**
> We are pleased to offer you a product of the highest quality.

68.1.15 *Teria/Teríamos muito prazer em* + infinitive

Teria/Teríamos muito prazer em . . . 'I/We would be delighted to . . .' is another formal expression used to express an invitation:

> **Teríamos muito prazer em recebê-lo aqui para um coquetel.**
> We would be delighted to welcome you here for cocktails.

68.2 Accepting or declining an offer or invitation

68.2.1 The expressions normally used to accept an offer or invitation are as follows:

> **Muito obrigado/a.** (*formal/informal*)
> Thank you very much.

> **Então tá, obrigado/a.** (*informal*)
> OK then, thanks.

> **Falou.** (*very informal*)
> OK.

> **Combinado. / Fechado.** (*informal*)
> It's a deal.

> **Eu topo.** (*informal*)
> I'll take you up on that. / Count me in.

> **Vou adorar.** (*informal*)
> I'd love to.

> **Com muito prazer.** (*formal*)
> I'd/We'd be delighted.

> **É muita gentileza sua. / É muito gentil da sua parte.** (*formal*)
> That's very kind of you.

> **Claro.** (*neutral*)
> Of course.

> **Aceito o convite.** (*neutral*)
> I accept your invitation.

Invitations and offers can also be accepted by repeating the verb of wanting used in the question:

> **Você quer que eu te acompanhe? – Quero.**
> 'Do you want me to go with you?' – 'Yes, I do.'

> **Você aceita uma água? – Aceito.**
> 'Would you like a glass of water?' – 'Yes, please.'

68.2.2 The following expressions are used to decline an invitation or offer:

> **Obrigado/a.** (*neutral*)
> No thank you.

> **Quero não, obrigado/a.** (*informal*)
> No thanks.

> **Estou bem, obrigado/a.** (*neutral*)
> I'm good/fine, thanks.

> **Está bom, obrigado/a.** (*informal*)
> No, I'm good/fine thanks.

> **Sinto muito, mas não dá/não vai dar.** (*neutral*)
> I'm sorry, but I can't/won't be able to.

> **Sinto muito, mas não vai ser possível.** (*formal*)
> I'm sorry, but it won't be possible.

> **Infelizmente não dá/não vai dar.** (*neutral*)
> I'm afraid I/we can't/won't be able to.

> **Queria muito mas . . .** (*neutral*)
> I'd really like to but . . .

> **Adoraria mas . . .** (*informal*)
> I'd love to but . . .

> **Já tenho compromisso.**
> I have a prior engagement.

> **Tenho compromisso naquele dia/naquela noite/hoje à noite.**
> I'm busy that day/that night/tonight.

> **Estou fora.** (*very informal*)
> Count me out.

68.3 # Enquiring whether an invitation is accepted or declined

When enquiring whether an invitation is accepted or declined, use the present tense. Note that the verb **vir** 'to come' can only be used if you are currently in the place referred to, otherwise the verb **ir** 'to go' must be used instead:

> **Você vem para a nossa festa?**
> Are you coming to our party? (*if you are in the party venue, e.g. your home*)

> **Você vai para a nossa festa?**
> Are you coming to our party? (*if you are not in the party venue*)

> **Você vai comigo?**
> Will you come with me? (*i.e. to a different place from here*)

VI

Expressing temporal relations

69

Talking about the present

Like English, Portuguese has a present simple tense, e.g. **eu estudo** 'I study' and a present continuous tense, e.g. **eu estou estudando** 'I am studying'. When talking about actions in the present,[1] the use of the two tenses is largely the same in the two languages, apart from a few small differences mentioned below.

NOTE | 1 Note that the English present continuous can also be used to talk about the future, as in 'I'm flying to New York tomorrow'. The Portuguese present continuous tense is never used with future reference.

69.1 The present simple

▶ **15.3** (p. 144)

The present simple is used as follows:

(i)   To report facts that are generally true or true in the present:

Os brasileiros falam português.
Brazilians speak Portuguese.

O Brasil é muito maior do que a França.
Brazil is much bigger than France.

Ele é dono da loja.
He's the owner of the shop.

(ii)   To express timeless ideas or emotions:

O Rio de Janeiro é lindo.
Rio de Janeiro is beautiful.

Eu gosto de jazz.
I like jazz.

É uma ótima ideia.
It's a great idea.

(iii) Talking about ongoing actions:

Eles moram em Curitiba.
They live in Curitiba.

O que você faz na vida?
What do you do for a living?

> **Trabalho num banco.**
> I work in a bank.

(iv) Talking about habitual actions. Such statements are often qualified with an adverb indicating frequency, such as **geralmente** 'usually', **sempre** 'always', **nunca** 'never', **quase nunca** 'hardly ever', **muitas vezes** 'often', **raramente** 'rarely, seldom'. These adverbs are placed immediately before the verb as in English:

> **Eu geralmente assisto o jornal das dez.**
> I usually watch the ten o'clock news.

> **Ele nunca atrasa.**
> He's never late.

> **Raramente saímos à noite.**
> We seldom go out in the evening.

(v) Describing present states or conditions with the verb **estar** 'to be':

> **Está frio hoje.**
> It's cold today.

> **Estamos muito cansados.**
> We're very tired.

69.2 The present continuous

The present continuous is used as follows:

(i) Describing an action that is happening at the time of speaking:

> **Estou tentando abrir essa gaveta.**
> I'm trying to open this drawer.

> **O telefone está tocando.**
> The phone's ringing.

> **Os vizinhos estão fazendo muito barulho.**
> The neighbours are making a lot of noise.

(ii) Describing an action that is ongoing but not happening right now:

> **Estou estudando japonês.**
> I'm studying Japanese.

> **Eles estão montando um negócio.**
> They're setting up a business.

> **Estamos construindo uma casa na praia.**
> We're having a house built at the beach.

(iii) To emphasize the temporary nature of what is normally an ongoing action:

> **Estamos morando na casa dos meus pais.**
> We're living at my parents' place.

> **Ela está trabalhando numa loja.**
> She's working in a shop.

> **Estou nadando três vezes por semana.**
> I'm going swimming three times a week.

(iv) To emphasize the temporary nature of what is normally a timeless or ongoing emotion. In English, the present continuous is sometimes used in such circumstances, but the present simple is often preferred:

> **Você está gostando do novo emprego?**
> Are you liking/enjoying your new job?

> **Estou achando que eles esqueceram.**
> I think (= *I'm starting to think*) they've forgotten.

> **Essa planta está precisando de água.**
> That plant needs (= *is in need of*) water.

> **Ela está querendo sair da empresa.**
> She wants (*at this particular time*) to leave the company.

(v) To describe present states and circumstances with verbs other than **estar**:

> **Por que você está sendo tão agressivo?**
> Why are you being so aggressive?

> **Está fazendo calor lá fora.**
> It's hot outside.

> **Está ventando muito.**
> It's very windy.

69.3 Expressing habitual action with *costumar* + infinitive

Habitual action in the present can be expressed using the present tense of the verb **costumar** 'to be in the habit of, to usually . . .':

> **Costumo correr de manhã.**
> I usually go running in the mornings.

> **O ônibus costuma atrasar.**
> The bus is quite often late.

> **Eles costumam jantar fora de vez em quando.**
> They are in the habit of going out for dinner occasionally.

69.4 Saying how long one has been doing something

69.4.1 Present simple/present continuous + *há/faz* + time phrase

Sentences such as 'I've been waiting a long time', 'We've lived here for five years', 'How long have you been here?' express a continuous action or state that started in the past and continues in the present. Such actions or states are expressed with the perfect simple or perfect continuous tense in English, whereas Portuguese uses the present tense followed by an expression of time (e.g. **muito tempo** 'a long time') introduced with **há** or **faz**, which, in this context, translate as 'for'[2]. Note that **faz** is less common than **há** in this position and sounds informal, while **há** is used in all registers. The present simple is used to talk about general, longer-term actions or states and the present continuous to talk about more momentary, shorter-term actions or states:

NOTE 2 The preposition 'for' can be omitted in English, but **há** or **faz** must be included in such time expressions in Portuguese.

Estou esperando faz um tempão.
I've been waiting (for) ages.

Moramos aqui há cinco anos.
We've lived/been living here for five years.

Você está aqui há quanto tempo?
How long have you been here?

69.4.2 *faz* + time phrase + *que* + present simple/present continuous

This construction means the same as the previous one,[3] but with a difference of emphasis. Here the emphasis is on the period of time rather than the action itself:

Faz duas horas que estou esperando!
I've been waiting for two hours!

Faz quanto tempo que você estuda português?
How long have you been studying Portuguese?

Já faz cinco anos que moramos aqui.
It's five years we've been living here now.

Faz mais de uma hora que ele está assim.
He's been like that for over an hour.

NOTE

3 Note that **há** can also be used in this construction, in place of **faz**, but is less common, especially in speech.

When the period of time refers to an action that has not yet taken place, a translation with 'it's . . . since . . .' is also possible:

Faz seis meses que não vejo a Cristina.
I haven't seen Cristina for six months. / It's been six months since I saw Cristina.

69.4.3 *estar* + *há* + time phrase + *sem* + infinitive/*estar sem* + infinitive + *há* + time phrase

This expression can also be used to say how long it is that you have not done something:

Estou há seis meses sem ver a Cristina. / Estou sem ver a Cristina há seis meses.
I haven't seen Cristina for six months.

Você está há quanto tempo sem fumar? / Você está sem fumar há quanto tempo?
How long is it since you smoked? (= *How long have you not been smoking?*)

69.4.4 *continuar* + gerund

This construction with the gerund describes an action or series of repeated actions that started in the past and is still going on, although the exact length of time is not specified:

Continua chovendo.
It's still raining.

Eles continuam se vendo de vez em quando.
They still see each other occasionally.

69.4.5 *continuar + sem + infinitive*

This construction describes an action that still has not taken place at the present moment:

O paciente continua sem comer.
The patient is still not eating.

Eles continuam sem se falarem.
They're still not speaking to one another.

70

Talking about the future

In English you can talk about the future in a number of different ways. You can use the future with 'will', as in 'I'll call you later'; a construction with 'going to', as in 'It's going to rain'; the present continuous, as in 'I'm seeing Sue tomorrow' or even the present simple, as in 'I leave for Brazil in the morning'. In Portuguese, the options are to use the verb **ir** 'to go' followed by an infinitive, the present simple or the inflected future tense. The last is almost entirely restricted to the written language, narrowing the options down to two in the spoken language. In some cases these two forms are interchangeable, in others they are not. This chapter also considers expressions of intent with regard to the future.

70.1 Talking about future events

This section considers the Portuguese equivalents of the English future with 'will' and 'going to' when talking about actions and events that will occur in the future as opposed to premeditated plans or arrangements.

70.1.1 Present of *ir* + infinitive

In the spoken language and informal written style, the present of the verb **ir** 'to go' is used with an infinitive to talk about future actions and events:

> **A casa vai ser vendida para quitar a dívida.**
> The house will/is going to be sold to pay off the debt.

> **Vamos precisar de mais leite.**
> We'll/We're going to need more milk.

> **A festa vai começar quando todo mundo estiver aqui.**
> The party will start when everyone's here.

> **Vai chover a qualquer momento.**
> It's going to rain any minute now.

70.1.2 Present simple

The present simple is used in speech to express spontaneous statements about the future, usually in reponse to the actual situation or a posited one. English uses 'will' in these cases:

> **Te ligo mais tarde.**
> I'll call you later.

Eu levo para você.
I'll carry it for you.

É o telefone. Eu atendo.
There's the phone. I'll get it.

A Laura nos leva, não é, Laura?
Laura will take us, won't you, Laura?

Se eu precisar de ajuda, te aviso.
If I need help, I'll let you know.

70.1.3 Inflected future tense

The inflected future tense is normally only used in the written language and corresponds to the use of **ir** + infinitive, presented in **70.1.1**:

A casa será vendida para quitar a dívida.
The house will be sold to pay off the debt.

O presidente se pronunciará amanhã.
The president will make a statement tomorrow.

As crianças voltarão às aulas na semana que vem.
The children will go back to school next week.

70.1.4 Present subjunctive

The 'will' future is sometimes rendered using the present subjunctive when the grammar of the sentence requires it:

Espero que você me perdoe.
I hope you will forgive me.

Estou com medo que ele caia.
I'm afraid he'll fall.

70.2 Talking about scheduled events in the future

When talking about actions or events that are scheduled for a specific time in the future, Portuguese, like English, uses the present simple:

Vou embora para o Brasil amanhã.
I leave for Brazil tomorrow.

O jogo começa às 20h00.
The game starts at 8 p.m.

Eles voltam em setembro.
They're back in September.

70.3 Talking about plans and intentions for the future

The section presents the Portuguese equivalents of the future expressed with 'going to' or with the present continuous in English, as well as other ways of expressing plans and intentions.

70.3.1 Present of *ir* + infinitive

In all registers, the present tense of the verb **ir** 'to go' is used with an infinitive to express planned and intended actions or events in the future. Planned and intended actions are those thought about in advance and planned by the subject of the sentence; this is different from the scheduled actions described in **70.2**, where the action is imposed upon the subject by external forces.

> **Vou comprar um computador novo.**
> I'm going to buy a new computer.

> **Vou ver o Davi amanhã.**
> I'm seeing Davi tomorrow.

> **Uma vez o telhado consertado, vão pintar a casa inteira.**
> Once the roof is repaired, they're going to paint the whole house.

> **Você vai sair hoje à noite?**
> Are you going out tonight?

70.3.2 Present simple of *ir* 'to go' referring to the future

When it is used with its full meaning of 'to go', the verb **ir** cannot be preceded by the auxiliary **ir**, so it is used in the present simple to refer to the future. Thus, **eu vou** can mean 'I go', 'I will go', 'I'm going' or 'I'm going to go':

> **Vou para São Paulo amanhã.**
> I'm going to São Paulo tomorrow.

> **Vamos para casa primeiro.**
> We're going to go home first.

> **Eles vão embora semana que vem.**
> They're leaving next week.

70.3.3 *pretender* + infinitive; *planejar* + infinitive

Another way of expressing a future intention is to use the verb **pretender** 'to intend to, plan to', usually in the present simple, followed by an infinitive:

> **Pretendo cursar Medicina.**
> I intend to study medicine.

> **O que é que você pretende fazer com essa roupa velha?**
> What are you planning to do with those old clothes?

> **Ele pretende passar um ano no Brasil.**
> He plans to spend a year in Brazil.

> **Pretendemos voltar amanhã.**
> We're planning to come back tomorrow.

The verb **planejar** 'to plan' can also be followed by an infinitive, but it is not usually used to talk about personal plans and intentions, and therefore rarely occurs in this construction in everyday conversation. It is more commonly used in contexts where an actual plan has been devised and is to be implemented:

> **O governo planeja cortar os gastos em 25%.**
> The government plans to cut spending by 25 per cent.

A empresa planeja dobrar seu faturamento até o final do ano.
The company plans to double its turnover by the end of the year.

70.3.4 *estar pensando em* + infinitive

The phrase **estar pensando em** ... 'to be thinking of . . .' with an infinitive is another way of expressing a more thoughtful intention:

Estou pensando em fazer uma faculdade.
I'm thinking of doing a university degree.

Quem é que você está pensando em convidar para a festa?
Who are you thinking of inviting to the party?

Já estou pensando em desistir.
I'm already considering giving up.

70.4 Expressing the future from a past perspective

When recounting past events, it is often necessary to refer to actions and events that are in the future in relation to the time you are referring to, as in 'He said *he would call*', '*They were going to depart* the next morning', '*We were planning to stay* for a week'.

70.4.1 Imperfect of *ir* + infinitive

The most common way of expressing the future from a past perspective is to use the imperfect of the verb **ir** 'to go' followed by an infinitive. This corresponds to the English 'would' or 'was/were going to':

Ele disse que ia ligar.
He said he would call.

Eles iam partir na manhã seguinte.
They were going to depart the next morning.

The verb **ir** can also be in the imperfect subjunctive if the grammar of the sentence calls for it:

Pensei que fosse chover.
I thought it was going to rain.

Eu não acho que ela fosse fazer uma coisa dessas.
I don't think she would do something like that.

70.4.2 Conditional tense

The conditional tense can be used to express the idea of 'would' when referring to the future from a past perspective. The conditional has a rather ponderous and formal ring to it and therefore tends to be avoided in the spoken language and hardly used at all in colloquial speech. Its place is taken by the imperfect of **ir** + infinitive (see **70.4.1**) or the imperfect tense (see **70.4.3**):

Ele disse que voltaria ainda hoje.
He said he would be back today.

Ela sabia que o chefe não estaria naquele dia.
She knew the boss wouldn't be in that day.

70.4.3 Imperfect indicative

In colloquial speech, the imperfect indicative is usually used in place of the conditional tense. The wider context and the sense of the sentence usually make it clear that the imperfect is being used with reference to future time:

> **Ele disse que voltava ainda hoje.**
> He said he would be back today.

> **Ela sabia que o chefe não estava naquele dia.**
> She knew the boss wouldn't be in that day.

70.4.4 Imperfect subjunctive

When the grammar of the sentence calls for it, 'would' with reference to a future action or event may be rendered by the imperfect subjunctive:

> **Ela estava com medo de que ele descobrisse a verdade.**
> She was afraid he would find out the truth.

> **Esperávamos que eles fossem compreensivos.**
> We hoped they would be sympathetic.

70.4.5 Imperfect of *pretender/estar pensando em* + infinitive

Past expressions of intent can be expressed with the imperfect of **pretender** 'to intend to, plan to' or **estar pensando em** 'to be thinking of', followed by an infinitive:

> **Eu não pretendia ficar tanto tempo assim.**
> I wasn't planning to stay as long as that.

> **A gente estava pensando em viajar esse fim de semana.**
> We were thinking of going away this weekend.

> **Quando é que você pretendia voltar?**
> When were you intending to come back?

70.5 Other ways of expressing the future

70.5.1 *estar prestes a* + infinitive

This expression means 'to be about to' referring to an imminent action:

> **Eu estava prestes a sair quando o telefone tocou.**
> I was about to go out when the phone rang.

70.5.2 *estar para* + infinitive

This expression means 'to be due to, to be soon to, to be meaning to':

> **O bebê dela está para nascer a qualquer dia.**
> Her baby's due any day now.

> **Estou para te ligar há duas semanas.**
> I've been meaning to phone you for two weeks.

70.5.3 *estar a ponto de* + infinitive

This expression means 'to be on the point of':

Ele estava a ponto de se afogar quando o salva-vidas chegou.
He was on the point of drowning when the lifeguard got to him.

70.5.4 *haver de* + infinitive

This is a formal/literary construction which, in addition to futurity, expresses a kind of wish, 'will surely'. The verb **haver** is often in the future tense:

Com o apoio do povo, haveremos de vencer essa batalha.
With the support of the people, we will surely win this battle.

Você há de convir que isso não é normal.
You will surely agree that this is not normal.

71

Talking about the past

71.1   Talking about events that are past and complete

71.1.1   The preterite

To talk about actions or events that took place in the past and ended in the past, as in 'I had dinner and went to bed', 'Cabral arrived in Brazil in 1500', 'We didn't find the restaurant', Portuguese uses the preterite tense:

> **Jantei e fui para a cama.**
> I had dinner and went to bed.

> **Cabral chegou ao Brasil em 1500.**
> Cabral arrived in Brazil in 1500.

> **Não encontramos o restaurante.**
> We didn't find the restaurant.

71.1.2   The present or historic present

In narrative contexts, ranging from telling a friend about a recent incident to written accounts of historical events, the present tense is often used to make the account more vivid and to add dramatic quality. This also occurs in English, but to a lesser extent than in Portuguese:

> **Aí ele olha para mim e diz assim: 'Me dá seu telefone.'**
> Then he looks at me and says, 'Give me your phone number.'

> **Nos próximos anos, os portugueses desbravam e colonizam o país.**
> In the years that followed, the Portuguese opened up and colonized the country.

71.2   Saying how long ago something happened

Using **há** with a time phrase in combination with a verb in the preterite serves to indicate how long ago something happened:

> **O escritor morreu há quinze anos.**
> The writer died fifteen years ago.

> **Recebemos a notícia há alguns minutos.**
> We got the news a few minutes ago.

Another way of expressing the same idea is with the word **atrás** 'back' after the time phrase:

> **A gente se conheceu dez anos atrás.**
> We met ten years ago.

It is extremely common to use both **há** and **atrás** together, although prescriptive gram-marians argue that this is pleonastic and should not be used in writing:

> **Ela me ligou há dois dias atrás.**
> She called me two days ago.

> **Isso aconteceu há algum tempo atrás.**
> This happened some time ago.

71.3 Talking about long-lasting past events

A sentence such as 'We lived in Brazil for five years' refers to a past event that lasted for a considerable period of time, 'five years', but that is nevertheless over at the time of speaking. In such cases, Portuguese uses the preterite tense:

> **Moramos no Brasil durante cinco anos.**
> We lived in Brazil for five years.

> **Ela passou seis meses na Itália.**
> She spent six months in Italy.

> **Fiquei duas horas esperando o ônibus.**
> I was there for two hours waiting for the bus.

71.4 Talking about past events related to the present

In sentences such as 'He's drunk too much', 'I've finished the book', 'She's broken her leg', English uses the perfect tense to describe a past event that has a bearing on the present. Portuguese uses the preterite in such cases:

> **Ele bebeu demais.**
> He's drunk too much.

> **Terminei o livro.**
> I've finished the book.

> **Ela quebrou a perna.**
> She's broken her leg.

The context usually makes it clear whether the preterite corresponds to the English simple past or perfect tense in a particular situation. Compare:

> **Ela foi esquiar ano passado e quebrou a perna.**
> She went skiing last year and broke her leg.

> **Acho que ela quebrou a perna. Vamos chamar a ambulância.**
> I think she's broken her leg. Let's call an ambulance.

The sense of the English perfect tense is often implied by using the adverb **já**. The basic meaning of this adverb is 'already', 'ever' or 'yet', but it would often be left untranslated in English:

> **Você já leu Harry Potter?**
> Have you (ever) read Harry Potter?

> **Já molhei as plantas.**
> I've (already) watered the plants.

> **Vocês já almoçaram?**
> Have you had lunch (yet)?

Portuguese also uses the preterite in sentences such as 'I haven't finished yet', 'He's always wanted to be an actor', 'I've been to the bank twice today', referring to events that have occurred over a period of time including the present:

> **Não terminei ainda.**
> I haven't finished yet.
>
> **Ele sempre quis ser ator.**
> He's always wanted to be an actor.
>
> **Já fui ao banco duas vezes hoje.**
> I've been to the bank twice today.

71.5 Referring to a prolonged or repeated action that began in the past and is still in progress

In sentences such as 'He's been reading the whole morning', 'We've been living here since 2002', 'He's been complaining since he got here', referring to prolonged or repeated action that began in the past and is still going on, Portuguese uses the present tense:

> **Ele já está a manhã inteira lendo.**
> He's been reading the whole morning.
>
> **Moramos aqui desde 2002.**
> We've been living here since 2002.
>
> **Ele está reclamando desde que chegou aqui.**
> He's been complaining since he got here.

Notice that the present simple is used for longer-term actions and the present continuous for shorter-term actions. Compare:

> **Ele reclama desde que chegou aqui há dois anos.**
> He's been complaining since he arrived here two years ago.
>
> **Ele está reclamando desde que chegou aqui há uma hora.**
> He's been complaining since he got here an hour ago.

71.6 Referring to the immediate past

71.6.1 *acabar de* + infinitive

The preterite of **acabar** is used in combination with the preposition **de** and an infinitive to express the idea of 'have/has just' as in the sentence 'He's just arrived':

> **Ele acabou de chegar.**
> He's just arrived.
>
> **Acabamos de jantar.**
> We've just had dinner.
>
> **Acabei de limpar essa cozinha!**
> I've just cleaned this kitchen!

To refer to a recent action from a past perspective, as in 'They had just arrived', use the pluperfect of **acabar** instead of the preterite:

> **Eles tinham acabado de chegar.**
> They had just arrived.

Eu tinha acabado de limpar a cozinha.
I had just cleaned the kitchen.

Note that, in more formal written language, 'have/has just' is expressed with the present of **acabar** and 'had just' with the imperfect:

O livro acaba de ser lançado.
The book has just come out.

Cabral acabava de chegar ao Brasil.
Cabral had just arrived in Brazil.

71.6.2 *agora (mesmo)* + preterite

Actions in the recent past can also be expressed using the preterite with the adverb **agora** 'just now' or, more emphatically, **agora mesmo** 'just this minute':

Eu cheguei agora.
I've just got here. / I got here just now.

Falei com o Cláudio agora mesmo.
I've just this minute spoken to Claudio. / I spoke to Claudio just a minute ago.

71.7 Referring to actions and developments that have been happening in the recent past

71.7.1 The perfect tense

To refer to actions and developments that have been taking place in the recent past, as in 'I've been studying hard lately', 'The market has been growing in recent years', Portuguese uses the perfect tense:

Tenho estudado muito ultimamente.
I've been studying hard lately.

O mercado tem crescido muito nos últimos anos.
The market has been growing substantially in recent years.

Note that the perfect tense is not used in Portuguese when the length of time is specified, as in 'He's been working here for two years.' In such cases, the present tense is used (see **69.4.1**).

71.7.2 *vir/andar* + gerund

The present tense of the verbs **vir** 'to come' and **andar** 'to go' can be combined with a gerund to describe what has been taking place in the recent past. Of the two, **andar** is more often used in less formal contexts:

A empresa vem crescendo a cada ano.
The company has been growing year by year.

O que é que você anda fazendo ultimamente?
What have you been doing lately?

Both verbs may also be used in the imperfect from a past perspective:

A situação vinha melhorando aos poucos.
The situation had gradually been improving.

Ele andava dizendo que ia casar.
He'd been saying he was going to get married.

71.8 Describing background states or actions in progress over an unspecified period of time in the past

In sentences such as 'I was tired', 'We used to live there', the beginning or the end of the state and the action are not specified. To describe states which 'set the scene' or actions in progress in an open period of time which provide the background to the main action, as in these examples, Portuguese uses the imperfect:

Desisti de ir na festa porque estava cansado.
I decided not to go to the party because I was tired.

O homem era alto e magro, e aparentava ter uns 50 anos.
The man was tall and slim, and looked about 50.

Eu me lembro que fazia muito calor no dia do casamento.
I remember that it was very hot on the day of the wedding.

O Jaime estava doente naquele dia e não foi trabalhar.
Jaime was sick that day and didn't go to work.

Naquela época ela trabalhava no centro da cidade.
At that time she worked/used to work/was working in the city centre.

Morávamos lá na época.
We used to live there then. / We were living there at the time.

In contrast to the preterite, the imperfect cannot refer to states or actions that took place in a closed period of time, even when these may have been prolonged or repeated. Compare the last four sentences above with the ones below, which contain verbs in the preterite:

Fez muito calor ontem.
It was very hot yesterday.

O Jaime esteve doente a semana inteira.
Jaime was sick the whole week.

Ela já trabalhou no centro da cidade.
She has worked in the city centre. (*before now*)

Moramos lá durante cinco anos.
We lived there for five years.

71.9 Talking about past habitual actions

71.9.1 The imperfect

To ask and give information about actions that occurred regularly in the past, over an unspecified period, the imperfect is used. This may sometimes be accompanied by a time phrase indicating frequency, such as **todo dia** 'every day', **muitas vezes** 'often', **nunca** 'never', **de vez em quando** 'occasionally, from time to time', etc.:

Ele vinha aqui todo dia.
He used to come here every day.

Meus avós falavam italiano.
My grandparents spoke Italian.

Eu corria de vez em quando.
I used to go running occasionally.

71.9.2 Imperfect of *costumar* + infinitive

Past habits can also be referred to by using the imperfect of the verb **costumar** 'to be in the habit of' followed by an infinitive. This construction sounds rather formal/literary and is not often used in colloquial speech:

Como meu pai costumava dizer, o gosto não se discute.
As my father used to say, there's no accounting for taste.

Ela costumava acordar todos os dias às cinco horas da manhã.
She used to get up at five o'clock in the morning every day.

71.10 Talking about actions that were taking place when something else happened

71.10.1 Imperfect of *estar* + gerund + preterite

To refer to an action that was in progress when some other event happened, e.g. 'We were having dinner when the police arrived', the action in progress is described using the imperfect of **estar** followed by a gerund, and the action that intervened is expressed using the preterite:

Estávamos jantando quando a polícia chegou.
We were having dinner when the police arrived.

Eu estava dormindo quando você ligou.
I was sleeping when you called.

The intervening action may be unstated but implied by the context:

Então, estava falando do meu encontro com a Sílvia.
Yes, so I was talking about when I met Silvia. (*i.e. before I was interrupted*)

71.10.2 The imperfect

In more formal and literary style, the simple imperfect may be used instead of the construction with **estar**:

A família jantava quando o telefone tocou.
The family were having dinner when the telephone rang.

But in speech and informal writing, the construction with **estar** is preferred, apart from a few fixed phrases:

O que é que eu falava mesmo?
What was I saying again?

> **Desculpe, o senhor dizia?**
> Sorry, you were saying?

71.11 Talking about a past event or action that occurred before another past event or action

71.11.1 The pluperfect

The pluperfect is used as in English to refer to an event or action that occurred before the main past events and actions described in the sentence:

> **Ele tinha esquecido a carteira e estava sem dinheiro.**
> He'd forgotten his wallet and had no money on him.

> **Eu tinha ligado antes de ir para lá.**
> I had called before going there.

71.11.2 The preterite

The preterite is often used in Portuguese where a pluperfect would be used in English, especially when the time relations are clear from the context:

> **Comi o sanduíche que trouxe de casa.**
> I ate the sandwich I had brought from home.

> **Ele percebeu que esqueceu a carteira.**
> He realized he had forgotten his wallet.

71.12 Referring to a prolonged or repeated action that began at an earlier time and was still in progress at a point in the past

In sentences such as 'He had been watching TV the whole day', 'They had been living there since 1950', 'I had been surfing for as long as I could remember', referring to a prolonged or repeated action that began at an earlier time and was still in progress at the point in the past you are describing, Portuguese uses the imperfect tense:

> **Ele já estava o dia inteiro assistindo TV.**
> He had been watching TV the whole day.

> **Eles moravam lá desde 1950.**
> They had been living there since 1950.

> **Eu pegava onda desde que me entendia por gente.**
> I had been surfing for as long as I could remember.

Notice that the imperfect simple is used for longer-term actions and the imperfect continuous for shorter-term actions (see **71.5**).

When the length of time is specified, the imperfect tense is used in combination with **havia**[1]/**fazia**, which, in this case, translates as 'for' (see **69.4.1**, **69.4.2**):

---

1   In speech, people often use the present tense **há** instead of **havia** in such cases despite the past reference.

Eles não se viam havia dois anos.
They hadn't seen each other for two years.

Fazia quatro meses que ela trabalhava lá.
She'd been working there for four months.

Appendices

Appendix I: Regular verb forms
▶ Chapter 15

		-ar	-er	-ir
		falar	comer	decidir
Present indic.	eu	falo	como	decido
	você, ele/ela	fala	come	decide
	nós	falamos	comemos	decidimos
	vocês, eles/elas	falam	comem	decidem
Imperf. indic.	eu	falava	comia	decidia
	você, ele/ela	falava	comia	decidia
	nós	falávamos	comíamos	decidíamos
	vocês, eles/elas	falavam	comiam	decidiam
Preterite	eu	falei	comi	decidi
	você, ele/ela	falou	comeu	decidiu
	nós	falamos	comemos	decidimos
	vocês, eles/elas	falaram	comeram	decidiram
Pluperf.	eu	falara	comera	decidira
	você, ele/ela	falara	comera	decidira
	nós	faláramos	comêramos	decidíramos
	vocês, eles/elas	falaram	comeram	decidiram
Future	eu	falarei	comerei	decidirei
	você, ele/ela	falará	comerá	decidirá
	nós	falaremos	comeremos	decidiremos
	vocês, eles/elas	falarão	comerão	decidirão
Conditional	eu	falaria	comeria	decidiria
	você, ele/ela	falaria	comeria	decidiria
	nós	falaríamos	comeríamos	decidiríamos
	vocês, eles/elas	falariam	comeriam	decidiriam
Present subj.	eu	fale	coma	decida
	você, ele/ela	fale	coma	decida
	nós	falemos	comamos	decidamos
	vocês, eles/elas	falem	comam	decidam

Imperf. subj.	eu	falasse	comesse	decidisse
	você, ele/ela	falasse	comesse	decidisse
	nós	falássemos	comêssemos	decidíssemos
	vocês, eles/elas	falassem	comessem	decidissem
Future subj.	eu	falar	comer	decidir
	você, ele/ela	falar	comer	decidir
	nós	falarmos	comermos	decidirmos
	vocês, eles/elas	falarem	comerem	decidirem
Personal infinitive	eu	falar	comer	decidir
	você, ele/ela	falar	comer	decidir
	nós	falarmos	comermos	decidirmos
	vocês, eles/elas	falarem	comerem	decidirem
Imperative	familiar	fala	come	decide
	formal	fale	coma	decida
	plural	falem	comam	decidam
Past participle		falado	comido	decidido
Gerund		falandò	comendo	decidindo

Appendix II: Principal irregular verbs

► Chapter 16

NB: Tenses that are not shown here follow the regular pattern for the particular conjugation, **-ar**, **-er** or **-ir**. In all verbs, the pluperfect, imperfect subjunctive and future subjunctive can be derived from the third person plural of the preterite.

Forms shown: first person singular, third person singular, first person plural, third person plural.

caber 'to fit'	*Pres. indic.*	**caibo, cabe, cabemos, cabem**
	Preterite	**coube, coube, coubemos, couberam**
	Pres. subj.	**caiba, caiba, caibamos, caibam**
dar 'to give'	*Pres. indic.*	**dou, dá, damos, dão**
	Preterite	**dei, deu, demos, deram**
	Pres. subj.	**dê, dê, demos, deem**
dizer 'to say'	*Pres. indic.*	**digo, diz, dizemos, dizem**
	Preterite	**disse, disse, dissemos, disseram**
	Pres. subj.	**diga, diga, digamos, digam**
	Fut./Cond.	**direi/diria**, etc.
	Past part.	**dito**
estar 'to be'	*Pres. indic.*	**estou, está, estamos, estão**
	Preterite	**estive, esteve, estivemos, estiveram**
	Pres. subj.	**esteja, esteja, estejamos, estejam**
fazer 'to do'	*Pres. indic.*	**faço, faz, fazemos, fazem**
	Preterite	**fiz, fez, fizemos, fizeram**
	Pres. subj.	**faça, faça, façamos, façam**
	Fut./Cond.	**farei/faria**, etc.
	Past part.	**feito**

haver 'to have'	*Pres. indic.*	**hei, há, hemos, hão**
	Preterite	**houve, houve, houvemos, houveram**
	Pres. subj.	**haja, haja, hajamos, hajam**
ir 'to go'	*Pres. indic.*	**vou, vai, vamos, vão**
	Preterite	**fui, foi, fomos, foram**
	Pres. subj.	**vá, vá, vamos, vão**
poder 'to be able to'	*Pres. indic.*	**posso, pode, podemos, podem**
	Preterite	**pude, pôde, pudemos, puderam**
	Pres. subj.	**possa, possa, possamos, possam**
pôr 'to put'	*Pres. indic.*	**ponho, põe, pomos, põem**
	Imperf. indic.	**punha, punha, púnhamos, punham**
	Preterite	**pus, pôs, pusemos, puseram**
	Pres. subj.	**ponha, ponha, ponhamos, ponham**
	Fut./Cond.	**porei/poria**, etc.
	Past part.	**posto**
querer 'to want'	*Pres. indic.*	**quero, quer, queremos, querem**
	Preterite	**quis, quis, quisemos, quiseram**
	Pres. subj.	**queira, queira, queiramos, queiram**
saber 'to know'	*Pres. indic.*	**sei, sabe, sabemos, sabem**
	Preterite	**soube, soube, soubemos, souberam**
	Pres. subj.	**saiba, saiba, saibamos, saibam**
ser 'to be'	*Pres. indic.*	**sou, é, somos, são**
	Imperf. indic.	**era, era, éramos, eram**
	Preterite	**fui, foi, fomos, foram**
	Pres. subj.	**seja, seja, sejamos, sejam**
ter 'to have'	*Pres. indic.*	**tenho, tem, temos, têm**
	Imperf. indic.	**tinha, tinha, tínhamos, tinham**
	Preterite	**tive, teve, tivemos, tiveram**
	Pres. subj.	**tenha, tenha, tenhamos, tenham**
trazer 'to bring'	*Pres. indic.*	**trago, traz, trazemos, trazem**
	Preterite	**trouxe, trouxe, trouxemos, trouxeram**
	Pres. subj.	**traga, traga, tragamos, tragam**
	Fut./Cond.	**trarei/traria**, etc.
ver 'to see'	*Pres. indic.*	**vejo, vê, vemos, veem**
	Preterite	**vi, viu, vimos, viram**
	Pres. subj.	**veja, veja, vejamos, vejam**
	Past Part.	**visto**
vir 'to come'	*Pres. indic.*	**venho, vem, vimos, vêm**
	Imperf. indic.	**vinha, vinha, vínhamos, vinham**
	Preterite	**vim, veio, viemos, vieram**
	Pres. subj.	**venha, venha, venhamos, venham**
	Past part.	**vindo**

Appendix III: Verbs with irregular past participles

▶ 17.2.2

abrir 'to open'	**aberto**
cobrir 'to cover'	**coberto**
dizer 'to say'	**dito**
escrever 'to write'	**escrito**
fazer 'to do'	**feito**
pôr 'to put'	**posto**
ver 'to see'	**visto**
vir 'to come'	**vindo**

Derivatives of these verbs show the same irregularity. Examples: **entreabrir** 'to half-open' > **entreaberto, encobrir** 'to cover up' > **encoberto, contradizer** 'to contradict' > **contradito, descrever** 'to describe' > **descrito, satisfazer** 'to satisfy' > **satisfeito, expor** 'to expose' > **exposto, antever** 'to foresee' > **antevisto, provir** 'to originate' > **provindo,** etc.

Appendix IV: Verbs with both a regular and an irregular past participle

▶ 17.2.3

Basic rule: the longer form shown first is used after the verbs **ter** and **haver** to form the perfect tenses; the shorter form shown second is used after the verb **ser** to form the passive, after **estar** and **ficar** expressing a resultant state or as an adjective qualifying a noun.

Exceptions to the basic rule:

1. Those regular participles marked with an asterisk (*) are also used after **ser** to form the passive.
2. Those irregular participles marked with an asterisk (*) are also commonly used as an alternative to the regular form after **ter** and **haver**.
3. Those irregular participles shown in parentheses are rarely used at all, even as adjectives, the regular form being preferred in all cases.

aceitar 'to accept' > **aceitado, aceito***
acender 'to light, turn on' > **acendido, aceso**
benzer 'to bless' > **benzido*, bento**
concluir 'to complete' > **concluído, (concluso)**
dispersar 'to disperse' > **dispersado*, disperso**
eleger 'to elect' > **elegido, eleito*** (similarly: **reeleger** 'to re-elect')
entregar 'to hand over, deliver' > **entregado, entregue***
envolver 'to involve, wrap' > **envolvido, (envolto)**
enxugar 'to dry, trim down' > **enxugado*, enxuto**
excluir 'to exclude' > **excluído, (excluso)**
expressar 'to express' > **expressado, expresso**
exprimir 'to express' > **exprimido, expresso**
expulsar 'to throw out, expel' > **expulsado, expulso***
extinguir 'to extinguish' > **extinguido, extinto***
fritar 'to fry' > **fritado, frito**
ganhar 'to win, earn' > **ganhado, ganho***

gastar 'to spend, wear out' > **gastado, gasto***
imergir 'to immerse' > **imergido, imerso**
imprimir 'to print' > **imprimido, impresso*** (similarly: **reimprimir** 'to reprint')
incluir 'to include' > **incluído, (incluso)**
inserir 'to insert' > **inserido, (inserto)**
isentar 'to clear, exempt' > **isentado*, isento**
libertar 'to free' > **libertado, (liberto)**
limpar 'to clean' > **limpado, limpo**
matar 'to kill' > **matado, morto**
morrer 'to die' > **morrido, morto**
pagar 'to pay' > **pagado, pago***
pegar 'to get' > **pegado, pego***
prender 'to fix', 'to arrest' > **prendido, preso**
restringir 'to restrict' > **restringido*, restrito**
romper 'to break' > **rompido, (roto)**
salvar 'to save' > **salvado, salvo***
soltar 'to release' > **soltado, solto**
submergir 'to submerge' > **submergido, submerso**
suprimir 'to do away with' > **suprimido, (supresso)**
surpreender 'to surprise' > **surpreendido*, surpreso**
suspender 'to suspend' > **suspendido, suspenso*.**

Appendix V: Second person verb forms

▶ 7.9

Although not in common use, second person verb forms are occasionally encountered, e.g. in poetry, songs, other works of literature and in religious texts. Here is an overview of the **tu** and **vós** forms of regular and irregular verbs:

Regular verbs		falar	comer	decidir
Present indic.	tu	falas	comes	decides
	vós	falais	comeis	decidis
Imperf. indic.	tu	falavas	comias	decidias
	vós	faláveis	comíeis	decidíeis
Preterite	tu	falaste	comeste	decidiste
	vós	falastes	comestes	decidistes
Pluperf.	tu	falaras	comeras	decidiras
	vós	faláreis	comêreis	decidíreis
Future	tu	falarás	comerás	decidirás
	vós	falareis	comereis	decidireis
Conditional	tu	falarias	comerias	decidirias
	vós	falaríeis	comeríeis	decidiríeis
Present subj.	tu	fales	comas	decidas
	vós	faleis	comais	decidais
Imperf. subj.	tu	falasses	comesses	decidisses
	vós	falásseis	comêsseis	decidísseis

Future subj.	tu	falares	comeres	decidires
	vós	falardes	comerdes	decidirdes
Personal infinitive	tu	falares	comeres	decidires
	vós	falardes	comerdes	decidirdes
Imperative	(tu)	fala	come	decide
	(vós)	falai	comei	decidi

Radical-changing verbs (see **16.1**): **tu** form is the same as the third person + **s**, e.g. **tu sobes**; **vós** forms are regular.

Semi-irregular verbs (see **16.2**): **tu** form is the same as the third person + **s**, but note: **tu produzes** 'you produce'; **vós** forms regular, but note: **vós credes** (< **crer**), **vós ledes** (< **ler**), **vós rides** (< **rir**).

Irregular present tenses: **dar** > **tu dás, vós dais**; **estar** > **tu estás, vós estais**; **haver** > **tu hás, vós haveis**; **ir** > **tu vais, vós ides**; **pôr** > **tu pões, vós pondes**; **ser** > **tu és, vós sois**; **ter** > **tu tens, vós tendes**; **ver** > **tu vês, vós vedes**; **vir** > **tu vens, vós vindes**. NB also: **tu dizes, fazes, queres, trazes**.

Irregular imperfects: **pôr** > **tu punhas, vós púnheis**; **ser** > **tu eras, vós éreis**; **ter** > **tu tinhas, vós tínheis**; **vir** > **tu vinhas, vós vínheis**.

Irregular preterites: **tu** form is the same as the first person singular + **(e)ste**, e.g. **tu fizeste** (< **fazer**), **tu disseste** (< **dizer**); **vós** form is the same as the first person singular + **(e)stes**. Exceptions are: **dar** > **tu deste, vós destes**; **ir/ser** > **tu foste, vós fostes**; **vir** > **tu vieste, vós viestes**.

Irregular present subjunctives: **tu** form is the same as the first/third person form + **s**, e.g. **tu digas** (< **dizer**); **vós** form: replace -**a** of first/third person form with -**ais**, e.g. **vós digais**. Exceptions are: **dar** > **tu dês, vós deis**; **ir** > **tu vás, vós vades**.

Imperative: **tu** form is the same as the third person singular of the present indicative; **vós** form is the same as the **vós** form of the present indicative without the final **s**, e.g. **ide!** 'go!'. Exception is: **ser** > **(tu) sê, (vós) sede**.

Bibliography

Academia Brasileira de Letras, *Vocabulário ortográfico da língua portuguesa*, 5th edn, Global Editora, São Paulo, 2009.

Bechara, Evanildo, *Moderna Gramática Portuguesa*, 37th edn, Nova Fronteira, Rio de Janeiro, 2009.

Cegalla, Domingos Paschoal, *Nova Minigramática da Língua Portuguesa*, 3rd edn, Companhia Editora Nacional, São Paulo, 2008.

Houaiss, A. and Villar, M., *Minidicionário da Língua Portuguesa*, 3rd edn, Editora Objetiva, Rio de Janeiro, 2008.

Kattán-Ibarra, J. and Pountain, C.J., *Modern Spanish Grammar: A practical guide*, 2nd edn, Routledge, London, 2003.

Perini, Mário A., *Modern Portuguese: A reference grammar*, Yale University Press, 2002.

Corpus of Brazilian Portuguese:

CETENFolha/NILC: Corpus of Electronic Text Extracts from the *Folha de S. Paulo* newspaper, part of the NILC/São Carlos corpus compiled by the Núcleo Interinstitucional de Linguística Computacional (NILC) of the University of São Paulo available at: http://acdc.linguateca.pt/cetenfolha.

Index

Portuguese words and phrases are listed in bold, and their English equivalents in italic; general topics are listed in roman type; *n* or *nn* after a section reference indicates that the topic will be found in a note or notes.

INDEX

INDEX